Investment Analysis for Real Estate Decisions

NINTH EDITION

Dearborn
Real Estate Education

BENNIE D. WALLER JR., PHILLIP T. KOLBE, AND GAYLON E. GREER

This publication is designed to provide accurate and authoritative information in regard to the subject matter covered. It is sold with the understanding that the publisher is not engaged in rendering legal, accounting, or other professional advice. If legal advice or other expert assistance is required, the services of a competent professional should be sought.

President: Dr. Andrew Temte
Executive Director, Real Estate Education: Toby Schifsky
Development Editor: Adam Bissen

INVESTMENT ANALYSIS FOR REAL ESTATE DECISIONS NINTH EDITION
©2019 Kaplan, Inc.
Published by DF Institute, Inc., d/b/a Dearborn Real Estate Education
332 Front St. S., Suite 501
La Crosse, WI 54601

All rights reserved. The text of this publication, or any part thereof, may not be reproduced in any manner whatsoever without written permission from the publisher.

Printed in the United States of America

ISBN: 978-1-4754-8417-5

CONTENTS

DEDICATION xv
ACKNOWLEDGMENTS xvi
ABOUT THE AUTHORS xvii
PREFACE xviii

PART ONE
Fundamental Issues in Real Estate Investment Analysis 1

UNIT 1
The Real Estate Investment Decision 2

Investment Analysis: Art and Science 4
Who Are Real Estate Investors? 4
Why Invest in Real Estate? 7
How Have Real Estate Investments Performed? 8
Concepts and Definitions 10
Investment Value: An Overview 13
Summary 22
Recommended Reading 23
Internet References 24
Review Questions 24
Discussion Questions 25

UNIT 2
Investment Strategy and Market Efficiency 26

Supply, Demand, and the Price of Real Estate Assets 28
Market Efficiency and Profit Opportunities 37
Strategy Implications 42
Summary 45
Recommended Reading 46
Internet References 46
Review Questions 46
Discussion Questions 47

UNIT 3
Land Utilization and the Rental Value of Real Estate 48

Economic Factors in Land Utilization 50
Linkages and "Natural" Zoning 54
The Market for Rental Space 57
Why Investors Need Market Research 58
Summary 59
Recommended Reading 60
Review Questions 61
Discussion Questions 61
Part One: Case Problem 62

PART TWO

Market Research and Cash-Flow Forecasting 65

UNIT 4
Market Research Tools and Techniques 66

Why Market Research is Needed 68
The Extent of Market Research 69
Market Research Design 71
Preparing a Research Report 75
Data Sources 76
Descriptive Research 79
Geographic Information Systems 80
Summary 85
Recommended Reading 86
Review Questions 87
Discussion Questions 87
Data Sources 88

UNIT 5
Reconstructing the Operating History 92

Introducing the Operating Statement 94
Types of Leases 95
Estimating the Ability to Command Rent 95
Estimating Operating Expenses 101
An Apartment Building Example 101
From Reconstruction to Forecast 106
Summary 108
Recommended Reading 108
Internet References 108
Review Questions 109
Discussion Questions 109
Problems 110

UNIT 6
Forecasting Income and Property Value 112

Gross Income Forecasting 114
Forecasting Operating Expenses 117
Forecasting Net Operating Income 119
Estimating Future Market Value 122
Additional Information Needed 124
Summary 124
Recommended Reading 126
Internet References 126
Review Questions 127
Discussion Questions 127
Problems 128
Part Two: Case Problem 129

PART THREE
Using Borrowed Money 131

UNIT 7
Financial Leverage and Investment Analysis 132

The Reasons Why Leverage Is So Popular 134

Measuring Financial Leverage 137

What Is the Right Amount of Financial Leverage? 139

Today's Lenders 143

Summary 145

Recommended Reading 146

Internet References 146

Review Questions 146

Discussion Questions 147

Problems 147

UNIT 8
Credit Instruments and Borrowing Arrangements 150

The Instruments for Credit 152

Mortgage Restructuring 155

Alternative Financing Strategies 158

Government-Sponsored Credit 160

Summary 161

Recommended Reading 162

Internet References 162

Review Questions 162

Discussion Questions 163

Problems 163

UNIT 9
The Cost of Borrowed Money 164
Interest Costs and Rates 166
Comparison of Financing Alternatives 172
Incorporating Leverage into the Operating Projection 178
Summary 182
Recommended Reading 182
Internet References 183
Review Questions 183
Discussion Questions 183
Problems 184
Part Three: Case Problem 186

PART FOUR

Income Tax Considerations 187

UNIT 10
Fundamental Income Tax Issues 188
The Tax Basis: Its Nature and Significance 190
The Initial Tax Basis 190
Allocation of the Initial Tax Basis 191
Adjustment of the Basis for Cost Recovery 193
Other Adjustments to the Tax Basis 196
Forecasting After-Tax Cash Flows 197
Tax Consequences of Ownership Form 199
Tax Consequences of Financial Leverage 203
Income Tax Credits for Property Rehabilitation 204
Limitations on the Deductibility of Losses 205
An Exception for Small-Scale Operators 206
Taxation of Foreign Investors 207
The Alternative Minimum Tax 207
Tax Consequences of Property Sales 208
Summary 208
Recommended Reading 209
Internet References 209
Review Questions 210
Discussion Questions 210
Problems 211

UNIT 11
Tax Consequences of Property Disposal 212

Computation of Realized Gain or Loss 214
Tax Treatment of Realized Gain or Loss 214
Estimating Cash Flow From Selling Maegan's Magic Manor 218
When are Realized Gains or Losses Recognized? 219
Use of the Installment Sales Method 220
Like-Kind Exchanges (1031 Exchanges) 224
Section 1033 Rollover: Casualty and Eminent Domain 226
Gifts of Property 226
Summary 228
Recommended Reading 229
Internet References 229
Review Questions 229
Discussion Questions 230
Problems 230
Part Four: Case Problem 231

PART FIVE
Measures of Investment Performance 233

UNIT 12
Traditional Measures of Investment Worth 234

Ratio Analysis 236
Traditional Profitability Measures 238
Adjustments for More Rational Analysis 243
Summary 244
Recommended Reading 244
Internet References 244
Review Questions 245
Discussion Questions 245
Problem 246

UNIT 13
Discounted Cash-Flow Analysis 248

Present Value   250

Net Present Value   251

Internal Rate of Return   252

Comparing Net Present Value and Internal Rate of Return   260

Approaches to Shore Up Internal Rate of Return   260

Summary   265

Recommended Reading   265

Internet Reference   265

Review Questions   265

Discussion Questions   266

Problems   266

UNIT 14
Investment Goals and Decision Criteria 268

The Choice of a Discount Rate   270

Investment Decisions and Decision Rules   272

Investment Value and Investment Strategy   275

Application of the Discounted Cash-Flow Technique   277

Summary   282

Recommended Reading   283

Internet Reference   283

Review Questions   283

Discussion Questions   284

Problems   284

Part Five: Case Problem   285

PART SIX
The Risk Element 289

UNIT 15
Risk in Real Estate Investment 290
Key Risk Elements 292
Controlling Risk 297
Risk Preferences and Profit Expectations 301
Measuring Risk 303
Summary 304
Recommended Reading 304
Internet Reference 304
Review Questions 304
Discussion Questions 305

UNIT 16
Traditional Risk-Adjustment Methods 306
The Payback-Period Approach 308
The Risk-Adjusted Discount Rate 308
The Certainty-Equivalent Technique 311
Partitioning Present Values 311
Sensitivity Analysis 316
Summary 320
Recommended Reading 321
Review Questions 321
Discussion Questions 322

UNIT 17
Contemporary Risk Measures 324
Probability as a Risk Measure 326
Interpreting Risk Measures 331
Standard Deviation and the Discounted Cash-Flow Model 338
Dealing With More Complex Cash-Flow Patterns 344
Summary 349
Recommended Reading 350
Review Questions 350
Discussion Questions 350

UNIT 18
Risk Management in a Portfolio Context 352

Modern Portfolio Theory and Risk Management 354
The Role of Real Estate in the Efficient Portfolio 358
Diversification Strategies for Real Estate 358
Summary 360
Recommended Reading 360
Internet References 361
Review Questions 361
Discussion Questions 361
Part Six: Case Problem 362

PART SEVEN

The Real Estate Investment Analysis Process Illustrated 363

UNIT 19
Investment Feasibility Analysis 364

The Nature of the Feasibility Question 366
Steps in the Feasibility Analysis Process 368
Preliminary Financial Feasibility 369
Format for a Feasibility Report 376
Summary 379
Recommended Reading 379
Internet References 380
Review Questions 380
Discussion Questions 380
Problems 381

UNIT 20
Subdivision Proposal Analysis 382

The Subdivision Process 384
Industrial Subdivision: A Case Study 386
Summary 395
Recommended Reading 395
Internet References 395
Review Questions 396
Discussion Questions 396

UNIT 21
Development and Rehabilitation   398

Overview of Real Estate Development   400
A Development Case Study   403
Rehabilitation   407
Commercial Rehabilitation: A Case Study   409
Summary   414
Recommended Reading   414
Internet References   415
Review Questions   415
Discussion Questions   415

UNIT 22
Industrial Property, Office Building, and Shopping Center Analysis   416

Industrial Building Investments   418
An Industrial Building Case Study   420
Office Building Investments   424
An Office Building Case Study   425
Shopping Center Investments   432
A Shopping Center Case Study   434
Summary   441
Recommended Reading   442
Internet References   442
Review Questions   442
Discussion Questions   443
Part Seven: Case Problem   444

PART EIGHT

Real Estate as a Security 447

UNIT 23
Real Estate Investment Trusts 448
REIT Regulation 450
REIT Management 451
REIT Assets 452
REITs as Investment Vehicles 452
REIT Mutual Funds 456
How REITs Are Evaluated 457
Sources of REIT Information 457
Summary 458
Recommended Reading 459
Internet References 459
Review Questions 460
Discussion Questions 460
Part Eight: Case Problem 461

APPENDIX A
Mathematics of Compounding and Discounting 463

APPENDIX B
Compounding and Discounting with Financial Calculators 485

APPENDIX C
Normal Distribution Table 493

APPENDIX D
A Closer Look at Like-Kind Exchanges 495

GLOSSARY 508
INDEX 534

DEDICATION

To our beautiful brides and children, whose love and understanding were felt and appreciated during the many hours of writing and rewriting.

ACKNOWLEDGMENTS

Previous editions of *Investment Analysis for Real Estate Decisions* were reviewed by Joseph Albert, James Madison University; Jaime R. Alvayay, California State University; Roger Cannaday, University of Illinois; Charles P. Edmonds III, Auburn University; Charles Floyd, University of Georgia; William Goolsby, Washington State University; Hans R. Isakson, University of Northern Iowa; Robert Mendelson, then of Southern Illinois University; Wade Ragas, University of New Orleans; James Vernor, Georgia State University; Leonard Zumpano, University of Alabama; Wayne Archer, University of Florida; Jerome Dasso, University of Oregon; Edwin E. Morgan, Baldwin-Wallace College; R. Keith Preddy, University of Tulsa; Linda Simms, then of DePaul University; Andy Do, San Diego State University; Paul R. Goebel, Texas Tech University; Samuel Goldman, New Mexico State University; Joseph J. Virostek, Duquesne University; Marcus T. Allen, Florida Gulf Coast University; Waldo Born, Eastern Illinois University; William J. Cahaney, Jefferson Community College; J. Douglas Timmons, Department of Economics and Finance, Middle Tennessee State University; William Voelker, University of Illinois; Robert Kaczmarek, ABR, Eclipse Realty, LLC; Deborah H. Long, EdD, DREI; Dr. Greg Smersh, Florida State University; H. Shelton Weeks, Florida Gulf Coast University, and Mark Sunderman, The University of Memphis. Additional consultation was provided by Victor Abraham, University of California at Los Angeles; Fred A. Forgey, University of Texas at Austin; Jonathan C. Keefe, Boston University; Michael J. Murray, Winona State University; Ronald C. Rogers, University of South Carolina; and Jeffrey J. Rymazewski, School of Business Administration, University of Wisconsin, Milwaukee. (Note: All professional and school designations are current as of the time of the review.)

The authors would also like to thank Professor Chris Manning, Loyola Marymount University for his valuable input and suggestions.

ABOUT THE AUTHORS

Bennie D. Waller, PhD, is a professor of Finance and Real Estate at Longwood University in Farmville, Virginia. He is also the Director for Center for Financial Responsibility. Waller earned his undergraduate degree from Longwood University, his MBA from the University of North Carolina-Wilmington, and doctoral degrees in Finance and Information Systems from the University of Mississippi. At Longwood, he has created a thriving undergraduate and graduate real estate program that uniquely allows opportunities for student research. Waller's research focus is on real estate brokerage, housing externality issues and valuation. Dr. Waller consults on such issues as principal/agent conflict, property valuation, and housing externality issues. He has published numerous articles in the top real estate journals, including the *Journal of Real Estate Research* and *Journal of Real Estate Finance and Economics, Journal of Housing Economics*, and *Real Estate Economics*.

Phillip T. Kolbe, PhD, is an author, teacher, and consultant. He was the Director of Graduate Studies in Real Estate at the University of Memphis, one of the few schools in the country to offer a master's degree in real estate. He has taught for more than 30 years, starting at the University of Arizona while he was the president of a real estate research corporation and CEO of a real estate market research firm. Kolbe has twice received the University of Memphis's Distinguished Teaching Award and was the first recipient of the Thomas W. Briggs Foundation Excellence in Teaching Award. In total, he has received 10 teaching awards during his academic career. He serves as a consultant to a wide variety of real estate companies and has published numerous articles and several books on real estate and investing. Kolbe also teaches companies, "Executive Leadership Lessons from General Ulysses S. Grant," in which he portrays the Civil War general. His website is *www.usgrantleadership.com*.

Gaylon E. Greer, MAI, PhD, is a real estate consultant, writer, and educator. He holds the MAI designation from the Appraisal Institute, is a Certified General Appraiser in Tennessee, and has served on that state's appraiser regulatory commission. Greer has written several books related to real estate, contributes regularly to professional journals, and is active in the American Real Estate Society and other professional organizations. Greer lectures nationwide to investors and professional practitioners. He resigned from the Morris S. Fogelman Chair of Excellence in Real Estate at the University of Memphis to devote full time to writing and consulting.

PREFACE

The three most important things in real estate are still location, location, location, but the industry is going through many transformations including changes in the tax code brought about by the 2018 Tax Cuts and Jobs Act (TCJA). The ninth edition of this text reflects such changes. This edition of *Investment Analysis for Real Estate Decisions* also takes into account the feedback of the many students and professors who have used earlier versions. We took the given advice on how to improve the text and incorporated it when appropriate. However, we have been careful not to fix what isn't broken. The ninth edition retains the structure, format, and tone that proved comfortable to users of earlier editions. The general organization has been retained: eight parts, with each part followed by case problems designed to illustrate the operation of principles explained in that part. The case problems, structured to reflect situations that occur in the real world of real estate, are coordinated so that a continuing case runs throughout the text. Yet the cases are still designed so that they can be used individually. An answer key for textbook questions is provided online.

KEY CHANGES IN THE NINTH EDITION

The most important change in this edition is the updating of material reflecting the Tax Cuts and Jobs Act. Current real estate market data were incorporated throughout. The increased production of real estate research, including that in several new real estate journals, is reflected in the recommended readings at the end of each unit. We have continued to expand the internet references because of its growing relevance and ease of use. Problems, examples, and review questions have been updated to reflect new tax laws. The use of calculator boxes was expanded where applicable to illustrate the use of financial calculators in problems. The keystrokes illustrated are those for the most common financial calculators, such as the HP-12C, HP-10B II, and HP-17BII, from Hewlett-Packard; the BA-II Plus and BA-35, from Texas Instruments; and the EL-733A and EL-1071S, from Sharp.

Student Spreadsheet Software

To facilitate the use of computerized spreadsheets in solving the end-of-part case problems, a spreadsheet template is available to all schools using this text via Dearborn's Instructor Resources website at *www.dearborn.com*. To access these files, please go to the instructor resources section there and click on *Investment Analysis for Real*

Estate Decisions, Ninth Edition. An icon appears in the margin next to those case problems with which the student spreadsheet software can be used.

Rational Organization

To guide students through the material, each of the text's eight parts begins with a brief explanation of purpose. Each part covers a subject that is fundamental to informed investment decision making:

- Part One sets the stage by explaining fundamental terms and concepts used throughout the text. It describes a widely accepted analytical framework and introduces relevant basic economic ideas.
- Part Two emphasizes the essential nature of market research, introduces key marketing concepts, and shows how market research is used to estimate future benefits from ownership.
- Part Three introduces the environment of mortgage lending, demonstrates the likely consequences of using borrowed money, and discusses commonly used credit instruments.
- Part Four explains relevant income tax provisions.
- Part Five covers ratio analysis and discounted cash-flow analysis and shows how to apply modern decision criteria to investment analysis.
- Part Six introduces traditional and modern risk analysis. The units provide for choice in one's degree of immersion in this complex yet essential subject.
- Part Seven illustrates the use of discounted cash-flow analysis to make investment decisions regarding several major categories of real estate.
- Part Eight addresses the growing dimension of real estate as a security.

A Book of Many Teaching Paths

Investment Analysis for Real Estate Decisions has been extensively adopted for both graduate and undergraduate use. While crafting the ninth edition, we kept that dual role in mind. We also communicated with professors who use the text in a variety of real estate courses. As a consequence, *Investment Analysis for Real Estate Decisions* continues to accommodate many teaching paths. Instructors who stress the discipline's theoretical aspects can omit Parts Six and Seven. Those who prefer to emphasize practical applications can omit Units 2, 3, 14, 17, and 18. Many schools offer a course that combines real estate investment and finance. Dearborn offers a package with both *Investment Analysis for Real Estate Decisions* and *Real Estate Finance.* The instructor's manual maps several alternative paths and provides additional suggestions for using the book.

PART ONE

Fundamental Issues in Real Estate Investment Analysis

When real estate assets are considered for investors' portfolios, these investors face a bewildering collection of alternatives. They must select from among countless combinations of opportunities that differ not only in the amount and timing of expected investment benefits but also in the degree of confidence with which investors hold their expectations.

Rational decision making under such circumstances challenges even the most educated and experienced investment analysts. Approaches range from impulsive judgments based on little more than intuition or "hot tips" to carefully calculated decisions backed by research and sophisticated analysis. These first three units lay the groundwork for the latter approach. The nature of the investment decision, the dynamic market environment in which decisions must be made, and basic considerations incorporated into rational investment analysis are all addressed in Part One.

UNIT 1

The Real Estate Investment Decision

UNIT PREVIEW

An attorney purchases a $200,000 interest in a condominium on the beach; a doctor puts $10,000 into a real estate investment trust (REIT); a real estate broker buys an $800,000 apartment building; a manufacturing firm invests millions in a new plant; the U.S. government spends billions to create a dam and reservoir system. All have made real estate investment decisions. As diverse as they appear, all these decisions have a common element: each requires giving up something now in expectation of future benefits. The sacrifice is immediate and certain; rewards will be received in the future, if at all.

The situation is compounded because investors generally have more opportunities than they have resources. They must choose, and always with incomplete information. The only way to avoid getting lost in a maddening maze of alternatives is to rank them by their probable contribution to investment objectives, subject to liquidity constraints and risk tolerance.

INVESTMENT ANALYSIS: ART AND SCIENCE

Real estate investment analysis thought has consistently lagged behind mainstream finance and investment thought. It wasn't until the late 1960s and early 1970s that analytical tools and techniques pioneered by economists and corporate financial analysts began to appear in real estate literature. Writing for the Appraisal Journal in 1970, Richard Ratcliff and Bernhard Schwab decried the virtual absence from real estate appraisal and investment literature terms such as *probability*, *utility function*, and *time value of money*, which were used routinely by investment decision theorists.[1]

More recently, modern decision theory has been imbedded into traditional real estate analysis, and the equity valuation technique explained in later units has been widely adopted. Computerized modeling to forecast after-tax cash flows and explore the impact of variance from expected operating results or changes in the operating environment (e.g., altered tax law, new government regulations, or shifts in the economic climate) are now commonplace.

State-of-the-art investment analysis treats real estate as a capital asset desired for the stream of benefits it generates. In this context, real estate becomes a special case of modern capital budgeting. Its analysis can use discounted cash-flow techniques and incorporate risk adjustments.

WHO ARE REAL ESTATE INVESTORS?

Personal success stories and how-to-books have conditioned us to think of real estate investment as the province of individual investors. Yet, real estate has become a major asset in the portfolios of many institutions, and foreign investors have found U.S. real estate equities to be increasingly attractive.

Institutional Investors

Real estate investment trusts and pension funds have become major investors in real estate equities. This is due in large part to changes in federal law: a 1961 Internal Revenue Code revision exempted distributed REIT earnings from taxation at the corporate level. Subsequent tax law changes liberalized REIT operating rules: the Employee Retirement Income Security Act of 1974 (ERISA) directed pension fund managers to diversify their portfolios and thus encouraged them to move more aggressively into real estate equities.

---

1 Richard U. Ratcliff and Bernhard Schwab, "Contemporary Decision Theory and Real Estate Investment," *Appraisal Journal* (April 1970), reprinted in *Readings in Real Estate Investment Analysis*, vol. 1 (Cambridge, Mass.: Ballinger Pub. Co., 1977).

Pension funds

Because of their steady and predictable streams of cash flow, pension funds are ideal real estate investors. Yet, their investment in real estate was minor until the 1970s. They moved in aggressively, however, when ERISA mandated more portfolio diversification. After retreating somewhat following market reverses of the late 1980s, they were back in force by the mid-1990s. In 2016, aggregate pension fund capital in real estate exceeded $3.1 trillion.[2] Because real estate represents just over 6% of total pension funds' assets, there is considerable room for growth for real estate in pension funds.[3]

Real estate investment trusts

In 2016, the National Association of Real Estate Investment Trusts reported that 184 member REITs that invest primarily in real estate equities had a market capitalization (aggregate market value of all shares) of approximately $960 billion.[4] Many specialize in certain types of real estate, such as apartments, shopping centers, or office or industrial buildings. Others prefer to hold diversified portfolios. Figure 1.1 shows the capitalization of real estate equity investments by REITs in 2018, by type of property held.

FIGURE 1.1: REIT Property Capitalization in 2012 by Property Type

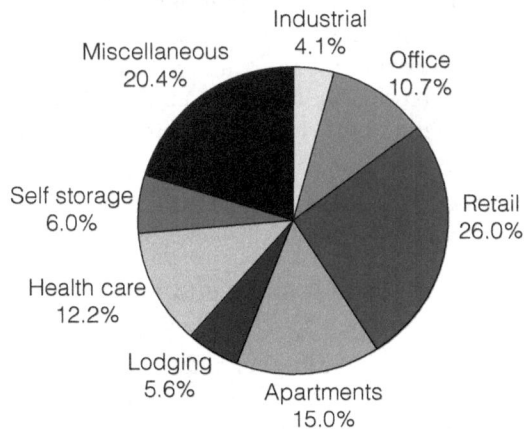

Source: Based on data from National Association of Real Estate Investment Trusts

---

2   Farhaz Miah, "US Public Pension Funds Investing in Real Estate," May 2, 2012, Prequin, *www.preqin.com/blog/101/5129/us-public-pension-real-estate*.
3   Ibid.
4   National Association of Real Estate Investment Trusts, "Historical REIT Industry Market Capitalization: 1972–2017," *www.reit.com/DataAndResearch/US-REIT-Industry-MarketCap.aspx*.

Foreign Participation in U.S. Real Estate Markets

Foreigners directly own a very small percentage of U.S. real estate—about 10% of its dollar value in 2016, according to one estimate.[5] The impact of these non-native property owners is distorted by disproportionate representation in certain parts of the country and in specific types of property. For example, the National Association of Realtors® (NAR) reports that in 2017, three states accounted for 50% of international sales—Florida, California, and Texas. Chinese investors remain as the top international investor followed by Canada, the United Kingdom, Mexico, and India. Government studies, though inconclusive, indicate that foreign direct investment surged during the early 1980s, then stabilized by the middle of that decade but—at least through 1987— remained high by historical standards.[6] Real estate equities fell into widespread disfavor among foreign investors in the late 1980s, but the market heated up again in the early 1990s and at the beginning of this century. The percentage of real estate investments held by foreign interests more than doubled from 4% in 2001 to 8.9% in 2012.

The influence of exchange rates

When shifts in foreign exchange rates make dollars relatively less expensive to holders of a foreign currency, as they have recently, U.S. real estate also becomes less costly to acquire. Suppose, for example, the euro sells for $1.23 on the foreign exchange market; a $9 million office building in Chicago will cost 7.32 million euros. If this and a comparable building in Paris generate the same operating income and have the same appreciation potential, investors might be indifferent between them. But suppose the euro climbs in value so that it trades at $1.50. Now, the $9 million Chicago property costs only 6 million euros, while the comparable building in Paris still costs 7.32 million euros; holders of euros will be inclined to invest in the United States.

The currency of a country tends to appreciate on foreign exchange markets when that country's economic and political prospects appear particularly sound. Thus, prosperity and political stability create a lure for foreign investors.

The relevance of relative interest rates

When interest rates in a country are higher than those in the country with whom one is trading, the higher rates tend to depress real estate prices, while lower rates elsewhere tend to inflate property prices there. The disparity makes real estate in the high-interest-rate country relatively more attractive.

Factors other than relative cost can influence the decision to invest in foreign real estate. Due to relative economic conditions, foreign real estate may offer the prospect of greater returns relative to risk, or it might reduce overall portfolio risk. Furthermore, investors might consider foreign real estate as a way to hedge against political risk.

---

5 Nick Timiraos, "Foreigners Snap Up Properties in the U.S.," *The Wall Street Journal,* 12 June 2012, *http://online.wsj.com/article/SB10001424052702303901504577460550067846454.html.*

6 U.S. Department of Commerce, *op. cit.*, various issues.

WHY INVEST IN REAL ESTATE?

Real estate investors, either directly or indirectly, purchase rights to a stream of future cash flows that are expected to be generated by the real estate. The cash flows might come from rental income, from using the property as loan collateral, from cash savings through offsetting otherwise taxable income with tax-deductible losses from the real property interest, or from net profits upon resale of the property interest.

The price an investor is prepared to pay for a defined property interest depends in part on the amount and the timing of these anticipated cash flows; how much will be received, and when? It depends also on the degree of confidence with which expectations are held and the investor's tolerance for bearing risk. The final variable is the attractiveness of alternative investment opportunities.

Virtually any investment goal can be accommodated with a position in real estate. Speculators can deal in real estate futures (by buying and selling purchase options); developers can reduce risk exposure by using standby loan commitments or taking a position in interest-rate futures; investors can buy fixed-income assets such as mortgage loans or net-leased properties. Real estate may be even more attractive when approached not as a simple investment, but rather as a business opportunity.

In short, the possibilities are constrained primarily by limits on investors' ability to conceive of alternatives. In Figure 1.2, investors are categorized in four ways: by the nature of their claims (*debt* or *equity*) and according to their degree of involvement in operations (*passive* or *active*).

FIGURE 1.2: Variety in Real Estate Investments

	Debt	**Equity**

Active	Loan origination
	    Construction lending
	    Permanent loans
	Loan purchases on secondary mortgage market
		Direct ownership of rental property; purchase or development

Passive	Pass-through certificates
	Mortgage real estate investment trust
	Mortgage-backed securities
	    Residential
	    Commercial
		Shares in real estate corporation
		Limited partnership shares
		Equity real estate investment trust

Passive and Active Investors

Many investors acquire direct title to real estate in which they invest, and they either oversee its operation themselves or hire professional property management firms to handle day-to-day operations. In Figure 1.2, they are characterized as *active investors*. Their key distinguishing characteristic is that they make decisions—selecting on-site management personnel, negotiating maintenance contracts, making rental rate decisions, approving leases, and so forth—that directly affect operating results.

In contrast, *passive investors* make no operating decisions. They turn their wealth over to professional asset managers, who in turn acquire interests in real estate, or they acquire shares in corporations, partnerships, or trusts that hold extensive real property interests. In any event, their decisions have little direct impact on the outcome of real estate operations.

Investment in Equity and Debt

Also in Figure 1.2, distinctions are made between investment in real assets, such as land and buildings, and in real estate–related financial assets, such as mortgage-backed promissory notes. Both involve exchanges of certain and immediate assets for uncertain expectations of future gain, but expectations regarding yield and risk may differ radically.

Consider a development such as an office building or an apartment complex. The institution or individual that buys the real property interest is an *equity investor*. Usually, though, most of the purchase money comes from a mortgage lender: a *debt investor*. Lenders often sell their mortgage-secured promissory notes to still other investors who prefer debt to equity positions.

The benefits to equity investors are less predictable than those to holders of debt because an equity investor gets no cash until the debt holder's periodic claims to payment on the promissory note are satisfied. Equity investors also reap the consequences of increases or decreases in property value.

HOW HAVE REAL ESTATE INVESTMENTS PERFORMED?

Returns on real estate investments and those on stocks, bonds, or other assets cannot be reliably compared because the yield data for real estate are sparse and contradictory. Unlike stock and bond markets, where minute-by-minute trading data generate enough information to crash a computer, real estate yield indices typically are computed using quarterly appraisal estimates. This causes a smoothing of trend indicators and makes real estate yields seem less volatile than they might with more frequent and more reliable information about value fluctuations. Yet comparisons, flawed as they are, are essential for rational portfolio decisions.

Surging interest in real estate ownership by institutional investors and the phenomenal growth in public offerings by REITs, described earlier, have contributed immensely to our knowledge about comparative yields. Research results, however, are heavily influenced by the period from which data are drawn.

Real estate became a darling of pension funds during the 1970s. An offspring of this relationship, the commingled real estate fund (CREF) acquires real estate and monitors its operation on behalf of institutional investors. CREFs have become treasure troves of information about real estate investment performance.

William Brueggeman, A. H. Chen, and T. G. Thibodeau analyzed asset performance data from two CREFs from 1972 through 1983. They broke the data, which at the time accounted for about 25% of all CREF assets, into various subperiods to see whether comparative results varied significantly through time. They found that on a risk-adjusted basis, real estate outperformed the Standard & Poor's index of 500 stocks and the Ibbotson Associates bond index for the entire period and for each subperiod. The real estate portfolio's superior performance differed considerably, however, among subperiods.[7]

For the entire period, and for the subperiod from 1972 through 1977, the researchers concluded that the CREF portfolio had higher yields than those of the Standard & Poor's 500 stock index, before and after adjusting for risk. For 1978 through 1983, average yields on the Standard & Poor's index exceeded the CREF yields by a narrow margin before adjusting for risk. The real estate portfolios were less risky, however, and after adjusting for relative risk the advantage shifted back to the CREF portfolio.

Other studies show conflicting results. Michael Giliberto compared total returns for an index of more than 1,200 large REITs with Standard & Poor's 500 stock index for 1978 through 1989 and found that the advantage had shifted decisively to common stocks.[8] In a 1984 analysis of 17 previous comparative yield studies, Robert Zerbst and Barbara Cambon concluded that real estate assets have shown returns roughly similar to common stocks since 1950, but they also found that real estate tends to outperform stocks during periods of inflation.[9] A study of data from 16 countries suggests that real estate is a good long-term hedge against inflation and that real estate values and rents are significantly related to stock returns.[10] F. Neil Myer and James Webb looked at returns to REITs and concluded that returns are more closely related to those on common stocks and closed-end mutual funds than they are to returns on unsecuritized real estate.[11] A more recent study, by Jim Clayton and Greg MacKinnon, drew similar

---

[7] William Brueggeman, A. H. Chen, and T. G. Thibodeau, "Real Estate Funds: Performance and Portfolio Considerations," *AREUEA Journal* 12, no. 3 (1994): 333–54.

[8] S. Michael Giliberto, "Equity Real Estate Investment Trusts and Real Estate Returns," *The Journal of Real Estate Research* 5, no. 2 (Summer 1990): 259–63.

[9] Robert H. Zerbst and Barbara Cambon, "Real Estate: Historical Returns and Risk," *The Journal of Portfolio Management* (Spring 1984): 5–20.

[10] Daniel C. Quan and Sheridan Titman, "Do Real Estate Prices and Stock Prices Move Together? An International Analysis," *Real Estate Economics* 27, no. 2 (1999): 183–207.

[11] F. Neil Myer and James R. Webb, "Return Properties of Equity REITs, Common Stock, and Commercial Real Estate: A Comparison," *Journal of Real Estate Research* 8, no. 1 (1993): 87–106.

conclusions but indicated that the relationship has changed over time. REIT returns are less related to returns on large capitalization stocks than they were in earlier years and more closely correspond to returns on small capitalization stocks.[12]

CONCEPTS AND DEFINITIONS

The investment perspective requires a slightly different view of real estate from the one to which many are accustomed. An investor must develop a perception of the property's worth as a portfolio asset and compare this with an estimate of the probable price at which the real estate can be acquired. Neither of these values can be determined with certainty. Investors must work with ranges within which they expect the values to lie. This brings us to three key definitions: most probable selling price, investment value, and transaction range.

Investment Value

A property's *investment value* is its worth to a specific owner. Investment value is unique to the individual and need not be closely related to most probable selling price. It is the value today, to the specific investor, of anticipated future benefits of ownership. It reflects the investor's assumptions about the asset's future ability to produce revenue, about the likely holding period, selling price, tax consequences, available financing, and all other factors that affect net benefits of ownership. Because there will not be precise agreement on all these factors or on the appropriate adjustment for waiting and for uncertainty, everyone's investment value is inevitably unique.

Most Probable Selling Price

The most likely amount at which a property will sell, given the prevailing market conditions and available financing arrangements, is commonly called *most probable selling price*. This is not to be confused with *market value,* which is defined by appraisers as the most probable price when a property is exposed to the market under specific, rigidly prescribed conditions that often do not prevail in the marketplace.

Transaction Range

The price range within which a transaction can occur and leave both the buyer and the seller better off than before is the *transaction range*. The present owner's investment value sets the lower end of the range; the prospective buyer's sets the upper end. The actual transaction price will fall somewhere between these extremes.

---

12 Jim Clayton and Greg MacKinnon, "The Time-Varying Nature of the Link Between REIT, Real Estate, and Financial Asset Returns," *Journal of Real Estate Portfolio Management* 7, no. 1 (2001): 43–54.

The current owner (prospective seller) establishes a minimum acceptable price based on assumptions about future benefits of continued ownership. This is shown as V_s in Figure 1.3. To be motivated to sell, the owner must conclude that the most probable selling price (shown as V_p in Figure 1.3) is greater than investment value.

FIGURE 1.3: Value Relationships—Seller's Perspective

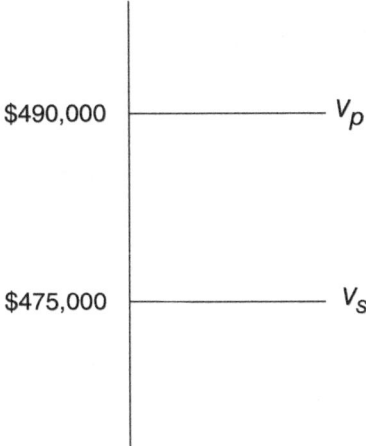

As we have observed, the property also has an investment value from the prospective buyer's point of view. That value, too, is based on assumptions about future benefits of ownership. It is the maximum amount the prospective buyer is justified in paying for the property. This relationship is illustrated in Figure 1.4. To be motivated to buy, the prospective buyer must conclude that investment value (V_b in figure 1.4) is greater than the most probable selling price, V_p.

FIGURE 1.4: Value Relationships—Buyer's Perspective

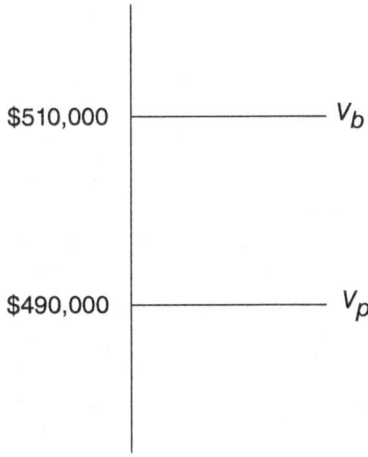

Within the range of possible prices set by the owner's and the prospective buyer's investment values (net of transaction costs), both will gain by getting together. Owners will not take less than a property's investment value to them, and buyers will not pay more than their investment value. This creates a transaction range, as shown in Figure 1.5. The exact price within this range will depend upon the parties' relative bargaining skills.

FIGURE 1.5: Value Relationships—Transaction Range

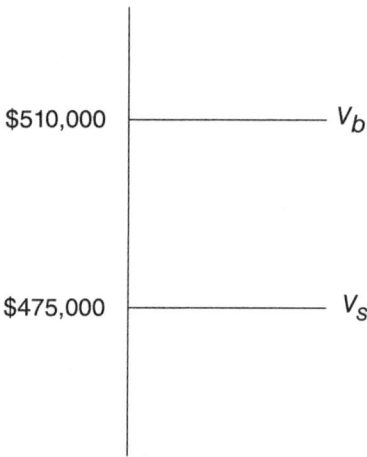

In Figures 1.3 through 1.5, it is assumed that buyer and seller agree on the most probable price, but that need not be the case. For a transaction to be possible, all that is needed is a transaction range—a difference between buyer's and seller's investment values—sufficient to absorb transaction costs.

Market Value

An early step in lender analysis is an appraisal of a property to determine current market value: the most probable price at which the property would sell for in a competitive market as of the date of the appraisal given exposure to the market for a reasonable time before that date. The estimate assumes reasonably informed parties acting in their own individual best interest and with neither subject to undue influence.

An analyst usually starts by analyzing the economic environment of the property being appraised. A typical first step is observations about the relationship between the national or regional economy and that of the city or community in which the property is located. The analysis proceeds from the wider or more general to the narrow and more specific—from the general economy to the neighborhood. Although this part of an appraisal report is often skipped by the mortgage loan analysis, it should, in fact, be studied intensely. Because the property is immovable, its value is acutely influenced by favorable or unfavorable neighborhood trends.

The use of a site will be concerned with convenience and accessibility. Neighborhood issues (e.g., the view from the property and unfavorable exposure) that can detract from market value might also be a concern. Locations near objectionable or incompatible uses often have a depressing impact on desirability and thus, on value. Examples include noise from traffic or activity at other sites, smoke, odors, congestion or a more recent concern of sex offenders and/or drug rehab facilities. Brastow, Waller, and Wentland (2014, 2018) find that sex offenders living near the subject property have a negative impact on the property's selling price as well as an extended marketing duration.[13,14,15] Similarly, Laroche, Waller, and Wentland (2014) find that residential rehabilitation centers located in residential neighborhoods also have a detrimental effect on neighboring properties which are being marketed.

The focus of the physical basis of market value should be on the functional efficiency of the layout, the durability of the construction, and the structure's aesthetic appeal.

INVESTMENT VALUE: AN OVERVIEW

Investment value (the most a would-be seller is justified in taking for a property or the maximum a prospective buyer is justified in paying) is at best difficult to estimate, requiring analysis of a wide range of disparate yet interwoven elements. The chore is greatly simplified when reduced to a system. This book presents such a system, sometimes called a *decision process*, which is widely used for evaluating real estate investment proposals.

This process is not unique to real estate. In spite of its complexity, real estate investment analysis is not fundamentally different from other investment decision making. Whatever the exact nature of the investment vehicle, for those schooled in modern financial analysis, the decision process does not vary.

Steps in the Investment Decision Process

1. *Estimate the stream of expected benefits.* Investment assets are desired only for the benefits that ownership is expected to bestow. Investors, in effect, purchase a set of assumptions about the property's ability to produce income over the proposed ownership period.

2. *Adjust for timing differences among expected streams of benefits flowing from investment alternatives.* As a rule, the sooner benefits are expected to be received, the more highly valued they are by investors.

---

13 Wentland, Scott, Bennie Waller, and Raymond Brastow. "Estimating the effect of crime risk on property values and time on market: Evidence from Megan's law in Virginia." *Real Estate Economics* 42.1 (2014): 223-251.
14 Dynamic Spatial Externalities and Real Estate Liquidity, Ray Brastow, Bennie D. Waller, and Scott Wentland. *Journal of Real Estate Research*, forthcoming
15 Laroche, Waller, and Wentland (2014) article, "Not in My Backyard: The Effect of Substance Abuse Treatment Centers on Property Values." Claire LaRoche, Scott Wentland and Bennie D. Waller. *Journal of Sustainable Real Estate*, 2014, 6:1, 63–92.

3. *Adjust for differences in perceived risk associated with the alternatives.* Just as investors are not indifferent to the timing of expected benefits, neither are they indifferent to the degree of certainty with which expectations are held.

4. *Rank alternatives according to the relative desirability of perceived risk-return combinations they embody.* Attitudes toward risk differ, but rational investors seek financial return as a reward for bearing the risk. Investors demand greater expected returns for higher risk. Most investors set a limit at which they will not shoulder additional risk, no matter what the potential return.

The investment analysis system explained in this book represents an application of this four-step process. It is an adaptation of capital budgeting techniques long used among corporate financial analysts. Three concerns—amount of benefit, and the timing and certainty of their receipt—determine the relative value of all investment alternatives.

The Value of the Benefit Stream

The benefits expected to be received in the far distant future add less to a property's investment value than do those whose anticipated receipt is more imminent. In general, the further in the future expected receipts lie, the less is their value today. The exact nature of the trade-off will differ among investors, depending on each individual's time preference for money.

Financial analysts have long recognized that the value of a business enterprise is the sum of the value of the outstanding debt plus the value of the equity. Real estate valuation theory also recognizes value of an investment property as the sum of the debt and equity positions. This is evidenced in appraisal techniques in which market value is estimated by capitalizing the property's expected net operating income (NOI) by the weighted average cost of debt and equity capital.

Investment value can, therefore, be expressed as the present value of the equity position plus the present value of the debt position. This is illustrated in Figure 1.6, which starts with the property's NOI: operating revenue minus operating expenses (these terms are defined and illustrated in Part Two). Holders of mortgage-secured debt have a senior claim on the property's NOI; their portion—annual debt service—flows down the left side of Figure 1.6. The remainder accrues to equity investors, but part of this will be siphoned off as income taxes. The residual is the after-tax cash flow to the equity investors, as shown on the right side of Figure 1.6. The bottom of the diagram illustrates the transformation of these expected cash flows into lump-sum equivalents: the investment value of each position.

The present value of the debt position is the amount of available mortgage financing or (in the case of present owners' investment values) the outstanding mortgage loan balance. Present value of the equity position is the value today of the anticipated after-tax cash flow during a prospective ownership period and of the anticipated proceeds from disposal. Investment value can be expressed algebraically as follows:

$$PV_e = \sum_{i=1}^{n} \frac{CF_i}{(1+r)^i} + \frac{CF_d}{(1+r)^n}$$

$$PV_i = PV_d + PV_e$$

where:

PV_i = Present value of total investment position

PV_e = Present value of the equity position

PV_d = Present value of the debt position

CF_i = After-tax cash flows to the equity investor occurring in year i (i = 1, 2, 3 . . . n)

CF_d = After-tax cash flow to the equity investor from property disposal at the end of year n

r = Discount rate

FIGURE 1.6: Cash-Flow Distribution and Value Relationships

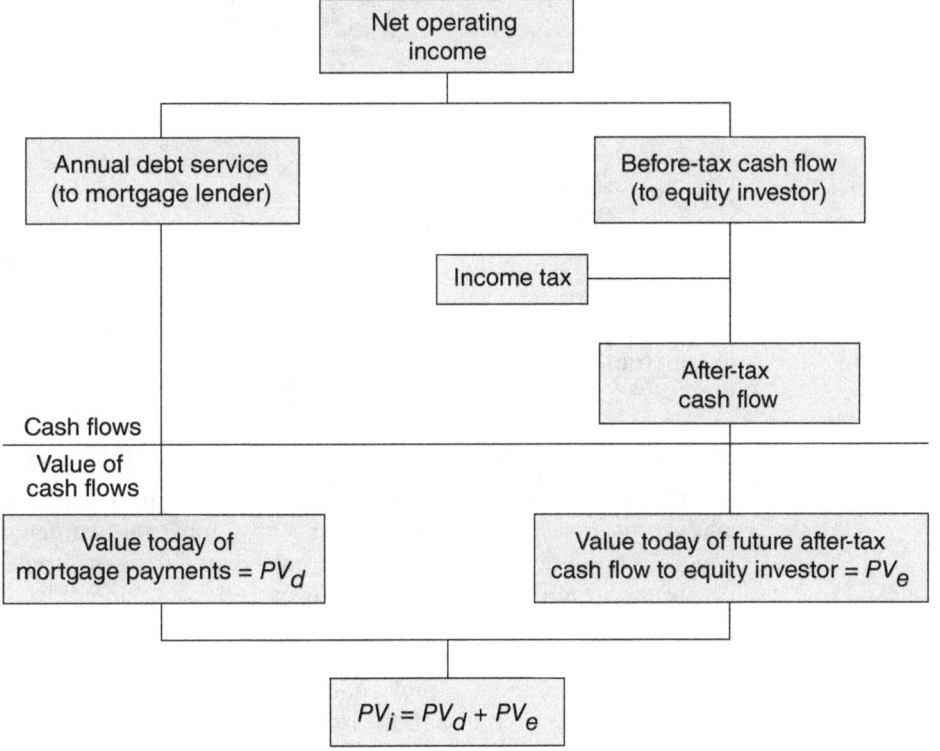

Estimating present value of the equity position requires assumptions about income, operating expenses, amount and terms of financing, sales price, and income tax. It also depends on the investor's opportunity cost of capital (the yield available on equally risky alternative opportunities).

To illustrate, consider an investment proposal for an apartment complex. A prospective investor notes that the property is expected to generate $1,265,700 of NOI the first year (don't worry about how the information is gathered, we will address that in later units) and is subject to a mortgage loan that requires annual payments (debt service) of $803,000. The remaining $462,700 of NOI will accrue to the equity investor, but part of it will be diverted to pay income taxes, which are estimated to be $123,100 for the first year. This leaves an estimated $339,600 in after-tax cash flow for the equity investor. Figure 1.7 replicates a portion of Figure 1.6, but it applies only to the first year, and cash-flow estimates have been entered in the boxes.

FIGURE 1.7: First-Year Cash Flows and Value Relationships

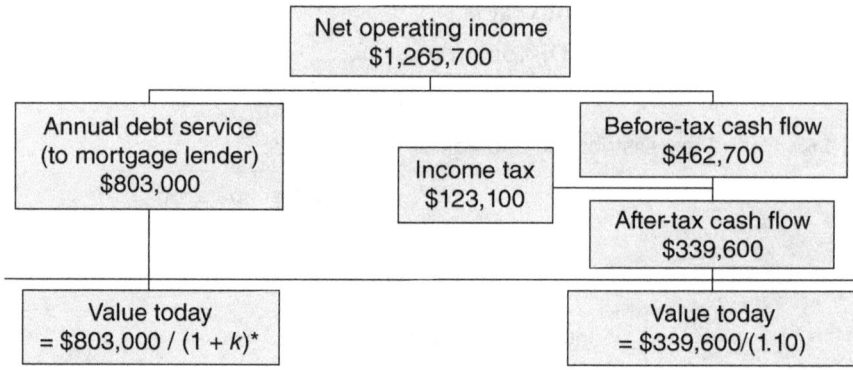

*k = lender's rate of return

Numbers below the line on Figure 1.7, the value of the cash flows, will depend on the appropriate discount rate and the amount of time the investor must wait to receive the cash. (Unit 13 explains discounted cash-flow analysis in greater detail.) If the appropriate discount rate for this investor is 10%, the value of the first year's cash flow to the equity investor will be $339,600 / 1.10, as shown in the bottom-right box of Figure 1.7, or $308,727. The cash flows to the lender are discounted at the lender's expected rate of return and would be placed in the bottom-left box of Figure 1.7.

Of course, cash is expected to continue flowing beyond the first year. To properly analyze an investment proposal, cash flow must be estimated for every year of the expected holding period and for the anticipated year of property disposal. Figure 1.8 illustrates a multiple-year forecast of cash flows to an equity investor who expects to hold the apartment complex for six years. Derivation of these numbers is explained in later units, and the numbers are used to further illustrate how investment decisions are made. For the moment, simply note the relationship between the numbers in the first column of Figure 1.8 and those in Figure 1.7. Also note that borrowing more money would increase the debt-service component and thereby reduce the expected after-tax cash flow to the equity investor. However, it would also reduce the amount of equity capital that must be invested.

Let us revisit our equation for determining the present value of the equity position, using the bottom line of Figure 1.8 for annual after-tax cash flow from operations. Assume further that the investor expects to sell near the end of the sixth year and to receive $7,828,100 in after-tax cash flow from the sale. (Unit 11 explains how to estimate the tax consequences of selling.) With these numbers, and continuing our assumption that 10% is the appropriate discount rate for the equity investor, our equation for determining the present value of the equity position becomes:

$$PV_e = \sum_{i=1}^{n} \frac{CF_i}{(1+r)^i} + \frac{CF_d}{(1+r)^n}$$

$$\frac{260,300}{(1+0.10)^1} + \frac{364,200}{(1+0.10)^2} + \frac{414,500}{(1+0.10)^3} + \frac{368,600}{(1+0.10)^4} + \frac{398,600}{(1+0.10)^5} + \frac{422,800}{(1+0.10)^6} + \frac{7,828,100}{(1+0.10)^6}$$

$$= \$236,636 + \$300,992 + \$311,420 + \$251,554 + \$247,499 + \$238,660 + \$4,418,758$$

$$= \$6,005,519$$

FIGURE 1.8: Projected After-Tax Cash-Flow Operations: Maegan's Magic Manor Apartments*

	Year 1	Year 2	Year 3	Year 4	Year 5	Year 6
Potential gross rent	$2,346,100	$2,463,400	$2,586,600	$2,677,100	$2,770,800	$2,867,800
Less: Vacancy allowance	176,000	98,500	103,500	160,600	166,200	172,100
	$2,170,100	$2,364,900	$2,483,100	$2,516,500	$2,604,600	$2,695,700
Add: Other income	102,000	111,200	116,700	118,300	122,400	126,700
Effective gross income	$2,272,100	$2,476,100	$2,599,800	$2,634,800	$2,727,000	$2,822,400
Less: Operating expenses						
Management fee	113,600	123,800	130,000	131,700	136,400	141,100
Salary expense	204,000	211,100	218,500	226,200	234,100	242,300
Utilities	109,000	112,800	116,800	120,900	125,100	129,500
Insurance	36,700	38,000	39,300	40,700	42,100	43,600
Supplies	21,700	22,500	23,300	24,100	24,900	25,800
Advertising, legal, misc.	33,100	34,300	35,500	36,700	38,000	39,300
Maintenance, repairs, and replacement	188,300	194,900	201,700	208,800	216,100	223,700
Property taxes	300,000	300,000	300,000	375,000	375,000	375,000
Total expenses	$1,006,400	$1,037,400	$1,065,100	$1,164,100	$1,191,200	$1,220,300
Net operating income	$1,265,700	$1,438,700	$1,534,700	$1,470,700	$1,535,300	$1,602,100
Less: Interest expense	752,700	736,100	718,000	698,500	677,300	654,400
Depreciation	383,300	400,000	400,000	400,000	400,000	383,300
Taxable income (loss)	$129,700	$302,600	$416,700	$372,200	$458,000	$564,400
Times: Marginal tax rate	0.40	0.40	0.40	0.40	0.40	0.40
Income tax (tax savings)	$51,900	$121,000	$166,700	$148,900	$183,200	$225,800
Net operating income	$1,265,700	$1,438,700	$1,534,700	$1,470,700	$1,535,300	$1,602,100
Less: Debt service	953,500	953,500	953,500	953,500	953,500	953,500
Before-tax cash flow	$312,200	$485,200	$581,200	$517,200	$581,800	$648,600
Less: Income taxes	51,900	121,000	166,700	148,900	183,200	225,800
After-tax cash flow	$260,300	$364,200	$414,500	$368,300	$398,600	$422,800

*All numbers have been rounded to the nearest $100.

> **CALCULATOR APPLICATIONS**
>
> $FV = 260{,}300$
> $n = 1$
> $i = 10$
>
> ***Solve for present value:***
>
> $PV = 236{,}636$
> Continue for each year
> Change *n* and *FV* for each year

If a prospective purchaser places a higher investment value on a property than the acquisition cost, buying it will increase the buyer's net worth. In like manner, selling a property that has a higher market value than its investment value enhances the seller's total wealth position.

Alternative investment strategies regarding a specific property can also be evaluated using the investment value model. Holding financing constant, the investor varies other investment criteria (such as alternative income tax treatments, as discussed in Part Four, or proposed remodeling or rehabilitation) and notes the impact on investment value. Financing or refinancing alternatives can be evaluated by holding all other factors constant and determining the effect of each financing plan on the value of the equity position. The investor accepts the alternative that produces the highest value of equity per dollar of required equity investment, provided each alternative is perceived as entailing equal risk.

We all interpret information according to our own frames of reference, which result from our unique history. For this reason, individuals reviewing the same information will usually draw different conclusions. There will likely be disagreement about the future stream of rental revenue and operating expenses associated with a property. Individuals will also differ in the degree of certainty with which they hold their expectations; they will perceive differing levels of risk associated with expected outcomes. For these reasons, there will seldom be general agreement about investment value.

Income tax situations are seldom exactly comparable. Consequently, most investors will anticipate different after-tax cash-flow streams even when they generally agree about the before-tax cash flows.

People also differ in their willingness to defer immediate consumption in the interests of even greater benefits in future years. Those with a high preference for present consumption will require a greater incentive to defer after-tax cash flows. Investment value for such investors will be relatively high for investments with a short-term payoff and relatively low for those requiring greater patience. This subject is pursued at length in Part Three.

We do not all have the same tolerance for risk. Those who are less bothered by the possibility of variance between expected and actual investment outcomes will be inclined to place a greater investment value on risky ventures than will those who prefer to face a more precisely determinable future. Other things being equal, almost all investors will prefer less risk to more risk; they differ greatly regarding the risk premium they attach to proposed investment ventures (i.e., the reduction in investment value due to possible variations between expected and actual after-tax cash flows).

Investor Objectives and Risk

Any attempt to discuss investor objectives quickly runs afoul of the nebulous term *investor*. Like Humpty Dumpty, we choose to let the expression mean just what we choose it to mean, and we mean it to include any person or entity that takes a debt or an equity position in real estate. This definition could mean something entirely different—it frequently does when used elsewhere.

Given the diverse entities—corporations, partnerships, trusts, pension funds, and so forth—that fit our definition of the term, there can be no doubt that investors will have varied objectives. Some (e.g., REITs, pension funds, and commercial banks) are constrained by law and regulatory agencies. Others, because of their relatively high-income tax obligations, seek tax shelter situations. Some view real estate as an opportunity to diversify their portfolios. Others seek fixed incomes. Some take speculative positions in search of enormous capital appreciation. Others consider real estate as their inventory in a basic merchandising sense.

Most investors, however, do hold in common certain basic traits, regardless of their motivations or personal objectives. All rational investors seek financial return as a reward for committing resources and as compensation for bearing risk. The amount of expected compensation and the acceptable degree of risk depend on specific investor objectives and individual attitudes toward risk.

Emotional temperament plays a large role in an investor's attitude toward risk. Some people are risk takers by nature; they not only accept it but go out of their way to incur it. This risk-seeking behavior is typified by gambling. These people gamble even when they know the game favors the house. They seem to revel in defying the odds. For them, the long shot is worth courting failure. Although there are people who are addicted to gambling, most risk seekers are mentally healthy people who wager only modest amounts relative to their total wealth.

Other people avoid risk at almost any price. They sacrifice expected returns to hedge their bets, even where the cost of hedging is disproportionate to the relatively small associated risk. As investors, these people favor fixed-income securities that carry a high degree of safety of principal, such as government bonds or insured certificates of deposit at commercial banks.

Most investors probably are somewhere in between these extremes. They tend to minimize risk exposure, preferring the relatively low-return certainty to the higher-return long shot. Moreover, they tend to become progressively more risk-averse as their total wealth increases. These propositions about investor behavior have been explored at length in the economic and financial literature and are not generally a matter of serious dispute.

It is generally agreed that, to the extent they are motivated by rational financial considerations, most investors have the attitude toward risk and expected return depicted in Figure 1.9. They prefer a higher return for a given perceived risk, they prefer less risk for a given expected return, and they accept additional perceived risk only if accompanied by additional expected return.

FIGURE 1.9: Relationship Between Perceived Risk and Expected Return for a Risk-Averse Investor

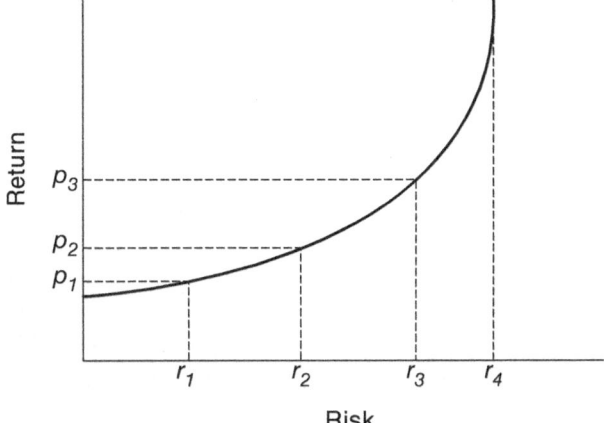

An additional investor characteristic demonstrated in Figure 1.9 is the tendency to become increasingly averse to additional risk as total perceived risk increases. Thus the investor whose attitude is depicted can be induced to accept the additional risk indicated by the distance r_1 to r_2 by the promise of an increase in total reward indicated by the distance p_1 to p_2. But to be induced to accept an identical additional risk increment (from r_2 to r_3), the investor must be able to anticipate a substantially greater reward increment (from p_2 to p_3). In addition, as indicated in the illustration, there is some level of perceived risk (r_4) beyond which the investor cannot be induced to venture, regardless of the possible benefits.

Of course, the exact shape and location of the curve depicted in Figure 1.8 depend on an investor's personal attitude toward risk. A more risk-averse attitude would be depicted by a much more steeply inclined curve, while a less risk-averse attitude would be depicted by a shallower curve. Someone who loves risk would actually trade expected return for additional risk. These various attitudes are shown in Figure 1.10. Moreover, investors will react differently to various types of risks. These issues are addressed in later units.

FIGURE 1.10: Diverse Attitudes Toward Risk

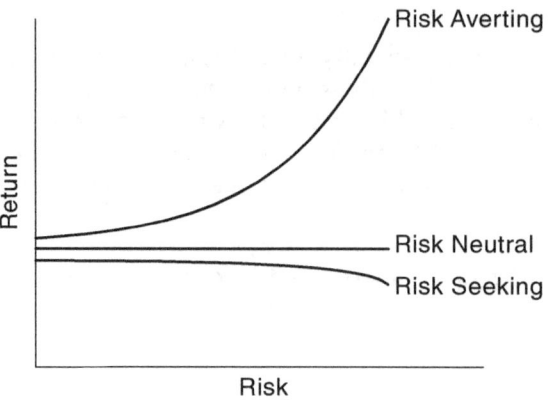

SUMMARY

Real estate investors make an immediate and certain sacrifice of current purchasing power in expectation of future economic benefit. Investment proposals are evaluated by comparing the magnitude of the sacrifice with the quantity and timing of expected benefits and by considering the level of certainty with which expectations are held. Adjusting for time and uncertainty permits comparison among competing alternatives.

Attempts to measure and compare real estate investment returns with those on other investments have been inconclusive. Outcomes are heavily influenced by the dates over which performance is measured. The preponderance of evidence seems to suggest that real estate and common stocks offer roughly equal long-term yield prospects but that real estate performs better during periods of high inflation. Research suggests that real estate prices are less volatile, but this may be an illusion due to real estate market inefficiencies.

Institutions as well as individuals find real estate an attractive investment medium. Changes in federal laws and regulatory attitudes have in recent years enhanced its appeal to pension funds. Equity REITs have multiplied in the more benign income tax environment.

Foreign direct investment in U.S. realty became a major public issue when its volume grew dramatically during the early 1980s; concern abated when the net flow of foreign equity capital ebbed at the end of the decade. The market heated up again in the early 1990s and in the beginning of the 21st century. Foreign investors' interest in U.S. realty is heavily influenced by foreign exchange rates and by comparative interest rates.

Investment analysis follows a consistent pattern regardless of the investment vehicle or investor entity: The streams of benefits from alternative proposals are forecast and are adjusted for timing and risk differences. Alternatives are then ranked according to their desirability, in terms of the trade-off between perceived risk and anticipated return. Rankings will differ according to the discount rate used for timing adjustments and with varying investor attitudes toward risk.

Investment value is the highest price a prospective buyer is justified in paying for a property or the lowest price a prospective seller is justified in accepting. It is a function of available financing, the investor's income tax position, the yield available on alternative investments, and the timing and amount of anticipated benefits flowing from the investment under consideration. The investment decision is subjective, and investment value will be different for each investor.

Investment value can be estimated by summing the present values of the equity position and the debt position associated with a proposed venture. Present value of the equity position is the discounted value of all anticipated future cash flows to the equity position. Present value of the debt position is the available loan or the remaining balance on an existing loan.

Investors differ in both their perceptions of and their attitudes toward risk. The difference among attitudes is sometimes expressed as degrees of risk aversion. The more risk-averse the investor, the greater the expected reward will have to be to induce investment in a given project.

RECOMMENDED READING

Bacow, Lawrence S. "Foreign Investment, Vertical Integration, and the Structure of the U.S. Real Estate Industry." *Real Estate Issues* 15, no. 2 (Fall–Winter 1990): 1–9.

Barrett, G. Vincent, and John P. Blair. *How to Conduct and Analyze Real Estate Market and Feasibility Studies*, 2nd ed. New York: Van Nostrand Reinhold Company, 1988, 71–82.

Conover, C. Mitchell, H. Swint Friday, and G. Stacy Sirmans. "Diversification Benefits from Foreign Real Estate Investments." *Journal of Real Estate Portfolio Management* 8, no. 1 (January–April 2002): 17–25.

Crumley, Ryan, and Donna K. Fisher. "Analysis of International Joint Ventures within Real Estate Investment Trusts." *Briefings in Real Estate Finance* 4, no. 3 (January 2005): 217–28.

Eichholtz, Piet M. A. "Does International Diversification Work Better for Real Estate than for Stocks and Bonds?" *Financial Analysis Journal* (January–February 1996): 56–62.

Hudson-Wilson, Susan. "Why Real Estate?" *The Journal of Portfolio Management* (Fall 2001): 20–32.

Kolbe, Phillip T., and Gaylon Greer. "Recent Changes in Individual Investors' Attitudes Toward Real Estate." *Real Estate Issues* 16, no. 1 (Spring–Summer 1991): 6–10.

Maurer, Raimond, and Frank Reiner. "International Asset Allocation with Real Estate Securities in a Shortfall Risk Framework: The Viewpoint of German and U.S. Investors." *Journal of Real Estate Portfolio Management* 8, no. 1 (January–April 2002): 27–44.

McMahan, John. "Foreign Investment in U.S. Real Estate." *Real Estate Issues* 15, no. 2 (Fall–Winter 1990): 48–50.

Rehring, Christian. "Real Estate in a Mixed-Asset Portfolio: The Role of the Investment Horizon." *Real Estate Economics* 40:1, 65–95.

Swanson, Peggy E. "An Economic Rationale/Empirical Tests of Foreign Investment in United States Real Estate." *Real Estate Issues* 13, no. I (Spring–Summer 1988): 40–46.

Worzala, Elaine, and Vickie L. Bajtelsmit. "Real Estate Asset Allocation and the Decision-Making Framework Used by Pension Fund Managers." *The Journal of Real Estate Portfolio Management* 3, no. 1 (1997): 47–56.

INTERNET REFERENCES

For numerous links and articles on real estate investment:
http://www.creonline.com/

For a real estate directory on many real estate topics:
www.reals.com

For links to over 20,000 investment sites and definitions of investment terms:
www.investorwords.com

REVIEW QUESTIONS

1. What are investors really looking for when they invest in real estate?
2. Who are the major participants in real estate investments?
3. What are some major determinants of foreign investment in U.S. real estate?
4. Describe the differences between passive and active investors.
5. What are the major steps in modern investment decision analysis?
6. Distinguish between the most probable selling price and the market value.
7. Explain how the transaction range for a given property is set. What is the role of investment value in arriving at the transaction range?
8. When estimating investment value, what factors are of concern to the investor?
9. What effect does the timing of cash flows have on investment value?
10. What is the relationship between the amount of risk to which an investor feels exposed and the investor's attitude toward additional risk?

DISCUSSION QUESTIONS

1. What difficulties might a researcher face when trying to compare the long-term investment performance of real estate and securities portfolios? Discuss problems in measuring yield and in comparing risk.

2. Real estate equity and debt markets are closely intertwined: Most new properties are financed in part with mortgage-secured notes, and there is an active secondary market for both mortgage notes and real estate equity interests. Under what circumstances would prices in these markets most likely move in opposite directions?

3. Under what circumstances would the most probable selling price of a property and its market value be essentially the same? Under what circumstances might they differ significantly?

4. To better determine just what a property is worth in the marketplace, would it make sense to ask an exorbitant price and wait for a series of offers, then accept the first subsequent offer that is higher than any received during the trial (information-gathering) period? What problems do you see with such a procedure?

5. Gambling is risk-seeking behavior and buying insurance is a risk-avoidance measure. Yet many people who gamble also buy insurance. How can these contradictory actions be reconciled?

6. If the U.S. dollar continues to weaken, how will that affect the U.S. real estate market?

UNIT 2

Investment Strategy and Market Efficiency

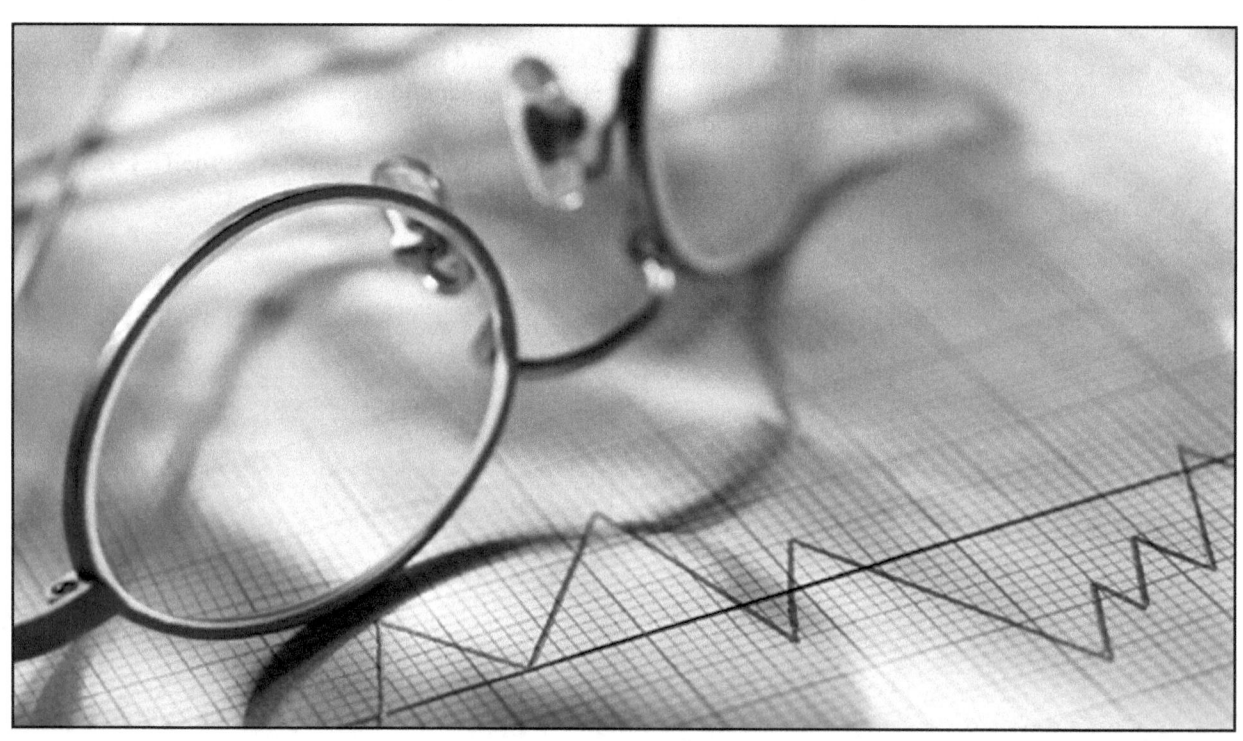

UNIT PREVIEW

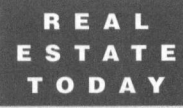

Unit 1 explains that investment value (the value of an asset to a specific individual) depends on the extent of future benefits investors expect, the anticipated timing of the benefits, the degree of confidence with which expectations are held, attitudes toward risk, and expected yields from available alternatives. If any of these key factors change, so does investment value.

Most probable price (the midpoint of a probability distribution of possible prices) is also discussed in Unit 1. Buying opportunities occur when the most probable price drops below investment value; seller motivation is increased when the most probable price rises above investment value.

The wider the gap between the most probable price and an individual's investment value, the greater the profit potential from buying or selling. However, the factors that affect investment value (rental rates, operating expenses, income tax rates, tax benefits, cost of capital) also affect most probable price. Expressed differently, when the investment values of market participants go up or down, their market activities—buying or selling—move prices in general, and thus each property's most probable price, in the same direction. When factors that affect investment value cause immediate changes in market price, the opportunities for extraordinary profits are rare and short-lived. If the most probable price lags changes in investment value, the opportunities will be more frequent and more lasting. The speed with which market prices react to altered circumstances, new information, or revised attitudes is a measure of the market's *efficiency*, and efficiency often differs radically between markets.

SUPPLY, DEMAND, AND THE PRICE OF REAL ESTATE ASSETS

To understand the nature and role of market efficiency in investment strategy, we need first to master the concepts of supply and demand and to understand how their interrelation determines market prices. It then becomes clear how changes in supply or demand alter market prices.

The Demand for Real Estate Assets

Economics defines *demand* as the relationship between market price and the quantity of a good or service that will be bought during a time period, over the entire range of possible prices. The relationship is illustrated in Figure 2.1 as a *demand schedule* for prime downtown office space.

FIGURE 2.1: Hypothetical Demand Schedule for Downtown Office Space

Purchase Price (per sq. ft.)	Square Feet Demanded (millions)
$120	2.3
$115	2.5
$110	2.8
$105	3.2
$100	3.7
$95	4.3

A *demand curve* presents the same information in graphic form. Figure 2.2 illustrates the demand schedule from Figure 2.1 as a demand curve. Quantity of office space is on the horizontal axis; price per square foot is on the vertical axis. The first line in Figure 2.1 indicates that at $120 per square foot, investors will buy 2.3 million square feet per annum. The same information is plotted as point A on Figure 2.2 at $120 along the vertical axis and at 2.3 million units along the horizontal. In like manner, the second entry in Figure 2.1 is plotted as point B in Figure 2.2, the third is plotted as point C, and so on.

The downward slope of the demand curve in Figure 2.2 (sometimes called a *demand function*, denoting that quantity demanded is a function of price) is representative of the usual relationship between price and quantity demanded; when prices increase, the quantity demanded falls. As prices rise, some potential purchasers opt for less expensive substitutes (suburban office space, perhaps, in our example) or drop out of the market altogether. As prices fall, buyers switch from relatively more expensive substitutes, and quantity demanded increases.

FIGURE 2.2: Hypothetical Demand Curve for Downtown Office Space

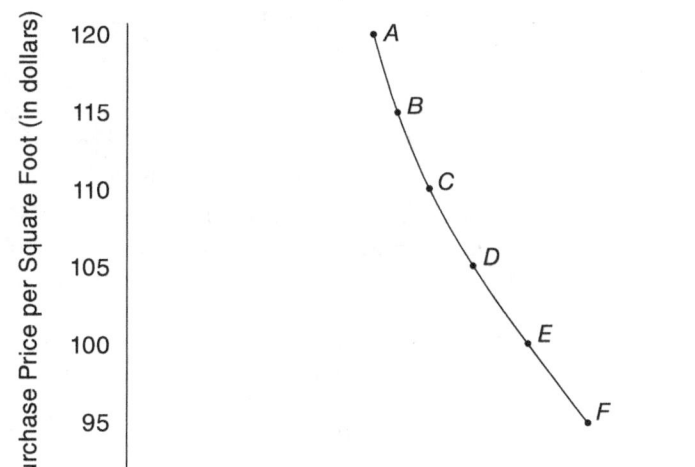

The determinants of demand

Among the more significant determinants of the location and shape of demand curves for real estate assets are variations in the number of prospective tenants, changes in operating expenses, changes in tax codes, yields available on other assets, technology, and tastes. A change in any of these may cause a shift in the demand curve.

- *Variation in the number of prospective tenants.* If population growth or economic expansion increases the number of businesses or professionals desiring to rent, competition for available office space will drive rental rates up and push vacancies down. The net operating incomes (NOIs) of buildings increase, and at prevailing prices, real estate becomes relatively more attractive. Investors shift out of other assets and into real estate, increasing the quantity demanded at every possible price. Conversely, a decline in the need for office space will push vacancies up and drive down the general level of rents; real estate investment becomes relatively less desirable, and resources are shifted elsewhere.

- *Changes in operating expense levels.* If the general level of building operating expenses increases or decreases relative to rental revenue, net profits are altered accordingly. This variation in profitability changes the desirability of real estate relative to other investments, and the demand schedule shifts.

- *Yields available on other assets.* If yield expectations on investments, that are considered to be acceptable substitutes for real estate, it will change their relative desirability and cause a transfer of resources. This moving into or out of real estate investment shifts the demand schedule.

- *Technology.* Technology changes can alter the need for rental space and thereby, the derived demand for land and buildings, even with no change in the level of business activity. Computerized data processing, for example, has greatly reduced the time and cost of generating business information and has whetted management's thirst for reports. Many businesses have taken additional office space to accommodate equipment that generates a veritable flood of data.

- *Tastes.* Changes in consumer tastes will alter the demand for goods and services produced by tenants and thereby shift the demand curve for productive space. As vacancy and rental rates adjust to new social and business conditions, the profitability of real estate (at prevailing prices) makes ownership more or less desirable than before. Tastes in residential rental space affect demand for apartment building ownership in the same manner and even more directly. For example, Gary Pivo and Jeff Fisher find that walkability, defined as the area within walking distance of a property for recreation or other functional purposes, increases the value of commercial real estate by as much as 9%.[1]

Shifts in demand

A specific demand schedule applies only so long as factors other than price that influence buyer behavior remain constant. As time passes, however, other things change. For our office space illustration, variation in the general level of business activity will affect rental rates, vacancy levels, and operating expenses. The rate of return on property purchased at a given price will change, and investors will revise their responses to posted prices. This represents a shift of the entire demand curve, as illustrated in Figure 2.3.

Movement along a demand curve—buyer responses to price changes, all else remaining constant—represents a change in *quantity demanded*; a shift in the curve's location or slope—a change in causal factors other than price—is a change in *demand*. If the altered relationships in Figure 2.3 make real estate investment less attractive, the depicted shift in demand will be inward to the left, resulting in less space demanded at each possible price. Were the relationships altered in the opposite direction, the shift would be outward to the right, representing greater quantities demanded at every possible price.

---

[1] G. Pivo and Jeffrey D. Fisher, "The Walkability Premium in Commercial Real Estate Investments," *Real Estate Economics* 39:2, 2011, 185–219.

FIGURE 2.3: Shifts in Demand and Changes in Quantity Demanded

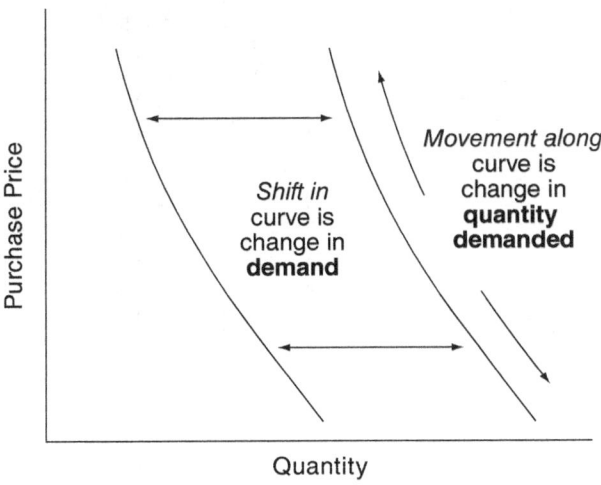

Demand shifters at work: An illustration

To see how demand shifters affect demand, consider the demand schedule for rental space in downtown offices, as illustrated in Figure 2.4. Note carefully that this is *not* demand for building and land ownership. For the moment, we are looking at the demand of tenants for rentable space. We will return later to the demand for ownership interests.

The curve labeled D in Figure 2.4 indicates the quantity of space that tenants will want to rent per time period, at every relevant rental rate. The vertical line labeled *supply* in Figure 2.4 indicates the total amount of office space that exists in the downtown area. It is vertical because no matter what rental rate prevails, over the short term, the physical quantity of rental space will be unchanged.

At price p (read off the vertical axis), the total supply of rental space (read as q on the horizontal axis) will be taken by tenants. Remember that the graph assumes everything except price (in this case, rent—the price of the right to occupy space) remains constant.

But suppose the level of downtown business activity declines, due perhaps to a general economic downturn or a movement of business to the suburbs. As a consequence, less space will be leased by tenants at each possible price per square foot. This is illustrated in Figure 2.4 as a shift from demand curve D to curve D'.

At the previously prevailing rental rate, p, there will be a temporarily vacant space, as indicated by the distance on the quantity (horizontal) axis from q to q'. Rental concessions will drive the prevailing rate from p to p', a price at which all available space will be taken. This represents a movement along the new demand curve D' from point a to point b.

FIGURE 2.4: Rental Rate Consequences of a Shift in Demand for Office Space

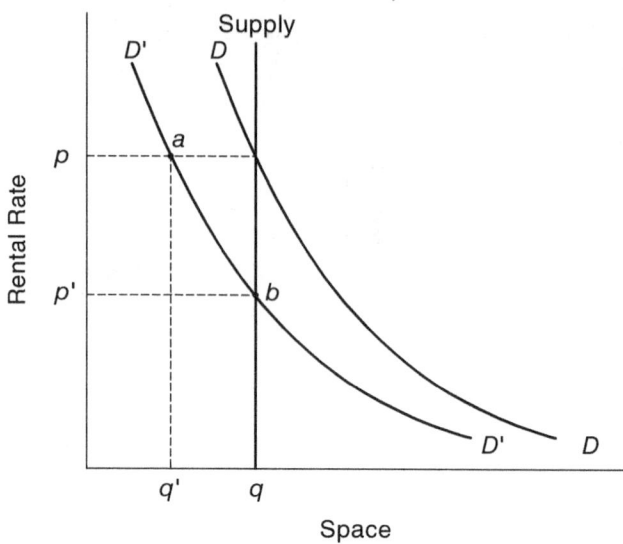

The Supply of Real Estate

Relative scarcity is also a factor in the power of a product or service to command value in exchange. Many items from which we derive great satisfaction have little or no exchange value, while others with little practical utility are precious.

Obvious examples are water and diamonds. Water, a basic requirement of life, has as much want-satisfying power as can be imagined; diamonds bear no relation to survival needs. Why doesn't water cost more than diamonds?

Relative scarcity is the missing element. No matter how useful an item is, it will command little value in exchange if it is relatively abundant. In desert regions or during periods of drought, water may well become more precious than diamonds.

This can be seen by revisiting Figure 2.4. The vertical supply function indicates the total quantity of office rental space that exists in the market area during a specified time period. As demand shifts, price moves to allocate the fixed quantity among prospective tenants. But suppose a large new block of office space comes into existence (a new development, perhaps, or space vacated by an owner-occupant). This will reposition the supply function on Figure 2.4, farther out on the horizontal axis. The new, greater quantity of space will be allocated to prospective tenants at a lower rental rate; the consequence of a reduction in scarcity is a decline in value, manifested as lower rates.

A key phrase in this definition is *during a specified time period*. The supply function differs rather drastically as the time period under consideration is lengthened or shortened.

Equilibrium price

Individual efforts to adjust to the market will result in an *equilibrium price* (rent) for space of a particular type within a specific market. Equilibrium denotes a stable, balanced, or unchanging system. Equilibrium price, therefore, is the price at which there will be sufficient quantity of a product to satisfy desires of all consumers at that price but with no surplus remaining on the market. It represents a consensus of value. In the context of our example, it is the rental rate that results in zero vacancies.

If there are no prospective tenants desiring to rent additional space at the prevailing rate, there will be no competitive bidding to drive the rate still higher. With no significant amount of vacant space on hand, landlords have no incentive to offer rental concessions. At lower rates, however, prospective tenants will put upward pressure on rental rates. At higher rates, tenants' efforts to economize on space use or to shift to a lower-rent market will place downward pressure on rates.

The time element in supply analysis

The illustration of market adjustments to allocate rental space when demand shifts (Figure 2.4) presupposes a fixed quantity of space available for rent. This is a reasonable assumption so long as the time period being considered is too short for additional space to be built. Over a longer term, though, more space can be developed and offered for rent. Then supply, like demand, will be responsive to changes in price.

Panel A in Figure 2.5 illustrates the distinction. Supply, the entire range of relationships between price and quantity supplied, is indicated by the curve labeled s. Because the time period is long enough for additional quantities to be developed, the curve slopes upward to the right, indicating that at higher rental rates more space will be developed and offered for rent.

Quantity supplied, the amount of space that will be available per time period at a specified rental rate, is measured at the intersection of the supply curve s and the demand curve D, and is read off the horizontal axis. Price, the rental rate at which all available space will be taken, is also measured at the intersection of the supply and demand curves, and is read off the vertical axis. Thus, for the supply curve s and the demand curve D, the equilibrium rental rate is p and the equilibrium quantity is q. A shift in demand from D to D' in panel A of Figure 2.5 changes the quantity supplied as indicated by movement along the supply curve from point a to point b.

A shift in supply, illustrated on panel B of Figure 2.5 as a jump from curve s to s', alters the entire relationship and prompts movement along the demand curve to the new equilibrium price p' and new equilibrium quantity q'. This might be caused, in our office rental space example, by a change in the cost of construction or by altered levels of optimism among real estate developers.

FIGURE 2.5: Movement Along a Supply Curve and Shift in Supply Curve

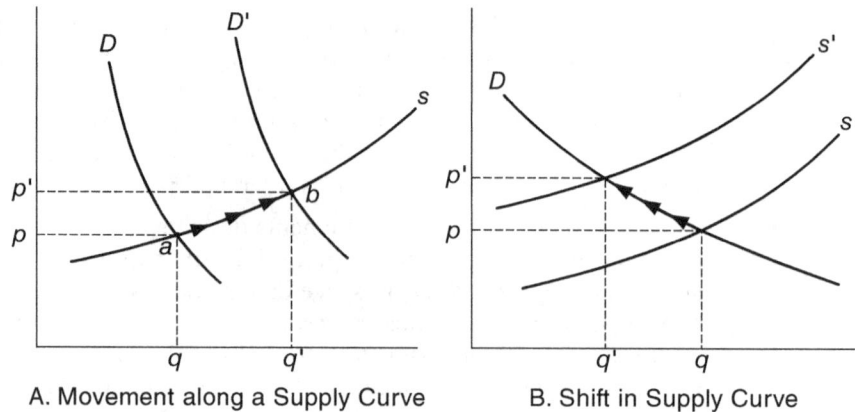

A. Movement along a Supply Curve   B. Shift in Supply Curve

The Market for Real Estate Assets

The role of time in supply analysis was illustrated using the market for rental space. Even over the short run, however, the supply of real estate assets (ownership interests in real estate) is responsive to price variations. This is because current owners will enter the market as sellers or as buyers, depending on their perceptions of the relationship between market prices and investment value.

To see this, consider a market for ownership interests in which only six people participate (we limit the number of participants to keep the illustration manageable—it could be expanded to any size). Assume that all rental units are completely substitutable (i.e., interchangeable) and that each participant's desire to own units is as indicated in Figure 2.6. Suppose that only 16 rental units exist in this market and that two are held by A, four by B, four by C, three by D, three by E, and none by F. These ownership quantities are shown at the bottom of Figure 2.6.

At various possible prices, participants will enter the market as buyers or sellers to adjust their portfolios to reflect the new market realities. In Figure 2.7, desired adjustments by all parties are shown at various possible prices. The difference between the amount each participant currently owns (shown at the bottom of Figure 2.6) and the amount each prefers at different prices are the aggregate quantities demanded (desired for purchase) or supplied (offered for sale) at each price.

FIGURE 2.6: Desired Portfolio of Rental Units

Price (per sq. ft.)	Desired Ownership Quantities (units per market participant)						
	A	B	C	D	E	F	Total
$95	3	0	2	0	0	0	5
$90	4	1	3	0	1	0	9
$85	5	2	4	0	1	0	12
$80	5	3	4	0	1	1	14
$75	5	3	4	1	1	2	16
$70	6	4	5	1	1	2	19
$65	6	5	5	1	2	3	22
$60	6	6	6	2	2	4	26

Current Ownership Quantities						
A	B	C	D	E	F	Total
2	4	4	3	3	0	16

The schedule in Figure 2.6 shows that at a price of $70, participant B wants to own four units, which is the number in that investor's current portfolio. Participant B therefore will not enter the market at that price. This is shown on Figure 2.7: quantity demanded by participant B at a price of $70 is zero. At a higher price such as $90, Figure 2.6 shows that B wants to own only one unit. But we see at the bottom of Figure 2.6 that B's portfolio contains four units; Figure 2.7 shows that at this price B will offer to sell three excess units. At a lower price, perhaps $65, the desired portfolio of five units (shown in Figure 2.6) will lead B to enter the market as a purchaser of one unit, as shown in Figure 2.7. In like manner, Figure 2.7 shows purchases or sales for all participants to adjust their portfolios to the amounts Figure 2.6 shows they desire at various market prices.

If at each price we add together all the negative amounts in Figure 2.7, we obtain the aggregate quantity supplied at that price. Adding the positive amounts yields the aggregate quantity demanded at each price. These amounts are shown in the last two columns of Figure 2.7. The price at which aggregate demand and aggregate supply are equal ($75 per unit) is the price that will permit all mutually advantageous exchanges to occur. At that price, Figure 2.6 shows that the total desired ownership quantity is 16, exactly the number that exists. This represents the short-term equilibrium price of rental units in this particular market. Figure 2.8 shows these relationships in graphic form.

FIGURE 2.7: Quantity of Rental Units Demanded or Supplied at Various Market Prices

Price (per sq. ft.)	Market Participants						Aggregate Quantity	
	A	B	C	D	E	F	Demanded	Supplied
$95	+1	−4	−2	−3	−3	0	1	12
$90	+2	−3	−1	−3	−2	0	2	9
$85	+3	−2	0	−3	−2	0	3	7
$80	+3	−1	0	−3	−2	+1	4	6
$75	+3	−1	0	−2	−2	+2	5	5
$70	+4	0	+1	−2	−2	+2	7	4
$65	+4	+1	+1	−2	−1	+3	9	3
$60	+4	+2	+2	−1	−1	+4	12	2

FIGURE 2.8: Demand and Supply in a Closed Market System

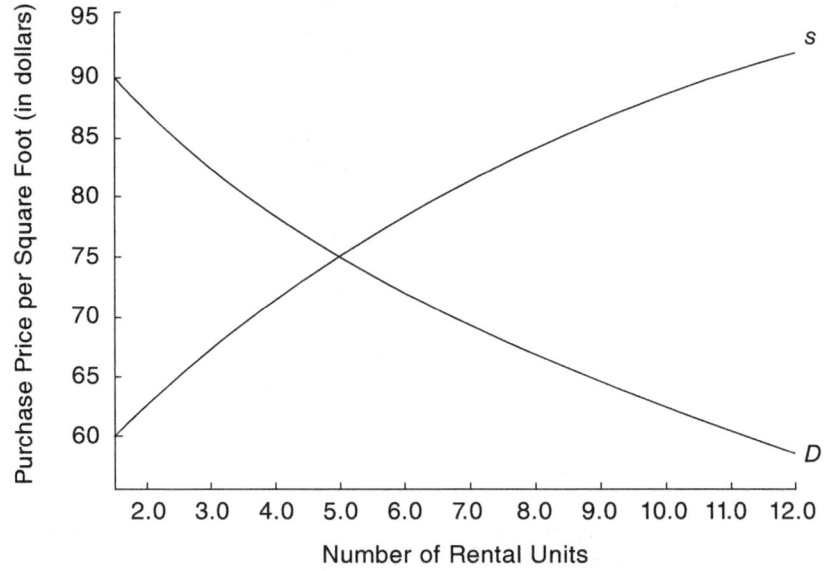

Over longer periods, supply curves of ownership interests, like those for rental space, are influenced by the cost of construction. When prices of existing improved property move above the cost of new construction, real estate developers have an incentive to build. The higher the market price, the greater the incentive and—other things remaining constant—the rate of construction. As a consequence, long-term supply is considerably more responsive to changes in price.

The longer the time period under consideration, the more responsive the supply function will be. Over the very long term, not only can additional structures be built on available land but also additional raw land can be developed for alternative uses. This relationship between the length of the time period involved and the responsiveness of supply to price changes is depicted in Figure 2.9.

FIGURE 2.9: Relationship Between Time and the Supply Function

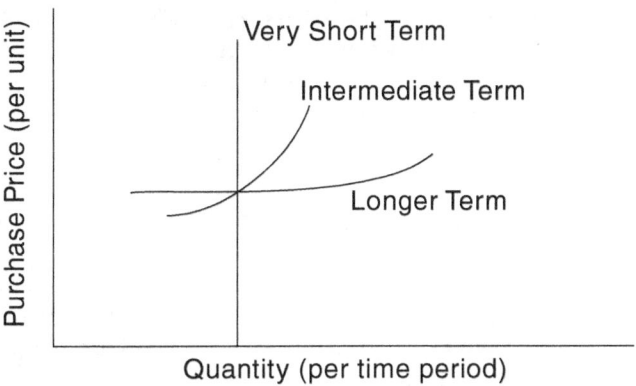

MARKET EFFICIENCY AND PROFIT OPPORTUNITIES

We have just seen that in a market economy, scarce resources go to those willing and able to pay the most for them. If the market works efficiently (if all relevant information is immediately available at little or no cost, and if there is little cost associated with buying and selling), the highest bidders will be those who reap the greatest utility from consumption. However, markets do not always work well, and all are not equally efficient. Before investigating the causes and implications of market imperfections, though, we need to more carefully define our terms.

Defining the Market

In general, *markets* are institutional arrangements or mechanisms that enable buyers and sellers to get together. They are not necessarily physical entities or geographic locations. There is, for example, a market for national currencies that is composed of an informal worldwide network of dealers connected by telephone and computer.

A market might be defined in terms of commonality of product. This leads to a description of a real estate market for industrial property, another for farmland, another for commercial sites, and so on. With notable exceptions for large industrial and commercial sites, the market in each of these segments is fragmented geographically because of the tendency of participants to concentrate in the locale with which they are most familiar. As a consequence, there is no truly national market for most real estate.

Within a geographically localized area, for example, one might find the following distinct markets for residential real estate:

- The single-family house, owner-occupant market
- The single-family house, renter-occupant market
- The multifamily rental market

Within each of these broad categories, it is necessary to define submarkets within which determinable market forces work more or less uniformly. William Kinnard has described these submarkets as *neighborhoods*.[2] A neighborhood, he explained, is a geographic area within which change has a "direct and immediate effect" on the property under analysis. Delineating neighborhoods this way permits direct investigation of market forces affecting prices of real estate services and real estate assets.

Of course, the "neighborhood" for some types of property might be national in scope. Furthermore, the distinction between market segments gets fuzzy at its edges. Though a mammoth industrial site might clearly appeal to a national or international market and a little welding shop only to local buyers, at some point between, an industrial plant will appeal to some potential buyers both locally and regionally or perhaps nationally and internationally. Whatever framework one chooses, some properties will refuse to fit neatly into the boxes. The relationship between broader and more localized markets is illustrated in Figure 2.10.

FIGURE 2.10: Markets Within Markets

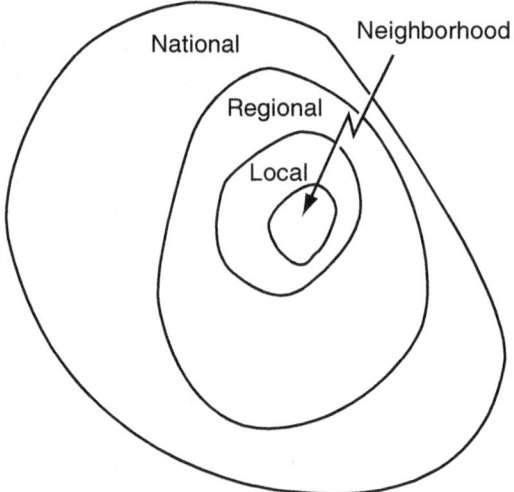

Consider the market area from which regional shopping centers draw customers. Such centers are generally widely separated, and each tends to capture almost all customers from its immediate vicinity. Even though a center's attractive power declines geometrically with required travel time, it occasionally pulls in some customers who

---

2 William N. Kinnard, Jr., *Income Property Valuation* (Lexington, Mass.: Lexington Books, 1971), 302.

frequent other relatively nearby centers. Consequently, two or more regional centers may draw substantial clientele from one large geographic area.

Even so, defining the market as best one can is an early step in market analysis, an issue pursued more fully in the next section of the book. Frustration with indistinct categories should be tempered by reassurance that this makes the analyst's intellect a more essential ingredient in the investment selection process.

Market Structures

Perhaps nowhere has economic modeling been more useful than in studying the structure of markets. Having propounded a market where all relevant information is instantly reflected in prices and another where prices are set by the seller, economists classify all other market structures in terms of where they fall on the spectrum between these extremes.

Absolute monopoly

In markets characterized by *absolute monopoly*, there is only one supplier of a good or service for which there is no reasonably acceptable substitute. The lower the price per unit, the greater will be the sales volume per time period: the monopolist selects the price, and buyers decide how much of the good they are willing to take off the market at the posted price.

Markets most nearly characterized by absolute monopoly are those so designated by government fiat. Even here there are substitutes, however flawed. What if a country has only one telephone company? If telephone rates are set too high, hiring messengers, sending telegrams, or writing letters becomes economical. Some state governments operate a monopoly in the sale of packaged alcoholic beverages, but their freedom to set prices is circumscribed by actual or potential bootleg or black market competition, as well as competing stores in neighboring states. Even in the printing of money, governments haven't been able to maintain an absolute monopoly. Entrepreneurs have created a number of financial instruments that are such good substitutes that they are popularly known as "near money" and are included in the supply equations economists use to measure monetary aggregates.

Atomistic markets

Atomistic markets are so large and diverse that individual participants, regardless of the scale of buying and selling, have no perceptible effect on price. Buyers can purchase as much as they desire, and sellers can sell as much as they wish. There are never shortages or market surpluses; there is no need for special "discount" prices to clear away unwanted inventory or for any government-mandated rationing schemes. Sellers do not need to advertise or to maintain an inventory to meet future needs.

Economic literature more frequently uses the terms *pure competition* or *perfect competition* to describe atomistic markets because these names are meaningful to economists. However, they are misleading to everyone else because competition in atomistic markets is neither more nor less intense than in other markets.

Reducing the quantity offered for sale in an atomistic market does not enable a seller to command higher prices because no buyer will respond to above-market price quotes. Buyers are in a similar position of not being able to bargain for better prices. All are simply price takers, in that their only choice is to accept prevailing prices or not participate.

Perhaps the most nearly atomistic are markets for unprocessed agricultural commodities or for ownership shares in large publicly held corporations. In each case, the units of product are completely undifferentiated and a host of market participants act with roughly equal knowledge of market conditions. These products are sold in auction markets, where each bidder instantly knows the bids of competitors.

Price searcher markets

Buyers and sellers in atomistic markets were earlier characterized as *price takers*. In contrast, sellers in pure monopoly markets are *price makers*. Between lies a host of markets where participants recognize that they cannot completely control prices but also understand that they do affect them. Each seller must be constantly aware of the impact that pricing decisions will have on the decisions of competitors, and every buyer searches for the best deal. Participants in such markets might best be described as *price searchers*.

In an effort to make finer distinctions, economists have classified price searchers' markets into subcategories. *Monopolistic competition* exists when any number of competitors produces goods or services that are sufficiently differentiated that consumers will not be entirely indifferent about which product they choose. *Oligopoly* implies that there are only a few sellers and that market conditions render entry by new purveyors extremely difficult. Economic policymakers consider these to be important distinctions. We need only note that real estate markets fall within the range characterized as either monopolistic competition or oligopoly and that in both categories buyers and sellers exhibit price-searching behavior.[3] Figure 2.11 illustrates the relationships.

FIGURE 2.11: Participants' Reactions to Market Structure

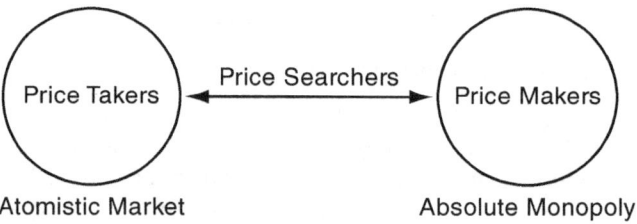

---

[3] For an excellent discussion of markets characterized in this fashion, see Armen A. Alchian and William R. Allen, *Exchange and Production Theory in Use* (Belmont, Calif.: Wadsworth, 1969).

Market Efficiency and Price Searchers

If a price searcher had full knowledge of asset supply and demand (i.e., of competitors' plans and consumers' desires) and knew the costs of all alternatives, profit-maximizing behavior would be simple. In fact, however, decisions have to be made without perfect foresight and without complete knowledge about current market conditions.

An important economic function of markets is to transmit information so that participants can make rational, informed buying and selling decisions. A market in which information is transmitted quickly and at low cost, and in which the information is immediately reflected in market prices, is said to be efficient. The time required for new information to be reflected in market prices is a measure of market efficiency. Information takes longer to be disseminated in less efficient markets, and some information might never be reflected in market prices.

The less efficient the market, the greater will be the degree of price-searching behavior. Participants can obtain intelligent insights of market-clearing prices in inefficient markets only by expending time and effort on research. The fact that real estate markets have infrequent transactions, relative to other financial markets, increases the search costs associated with real estate investment.

The market for real estate equities is characterized by significant inefficiencies. Many real estate transactions occur at prices that reflect little more information than past prices of similar properties. Moreover, because transactions are infrequent and information is difficult and costly to generate, there typically is a considerable lag between the time comparable transactions occur and the time when the informational content of those transactions is fully reflected in market prices. Even the sale of real assets can be volatile due to factors of liquidity, investor's private demands, and bargaining inefficiencies brought about as the result of non-dealer-intermediated markets.[4]

Sources of Inefficiency

The concept of a market-clearing price is unambiguous when applied to a public auction where bids are immediately revealed to all participants. Everyone is immediately aware of all offers so that currently available information is almost certain to be reflected in prices. Real estate transactions, in contrast, are typically a matter of personal negotiation between buyer and seller. The prospective buyer does not know who else might be bidding on the property or what offers they are prepared to make. The seller must accept or reject offers without knowing whether others are forthcoming.

As a consequence, real estate markets may never "clear" in the sense of all parties being able to adjust their portfolios at a stated price. Numerous factors inhibit market adjustments from fully reflecting actual supply and demand conditions.

---

4 D. C. Quan and J. M. Quigley, "Price Formation and the Appraisal Function in Real Estate Markets," *Journal of Real Estate Finance and Economics* 4 no. 2, 1991, 127–146.

Information is costly and difficult to obtain

Information that is too costly to be purchased (i.e., the costs of obtaining the information are exceeded by the benefits) will not be reflected in market prices. Real estate market information is relatively costly and difficult to obtain, due to the fragmented character of the market, the difficulty in making meaningful price comparisons among properties, and the virtual absence of disclosure requirements.

Transaction costs are high

Transaction costs associated with real property markets are considerably greater than those encountered in securities markets. This inhibits real estate portfolio adjustments and thereby increases the time required for new information to be reflected in market prices.

The product is differentiated

Product substitutability contributes to the efficiency of markets. We have noted that every real estate parcel is unique in at least one respect: its location. Even when reasonably acceptable substitutes exist, buyers have specific preferences; in many instances, there are no good substitutes. This gives prospective sellers a degree of monopolistic control, and the traditional model of a market-clearing price does not fit.

STRATEGY IMPLICATIONS

Earlier, we observed that the supply curve for new property improvements (i.e., the production of new buildings) depends on the relationship between production cost and rental rates. In every undergraduate course in microeconomic theory, economists demonstrate that the supply curve (the schedule of quantities that will be produced at various prices) is the same as the schedule of marginal cost of production (the cost of producing one more unit of a good or service).

So long as marginal revenue (the revenue from selling one more unit of good or service) is equal to or greater than marginal cost (the cost of producing the unit), producers in search of profit will expand the market. If the cost of producing another unit (marginal cost) exceeds marginal revenue (the selling price), it makes no sense to expand production. When the market is in equilibrium (i.e., when the product is selling at its market-clearing price) in an atomistic market, the average cost per unit will be the same as the marginal cost. Because marginal revenue is the same as the average revenue (the price is not affected by one individual's production decisions), the average cost of producing units is the same as the market price. This concept is illustrated in Figure 2.12.

Cost, it is important to remember, includes sufficient profit to induce businesses to operate. Management or entrepreneurship is a factor of production, and its cost is called *profit*. Thus, in Figure 2.12, the firm is earning a sufficient return to induce it to keep producing at this level but not enough to cause it to expand. Similarly, there is enough profit to keep competitors producing at current levels but not enough to make them expand or to lure additional competitors into the market.

FIGURE 2.12: Equilibrium Revenue-Cost Relationship in Atomistic Market

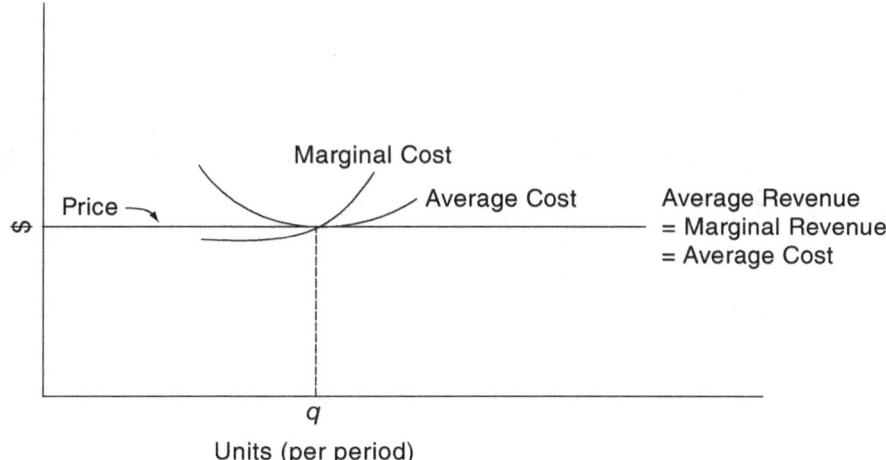

In the case of a real estate firm operating in an atomistic market, marginal revenue will remain constant over the relevant range of production and will be the same as average revenue; it is simply the product's price. This is shown in Figure 2.12 by the flat marginal revenue function.

Costs behave differently from revenue. Beyond some relatively modest level of production, the cost per additional unit produced grows as the rate of production is increased. Economists refer to this as *diseconomies of scale*, by which they mean per-unit cost grows when the number of units per time period increases. As the firm gets larger, for example, overhead grows disproportionately. Speeding up production means hiring more people, possibly some who are less qualified than those hired earlier.

As marginal cost escalates, it pulls average cost—more slowly, but inevitably—upward. If the firm in Figure 2.12 expands output further, average cost will exceed average revenue. There is no profit potential to encourage expansion.

When firms earn more profit than is needed to keep them in business, the excess is called *economic rent*. In real estate, that term means something entirely different; so let's just think of the phenomena as *extra profit*, by which we mean "more than is necessary to sustain current levels of output." In an efficiently functioning atomistic market, extra profit is short-lived.

Figure 2.13 illustrates the adjustment process. Panel A shows a situation where average cost (including enough profit to induce businesses to operate) is less than average revenue. The result is extra profit. This might happen in the market for rental space, for example, because the firm's market research revealed a special amenity that induces tenants to pay more rent per square foot.

FIGURE 2.13: How Markets Adjust

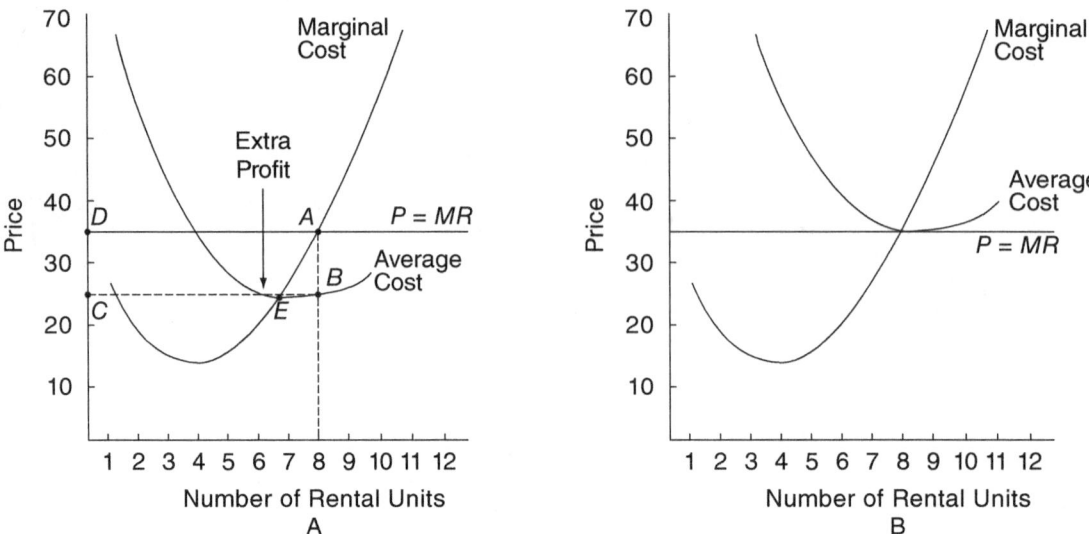

In an efficient market, competitors will quickly follow suit. The extra amenity will become standard, and the increased quantity supplied will drive market rent down (remember the impact of an outward shift in aggregate supply—it results in a lower equilibrium price) until the extra profit disappears.

The less efficient the market, the longer the adjustment will take and the more lasting will be the reward for innovating. By seeking out pockets of market inefficiency, market niches where there are some monopoly elements or where entry is difficult for other reasons, the extra profit can be reaped even longer. To keep reaping higher-than-average profits in a fairly efficient market, firms have to constantly innovate.

Investors who have differential access to information—they get the information sooner, or at less cost than do most investors—or whose transaction costs are atypically low, need not innovate to prosper. Those who get information sooner can exploit market inefficiencies by acting on the information before its impact is fully reflected in prices. If they are able to reduce their average information search costs—perhaps due to the volume of their transactions—or their transaction costs, they can act on information that does not move the market far enough to justify portfolio adjustments for most participants.

To demonstrate key concepts, economists often illustrate the outcome, assuming that nothing changes except the variables under analysis. People who must contend with the less tractable behavior of real-world variables often find this frustrating. In a dynamic market environment, everything is in constant flux. Shifts can occur with lightning-like rapidity and in unexpected directions.

The economists' calm assumptions of order and predictability are useful, though, because they let us peer through the fog of commercial business and see the underlying cause-and-effect relationships. Real estate investment analysts need to understand the economic concepts of supply and demand because these forces determine the outcomes of multiple-year investment ventures such as those we will be investigating. The balance of Part One of the text investigates the determinants of vacancy and rental rates and explores relevant dimensions of market research. These are nothing more than the application in a real-world environment of the dry concepts of supply and demand.

SUMMARY

Real estate is one of a wide range of assets available for inclusion in investors' portfolios. The lower the price at which an asset can be acquired relative to the price of competing assets of the same income and risk category, the greater the relative yield on the asset in question. Therefore, the lower-priced asset will be relatively more desirable, other things being equal. Translated into traditional supply and demand language, this means that the lower the price, the greater the quantity of an asset or service buyers stand ready to take off the market.

For a given level of demand for real estate (i.e., at existing rent levels), each real estate investor develops a perception of appropriate prices for real estate assets. When market prices are below this perceived value, they will be inclined to add to their portfolios. Conversely, they will be inclined to sell when market prices move above the perceived value. Thus, while the supply of space available for rent is relatively fixed over the short term, the supply of property interests is highly responsive to price even over the short term.

Markets are institutional arrangements or mechanisms that bring buyers and sellers together. Markets are often defined in terms of commonality of product, such as the residential real estate market or the market for industrial buildings. They are also frequently defined in geographic terms. In this respect, *neighborhood* is a term sometimes used to describe an area in which specific phenomena have a direct and immediate influence on all real estate. Market boundaries are difficult to define, because submarkets tend to overlap.

Economics classifies market structures according to the extent to which individual buyers and sellers can influence prices and according to the degree to which relevant market information is readily reflected in prices. Markets in which there is only one supplier of a good or service are called *monopolies*. Those having so many participants that no one person or firm has any discernible impact on price are called *atomistic*. Most markets fall between these extremes.

In efficient markets all relevant information is quickly reflected in market prices. Participants in less efficient markets can benefit by searching for the best available price. Because information in inefficient markets is scarce and expensive, participants with monopolistic access to information may be able to consistently outperform the market.

RECOMMENDED READING

Alchian, Armen A., and William R. Allen. *Exchange and Production: Competition, Coordination, and Control.* Belmont, Calif.: Wadsworth Publishing Company, Inc., 1983.

Childs, Paul D., Steven H. Ott, and Timothy J. Riddiough. "Optimal Valuation of Noisy Real Assets." *Real Estate Economics* 30:3, 2002, 385–414.

DePasquale, Denise, and William C. Wheaton. *Urban Economics and Real Estate Markets.* Englewood Cliffs, N.J.: Prentice Hall, 1996, chap. 2.

Fanning, Stephen F. *Market Analysis for Real Estate: Concepts and Applications in Valuation and Highest and Best Use.* Chicago: Appraisal Institute, 2005.

Fullerton, Thomas M. Jr. "Urban Economics and Real Estate Markets." *Business Economics* 31, no. 4 (October 1996): 69–71.

Smith, Lawrence B. "Urban Economics and Real Estate Markets." *Regional Science and Urban Economics* 28, no. 3 (May 1998): 379–85.

INTERNET REFERENCES

For news, trends, and research on commercial real estate:
www.reis.com

For current real estate news:
www.GlobeSt.com

For information on indexes and rates:
www.bls.gov/cpi

For current news and research on real estate:
www.irei.com

REVIEW QUESTIONS

1. How are price and demand for an economic good related?
2. What conditions might cause a shift in demand for office space in a downtown area?
3. What is the relationship between price and the quantity supplied of an economic good?
4. Compare short-term and long-term supply functions in real estate markets.
5. How are real estate markets categorized, and how are they defined?
6. Explain the difference between atomistic and monopolistic markets.
7. What are some of the factors inhibiting market adjustments from readily reflecting supply and demand conditions in real estate markets?

8. Look at Figure 2.6. Suppose there are 16 units in the market and the market has reached the equilibrium position where the price is $75 per square foot; A holds five units, B holds three units, and so on. Now, suppose that an additional three rental units are added to the supply (due to development activity). With everything else remaining as before, who will acquire the additional units, and what will be the new equilibrium price?

9. What is the relationship between demand for rentable space and demand for land and buildings?

10. Why do supply curves generally become less nearly vertical as the time period under consideration grows longer?

DISCUSSION QUESTIONS

1. Are the price and quantity demanded always inversely related? Can you think of circumstances under which increasing the price of a good or service might cause the quantity demanded to increase? Can you think of circumstances under which decreasing the price might cause quantity demanded to decrease?

2. In a dynamic, constantly changing economy, would you expect most markets ever to reach an equilibrium price? What about markets for various classes of real estate?

3. In highly concentrated markets, competition is likely to be just as furious as in atomistic markets, but it is often in arenas other than price. What are some prominent examples of nonprice competition?

4. How might modern technology and modern management techniques be used to reduce real estate brokerage costs? What barriers might inhibit introduction of such cost-saving measures?

5. Many companies are decreasing costs by having their employees work from home. How will such a management technique affect the demand for office space? How will it affect the supply of office space over the short term? How will it affect the supply over the long term?

UNIT 3

Land Utilization and the Rental Value of Real Estate

UNIT PREVIEW

REAL ESTATE TODAY

You will recall Unit 1 discussed that real estate investors, in effect, buy a set of assumptions about a property's ability to generate a stream of benefits. For investment property, a substantial portion of the benefit stems from net operating income (NOI) generated by tenants. The balance is in the form of cash flow when the property is sold, which is heavily dependent on the property's ability to generate rental income after the sale. The property's rent-generating ability, then, is a key factor in its investment value.

The Unit 3 investigates factors affecting a location's appeal and, thus, the rental value of real estate at that location. It demonstrates how competitive bidding allocates the most desirable locations to tenants who benefit sufficiently to be able to pay the most rent. Those who are unable to secure the most desirable locations settle for the best affordable alternatives. A pecking order results with the hierarchy being characterized by a descending order of density of land use and of declining rents as one locates farther from the ideal location.

As society's characteristic way of carrying on social and economic activities changes, so does the relative allure of various locations. However, the cityscape does not readily adapt to altered needs. Its structure yields only grudgingly to changes resulting from individual economic decisions. As a consequence, cities reflect a hodgepodge of development patterns, some created to meet contemporary needs and some that are simply artifacts of a bygone era. In every city, however, individual location decisions have resulted in logical, systematic development patterns whose orderliness may be hidden from untrained eyes.

ECONOMIC FACTORS IN LAND UTILIZATION

Choosing a location is primarily an economic decision, although it is constrained by collective values expressed in zoning and building codes. For this reason, the pattern of urban development, through an overlay of politically imposed restrictions, reflects basic economic forces. One such force that becomes increasingly evident as cities grow and mature is *specialization of function*. As hamlets become towns and towns evolve into cities, real estate uses of like character increasingly tend to be concentrated in specific functional zones.

This tendency is evident not only among broad categories of use such as residential, industrial, and commercial, but within these categories as well. Residential users tend to segregate themselves by social and economic class, resulting in distinct neighborhoods with highly stratified levels of housing size and quality. Within commercial districts, there is also notable clustering of similar uses, and the data reflect significant spatial specialization in office activity based on industry type.[1]

Segregation of uses and market-directed specialization are, however, never absolute. Decisions about location are often a matter of trial and error, and mistakes are difficult to correct, owing to the high cost of altering prior choices. Moreover, variations in the level of economic activity, combined with perpetual change in technology and life- styles, constantly give birth to new economic motivations, rendering old choices sub- optimal and creating maladjustments that lead to reassessment of previous decisions.

Subject to inconsistencies and anomalies induced by the prohibitive cost of making small adjustments, by errors in judgment, and by the irrational element in human nature, land utilization in a market system is determined by efforts to extract economic returns. Space is leased to those who can pay the highest rent, and more-productive users can outbid their rivals. The ultimate consequence is an orderly pattern of land use that generates the greatest aggregate economic benefit for the community.

Of course, not all potential users compete directly for the same land. For example, although railroads and freeways detract from the desirability of adjacent locations as residential neighborhoods, factories and warehouses benefit from proximity to these transportation facilities. Low-priced homes are preferably built on level terrain to minimize construction costs, but buyers of higher priced houses might pay a premium for the excellent view from a hillside location.

However, within broad ranges of potential uses, direct competition does take place. Where the competition is based primarily on economic considerations, the use that results in the greatest rent-paying capacity is that which exacts the most economic benefit from a site.

Although concentration is a natural adaptation to the need and desire to overcome the "friction" of space, decentralization is a normal and continuing counterforce necessitated by market forces. Low-intensity land users are forced out of central locations

---

[1] John M. Clapp, Henry O. Pollakowski, and Lloyd Lynford, "Intrametropolitan Location and Office Market Dynamics," *Journal of the American Real Estate and Urban Economics Association* 20:2 (now *Real Estate Economics*) (1992).

by those who benefit most from proximity to the center and can therefore afford to pay higher rental rates. Land-use density thus tends to be highest at the center of development activity, the spot we characterize here as the "100% location." Progressively lower densities are encountered toward the development fringe.

Development Patterns

Academicians are fond of creating abstract models to isolate key elements in economic relationships. These simplified representations of a complex world permit uncluttered concentration on issues chosen for closer examination. The classic example is Johann Heinrich von Thünen's analysis, more than 175 years ago, of the effects of location on land utilization. In his book *The Isolated State*, he demonstrated how transportation costs affect land use, by assuming an isolated economic area comprising an urban core surrounded by a flat rural plain. By assuming that climate, soil fertility, and transportation facilities are uniform, von Thünen freed his model from complications such as competing urban areas, aesthetic considerations, and differential transportation costs per unit of distance traveled. His analysis held constant all factors except choice of market and land use. Under these circumstances, he demonstrated that land-use choices are directly attributable to variations in transportation costs. He showed that the closer land lies to the central market, other things remaining constant, the more intensively it will be used.[2]

Reasoning similar to Von Thünen's led early urban economists to describe idealized urban development in terms of concentric rings of relatively homogeneous uses, with progressively less intensive land use in the outer rings. Ernest W. Burgess attempted to fit this concentric ring model to the pattern of development existing in Chicago in the early 1920s.[3] Basing his argument on intensity of land use, Burgess wrote that the central area will be dominated by financial firms and major retail stores. Outside the central zone will be found wholesaling and light manufacturing businesses, somewhat overlapping a third zone containing the homes of low-income residents. Beyond this will be a zone occupied by heavy manufacturing, which needs ready access to transportation routes to the outside world. Outer rings, he said, will be reserved for residential use, serving progressively wealthier users as distance from the center increases.

Burgess's version of the concentric ring model is designed to explain urban development as it existed in the 1920s, and readers will be hard-pressed to find the patterns today that Burgess detected. His fourth ring, the "zone of transition" in cities such as Chicago, no longer contains a significant number of factories, comprising, instead, a mixture of abandoned buildings and redevelopment into middle-class residential structures. Much of industry has moved into what he categorized as the commuter's zone, leaping over residential areas that blocked the expansion of previous manufacturing facilities.

---

2 Johann Heinrich Von Thünen, *Der Isolierte Staat*, 1826. For an English translation, see Peter Hall, ed., *Von Thünen's Isolated State* (London, England: Pergamon Press, 1966).

3 Ernest W. Burgess, "The Growth of the City," in Robert Park et al., *The City* (Chicago: University of Chicago Press, 1994).

Limitations of the concentric ring model are obvious. Topography and specialized transportation corridors distort the circular pattern. Technology and lifestyle changes alter the relative intensity of land uses among various categories, thereby varying competitors' ability to bid for highly valued sites. Inner-circle users find their expansion needs frustrated by users in the next zone, and they are forced to leapfrog to areas beyond.

Another model that explains development is central place theory, first proposed by Walter Christaller.[4] The theory explains development by a hierarchy of centers as near as possible to the customers they serve. The distribution of central places is determined by the size of the service area for each central place because specialized central places are assumed to not overlap.

Later work of W. L. Garrison and B. J. L. Berry explained that two factors control the distribution of central places: the range of a good and the threshold.[5] The range of a good or service is the distance over which people will travel to obtain it. The threshold is the minimum number of purchasers necessary to support a good or service from a central place. These theories still apply to modern development, especially in retail real estate.

Business Location Decisions

Imperfections in the market create substantial deviation from the pattern of land uses dictated by the need for efficiency in human affairs. But a systematic pattern suggestive of earlier models is nonetheless discernible in every urban area, reflecting the history of rational use decisions over a period of years.

As the single most convenient spot for the greatest number of people, the central business district is the logical place for firms drawing customers from throughout an area. Financial offices are sufficiently land-intensive to justify this area of highest land rents.

Outside the central business district, retail locations create divergent patterns of city structure. Many profit from locating along major traffic arteries and create business thoroughfares at various locations throughout the city. Others benefit from mutual proximity; they cluster and thus create multiple nuclei or miniature downtowns throughout metropolitan areas.[6]

Businesses locating along major arterial streets create what has been described as a radial or axial development pattern, as illustrated in Figure 3.1. Thus, towns expand first along their major transportation arteries and then "flesh out" with residential and further commercial development in the interstices between these ribbons of growth.

---

4   Walter Christaller, *Die Zentralen Orte in Suddeutschland* (Jena, 1933).
5   B. J. L. Berry and W. L. Garrison, "Functional Bases of the Central Place Hierarchy," *Economic Geography* 34:2 (1958): 145–54.
6   Richard U. Ratcliff describes these patterns as string street developments and nucleation. See Richard U. Ratcliff, *Real Estate Analysis* (New York: McGraw-Hill, 1961).

Mutual proximity benefits many businesses. Convenience shops seek locations adjacent to stores featuring shopping goods to capture business from customers drawn by their neighbors. Stores carrying similar lines of merchandise frequently benefit from clustering because they collectively draw a larger crowd of shoppers than could any one of them in isolation. Since the early 1950s, real estate entrepreneurs have catered to these special needs of merchants by developing shopping centers that take on the dimensions of modest central business districts.

FIGURE 3.1: Radial and Nodal Development Extends Outward From Central Area

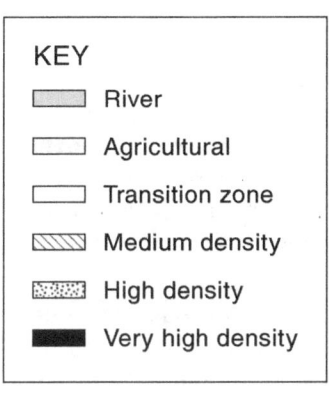
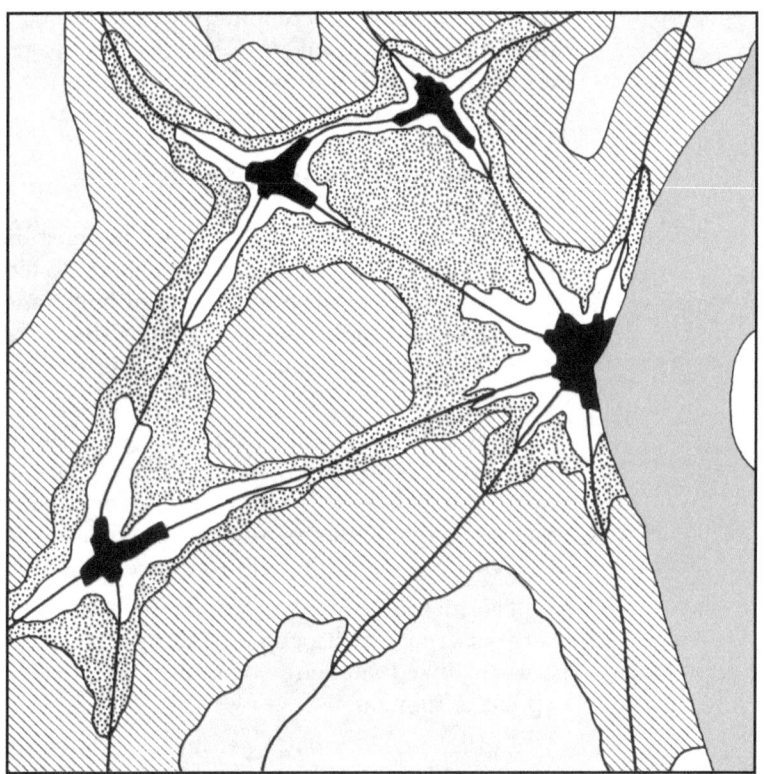

The reasons for clustering of stores to form multiple nuclei at particular locations depend on such diverse factors as prevailing transportation patterns, the socioeconomic status of potential customers, and even the availability of sufficient space. Once formed, the nuclei create peaks in local land values and frequently spawn axial developments of their own.

Another set of factors influencing development was published by Charles C. Colby in 1933 suggesting that centrifugal forces move one group away from the central zone to the periphery, while centripetal forces will attract another group toward the central area.[7] Two groups of factors still influence the location of centers and the development of real estate. Centripetal forces attract specialized land uses because of the accessibility to related activities and to customers. Probably the most influential centripetal force is jobs, as people move from an agricultural area into an urban center in search of employment. On the other hand, centrifugal forces, such as crime and congestion, drive certain land uses out to other areas.

LINKAGES AND "NATURAL" ZONING

If rental charges were absent, every business firm would seek a location that minimizes the costs of overcoming the friction of space. The need to move people and things between sites creates costs that tend to reduce a location's desirability. Ideally, closely linked activities would take place at the same site, thus reducing transfer costs to zero. This, of course, is seldom possible.

Linkages and Transfer Costs

As a part of their daily lives, people must constantly travel between various locations. Children travel from home to school, to the playground and entertainment facilities, and so on. Adults travel between home and work. For many people, work itself takes place at a multitude of different sites. Entire families must travel for medical, dental, and legal services; for shopping and entertainment; and for a host of other activities.

Similarly, *things* must constantly be shuffled between various locations. Food moves from farms to processing plants to storage, then to retail outlets and finally to homes or restaurants. Manufacturing processes start at farms or mines, from which raw materials might undergo processing at a variety of different locations before a finished product is moved to a retail location and finally to the site of consumption.

The relationships that require such movement are called *linkages*, and the locations between which people or things move are *linked sites*. Costs of transportation between linked sites are sometimes referred to as *transfer costs* and may be either explicit or implicit.

Explicit transfer costs get the most attention, perhaps because they are easier to determine. These are costs measurable in dollars: cost per mile of the chosen transportation medium plus the dollar value of time spent en route.

Analysts sometimes err by ignoring or underestimating the importance of *implicit* transfer costs. Although more subtle and difficult to identify, they are no less significant than their explicit counterparts. They include the disutility of moving between linked sites, a cost that is not reflected on accounting statements. Examples include the fear of traveling through areas considered dangerous and the aggravation and discomfort of coping with congested highways or public transportation facilities.

---

7   Charles C. Colby, "Centrifugal and Centripetal Forces in Urban Geography," *Annals of the Association of American Geographers* 23 (1933): 1–20.

Linkages and Location of Industry

In addition to affecting the level of transfer costs, a firm's location decision might also affect processing costs. This occurs when a site has natural advantages due to soil fertility, a benign climate, or some other natural endowment. Where processing costs are a major consideration, firms might accept considerable additional transfer costs to reduce their processing costs. Where processing costs are relatively minor or are not greatly affected by location, transfer costs become the prime factor in industrial location decisions. The key issue is that a wisely chosen location will minimize the sum of processing and transfer costs.

Figure 3.2 illustrates a 100% location in the absence of differential rents and the effect on operating costs other than rent as a business moves farther from the 100% location. Earlier, we observed that the 100% location is usually the center of development activity, where land is most intensely used. More precisely, we define it for any activity as the location where the net benefit would be greatest in the absence of rent (in the case of owner-occupants, in the absence of occupancy costs).

FIGURE 3.2: Industrial Location Decisions with Constant Rent or No Rent

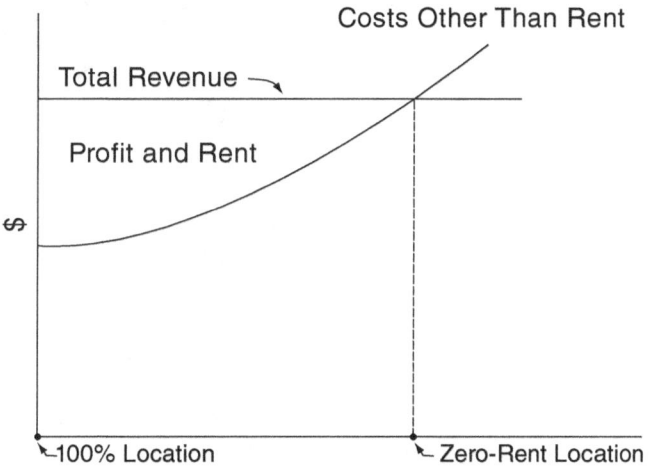

Variation from 100% Location

If revenues were unaffected by location, a convenient fiction we have incorporated into Figure 3.2, then the best location would be the one that minimizes all costs. Were no rental charges levied, the best location would be at the 100% location, the intersection of the axes on Figure 3.2. At that point, the excess of revenue over costs other than rent would be maximized.

Continuing the assumption that revenues are not affected by location, but dropping the assumption that all locations are either free or equally costly, location decisions hinge on determining what variation from the 100% location will minimize the sum of rental charges and all other costs. Other costs include additional expenses because of such issues as physical limitations, regulatory requirements, and environmental problems. Rent differentials are created by competition for space at or as close as possible to the 100% location. Firms that can benefit the most from the 100% location are able to outbid all others, forcing their competitors out into the area of Figure 3.2 between the 100% location and the zero-rent location.

A location decision for an industrial use at a given rent gradient is illustrated in Figure 3.3. The firm's total cost at each location is the sum of costs other than rent plus the rent charged at that site. The sum of these charges is illustrated by the total cost curve at the top of the figure. The optimum location for the firm depicted in Figure 3.3 is the one that minimizes total costs, including rent.

FIGURE 3.3: Industrial Location Decisions with Rent Differentials

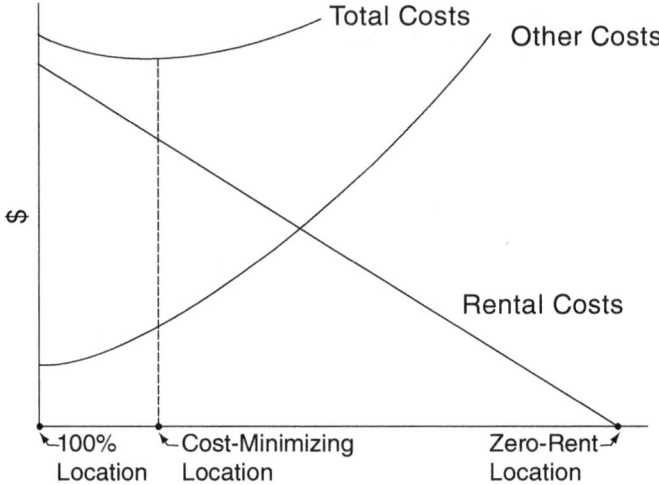

Commercial Location Decisions

Businesses whose sales are greatly affected by location decisions have more variables to consider. They must factor in transfer costs borne by their customers, shoppers who consider travel time and inconvenience when deciding which stores to visit. Even so, total transfer costs (regardless of who incurs them) determine the relative desirability of various sites. As with industrial firms, in the absence of rent (or the cost of property ownership), commercial firms will want the 100% location. But competition for that location drives up the rent there, and that results in a declining rent schedule as one moves farther from the location that would be most desirable in the absence of rent (the 100% location). This is illustrated in Figure 3.4, which shows rent and profit before rent declining with distance from the 100% location. The optimum location is the one that maximizes net profit: profit before rent, minus rent.

FIGURE 3.4: Retail Location Decisions

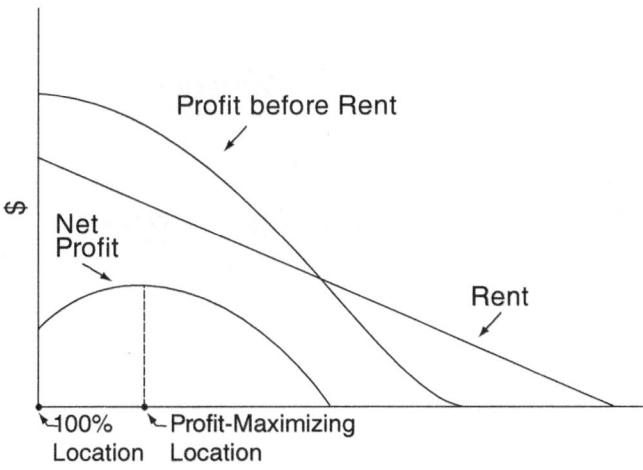

THE MARKET FOR RENTAL SPACE

We saw in Unit 2 that markets perform the basic function of allocating resources among various users. Thus, the interaction of supply and demand forces in the market for real estate assets channels property rights to the highest bidders. And to the extent that bid prices are based on accurate appraisal of the stream of future benefits flowing from ownership, assets are acquired by users who can wring the greatest net benefit from their use.

Just as there is a market that allocates available ownership interests among various would-be users, so too is there a market that allocates real estate services (shelter and location benefits from occupancy). Competitive bids create the highest rents at what would otherwise be the most desirable location (the 100% location), and rents tend to decline as distance from the 100% location increases.

Market Adjustments

Look again at Figure 3.4. The curve labeled "Profit before Rent" represents the absolute maximum rent a firm with such a profile can pay and still find it worthwhile to remain in business. Where profit before rent drops below the rent gradient, commercial users are priced out of the market by others who can generate greater profit from the locations. Therefore, only the segment of the profit-before-rent curve that is above the rent gradient represents viable commercial locations. This segment is reproduced in Figure 3.5 and labeled "Commercial Bid-Rent Curve." Were there no other bidders, commercial firms whose profit profiles are represented by this curve would occupy locations ranging from the 100% location outward to the point where the commercial bid-rent curve intersects the horizontal axis.

FIGURE 3.5: Bid-Rent Curves and Natural Zoning

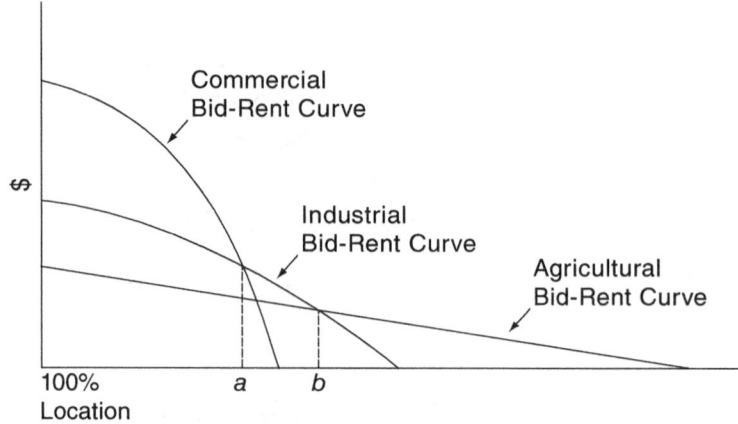

Distance from 100% Location

But, of course, there are other contenders for available sites. Firms whose revenues are less dependent on being near the 100% location will not be able to outbid commercial endeavors for nearby locations. But the other firms' bid-rent curves will decline less abruptly with distance, so they will place winning bids for more distant sites. Figure 3.5 depicts the bid-rent curve for such an industry, labeled "Industrial Bid-Rent Curve." A third economic group might have a profit profile that generates bid-rent curves such as the one labeled "Agricultural Bid-Rent Curve."

Figure 3.5 reveals that commercial firms will outbid alternative users for space between the 100% location and point *a*, whereas industrial users will submit winning bids for the area between point *a* and point *b*. Beyond point *b*, other pursuits can afford to pay higher rents than either commercial or industrial firms. Thus, economic considerations will tend to segregate activities even without the formal zoning regulations adopted by most municipalities.

Because the market is not a perfect allocator of resources, there will be some overlapping of uses, particularly near points *a* and *b* in Figure 3.5. These points represent the locus of zones of transition between predominant uses. This is the economic rationale underlying the concentric ring and the multiple nuclei patterns of urban development discussed earlier.

WHY INVESTORS NEED MARKET RESEARCH

If the real estate market were atomistic (if buyers and sellers, landlords and tenants, were all price takers), there would be little need for market research. Energy would be expended primarily on cost control.

In at least one aspect, though, all real estate is a differentiated product; each site is unique with respect to its exact location. The significance of this distinction differs from situation to situation. Parcels that are somehow unique might command a considerable rent premium. Conversely, properties that are atypical may transact at a discount. The difference may lie in architectural aesthetics, construction quality, luxurious appointments, or any other element that creates a compelling image for tenants.

Distinctions that exist only in the perception of tenants may be far more valuable than actual physical differences. Styling, quality of construction, and functional features can be duplicated by competitors, but reputation is unique to individual properties and often is generated consciously to appeal to a specific class of tenant. Depending on the image associated with the address, a property may command premium rents or sell at a discount from prevailing rates for similarly located and outfitted space.

Price searchers who have access to better market intelligence than that available to their competitors may benefit substantially. If they can discern what locations will afford competitive advantages to tenants in the near future, they can acquire title to appropriate parcels before such information is reflected in prices. If they are able to forecast changes in location advantage accurately over the years, they can more precisely estimate a new property's investment value. Comparing investment value with market values that do not yet reflect all pertinent information will enable astute researchers and analysts to consistently outperform the market. It is for this reason that Part Two of the book is devoted to market research.

SUMMARY

Real estate owners who rent their space to users are in effect selling a service that comprises shelter and location. In many cases, the rental rate a property commands is substantially determined by its location; the more desirable the location, the greater the rent per square foot. At progressively more remote locations, both density of use and rental rates tend to decline. This pattern is distorted by the fact that, once a building has been constructed, the most economically advantageous use of the site might be entirely different from a still vacant site.

The relationships requiring movement of people or things between sites are called *linkages*. Sites between which movement occurs are said to be *linked*, and the cost of movement is called *transfer costs*. Space users strive to locate in order to minimize the total cost of rent plus aggregate transfer costs.

Because the market for real estate rental space is relatively inefficient, property owners or managers, who are more adept at market research, frequently are able to consistently differentiate their product and thereby command premium rents. They are thus able to reap above-average profits. The advantage tends to disappear as competitors become aware and rush to produce close substitutes for the space noted to be in high demand. Constant market research is needed, therefore, to find new sources of product differentiation to perpetuate high yields.

RECOMMENDED READING

Berke, Philip R., David R. Godschalk, Edward J. Kaiser, and Daniel A. Rodriguez. *Urban Land Use Planning*, 5th ed. Champaign-Urbana, Ill.: University of Illinois Press, 2006.

Bradley, David M. "The Laws of Real Estate Dynamics." *The Appraisal Journal* 54, no. 3 (July 1990): 314–23.

Cutter, Bowman, and Autumn DeWoody. "Parking Externalities in Commercial Real Estate." *Real Estate Economics* 38:2, 2010, 197–223.

DePasquale, Denise, and William C. Wheaton. *Urban Economics and Real Estate Markets*. Englewood Cliffs, N.J.: Prentice Hall, 1996, chapters 2 through 65.

Fenker, Richard M. *The Site Book*. Ft. Worth, Tex.: Mesa House Publishing, 1996.

Fullerton, Thomas M. Jr. "Urban Economics and Real Estate Markets." *Business Economics* 31, no. 4 (October 1996): 69–71.

Godschalk, David R. "Land Use Planning Challenges: Coping With Conflicts in Visions of Sustainable Development and Livable Communities." *Journal of the American Planning Association* 70, no. 1 (Winter 2004): 5–14.

Haurin, Donald. "The duration of marketing time of residential housing." *Real Estate Economics* 16, no. 4 (1988): 396-410.

Haurin, Donald R., Jessica L. Haurin, Taylor Nadauld, and Anthony Sanders. "List Prices, Sale Prices and Marketing Time: An Application to US Housing Markets." *Real Estate Economics* 38, no. 4 (2010): 659-685.

Levy, John M. *Contemporary Urban Planning*. 8th ed. Englewood Cliff, N.J.: Prentice Hall, 2008.

Mayhew, Judith. "Strategies for Managing Urban Growth and Revitalization." *Journal of Real Estate Portfolio Management* 8, no. 4 (2002): 25–30.

Pittman, Robert H., and Maury Seldin. "Real Estate Analysis Using Geographic Data." *Real Estate Issues* 15, no. 1 (Spring–Summer 1990): 32–38.

Ratcliff, Richard U. *Real Estate Analysis*. New York: McGraw-Hill, 1961, 13–41.

Valuation for Real Estate Decisions. Santa Cruz, Calif.: Democrat Press, 1972, 15–48.

Ratcliffe, John, and Michael Stubbs. *Urban Planning and Real Estate Development,* Natural and Built Environment Series, No. 8. New York: Taylor and Francis Group, 1996.

Smith, Lawrence B. "Urban Economics and Real Estate Markets." *Regional Science and Urban Economics* 28, no. 3 (May 1998): 379–85.

Song, Yan. "Smart Growth and Urban Development Pattern: A Comparative Study." *International Regional Science Review* 28, no. 2 (April 2005): 239.

Weber, Bruce R. "Application of Geographic Information Systems to Real Estate Market Analysis and Appraisal." *The Appraisal Journal* 58, no. 1 (January 1990): 127–32.

REVIEW QUESTIONS

1. What are the limitations of the concentric ring hypothesis as developed by von Thünen and Burgess?
2. Explain the concept of linkages.
3. How is land utilization determined in a market system?
4. Explain the axial development pattern of cities and the multiple nuclei pattern.
5. What are explicit and implicit transfer costs?
6. What should an industry consider in selecting a location?
7. How do transfer costs affect commercial location decisions?
8. What is the effect on the quantity of rental space in a market area and prevailing market rents, over the short run and the long run, of shifts in demand for rentable space?

DISCUSSION QUESTIONS

1. If you were designing a city to be built on virgin land, to what extent might you copy the pattern suggested by von Thünen and Burgess? Why might you choose a different pattern, and what would your alternate pattern be?
2. What centrifugal factors today are forcing development out of cities? What centripetal factors are now attracting development?
3. Think of a regional or superregional shopping mall in your city as a central business district and try to apply what you have read to explain the pattern of adjacent development since the mall was created.
4. By their influence on land values, market forces tend to create "zones" of specialized land uses. Therefore, what purpose is served by legal zoning? What are some reasons citizens might prefer regulated rather than market-determined land-use patterns?
5. A land acquisition specialist for a discount store chain said that when his firm decides to enter a new market, it buys or leases the three best store locations in the area, uses the best one for its new store, and makes certain that the other two sites are used only for noncompeting purposes. Discuss this in terms of the text's explanation of bid-rent curves and natural zoning.
6. How do past land-use theories explain the development of your local market? Are there development patterns that cannot be explained by these theories?

PART ONE

Case Problem

1. Suppose the demand curve for Class A office space in the metropolitan area is as follows:

Rental rate (per sq. ft.)	Quantity demanded (millions of sq. ft.)
$30	3.0
$31	2.9
$32	2.8
$33	2.7
$34	2.6
$35	2.5
$36	2.4

   Suppose also the quantity of Class A office space in the area is 2.9 million square feet. If no market participant is in a position to affect the market price, and all relevant information is readily available to all market participants, what will be the generally prevailing rental rate per square foot for office space of this class over the short term?

   Suppose a new investor enters the market, buys several office buildings, and announces that rent will be $33 per square foot for all new tenants and for all lease renewals. What will be the short-term impact on his gross rental income?

   a. If he controls 3% of the office space in this market area?
   b. If he controls 50% of the office space in this market?

2. Steve Silver purchased a parking lot 10 years ago for $100,000. He has earned an average annual NOI of $14,000 and is now considering selling the parking lot. Manny Mumford likes the parking lot's location and initiates negotiation for its purchase. Silver points out that the city has recently increased parking fees at municipal lots and observes that fees can now be raised on this lot sufficiently to move the NOI to about $20,000 annually. He notes that the $14,000 per year he has been earning represents a 14% per annum return on his investment. He thinks this is a good yield and states that Mumford can do equally well, based on the anticipated $20,000 per annum NOI, by paying about $144,000 for the lot. Mumford retorts that Silver will have an assured rate of return once the lot is sold but that Mumford will be taking a risk that the anticipated cash flow will not materialize. Therefore, says Mumford, she should earn a premium. She suggests an 18% yield and offers a price of about $111,000. Both parties earnestly state their desire to be fair and equitable in establishing a price for this property, but they are at odds as to how a price might best be determined. What do you suggest?

3. An office park manager experiments with rental rates and finds that every 1% change in per-square-foot rental rates induces a 4,500-square-foot change (in the opposite direction) in the amount of rented space. Rents are currently $18 per square foot and occupancy is at 90%. Fixed operating expenses (those that do not vary with occupancy level) are $7 per square foot; variable operating expenses (assume they vary directly with occupancy level) are $2 per square foot of occupied space. Total space available is 100,000 square feet.

Assuming the relationship between rental rates and occupancy levels remains invariant at all levels, what rental rate will maximize NOI (revenue minus operating expenses)?

PART TWO

Market Research and Cash-Flow Forecasting

Real estate investment is an expression of belief in a property's income-generating potential. Cash from operations and from eventual resale are the investor's only real benefits; both are dependent on the property's ability to generate rent. If rental income proves short-lived, market value will plummet and there will be little cash from either source. Thus, in a very real sense, investors buy a set of assumptions about a property's ability to produce income.

For that reason, successful investment decisions require an accurate perception of the property's ability to command rent, and reliable analysis incorporates a healthy dose of market research. Part One laid the foundation for such research by explaining how economic forces determine supply and demand relationships, the interaction of which sets market-clearing rental rates and property values. Part Two relates these concepts to discrete real estate parcels and the expectations of specific real estate investors.

Unit 4 introduces the tools and techniques for market research, and gives examples of supply and demand analysis. Unit 5 explains the typical format for reconstructing a property's operating history and extending the analysis into an operating forecast. The payoff, presented in Unit 6, is a multiple-year forecast of net operating income (NOI) and an estimate of market value at the end of the forecast period.

UNIT 4

Market Research Tools and Techniques

REAL ESTATE TODAY

UNIT PREVIEW

Decision making for real estate investments is essentially a matter of interpreting information about the real estate market in general, the subject parcel in particular, and the investor who must make a decision. First, however, the information must be collected and organized in a logical manner. G. Vincent Barrett and John P. Blair have called market research both the most difficult and the most consequential part of the real estate development planning process.[1] Their observation is equally true for the real estate investment decision-making process.

---

1 G. Vincent Barrett and John P. Blair, *How to Conduct and Analyze Real Estate Market and Feasibility Studies*, 2nd ed. (New York: Van Nostrand Reinhold, 1988), 10.

WHY MARKET RESEARCH IS NEEDED

Market information is needed by investors and portfolio managers at every stage in the decision-making process. They must, for example, estimate the most probable cash flow from each investment alternative and each potential deal structure. They need to know yields available in the marketplace so that cash-flow estimates can be adjusted intelligently for differences in the timing and certainty of expected receipt.

Market Research for Portfolio Decisions

Every portfolio should be reevaluated often and adjusted based on market information. Managers must decide whether to keep the properties that are now in the portfolio or to adjust the mix. If their decision is to adjust, they must decide how to divest themselves of existing assets (e.g., an outright sale, a sale and leaseback, or an exchange). If no divestiture is indicated, they must nevertheless judge whether to refinance, refurbish, or convert property to a different use. All these decisions depend on the same variables as acquisition decisions, and all require market information.

Market Research for Better Property Management

Market research is also needed to facilitate operating management decisions. Gilbert A. Churchill, Jr., notes that research information is used by operating management for planning, problem solving, and control purposes.[2]

As a planning tool, market research can identify opportunities and potential problems. Property managers need to know basic trends in the economic environment within which they must lease and administer rental space, so they can estimate how the trends will affect their operations. Research might reveal, for example, that changing income levels, consumption patterns, and work practices will radically alter space needs. This information, in tandem with data on competitive rents, will aid in setting appropriate rent schedules and advertising budgets.

Market research assists in identifying modifications that will enhance a property's rentability. Information about the needs and preferences of present and potential tenants might reveal that some amenities should be eliminated because they do not generate enough additional rent to cover their operating and maintenance costs, while others should be added to make the building more competitive. Research helps in deciding whether to lease space on a long-term or a short-term basis, and which lease clauses are likely to be met with the least tenant resistance. It indicates what tenant mix will maximize a property's ability to command rents. Should an office building cater to tenants in a specific profession, such as law or medicine, for example, or will a more diverse tenant mix lead to lower vacancy rates and greater operating income?

---

[2] Gilbert A. Churchill, Jr., *Marketing Research: Methodological Foundations*, 5th ed. (Ft. Worth, Tex.: The Dryden Press, 1994).

Control-oriented market research permits early identification of existing and potential management trouble spots. Good research helps management assess the quality of current building operations and evaluate proposed changes. By comparing building rental and vacancy rates with those of comparable properties, for example, management can evaluate its marketing program; comparing tenant turnover rates will highlight the degree of tenant satisfaction. Comparative operating expense ratios (expenses as a percentage of gross rents) help management spot operating inefficiencies and permit early corrective action.

THE EXTENT OF MARKET RESEARCH

Three key factors determine the extent to which market research will be worthwhile for investment decision making: the stability of market conditions, the complexity of the property involved, and investors' tolerance for risk. The more stable the market, the less the need for data collection and analysis; the larger and more complex the property, the greater the need. The exact trade-off between spending time and money to refine the analysis and economizing by accepting greater uncertainty depends on the investors' risk tolerance.

Costs vs. Benefits

Carefully planned and appropriately executed market research will always push back the curtain of uncertainty. Its value depends to a large extent on the investor's attitude toward risk. Investors who are more comfortable with ambiguity will make decisions with less information. Those who find uncertainty unsettling will expend more resources in search of predictability, even though the cost of the effort might reduce their portfolios' ultimate profitability. Either strategy is reasonable, provided investors understand the relationship between incremental research costs and benefits.

The issue is illustrated in Figure 4.1. Expected total costs of research and its expected total value are measured on the vertical axis; the vertical distance between the cost and benefit functions represents net benefit derived (benefit minus cost). Maximum net benefit results from the amount of research and analysis represented by point m on the horizontal axis. Additional data gathering and analysis beyond this point cost more than its incremental benefit and reduces the net benefit from market research.

FIGURE 4.1: Cost, Benefit, and Optimum Level of Research Effort

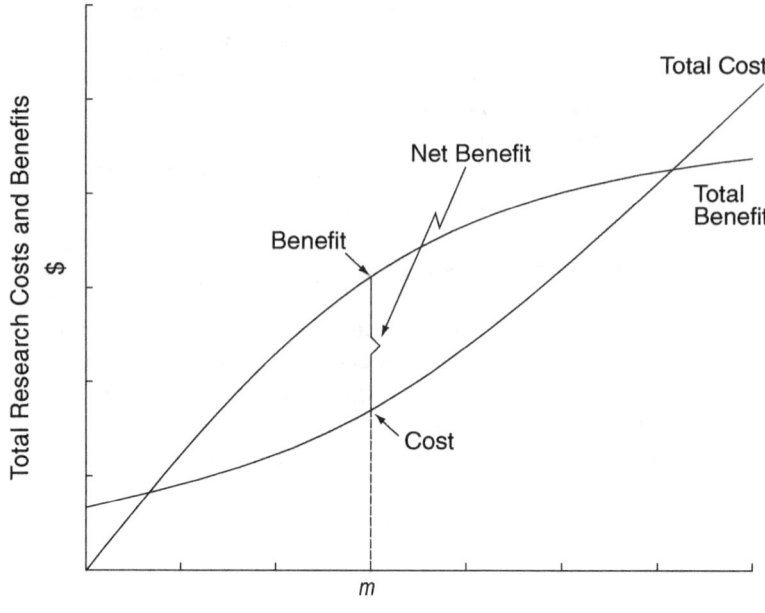

The Role of Prevailing Market Conditions

If supply and demand are in equilibrium in a market, very little market research would be warranted; perhaps nothing more than reference to current rental and vacancy rates and some analysis of the relationship between NOI and market values would be needed. All these factors can be expected to change over time, but if the changes proceed smoothly and thus predictably, the refinement that additional research permits may not be worth the cost.

However, suppose the neighborhood is undergoing change, perhaps a transition from predominantly residential to mixed residential and commercial use. The pace of the change and its likely impact on ability to command rent must be analyzed. The likelihood of a successful transition for the subject property and its most appropriate commercial use must be investigated.

When vacancy rates are near historically high or low levels, a trend reversal may be sudden and sharp; investors need market information to gauge the likelihood of such a reversal and its probable severity. When construction activity is proceeding at a frenetic pace, national or local politics are in a state of flux, or internal migratory patterns are changing noticeably, it may be necessary to collect a substantial amount of data and to analyze those data extensively to estimate impacts of local real estate markets.

The Role of Complexity

For a fairly simple investment proposition, such as a small and smoothly operating apartment building in a stable community, the need for market analysis may be minimal. The operating history of the property might be an adequate guide to its future, and prevailing relationships between operating income and market values might be all that one needs to estimate market value at the end of the proposed investment period.

But, suppose the investor must choose between buying and trading. Perhaps, the seller is offering a property that has more than one prospective use, and the most profitable use is uncertain. A seller might offer a mortgage loan where the credit terms will affect the transaction price. In such instances, market data and extensive analysis will be needed. The general rule is, the more complex the proposed arrangement, the greater is the need for market research.

Complexity is often correlated with property size. Investment in a small strip shopping center that has been fully developed and is 100% leased justifies less attention to data collection and analysis than investment in a regional shopping center that is still in the proposal stage and is to be developed in an untested market.

Avoiding Analysis Paralysis

Because the payoff from research is not objectively measurable, decision makers will be sorely challenged to identify the optimum level. James D. Vernor has observed that research proceeds in successive iterations, with each round becoming increasingly more complex and costly.[3] Beginning with readily available information incorporated into crude financial synthesis, such as first-year ratio analysis, the investigation progresses to successively more detailed data collection and elaborate financial analysis.

However the dilemma is confronted, some market intelligence must be gathered before substantial resources are committed to an uncertain venture. But there is some point beyond which research and analysis must cease and a "go or no-go" decision must be made. The problem is phrased succinctly by George Bernard Shaw: "When we have done our utmost to arrive at a reasonable conclusion, we . . . must close our minds for the moment with a snap, and act dogmatically on our own conclusion. The man who waits to make an entirely reasonable will dies intestate."

MARKET RESEARCH DESIGN

Because investment dilemmas are not uniform, research procedures must be customized. Yet, even though each project has its own special emphasis, all share a common sequence of steps. The problem to be solved or the question to be answered should be carefully formulated before any data are gathered because the nature of the problem will largely determine the information to be assembled. Data collection and analysis then proceed from a broad macro level to an increasingly specific micro level.

---

[3] James D. Vernor of Georgia State University, in private correspondence.

Problem Formulation

As with most of life's dilemmas, carefully defining the investment problem takes one a long way toward its solution. Gilbert Churchill summarized the importance of problem formulation this way.[4]

One of the more valuable roles marketing research can perform is helping to define the problem to be solved. Only when the problem is carefully and precisely defined can research be designed to provide pertinent information. Part of the process of problem definition includes specifying the objectives of the specific research project or projects that might be undertaken. Each project should have one or more objectives, and the next step in the process should not be taken until these can be explicitly stated.

Data Collection and Analysis

The broadly recommended research approach is to work from the general to the specific, starting with an analysis of national and international economic trends (to the extent their consideration is relevant) and working down through metropolitan and neighborhood trends to an analysis of the prospects for the specific property that is the subject of the effort. This sequence is illustrated in Figure 4.2.

FIGURE 4.2: Sequential Components of Market Analysis
1. Analyze national and international economic trends (especially inflation, interest rates, and the rate of economic growth) that influence local real estate investment conditions.
2. Consider regional and metropolitan economic, demographic, and political trends that are relevant to the investment opportunity.
3. Delineate specific geographic boundaries of the neighborhood, trade, or market area within which the subject property will directly compete with peer-group properties.
4. Analyze potential tenant demand within the neighborhood, trade, or market area for the specific type of rental property under consideration. Project demand over the forecast period.
5. Identify and analyze competitive (peer group) properties in the neighborhood, trade, or market area.
6. Estimate potential additions to the supply of competing properties in the neighborhood, trade, or market area over the forecast period. Estimate the subject property's *fair share* of projected demand (projected submarket supply divided by projected submarket demand).
7. Compare the subject property's characteristics with tenant needs and with the characteristics of present and projected competing properties to estimate probable changes in market share over the forecast period. (This is an estimate of the *capture rate*, the percentage of total submarket demand that the subject property is likely to secure.)

---

4 Churchill, *op. cit.*, 21–24.

The first level involves collecting and analyzing relevant national and international economic trends. This involves assessing the impact of economic aggregates such as Federal Reserve monetary policy and government fiscal policy. These should be related to regional and metropolitan economic indicators, to see how local and metropolitan trends might deviate from national trends over the forecast period.

On the regional and metropolitan level, in addition to economic aggregates, the analyst should collect demographic trend data: information on such factors as population, employment, household size, and purchasing power that will have an impact on the demand for real estate. Political data that have an impact on real estate supply and demand (e.g., local officials' attitudes toward economic growth, business location incentives, local tax policy, and the threat of rent controls) become important at this level. For example, the TCJA, signed December 22, 2017 by President Trump has placed limitations on the purposes of home equity loans or home equity lines of credit.

The aim is to recognize patterns and to spot clues as to how these patterns might change and to relate these patterns to likely future trends. For this, real estate market analysts will generally rely on forecasts produced by individuals and firms that specialize in broad market analysis. Such forecasts are widely available at modest cost; often they are free.

As the focus shifts from overall macro level analysis to an increasingly specific micro level, reliable information becomes progressively scarce. At this point, the analyst works with the observed relationships between available trends and projections for wider market areas to derive estimates for the neighborhood, trade, or market area within which the specific property will compete for tenants.

Research objectives at the submarket level are to determine supply and demand relationships as they currently exist for the type of rental property under analysis and to forecast them over the period of the proposed investment. Relationships for the wider regional or metropolitan market are of little direct use because a specific property will compete with only a limited portion of the wider market. Strip shopping centers, for example, do not compete with large regional malls, and a small suburban office building will seldom compete with office high-rises in the central business district. Submarkets exist because tenants and investors perceive differences in property location, rental rates, property size, building age, condition or design, or other characteristics that make one property more or less desirable than others, and decide which are reasonable substitutes.

A Four-Quadrant Forecasting Matrix

The quandary is that a wealth of data are available regarding current conditions and for forecasting future conditions in the wider (macro) market, but the goal is to estimate future conditions as they affect a specific property, which may be influenced by only a limited portion of the wider market. We need a technique for proceeding from available regional and metropolitan market data to a forecast regarding that limited portion of the market in which the subject property directly competes.

A four-quadrant matrix such as that illustrated in Figure 4.3 is often used to illustrate the problem. Information about present and historical market conditions in the region or the metropolitan area will generally be available; it fills in the upper-left quadrant. More often than not, similar data have been incorporated into forecasts, and this goes in the upper-right quadrant.

FIGURE 4.3: Four-Quadrant Forecasting Model

	Present	**Future**
Regional or citywide	C Current and historical Economic and demographic Vacancies, rent	A/D Forecast Economic and demographic Vacancies, rent
Specific property and immediate market area	B Physical characteristics Demand characteristics Rent and vacancies Market share estimate	E Property performance forecast

Data for the lower-left quadrant, the subject property's share in market rental revenue, its physical characteristics and those of peer-group properties, as well as demographic and socioeconomic characteristics of tenants, are less readily available but can be collected. The challenge is to use the data that relate directly to the property and its market area, which are directly applicable but incomplete, and the data from the region or metropolitan area, which are more extensive but not directly applicable, to develop a micro level forecast in the lower-right quadrant. Dowell Myers and Kenneth Beck have suggested a detailed approach for navigating the matrix to generate a usable forecast of relevant supply and demand variables in the lower-right quadrant.[5] A synopsis of their strategy is presented here, and is related to Figure 4.3 by using alphabetical indicators for each step.

A. Macro-forecasts of economic aggregates such as regional or metropolitan employment, income, growth rates, and demographic composition have often been generated by other researchers, and the investment analyst will seldom have the resources to prepare a more reliable forecast. These provide the initial market forecast for the upper-right quadrant.

B. Collect physical, economic, and demographic information relating to the subject property and peer-group properties (data for the lower-left quadrant) and organize it in a fashion that relates it directly to the available macro level forecast. Vacancy rates and the rate of change in rental rates,

---

[5] Dowell Myers and Kenneth Beck, "A Four-Square Design for Relating the Two Essential Dimensions of Real Estate Market Studies," included in James R. DeLisle and J. Sa-Aadu, eds., *Appraisal, Market Analysis, and Public Policy in Real Estate* (Boston: Kluwer Academic Publishers, 1994), 259–88.

for example, are likely to be functionally related to construction activity and population change.

C. Link the reorganized data for the subject and peer-group properties (the lower-left quadrant data) to similar data for the region or metropolitan area (the upper-left quadrant). For example, relate metropolitan rental and vacancy rates to rental and vacancy rates for the subject and the peer-group properties; when market-wide vacancy or average rental rates change, do the same measures for the subject and its peers change by a lesser or a greater amount? Quantify the observed relationship.

D. Forecast relevant regional or metropolitan variables such as rental and vacancy rates by using observed past relationships between these and other regional or metropolitan variables (such as construction activity and demographic and economic trends) that have been included in available macro-forecasts. This pushes the relevant variables out of the upper-left into the upper-right quadrant.

E. Relate the forecast of relevant regional or metropolitan variables, such as vacancies and rental rates, that have been pushed into the upper-right quadrant, to the same variables for the subject and its peer-group properties, by using the observed past relationship and incorporating any observed trend in the relationships. This pulls the relevant property-specific variables into the lower-right quadrant.

PREPARING A RESEARCH REPORT

A research report summarizes procedures and reports conclusions. It must be clear, complete, accurate, and precise. The report will be only as good as the underlying data and analysis, but no matter how thorough the research or insightful the analysis, it will not be successful unless effectively communicated.

The temptation exists to concentrate on regional or metropolitan data, which are likely to be plentiful, and to skimp on project-specific analysis, where data are generally lacking. One result is reports that bulge with national, regional, and metropolitan data, with little or no explanation of how the data relate to the impending investment decision.

At the broadest level, most reports should be limited to bare-bones reporting of trends that will have an impact on supply or demand variables for the subject property (those incorporated into the four-quadrant analysis illustrated in Figure 4.3). As the analysis proceeds to progressively disaggregated levels (from national to submarket and property-specific considerations), it should become progressively more detailed. At every level, all data included in the report should be directly related to the problem the analysis is designed to solve or the question it is designed to answer.

There is no such thing as *the* correct report format. Appropriate organization and presentation depends on the nature of the problem and the user's needs. Many variations are possible; Figure 4.4 presents a general outline of what a complete market analysis report might contain.

FIGURE 4.4: Outline for a Market Analysis Report

I. *Executive Summary.* Concisely state the objectives of the analysis and the analytical methods, data sources, assumptions, and conclusions. The executive summary will be the only part of a report that many decision makers will read. It should be sufficiently specific to alert readers to the key issues and explain how findings were derived.

II. *Overview.* Present an analysis of relevant economic and demographic trends at the national, regional, and metropolitan levels, and explain how they relate to demand and supply in the submarket area.

III. *Submarket Delineation and Site Analysis.* Define submarket boundaries and summarize site-specific data (a physical description of site attributes such as the desirability of the location relative to competing properties, the site's geographic orientation and physical features, and the nature, age, and condition of the improvements) that may have an impact on the property's competitive position.

IV. *Analysis of Demand.* Project overall demand in the submarket area for property such as the subject. Draw conclusions about absorption rates—the rate at which new and existing vacant space will be taken by tenants.

V. *Analysis of Supply.* Survey the existing stock of competing space and analyze past trends, the current environment, and likely future changes to derive a forecast of the future supply.

VI. *Competitive Analysis.* Compare the subject property's features and advantages with those of existing and projected future competitive properties.

VII. *Forecast Rental Revenue.* Draw conclusions about competitive strengths and weaknesses over the forecast period, and estimate changes in rental rates and market share. Present final estimates of rental rates, vacancy factors, and gross rental revenue. If the project is new or is to be rehabilitated, estimate the total marketing time required to achieve stable occupancy levels.

DATA SOURCES

Once the problem is properly defined and clearly specified, researchers next turn their attention to data collection. At this point, a decision must be made whether to rely on primary or on secondary sources. Primary data are gathered by the researcher precisely for the problem at hand. Secondary data, in contrast, have been previously gathered (by the researchers or by others) for some other purpose. A good operating rule is to rely on primary sources only if secondary data are not available.

Secondary Data Sources

Where available, secondary data are almost certain to be less costly and less time-consuming to obtain than primary data. Information that is readily available free of charge in nearby libraries or at modest cost from research firms might cost thousands of dollars and require weeks of effort for a primary researcher to gather. Because this information can be used an infinite number of times until it becomes dated, firms that collect and sell it can reap a tidy profit while charging a small fraction of what it would cost their customers to do their own primary research.

A key disadvantage of secondary sources, and a major cause of users' frustration, is that the data are seldom available in precisely the desired form. Units of measure may be inappropriate for the intended purpose, class definitions seldom exactly fit analysts' needs, and the information is seldom as current as one would like. None of these shortcomings are necessarily fatal; reorganizing and updating the information is usually less costly and less time-consuming than starting from scratch.

Secondary data are frequently available in raw form from sources that gather them. These include government agencies, universities, and private firms (real estate appraisers, brokers and counselors, market research firms, architects, accounting firms, and so forth) whose data needs lead them to investigate phenomena of interest to real estate investment analysts. Their data files can save many days of tedious work and costly hours of field investigation. Large commercial data banks (companies that specialize in collecting and reselling information) often have computerized storage and retrieval facilities that permit them to provide information in almost any format and in a variety of classifications at modest cost.

At the national, regional, and metropolitan levels, information overload is more likely than information starvation. A flood of data makes it difficult to decide what is appropriate and what is mere window dressing. The sheer volume of statistical information from government and private sources is intimidating. One's best ally is likely to be a research librarian on the staff of a metropolitan or university library. Having made a career of navigating the data thicket, librarians can aim researchers at the right sources. Because the librarian might provide an overwhelming source of general information yet know nothing about real estate, the researcher must be prepared to clearly outline the search parameters. A mismatch between the analyst's needs and what a librarian thinks is needed can initiate a frustrating trip through a madhouse of useless information, a data inundation in which one might metaphorically drown.

The U.S. Bureau of the Census, under the Department of Commerce, is the largest data-gathering agency in the nation. Census data are generally of high quality and are available in a variety of formats, permitting researchers to create their own formats and classifications. Census data tapes or compact discs (CD-ROM) can be purchased from the Bureau of the Census. They are available for use free of charge at most larger metropolitan and state university libraries.

While less prolific than the Census Bureau, other federal agencies are also hooked on data generation. The Department of Labor, the Department of Housing and Urban Development, the various Federal Reserve Banks, Bureau of Labor Statistics, and a host of other taxpayer-supported institutions are data-generating engines.

State and metropolitan governments' data collection brooms have a narrower sweep, but they are no less thorough. School enrollments, sales tax collections, building permits, highway traffic volume—these are representative data series that have tremendous research value in real estate and are readily available from government agencies. Much of this information is available in online databases. All data will be cataloged and made available for fingertip retrieval under the guidance of a competent research librarian.

Private information storehouses rival those of government agencies and are often in a more useful format for real estate market analysis. Once again, it helps to know exactly what one wants before contacting a prospective source. Unlike the government, private sources are under no obligation to make their data public. They are likely to do so only as a professional accommodation or for a fee.

A host of data storage and retrieval firms earn a living off the mountain of data generated by government and private sources. They do this by reorganizing the information and offering it in more usable form, often coupled with a forecast generated by extending observed trends. Computerized data storage, processing and retrieval efficiencies, and their large volume of business enable many of the firms to sell custom-ordered reports at relatively modest prices. The reliability of their small-area forecasts varies widely, however.

Offering to share data with firms active in the submarket area of interest might shake loose information from initially reluctant sources. While raw data might be confidential, and sharing it a violation of confidence from the various sources, researchers can offer to provide a summary of their findings. The key is to know where the information is likely to be located, and then to have the interpersonal skills and investigative persistence to ferret it out.

Primary Data Sources

Secondary sources sometimes prove inadequate. The data may be hopelessly outdated, unreliable, or inappropriately classified. It then becomes necessary to resort to primary data sources to update, supplement, validate, or supplant the secondary sources.

Primary data may be gathered by communication or by observation, with the choice usually dictated by the nature of the intelligence desired. Communication involves asking questions. These may be oral or written and can elicit responses in either form. They may be short and to the point, or they might involve in-depth interviews. Observation means checking and recording relevant facts or behavior. For example, a researcher might estimate the boundaries of a store's trade area by checking customers' license plates and noting their counties of origin.

Communication is a more versatile technique than observation. Whatever it is the researchers want to know, all they have to do is ask. This makes communication faster and more cost-effective for most purposes. Researchers are not forced to wait for events to occur so that they can be observed.

Accuracy of responses is, of course, a constant concern. Respondents may be inclined to say what they believe their interrogators want to hear. Responses are also influenced by how questions are structured, and sometimes by the interviewer's demeanor.

Data collected by observation are more likely to be objective and factual. The subject's perceptions play less of a role, and conclusions are likely to be more reliable. Observation tends to be more time-consuming, however, and therefore more expensive. For example, a researcher can calculate an accurate vacancy rate for a retail market by conducting an exhaustive search of all retail properties in the market area and observing which spaces are vacant.

DESCRIPTIVE RESEARCH

Much of the primary research data needed by real estate investment analysts are descriptive in nature. Examples include the following:

- *Tenant profile.* Based on information gathered from tenants in similar buildings, one might attempt to describe the profile of a most likely tenant for a proposed structure, characterizing the tenant with respect to amenities desired, amount of space taken, and special facilities required.
- *Consumer/resident profile.* One may wish to estimate the proportion of people in a specific population who behave in a particular manner. To illustrate, it might be necessary to estimate the percentage of residents within a certain radius of a proposed shopping center who would shop at the complex.
- *Estimated reactions to proposed alterations in rental terms.* This could include changes in the length of leases or the relative degree to which rent depends on a flat fee versus a percentage lease clause. One might also wish to estimate typical reactions to separating rental rates for basic facilities and rates for special amenities, such as swimming pools and health club facilities.

Planning for Research

Prior to starting the collection process, clearly specify who is to contribute information, what information is to be collected, and when it is to be solicited. Decide in advance where and how interviews will be conducted. Also, in advance, work out an efficient cataloging system.

Conducting all this work in advance often unearths analytical problems that might otherwise surface during data collection or after all the interviews have been conducted. A dummy table of cataloged variables (or a computer data storage and retrieval program), previously worked out, leaves only the task of collecting the information and recording it in the catalog space or the computer data bank provided. With this precaution, for example, researchers are less likely to overlook a crucial variable that should have been included in the data program; they are even less likely to fall into the common trap of gathering information that may be interesting in its own right but does not prove useful for solving the research problem.

Cross-Sectional and Time Series Data

Descriptive surveys may be *cross-sectional* or *time series*. Cross-sectional surveys, which involve one-time sampling from a population of research interest, are by far the most frequently encountered type of data collection assignment. All elements are measured at a single point in time. The cross-sectional survey thus provides a snapshot of the variables under observation at the time of the survey.

Time series, in contrast, measure changes over time. Sometimes called *longitudinal studies*, they involve repeated measures of the same phenomena, recording any variation through time. Time series analysis in no way implies that time itself is a causal factor in observed change. Rather, the analyst observes changes in both the phenomena of interest and other factors presumed to bear a causal relationship. Time series or longitudinal studies can help the analyst see trends and make better estimates of how long it will take to achieve a level of growth in such items as population, traffic, or housing.

Inferential Analysis

Modern statistical techniques are a powerful addition to the analyst's repertoire of analytical tools. They permit rapid and inexpensive analysis and synthesis of masses of data. They also permit reliable generalizations to be drawn from a limited sample.

Statistics have received an undeserved reputation for requiring high-order mathematical skills. Deriving or proving fundamental rules (mathematicians call them *theorems*) may require daunting degrees of knowledge; applying generally accepted techniques is an entirely different matter. The most commonly used statistical tools require no more knowledge of arithmetic than typically acquired in high school. What is needed is an understanding of the statistical relationships themselves: their strengths and weaknesses, their uses and potential misuses.

This makes statistical analysis particularly valuable for market research, where conclusions about consumer preferences must be drawn from questionnaires distributed to only a small proportion of the total market or where predictions about the future must be based on past trends.

Statistical applications are divided conveniently into two broad categories. *Descriptive statistics* involve measuring characteristics that are important to a problem and bringing them together in summary form. Descriptive statistics use quantitative expressions to describe characteristics of a sample or an underlying population. Knowledgeable and busy analysts appreciate the inexpensive and timely reduction of large masses of data to essentials.

Inferential statistics involve drawing conclusions from evidence contained in the data. Real estate analysts frequently use such techniques to draw inferences about a general class of phenomena from a sample or to estimate future occurrences by studying data from the recent past.

GEOGRAPHIC INFORMATION SYSTEMS

Much of the data used in real estate investment analysis are *spatially related*: analysts are concerned not simply with *how much* or *what kind*, but also with *where*. Examples of spatially related data of interest include topological features such as streets, zoning, traffic density, population density, income levels, spending patterns, population age distribution, household size, and so forth.

The traditional way of presenting spatially related information has been with transparent overlays that are layered one after another on a map of the market area. This cumbersome but effective technique lets analysts see how each key variable relates spatially to the property under analysis, and permits limited "what if" speculation by using overlays with various trend projections. In recent years, the technique has been rendered more versatile and more effective by the advent of powerful and relatively inexpensive computers.

Computerization has also given this technique a new name: *geographic information systems*, or GIS. The computerized technique, called *spatial modeling*, permits layered data to be retrieved from a data storage system and directly displayed on a computer screen or a printed map. An example is illustrated in Figure 4.5.

FIGURE 4.5: GIS: Map Overlays, Referenced to an Underlying Grid

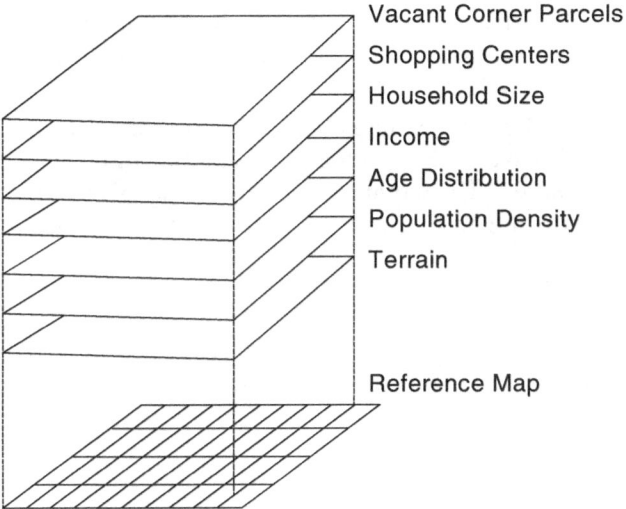

A spatially related model might, for example, display all geographic areas where residents live more than 10 minutes' driving time from a shopping center and show population densities in each area. Or all vacant commercial-zoned parcels of more than 12,000 square feet that face a major traffic artery might be displayed if they are within one mile of population concentrations that contain at least, for example, 1,000 households.

These same data could be displayed on a map with population growth and the growth in traffic density projected forward for a number of years. This would highlight sites with potential for significant market improvement, in many cases before the potential is reflected in market prices.

Until very recently, the technology for GIS required expensive computer systems and operators that were highly trained specialists. Moreover, accumulating relevant data and loading it into computer memory were expensive and time-consuming. Simpler programs, coupled with expanded computer speed and capacity, now permit GIS to be run on personal computers. Many of the programs written for personal computers can import data files from the Census Bureau's TIGER (Topologically Integrated Geographically Encoded Reference) System, which contains spatially related information on income, age, race, sex, households, and so forth. TIGER System data are available for download or on CD-ROM discs and can be purchased from the Bureau of the Census.[6] They are also available at most major libraries.

Many commercial vendors sell related information sets that are decomposed to the level of census tracts and blocks or post office ZIP codes. For larger metropolitan areas the data are often further available for ZIP code plus an additional four-digits that further decompose the geographic area. These data sets are compatible with most widely available GIS software packages such as ArcGIS.

Beyond specific site analysis, area markets can be analyzed by integrating TIGER file data with other information to identify economic and social characteristics and key linkages within a market area. The systems are particularly valuable for analyzing linkages where distances must be measured along road networks rather than in straight lines and where traffic congestion and bottlenecks must be factored in.

Data for different time periods can be overlaid on a market area or metropolitan map to create a graphic representation of change through time. In this manner, analysts can identify neighborhoods by stages of growth and determine which are in an early growth phase, which are at or near maturity, and which are in decline.

---

[6] *https://www.census.gov/geo/* (last visited on 4-29-2018)

Example 4.1

An investment enterprise interested in constructing a large shopping mall within the perimeter of the town of Anysville has decided that the potential location should meet the following requirements:

A. The site must be within a half-mile zone outside the urban area.
B. The site should be located no more than 200 yards from existing high-traffic roads or no more than 100 yards from medium-duty or light-duty roads.
C. The site should be located in an area that does not infringe on existing forested lands.
D. Selected parcels must be at least 12 acres in size.

From map layers of Anysville, a half-mile buffer zone surrounding the town is identified (A); 200-yard and 100-yard buffer zones are generated along existing heavy-duty and medium/light-duty roads (B). By overlaying these two map layers, the desired areas are identified (C). The forested areas are introduced and "removed" from the selected areas (D). Areas below the required size of 12 acres are eliminated to provide the potential mall sites (E).

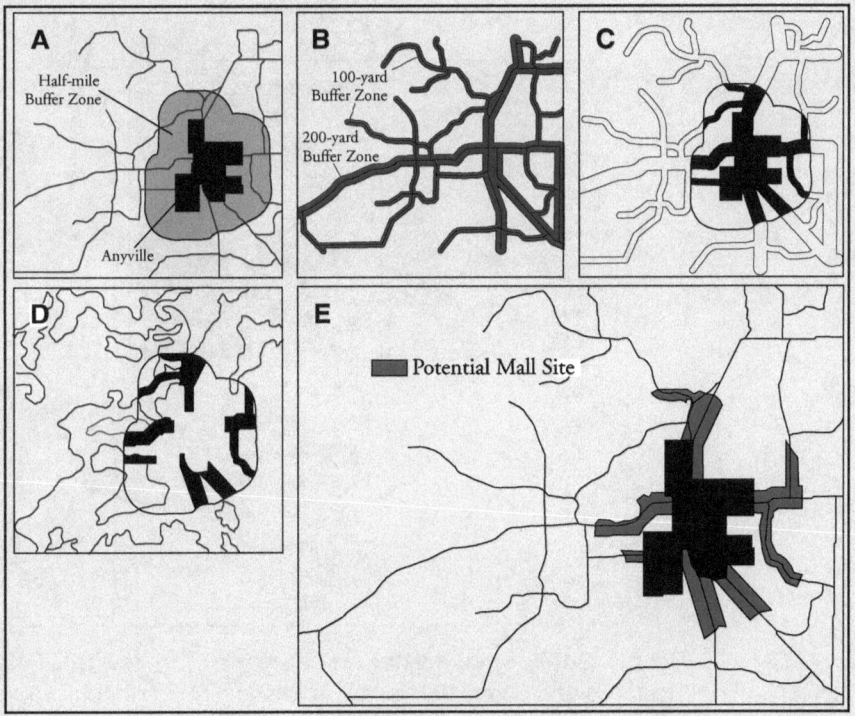

Source: Devlin Fung, "Managing by the Map," in *Business Perspectives*, Bureau of Business and Economic Research, University of Memphis, 8(2): 15–17.

Example 4.2

A real estate company wants to investigate the average cost of houses sold in Shelby County in 1980 and 1990, and the change within that period. Data needed include houses sold during the two periods, the street/road map, and the housing zones based on the multiple listing service (MLS). The location of each house can be identified on the street map using the address-matching function of the GIS software (A). The average prices of houses for the two respective years are summarized, based on the MLS zones (B and C). Finally, by overlaying the two maps, the changes in price for each zone can be computed and displayed (D). The resulting map helps identify the spatial distribution and the magnitude of changes in average home prices within the period in Shelby County.

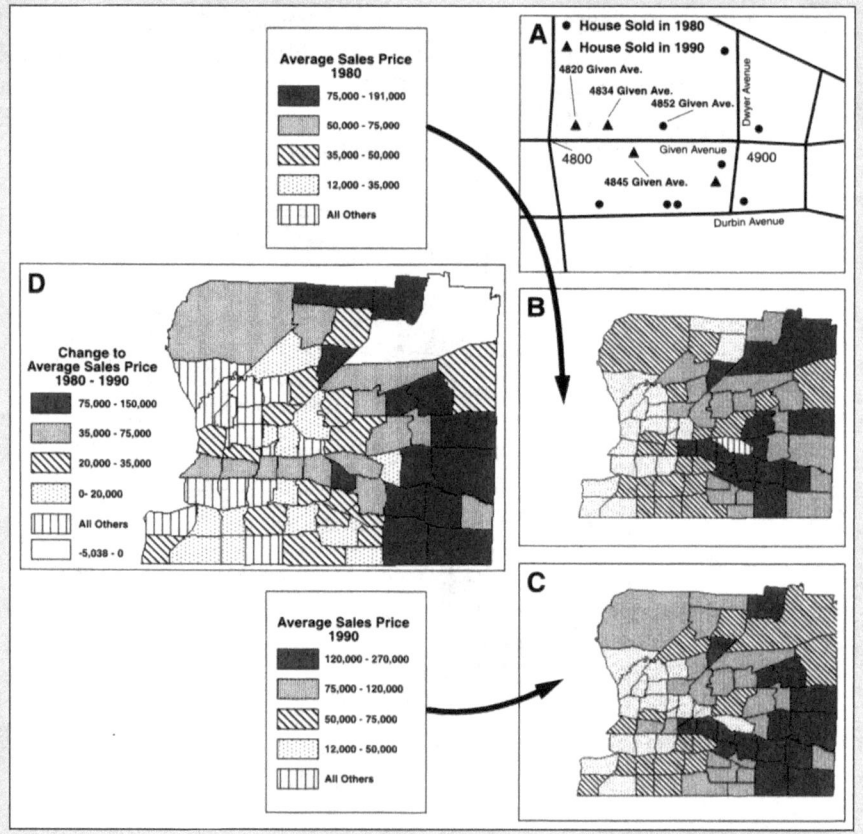

Source: Devlin Fung, "Managing by the Map." *In Business Perspectives*, Bureau of Business and Economic Research, University of Memphis, 8(2): 15–17.

SUMMARY

Market research is an essential element in rational investment decision making. Reliable revenue and expense forecasts and estimates of future market values require market research and analysis. Market data permit evaluation of management performance and identification of potential areas of performance improvement. Research should be pursued to the point where incremental research and analysis costs equal incremental benefits anticipated.

To a significant extent, market research programs are dictated by the nature of the research problems. Generally, however, the program will start with a definition of the problem and proceed to selection of data collection methods and research design. Data are collected, analyzed, and interpreted, and the research report is prepared.

Usually, the most useful approach is to proceed from the general to the particular, from wide-area market and demographic forecasts to projections about a specific property. Because wide-area data are generally more readily available and more amenable to reliable forecasting, analysts depend heavily on identifying consistent relationships between regional and neighborhood phenomena. They exploit observed relationships to generate useful estimates of a property's prospects, based on the relationship and an aggregate forecast.

Sources for data are designated as primary or secondary, depending on whether data are collected specifically for a current research problem or for some other purpose. Secondary data (collected for other uses) are generally more convenient and less costly to collect but are likely to be in a format or in units other than those needed. Primary data should be collected only after exhausting all available sources of secondary data.

Primary data are gathered by communicating with research subjects or by observing and reporting on their actions. Communication is more versatile and, where practical, tends to be faster and more cost-effective. Subjectivity is sometimes introduced, however, by the tendency of respondents to give answers they believe researchers expect.

The majority of market research is descriptive in nature. Descriptive studies may involve a one-time sampling from a population of research interest (cross-sectional data) or repeated measures of the same phenomena to detect changes over time (time series data).

Inferential statistics permit conclusions to be drawn about an entire class of phenomena from observing a sample of the population. Where possible, samples from which inferences are to be drawn are collected on a random basis. Generally, however, real estate data represent judgment samples in which observations are judged to be representative of the underlying population of interest.

Computerized GIS permit data to be displayed in an endless variety of combinations, all spatially related. Maps can display the data as they exist currently or, based on forecasts, as they are likely to exist at specified future dates.

RECOMMENDED READING

Birkin, Mark, et al. *Intelligent GIS: Location Decisions and Strategic Planning.* New York: Wiley, 1996.

Brandon, Plewe. *GIS Online: Information Retrieval, Mapping, and the Internet.* Santa Fe, N.M.: OnWord Press, 1997.

Clapp, John, and Mauricio Rodriguez. "Using a GIS for Real Estate Market Analysis: The Problem of Spatially Aggregated Data." *The Journal of Real Estate Research* 16, no. 1 (1998): 35–56.

Dueker, Kenneth J., and P. Barton DeLacy. "GIS in the Land Development Planning Process." *Journal of the American Planning Association* 56, no. 4 (Autumn 1990): 483–92.

Farragher, Edward J. and Arline Savage. "An Investigation of Real Estate Investment Decision-Making Practices." *The Journal of Real Estate Practice and Education* 11, no. 1 (2008): 29-40.

Fotheringham, Stewart A., ed. *Spatial Models and GIS: New and Potential Models.* Boca Raton, FL: CRC Press, 1999.

Hohl, Pat, ed. *GIS Data Conversion: Strategies, Techniques, and Management.* Santa Fe, N.M.: OnWord Press, 1998.

Jennen, Maarten G.J. and Dirk Brounen. "The Effect of Clustering on Office Rents: Evidence from the Amsterdam Market." *Real Estate Economics*, 37:2, 2009, 185-208.

Kennedy, Heather, ed. *The ESRI Press Dictionary of GIS Terminology.* Redlands, Calif.: ESRI Press, 2001.

Korte, George. *The GIS Book.* 5th ed. Santa Fe, N.M.: OnWord Press, 2000.

Mitchell, Andy. *The ESRI Guide to GIS Analysis.* Redlands, Calif.: ESRI Press, 2005.

Molenaar, Martien. *An Introduction to the Theory of Spatial Object Modeling for GIS.* Bristol, Pa.: Taylor & Francis, 1998.

Ormsby, Tim, and Jonell Alvi. *Extending ArcView GIS: Teach Yourself to Use ArcView GIS Extensions: Network Analyst, Spatial Analyst, 3D Analyst: Self-Study Workbook for ArcView GIS Users.* Redlands, Calif.: ESRI Press, 1999.

Pickles, John, ed. *Ground Truth: The Social Implications of Geographical Information Systems.* New York: Guilford Press, 1995.

Pittman, Robert. "Geographic Information Systems: An Important New Tool for Economic Development Professionals." *Economic Development Review* 8, no. 4 (Fall 1990): 4–7.

Sappington, Nancy, ed. *Applications of Geographical Information Systems.* Redlands, Calif.: ESRI Press, 2000.

Thrall, Grant I. *Business Geography and New Real Estate Market Analysis.* Cary, N.C.: Oxford University Press, 2002.

Weber, Bruce. "The Use of GIS and OLAP for Accurate Valuation of Developable Land." *Journal of Real Estate Portfolio Management* 7, no. 2 (July–September 2001): 253–81.

Wofford, Larry E., and Grant Thrall. "Real Estate Problem Solving and Geographic Information Systems: A Stage Model of Reasoning." *Journal of Real Estate Literature* 5, no. 2 (July 1997): 177–202.

Wong, David W. S., and Jay Lee. *Statistical Analysis of Geographic Information with ArcView GIS and Arc GIS.* New York: Wiley, 2005.

REVIEW QUESTIONS

1. Why is there a need for market research in real estate investment decisions?
2. How much market research should be done?
3. What steps are customarily used in research procedures?
4. Which are preferable, primary or secondary data sources?
5. Describe some methods of collecting primary data.
6. Describe the four-quadrant research model for deriving a property-specific market forecast.
7. How can time series/longitudinal studies be most helpful in a feasibility study?
8. How is GIS useful in feasibility studies?

DISCUSSION QUESTIONS

1. One of your investment clients intends to put virtually all of her capital into a large apartment complex. Another client is acquiring a portfolio that will eventually include more than 100 duplex apartments, which he says will be scattered more or less randomly over the cityscape. In what ways might your recommended market analysis for these two clients differ?
2. What are some local sources of secondary market data that might prove useful for real estate investment analysis, and how might one go about gaining access to these data?
3. Existing vacancy rates are critical data for market analysis. How might one obtain vacancy rate data on office buildings in a metropolitan area? What methods could be used to collect primary data? What secondary data sources could be used?
4. How have feasibility studies changed recently in light of environmental problems and changes in laws or regulations?
5. How could you best use GIS in a feasibility study for a high-end retail development?
6. Where have you avoided analysis paralysis when making a decision? What was the point at which you made a decision even though other analysis could still be conducted?

DATA SOURCES

Census Data

There are in fact 10 different censuses, all of interest to real estate analysts to a greater or lesser extent.

- *Population.* Every 10 years, the entire population is counted. The result is a detailed breakdown of population statistics by characteristics such as age, sex, marital status, race, education, family size, occupation, income, and so forth. Data are provided on a regional basis within each category. Annual Current Population Reports update the census data by incorporating the latest information on changes in population characteristics.

- *Housing.* Since 1940, the decennial census has reported detailed data on housing, including the size, condition, and type of structures; number of occupants per household; average market value; average rents and facilities such as plumbing and major kitchen appliances. Current Housing Reports are issued annually to update these data.

- *Retail trade.* The Census of Retail Trade, conducted every five years, reports detailed data on the number of stores of various types, total sales, and number of employees. Data are reported by relatively small geographic areas, such as counties, cities, and standard metropolitan statistical areas. Monthly Retail Trade Reports provide the current data.

- *Service industries.* Taken every five years, the Census of Service Industries provides data on receipts, number of firms, employment, and types of business within the service industries. Current data are published in monthly Selected Services Reports.

- *Wholesale trade.* Wholesalers are classified into more than 150 separate business groups in the Census of Wholesale Trade. The census reports are published every five years and contain statistics on sales volume, warehouse space, expenditures, employment, and so forth. Current data are reported in monthly Wholesale Trade Reports.

- *Manufacturers.* Every five years the Census of Manufacturers is authorized to report manufacturing data in about 450 different classifications of manufacturing activity. Detailed data are generated on the number of firms, their output, employment, wages, sales and value added, and a number of additional measures. Supplementary data are found in the Annual Survey of Manufacturers and in Current Industrial Reports, published monthly.

- *Mineral industries.* Also intended to be generated every five years, the Census of Mineral Industries provides information similar to the Census of Manufacturers but reports on mineral industries in approximately 50 separate categories. Annual data similar (but not directly comparable) to those contained in the Census of Mineral Industries are reported annually in the Minerals Yearbook (Bureau of Mines, Department of the Interior).

- *Transportation.* Also published at five-year intervals, the Census of Transportation provides statistics on passenger travel, truck and bus use, and commodities shipped by various categories of carriers.

- *Agriculture.* The Census of Agriculture offers detailed information on land uses, employment, quantity and value of products, and land-use practices every five years. Data are presented by county within each state. Annual publications, *Agriculture Statistics* and *Commodity Yearbook*, provide current information.

- *Government.* General characteristics of state and local governments (employment, payroll, indebtedness, revenues and operating expenses, and so forth) are reported every five years in the Census of Government.

Private Data

Many private publishers provide information of special interest to real estate analysts. Here are eight that are particularly useful:

- *Dollars and Cents of Shopping Centers.* Published every two or three years by the Urban Land Institute, 1025 Thomas Jefferson Street N.W., Suite 500 W., Washington, DC 20007, *www.uli.org*. Contains statistical data on operation of superregional, community, and neighborhood shopping centers. Presents operating results by geographic location and shopping center age. Also contains tenant information and characteristics. Some information is provided for Canadian centers.

- *Downtown and Suburban Office Building Experience Exchange Report.* Published annually by the Building Owners and Managers Association International, 1201 New York Ave. N.W., Suite 300, Washington, DC 20005, *www.boma.org*. Provides statistical data about income and expenses for office building operations. Data are divided into downtown and suburban categories. Information is further subdivided according to building age, geographic location, size, and height. The publication includes some time series data.

- *Expense Analysis: Condominiums, Cooperatives, and PUDs.* Published annually by the Institute of Real Estate Management, 430 N. Michigan Ave., Chicago, IL 60611, *www.irem.org*. Provides expense data for condominiums, cooperatives, and planned unit developments. Data are classified by building age, geographic location, and price range. This includes statistical series on interior and exterior common area maintenance costs, utilities expense breakdown, and a summary of building amenities.

- *Income-Expense Analysis: Conventional Apartments.* Published annually by the Institute of Real Estate Management, 430 N. Michigan Ave., Chicago, IL 60611, *www.irem.org*. It provides income and expense data for apartment buildings in each of the following categories:
    - Garden-type, unfurnished
    - Furnished elevator buildings
    - Lowrise, 12 to 24 units, unfurnished
    - Lowrise, 25 or more units, unfurnished
    - Furnished units

    Data are presented by region, location, and building age. Separate series are provided for major metropolitan areas. Includes vacancy losses, tenant turnover, bad-debt losses, and parking revenue. Some trend data are provided.

- *Income-Expense Analysis: Office Buildings.* Published annually by the Institute of Real Estate Management, 430 N. Michigan Ave., Chicago, IL 60611, *www.irem.org*. Income and expense data for suburban office buildings are provided on national, regional, and major metropolitan area bases. Data are divided according to building size, age, rental range, and building type. Utility cost analysis and trend data are included.

- *Income-Expense Analysis: Shopping Centers.* Published annually by the Institute of Real Estate Management, 430 N. Michigan Ave., Chicago, IL 60611, *www.irem.org*. Income and expense data for shopping centers are provided on national, regional, and major metropolitan area bases, and are provided separately for open and enclosed malls. Data are divided according to building size and age group. Analysis and trend data on expansion and renovation activity, property taxes, sales, marketing, leasing, food courts, and ownership interests are included.

- *Trends in the Hotel Industry.* Published annually by CBRE Hotels' Americas Research (formerly PKF Consulting USA), *www.cbre.us*. Provides revenue and expense data separately for hotels and motels, transient hotels, resort hotels, motels with restaurants, and motels without restaurants. This includes data on occupancy rates, room rental rates, total revenues and expenses, energy costs, and property taxes.

- *U.S. Lodging Industry.* Published annually by PricewaterhouseCoopers (PwC), LLP, 1301 Avenue of the Americas, New York, NY 10019, *www.pwc.com*. Contains descriptive information about the lodging industry around the nation. Also provides income and expense data. Facilities are listed according to location as center city, airport, suburban or highway, and resort. Buildings are classified into four different size categories. Includes occupancy-rate data, food and beverage sales data, and ratios of sales per room.

Internet GIS Data

- *www.census.gov*—includes maps of demographic data
- *www.ed.ac.uk/geosciences*—GIS dictionary
- *www.esri.com*—GIS (ARC information)
- *www.usgs.gov/products/maps/gis-data*—part of U.S. Geological Survey site; explains GIS and applications
- *www.gisportal.com*—links to more than 1,000 GIS-related links
- *www.logic.org*

Internet Real Estate Data

- *www.uli.org*—list of real estate data sources
- *www.realtor.com*—real estate sales data from the National Association of REALTORS®
- *www.irr.com*—Integra Realty Resources provides a wide range of commercial real estate data

UNIT 5

Reconstructing the Operating History

UNIT PREVIEW

Real estate investors are interested in the physical aspects of their property because of the economic benefits that ownership bestows. (This is not to contend that nonfinancial aspects of ownership are unimportant. Aesthetics may well be valued as an end in itself, apart from the question of economic worth. Such issues, however, transcend the investment decision.) As an investment medium, real estate is only a means to the ultimate end of financial gain; its desirability is strictly a function of the amount, timing, and certainty of economic benefits, net of federal, state, and local income taxes.

The beginning point for forecasting benefits from a proposed venture is the property's immediate past operating history and the recent history of comparable properties. This experience is incorporated into a forecast by considering how anticipated changes in the economic, social, and political environment will impact the property's ability to generate rents and how they will affect the cost of maintaining and operating the property. Rational analysis must also include a forecast of the likely change in a property's market value over the anticipated holding period.

INTRODUCING THE OPERATING STATEMENT

Different from traditional income statements, which show revenues and expenses when earned or incurred whether or not payments have been made, real estate operating statements report cash receipts and disbursements. The cash flows can stem from rental operations, or from nonoperating transactions such as borrowing and repaying debt, interest payments on outstanding indebtedness, income taxes, or capital expenditures. All are reported on the operating statement. A typical income property operating statement is illustrated in Figure 5.1.

Potential gross rent/income is the amount of rental revenue/income a property would generate with no vacancies or uncollectible accounts. Adjusting potential gross rent to reflect losses from vacancies and uncollectible accounts and to include income from sources other than rents results in *effective gross income*. Other sources of income may include such items as parking fees or vending machine revenue. On a historical basis, this is the gross revenue a building has actually produced.

Operating expenses, shown in the next section of the operating statement in Figure 5.1, include all cash expenditures required to maintain and operate the property so as to generate the gross rent. *Net operating income (NOI)* is simply the difference between effective gross income and operating expenses. If there were no income taxes or other nonoperating transactions (such as debt repayment), this would also be the net cash flow to the equity investors.

FIGURE 5.1: Rental Property Annual Net Operating Income

Potential gross rent		$1,500,000
Less: Allowance for vacancies and rent loss		75,000
		$1,425,000
Plus: Other income (parking)		9,000
Effective gross income		$1,434,000
Less: Operating expenses		
Management fee	72,750	
Salary expense	133,900	
Utilities	77,700	
Insurance	54,400	
Supplies	19,000	
Advertising, legal, misc.	29,000	
Maintenance, repairs, and replacements	116,000	
Property tax	183,000	685,750
Net operating income		$748,250

TYPES OF LEASES

The potential cash flow from rent is affected by the type of leasehold estate for the property. An estate or tenancy for years is for a definite period of time, and the tenant is legally obligated to pay the rent for the entire term until the expiration date. A periodic estate or periodic tenancy has no expiration date and automatically renews until the tenant or landlord gives notice to end it. A month-to-month lease is a common example. The amount of required notice to end the lease is either dictated in the lease or by legislation. A tenancy at will has no specific term and ends with notice given.

Lease types also determine the rent cash flows. Gross or service leases are common on residential property where the tenant only pays rent and the landlord is responsible for property maintenance and all property charges, such as real estate taxes. Many commercial property leases are net leases where the tenant also pays such property charges as real estate taxes, insurance, maintenance, and repairs in addition to the rent payments. Rents do not vary with fixed/flat/straight leases, but the rents in variable leases will change over time. Fixed leases are common for short-term leases, such as a one-year apartment lease. Long-term commercial leases will vary with an established graduation (e.g., 4% per year) or with an index, such as average rent for that type of property in that market. Many retail leases will be percentage leases, where the tenant pays a base each period plus a percentage of income (sales). Obviously, the type of lease will have much to do with the likelihood and magnitude of future rent cash flows.

ESTIMATING THE ABILITY TO COMMAND RENT

The normal starting point for estimating effective gross income is the property's operating records. But unless they are prepared by a reliable and disinterested party using information from original source documents, these records can be suspect. Analysts seek to verify them, and test their reasonableness by comparing them with rents from comparable properties.

Collecting Data from the Subject Property

In order to estimate recent gross income, inspect the property's rent roll. If properly maintained, it will show actual rental collections, delinquent rents, and vacant rental space. Review individual leases to determine contract rental rates (the rates tenants were contractually obligated to pay) and *concessions* (agreements between landlords and tenants, such as a month's free rent to attract new tenants during a period of high vacancies that make effective rents less than contract rates). Verify the information, if possible, by conversing with the building's manager and tenants.

Compare with Peer-Group Properties

Comparable properties are frequently the most valuable source of data for verifying a property's recent operating history. The challenge is to find properties that are truly comparable. For estimating ability to command rents, a comparable property must function as a close substitute for the subject property. This economic means of substitution must appeal to the same subset of prospective tenants (the market segment) and must be considered equally desirable. Its location must be equally appealing, and offer approximately the same amenities. First, define the market area. Then identify property in the area that competes directly with the subject.

Determining of the market area

The property's *market area* is the geographic area from which tenants will be drawn. Properties that are close substitutes in the minds of prospective tenants will involve roughly similar linkages and transfer costs. They will have equally desirable environments, or environmental effects will offset differences in transfer costs.

- *Linkages will be similar.* Economic specialization creates interdependence among sites and requires movement of people or things between them. Relationships that create such movement are called *linkages*, as explained in Unit 3, and properties between which the movement occurs are said to be linked. Examples include travel between places of residence and work, school, or shopping; movement of raw material from place of origin to manufacturing locations; transport of semifinished and finished goods from manufacturer or processor to wholesalers and through retail outlets to points of consumption.

- *Transfer costs will be comparable.* The costs of moving people and things between linked sites are called *transfer costs*. We learned in Unit 3 that these may be *explicit* (accounting costs per trip, multiplied by the number of trips) or *implicit* (frustration and worry from moving along congested transportation arteries or across dangerous terrain). Sites that offer greater transfer-cost economies, perhaps because of shorter distances or more convenient transport links (freeway interchanges, airport or river terminals, for example), have a competitive advantage that enhances their ability to command rent. Peer-group properties will have roughly equal transfer costs, or the property with higher costs will offer offsetting advantages such as more desirable neighborhood influences.

- *Neighborhood influences may offset higher transfer costs.* Other things being equal, sites with lower transfer costs will be more desirable. Some tenants, however, choose locations that increase transfer costs because they like the neighborhood. Desirable neighborhood factors—environmental influences that increase a site's value due to their attractiveness—include aesthetic or prestige considerations, a perception of safety, or neighbors whose activities somehow complement one's own.

Defining a market area for housing

A residential market area has been defined as the area "within which all dwelling units are linked together in a chain of substitution.[1]" Within such an area, housing that is physically comparable and similarly priced will be mutually substitutable by prospective renters.

Many times, precise market area boundaries are impossible to define, but they can be approximated. One need only establish the most probable linkages with respect to a particular category of tenants. A major linkage, for example, is place of employment, and the range of possible employment from any given residential site is determined by the time, expense, and difficulty of the journey to work. Whether this is measured in terms of automobile driving time and distance or in terms of accessibility and cost of public transportation depends on the characteristic transportation mode of the market segment most likely to find the housing affordable and otherwise desirable.

To determine commuting patterns, one can distribute brief questionnaires at nearby employment centers. Responses will reveal tolerable commuting time and expense, and a map can be drawn to show the geographic area of employment from which an apartment building's tenants are likely to be drawn. Major employment centers within these boundaries constitute the employment base for prospective tenants. Other residential areas that are equally accessible to these employment centers form the competitive market area; apartment buildings within this area that offer similar amenities and are of equal quality will be peer-group properties. Figure 5.2 shows maps of a market area and the area of competing rental units.

---

[1] The Institute for Urban Land Use and Housing Studies, Columbia University, *Housing Market Analysis: A Study of Theory and Methods* (Washington, D.C.: Housing and Home Finance Agency, 1953).

FIGURE 5.2: Estimating the Market Area

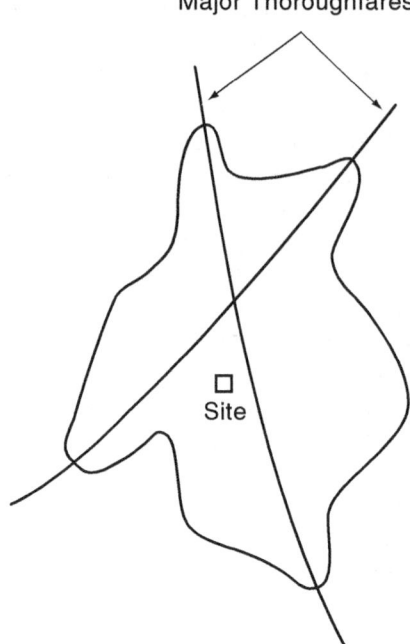
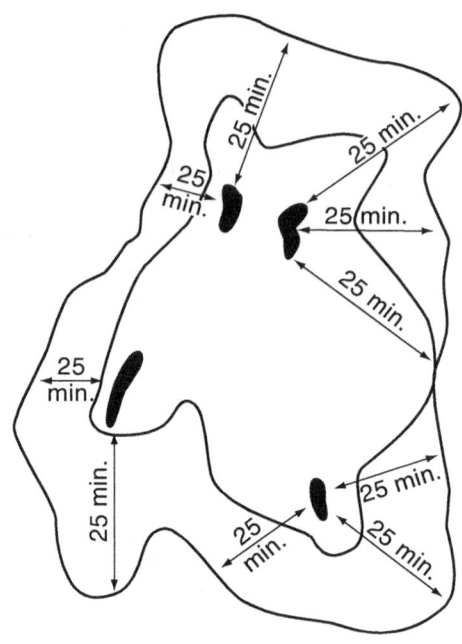

Panel A
Market Area = 25-Minute
Travel Time from Site

Panel B
Competitive Area = 25-Minute
Travel Time from Major Employment Nodes

Determining Retail Trade Area Boundaries

The trade area of a retail store is the geographic area from which the major portion of patronage is drawn. Within the trade area, the strongest drawing power is felt close to the site itself; drawing power diminishes as travel time increases.

A number of techniques have been recommended for estimating trade area boundaries for various types of retail or service establishments, and analysts will need specialized study to appreciate the strengths and weaknesses of each. John McMahan advises estimating trade area boundaries by the time required for potential customers to reach the facility. He further suggests the following rough rules of thumb[2]:

- Neighborhood shopping centers: 5 to 10 minutes
- Community shopping centers: 10 to 15 minutes
- Regional malls: 15 to 30 minutes

---

2 John McMahan, *Property Development: Effective Decision Making in Uncertain Times* (New York: McGraw-Hill, 1976), 161.

McMahan's rules of thumb correspond closely to advice from the Urban Land Institute, which labels trade areas as primary, secondary, and tertiary. The primary trade area is viewed as that requiring not more than about five minutes of travel to reach stores offering convenience items and 10 minutes of travel time to those offering big-ticket items for which consumers will do comparative shopping. The Urban Land Institute estimates that about 60% to 70% of ultimate sales volume will come from populations within this area. The balance will be drawn from the secondary and tertiary areas, which are farther away and for which the store or shopping center is less accessible. The institute characterizes the tertiary trade area as the farthest from which even major regional shopping centers can expect to draw customers. It sets the outer distance in travel time at about 25 to 30 minutes.[3] *Outlet malls* do not fit into the traditional three-category classification used by McMahan. They draw customers from much greater distances.

Estimating office market boundaries

The size and nature of a proposed office project determine the extent of the competitive survey. Office buildings tend to be developed in clusters or local nodes within a metropolitan area.[4] Figure 5.3 illustrates a typical nodal development pattern. Small- to medium-size office buildings intended as general office space compete primarily with other buildings in the same node. Larger buildings or those catering to specialized users may compete with buildings throughout an entire metropolitan area. In each instance, the survey will encompass the area within which major competitive buildings are located.

---

3   The Urban Land Institute, *Shopping Center Development Handbook*, 2nd ed. (Washington, D.C.: The Urban Land Institute, 1985): 22–23.

4   McMahan, *op. cit.,* 182.

FIGURE 5.3: Nodal Pattern of Office Building Development

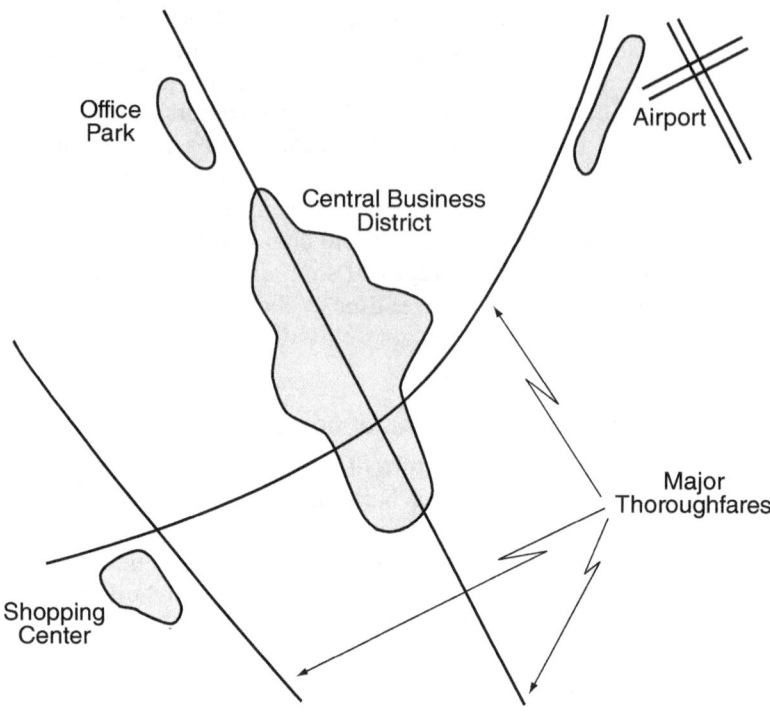

Identifying Peer Properties within the Market Area

Peer/comparable properties within the market area will be physically similar to the property under analysis, to the extent physical structure affects the ability to command rent. Analysis is facilitated by classifying buildings and other property improvements in terms of their functional efficiency and physical durability.

Determining functional efficiency

How well a property is designed to do the job it is intended to perform is the measure of its *functional efficiency*. Even though properties are intended for the same use and are located in the same market area, they are unlikely to be directly competitive if their functional efficiency differs significantly.

Functional efficiency is related to specific property uses and can be evaluated only in that context: houses are compared with design needs for modern family lifestyles, warehouse design is evaluated in terms of compatibility with modern storage and transportation technology, and office buildings are judged according to modern business needs.

When first put into service, well-designed structures may be very functionally efficient but may be rendered less appropriate for their tasks as lifestyles, taste, and technology alter use patterns. Less well-designed buildings may be functionally inefficient from the outset. Older warehouses, for example, may have load-bearing columns that are too close together to facilitate the use of modern forklift vehicles, or their ceilings may be too low to accommodate up-to-date storage and distribution technologies. Three-bedroom apartments will be functionally less efficient if the average family size in the market area contracts. Older office buildings might not accommodate contemporary requirements for telecommunications capability. Loss of efficiency due to defective or dated design (*functional obsolescence*) diminishes a building's competitive position and may eventually lead to abandonment or to an alternative use.

Determining physical durability

The remaining physical life and the extent of deferred maintenance of a structure is the measure of its *physical durability*. This is a function of soundness of design plus the extent to which routine maintenance has forestalled structural deterioration. Buildings that differ radically in physical durability are not likely to appeal to the same market segment, even when their intended use is the same.

Some indications of life-shortening defects can be noted by comparing the building's physical appearance with others of similar age. Past abuse leaves physical traces (foundation cracks, dry rot, termite infestation, and so on) that suggest whether future deterioration is likely to proceed more or less rapidly compared with competing buildings. Another frequent tip-off is maintenance and repair expenses that are high when compared with buildings of similar age.

ESTIMATING OPERATING EXPENSES

As is true for gross income, the starting point for estimating operating expenses is the property's operating history. The experiences of peer-group properties are often more reliable indicators; however, because the influence of above-standard or below-standard management tends to offset when the experiences of several properties are being compared.

Published sources that give average operating expenses for various types and sizes of properties are readily available.[5] These data are drawn from samples reported by members of trade groups, and they give little or no information about the dispersion around the mean of the sample. For this reason, while they constitute informative benchmarks against which to compare tentative conclusions for reasonableness, they are a poor substitute for detailed information drawn from the subject or from peer-group properties. The most frequently used sources are listed in the Data Sources section at the end of Unit 4.

AN APARTMENT BUILDING EXAMPLE

Maegan's Magic Manor is a 280-unit apartment complex consisting of 50 two-bedroom units, each having 1,100 square feet of living area; 150 one-bedroom units, each containing 800 square feet of living area; and 80 studio-type units, each with 600 square feet of living area. The owner provides a statement of the property's most recent operating results, which is presented in Figure 5.4.

---

5   McMahan, *op. cit.,* 182.

FIGURE 5.4: Maegan's Magic Manor Prior Owner's Operating Statement for Year Ended December 31, 20xx

Gross revenue		
Rent receipts		$2,140,000
Parking fees		<u>99,000</u>
Total		$2,239,000
Expenses		
Management fees (5% of effective gross)	112,000	
Salaries	197,100	
Utilities	201,900	
Insurance	67,400	
Supplies	20,000	
Advertising, legal, misc.	33,000	
Maintenance, repairs, and replacements	149,000	
Property taxes	<u>180,000</u>	<u>960,400</u>
Net income for the year		<u>$1,278,600</u>

Reconstructing Effective Gross Income

By inspecting the rent roll, analysts discover that some tenants are on 24-month leases, some are on 12-month leases, and some are renting on a month-to-month basis. While talking with tenants and reading leases, they note that several tenants received special inducements (concessions) such as decorating allowances or discounts on parking fees at a nearby garage operated by the same management company. The concessions seem to be related to periods when vacancies were particularly high, but impossible to verify because both the owner and the management firm refuse to confirm concessions reported by tenants but not included in leases.

Fortunately, a number of apartment buildings in the immediate neighborhood offer similar accommodations. Services provided by these other properties are essentially the same as those of the subject property. All the units chosen as sources of comparable market data offer single baths and kitchen–dining room combinations, which conforms to the profile of units in the property under analysis. The data on comparable properties are as follows:

- Property A contains a total of 250 units: 175 two-bedroom units with 990 square feet of living area rent for $770 per month, 50 single-bedroom units with 725 square feet rent for $645 per month, and 25 studios with 590 square feet rent for $525 per month. Currently, five two-bedroom units and seven studios are vacant. All the one-bedroom units are under lease.

- Property B is a 185-unit building with 75 two-bedroom, 75 one-bedroom, and 35 studio units. The two-bedroom units have 1,025 square feet of living area and rent for $810 per month. The single-bedroom apartments have 750 square feet of living area and rent for $660. The studios contain 610 square feet and command rents of $535. Currently, 10 one-bedroom and five studio units are vacant. All the two-bedroom units are occupied.

- Property C has 360 units, of which 225 are two-bedroom and 75 are one-bedroom apartments. The remaining 60 units are studios. Two-bedroom units contain 980 square feet of living area and rent for $765. One-bedroom units have 735 square feet of living area and rent for $645. Studios, which have 595 square feet of living area, rent for $525. This complex currently has two vacant two-bedroom units and 15 vacant studios. All one-bedroom units are rented.
- Property D is a 300-unit building containing 100 two-bedroom, 125 one-bedroom, and 75 studio apartments. Two-bedroom units each have 995 square feet of living area and rent for $775. The one-bedroom units have 755 square feet of living area and rent for $655. Studios rent for $575 and have 650 square feet of living area. There are 10 vacant one-bedroom and 10 vacant studio apartments.

Gross rental data from the comparable rental units are consolidated in Figure 5.5. Expressing gross rents on a per-square-foot basis by type of rental unit eliminates differences due to variation in the unit size or type. The data suggest that if the building's two-bedroom units were vacant and available, they would rent for about $0.78 per square foot. About $0.88 per square foot appears the best estimate for one-bedroom units and studios. Studio apartments renting for no more per square foot than one-bedroom units is cause for reflection, but the conclusion is reinforced by the higher vacancy rate for studios.

FIGURE 5.5: Derivation of Market Rental Rates on Properties Deemed Comparable to Maegan's Magic Manor

	Comparable Property			
	A	B	C	D
Two-bedroom units				
Monthly rental	$770	$810	$765	$775
Square feet	990	1,025	980	995
Rent per square foot	$0.78	$0.79	$0.78	$0.78
One-bedroom units				
Monthly rental	$645	$660	$645	$655
Square feet	725	750	735	755
Rent per square foot	$0.89	$0.88	$0.88	$0.87
Studio units				
Monthly rental	$525	$535	$525	$575
Square feet	590	610	595	650
Rent per square foot	$0.89	$0.88	$0.88	$0.88

Vacancy data for the comparable apartments are consolidated and arrayed on Figure 5.6. Comparable property B has an unusually high vacancy rate in its one-bedroom units, and this has a disproportionate impact on the average for the group. An uncharacteristically high rate in one property might be attributable to a transient difficulty (a malfunctioning heating or cooling system perhaps, or a disruptive tenant that has since been evicted) or to incompetent management. For Maegan's Magic Manor apartments, the analysts conclude that market estimates in fact reflect most likely experience under typically competent management.

Data concerning market rental rates and most probable vacancy experience, drawn from the comparable properties and exhibited in Figures 5.5 and 5.6, are used to arrive at estimates of potential gross rent and allowance for vacancy losses for Maegan's Magic Manor. Final conclusions are computed in Figure 5.7 and are incorporated into the reconstructed operating report, which is shown in Figure 5.8.

FIGURE 5.6: Derivation of Market Vacancy Factors Applicable to Maegan's Magic Manor

	Comparable Property				
	A	B	C	D	Total (Weighted Average)
Two-bedroom units					
Number of units	175	75	225	100	575
Vacancies	5	0	2	0	7
Percent vacant	2.9	0	0.9	0	(1.2)
One-bedroom units					
Number of units	50	75	75	125	325
Vacancies	0	10	0	10	20
Percent vacant	0	13.3	0	8.0	(6.2)
Studio units					
Number of units	25	35	60	75	195
Vacancies	7	5	15	10	37
Percent vacant	28.0	14.3	25.0	13.3	(19.0)

FIGURE 5.7: Estimated Gross Revenue and Vacancy Rates for Maegan's Magic Manor

	Two-Bedroom	One-Bedroom	Studio
Estimated potential gross monthly income			
Market rent per square foot	0.78	0.88	0.88
Square feet per unit	× 1,100	× 800	× 600
Rent per unit	$858	$704	$528
Number of units	× 50	× 150	× 80
Total potential monthly rent	$ 42,900	$ 105,600	$ 42,240
Annual (monthly × 12)	$514,800	$1,267,200	$506,880
Estimated vacancy factor			
Annual potential gross	$514,800	$1,267,200	$506,880
Vacancy Factor (from Figure 5.6)	× 0.012	× 0.062	× 0.190
Vacancy loss estimate	$ 6,178	$ 78,566	$ 96,307

Total annual potential gross revenue (rounded to nearest $100) = $2,288,900

Total annual vacancy loss estimate (rounded to nearest $100) = $181,100

FIGURE 5.8: Reconstructed Prior-Year Operating Statement for Maegan's Magic Manor

Potential gross rent		$2,288,900
Less: Allowance for vacancies		181,100
		$2,107,800
Plus: Other income		99,000
Effective gross income		$2,206,800
Less: Operating expenses		
Management fee (5% of effective gross)	110,300	
Salary expense	197,100	
Utilities	105,300	
Insurance	35,500	
Supplies	21,000	
Advertising, legal, misc.	32,000	
Maintenance, repairs, and replacements	181,900	
Property taxes	300,000	983,100
Net operating income (annual)		$1,223,700

Reconstructing Current Operating Expenses

Remember that operating expenses are cash expenditures required to maintain properties in sufficient condition to generate the effective gross revenue. A first step toward estimating a property's current operating expenses is to convert the current owner's statement to a more useful format. The present owners reported operating results for Maegan's Magic Manor are shown in Figure 5.4.

By questioning the owner about reported maintenance and repair charges, the analysts learn that the owner and her sons held other expenses down by doing much of the maintenance work themselves. Comparison with similar buildings in the area reveals that a proper maintenance, repair, and replacement program would have consumed between 8.0% and 8.5% of effective gross income.

The owner's operating statement also shows property taxes that are too low and utilities that are too high. A check with the county assessor's office reveals that last year's taxes were $300,000 and that they are unlikely to change before the next reassessment, which is scheduled in two years. The reported utilities expenses were actually for two years. The corrected number, based on the most recent 12 months, is $105,300.

All other reported expense items appear reasonable for a building of this size and age, based on the analyst's experience with comparable properties and on reference to published standards. Therefore, no other adjustments are indicated except for the management fee, which is lower because of the revised effective gross income.

Revised Operating Statement

The effective gross income for the preceding year, after including revised estimates of vacancy losses and parking income, is $2,206,800. Revised operating expenses total $983,100. These adjustments yield reconstructed NOI of $1,223,700. The reconstructed operating statement is shown on Figure 5.8.

FROM RECONSTRUCTION TO FORECAST

Some commercial projects may require complex calculations on a lease-by-lease basis. Specially designed computer spreadsheet software is available to perform this detailed analysis. One such software is ARGUS, available from Realm Business Solutions, Inc. (https://argus.altusgroup.com/). An excellent case study using ARGUS is presented in Unit 13 of *Income Property Valuation*. Figure 5.9 is a copy of a printout of an ARGUS worksheet illustrated in *Income Property Valuation*.[6]

The sole purpose of reconstructing the property's operating history is in the anticipation that the history will serve as a guide to the immediate future. In the absence of any changes in the property itself or in its operating environment, there is no reason to expect that the operating results will change over time.

---

[6] Jeffrey D. Fisher and Robert S. Martin, *Income Property Valuation* (Chicago: Dearborn Real Estate Education, 2008), Chapter 13.

But, of course, changes do occur. Change is a constant factor that must always be incorporated into the analysis. Forecasting, therefore, represents an attempt to estimate the nature of change in the factors that affect operating results and to determine the impact those changes will have on the property's future operations. Estimating the changes and their impact is the subject of Unit 6.

FIGURE 5.9: Cash-Flow Summary

SCHEDULE OF PROSPECTIVE CASH FLOW
In Inflated Dollars for the Fiscal Year Beginning 6/1/2000

For the Years Ending	Year 1 May-2001	Year 2 May-2002	Year 3 May-2003	Year 4 May-2004	Year 5 May-2005	Year 6 May-2006
POTENTIAL GROSS REVENUE						
Base Rental Revenue	$733,500	$735,000	$754,224	$760,189	$772,145	$808,622
Absorption & Turnover Vacancy	(36,000)		(18,911)	(77,912)	(160,500)	(41,329)
Scheduled Base Rental Revenue	697,500	735,000	735,313	682,277	611,645	767,293
Base Rental Step Revenue	1,875	22,500	20,625			
CPI & Other Adjustment Revenue	900	11,783	15,844	3,309	16,001	22,352
Expense Reimbursement Revenue						
Property Taxes	17,500	18,271	13,452	11,819	4,732	1,460
Property Insurance	2,500	2,611	1,922	1,688	675	209
Utilities	17,850	19,878	9,406	5,544	3,309	3,099
Janitorial	15,500	16,484	11,023	9,205	4,013	1,709
Maintenance	5,000	5,551	2,109	942	880	1,044
Total Reimbursement Revenue	58,350	62,795	37,912	29,198	13,609	7,521
Other Income	10,000	10,300	10,609	10,927	11,255	11,593
TOTAL POTENTIAL GROSS REVENUE	768,625	842,378	820,303	725,711	652,510	808,759
EFFECTIVE GROSS REVENUE	768,625	842,378	820,303	725,711	652,510	808,759
OPERATING EXPENSES						
Property Taxes	35,000	36,050	37,131	38,245	39,393	40,575
Property Insurance	5,000	5,150	5,305	5,464	5,628	5,796
Utilities	74,250	77,250	79,170	80,315	81,037	86,076
Janitorial	40,000	41,400	42,849	44,349	45,901	47,507
Maintenance	25,000	25,750	26,522	27,318	28,138	28,982
Management Fee	38,431	42,119	41,015	36,286	32,626	40,438
Reserves	10,000	10,300	10,609	10,927	11,255	11,593
TOTAL OPERATING EXPENSES	227,681	238,019	242,601	242,904	243,978	260,967
NET OPERATING INCOME	540,944	604,359	577,702	482,807	408,532	547,792
LEASING & CAPITAL COSTS						
Tenant Improvements	150,000		53,045	245,864		365,172
Leasing Commissions	13,500		8,825	32,724		44,883
Capital Expense	24,000					
TOTAL LEASING & CAPITAL COSTS	187,500		61,870	278,588		410,055
CASH FLOW BEFORE DEBT SERVICE & TAXES	$353,444	$604,359	$515,832	$204,219	$408,532	$137,737

SUMMARY

The beginning point for forecasting the stream of benefits that will flow from a rental property is to reconstruct the operating history. Past trends are projected into the future, with revisions to reflect perceived changes in the economic, political, and social environment that are likely to affect the property's ability to generate future benefits.

All benefits are expressed on a cash-flow basis. A typical operating statement starts with an expression of the gross rent the property would generate if fully rented. This is adjusted for vacancies and rent losses, plus revenue from sources other than rent, to arrive at effective gross revenue. Subtracting operating expenses from the effective gross revenue yields NOI. Further adjustments, for financing costs, income taxes, and other nonoperating cash flows, yield an estimate of net cash flow to the equity investor.

The sources of information regarding rental revenue and operating expenses include the past operating history of the property itself, the operating records of comparable properties, and data from published sources. The last source provides benchmarks against which to gauge the reasonableness of conclusions.

RECOMMENDED READING

Collett, David, Colin Lizieri, and Charles Ward. "Timing and the Holding Periods of Institutional Real Estate." *Real Estate Economics* 31:2, 2003, 205–222.

INTERNET REFERENCES

For economic data:
www.economy.com/freelunch
www.bls.gov
www.bea.gov

For office and industrial data:
www.cbre.com//research-and-reports

For unbiased information and analysis of a variety of properties:
https://www.msci.com/real-estate

For information on properties in Tokyo:
www.realestate-tokyo.com

For data on places to live:
www.bestplaces.net

REVIEW QUESTIONS

1. How do income and expense statements prepared by accountants differ from operating statements used by real estate investment analysts?
2. What items should be considered when forecasting income and expenses over an investor's anticipated holding period?
3. Carefully inspect the prior owner's operating statement for Maegan's Magic Manor apartments (Figure 5.4). Do you see any problems with the owner's presentation of income and expenses?
4. Describe the process used to estimate rentals for Maegan's Magic Manor.
5. List some of the considerations inherent in the expense items as presented by the current owner of Maegan's Magic Manor.
6. What is the value of published data in developing an estimate of the operating history of a property?
7. What are some of the forces affecting the ability of a property to generate rents?

DISCUSSION QUESTIONS

1. Offering brochures for the purchase of rental property frequently state that current rental rates can be raised. Comment on such claims.
2. How does our concept of gross income and operating expenses differ from those you studied in accounting? Which is the correct definition?
3. You are analyzing a new apartment complex (the only one of its kind) recently constructed on the fringe of an urban area. Because of its access to open areas and freedom from congestion, noise, and so forth, the units are in great demand. In fact, NOI per rental unit is almost 50% above that of slightly older but otherwise comparable units that are clustered in an area closer to the central city. Because of the high rents and virtual zero vacancies that yield a 50% premium in NOI, the owner argues that his property is worth 50% more than the other units. Comment on this assertion.

110   UNIT 5   Reconstructing the Operating History

PROBLEMS

1. Construct the effective gross income for Hammond Harmony Apartments, a 225-unit complex, all two-bedroom apartments of 1,000 square feet each. Five complexes of similar accommodations and services are in the immediate neighborhood, all with only two-bedroom units.
   - Kelvin Knights has 200 units, each with 1,000 square feet, renting for $800. There are 12 vacant units.
   - Griggs Grove has 150 units, each with 975 square feet, renting for $790. There are 11 vacant units.
   - Kennedie Village has 250 units, each with 990 square feet, renting for $800. There are 16 vacant units.
   - Esther's Eden has 100 units, each with 1,025 square feet, renting for $830. There are seven vacant units.
   - Ginny Gallery has 300 units, each with 1,030 square feet, renting for $840. There are 18 vacancies.
   - Hammond Harmony parking fees and washer/dryer rental income is $90,000 per year.

2. Construct the net income for Hammond Harmony Apartments if the management fee is 4.5% of EGI, annual salaries are $195,500, insurance is $68,200, supplies cost $22,400 per year, advertising/legal is $33,100, maintenance is $70,000, and repairs and replacements are $80,000 per year. Property taxes are projected to be $290,500 next year. Utilities average $9,075 per month.

UNIT 6

Forecasting Income and Property Value

UNIT PREVIEW

REAL ESTATE TODAY

As explained and illustrated in the previous unit, the starting point for estimating cash flows over the investment period is the reconstruction of a property's operating history as well as the estimation of the results of current operations as they would have been with competent management. Rational investment decisions require this estimate. And to get there, one must first forecast operating results and market value at some point in the future. Those forecasts are the objective of this unit.

In order to develop an operating forecast, one must first project changes in key variables that determine gross income, and then estimate related operating expenses to derive a net operating forecast. With the operating forecast in hand, projecting future market value is a matter of measuring the relationship between net operating income (NOI) and value, then projecting changes in that relationship over the forecasting period. This unit addresses each of these steps in the indicated sequence.

GROSS INCOME FORECASTING

The income-generating potential of a property depends on (1) the interaction of supply and demand in its market area, which determines market-clearing rental rates and the amount of rental space that will be occupied, and (2) its desirability relative to competing properties in the market area, which determines its share of the market. Forecasting gross rental income, therefore, requires estimating future changes in supply and demand relationships and changes in a property's market share.

Supply and demand, and their role in setting market-clearing prices, were introduced in Unit 2; Unit 4 explained a technique for translating theory into a gross income forecast for a specific property. If the property's proportional share of market rent remains stable, the technique works beautifully. The missing link is how to gather evidence and exercise judgment to determine likely changes in market share.

Competitive weapons in the battle for market share are location and a specific set of physical amenities. The final step in forecasting future rent-generating capacity is to anticipate changes in these variables and in their desirability to prospective tenants.

The Impact of Physical Characteristics

A property's physical characteristics—buildings and other site improvements—by their very nature have limited useful lives. As its usefulness wanes, a facility becomes less desirable relative to competing properties that are newer or have been better maintained. Estimating the extent of this unavoidable decline in competitive posture is a crucial element in accurately projecting market share. The task is simplified by considering the functional efficiency and physical durability of the physical characteristics.

Declining functional efficiency

The appropriateness of a facility's design or engineering for its intended use is the measure of its functional efficiency, as explained in Unit 5. Diminished usefulness due to declining conformity with current standards leads inevitably to a decreasing share of rental revenue. This loss of competitive position due to defective or dated design or engineering is called *functional obsolescence*. In many cases it leads to abandonment or recycling into alternative uses.

Updates in manufacturing, transportation, and storage technology, for example, inject obsolescence into factories and warehouses and cause them to be abandoned, demolished, or converted. Modern industrial techniques that favor single-story manufacturing plants render older, multistoried facilities obsolete. Warehouses lose competitive position because of ceilings with insufficient clearance, floors with inadequate load-bearing capacity, and load-bearing columns with bay widths that hamper the movement of materials-handling machinery.

Declining physical durability

In Unit 5, *physical durability* is defined as the measure of how long a structure will continue to be productive. In-depth evaluation of this factor is usually beyond a real estate analyst's technical capabilities and requires the services of a building design or construction engineering consultant.

Environmental risk

The investment value of a property can be greatly diminished by environmental problems. State and federal laws impose liability on owners of contaminated property without regard to fault or cause of contamination. Costs to mitigate environmental problems can be substantial. Investors should hire experts to conduct an environmental audit (Phase 1) before purchasing property. In order to ensure that there are no environmental problems on the property, lenders often require environmental audits before they will approve loans.

The Impact of Locational Characteristics

A property's location relative to prospective tenants' needs and to the locations of competing sites is a primary determinant of its market share. Some elements of locational desirability are property-specific, a function of the relationship between the site and locations with which it is linked. Others are environment-related, dependent on the relationship between the site and surrounding geography. Unlike physical features, which can be altered more or less at will, locational elements are generally not amenable to manipulation and control.

Locational analysis is always important. It becomes more so when investment success hinges on anticipated changes in locational factors. Examples include acquiring vacant land in the path of expected urban expansion or rehabilitating property in older neighborhoods with the expectation of imminent urban economic revival.

Analysis of Linkages and Transfer Costs

Identifying linkages—relationships that require movement of people or things between linked sites—that result from existing or intended land use is the first step in locational analysis. This involves studying present or planned economic activity at the site to determine major geographic points to or from which there will be movement of people or products.

The analyst then judges the relative importance of each linkage and estimates transfer costs—the costs of movement between the linked sites. Comparing these costs with those incurred by people engaged in the same activity at competing locations yields an estimate of the location's contribution to a property's ability to command rent.

Linkages and transfer costs are discussed at length in Unit 3. Recall that transfer costs might be explicit or implicit and that total transfer cost is the product of the cost per trip, both implicit and explicit, and the number of trips made per period of time. A significant change in the relative importance of linkages or in the relative dimensions of transfer costs will alter a site's competitive position.

Linkages may change

Altered lifestyles, emerging business patterns, or shifts in technology can sever existing linkages and create new ones. The transition from urban to suburban living, for example, created linkages between communities and regional shopping centers while reducing the significance of old linkages between residential neighborhoods and the central business district. Concurrently, increasing congestion in urban areas has added value to industrial sites that are outside yet convenient to major urban concentrations.

Relative transfer costs may be altered

Supplanting or modifying existing transportation networks can drastically alter relative transfer costs. Contemporary examples include the rerouting of major highways, the closing of railway spurs, and alterations in the cost and availability of parking facilities. Such changes may sever ready access to linked sites and thereby destroy the locational value of proximity to places of work or shopping. A bridge over a previously impassable river or a new limited-access highway can diminish a site's locational advantage by providing ready access to competing sites. Freeway construction in many areas has altered traffic patterns and shifted the relative advantages of locations that share common linkages.

Analysis of Neighborhood Environmental Factors

A site's desirability relative to competing properties is influenced by the economic and social status of the immediate neighborhood. These are subject to change, so analysts should assess the neighborhood's ability to retain its attractiveness over the projection period and adjust revenue forecasts to reflect the consequences of expected changes.

Relocating or closing support facilities such as schools, churches, playgrounds, medical facilities, or police substations may significantly affect a residential neighborhood's desirability. Demolishing physical barriers such as a railroad embankment or a large public building or creating new ones can have the same effect. Altering barriers that are more psychological than physical, such as a small park or an architecturally distinctive building that has become a symbol of neighborhood solidarity or uniqueness, for example, can have the same outcome.

Changes in zoning laws can accelerate a locale's incipient transition from one predominant use to another. The process might enhance or diminish the desirability of existing rental space, even while pushing land value in the opposite direction. Rezoning from residential to commercial use, for example, might make an area less desirable to residential tenants and thereby reduce the competitive strength of existing residential rental properties, while making the land more valuable because it can be developed with strip shopping centers, fast-food outlets, and so forth.

The Supply Factor

As explained in Unit 2, a site's desirability interacts with the relative scarcity and price of close substitutes to determine its value. A forecast of changes in the supply of comparable rental space is, therefore, an essential element in the analysis of a property's ability to command rent over the projection period.

Land availability and supply analysis

The four-quadrant matrix analysis investigated in Unit 4 indirectly takes into account demographic and economic factors that affect supply; it does not directly address the question of whether land is available to expand the quantity of rental space in a market area. The inventory of developable land includes previously developed sites whose buildings are nearing the end of their useful economic lives and thus are candidates for razing and redevelopment, as well as vacant sites that are properly zoned and currently available. It also includes advantageously located sites that are not appropriately zoned, if there is a reasonable likelihood of their being rezoned during the forecast period. Additionally, land may become available because previously reluctant owners may now have financial needs and, therefore, may be more willing to sell than the previous owners.

Product differentiation and supply analysis

Real estate that has unique features can command premium rents. In marketing terms, the differences—whether real or spurious—desensitize tenants to price differentials. The distinction may lie in unique architecture, high-quality construction, luxurious appointments, or other elements that create a compelling image for potential tenants.

Physical differences may be less significant than those that exist only in the perception of tenants. Styling, quality, and functional features can be duplicated by competitors. Image, in contrast, is unique to individual properties and is often generated consciously to appeal to a specific market segment. Due solely to its reputation, a property may consistently command a premium price or sell at a discount from prevailing rates for similarly located and outfitted competitors. By successfully cultivating and protecting a uniquely desirable property image, one can capture some of the monopoly advantages associated with unique location. Such a property is far less vulnerable to competition from otherwise comparable rental space.

FORECASTING OPERATING EXPENSES

In at least one respect, projecting operating expenses is a simpler task than projecting gross revenue: expenses are less sensitive to minor variations in a property's location. Operating costs for a particular class of property will, of course, vary from one part of the country to another because of the influence of such factors as climate and prevailing wage scales. Snow removal, for example, is a major item for properties in some parts of the country, while air-conditioning looms large in others. Within a single metropolitan area, though, the cost of operating similar properties and maintaining them at reasonably similar levels of repair should be closely related.

Therefore, analysts can look farther distances in search of peer-group properties to derive operating expenses estimates. Buildings of similar age and construction quality, housing tenants of roughly similar socioeconomic class, should cost about the same to operate and maintain anywhere in the city.

If the age or quality of buildings' construction differ significantly, operating costs may vary widely. Other things being equal, older buildings will be more expensive to operate, and operating expenses will consume a larger portion of the gross income. Poorly constructed buildings of any age generally require more extensive maintenance than better quality buildings, and those with less insulation will cost more to heat and cool.

The main impact that tenants will have on operating costs is the extent to which they exercise responsibility in using the facility. Some residential neighborhoods, for example, might be characterized by apartment tenants who are less responsible and who include vandals among their families or friends. Some office and retail complexes will be occupied by tenants whose clients or customers create higher-than-average wear and tear on facilities.

For that reason, published averages are likely to be poor indicators of an individual property's operating expenses. The trade groups that collect and report such data (the most widely distributed publications are listed at the end of Unit 4) make only a limited effort to discriminate their samples by quality of construction or by socioeconomic characteristics of tenants or users.

Multiple years of operating expense data are useful in establishing a trend. Based on the trend, analysts can estimate future expenses by noting indicated political, economic, or social changes that might alter the trend during the forecasting period. These changes might occur at the national, state, or metropolitan level. A shift in Federal Reserve monetary policy will affect future inflation rates, and thus the cost of operating and maintaining a rental property. A shift in federal fiscal policy might have similar implications because of its impact on employment and wage levels. Impending changes in taxes and/or federal minimum wage laws might have a measurable effect on operating expenses, and these are also frequently signaled by earlier shifts in national political alignments.

Other examples of regional or metropolitan economic phenomena that signal a change in operating costs are shifts in the labor market, a trend to or away from unionization, or changes in supply and demand relationships for key materials or supplies. If a booming local economy threatens labor shortages, analysts might project labor costs to rise faster than the overall operating expense trend; if the regional or metropolitan economy is softening, the estimated growth in labor cost might be lower than the overall operating expense trend line.

FORECASTING NET OPERATING INCOME

To illustrate how a reconstructed operating statement might be transmuted into a multiple-year forecast, please study Figure 5.8, which presents the prior year's reconstructed operating results for an apartment complex, Maegan's Magic Manor, to show what the results would have been with competent management. The analyst notes that, as a consequence of abnormally high vacancies and stagnant rents, there has been no significant new construction in the market area for the past three years. Further investigation reveals a steady drop in vacancy rates, from a high of 14% three years back to about 7.9% in the past year.

Although the overall simple vacancy rate for the other four complexes in the market area is 5.8% (64 vacant units out of a total inventory of 1,095), the effective rent vacancy for Maegan's Magic Manor is 7.9%. This rent vacancy is higher because Maegan's Magic Manor has a higher percentage of studio and one-bedroom units than the other market area complexes. These studios and one-bedroom units have much higher vacancy rates than the two-bedroom units. One-bedroom units (with a 6.2% vacancy) comprise 30% of the other four complexes' units, but they are 54% of Maegan's Magic Manor. Studios (with a 19% vacancy) make up only 18% of the other complexes but are 28.5% of Maegan's Magic Manor. In contrast, the low vacancy rate for the two-bedroom units (1.2%) is much more beneficial for the other complexes where they comprise 52.5% of the apartments versus 18% of Maegan's Magic Manor. This underlines the importance of using unit-type vacancies when calculating gross revenue as we did in Figure 5.7.

Coincident with the decline in vacancies to a rate close to the long-term average, our analyst notes that market rents began moving up about six months ago. The tightening rental market will be increasingly reflected in the rent roll of Maegan's Magic Manor as leases expire and are renewed or new tenants are signed. After including revised estimates of vacancy losses and parking income, the analyst anticipates that potential gross rent during the first year of the forecast period will be about $2,346,100, representing an increase of 2.5% above last year's reconstructed amount.

The analyst could have calculated average rent increases from historical data during the recent period of relatively high vacancy rates. An observed decline in vacancy rates with the growth of job opportunities in a nearby market could be used by the analyst to estimate a variation in the historical trend. With no increased supply of apartment units, increased job opportunities nearby will result in increased occupancy and decreased vacancies. Vacancies are expected to decline to an average of 7.5%. Based on past experience and other comparable properties, operating expenses other than management fees and property taxes are expected to grow at about 3.5% per annum. Management fees are expected to be 5% of the effective gross income. Property taxes should remain at the current $300,000 until the next scheduled reassessment by the county tax assessor. The estimated first-year NOI, therefore, is $1,265,700. These revenue and expense estimates are shown on the operating forecast in Figure 6.1.

FIGURE 6.1: First-Year Operating Forecast for Maegan's Magic Manor

Potential gross rent		$2,346,100
Less: Allowance for vacancies and rent loss (7.5%, rounded)		176,000
		$2,170,100
Plus: Other income		102,000
Effective gross income		$2,272,100
Less: Operating expenses		
Management fee (5% of EGI)	113,600	
Salary expense	204,000	
Utilities	109,000	
Insurance	36,700	
Supplies	21,700	
Advertising, legal, misc.	33,100	
Maintenance, repairs, and replacements	188,300	
Property taxes	300,000	1,006,400
Net operating income (annual)		$1,265,700

The 2.5% increase in potential gross rents forecasted for the first year reflects growth that has occurred almost exclusively during the past six months, representing an annual rate of 5%. With local employment booming, vacancy rates declining precipitously, and no new construction pending, a shortage of apartment space seems to be looming.

Maegan's Magic Manor apartments are advantageously located near the periphery of a major office-zoned district that has been heavily developed. The analyst concludes that with competent management, Maegan's Magic Manor should experience an occupancy level and command rents at least equal to the average for the market area: occupancy should hit 96% (a 4% vacancy rate) by the second year of the forecast, and rents should grow at about 5% per annum until new apartments are built.

When vacancies drop below their historical average (about 6% in this market area), developers become interested. The analyst notes that several local developers have recently bought apartment-zoned land, indicating plans for imminent development. By the fourth year of the forecast, additions to supply should drive vacancy rates back to their historical average of about 6%. Rental increases will moderate and are expected to grow at the projected 3.5% inflation rate after the third year. Other income (primarily parking fees) is expected to hold fairly constant at about 4.7% of rental collections.

Stagnant rental rates and high vacancies have not hindered the growth in operating expenses, most of which are not radically affected by occupancy levels. In recent years, operating expenses for peer-group apartment complexes have grown at about 3.5% per annum, approximately at the general rate of inflation. Except for management and property taxes, Maegan's Magic Manor's expenses are expected to keep pace with inflation, which is expected to remain stable at around 3.5% per annum over the forecast period. Management fees will remain at 5% of effective gross income. Property taxes are scheduled for reassessment in three years (the increased rate will apply in the fourth year of the forecast). Based on the anticipated changes in revenue and expenses, the tax assessment will probably increase by about 25%.

By incorporating these expectations into the analysis, and starting with the one-year forecast from Figure 6.1, the analyst constructs a six-year operating forecast for Maegan's Magic Manor apartments. The forecast is shown in Figure 6.2.

FIGURE 6.2: Six-Year Operating Forecast for Maegan's Magic Manor Apartments*

	Year 1	Year 2	Year 3	Year 4	Year 5	Year 6
Potential gross rent	$2,346,100	$2,463,400	$2,586,600	$2,677,100	$2,770,800	$2,867,800
Less: Vacancy allowance	176,000	98,500	103,500	160,600	166,200	172,100
	$2,170,100	$2,364,900	$2,483,100	$2,516,500	$2,604,600	$2,695,700
Add: Other income	102,000	111,200	116,700	118,300	122,400	126,700
Effective gross income	$2,272,100	$2,476,100	$2,599,800	$2,634,800	$2,727,000	$2,822,400
Less: Operating expenses						
Management fee	113,600	123,800	130,000	131,700	136,400	141,100
Salary expense	204,000	211,100	218,500	226,200	234,100	242,300
Utilities	109,000	112,800	116,800	120,900	125,100	129,500
Insurance	36,700	38,000	39,300	40,700	42,100	43,600
Supplies	21,700	22,500	23,300	24,100	24,900	25,800
Advertising, legal, misc.	33,100	34,300	35,500	36,700	38,000	39,300
Maintenance, repairs, and replacement	188,300	194,900	201,700	208,800	216,100	223,700
Property taxes	300,000	300,000	300,000	375,000	375,000	375,000
Total expenses	$1,006,400	$1,037,400	$1,065,100	$1,164,100	$1,191,700	$1,220,300
Net operating income	$1,265,700	$1,438,700	$1,534,700	$1,470,700	$1,535,300	$1,602,100

*All numbers have been rounded to the nearest $100.

As a check on the forecast's reasonableness, our analyst computes the ratio between forecasted operating expenses and effective gross income (this is the *operating expense ratio*, which is explained further in Unit 12). The ratio, shown in Figure 6.3 for each year of the forecasting period, is derived by dividing total expenses by effective gross income.

Consulting the most recent annual edition of *Income/Expenses Analysis, Conventional Apartments* (Lisle, Ill.: Institute of Real Estate Management), the analyst compares the forecast operating ratios shown in Figure 6.3 with the average for lowrise apartments built since 1978 and containing more than 25 units—the reported category that fits Maegan's Magic Manor—in the metropolitan area. The reported ratios have grown gradually during recent years, approximately in tandem with increasing vacancy rates, so our analyst considers it reasonable to expect them to drop back to their historical level of about 44% as average vacancies drop and rents escalate. Because that is the pattern reflected by the forecast on Figure 6.3, it tends to validate the forecast.

FIGURE 6.3: Forecasted Operating Expense Ratios for Maegan's Magic Manor Apartments

Forecast Year	Operating Expense Ratio
1	44.3
2	41.9
3	41.0
4	44.2
5	43.7
6	43.2

ESTIMATING FUTURE MARKET VALUE

Investors usually plan on selling the property at some future time, and the value of the expected after-tax proceeds from selling may constitute a substantial portion of the property's investment value. Income tax consequences of selling are addressed in Unit 11. First, though, it is necessary to estimate the eventual selling price. A convenient way to approach this is to forecast the relationship between NOI and market value, and to apply the forecasted relationship to the NOI projected for the final year in the forecasting period.

The capitalization rate or cap rate is the ratio of a property's NOI to its market value. The relationship is

$$R = \frac{\text{NOI}}{\text{value}}$$

where R is the capitalization rate and *NOI* is the net operating income (this can be the most recent income or the projected income).

Capitalization rates change with the cost of capital and with investors' perceptions of future cash flows from investment. At best, therefore, we can only estimate what the rate will be at the end of the expected holding period. Fortunately for our purposes, these changes tend to be modest and to occur gradually.

To illustrate, Figure 6.4 charts nationwide average capitalization rates for apartment properties on an annual basis from 1992 through 2017. They range from a high of 9.66% to a low of 7.94% over a 25-year period that encompasses a variety of market and economic conditions. The arithmetic mean for the period is approximately 8.82%. Similar patterns are reported for other categories of rental property.

FIGURE 6.4: Apartment Building Capitalization Rates 1992–2017

Year	Rate (%)	Year	Rate (%)
1992	9.66	2005	9.14
1993	9.15	2006	9.26
1994	9.15	2007	8.81
1995	9.22	2008	8.77
1996	8.47	2009	8.85
1997	8.45	2010	8.89
1998	8.71	2011	8.6
1999	7.94	2012	8.25
2000	8.97	2013	8.39
2001	9.61	2014	8.24
2002	9.21	2016	8.15
2003	9.19	2017	8.16
2004	9.00		

Source: www.RealtyRates.com

One can legitimately object that these national averages can mask a multitude of variations in specific markets. Investigation reveals, however, that rates in most metropolitan areas exhibit similar stability.

Anticipating similar stability in the relationship between NOI and market value in the market area that includes Maegan's Magic Manor, our analyst estimates what the market value will be after six years by applying the average capitalization rate for similar properties in this market area. The long-term average rate has been 8.82%, so the forecasted market value at the end of the anticipated six-year holding period is the expected sixth year's income divided by 0.0882. This is $18,164,399, or rounded, $18,200,000:

$$\$1,602,100 / 0.0882 = \$18,164,399$$

Even where an investor's plan does not include eventual property disposal, the income capitalization technique is useful. It enables one to place a value, at any point in time, on an infinite series of future cash flows. This topic is explained in Appendix A.

The future sales price could also be estimated by using the relationship between the current market value and the current or forecasted gross income. This ratio, called the *gross income multiplier*, is determined by dividing the market price by the effective gross income:

gross income multiplier = market price / effective gross income

If the ratio is expected to remain reasonably stable, future market values can be estimated by applying the computed multiplier to the forecasted effective gross income. If the ratio is not expected to remain stable, it can still be used by first estimating how it is likely to change. Refinements to gross income multiplier analysis (such as deciding between effective gross income and potential gross income as the denominator in the equation, and whether to use the most recent year's operating results or the results forecasted for the ensuing year) are explored in Unit 13.

Another technique for estimating future market values is *trend extrapolation*. If properties similar to the subject have been increasing in market value at, for example, 5% per annum in recent years, a similar rate of increase for the subject property is a reasonable expectation. Trends shift through time, however, so a simple straight-line extrapolation over several years might generate an unreliable forecast.

ADDITIONAL INFORMATION NEEDED

We have come a long way since the beginning of this book, but rational investment analysis requires still more information. To move from the operating forecast developed in Figure 6.2 to a rational investment decision, we must use our estimate of future NOI and future market value to derive a forecast of after-tax cash flow to the equity investor. Recall from Unit 1 that the value placed on those after-tax cash flows comprises the value of the equity position. Adding the estimated mortgage loan gives us an estimate of investment value, as described in Unit 1 and illustrated in Figure 1.6.

To derive a forecast of after-tax cash flows from the operating forecast, we must incorporate the following:

- *Consequences of using borrowed money.* Using borrowed money wisely gives investors more mileage from their personal (equity) funds. This topic is addressed in Part Three.
- *Income tax consequences.* Tax collectors have first dibs on investment income. Relevant aspects of the Internal Revenue Code are discussed in Part Four.

SUMMARY

Revenue forecasting is essentially a marketing research problem. Demand for rental space at a specific location depends on the level of demand in the market area and on the desirability of amenities and locational factors the site confers. It depends also on the price and availability of competing sites that offer about the same level of want-satisfying power. Thus, both physical and locational characteristics affect a property's ability to command rents. Physical characteristics include both geological features and improvements such as landscaping and buildings; locational characteristics relate to how well a location is suited for its intended use.

The contribution that physical characteristics make to a property's competitive position changes over time. These changes are attributable both to physical deterioration and to altered needs or tastes on the part of prospective tenants. Improvements become less suitable with age, as a result of decline in their attractiveness and because of increased maintenance costs. Technological innovation or variation in style and tastes may render existing physical structures less desirable than before, even without the factor of physical deterioration.

Linkages, neighborhood influences, and institutional factors all contribute to relative locational desirability. Linkages require movement of goods or people between properties and give rise to transfer costs. The importance of locations that minimize transfer costs increases with the relative importance of these costs to the total cost of a tenant's use of the site. Both explicit and implicit transfer costs must be factored into location decisions.

Linkages are almost certain to change over time. Altered lifestyles, new technology, shifts in consumer tastes—these and a host of other phenomena may promote the emergence of important new linkages, as well as a decline in the significance of old ones. Because linkages play such a dominant role in determining a property's ability to command rent, accurate perception of emerging trends is a major factor in reliable income forecasting.

Even if linkage relationships remained virtually constant, their impact on a property's income-generating capacity might shift due to changes in relative transfer costs. As the cost of moving people or goods between linked sites is increased or decreased by modification of transportation facilities or other economic shifts, the linkage's impact on a site's ability to command rent may be altered.

Sites are subject to both desirable and undesirable neighborhood influences. Such influences are particularly important in real estate decisions because site immobility prohibits moving to escape the influence of neighborhood factors. Building and zoning ordinances, fire codes, and federal, state, and local land-use laws are frequently designed to protect against the encroachment of neighborhood factors deemed undesirable. Private agreements are often designed with the same objective.

Supply and demand considerations must be factored into revenue forecasts. This involves estimating probable changes in site linkages, in neighborhood influences, and in institutional factors that may influence demand or supply. Supply is a less troublesome consideration when significant monopoly elements are present. Monopoly elements may result from unique physical or locational factors or they may exist only in the perception of potential tenants. Regardless of their origin, they reduce the property's vulnerability to competitive inroads from comparable property.

RECOMMENDED READING

American Institute of Real Estate Appraisers. *The Appraisal of Real Estate*, 14th ed. Chicago: Appraisal Institute, 2013.

Aydin, Recai, and Barton A. Smith, "Evidence of the Dual Nature of Property Recovery Following Environmental Remediation." *Real Estate Economics* 36:4, 2008, 777–812.

Barrett, G. Vincent, and John P. Blair. *How to Conduct and Analyze Real Estate Market and Feasibility Studies,* 2nd ed. New York: Van Nostrand Reinhold Company, 1988.

Clapp, John, and Mauricio Rodriguez. "Using a GIS for Real Estate Market Analysis: The Problem of Spatially Aggregated Data." *The Journal of Real Estate Research* 16, no. 1 (1998): 35–56.

Dueker, Kenneth J., and P. Barton DeLacy. "GIS in the Land Development Planning Process." *Journal of the American Planning Association* 56, no. 4 (Autumn 1990): 483–92.

Fanning, Stephen F., Terry V. Grissom, and Thomas D. Pearson. *Market Analysis for Valuation Appraisals*. Chicago: Appraisal Institute, 1995.

Miles, Mike E., Gayle Berens, Mark J. Eppli, and Marc A. Weiss. *Real Estate Development: Principles and Process,* 4th ed. Washington, D.C.: The Urban Land Institute, 2007, Units 11 and 12.

Pittman, Robert. "Geographic Information Systems: An Important New Tool for Economic Development Professionals." *Economic Development Review* 8, no. 4 (Fall 1990): 4–7.

Weber, Bruce. "The Use of GIS and OLAP for Accurate Valuation of Developable Land." *Journal of Real Estate Portfolio Management* 7, no. 3 (July–September 2001): 253–281.

White, Michelle, J. "Commuting and Congestion: A Simulation Model of a Decentralized Metropolitan Area." *Journal of the American Real Estate and Urban Economics Association* (now *Real Estate Economics*) 18:3, 1990, 335–368.

Wofford, Larry E., and Grant Thrall. "Real Estate Problem Solving and Geographic Information Systems: A Stage Model of Reasoning." *Journal of Real Estate Literature* 5, no. 2 (July 1997): 177–202.

INTERNET REFERENCES

For valuation information from the Appraisal Institute:
www.appraisalinstitute.org

For information on trends in building valuation:
www.buildings.com

For information on appraisal:
www.appraisers.org

For GIS links, references, and publications:
www.mrsc.org

REVIEW QUESTIONS

1. List some of the key physical characteristics that influence a property's income-producing capability.
2. List some of the locational factors that will influence a property's ability to command rents.
3. What future trends must be considered in forecasting the rent-generating ability of a property?
4. How does supply affect the rent-generating capability of property?
5. List the relationship between price and supply of rental property.
6. The text distinguishes between the responsiveness of short-run and long-run supply curves to changes in rental rates. What determines the length of time that defines the *long* rather than the *short* run?
7. What is functional obsolescence and how does it affect a property's ability to command rent?
8. What are linkages and how do they influence tenants' location decisions?
9. How do explicit and implicit transfer costs differ? Give some examples of both.
10. Give at least two examples of institutional arrangements that can either enhance or detract from a property's ability to command rent.

DISCUSSION QUESTIONS

1. In an inflationary environment, cash flows in future years will have less purchasing power than those in earlier years. Thus, a multiple-year cash-flow forecast is not a consistent measure of a property's performance. How might this difficulty be addressed?
2. Operating expenses cannot be estimated based on experience and are totally unrelated to revenue projections. Do you agree? Discuss.
3. What examples (other than those in the text) can you think of where significant new linkages have emerged or the importance of existing linkages has shifted significantly to alter the relative value of properties that are imperfect substitutes?
4. Give some examples from your community where relative transfer costs have been altered enough to shift the competitive positions of properties in the area.
5. Give examples from your community where a site has been differentiated from the competition through imaginative marketing or by controlling a unique location.

PROBLEMS

1. Craine Crossroads has 100 two-bedroom apartments that currently rent for $900 per month. The complex currently has five vacant units, matching the vacancy rate for two-bedroom units in the market area. Additional other income from recreation room fees and parking is $40,000 per year. Next year, two new apartment complexes will be completed in the market area, causing the vacancy rates for the existing complexes to rise to 7.5%. Other income will remain flat and rent at Craine Crossroads will rise only 2%. Management fees are 5% of effective gross income. Property taxes are scheduled to go up to $140,000 from the current $130,000. Maintenance, repairs, and replacements are 8% of EGI. The other operating expenses are expected to cost 3% more next year. Those current expenses are as follows:

Salaries	$95,200
Utilities	$50,800
Insurance	$19,100
Supplies	$9,900
Advertising, legal, misc.	$14,700

    Reconstruct this year's and next year's operating statements for Craine Crossroads.

2. Calculate the next year's operating statement for Craine Crossroads if the vacancy rate drops to 4% next year because of the transfer of troops to the army post nearby. All other projected figures will remain the same.

PART TWO

Case Problem

Allen Benedict is thinking of buying an apartment complex that is offered for sale by the firm of Getz and Fowler. The price, $2.25 million, equals the property's market value. The following statement of income and expense is presented for Benedict's consideration:

The St. George Apartments Prior Year's Operating Results, Presented by Getz and Fowler, Brokers

30 units, all two-bedroom apartments, $975 per month		$351,000
Washer and dryer rentals		10,000
Gross annual income		$361,000
Less operating expenses:		
Manager's salary	10,000	
Maintenance staff (one person, part-time)	7,800	
Seedy landscapers	1,300	
Property taxes	13,500	32,600
Net operating income		$328,400

By checking the electric meters during an inspection tour of the property, Benedict determines the occupancy rate to be about 80%. He learns, by talking to tenants, that most have been offered inducements such as a month's free rent or special decorating allowances. A check with competing apartment houses reveals that similar apartment units rent for about $895 per month and that vacancies average about 5%. Moreover, these other apartments have pools and recreation areas that make their units worth about $20 per month more than those of the St. George, which has neither.

The tax assessor states that the apartments were reassessed 12 months ago and that the current taxes are $71,400.

Benedict learns that the resident manager at St. George, in addition to a $10,000 salary, gets a free apartment for her services. He also discovers other expenses: insurance will cost $6.50 per $1,000 of coverage, based on estimated replacement cost of about $1.8 million; workers' compensation ($140 per annum) must be paid to the state; utilities, incurred to light hallways and other common areas, cost about $95 per month for similar properties; supplies and miscellaneous expenses typically run about 0.25% of effective gross rent. Professional property management fees in the market area typically are about 5% of effective gross income.

Case Problem

1. Develop a prior year's reconstructed operating statement, assuming typically competent, professional management. Based on the reconstructed NOI and the current market value, determine the capitalization rate.
2. Develop a seven-year forecast of NOI for the St. George Apartments, incorporating the following assumptions:
    a. Potential gross rent and miscellaneous other income will grow at 2.5% per annum over the forecast period.
    b. Vacancies in the market area will remain constant over the forecast period.
    c. Operating expenses other than management fees and property taxes will grow at 2.5% per annum over the forecast period.
    d. Management fees as a percent of effective gross income will remain constant over the forecast period.
    e. Property taxes are expected to increase to $76,048 in the third year of the forecast and to $85,039 in the seventh year.
3. Assuming that the capitalization rate will remain constant, develop an estimate of the property's market value at the end of the projected holding period.
4. Suggest some reasons why the capitalization rate might not remain constant. Why might it become larger or smaller that the currently prevailing rate?

Save your work. It will be needed to solve case problems for Part Three.

PART THREE

Using Borrowed Money

Often, the narrative surrounding real estate tells of fortunes made using other people's money. Tales of investors and developers building real estate empires on financial shoestrings are fascinating and inspirational, but they can bewilder and discourage those who have just been denied credit at a local lending institution. It sounds easy in the wheeler-dealer biographies, popular get-rich-quick books, and infomercials that fill late-night television. Yet, it can become very complicated in practice.

Programs and books that are intended for popular consumption may overstate the benefits of borrowing and short-change the risk, but the fact is that few real estate deals are consummated without at least some borrowed money. If no third-party lender is involved, it is usually because the seller agrees to take back a promissory note for a substantial part of the consideration. Financing arrangements are often a more critical issue than price, and languishing projects can sometimes be resuscitated by restructuring the financing. Real estate–related borrowing is an intricate, frequently arcane, craft. Its mastery is eagerly sought by investors who appreciate the value of favorable financial leverage.

Sophisticated investors understand the importance of an unusually keen grasp of financial markets, arrangements, and procedures. These markets, arrangements, and procedures are the topic of Part Three. We begin with Unit 7, which introduces the concept and the consequences of borrowing. Unit 8 describes common credit instruments and borrowing arrangements. Part Three concludes with Unit 9, which explains the cost of borrowing and describes ways to compare alternative financing arrangements.

UNIT 7

Financial Leverage and Investment Analysis

UNIT PREVIEW

Unit 1 introduced the concept of cash flow as the source of value for rental real estate. Figure 1.6 illustrated how the cash flows from operations are divided between the debt position and the equity position. Unit 6 explored ways to estimate the cash flows from operations. This unit addresses the issue of using borrowed funds, thereby creating a debt position and earmarking a portion of the operating cash flows for a lender.

Most real estate transactions involve debt financing, and borrowing is usually the major source of funds. Sometimes this is the only way to gain control of a project. But even where it is not necessary for control, investors borrow to enhance the expected yield on equity resources.

This unit explains the popularity of borrowing in connection with real estate investments by exploring the concept of financial leverage. The unit then addresses the question of determining how much borrowing is appropriate. It concludes with a survey of the most common sources of borrowed funds.

THE REASONS WHY LEVERAGE IS SO POPULAR

Financial leverage is created by mixing borrowed funds with equity. The higher the ratio of borrowing to equity, the greater the degree of leverage. When the rate of return on assets exceeds borrowing costs, leverage is said to be favorable, or positive. If the cost of borrowing is greater than the return on assets, leverage is unfavorable, or negative.

A great number of books highlight the concept of *leveraging out*, buying entirely with borrowed funds. However, these books fail to mention that such benefits are associated with increased risk. The popularity of mortgage borrowing stems from its potentially positive impact on equity investment: favorable leverage magnifies the yield on equity funds, multiplies the tax deduction for depreciation expense (by permitting the purchase of more property with available equity funds), and amplifies the benefit from favorable tax rates applicable to capital gains.

The Spread

The difference between the rate of return on assets and the cost of borrowing is called the spread. In a highly leveraged investment, even a small favorable spread greatly magnifies the return on equity. Leverage cuts both ways, though. A small negative spread (unfavorable leverage) on a high-leverage deal will devastate the yield to equity investors. It can make what would otherwise have been a modestly successful investment venture a total disaster.

The potential impact of financial leverage is illustrated in Example 7.1. In the example, NOI is 14% of the property's market value. If the equity investors decide against financial leverage, their equity investment will be $1.5 million and they will expect to receive the full $210,000 per annum NOI, a current yield of 14%. (*Total yield*, the current yield plus the benefits of appreciation, will be even greater if the property's value increases. It will be lower if value declines.) This information is summarized in the first column of Figure 7.1.

> **Example 7.1**
>
> A property that has a market value of $1.5 million is expected to generate annual NOI of $210,000. A $1 million mortgage loan that will be repaid in equal monthly installments over 20 years, with interest at 9% per annum, is available. The monthly payments of $8,997.26 include accrued interest and sufficient principal to retire the loan over its 20-year term. Annual debt service is simply 12 times this amount, or approximately $107,964.

If the investors elect to borrow the $1 million, approximately $107,967 of the NOI will be siphoned off as debt service (principal and interest payments on the mortgage loan). Only the remaining $102,033 will flow to the equity investors. The impact on before-tax cash flow and current yield on the equity investment is shown in the second column of Figure 7.1.

> **CALCULATOR APPLICATIONS**
>
> PV = 1,000,000
> h = 240 (12 months × 20 years)
> i = 0.7500 (9 / 12)
>
> **Solve for present value:**
> PMT $8,997.26
> Debt service = 12 × PMT = $107,967

See what happens when even greater financial leverage is used. Assume that an 80% loan ($1.2 million) is also available on the investment in Example 7.1. This loan will be for the same period (20 years) and at the same interest rate (9%) as the lesser loan set forth in the example. The larger loan reduces both the required equity investment and the cash flow to the equity position: the monthly payment required by the alternative loan will be $10,796.71 and the annual debt service will be 12 times this amount, or approximately $129,561. Expected cash flow to the equity investors drops to $210,000 minus $129,561, or $80,439, while the equity investment is reduced to $300,000. The impact on cash flow to the equity position, expressed as a percentage of the initial equity investment, is summarized in the third column of Figure 7.1.

FIGURE 7.1: Cash-Flow Consequences of Financing Alternatives in Example 7.1

	No Loan	$1,000,000 Loan	$1,200,000 Loan
Net operating income	$ 210,000	$ 210,000	$ 210,000
Less: Annual debt service	0	107,967	129,561
Before-tax cash flow	$210,000	$102,033	$80,439
Purchase price	$1,500,000	$1,500,000	$1,500,000
Less: Loan amount	0	1,000,000	1,200,000
Equity Invested	$1,500,000	$500,000	$300,000
Ratios			
Mortgage constant (debt service/loan amount)	n/a	0.108, or 10.8%	0.108, or 10.8%
Return on assets (net operating income/cost)	0.140, or 14.0%	0.140, or 14.0%	0.140, or 14.0%
Current yield (Before-tax cash flow/equity)	0.140, or 14.0%	0.204, or 20.4%	0.268, or 26.8%

The fundamental principle illustrated by Figure 7.1 is that as long as the debt-service constant (the annual debt service expressed as a percentage of the amount borrowed) is less than the rate of return on total assets, additional financial leverage increases cash flow to the equity position as a percentage of the equity investment. In Figure 7.1, the current yield on assets (NOI divided by market value) is seen to be 14%; the annual debt-service constant is only 10.8%.

Amplifying the Tax Shelter

Income tax law creates a major incentive to financial leverage. Interest payments are generally deductible from taxable income on a dollar-for-dollar basis. (Part Four of this text explores exceptions and special limitations on the deductibility of interest expense.) Yet, investors are also allowed an annual tax deduction (called an *allowance for depreciation* or *cost recovery*), even when properties are purchased with borrowed money. Thus, buying with borrowed funds greatly amplifies the amount of tax-deductible expenses an investor can claim with the same level of equity investment.

Amplifying the Gain on Disposal

When market values are increasing, favorable financial leverage will multiply the gain from appreciation. This is illustrated in Example 7.2 by assuming a current yield of zero; no benefits accrue other than from appreciation. Because the interest rate on the purchase-money mortgage in the example is less than the expected rate of increase in the market value of the property, financial leverage amplifies the expected yield impressively. The expected annual rate of return on equity (total return, the current yield—zero in this case—plus appreciation), calculated on a before-tax basis under both of the available financing alternatives, is presented in Figure 7.2.

Example 7.2

A parcel of land that is well situated to benefit from rapid urban growth can be acquired for $800,000. A prospective investor expects that the land will double in value over the next five years, after which time she plans to sell. During the interim, the land can be leased to a turnip farmer for an annual rental that just covers the property tax liability, so there will be zero annual cash flow before debt service and income taxes. (Because there are no improvements on or to the land—just raw farmland—there is no cost recovery allowance to consider.)

The land can be purchased for $800,000 cash, or the present owner will agree to accept a $200,000 down payment accompanied by a note and purchase-money mortgage for $600,000. Both the principal and the accumulated interest on the note will be due and payable at the end of the fifth year, with interest accumulating at a compound annual rate of 8%.

The $881,597 balance due on the purchase-money note in the *with leverage* calculation represents the value, after five years, of a $600,000 deposit (the face amount of the note) drawing interest at a compound rate of 9% per annum. The annual rates of return (29.14% and 14.87%) represent compound annual growth rates that will make the initial equity cash outlays under each alternative approximately equal to the net equity proceeds on sale after five years. Compound interest and discount calculations are explained in detail in Appendix A.

FIGURE 7.2: Cash-Flow Consequences of Financing Alternatives in Example 7.2

	With Leverage	Without Leverage
Proceeds from sale after 5 Years	$1,600,000	$1,600,000
Less: Balance due on loan	881,597	0
Net sales proceeds, before tax	$718,403	$1,600,000
Initial cash outlay	$200,000	$800,000
Approximate annual pretax rate of return	29.14%	14.87%

CALCULATOR APPLICATIONS

$PV = -200,000$ $\qquad$ $PV = -800,000$
$FV = 718,403$ $\qquad$ $FV = 1,600,000$
$n = 5$ $\qquad\qquad\quad$ $n = 5$

Solve for i: $\qquad$ *Solve for i:*
$i = 29.14\%$ $\qquad\quad$ $i = 14.87\%$

Because interest expense is deductible and the gain on disposal is taxable, both at the same incremental rate in our example, the after-tax rate of return on the equity investment is simply the before-tax rate times one, minus the incremental income tax rate. The positive consequences are further amplified when carrying costs (i.e., the interest on borrowed money) are tax deductible at the investor's incremental income tax rate, yet the gain on the sale is taxed at a lower rate applicable to long-term capital gains. These issues are addressed in Part Four, which explains federal income tax rules.

MEASURING FINANCIAL LEVERAGE

Financial leverage can be measured as the relationship between an equity investment and the total market value of assets acquired. Corporate financial analysts frequently express this relationship as a *debt-to-equity ratio*, the ratio between borrowed funds and equity funds. For reasons having to do more with its origin than with its usefulness, the ratio between borrowed funds and the market value of the asset being financed (a *loan-to-value ratio*) is more commonly used in real estate circles.

The loan-to-value ratio is a measure of the mortgage lender's margin of safety in the event of default, and it is for this purpose that the measure was initially devised. The ultimate cure for default is public sale of the mortgaged property, and the lender expects to recoup the loan balance from the sales proceeds. Should the sale bring less than the loan balance (plus costs associated with the sale), the lender is almost certain to suffer financial loss. The loan-to-value ratio is an expression of the risk of such a loss. The ratio for the property in Example 7.1 ($1,000,000 / $1,500,000 = 0.67, or 67%) expresses the fact that, in the event of immediate default, the property could sell for as much as one-third (1 − 0.67) below its current value before the lender would suffer a significant loss.

Loan-to-value ratios serve an entirely different function for investment analysts. They provide a measure of the dollar amount of real estate that can be controlled with a given amount of equity funds. If, for example, the available loan-to-value ratio is 0.67, then an investor can control [$1 / (1 − 0.67)], or $3 of real estate for every $1 of equity funds invested. This is the case in Example 7.1, where $500,000 of equity investment confers control of a $1.5 million asset. The loan-to-value ratio, therefore, serves as a measure of possible financial leverage.

The debt-to-equity ratio expresses the same relationship in a slightly different fashion. In Example 7.1, the debt-to-equity ratio is $1 million to $500,000, or two to one. This indicates that the investor can borrow $2 for every $1 of equity funds used.

Another ratio designed to express the risk associated with financial leverage is the *debt-coverage ratio*, also known as debt-service ratio, the ratio between NOI and the annual debt-service obligation. It is a measure of the extent to which NOI can fall below expectations before it becomes insufficient to service the debt. In equation form, it is as follows:

$$\text{debt coverage ratio} = \frac{\text{annual net operating income}}{\text{annual debt service}}$$

The debt-coverage ratio for the $1 million loan in Figure 7.1 is 1.95, calculated by dividing the $210,000 NOI by the $107,967 annual debt-service requirement. This expresses an expectation that annual cash flow before debt service will be approximately 1.95 times the amount required to service the debt. It indicates a substantial cushion for underestimated expenses or overestimated revenues before actual NOI falls below what is required to service the mortgage indebtedness. For the $1.2 million loan in Figure 7.1, the debt-coverage ratio is only 1.62. The ratio is smaller than with the $1 million loan, because a greater portion of the NOI will be needed to satisfy the debt-service obligation.

WHAT IS THE RIGHT AMOUNT OF FINANCIAL LEVERAGE?

Remember from Example 7.1 that the greater the amount of favorable leverage used, the greater the return on equity capital. This suggests that one can't have too much favorable financial leverage. Yet there does seem to be an optimal capital structure, and there are definite limits on the amount of debt financing lenders are willing to supply. Someone has suggested that financial leverage is like flavoring in a cake: too little or too much is disastrous, just the right amount creates a delicious concoction.

Debt-Coverage Ratios and Available Financing

Selecting the right amount of financial leverage assumes lenders' willingness to advance funds. The first question to be addressed, therefore, is how much leverage is available. Only then is it meaningful to ask how much of the available leverage should be used.

On all except very small investment properties, lenders can be confident that borrowers will honor their debt-service obligations only if the properties generate sufficient cash flow for this purpose. Moreover, because a property's value depends on its ability to generate income, the value of mortgaged property will decline if the anticipated income does not materialize. An important measure of the lender's security, therefore, is the relationship between annual NOI from a property and the debt-service obligation associated with a mortgage loan.

As described earlier, this relationship is expressed as a debt-coverage ratio. Mortgage lenders often specify minimum acceptable debt-coverage ratios as a constraint on the amount they are willing to lend. Dividing the estimated annual NOI by the minimum acceptable debt-coverage ratio yields the maximum amount of annual debt service a property will support. Dividing this by the annual loan constant for the most likely loan terms results in an estimate of the loan that the property will support as illustrated in Example 7.3.

The expected $400,000 income from the property in Example 7.3 must be at least 1.2 times as great as the annual debt-service obligation. The debt-service obligation, therefore, cannot exceed $400,000 / 1.2, or $333,333. A 9%, 20-year, fully amortizing loan requires monthly payments of $0.0089973 per dollar borrowed. The annual debt service per dollar borrowed is simply 12 times this amount, or $0.10797. Because the maximum debt service the NOI will support is $333,333, the property will support a maximum loan of $333,333 / 0.10797 = $3,087,274. Because amortization tables round to the fifth digit, financial calculators produce a more accurate number.

Example 7.3

Conversation with lenders results in an estimation that they will insist on a debt-coverage ratio of not less than 1.20 and will lend at 9% per annum, to be repaid in equal monthly installments of principal and interest over 20 years. The property is expected to yield first-year NOI of $400,000.

> **CALCULATOR APPLICATIONS**
>
> Debt service / 12 = monthly payment
> 333,333 / 12 = 27,777.75
> *PMT* = 27,777.75
> *n* = 240 (12 months × 20 years)
> *i* = 0.7500 (9/12)
>
> **Solve for present value:**
> *PV* = $3,087,357

Loan-to-Value Ratios and Available Financing

In addition to specifying minimum acceptable debt-coverage ratios, lenders usually specify maximum acceptable loan-to-value ratios. The actual loan they will make is the one that satisfies the most restrictive of these constraints.

For example, if the property whose income is given in Example 7.3 has a value of $4 million and the lender cites a maximum loan-to-value ratio of 70%, the maximum amount that could be borrowed is 0.7 times $4 million, or $2.8 million. This is true even though the debt-coverage constraint would permit a loan of slightly more than $3 million. Conversely, if the property was worth $5 million, the loan-to-value ratio would permit a loan of $3.5 million, yet the debt-coverage ratio constraint would limit the loan to a little more than $3 million.

Financial Leverage and Risk

Many people view lenders as tight-fisted money-mongers who will make a loan only when borrowers are so prosperous and wealthy they don't need the funds. Yet, toward the peak of each real estate investment cycle, when the competition to place loans is greater than borrowers' problems in qualifying, lenders sometimes engage in a veritable lending frenzy. Moreover, even in normal times, lenders' restrictions can often be circumvented by convincing the seller to provide supplementary financing.

Just because the money is available does not mean it should be borrowed, though. Two negative consequences can result from increasing dependence on borrowed funds: the venture becomes increasingly risky, and the cost of borrowing escalates.

Even if borrowing costs do not increase, the net benefit of borrowing will eventually be diminished by offsetting increases in financial risk. We saw earlier that the benefits are predicated on an assumption that leverage will be favorable. But this assumption is based on a forecast that is fraught with uncertainty. If the operating forecast proves overly optimistic and the total return on assets falls below the cost of borrowed money, the negative consequences of the flawed investment strategy grow directly with the degree of financial leverage used.

Examine Example 7.1 again. Recall that the $210,000 NOI is only an expectation. The actual operating income might be considerably less. Suppose it turns out to be only $150,000. The actual current yield on assets drops to 10%, which is less than the debt-service constant. Using financial leverage drops, rather than increases, the actual current yield on equity, and the greater the degree of financial leverage, the smaller the current equity yield. (Whether leverage is ultimately favorable or unfavorable depends on the total return on assets: current yield plus-or-minus the rate of change in asset value. It depends also on the income tax consequences). The impact on current yield to the equity investor when leverage is used and NOI falls below expectations is illustrated in Figure 7.3.

FIGURE 7.3: Cash-Flow Consequences of Financing Alternatives in Example 7.1 with Less-Than-Expected Net Operating Income

	No Loan	$1,000,000 Loan	$1,200,000 Loan
Net operating income	$150,000	$150,000	$150,000
Less: Annual debt service	0	107,967	129,561
Before-tax cash flow	$150,000	$42,033	$20,439
Purchase price	$1,500,000	$1,500,000	$1,500,000
Less: Loan amount	0	1,000,000	1,200,000
Equity invested	$1,500,000	$500,000	$300,000
Ratios			
Debt service/loan amount	n/a	0.108, or 10.8%	0.108, or 10.8%
Net operating income/cost	0.100, or 10.0%	0.100, or 10.0%	0.100, or 10.0%
Before-tax cash flow/equity	0.100, or 10.0%	0.084, or 8.4%	0.068, or 6.8%

Examine again at the investment described in Example 7.2. Figure 7.2 illustrates how financial leverage increases the expected yield on the investment, from 14.87% without financial leverage to 29.14% with financial leverage. But the example and the table assume that the property doubles in value over five years, a compound rate of appreciation of about 14.9% per annum. What if the property appreciates at a rate of less than 8% per annum (the cost of borrowed money)? Then, financial leverage will be negative rather than positive; it will reduce the rate of return on equity funds. For example, if the property appreciates at a compound annual rate of only 7%, proceeds from sale after five years would be $1,122,041, and the net sales proceeds (after paying off the loan) before taxes would be $240,444. This represents a rate of return on the equity investment of only 3.75% per annum. Note also that the balance due on the $600,000 loan (principal plus cumulative interest) will be $881,597. If the land sale nets less than that amount, there will not be sufficient cash flow to pay off the loan.

Financial Leverage and the Cost of Borrowing

In addition to increasing the range of possible outcomes to equity investors, increasing financial leverage also drives up the cost of borrowing. As leverage increases, lenders insist on additional effective interest as compensation for their additional risk exposure. The increase may take the form of larger front-end fees, higher interest rates, or both. The result is greater incremental borrowing costs, as illustrated in Figure 7.4.

Figure 7.4 depicts only the explicit costs: those charged by the lender. There is a second layer of cost, however, that borrowers must factor into their leverage decision. This is the implicit cost expressed as greater risk exposure. Earlier, we saw that the greater the amount of borrowed money relative to equity funds, the greater the range of possible outcomes for equity investors, and dispersion of possible outcomes around the expected outcome is a common way of measuring risk. As discussed in Unit 1, investors typically prefer less risk and expect to be compensated for assuming more. Risk bearing, therefore, can be thought of as an implicit cost of using borrowed money.

FIGURE 7.4: Incremental Cost of Borrowing

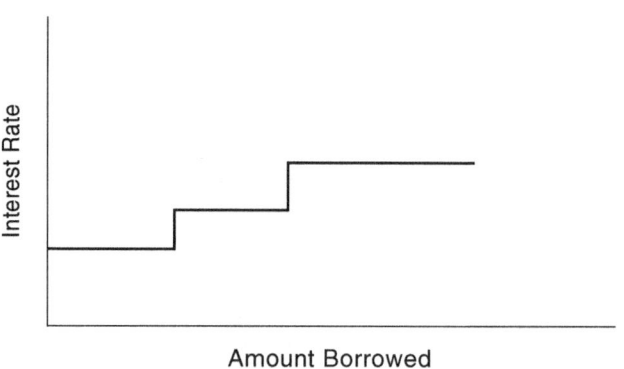

Figure 7.5 replicates Figure 7.4 but adds two elements. The flat, horizontal line depicts the expected rate of return on assets. Because the source of investment funds does not affect the return on assets, the marginal rate is the same at all levels of financial leverage.

Before considering risk, the optimal amount of financial leverage is $L1$, where the increment cost of borrowing exactly equals the incremental return on assets.

Additional leverage would cost more than the expected rate of return on assets, and so would pull down the expected rate of return to the equity investors.

When the implicit cost of additional risk associated with financial leverage is factored into the analysis, the incremental cost of borrowing is more appropriately depicted by the upward-sloping line in Figure 7.5. This is the explicit cost as depicted by the stair-step cost line, plus the implicit cost of added uncertainty. With consideration of risk, the optimal amount of financial leverage is reduced to $L2$, where the marginal return on assets equals the risk-adjusted marginal cost of borrowing.

FIGURE 7.5: Optimal Amount of Financial Leverage

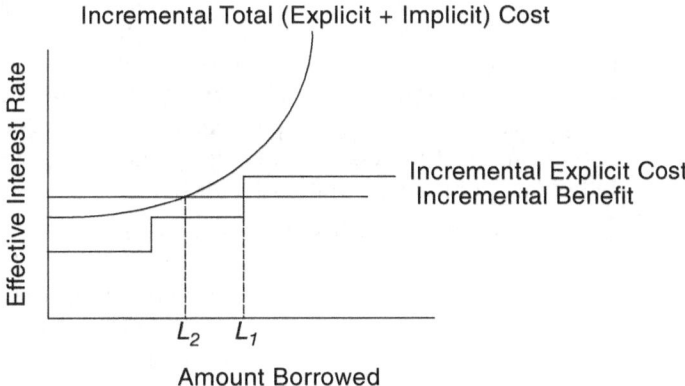

TODAY'S LENDERS

Investors in real estate depend on a different set of mortgage lenders than do homebuyers. The cast of players changes through time, and there has been a major realignment over the past decade. Today's most frequent sources are commercial banks, insurance companies, pension funds, and an odd mixture referred to as *conduits*.

Insurance Companies and Pension Funds

Insurance companies have long been a key source of mortgage funds for investment property. Their predictable inflow of investable funds and the long-term nature of most of their obligations make mortgage loans a particularly appropriate investment. Figure 7.6 shows the composition of the insurance industry's mortgage loan portfolio in 2015.

FIGURE 7.6: Composition of Life Insurance Industry's Mortgage Loan Portfolios

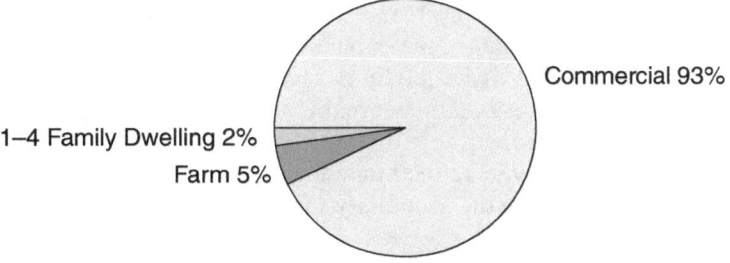

Source: American Council of Life Insurance

Life insurance companies' lending practices are regulated by state insurance agencies, which vary from state to state. The regulators typically set limits on the types of investments the insurance companies can make and the percentage of their investment portfolios that can be devoted to each category. Within the constraints set by regulators, the big insurance companies exhibit a preference for loans on very large ventures. They often acquire an equity participation interest (i.e., part ownership). Smaller insurers are inclined to reach farther down the mortgage loan feeding chain; some make individual home loans in their locale.

Pension funds' cash flows are very similar to those of life insurance companies in terms of predictability and term structure, yet they have not been a major player in commercial real estate mortgage lending until recently. They have moved aggressively into the market during the mid-1990s, and their growing presence has prompted Real Estate Capital Markets Report to begin showing them as a commercial mortgage source for the first time in 1995.

Commercial Banks

Because a substantial portion of their funds are from demand deposits, commercial banks have greater liquidity needs than most other commercial mortgage lenders, and commit only a modest portion of their portfolio to mortgage lending. Yet, the tremendous volume of deposits available to them makes them a major source of mortgage loan funds. They typically originate several times the dollar volume of commercial mortgage loans as the life insurance industry originates the second most significant source.

Banks face federally imposed limits on the amount they can loan relative to the dollar value of collateral. With certain specified exceptions, they cannot lend more than 85% of the market value of improved property other than one- to four-family residences. They are typically limited to 80% of the market value with respect to loans to finance nonresidential construction, 75% for land development loans, and 65% of value when financing acquisition of raw land.

Due to the liquidity needs of banks, real estate loans of short duration are more suitable for bank portfolios than traditional, long-term, fully amortizing mortgage loans. Consequently, they favor loans to finance construction (due dates typically are one to three years), and short-term loans (typically 6 to 12 months) to mortgage companies to finance the companies' mortgage loan portfolios until they can be sold. Also, they often make medium-term (10-year to 15-year) mortgage loans to favored commercial customers, but many of these loans are partially amortizing and shortened by a provision that the remaining balance must be paid after five or seven years. Banks are major players in the home loan origination business, but these loans are usually sold to investors in the secondary market.

Conduit Sources

A major source of real estate debt financing (approximately $315 billion was borrowed this way during 2007 according to one source) is funded with commercial mortgage-backed securities—CMBS, also known as conduit loans. The volume of this financing plummeted in 2008 to just over $29 billion as a result of the subprime mortgage debacle and to under $19 billion in 2010.[1] CMBS financing rebounded somewhat following the financial crisis to 76 billion in 2016 but still significantly lower than pre-crisis events.[2] These are securities that represent shares in a pool of mortgages. Holders of the securities get the scheduled cash flow from the mortgage pool, minus the servicing fee. Commercial mortgage-based securities are attractive investments for regulated institutions because, as securities, the instruments typically require a substantially smaller liquid reserve than do real estate or mortgage investments.

In the past, most CMBS were issued by lenders who originated the loans or by entities that acquired ownership of the originating institutions. In recent years, however, numerous lenders and investment bankers have formed partnerships that enable mortgage borrowers to tap the CMBS market by using conduits.

Because CMBS are so alluring to investors, lenders see them as an ideal way to replenish their loaned funds at a profit by accommodating the needs of a source of financing that seems to have an almost unlimited capacity to supply funding for quality real estate loans. Long-term lenders of all types have increasingly adapted their underwriting guidelines and loan requirements to meet the CMBS market. With so many traditional commercial mortgage lenders, such as life insurance companies, pension funds, commercial banks, and now new real estate lenders, such as GE Capital Real Estate and GMAC Commercial Mortgage, rushing to securitize and sell their loans, the needs, interests, and requirements of the CMBS investors are of paramount importance. An extensive discussion of CMBS is found in Unit 6 of *Real Estate Finance, Third Edition* by Kolbe, Greer, and Waller.

SUMMARY

Financial leverage, the use of borrowed money, enables investors to acquire a much more expensive property than would otherwise be possible. It also permits acquiring more separate properties and thus may reduce overall risk.

Financial risk is the risk that cash flow from an investment will be insufficient to meet associated mortgage-debt payments. Increasing financial leverage also increases financial risk. The borrowing decision involves weighing offsetting elements of enhanced earnings potential and increased financial risk.

Interest expense may be deducted from taxable income, thereby decreasing the after-tax cost of borrowing. Borrowing enables investors to control a much larger financial investment, with the consequent possibility of claiming greatly increased income tax deductions for cost recovery allowances. An increased probability of ultimately realizing a substantial gain on disposal of the property also results.

---

1   CRE Finance Council, 2010.
2   *www.cmalert.com/rankings.pl?Q=91*

RECOMMENDED READING

Downs, Anthony. *The Revolution in Real Estate Finance.* Washington, D.C.: The Brookings Institution, 1985.

Fascitelli, Michael D., Frank J. Walter, and Christopher C. Andrysiak. "The Role of the Investment Banker in Real Estate Development." Unit 15 of Alenick, Jerome B. *Real Estate Development Manual.* Boston: Warren, Gorham, and Lamont, 1990.

Kolbe, Phillip T., Gaylon E. Greer, and Bennie D. Waller Jr. *Real Estate Finance.* 3rd ed. Chicago: Dearborn Real Estate Education, 2012.

Marron, Edward W., Jr., and Robert S. Blumenthal. "Real Estate Merchant Banking: The Next Wave in Finance for the Real Estate Developer." Unit 16 of Alenick, Jerome B. *Real Estate Development Manual.* Boston: Warren, Gorham and Lamont, 1990.

Miles, Mike E., Gayle Berens, Mark J. Eppli, and Marc A. Weiss. *Real Estate Development: Principles and Process.* 4th ed. Washington, D.C.: Urban Land Institute, 2010.

Stein, Joshua. "Mortgage Loan Structures for the 1990s." *Real Estate Review* 24, no. 1 (Spring 1994): 15–20.

INTERNET REFERENCES

For articles and links on real estate finance:
www.mortgagemag.com
www.individual.com (enter mortgage type)

For information on interest rates:
www.bai.org
www.bloomberg.com
www.interest.com
www.newyorkfed.org

For information on commercial mortgages:
www.cmAlert.com

For information on insurance companies:
www.acli.com

REVIEW QUESTIONS

1. How do income tax laws create an incentive to borrow money?
2. When financial leverage is used, what is the potential impact on before-tax cash flow and the current before-tax yield to the equity position?
3. Explain the meaning of the loan-to-value ratio from a mortgage lender's perspective and from the viewpoint of an investor.
4. Describe financial risk in real estate investment and explain a useful method of measuring financial risk.

5. How can the debt-coverage ratio be used to determine the amount of available financing for a project?
6. Financial leverage can amplify the gain realized on the disposal of a property. Explain how this occurs.

DISCUSSION QUESTIONS

1. Some financial advisors advocate remaining debt-free and buying all investment assets with equity funds. Are there any disadvantages to this practice? Explain why or why not.
2. The initial interest rate charged on variable-rate mortgage loans is usually lower than that charged on fixed-rate loans of equal length.
   a. Why is this so?
   b. As a borrower, what are some factors you should consider in deciding whether to accept a variable-rate or a fixed-rate loan when the variable-rate is somewhat lower than the fixed-rate?
3. William Zeckendorf, a legendary real estate developer and promoter, is said to have commented during a real estate negotiation, "You can name the price if I can name the terms." What was the logic (if any) of Zeckendorf's position?

PROBLEMS

1. Replicate Figure 7.1 if the NOI dropped to $150,000, thereby producing a negative or unfavorable spread.
2. If operating expenses rose further to decrease the NOI to $120,000, calculate the current yield for Figure 7.1.
3. A property is expected to generate $300,000 of NOI over the next 12 months. Discussion with lenders leads to the conclusion that the minimum acceptable debt-coverage ratio will be 1.20 and that loan terms will be 8% per annum, with 20-year amortization (monthly payments).
   a. What is the maximum supportable annual debt service?
   b. What size loan does this imply?
4. Discussion with lenders indicates that a loan can be obtained for 75% of a property's market value. Loan terms will probably be 8% interest, 20-year amortization (monthly payments), with the rate renegotiable after 7 years. The property is estimated to be worth $200,000.
   a. How much can be borrowed?
   b. What will be the annual debt service?
   c. What is the expected annual loan constant?

5. An investor wishes to purchase a retail building that generates $42,000 in NOI. The purchase price for the building is $500,000, and the investor can obtain a 75% loan at 8.5% amortized over 25 years in monthly payments.
   a. What is the debt service?
   b. What is the debt-coverage ratio?
6. A piece of land can be purchased today for $200,000. If the investor can lease the land as a hunting preserve for annual rent that will pay all real estate taxes and insurance, should the investor take out a $160,000 loan at 12% to purchase the land? The investor predicts that she can sell the land in 10 years for triple the purchase price, at which time she will have to pay off the principal and interest ($496,936) on the loan. Is this a favorable spread?
7. A property that can be purchased for $1.7 million has an expected first-year NOI of $190,000. An investor is considering two loan alternatives:

   Loan A:
   A 70% loan-to-value ratio, with interest at 7.5% per annum. The loan will require level monthly payments to amortize the principal over 20 years.

   Loan B:
   An 80% loan-to-value ratio, with interest at 8% per annum. This loan will require level monthly payments to amortize the principal over 25 years.

   Required: For each loan, determine:
   a. The expected before-tax cash flow (NOI minus annual debt service) as a percentage of the equity investment.
   b. The actual before-tax cash flow as a percentage of the equity investment, if the actual NOI falls 10% below expectations.
   c. The percentage by which actual NOI can fall below expectations before it is just sufficient to provide for annual debt service.

UNIT 8

Credit Instruments and Borrowing Arrangements

UNIT PREVIEW

REAL ESTATE TODAY

The majority of real estate loans are coupled with promissory notes and secured by mortgages that pledge the realty as collateral. Standard interest and repayment provisions are many times modified in order to give lenders more attractive yields, shift risk from lenders to borrowers, or make loans more attainable. These modifications are often dependent on the lending environment. With the development of many alternative security instruments, the best alternative depends on the character of pledged property and on borrowers' and lenders' objectives.

THE INSTRUMENTS FOR CREDIT

State statutes and precedent have established strict procedures and extensive documentation requirements for real estate loans. These procedures and documents, evolved from ceaseless contention between borrowers and lenders, each vying for advantage, are designed to safeguard security interests and to assert claims against pledged property in the event an underlying debt obligation is not honored. Some reflect legislation aimed at protecting borrowers against greedy lenders; others comply with laws that give lenders greater recourse against deadbeat borrowers.

Promissory Notes

A promissory note is a written promise by the *obligor* to pay a specified sum of money to another person, called the *payee* or *obligee*, under terms and conditions agreed on by the parties. Notes used in real estate finance are generally referred to as *mortgage notes*. These notes differ from other promissory notes only in their reference to the real estate that serves as security for the promise to pay.

Because it documents a private agreement between contracting parties, a promissory note may contain any legal provision on which the parties agree. As a practical matter, most include basically the same provisions. The note must show the following:

- The amount of the debt
- The promise to pay
- The interest rate charged
- Payment terms (amount and timing of payments)
- A reference to the real estate pledged as collateral

Other provisions that are frequently incorporated, although they are not essential to create a legally binding obligation and security interest, include the following:

- An *acceleration clause*, which permits the lender to demand immediate repayment of the entire loan balance if the borrower defaults on any provision
- Default provisions, which usually include a waiver of certain legal rights that might exist in the absence of specific wording to the contrary
- Terms under which prepayment may be made, including prepayment penalties if applicable
- A promissory note's terms are commonly repeated in the accompanying security instrument, a mortgage or deed of trust. The note and security instrument together constitute the contract between borrower and lender, and in fact are often combined. Should provisions of the two documents (when they are not combined) conflict, those of the note prevail.

Mortgages

Notes and mortgages work together: the note acknowledges the debt and is a promise to pay; the mortgage pledges specific assets as security for the promise. Mortgages also specify the lender's rights in a borrower's estate in the event of default. If there is no default, a mortgage creates no interest in the pledged property.

Because laws vary, mortgage provisions differ from state to state. Mortgages are contracts and are subject to the same limitations as other contracts: they must involve competent parties, and there must be an offer and acceptance, consideration, and legality of purpose. Because they are subject to the *statute of frauds*, mortgages must be in writing and signed by all parties to be enforceable.

Fundamental mortgage provisions are determined by statute in the state where the mortgaged property is located, regardless of where the loan is originated. Because they are contracts between borrowers and lenders, mortgages may be adapted to suit any legal purpose. Beyond the basics, their provisions are governed by the intent of the parties.

A number of widespread mortgage innovations have evolved to suit special types of real property pledges. Of particular interest to real estate investors are purchase-money mortgages, blanket mortgages, and open-ended mortgages.

Purchase-money mortgages

A mortgage given by a buyer to a seller to secure a note in partial or full payment of the purchase price is called a *purchase-money mortgage* (also known as a *take-back mortgage or seller financing*). The major distinction between a purchase-money mortgage and a mortgage securing a later third-party loan lies in the order of priority of the underlying lien. If a purchase-money mortgage is executed and recorded simultaneously with the deed, it takes precedence over all the mortgagor's subsequent debts.

To protect the priority of a purchase-money mortgage, it must be recorded at the same time as the deed conveying the associated property.

Seller/Owner Financing

The practice of seller financing increased significantly after the housing and economic crisis of 2007, largely as the result of many lender's reluctance to lend during the housing crisis and that many properties didn't have the necessary equity in terms of loan-to-value (LTV) requirements. As a result, many residential homeowners who needed to sell their property resorted to using seller financing.

Seller financing may also be beneficial in that it may lower or eliminate some of the front-end fees, such as legal and appraisal fees. Furthermore, the credit approval process is likely to be less costly. Seller financing may also offer tax benefits to the sellers by allowing them to spread their tax liability over an extended period.[1]

---

1 Section 453 of the Internal Revenue Code permits sellers who take back a promissory note in part payment to defer recognition of the taxable gain on the sale. Instead of paying taxes in the year of the transaction, they recognize the gain on a ratable basis as they collect the principal portion of the note.

Blanket mortgages

Borrowers may at times pledge two or more parcels of property as security for a single loan. The mortgage thereby created is known as a *blanket mortgage* and may contain special clauses to meet specific borrower needs. A blanket mortgage might be used to finance a building that is to be converted to condominiums, for example. As each unit is sold, it must be released from the mortgage so that the buyer can pledge the property as security for a loan to finance the transaction. This requires a provision for partial release in the blanket mortgage. A *partial release clause* typically provides for segments of a mortgaged property to be released after specified lump-sum payments on the mortgage note. Blanket mortgages are commonly used by developers.

Open-ended mortgages

A mortgage can be written so that it will secure future as well as current loans. Even when the exact amount of the subsequent advances cannot be precisely forecast, a properly drawn open-ended mortgage enables the lender to make subsequent payout and have the lien securing these additional funds be senior to other liens that may have been created during the interval between payouts. Such mortgages are called *open-ended* or, more simply, *open* mortgages. They are often used to finance purchases and subsequent renovation or additional construction.

Deeds of Trust

Whereas a mortgage is a straightforward contract between two parties (borrower and lender), a *deed of trust* or *trust deed* also involves a third party designated to act as a trustee in the transaction. The borrower conveys the property to the trustee, who holds title for the lender's benefit. In several states, this procedure has largely supplanted mortgage arrangements.[2] In others, both mortgages and trust deeds are used.[3]

A trustee takes title via a deed accompanied by a *trust agreement* (sometimes incorporated into the deed itself), which sets forth terms of the security arrangement and instructs the trustee in the event of default. Trust agreements usually instruct the trustee to conduct a public sale of the property in the event of default (in some states, foreclosure on a deed of trust requires essentially the same proceeding as with a mortgage). Proceeds of the sale are distributed in accordance with the trust agreement, the terms of which are generally prescribed by statute. Funds generally are used first to cover the trustee's expenses, then to satisfy the balance of indebtedness plus accrued interest, with any remaining money going to the defaulting debtor.

Deeds of trust embody some advantages for lenders, even in states that require foreclosure to proceed in the same fashion as with a defaulted mortgage. Selling a note secured by a deed of trust, for example, involves less legal expense and bother than one secured by a conventional mortgage. Moreover, a note secured by a deed of trust can be held without ownership becoming a matter of public record, because the owner

---

2   California, Colorado, Connecticut, Mississippi, Missouri, Oregon, Tennessee, Texas, Virginia, West Virginia.

3   Alaska, Delaware, Idaho, Kansas, Kentucky, Nevada, South Carolina.

of record is the trustee rather than the lender. This is impossible with a mortgage note because the assignment of a mortgage needs to be recorded to protect the assignee (the person who receives the mortgage).

MORTGAGE RESTRUCTURING

Real estate lending practices had evolved only modestly from their roots in the post-Depression restructuring of the 1930s until the 1970s. The pace of change accelerated gradually but inevitably during the 1970s until, late in that decade, it reached a level that can safely be called revolutionary. Wildly fluctuating interest rates, lowered yields to equity capital, intensified competition among lenders, partial deregulation of financial markets, and frequent changes in federal income tax law dislocated the mortgage lending industry and caused restructuring on a scale unprecedented since the economic turmoil of the 1930s. The mortgage lending industry once again went through significant changes after the economic and housing crisis in 2007. Specifically, the enactment of the Dodd-Frank Act took aim at the mortgage industry by requiring increased lender accountability, greater consumer protections and legal assistance, as well as increased appraisal scrutiny.

Amortization Alternatives

From the late 1930s to the 1970s, real estate mortgage loans (other than those for construction and development) made by institutional lenders called for equal monthly payments of combined principal and interest sufficient to retire the loan over 25 to 30 years or longer. Such loans are said to be *fully amortizing*, and are still the norm in residential financing. In mortgage lending on investment properties, however, the fully amortizing long-term loan has been substantially replaced.

Partially amortizing mortgages

One of the most common arrangements today is the partially amortizing mortgage that requires equal periodic payments to retire the principal over 20 or 30 years. But, instead of running full term, though, the balance becomes due and payable in a much shorter time—perhaps five to ten years. The final payment, which includes the remaining principal amount, is called a *balloon payment* and is due at a predetermined date, known as a *stop*. This type of arrangement is also common with seller/owner financing, in which the seller agrees to finance the property for the buyer. Seller financing was once viewed very skeptically by sellers but gained popularity following the housing crisis in the mid to late 2000s as a result of the decreased liquidity of the housing markets. One type of such arrangement may be to amortize the selling price over 30 years, making the payments more affordable for the buyer, with a balloon payment due at the end of five years. The sellers can then analyze the situation to see whether or not they want to give the debtor another partially amortizing loan.

UNIT 8 Credit Instruments and Borrowing Arrangements

Interest-only loans

The *interest-only (IO) loan* requires periodic payments of accrued interest but no principal payments until the note matures. The entire principal amount then becomes due and payable in a lump sum. IO loans are also called *straight, term,* or *bullet loans*. A special variant of the IO loan, called a *bullet loan* or *gap financing*, is often used when a construction loan expires and long-term financing has not yet been procured. Typically, an IO loan is negotiated to run from two to ten years, with interest but no principal payments during the term, and no provision for early payment or loan renewal.

Example 8.1

A small office building can be purchased for $250,000. The investor can finance 75% on a 20-year loan. The lender has offered the investor the choice of a fully amortizing loan at 8.25%, a partially amortizing loan at 8.0% with a 6-year stop, or an IO loan at 8.5%.

Example 8.1 shows the divergent payments and balances for loans with different amortization alternatives. The fully amortizing loan pays off the entire balance at the end, while the partially amortizing loan has a large balloon payment at the stop and the IO loan has the entire principal due at the end.

CALCULATOR APPLICATIONS

Fully Amortizing	**Partially Amortizing**	**Interest-Only**
PV = 187,500	PV = 187,500	$187,500
n = 240 (20 years × 12)	n = 240	× 0.085
i = 0.6875 (8.25 ÷ 12)	i = 0.6667 (8 ÷ 12)	$15,937.50
		÷ 12
Solve for PMT:	**Solve for PMT:**	PMT = $1,328.13
PMT = $1,597.62	PMT = $1,568.33	
Balance in 20 years = 0	Balance in 6 years	Balance in 20 years = $187,500
	n = 168 (240 − 72)	
	i = 0.6667	
	PMT = 1,568.33	
	Solve for PV:	
	PV = $158,206.52	

Interest Rate Alternatives

Persistent price inflation and rising interest rates combined during the 1970s to ravage mortgage lenders' profitability and threaten their long-term survival. When interest rates escalated, lenders holding a portfolio of long-term, fixed-rate loans found the spread—the difference between interest rates earned on mortgage loans and rates paid to depositors—shrinking alarmingly. They responded with a wave of innovative financing arrangements designed to transfer interest-rate risk to borrowers.

Adjustable-rate mortgages

Mortgages with interest rates that vary with some market index, such as the average yield on Treasury securities, the average cost of funds to insured lenders, or average mortgage rates, are called *adjustable-rate mortgages* (ARMs). In some places, ARMs are called by other names, including *variable-rate mortgages* (VRMs), which actually include all types of mortgages with varying rates or payments to counteract the effect of changing market interest rates and inflation. Whatever the local name, the purpose is to shift from lender to borrower a portion of the risk of unanticipated changes in interest rates. The payments on ARMs are calculated just as they are for partially amortizing mortgages, except the stop is when the adjustment is made in the interest rate on the ARM. The balance is calculated and the new payment is recalculated using the new interest rate for the remaining period of the loan. Borrowers are sometimes attracted to an ARM as it enables them to borrow at lower rates and, therefore, to typically qualify for a larger loan. However, this can be a risky proposition in a volatile interest-rate environment because these adjustable rates are tied to some market index, such as the yield on Treasury securities or the LIBOR (London Interbank Offer Rate) rate, and the borrowers rate will fluctuate with changes in that index. This may cause significant increases in the mortgage payment, as was the case in 2007 with the housing crisis. In fact, ARMs are attributed with being a significant contributor to the subprime and housing crisis because borrowers were faced with increasing mortgage payments coupled with declining housing values.

Renegotiable-rate mortgages

Renegotiable-rate mortgages (RRMs) are fixed-rate, level-payment instruments with payments designed to amortize the loan over 20 to 30 years. After a relatively short period, however (typically, three to five years), the principal balance is due and payable. The balance is then refinanced by the lender over the remaining years at currently prevailing interest rates, with the remaining principal balance falling due once again in three to five years. In this manner, the interest rate is adjusted to the market periodically over the entire amortization term. This type of mortgage is sometimes called a *rollover loan*, and is used extensively in Canada. In some circles, it is referred to as a *Canadian rollover* loan. The key difference between the rollover and a partially amortizing loan is that, with a rollover, the lender guarantees refinancing when the rollover loan becomes due and payable.

Equity participation mortgages

Lenders, having observed developers and investors reaping the benefits of sustained inflation while financial institutions bore the brunt of risk associated with new projects, began experimenting with ways to share the wealth from successful projects while continuing to insulate themselves from the consequences of poor performance. Their experiments have spawned a covey of contract clauses that permit lenders to receive a portion of the economic benefit that previously accrued solely to borrowers; this is in addition to the lender's interest charges. The provisions are collectively referred to as *equity kickers.*

One common form of equity participation involves a share in gross property revenue above some specified base figure, plus a share in capital appreciation on ultimate sale of a project (or, if the project isn't sold, when the mortgage is retired). The instrument used to accomplish this is often called a *shared equity participation* (SEP) mortgage. The other common arrangement is for the lender to share only in the increase in market value during the loan term. This is accomplished with a *shared appreciation mortgage* (SAM). These arrangements do not involve actual ownership interests but are merely contingent interests. Investors are willing to give up part of that equity or appreciation in order to obtain a lower interest rate from the lender.

ALTERNATIVE FINANCING STRATEGIES

Third-party loans secured by mortgages or deeds of trust are by far the most common vehicles for generating financial leverage. However, they are not the only strategies available. Many investors further amplify financial leverage with installment sales contracts, through sale-and-leaseback arrangements, or by recourse to junior financing.

Installment Sales Contracts

Whenever sellers fund a portion of the transaction price, an *installment sales contract* may be used instead of a note and mortgage. Sometimes called *land contracts*, *contracts for deed*, or *articles of agreement*, installment sales contracts spell out terms and conditions under which sellers (*vendors*) are obligated to render deeds of conveyance to buyers (*vendees*) at some future date. During the interim, vendors retain title in their own names and continue as owners of record. The contracts remain *executory* (incomplete) until all preconditions have been met and the deeds are delivered.

Because the seller retains legal title under an installment sales contract, a buyer has only those rights granted by contract terms or by specific provisions of state statutes. Typical arrangements give buyers the right of possession during the term of their contracts and require them to pay all property taxes and assessments, to acquire and maintain hazard insurance, and to maintain the property in good repair. Sellers often are not required to have good title during the term of the contract, but they must acquire title in order to convey as the contract prescribes.

Installment sales contracts frequently stipulate that default extinguishes all of a vendee's rights in the property. Where such provisions are enforceable, defaulting vendees not only lose their rights to possession and collection of rents but also forfeit any equity accumulated due to debt retirement or increases in property value.

Buyers sometimes strengthen their positions in installment sales transactions by insisting that the seller provide title insurance and by recording the transaction. Title insurance ensures that the vendor has good title, or reveals exceptions as listed on the insurance document; recordation gives constructive notice to the world of the vendee's claim against the property.

Sales and Leasebacks

Although no credit is involved, sale-and-leaseback arrangements serve as an alternative means of financing and have become a popular strategy for generating development capital. By selling a site and leasing it back with a provision that the new landowner's interest will be subordinated to a mortgage taken out by the lessee (the tenant who was the seller), a developer can radically reduce the need for equity capital.

Developers and builders also use sale-and-leaseback arrangements to generate funds to retire construction loans. This might involve only the land under the project, or it might involve selling and leasing back the entire project on a long-term *net lease* (the lessee pays all operating expenses and remits a net amount to the owner). This gives investors an assured periodic cash flow with freedom from management responsibility and an income tax deduction for depreciation expense.

Junior Mortgages

Mortgage loans are characterized as senior or junior, according to the order of priority for repayment in the event of default. Should a foreclosure sale occur, the proceeds go first to satisfy claims secured by a first mortgage, then to those secured by a second mortgage, then to a third mortgage, and so on, until all secured loans are honored or until funds are exhausted. Generally, the order of priority is determined by the time documents are submitted to the county recorder or registrar of deeds. The mortgage loans that represent claims subordinate to the first mortgage are called *junior liens* or *junior mortgages*.

Junior mortgage loans are often extended by sellers in lieu of all or a part of the gap between the transaction price and a first mortgage loan available from an institutional lender. In addition to their primary goal of expediting the transaction, sellers may get a higher price for their property when they provide financing. Moreover, the interest rate on the junior mortgage might be higher than the rate of return on alternative investment opportunities. Sellers might also reap income tax advantages by reporting such sales using the installment sales method, as described in Unit 11.

Other sources of junior mortgage loans include REITs (see Unit 23), finance companies, and private individuals who make such loans as a regular line of business. Some financial institutions make a limited number of long-term second mortgage loans, though their ability to do so is constrained by regulatory provisions.

GOVERNMENT-SPONSORED CREDIT

Over the years, the federal government has experimented extensively with special incentives to encourage investment in rental housing for low-to-moderate income tenants. Many of the experiments are defunct, but some tax-exempt financing remains for low-income rental housing.

Department of Housing and Urban Development

The Department of Housing and Urban Development (HUD) has sponsored long-term, low-interest loans as an incentive for investing in low-income housing. HUD programs change with sufficient regularity to provide full-time employment for a host of researchers trying to track the red tape.

Private Activity Bonds

For a long time, state and local governments were empowered to issue bonds whose interest is exempt from federal (and, in some locales, state) income taxes. Local governments used the bonds, whose tax-exempt status permitted them to carry a much lower interest rate than conventional private-source bonds, to finance private business development.

Beginning in 1986, the Internal Revenue Code (in Section 142) restricted the use of tax-exempt bonds issued to finance private commercial activities. Code Section 142 exempts from these restrictions only qualifying bonds to finance specifically enumerated projects:

- Airports, docks and wharves, mass communication facilities, and high-speed intercity rail facilities owned by government units, though they may be leased to private companies under strictly limited conditions
- Water, sewage, and solid or hazardous waste disposal facilities, as well as local or district utilities that will provide services available to the general public
- Qualified residential projects—bonds to finance residential rental projects will qualify for tax exemption only if, during a "qualified project period," which may last for 15 years or longer, a prescribed portion of the tenants are sufficiently impoverished. At least 40% of the units must be occupied by tenants whose income does not exceed 60% of the area median, or at least 20% must be occupied by tenants whose income does not exceed 50% of the area median.

Redevelopment Bonds

Tax-exempt redevelopment bonds may be issued to finance land acquisition and preparation (razing existing structures and so forth), for relocating tenants out of the redevelopment area, and for rehabilitating buildings in areas designated as "blighted" by local government. The debt service on redevelopment bonds must be underwritten to a significant degree by local government, either by pledging general tax revenue or the incremental property tax revenue that will result from enhanced property values in the redeveloped area.[4]

Construction Bonds

Construction lending is perhaps the riskiest of real estate loans. Lenders provide funds for both labor and materials on security of nonexistent or incomplete structures. To reduce risk, lenders closely monitor construction activity and disburse money in stages as construction progresses. Lenders sometimes pass money directly to suppliers and subcontractors or require proof that claims have been satisfied before disbursing the next installment or draw.

Reflecting their higher risk and greater administrative burden, construction loans command a higher interest rate than permanent financing. Lenders also profit from significant fees and discounts levied on borrowers. Effective yields are enhanced by quick loan turnover since construction terms are relatively short. Construction loans are described in more detail with a case example in Unit 9 of *Real Estate Finance, Third Edition*, by Kolbe, Greer, and Waller.

SUMMARY

Promissory notes represent a promise to pay a debt and specify the terms and conditions. The promise may be secured or unsecured. If real estate is pledged as security for the promise, this is usually accomplished by a mortgage or a deed of trust. These appear to be actual transfers of ownership, but contain a defeasance clause that renders the transfer inoperative if the promissory note is honored by the borrower.

Common variations of security instruments include purchase-money mortgages, blanket mortgages, open-ended mortgages, and equity participation mortgages. Purchase-money mortgages secure notes given in part payment for property, while blanket mortgages pledge two or more parcels of property as security for a single loan. Open-ended mortgages are written so that additional funds can be advanced under the security of the same mortgage. Equity participation loans permit lenders to share in earnings or appreciation without relinquishing their positions as creditors.

Installment sales contracts are an alternative financing arrangement wherein the seller agrees to deliver a deed only after the buyer satisfies contractual arrangements—usually payment of the purchase price plus interest. Sale-and-leaseback arrangements also substitute conventional mortgage financing. In this arrangement, the financier buys the property and leases it back to the user.

State and local governments issued a spate of tax-exempt bonds as a real estate financing device. Income tax law revisions in the 1980s drastically curtailed the uses to which such bond financing can be put.

---

4 Internal Revenue Code Section 144(c).

RECOMMENDED READING

Alvayay, Jamie, R., Ronald C. Rutherford, and William S. Smith. "Tax Rules and the Sales and Leaseback of Corporate Real Estate." *Real Estate Economics* 23:2, 1995, 207-238.

Brougham, Sharen K. "Reminder: The Wrap Is Back." *Commercial Investment Real Estate Journal* 9, no. 1 (Winter 1990): 10–14.

Downs, Anthony. *The Revolution in Real Estate Finance*. Washington, D.C.: The Brookings Institution, 1985.

Fisher, Lynn, M. "The Wealth Effects of Sales and Leasebacks: New Evidence." *Real Estate Economics*, 32:4, 2004, 619-643.

Friedman, L.M. *A History of American Law.* 3rd ed. New York: Touchstone, 2005.

Greenberg, Alan. "Back to Basics: Negotiating Financing In the 1990s." *Real Estate Finance Journal* 7, no. 3 (Winter 1992): 33–37.

Hudsick, Clifford A. "A Tax-Exempt, Credit-Enhanced Bond Financing." *Real Estate Review* 25, no. 3 (Fall 1995): 32–37.

Kolbe, Phillip T., Gaylon E. Greer, and Bennie D. Waller, Jr. *Real Estate Finance.* 3rd ed. Chicago: Dearborn Real Estate Education, 2012.

Martindale-Hubbell Law Digest: United States Law Digests, 1992. Part I, Digest of the Laws of the States, The District of Columbia, Puerto Rico and The Virgin Islands. Martindale-Hubbell, a Division of Reed-Elsevier, Inc.

Pollack, Bruce. "Real Estate Loan Underwriting Revisited." *Real Estate Finance Journal* 7, no. 2 (Winter 1992): 63–68.

Stein, Joshua. "Cures for the (Sometimes) Needless Complexity of Real Estate Documents." *Real Estate Review* 25, no. 3 (Fall 1995): 63–67.

INTERNET REFERENCES

For information on mortgages and regulations:
www.federalreserve.gov

REVIEW QUESTIONS

1. How do mortgage notes differ from other promissory notes?
2. List five provisions that must be included in mortgage notes.
3. What functions do mortgages serve?
4. How do purchase-money mortgages differ from other mortgages?
5. What is an open-ended mortgage?
6. Describe the role of the trustee in a trust deed arrangement.
7. For what real estate uses can tax-exempt bond financing be used under current income tax regulations?
8. What is the attraction of adjustable-rate loans to borrowers? To lenders?

DISCUSSION QUESTIONS

1. Why is there so much variety in loan documentation among the various states? Would a uniform national system be useful? Explain why or why not.

2. It has been argued that the wording on loan documents favors lenders over borrowers, while courts' interpretations favor borrowers over lenders. Discuss.

3. What is to keep an unscrupulous seller under an installment contract from mortgaging the property after the installment contract has been negotiated, so that the buyer discovers a first mortgage lien on the property when the deed is eventually delivered?

4. Why might a business elect to dispose of its buildings in a sale-and-leaseback arrangement, even though it will continue to need the premises for an indefinite period? Why not keep ownership of the property as an additional investment, and thereby avoid having to pay rent?

5. There were very few successful mortgage loan innovations in this country during the 1950s and 1960s. Then, the following two decades witnessed a spate of innovations. What might have caused this abrupt shift in the rate of innovation?

PROBLEMS

1. An investor wants to purchase an office building for $200,000. If he can obtain a fully amortizing, 75% LTV loan for 20 years at 8.25%, what will be his monthly payment and balance at the end of the loan?

2. If the investor obtained a 25-year partially amortizing loan at 8% with a 5-year stop, what is his monthly payment? What would be the balance due at the end of the stop?

3. If the investor obtained an IO loan at 7.75 for 10 years, what would the monthly payment be? What would his balance be at the end of the loan?

UNIT 9

The Cost of Borrowed Money

UNIT PREVIEW

Unit 8 explored borrowing options but did not explain how cost is computed. Well-defined cost comparisons are the focus of this unit. We first examine the mechanics of computing payments and the annual debt service, then consider a way to compare the incremental costs and benefits of alternative debt structures.

REAL ESTATE TODAY

UNIT 9 The Cost of Borrowed Money

INTEREST COSTS AND RATES

The cost of using borrowed money is, of course, interest expense. Like so many costs and benefits, however, interest expense is not always what it seems. An early step in mastering mortgage finance issues is to understand the difference between nominal or contract interest, effective interest, and real interest.

Nominal and Effective Rates

Of all the aspects of interest, the easiest to understand is the *nominal rate*, or *contract rate*. This is simply the rate of interest stipulated in the promissory note. It is usually stated as an annual rate, even though payments are most often made monthly.

A little less simple is the *effective interest rate*. This is the rate actually paid for the use of borrowed funds, and it often differs strikingly from the contract rate. Effective rates are a function of the amount borrowed and the amount and timing of the required repayment.

It is common that there are differences between nominal and effective rates on term loans when the borrower pays a *loan origination fee* or *discount points*. The borrower has the use of only a fraction of the funds stipulated in the promissory note (the face amount of the note, minus the origination fee or discount points). Interest and principal payments, however, are based on the full face amount of the note. Interest expense computed on the funds that the borrower actually has available as a consequence of the loan—effective interest—is then higher than the nominal or contract rate.

To illustrate this, consider Example 9.1. Monthly payments on the $100,000 mortgage note are $599.55. This can be determined using a financial calculator or by referring to financial tables. However, the borrower has the use of only $98,000. This amount, called the *loan proceeds*, is determined by subtracting the loan origination fee from the face amount of the loan.

Example 9.1

A borrower signs a $100,000 mortgage note payable in equal monthly installments over 30 years, with interest at 6% per annum on the unpaid balance. The lender charges a loan origination fee equal to 2% of the face amount of the loan (2 points).

$$\begin{aligned}\text{loan proceeds} &= (\text{face amount of note}) - (\text{origination fee}) \\ &= \$100,000 - (0.02 \times \$100,000) \\ &= \$100,000 - \$2,000 \\ &= \$98,000\end{aligned}$$

Because the borrower must pay $599.55 per month but only has the use of $98,000, the effective interest rate is that which makes the monthly payments to amortize a $98,000 loan equal $599.55 for 30 years. To determine the effective rate, view the problem as a monthly annuity of $599.55 and solve for the internal rate of return

(IRR): the discount rate that makes the present value of the annuity stream equal to the $98,000 loan proceeds. This rate is 6.19%, determined as follows:

$$v_0 = \text{payment} \sum \left(\frac{1}{1 + \frac{e}{12}} \right)^{12t}$$

$$= \$599.55 \sum \left(\frac{1}{1 + \frac{e}{12}} \right)^{12t}$$

$$= \$98,000$$

where
V_0 = amount of the loan proceeds
t = ranges over the amortization period (in years)
e = effective annual interest rate

Solving for e in the equation is somewhat involved; it requires a logarithmic transformation. Alternatively, the solution can be found by successive approximations; using various possible values for e that are slightly in excess of the contract interest rate until the equation yields a present value of $98,000. The easiest approach, of course, is to use a financial calculator.

CALCULATOR APPLICATIONS

n = 360 (30 × 12)
PV = –98,000
PMT = 599.55

Solve for i:
i = 0.515789
Effective rate per annum = i × 12
= 6.19%

The problem can also be solved using loan amortization factors. An excerpt is presented here as Figure 9.1. Recall that when payments are unknown, they are determined from the table using the following equation:

payment = note amount × amortization factor

where the amortization factor is for the contract rate of interest. With known payments, the effective interest rate can be determined by restructuring the equation as follows:

payments = loan proceeds × amortization factor

where the amortization factor is for the effective interest rate rather than the contract rate. Substituting numbers applicable to Example 9.1 into the previous equation gives the following:

$$\$599.55 = \$98,000 \times \text{amortization factor}$$

Therefore:

$$\text{amortization factor} = \frac{\$599.55}{\$98,000} = 0.006117857$$

Reference to the 25-year row of Figure 9.1 reveals that this amortization factor lies between 6% and 7%. Interpolation in the manner described in Appendix A reveals that the effective rate is approximately 6.19%.

The computation presupposes that the note remains in effect until fully amortized. Thus, a borrower who anticipates no early payment will reasonably expect the effective interest rate, on a pretax basis, to be approximately 6.19%. This rate is the yield to the lender, the annual percentage rate (APR), which the lender must disclose. The prospective borrower will compare this loan with alternative proposals, based on the 6.19% rate.

Now suppose our investor expects to refinance in five years. Such anticipation might be reasonable in a market where values are growing rapidly, so that the investor anticipates borrowing a substantially greater sum in the future or an economic environment where interest rates are expected to decline. The prospective borrower will want to determine the effective interest rate based on amortizing the front-end fee over the abbreviated five-year borrowing period.

The proceeds from borrowing, as well as the annual debt service, will be unaffected by the altered time perspective. But after five years, there will be a lump-sum payoff equal to the outstanding balance of the loan.

As explained in Appendix A, the remaining balance is the value at that point of the remaining payments, when discounted at the contract rate. The contract rate in Example 9.1 is 6% per annum (6/12, or 0.50% per month) and, after 5 years, 25 years (12 × 25, or 300 months) of payments at $599.55 per month remain.

Using a financial calculator, one can determine that the present value of $599.55 per period for 300 periods (25 years times 12 months), discounting at 0.50% (6% per annum divided by 12), is $93,054.28.

The effective interest rate with a five-year holding period is the discount rate that makes the present value of $599.55 per month for 60 months plus the present value of $93,054.28 (the remaining loan balance) have a present value equal to the $98,000 loan proceeds (note the cumulative rounding error of $.08).

FIGURE 9.1: Monthly Payment to Amortize a One-Dollar Debt

Number of Years	Annual Interest Rate						
	6.0%	7.0%	8.0%	9.0%	10.0%	12.0%	14.0%
1	0.086066	0.086527	0.086988	0.087451	0.087916	0.088849	0.089787
2	0.044321	0.044773	0.045227	0.045685	0.046145	0.047073	0.048013
3	0.030422	0.030877	0.031336	0.031800	0.032267	0.033214	0.034178
4	0.023485	0.023946	0.024413	0.024885	0.025363	0.026334	0.027326
5	0.019333	0.019801	0.020276	0.020758	0.021247	0.022244	0.023268
6	0.016573	0.017049	0.017533	0.018026	0.018526	0.019550	0.020606
7	0.014609	0.015093	0.015586	0.016089	0.016601	0.017653	0.018740
8	0.023141	0.013634	0.014137	0.014650	0.015174	0.016253	0.017372
9	0.012006	0.012506	0.013019	0.013543	0.014079	0.015184	0.016334
10	0.011102	0.011611	0.012133	0.012668	0.013215	0.014347	0.015527
11	0.010367	0.010884	0.011415	0.011961	0.012520	0.013678	0.014887
12	0.009759	0.010284	0.010825	0.011380	0.011951	0.013134	0.014371
13	0.009247	0.009781	0.010331	0.010897	0.011478	0.012687	0.013951
14	0.008812	0.009354	0.009913	0.010489	0.011082	0.012314	0.013605
15	0.008439	0.008988	0.009557	0.010143	0.010746	0.012002	0.013317
16	0.008114	0.008672	0.009249	0.009845	0.010459	0.011737	0.013077
17	0.007831	0.008397	0.008983	0.009588	0.010212	0.011512	0.012875
18	0.007582	0.008155	0.008750	0.009364	0.009998	0.011320	0.012704
19	0.007361	0.007942	0.008545	0.009169	0.009813	0.011154	0.012559
20	0.007164	0.007753	0.008364	0.008997	0.009650	0.011011	0.012435
25	0.006443	0.007068	0.007718	0.008392	0.009087	0.010532	0.012038
30	0.005996	0.006653	0.007338	0.008046	0.008776	0.010286	0.011849

Months	Monthly Payments	Present Value When Discounting at the Effective Rate*
1–60	$599.55	$31,012.06
60 FV	$93,054.28	68,987.86
		$99,999.92

*Effective rate is 6.4842% per annum.

The effective rate can be quickly solved using a financial calculator.

> **CALCULATOR APPLICATIONS**
>
> PMT = 599.55
> FV = $93,054.28
> n   = 60
> PV = –98,000
>
> **Solve for *i*:**
> *i* = 0.540349066
> Effective rate per annum = *i* × 12
> = 6.484189%

Nominal and Real Rates

The real rate of interest is the effective rate, adjusted for inflation. The nominal rate is a real rate plus a premium for expected inflation. Inflation has a major impact on interest rates because the money that mortgage lenders receive back from borrowers (interest and principal payments) will buy less than the money they lend. If, for example, a $1,000 loan is to be repaid in one year with cumulative interest at 6%, the borrower receives the $1,000 loan proceeds and repays $1,060 in 12 months. The nominal rate is 6% (to keep the example simple, the nominal and the effective rates are the same) but the real rate depends on price level changes during the interim.

Suppose during the year the average level of prices increases by 3%. Using the time the loan proceeds were disbursed as the base year, the purchasing power of the principal and accumulated interest paid a year later is $1,060 / 1.03, or $1,029.13. The real interest (i.e., the amount of purchasing power paid for the use of money) has been only $29.13, and the real rate of interest (on a before-tax basis) has been ($29.13 / $1,000) × 100, or 2.913%.

Expressed generically, for any single compounding period, the real rate of interest (I_r) is as follows:

$$I_r = \frac{1+I_n}{1+P} - 1$$

where:

I_r = real rate of interest
I_n = nominal rate of interest
P = percentage change in the general price level

Applying the generalized formula to our example, we have:

$$I_r = \frac{1+0.06}{1+0.04} - 1 = 0.019231, \text{ or } 1.923\%$$

So far we have applied price-level adjustments on a before-tax basis. On an after-tax basis, the reduction in real interest rates as a consequence of inflation is even more dramatic. This is because the interest expense deduction is based on the nominal rather than the real interest. If the borrower in our continuing example (a $1,000, 6% loan for one year, with interest and principal due at year end) is in the 40% combined federal and state income tax brackets, and if the interest expense is fully deductible in the year incurred and paid, the after-tax real rate of interest is approximately 2.26%:

nominal after-tax rate = (before-tax rate) × (1 − tax rate)
= 0.06 × 0.60
= 0.036, or 3.6%

$$\text{real after-tax rate} = \frac{1+I_n}{1+P} - 1 = \frac{1.036}{1.06} - 1 = 0.22642, \text{ or } 2.26\%$$

At first look it seems from these computations that inflation is uniquely kind to borrowers. But lenders understand the impact of inflation and demand an interest rate premium for expected inflation. If the consensus about future price level changes is an accurate reflection of what actually happens, the real interest rate will be unaffected by price level changes because the actual changes will have been reflected in the nominal interest rate. If lender consensus overestimates inflation, the inflation premium embedded in nominal rates will cause the real rate to be higher than it otherwise would have been; if the consensus inflation forecast ends up on the low side, real rates will be lower than otherwise. If actual deflation (a decline in the general level of prices) occurs, the real rate will be higher than the nominal rate. Should that occur, the value of P in our equation will be *negative*, making $(1 + P)$ less than 1.

Before-Tax and After-Tax Borrowing Cost

Because interest payments are usually a tax-deductible expense in the year paid (see Unit 10 for details and for important exceptions), federal and state governments in effect pay part of the cost of borrowing. The only cost relevant to the borrower is the after-tax cost.

If interest expense is fully deductible in the year paid, the after-tax cost of borrowing is $i \times (1 - t)$, where i is the before-tax rate and t is the incremental income tax rate. Applying this formula to Example 9.1 and assuming that the borrower is in the 40% (combined state and federal) income tax bracket, the after-tax rate is $6 \times (1 - 0.40)$, or 3.6% per annum. If the loan is a straight-term loan (i.e., only the interest is paid currently), the annual after-tax debt service is $3,600 per annum:

Face amount of note	$100,000
Times: Contract interest rate	0.06
Annual interest payments	$6,000
Less: Tax savings (0.40 × $6,000)	2,400
After-tax cost of borrowing	$3,600

Paying loan origination fees or discount points complicates the math, but the premise remains unchanged: The after-tax cost is the before-tax cost minus the income tax savings. The complication stems from the way tax law requires prepaid interest to be handled. As explained in Unit 10, the prepaid amount (discount points or loan origination fees) on a loan to finance business or investment property must be deducted ratably over the term of the loan.

COMPARISON OF FINANCING ALTERNATIVES

Anyone who has ever shopped for a loan knows that borrowers face a bewildering array of alternatives. Different lenders quote various combinations of interest rates and front-end fees, and offer alternative rates coupled with different amortization periods. Figure 9.2 summarizes the results of inquiries at seven life insurance firms in the mid-1990s. Required occupancy levels that had to be achieved before the loan proceeds would be disbursed ranged from a low of 60% to a high of 90%. Four of the lenders were willing to commit themselves to a specific interest rate at time of application, two would commit at the time of loan approval, and one only would commit when a commitment letter was issued. Loan terms ranged from 10 to 12 years, with amortization over 20 to 30 years. Today the market is one of structured financing. While almost all lenders lock-in rates at application, the terms of the loan are customized depending on the needs of the client, hence amortization and terms vary greatly. No simple rule of thumb serves as a reliable guide through the loan alternative wilderness, but the concepts we have investigated in this unit provide the needed analytical tools.

FIGURE 9.2: Loan Quotes for a New Apartment Complex, from Seven Insurance Companies, Mid-1990s

Company	A	B	C	D	E	F	G
Required occupancy	60%*	84%†	90%	80%	90%	80%	n/a
Interest rate							
Lock-in:							
At application		X	X‡	X‡	X‡	X	
On acceptance	X						
At commitment							X
Amortization	25 years	30 years	20/25 years	25 years	25/30 years	30 years	25 years
Term	12 years	10 years	10/20 years	10 years	10/25 years	10 years	10/15 years

*Additional security via a letter of credit until occupancy reaches 93%.
†Loan can be funded before 84% occupancy, if letter of credit is provided.
‡Interest rate can be locked in at this point, for a fee.

Comparison of Effective Interest Rates

One particularly confusing issue is the range of interest rates offered, where they are coupled with different front-end fees. To estimate the effective interest rate together with loan alternatives, first estimate the amount and timing of debt-service payments for each. Then find the related effective rates. Next, arrange the effective rates and compare each with the related risk (however risk is measured) to determine which seems most appealing, given the borrower's attitude toward risk.

Example 9.2 presents three alternatives. The first step in analyzing them is to compare the loan proceeds. This, you should recall, is the face amount of the note minus the front-end charges. The net loan proceeds are shown on the third line of Figure 9.3.

Example 9.2

An investor is offered three alternative $1 million loan proposals. All the loans are fully amortizing and require monthly payments.

    a. There is a 2.5% origination fee for loan A. The interest rate is 7.5% per annum. The amortization period is 20 years, and there is no prepayment penalty.

    b. Loan B requires a 0.5% loan origination fee. The contract interest rate is 8% and the amortization period is 25 years. There is no prepayment penalty.

    c. Loan C requires no loan origination fee. The interest rate is 8% and the amortization period is 25 years. There is a prepayment penalty of 2% of the prepaid amount.

FIGURE 9.3: Effective Interest Rate with Three Borrowing Alternatives, When Loans Run Full Term

	Loan Proposal		
	A	B	C
Face amount of note	$1,000,000	$1,000,000	$1,000,000
Less: Front-end charges	25,000	5,000	0
Loan proceeds	$975,000	$995,000	$1,000,000
Monthly payment	$8,055.93	$7,718.16	$7,718.16
Effective pretax rate	7.84	8.06	8.00

In each case, the effective interest rate is that which makes the present value of the monthly payments equal to the loan proceeds. If the loan remains outstanding for its entire term, the best alternative is A. As shown in Figure 9.3, C is marginally less expensive than B, because their contract interest rates are the same and C entails no front-end fee.

If the expected period of the loan is only five years, however, the relative costs shift. The effective interest rate is the discount rate that makes the present value of the monthly payments plus the present value of the final balloon payment (discounting on a monthly basis) exactly equal to the loan proceeds. The first step toward a solution is to determine the amount of that final payment. The remaining balances after five years are shown in the first column of Figure 9.4.

CALCULATOR APPLICATIONS

Loan A	Loan B	Loan C
PMT = 8,055.93	PMT = 7,718.16	PMT = 7,718.16
n = 240 (12 months × 20 years)	n = 300	n = 300
FV = 0	FV = 0	FV = 0
PV = −975,000	PV = −995,000	PV = −1,000,000
Solve interest rate:	**Solve interest rate:**	**Solve interest rate:**
i = 0.652982286 × 12	i = 0.671540307 × 12	i = 0.666666391 × 12
= 7.84	= 8.06	= 8.00

Figure 9.4 also shows effective rates when the loans are paid off early. Amortizing loan A's hefty origination fee over just five years drives its effective rate above that for loan B, which has a smaller front-end fee to be amortized. Because of its prepayment penalty, however, loan C is most radically affected. After five years the remaining balance on that loan is still $922,739, and this amount is subject to the 2% prepayment penalty.

FIGURE 9.4: Effective Interest Rates for Three Loan Alternatives, with Prepayment after Five Years

	Loan Proposal		
	A	B	C
Remaining balance after five years	$869,021	$922,739	$922,739
Add: Prepayment penalty	0	0	18,455
Payoff amount	$869,021	$922,739	$941,194
Effective pretax rate	8.15	8.13	8.31

CALCULATOR APPLICATIONS

Loan A
PMT = 8,055.93
n = 180 (12 months × 15 years remaining)
FV = 0
i = 0.625 (7.5 ÷ 12)
Solve for balance/PV:
PV = 869,020.78

PMT = 8,055.93
n = 60 (12 months × 5 years)
FV = 869,020.78

PV = −975,000
Solve for interest rate:
i = 0.67888043 × 12
  = 8.15

Loan B
PMT = 7,718.16
n = 240
FV = 0
i = 0.6667 (8 ÷ 12)
Solve for balance/PV:
PV = 922,739.15

PMT = 7,718.16
n = 60
FV = 922,739.15

PV = −995,000
Solve for interest rate:
i = 0.677179862 × 12
  = 8.13

Loan C
PMT = 7,718.16
n = 240
FV = 0
i = 0.6667 (8 ÷ 12)
Solve for balance/PV:
PV = 922,739.15

PMT = 7,718.16
n = 60
FV = 941,193.93

PV = −1,000,000
Solve for interest rate:
i = 0.692425483 × 12
  = 8.31

Which Nominal Rate Is Applicable

When interest rates are changing, lenders are reluctant to quote a definite contract interest rate. Instead, many prefer to express rates in terms of a benchmark. By way of illustration, typical rates quoted by various categories of lending agents in the second quarter of 2018 were around 105 basis points (i.e., 1.05 percentage points) above the rate on U.S. Treasury notes of corresponding term. Thus, if a mortgage loan was to run for 10 years and 10-year U.S. Treasury notes were earning 2.93%, one might have been able to borrow at a nominal rate of 3.98%.

> **Example 9.3**
>
> A property owner still has 10 years to pay on a $250,000, 5%, 30-year first mortgage note. Monthly payments, including both principal and interest, are $1,342.05 and the remaining principal balance is approximately $126,530.

Wraparound Mortgages

One special category of junior mortgage, called a *wraparound* (WAM) or *all-inclusive mortgage* has become popular in recent years. The face amount of the wraparound note includes the balance due on an existing note in addition to any amount to be disbursed on the new note. The wraparound lender assumes responsibility for meeting debt-service obligations on the old mortgage note that has been "wrapped."

Wraparound loans—sometimes called *wraps* or *WAMs*—are frequently used to stretch out payments on an existing loan, thus reducing a borrower's periodic debt-service obligation, or they might be used to raise additional money. Sometimes a wraparound loan does both.

In order to see how a stretched-out payment wrap might work, consider Example 9.3. The borrower might reduce the monthly payments by negotiating a new, long-term wraparound mortgage loan for exactly the remaining balance of the existing note: $126,530.

If the wraparound note is payable in monthly payments over 25 years with interest at 7.5%, monthly payments will be only $935.05. No funds are actually disbursed as a consequence of the new note. Instead, the wraparound lender makes all further payments on the underlying first mortgage note. The original borrower will thereby have reduced the monthly payment obligation by $407 (the old payment of $1,342.05 minus the new payment of $935.05), at the cost of extending the payment period from the 10 years remaining on the old mortgage to the 25-year term of the new.

Remaining payments on the old loan ($1,342.05 monthly for 10 years) will become an obligation of the wraparound lender, who will incur a monthly net cash outflow of $407:

Monthly payment on "wrapped" loan	$1,342.05
Monthly receipt from wraparound note	395.05
Monthly net outlay for remaining life of "wrapped" note	$407.00

After 10 years, the old note is retired and the lender's monthly payment obligation ceases. Monthly receipts, however, will continue for another 15 years. The lender's cash-flow expectation at the time the wraparound note is negotiated is as follows:

Years	Monthly Cash Flow		
	Inflow	Outflow	Net
1–10	$935.05	$1,342.05	($407)
11–25	$935.05	0	$935.05

Assuming, for simplicity, that the lender receives no loan origination fee and charges no discount points, the average annual yield on funds actually extended will be the discount rate that makes the present value of the forecast cash flow exactly zero. This higher yield for the lender explains why lenders offer the wraparound at a lower rate than a standard mortgage and, especially, lower than a risky second mortgage. The yield rate is determined by solving for r in the following equation and multiplying by 12:

$$0 = \sum_{t=0}^{n} \frac{CF_t}{(1+r)^t}$$

$$\therefore \text{Yield} = 12.85\%$$

where:

CF = the monthly net cash flow
n = the number of months in the repayment period
r = the discount rate that satisfied the equality by making the present value of the negative flows exactly equal to that of the positive flows

The example is illustrated below using the cash-flow function on a financial calculator.

CALCULATOR APPLICATIONS

CF(0) = 0
CF(1) = –407.00
F(1) = 120 (F represents the frequency of payments)
CR(2) = 935.05
F(2) = 180

Compute IRR = × 12 = %

If, in addition to stretching out payments on existing indebtedness, the borrower in Example 9.3 wanted to raise additional funds, this could be accomplished with the same wraparound mortgage note. If an additional $75,000 were needed, then the amount of the wraparound note would include the $126,530 balance of the old mortgage plus $75,000. Monthly payments on a 7.5%, 25-year wraparound mortgage note for this amount would be $1,489, compared with $1,342 payments on the underlying first mortgage. The lender's monthly cash flow would then be as follows:

Years	Monthly Cash Flow		
	Inflow	Outflow	Net
Zero	0	$75,000	($75,000)
1–10	$1,489	$1,342	$147
11–25	$1,489	0	$1,489

The yield rate to the mortgage lender would then be 12 times the rate, r, which satisfies the equality in the following equation:

$$0 = \sum_{t=1}^{n}\left[\frac{CF_t}{(1+r)^t}\right] - \$75,000$$

$$\therefore \text{Yield} = 10.9\% \text{ (rounded)}$$

where the factors n and CF_t have the same meanings as before, and yield is 12 times the monthly rate that satisfies the equality.

The wraparound mortgage may be an attractive alternative for a borrower who is considering a second mortgage loan because the interest rate on the wraparound is usually lower than that for a conventional second mortgage. If the borrower in this example had obtained a new second mortgage for the $75,000, the lender would charge a higher interest rate to compensate for the additional risk. If that rate was at 10%, the combined payment on the first and the second mortgage notes ($1,342 plus $682, for a total of $2,024) would be substantially higher than the $1,489 payment on the wrap.

INCORPORATING LEVERAGE INTO THE OPERATING PROJECTION

In Unit 6, we developed a six-year operating forecast for a 280-unit apartment complex called Maegan's Magic Manor. We are now equipped to incorporate a projection of the consequences of using financial leverage and derive an estimate of the before-tax cash flow to the equity investor.

By checking with several lenders that are the most likely source of a mortgage loan, we conclude that the likely borrowing terms include interest at 5.5%, and level monthly payments to amortize the loan over 20 years. At this rate, we can avoid paying a loan origination fee. The lender will probably require the rate to be renegotiated after seven years, but this is beyond our 6-year projected holding period. We also conclude that the LTV ratio cannot exceed 70% and the debt-coverage ratio cannot be less than 1.2.

The loan requirements regarding the LTV ratio and the debt-coverage ratio (also known as the debt-service ratio) create constraints on the amount we can borrow. The more severe restraint is the LTV ratio.

Debt-Coverage Ratio

Lenders base the permissible debt-coverage ratio on the first-year operating projection. We expect the NOI to be $1,265,700, and it must comprise at least 1.2 times the annual debt service. This implies debt service of no more than $1,054,750.

$$\text{debt-coverage ratio} = 1.20 = \frac{NOI}{\text{debt service}} = \frac{\$1,265,700}{\text{debt service}}$$

Therefore:

$$\text{maximum debt service} = \frac{\$1,265,700}{1.20} = \$1,054,750$$

Because this constraint limits the annual debt service to $1,054,750, the monthly mortgage loan payment cannot exceed $1/12$ of that amount, or $87,895.83. Using a financial calculator and incorporating the expected 5.5% interest rate and 25-year amortization period, we determine this to imply a loan of no more than $12,777,649.62. The permissible loan amount will be rounded by the lender, probably to $12,800,000.

CALCULATOR APPLICATIONS

PMT = 87,895.83
n = 240 (20 years × 12)
i = 0.4583 (5.5 ÷ 12)

Solve for present value:
PV = 12,777,649.62

Loan-to-Value Ratio

In order to estimate the maximum loan that will satisfy the expected 70% loan-to-value (LTV) ratio, we must first estimate the market value of the property. We note that similar apartment buildings in the same market area have recently sold at around a 9% capitalization rate. As discussed in Unit 6, the capitalization rate, or cap rate, is the ratio of a property's NOI to its market value. Using simple algebra, we can find market value:

$$\text{value} = \frac{NOI}{R}$$

Using the reconstructed prior-year NOI from Figure 5.8, this implies a market value of $1,223,700 ÷ 0.09, or $13,596,667. The lender will probably lend no more than 70% of this amount: 0.70 × $13,596,667 = $9,517,667, rounded to $9.5 million.

Anticipated Loan Amount

Prevailing lending policies place constraints on the debt-coverage ratio and the LTV ratio. The more severe constraint will govern the amount that can be borrowed. We have estimated the amounts to be as follows:

Based on permissible debt-coverage ratio: $12.8 million

Based on permissible LTV ratio: $9.5 million

Because the more severe constraint governs, we estimate the most we can borrow on the strength of a first mortgage pledged as security is $9.5 million. Additional funds might be available by pledging additional collateral or, if the borrower assumes personal liability for the loan, based on a personal credit rating.

Before-Tax Cash Flow from Maegan's Magic Manor

Because the investor can expect to borrow $9.5 million at 5.5%, to be amortized by monthly payments over 20 years, a financial calculator can quickly reveal that the monthly payment will be $65,349.29. The annual debt service is simply 12 times this amount, or (rounded to the nearest whole dollar) $784,192.

If the only nonoperating cash flows are debt service and income taxes, the before-tax cash flow for each year will be the NOI minus the annual debt service. Figure 9.5 extends the forecast from Figure 6.2 to derive a six-year before-tax cash-flow projection.

Debt Amortization Schedule for Maegan's Magic Manor

The annual debt service will comprise, in part, interest payments and, in part, principal payments. Initially, most of the entire annual debt service will be consumed by the interest expense. Gradually, as the principal amount is whittled down, more and more of the debt service will be applied to reduce the loan balance. To extend the forecast to after-tax cash flow, we will have to divide the payments into principal and interest, because the interest payments are tax-deductible but the principal payments are not.

A table that divides the payments into interest and principal components is called an *amortization schedule*. Most financial calculators are programmed to develop such a schedule; their use is explained in Appendix B. Electronic spreadsheets will also produce amortization schedules. A more involved method, using the amortization tables, is described in Appendix A. However it is derived, the results (with minor differences due to rounding error if one uses amortization tables) will be as shown in Figure 9.6.

FIGURE 9.5: Projected Before-Tax Cash Flow from Operations: Maegan's Magic Manor Apartments*

	Year 1	Year 2	Year 3	Year 4	Year 5	Year 6
1. Potential gross rent	$2,346,100	$2,463,400	$2,586,600	$2,677,100	$2,770,800	$2,867,800
2. *Less*: Vacancy allowance	176,000	98,500	103,500	160,600	166,200	172,100
3.	$2,170,100	$2,364,900	$2,483,100	$2,516,500	$2,604,600	$2,695,700
4. *Add*: Other income	102,000	111,200	116,700	118,300	122,400	126,700
5. Effective gross income	$2,272,100	$2,476,100	$2,599,800	$2,634,800	$2,727,000	$2,822,400
6. *Less*: Operating expenses						
7. Management fee	113,600	123,800	130,000	131,700	136,400	141,100
8. Salary expense	204,000	211,100	218,500	226,200	234,100	242,300
9. Utilities	109,000	112,800	116,800	120,900	125,100	129,500
10. Insurance	36,700	38,000	39,300	40,700	42,100	43,600
11. Supplies	21,700	22,500	23,300	24,100	24,900	25,800
12. Advertising, legal, misc.	33,100	34,300	35,500	36,700	38,500	39,300
13. Maintenance, repairs, and replacements	188,300	194,900	201,700	208,800	216,100	223,700
14. Property taxes	300,000	300,000	300,000	375,000	375,000	375,000
15. Total expenses	$1,006,400	$1,037,400	$1,065,100	$1,164,100	$1,191,700	$1,220,300
16. Net operating income	$1,265,700	$1,438,700	$1,534,700	$1,470,700	$1,535,300	$1,602,100
17. *Less*: Interest expense	515,800	500,700	484,700	467,800	449,900	431,100
18. Depreciation	383,300	400,000	400,000	400,000	400,000	383,300
19. Taxable income (loss)	$366,100	$538,000	$650,600	$602,900	$685,400	$771,000
20. *Times*: Marginal tax rate	0.40	0.40	0.40	0.40	0.40	0.40
21. Income tax (tax savings)	$146,600	$215,200	$260,000	$241,200	$274,100	$308,400
22. Net operating income	$1,265,700	$1,438,700	$1,534,700	$1,470,700	$1,535,300	$1,602,100
23. *Less*: Debt service	784,200	784,200	784,200	784,200	784,200	784,200
24. Before-tax cash flow	$481,500	$654,500	$750,500	$686,500	$751,100	$817,900

*All numbers have been rounded to the nearest $100.

FIGURE 9.6: Loan Amortization Schedule for Maegan's Magic Manor Apartments*

Year	Debt Service	Interest	Principal	Loan Balance
1	$784,192	$515,802	$268,390	$9,231,610
2	$784,192	$500,662	$283,530	$8,948,080
3	$784,192	$484,670	$299,522	$8,648,558
4	$784,192	$467,773	$316,419	$8,332,139
5	$784,192	$449,926	$334,266	$7,997,873
6	$784,192	$431,070	$353,122	$7,644,751
7	$784,192	$411,151	$373,041	$7,271,710

*All numbers have been rounded to the nearest $1.

SUMMARY

Interest is the cost of borrowed money and is usually specified in the promissory note. This contract rate (called the *nominal rate*) will differ from the effective rate when borrowers pay a fee in connection with the loan or when the amount of money actually disbursed by the lender is less than the face amount of the loan. To determine the effective rate, find the discount rate that makes the present value of all payments to be made by the borrower exactly equal to the loan funds disbursed.

Because interest expense incurred to acquire or carry income-generating assets is tax-deductible, the after-tax cost of borrowing is reduced. The higher the borrower's marginal income tax rate, the lower the after-tax cost of borrowing.

A distinction must be made between the nominal rate and the real interest rate. The real rate is the nominal rate, adjusted for price inflation over the period between borrowing and paying the interest.

Borrowing decisions are complicated by the various loan terms offered. A key variable in the choice between alternatives is the comparative effective interest rates, the discount that makes the future payment obligation equal to the net loan proceeds.

A wraparound mortgage is a financing device that enables a junior lienholder to control payments to a senior lienholder. Depending on how it is structured, the wraparound might increase the lender's effective yield.

RECOMMENDED READING

Downs, Anthony. *The Revolution in Real Estate Finance*. Washington, D.C.: The Brookings Institution, 1985.

Kolbe, Phillip T., Gaylon E. Greer, and Bennie D. Waller, Jr. *Real Estate Finance*. 3rd ed. Chicago: Dearborn Real Estate Education, 2012.

Bo, Liu, and Sing, Tien Foo, "Unobservable Risks in Mortgage Contract Choice" Real Estate Economics 41:4, 2013, 958–985.

Rose, Morgan J. "Origination Channel, Prepayment Penalties, and Default." *Real Estate Economics* 41:3, 2012, 1-46.

Roulac, Stephen E., and Neil F. Dimick. "Real Estate Capital Markets Undergo Fundamental Changes." *Real Estate Finance Journal* 6, no. 3 (Winter 1991): 717.

Valachi, Donald J. "Installment Sales of Mortgaged Real Estate and the Wraparound Mortgage: An Update." *The Appraisal Journal* 61, no. 3 (July 1993): 426–30.

INTERNET REFERENCES

For calculations involving interest rates:
www.bai.org
www.interest.com

REVIEW QUESTIONS

1. Describe the difference between nominal and effective interest rates.
2. Under what circumstances might the nominal and effective rates be the same? What makes them differ?
3. Under what circumstances will paying off a loan balance before maturity cause the effective interest rate to be higher?
4. If financial leverage is favorable, why would an investor want to repay a loan before its due date?
5. Distinguish between nominal and real interest rates.

DISCUSSION QUESTIONS

1. Why would a lender charge a lower contract interest rate coupled with a front-end fee? Why not simply incorporate the effective rate into the contract rate?
2. Because inflation causes real interest rates to be lower, won't lenders simply factor inflation into their contract rates so that the real rate remains constant? With rational borrowers and lenders, shouldn't adjustments for anticipated inflation cancel out inflation's impact?
3. The deductibility of interest expense for federal income tax purposes radically alters the consequences of borrowing. Should interest expense be deductible? Why make interest expense (payment to the debt position) deductible when dividends or partnership payouts (payment to the equity position) are not?

184   UNIT 9   The Cost of Borrowed Money

PROBLEMS

1. Compute the effective interest rate on each of the following loans. Each is for $100,000, fully amortizing over 20 years, and the contract interest rate is 9%:
   a. A 6% front-end fee, with no prepayment anticipated
   b. A 5% front-end fee, with prepayment planned after five years (no prepayment penalty)
   c. A 4% front-end fee and prepayment planned after 10 years (a prepayment penalty equal to 2% of the unpaid balance)

2. A prospective borrower is offered a $500,000 first mortgage loan with interest at 8% per annum. Monthly payments will be required to amortize the loan over 25 years. Two alternatives are offered:
   a. A five-year loan with a 1% front-end fee
   b. A seven-year loan with a 1.5% front-end fee

   Required
   (1) Which loan alternative carries the lower pretax effective interest rate, assuming they run full term?
   (2) Which loan alternative carries the lower pretax effective rate if they are to be retired through refinancing after three years (assume there is no prepayment penalty)?
   (3) If the borrower intends to let the loan run full term, then refinance with another mortgage loan equal to the remaining balance, what consideration should be factored into the loan choice, other than the effective interest rate?

3. An investor seeks to borrow funds for a long-term investment. The investment is virtually certain to generate profits of 10% per annum but has no prospects for a higher yield or for appreciation. It is a one-time opportunity that will accommodate all the funds the investor can raise, and it can be liquidated at any time with no transaction costs. The investor has no cash available but can borrow on the following terms:
   a. A 25-year, 8.5% loan with a 2.5% origination fee and no prepayment permitted. The loan will be fully amortized over the 25-year term. Loan proceeds (net of the front-end fee) will be $50,000.
   b. A 25-year, 8% loan, fully amortizing, with no loan origination fee and no prepayment permitted. Loan proceeds will be $40,000.

   Required: Given that there is no other source of funds available for investment and that this is the only investment opportunity available, and assuming the investor is not a taxable entity (for computational convenience, ignore income taxes), if all other factors remain equal, which loan should the investor take?

4. You are considering three loan proposals to finance the purchase of investment property. The purchase price is $500,000 and the expected NOI is $60,000. The alternatives are as follows:
   a. LTV ratio is 90%, interest rate is 9%, and terms are 25 years, level amortizing with monthly payments.
   b. LTV ratio is 80%, interest is 8%, and terms are 25 years, level amortizing with monthly payments.
   c. LTV ratio is 80%, interest is 7.5% + three points, and terms are 25 years, fully amortizing with monthly payments.

   Determine

   (1) The effective interest rate for each loan, assuming the loan is outstanding for the full 25-year amortization term
   (2) The incremental rate of interest paid for the additional funds provided in Loan A over Loan B

5. A $750,000 mortgage loan that is being fully amortized with level payments over 20 years has 5 years remaining. The contract interest rate is 7%. The borrower refinances with a 15-year, fully amortizing wraparound loan that carries a contract interest rate of 8.25%. To keep the monthly payment below $3,000, over how many years must the wraparound be amortized? Round your answer to the nearest whole year.

6. If the borrower negotiates the wraparound loan described in problem 5, what will be the annual net cash flow to the wraparound lender (a) for the first five years of the new loan and (b) in subsequent years?

PART THREE

Case Problem

Please refer to the case problem for Part Two. Assignment 2 of that problem called for a seven-year forecast of NOI for the St. George Apartments. If you have not yet completed that assignment, please do so now.

Assignment:

1. Based on NOI projection for the first year, estimate the mortgage loan that will be available if the lender requires a debt-coverage ratio of not less than 1.20. Anticipated loan terms are interest at 8.5% per annum, and level monthly payments to amortize the loan over 20 years. No discount points or loan origination fee is anticipated.

2. Round your mortgage loan estimate from Assignment 1, to the nearest $100,000. Modify the St. George Apartments projection to derive a seven-year projection of before-tax cash flow, based on this loan.

3. Using the mortgage loan from Assignment 2, develop a seven-year amortization schedule for the St. George Apartments. Include an anticipated remaining mortgage balance at the end of seven years.

4. Using the forecasted future market value developed in Assignment 3 of the Case Problem for Part Two (rounded to the nearest $100,000), estimate before-tax cash flow from disposal, assuming the following:

    a. The property is sold at the end of the seventh year (i.e., before the first debt-service payment falls due for the eighth year).

    b. Transaction costs (brokerage, legal and accounting fees, and so forth) equal 8% of the selling price.

Save your work. It will be needed to solve Case Problem 1 for Part Four.

PART FOUR

Income Tax Considerations

Income taxes establish a claim superior to that of equity investors, whose right is a mere residual. The relevant measure of investment outcomes, therefore, is the value of after-tax cash flows, and expected income tax consequences are a vital part of the analysis. This section outlines major tax opportunities and tax traps associated with real estate investing.

Our perspective is that of the individual (noncorporate) taxpayer who holds real estate for use in a trade or business or for production of income. Tax rules affecting real estate held for personal use or for corporations differ radically. Tax advantages for real estate investors were retained in the 2017 American Tax Relief Act (ATRA). Investors also benefitted from lower tax rates and an exclusion for pass-through entities.

Federal income tax law is found in the Internal Revenue Code, frequently referred to as *the Code*, with more than 3,000 pages with 5,000 more pages of regulations to make its provisions comprehensible. All this is accompanied by a massive library of court decisions in settlement of disputes between tax collector and taxpayers.

In the next two units, we will cover only a portion of the tax issues addressed by this extensive material. Our concern is with these segments of the Code and implementing regulations that directly influence income tax consequences of real estate investment. Even so, we must limit ourselves to an overview of most issues in order to discuss, in greater detail, matters of overriding importance.

Lawmakers have become notorious for almost constant tinkering with the Internal Revenue Code, so some of these tax rules might have been superseded by the time you read about them. Court rulings will further define changes in the tax laws.

UNIT 10

Fundamental Income Tax Issues

UNIT PREVIEW

This unit outlines fundamental income tax issues that are of vital concern to real estate investors. Because the investor's tax basis in a property is so significant to investment outcomes, that is the first issue addressed. The unit then considers the tax consequences of ownership forms. It concludes with an introduction to the income tax consequences of disposal.

UNIT 10 Fundamental Income Tax Issues

THE TAX BASIS: ITS NATURE AND SIGNIFICANCE

From the time a property is acquired, owners have a tax basis in their property. During the period of ownership, the basis may be adjusted to reflect disinvestment or additional capital investment. This tax basis is a primary determinant of tax consequences during the holding period. Selling or exchanging a property generates a gain or loss equal to the difference between the sales price and the adjusted basis of the property at the time of disposal.

THE INITIAL TAX BASIS

The initial tax basis in a newly acquired property depends in part on how it is acquired. If the property is received as a gift, its initial tax basis will be the same as the adjusted tax basis of the donor, unless the donor incurs gift tax liability. In that case, the initial tax basis will include the portion of the donor's gift tax liability that was incurred because the property increased in value while it was owned by the donor. The initial tax basis in inherited property is its market value as determined for estate tax purposes (gift and estate taxes are explained in Unit 11).

The initial basis in property acquired by purchase is its cost of acquisition. This includes everything of value given in exchange. It also includes all costs incurred in obtaining and defending title. Thus, cost includes purchase commissions (if any), legal fees, title insurance, and other items that are incurred in connection with acquisition and are not deductible as current operating expenses. Example 10.1 illustrates the determination of a purchaser's initial tax basis.

Example 10.1

An apartment building is purchased on the following terms: $50,000 in cash at closing, with the purchaser taking title subject to an existing mortgage note, which has a remaining balance of $400,000, and signing a note and second mortgage for $60,000. The buyer also pays $2,000 into a property tax and insurance escrow account (escrow involves the holding by a third party, an escrow agent, of something of value that is the subject of a contract between two other parties, until that contract has been consummated), $240 for the seller's prepaid water bill, $250 for heating oil remaining in the building's tanks, $50 for document recording, and $90 for state documentary stamps (essentially, a sales or transfer tax). Other expenditures include $1,500 for legal representation, $210 for an owner's title insurance policy, $450 for a lender's title insurance policy, and $180 for a credit report.

Example 10.1 (continued)

The purchaser's initial tax basis is $512,350, determined as follows:

Purchase price		
Cash down payments	$50,000	
Second mortgage note	60,000	
First mortgage note	400,000	$510,000
Attorney's fee		1,500
Owner's title policy		210
Recording fee		50
Documentary stamps		590
Initial tax basis		$512,350

All other outlays represent costs of obtaining financing or are incidental to the purchase and, therefore, are not properly includable in the initial basis.

ALLOCATION OF THE INITIAL TAX BASIS

If two or more assets (e.g., land and buildings) are acquired as a single transaction, the initial tax basis must be allocated among them in accordance with their relative market values. This implies that relative values are known; in fact, they generally have to be estimated. The following techniques, if properly applied, will survive IRS scrutiny:

- Specify the price of each asset in the original purchase contract. If the purchase is an arm's-length transaction, such contractual determination forms a defensible cost allocation basis.

- Use the ratio of land value to building value estimated by the tax assessor, who usually assesses land and improvements separately. Although the assessor's estimate of total value might differ considerably from the investor's initial tax basis, the relative estimates nevertheless provide a generally acceptable way of allocating the basis. Because the tax assessor is a neutral third party, this is the technique most readily accepted by the IRS.

- Have an independent appraiser estimate the assets' relative values. If a third-party lender finances the transaction, an appraisal will usually be required. In addition to its intended purpose, the appraisal can be used to allocate the tax basis.

Example 10.2

The cost of a property, including all transactions that are appropriately includable in the initial basis, totals $800,000. The property includes land and two buildings. The values, based on the tax assessor's appraisal and an independent appraiser, are as follows:

	Assessor	Appraiser
Land	$125,000	$150,000
Building A	300,000	400,000
Building B	200,000	300,000
Total	$625,000	$850,000

Consider the property in Example 10.2. Neither the tax assessor's nor the independent appraiser's value estimate correspond to the actual purchase price. Yet, they can be used to allocate the initial tax basis among the three assets that the taxpayer has acquired in a single purchase. If the assessor's estimates are used, the initial tax basis will be allocated as follows:

	Assessor's Estimate	Percent of Total	Purchaser's Allocation
Land	$125,000	20	$160,000
Building A	300,000	48	384,000
Building B	200,000	32	256,000
Total	$625,000	100	$800,000

If the taxpayer elects to allocate based on the independent appraiser's value estimate, the allocation will be as follows:

	Assessor's Estimate	Percent of Total	Purchaser's Allocation
Land	$150,000	17.65	$141,200
Building A	400,000	47.06	376,480
Building B	300,000	35.29	282,320
Total	$850,000	100.00	$800,000

In Example 10.2, the taxpayer will prefer the allocation based on the independent appraiser's value estimate because he has a higher percentage of the tax basis in improvements to calculate the depreciation allowance.

ADJUSTMENT OF THE BASIS FOR COST RECOVERY

An allowance for recovery of invested capital can be deducted from otherwise taxable revenue. The allowance, called a *depreciation allowance*, is sufficient to recover the cost of buildings and land improvements, such as roads and walkways, over periods specified in the Internal Revenue Code. Land is not depreciable.

Only assets held for business or income purposes qualify for the depreciation allowance. Note that the determining factor is *intent* to produce income, rather than actual success in doing so. Thus, an owner of rental property may claim a depreciation allowance regardless of whether a tenant actually occupies the premises. But the IRS may insist on evidence of intent. For example, a house previously occupied by the owner will not qualify for a deduction when vacated and offered for sale. It will be considered income property and, therefore, qualify for a depreciation allowance only if the owner actively seeks to rent it after moving out.

Allowable Cost Recovery Periods

Congress adjusts allowable recovery periods from time to time with no apparent regard to actual useful lives of assets. The decision appears to be primarily conditioned on a need to enhance tax receipts (when recovery periods are lengthened) or encourage investment (when the periods are shortened). Currently, the tax basis of qualifying residential structures—buildings from which at least 80% of gross rents stem from residential tenants—is recovered over 27.5 years; that of nonresidential structures (if put into service after May 12, 1993) is 39 years. The tax basis of land improvements such as sidewalks, roads, sewers, gutters, and fences is recoverable over 15 years. These recovery periods were preserved in the most recent tax law.

Computation of the Allowance

The tax basis of a building is recovered in equal annual increments over the recovery period. If a property is owned for less than 12 months during a particular taxable year, the allowance during that year is permitted only for the number of months that it is owned. Half a month's allowance is permitted during the month in which a taxpayer first puts a property into service, regardless of how many days during that month the property is actually in service. Another half-month allowance is claimed in the month of disposition, again without regard to the actual number of days the property is owned that month. This half-month allowance is called the *mid-month convention*.

> **Example 10.3**
>
> During March 2016, a taxpayer who files tax returns on a calendar-year basis acquires a residential income property that she operates until November 2018, the month in which she sells. The portion of the purchase price (including applicable transactions costs) properly attributable to the building is $2.5 million.

To see how the allowance is computed, consider Example 10.3. Because the property is residential in nature, the $2.5 million initial tax basis of the building will be recovered over 27.5 years. The monthly allowance, therefore, will be $7,575.76:

$$\frac{\text{recoverable amount}}{12 \times \text{recovery period}} = \frac{\$2,500,000}{330} = \$7,575.76$$

During the year of acquisition, the depreciation allowance is $7,575.76 times the number of months held, including a half-month allowance for March. Therefore, our investor's first-year allowance, rounded to the nearest whole dollar, is $71,970:

$$\text{months in use} \times \text{monthly allowance} = 9.5 \times \$7,575.76 = \$71,970$$

During each whole year of this investor's ownership, the allowance will be 12 times $7,575.76, or $90,909. During the year of disposal, the taxpayer will claim the allowance for only 10.5 months. Thus, the final year's allowance will be 10.5 times $7,575.76, or $79,545.

Had the property in Example 10.3 been nonresidential—perhaps an office or a store building—the allowance would have been smaller. Because the recovery period for nonresidential properties is 39 years, the monthly allowance for this property would have been $5,341.88:

$$\frac{\text{recoverable amount}}{12 \times \text{recovery period}} = \frac{\$2,500,000}{468} = \$5,341.88$$

Under the revised assumption that the property in Example 10.3 is nonresidential, therefore, the first year's allowance will be 9.5 times $5,341.88, or $50,748. The annual allowance during each full year of ownership will be 12 times $5,341.88, or $64,103. In the year of disposal the taxpayer will claim an allowance of 10.5 times $5,341.88, or $56,090.

Improvements on and to the land, as previously noted, are recovered over 15 years. Taxpayers are permitted to use an accelerated technique, called the *150% declining balance method*, which permits larger allowances during earlier years offset by smaller allowances later. They may shift to the straight-line method for the remainder of the 15-year period when doing so will generate a higher annual allowance. Example 10.4 illustrates the use of this method.

Example 10.4

Assuming a $60,000 cost attributable to land improvements that qualify for the cost recovery allowance, the annual allowance for the first 5 years, using the 150% declining balance method over 15 years, is as follows:*

(1.5 × 1/15) × ($60,000, minus cumulative allowances)

Example 10.4 (continued)

During the first five full years, the annual allowance will be as follows:

Year	Declining Balance	×	Rate	= Allowance
1	$60,000 − $0 = $60,000	1.5 × 1/15 =	0.10 × 0.5	$3,000
2	$60,000 − $3,000 = $57,000		0.10	$5,700
3	$57,000 − $5,700 = $51,300		0.10	$5,130
4	$51,300 − $5,130 = $46,170		0.10	$4,617
5	$46,170 − $4,617 = $41,553		0.10	$4,155

*During the year of acquisition, the taxpayer gets only half a year's deduction (the mid-year convention).

A Depreciation Schedule for Maegan's Magic Manor

In Unit 5, we developed a reconstructed operating statement for a 280-unit apartment complex called Maegan's Magic Manor. The reconstructed statement is presented in Figure 5.8. Starting with that statement, we developed (in Unit 6) a six-year operating forecast. The forecast is presented in Figure 6.2. Then, in Unit 9, we extended the forecast to include before-tax cash flows. That projection is presented in Figure 9.5.

We can also develop a schedule of expected depreciation allowances for Maegan's Magic Manor, but first we must have an estimate of the purchase price and the relative value of land and improvements. In Unit 9, to estimate the size of the mortgage loan, we derived a market value estimate of $13,596,667. If our investor acquires the property at this price and incurs $150,000 of transaction costs that must be capitalized, the initial tax basis will be $13,746,667. From the assessor's percentage of value attributable to land, we calculate the land value to be $2,746,667. Therefore, the amount allocable to the improvements and recoverable via annual depreciation allowances is $11 million:

Initial tax basis of land and improvements
Purchase price $13,596,667
Add: Transaction costs   150,000
Total initial tax basis $13,746,667
Less: Tax basis of land   2,746,667
Amount to be recovered $11,000,000

The monthly depreciation allowance is an amount that will enable the investor to recover the $11 million over 27.5 years:

$$\text{monthly allowance} = \frac{\$11,000,000}{12 \times 27.5} = \$33,333.33$$

UNIT 10 Fundamental Income Tax Issues

The annual allowance (other than in the year of acquisition and the year of disposal) will be 12 times the monthly amount. During the year of purchase and the year of disposal, the allowance will be computed based on the number of months of ownership, including half a month's allowance during the initial month and the final month (without regard to the actual day of the month on which transactions occur). The computations are shown in Figure 10.1.

FIGURE 10.1: Projected Annual Depreciation Allowances for Maegan's Magic Manor Apartments

Year	Allowance*
1†	$383,300
2	$400,000
3	$400,000
4	$400,000
5	$400,000
6†	$383,300

Depreciable amount:	
Estimated purchase price	$13,596,667
Add: Estimated transaction costs	150,000
Initial Tax basis, land, and improvements	$13,746,667
Less: Amount allocable to land	2,746,667
Depreciable amount	$11,000,000
Recovery period: 27.5 years	
Monthly allowance: $\dfrac{11,000,000}{12 \times 27.5} = \$33,333.33$	

*Amounts rounded to nearest $100.

† Incorporates the half-month convention. Assumes purchase during the first month of taxable year and sale during the final month of taxable year.

OTHER ADJUSTMENTS TO THE TAX BASIS

A number of factors other than depreciation allowances result in adjustments to the tax basis. Some of these decrease the basis; others increase it.

The tax basis is reduced when a portion of an asset is sold or destroyed by casualties such as fire, flood, or storm. A partial sale requires that the tax basis be reduced by the portion of the basis properly attributable to the part sold. In the case of casualty losses, the basis must be reduced to reflect allowable loss deductions in the year of the casualty, plus any loss for which compensation is received.

Expenditures that significantly increase the value or useful life of an asset must be added to the tax basis. Generally, this includes any expenditure that is not deductible as a current expense. Examples include items such as a new central heating or cooling system, a new roof, or new wall-to-wall carpeting. Treasury Regulation 1.162-4 distinguishes between capital expenditures and currently deductible repairs and maintenance.

The cost of improvements, alterations, or additions that must be capitalized (i.e., added to the tax basis) will be written off via depreciation allowances in the same manner as the initial recoverable cost. But the deductions must be based on an entirely separate recovery schedule that begins with the month that the improvements, alterations, or additions are first placed in service.

Transaction costs associated with acquiring or disposing of property are also added to the adjusted basis. We saw earlier how transaction costs incurred to acquire property, but not those to get it financed, are added to the basis. In the same manner, transaction costs at disposal are added to the adjusted basis.

FORECASTING AFTER-TAX CASH FLOWS

Now we have enough information to extend the cash-flow forecast from Unit 9 to include income tax consequences. Figure 9.5 presents a six-year forecast of before-tax cash flows, Figure 9.6 presents an amortization schedule for the mortgage loan that is incorporated in the analysis, and Figure 10.1 shows the projected schedule of depreciation allowances. The only additional information we need to extend the analysis to after-tax cash flow is the investor's marginal income tax bracket. Figure 10.2 shows after-tax cash-flow projection, assuming the appropriate (combined federal and state) income tax bracket is 40%.

Lines 1 through 16 of Figure 10.2 are taken directly from Figure 9.5. Starting with line 17, we derive an estimate of taxable income by subtracting tax-deductible items that are not considered operating expenses and therefore do not reduce NOI. The items are interest expense (line 17 on Figure 10.2, taken from Figure 9.6) and the depreciation allowance (line 18 on Figure 10.2, taken from Figure 10.1). The result, on line 19, is taxable income.

Multiplying taxable income by the 40% marginal income tax rate (line 20) results in the expected income tax obligation, shown on line 21. Line 22 is simply a restatement of NOI, brought down from line 16. Line 23 adjusts for debt service to arrive at before-tax cash flow (line 24), which is the same as shown in Figure 9.5. Subtracting estimated income tax liability (or adding back expected income tax savings) due to the investment, as shown on line 25, yields line 26, the estimated after-tax cash flow from the investment.

FIGURE 10.2: Projected After-Tax Cash Flow From Operations: Maegan's Magic Manor Apartments*

	Year 1	Year 2	Year 3	Year 4	Year 5	Year 6
1. Potential gross rent	$2,346,100	$2,463,400	$2,586,600	$2,677,100	$2,770,800	$2,867,800
2. *Less:* Vacancy allowance	176,000	98,500	103,500	160,600	166,200	172,100
3.	$2,170,100	$2,364,900	$2,483,100	$2,516,500	$2,604,600	$2,695,700
4. *Add:* Other income	102,000	111,200	116,700	118,300	122,400	126,700
5. Effective gross income	$2,272,100	$2,476,100	$2,599,800	$2,634,800	$2,727,000	$2,822,400
6. *Less:* Operating expenses						
7. Management fee	113,600	123,800	130,000	131,700	136,400	141,100
8. Salary expense	204,000	211,100	218,500	226,200	234,100	242,300
9. Utilities	109,000	112,800	116,800	120,900	125,100	129,500
10. Insurance	36,700	38,000	39,300	40,700	42,100	43,600
11. Supplies	21,700	22,500	23,300	24,100	24,900	25,800
12. Advertising, legal, misc.	33,100	34,300	35,500	36,700	38,500	39,300
13. Maintenance, repairs, and replacements	188,300	194,900	201,700	208,800	216,100	223,700
14. Property taxes	300,000	300,000	300,000	375,000	375,000	375,000
15. Total expenses	$1,006,400	$1,037,400	$1,065,100	$1,164,100	$1,191,700	$1,220,300
16. Net operating income	$1,265,700	$1,438,700	$1,534,700	$1,470,700	$1,535,300	$1,602,100
17. *Less:* Interest expense	515,800	500,700	484,700	467,800	449,900	431,100
18. Depreciation	383,300	400,000	400,000	400,000	400,000	383,300
19. Taxable income (loss)	$366,600	$538,000	$650,000	$602,900	$685,400	$787,700
20. *Times:* Marginal tax rate	0.40	0.40	0.40	0.40	0.40	0.40
21. Income tax (tax savings)	$146,600	$215,200	$260,000	$241,200	$274,200	$315,100
22. Net operating income	$1,265,700	$1,438,700	$1,534,700	$1,470,700	$1,535,300	$1,602,100
23. *Less:* Debt service	784,200	784,200	784,200	784,200	784,200	784,200
24. Before-tax cash flow	$481,500	$654,500	$750,500	$686,500	$751,100	$817,900
25. *Less:* Income taxes	146,600	215,200	260,000	241,200	274,200	315,100
26. After-tax cash flow	$334,900	$439,300	$490,500	$445,300	$476,900	$502,800

*All numbers have been rounded to the nearest $100

TAX CONSEQUENCES OF OWNERSHIP FORM

Real estate investors face a bewildering array of ownership entity choices. Legal and financial distinctions among the alternatives may appear inconsequential; the reality is that the choice of title-holding entity is often crucial to a venture's outcome.

A decision to involve other investors in some form of pooling-of-equity arrangement vests the entity question with particular urgency. Outside investors generally insist on an arrangement that limits their personal financial liability.

Asset liquidity is interrelated with the issue of financial liability and is significantly affected by choice of ownership entity. The ability to liquidate a position at the investor's own volition is often a powerful determinant of willingness to enter into cooperative ventures. To enhance liquidity, cooperative ventures generally employ an entity that enables investment shares to be transferred in relatively small increments.

A continuous thread running through all deliberations concerning the entity question is the importance of maintaining decision-making control over operational matters. Sacrificing control to induce associates to contribute additional funds is self-defeating if the associates prove to be inept managers. The entity decision should be made only after careful consideration of its impact on operational control.

Ownership by Individuals

The least-complicated ownership alternative is title vested directly to an investor as an individual. This individual ownership is also known as a tenancy in severalty. Where more than one individual is to take an equity position, a possible alternative to individual ownership is a *cotenancy arrangement*.

Cotenancies are not taxpaying entities. All profits and losses accrue to the cotenants as individual taxpayers and are reported on their personal tax returns. Profits and losses are divided among the cotenants in accordance with their relative ownership interests in the property. With respect to a personal interest in the property, therefore, the investors are in the same tax position as if they held title to a part of the property as sole owners.

The cotenancy arrangements most commonly encountered are *tenancy in common* and *joint tenancy*. The exact wording in a deed of conveyance to create joint tenancy as opposed to tenancy in common differs among the states. In either case, agreements among cotenants regarding operational matters can be arranged as they please but should be in writing and signed by all parties to avoid misunderstanding and to serve as a guide for settling possible disputes. To ensure enforceability and access to legal remedies, any such agreement should be made under the guidance of legal counsel.

Tenants in common

When property is held as a tenancy in common, each investor's name appears on the deed, and each holds an undivided interest in the whole property. The interests need not be equal (e.g., one party might hold a 10% interest, another a 25% interest, and yet another a 65% interest), but they are necessarily undivided; unless there is a specific agreement to the contrary, each tenant in common has the use of the whole property. Substantial alterations or improvements require agreement among the owners, thereby effectively reducing the operational control of any one owner. The usual arrangement is to provide that one owner operates the property under a limited power of attorney from the others.

Joint tenancy

Joint tenancy has essentially the same characteristics as tenancy in common, with two important exceptions: (1) the joint tenants' property interests are always equal, and (2) in the event of a joint tenant's death, the deceased person's interest in the property goes to the other joint tenant or tenants rather than to the deceased tenant's heirs. Because of the right of survivorship, joint tenancy is obviously inappropriate unless the joint tenant is someone to whom you intend to bequeath your property interest in any case. Observations made earlier about control and special operating agreements among tenants in common apply also to joint tenants. Joint tenancy also requires one deed for all owners, who must receive title at the same time.

Ownership in General Partnerships

Unlike corporations, partnerships are not taxable entities. Income and losses are taxed directly to the individual partners, and the nature of the income and loss items (e.g., ordinary income or capital gains) is not affected by the partnership's existence. Partnerships must file tax returns, but these are purely informational. The return must show the amount and nature of income, expenses, and deductions and indicate how each item is allocated among the partners. Partners must in turn report these individual items on their personal income tax returns.

In the absence of specific contrary agreements, general partners share profits and losses equally and have equal authority over the partnership business. They are jointly and severally liable for all partnership obligations, even if the obligation is created as a consequence of one partner, having exceeded the authority granted under the partnership agreement.

Shared management authority, combined with unlimited joint and several liability, places severe limitations on the usefulness of general partnerships as real estate ownership entities. As a practical matter, general partnerships tend to be limited to a few business associates who are well acquainted and share a high degree of mutual confidence.

Limited Partnerships

Real estate investors who contribute capital but do not participate in day-to-day management may object to being personally liable for financial obligations arising from the venture. A limited partnership gives them freedom from personal liability without the double taxation that results from the corporate ownership entity.

Limited partnerships have one or more general partners who conduct partnership business and who have unlimited personal liability for partnership obligations. There will also be one or more limited partners who have no personal liability but who share in partnership profits and losses in the same way partners do in a general partnership. Limited partnerships were once popular, but income tax complications have driven the entity into disfavor.

Limited Liability Companies

To gain the income tax advantage of a partnership entity and the limited liability benefits of the corporate form, investors may consider a limited liability company (LLC). This ownership entity is relatively new, but is now authorized in most states. Instead of shareholders (as in corporations) or partners (as in partnerships), the LLC has members. The company is operated in accordance with an operating agreement that resembles corporate bylaws and is managed by designated parties who need not be members.

Limited liability for all members

Neither the members nor the managing parties of an LLC have personal liability. In this respect, the LLC is more like a corporation than a partnership.

Tax conduit treatment

If structured in compliance with IRS rulings, LLCs will be treated as pass-through entities in essentially the same manner as partnerships. As a consequence, members are taxed in the same way as partners in a partnership or shareholders in a subchapter S corporation discussed in the next section.

Corporate Ownership

Corporations are legal entities with an identity separate and distinct from that of their owners (shareholders). Corporations can buy or sell property and otherwise enter into contracts, sue and be sued, and transact business in the same manner as individuals.

Corporations are also taxable entities. They must file corporate income tax returns and pay taxes on their net earnings. For this reason, flow-through accounting treatment (as discussed later with respect to limited partnerships) is not available to corporate shareholders. The new tax law passed in 2017 reduced the corporate tax rate, thereby decreasing the taxes due. The new tax rate is now 21% versus the past rate of 35%.

Any distribution of corporate earnings in the form of cash dividends is taxable to corporate stockholders as regular income. (There is a special exception for corporations that qualify under Subchapter S of the Internal Revenue Code. These corporations, also called *tax option corporations*, are discussed in the next section.) This, in effect, results in double taxation of distributed earnings. Moreover, refusal to declare a cash dividend may result in an even higher tax on accumulated earnings that exceed the corporation's legitimate needs. This *excess accumulated earnings tax*, when added to the regular tax, is essentially confiscatory.

In spite of its obvious disadvantages, the corporate entity should not be casually dismissed. It does offer several offsetting advantages. Chief among these are the following:

- *Limited shareholder liability.* Unless they voluntarily enter into a contrary arrangement, stockholders are not liable for debts contracted by the corporation. Thus, they are personally exposed to risk only to the extent of their investments in the corporation.
- *Liquidity.* Fractional interests in the form of one or more shares of stock can be issued as a means of transferring small portions of ownership—a procedure that might be awkward or impossible if the real property were held in the names of corporate investors.
- *Simplified transactions.* Corporate ownership shares are personalty (personal property) rather than realty. Procedures for transferring ownership are different for personalty and, in most cases, less involved than for realty.
- *Simplified estate settlement procedures.* When the estate of a decedent owns realty in more than one state, there is the possibility that both states will try to collect death taxes based on the property's value. Because corporate shares are personalty rather than realty, using a corporate ownership entity avoids this complication.

Subchapter S Corporations

Owners of certain corporations may elect to have income from the corporation (other than certain specified capital gains) taxable directly to shareholders rather than to the corporation. Losses are also passed through to shareholders, but only to the extent of the shareholders' adjusted tax basis in the stock. Additional losses must be carried forward until the stockholder makes further contributions to the corporation. Unlike real estate partnership interests, the basis of stock is not increased by a pro rata share of mortgage debt. Corporations that qualify for and make this election are called *S corporations* (reflecting the location of the rules, in Subchapter S of the Code), or *tax option corporations.*

The process for qualifying for the special treatment afforded under Subchapter S can be quite complex. Success requires an intimate knowledge of the statute and implementing regulations.

Tax Exclusion for Pass-Through Entities

The Tax Act of 2017 provided a key advantage to pass-through entities, such as Sub S Corporations and LLCs. Before calculating the taxes due to the individual owners of these entities, 20% of the taxable income is excluded. Therefore, only 80% of the income is taxed at the new lower tax rates. The 20% deduction is subject to wage limits. Married individuals filing jointly may not earn more than $315,000 in order to take the exclusion. Figure 10.3 illustrates the tax ramifications for owners of Maegan's

Magic Manor Apartments. If the ownership was held in a pass-through entity, such as a Sub S corporation and the individual owners all had incomes below the $315,000 limit and their combined state and federal tax bracket was 40%, the investors could use the 20% exclusion and thereby reduce their tax liability by $29,300, a savings of 7.5%

FIGURE 10.3: After-Tax Cash Flow from Operations Maegan's Magic Manor Apartments Pass-Through Tax Treatment

Year 1

19. Taxable Income (Loss)	$366,600
Minus 20% exclusion	73,300
New Taxable Income	293,300
20. Times: Marginal Tax Rate	0.40
21. Income Tax	98,464
22. Net Operating Income	1,265,700
23. Less: Debt Service	784,200
24. Before-Tax Cash Flow	481,500
25. Less: Income Tax	117,300
26. After-Tax Cash Flow	364,200

TAX CONSEQUENCES OF FINANCIAL LEVERAGE

The act of borrowing or repaying money is not a taxable event—it neither increases, nor decreases tax liability. Interest on borrowed money secured by a mortgage on rental real estate, in contrast, is usually deductible in the taxable year that it is paid. The most significant exceptions to this general rule involve special treatment of prepaid interest and construction-period interest and deduction limitations incorporated into passive activity loss rules, discussed later.

Prepaid Interest Must Be Amortized

Prepaid interest is generally not deductible by the borrower until the interest is actually earned by the lender. Consequently, discount points and loan origination fees, both of which are explored in Unit 9, must be deducted ratably (amortized) over the term of the loan on which they were incurred. Loans to purchase or to finance improvements to a personal residence are exempted from this rule, providing the discount points are representative of those charged in the market area.

Construction-Period Interest Must Be Capitalized

Interest incurred during construction of real estate improvements is considered a part of the construction cost. Thus, it is a part of the initial tax basis of the improvements and figures into the cost recovery allowance.

Limits on the Deductibility of Interest

Deductions for interest incurred to acquire or carry portfolio assets such as stocks and bonds are limited to the amount of income earned by the portfolio. Any investment interest in excess of portfolio income is carried forward and claimed as offsets against portfolio income in subsequent years.

There are also overall limits on the amount of net losses from real estate that can be offset against income from other sources, if the real estate is deemed to be a passive investment (the passive asset limitation rules are explored later).

These limitations may prevent some interest expense from being deducted in the year incurred. Should that occur, the interest expense is carried forward and treated as interest expense incurred in the following year. There are no limits on the number of years that interest expense can be carried forward in this manner.

Investment Strategy Implications

Because selling a property may result in income tax liability, while borrowing against it does not, investors will often benefit from borrowing rather than selling. One's equity in a property is the difference between market value and the balance of mortgage indebtedness. Selling a property is often referred to as *liquidating the equity*, because it results in the equity interest being converted to cash. Borrowing does the same thing, by reducing the difference between market value and mortgage indebtedness, but—unlike selling—the borrowing is not a taxable event.

INCOME TAX CREDITS FOR PROPERTY REHABILITATION

Benefits from tax shelters, though extensively curtailed by legislation since 1986, are still available to investors involved in real estate renovation and rehabilitation. But not all opportunities are created equal. If they conform to rigorously detailed criteria, expenditures to renovate low-income housing or selected nonresidential properties generate special benefits in the form of tax credits. Tax credits for rehabilitating certified historic structures are even more generous. Many of such tax credits are to thwart gentrification in areas previously owned and/or occupied by low-income residents.[1]

How Tax Credits Work

Tax credits, dollar-for-dollar reductions in tax liability, are not to be confused with tax deductions. A credit is subtracted after the amount of income taxes is computed, then is subtracted from tax liability. Taxpayers in the 35% marginal income tax bracket, for example, would find their income taxes reduced by one dollar for every dollar of tax credits, but only $0.35 for every dollar of tax deductions.

---

1 Turnbull et al, forthcoming.

LIMITATIONS ON THE DEDUCTIBILITY OF LOSSES

The Internal Revenue Code, Section 469, requires taxpayers to report their income and losses separately from activities characterized as passive. With limited exceptions, net losses from passive activities cannot be offset against income from other sources. Instead, the net losses must be carried forward and offset against passive income in future years. Any remaining passive loss carryovers become deductible when the passive activity asset to which they apply is sold or otherwise disposed of in a taxable transaction.

Passive activities include ownership interests in most rental property and in any trade or business in which the taxpayer does not materially participate in management. *Material participation* is said to be lacking if the owner is not actively involved, year-round, on a "regular, continuous, and substantial basis." Figure 10.4 illustrates these provisions.

Limited Partners' Income and Expenses Are Always Passive

Limited partnership interests are specifically included in the passive activities category by the statute. Code Section 469(h)(2) says, "Except as provided in regulations, no interest in a limited partnership as a limited partner shall be treated as an interest with respect to which a taxpayer materially participates." Section 469(i)(6)(C) says, "No interest as a limited partner in a limited partnership shall be treated as an interest with respect to which the taxpayer actively participates." Taken together, these two provisions effectively foreclose any possibility that limited partnership interests might escape being characterized as passive activities.

Real Estate Rental Income and Expenses Are Sometimes Passive

Real estate held for rental purposes is defined as a passive activity by the wording of Code Section 469(c)(2), which states, "The term 'passive activity' includes any rental activity." Additional wording excludes the following:

- Rental income that is incidental to the primary business activity or where substantial personal service is involved (e.g., hotels, motels, and resorts). Elsewhere, the Code contains special provisions that exempt real estate under certain circumstances.

- Rental income when the taxpayer is actively engaged in a real property trade or business such as brokerage, development, or management. To be considered *actively engaged*, the taxpayer (or the taxpayer's spouse if they file a joint return) must have at least a 5% ownership interest in the business, and more than 50% of the taxpayer's working hours must be devoted to the activity, which must occupy more than 750 hours annually.

FIGURE 10.4: Determining the Character of Real Estate Rental Income

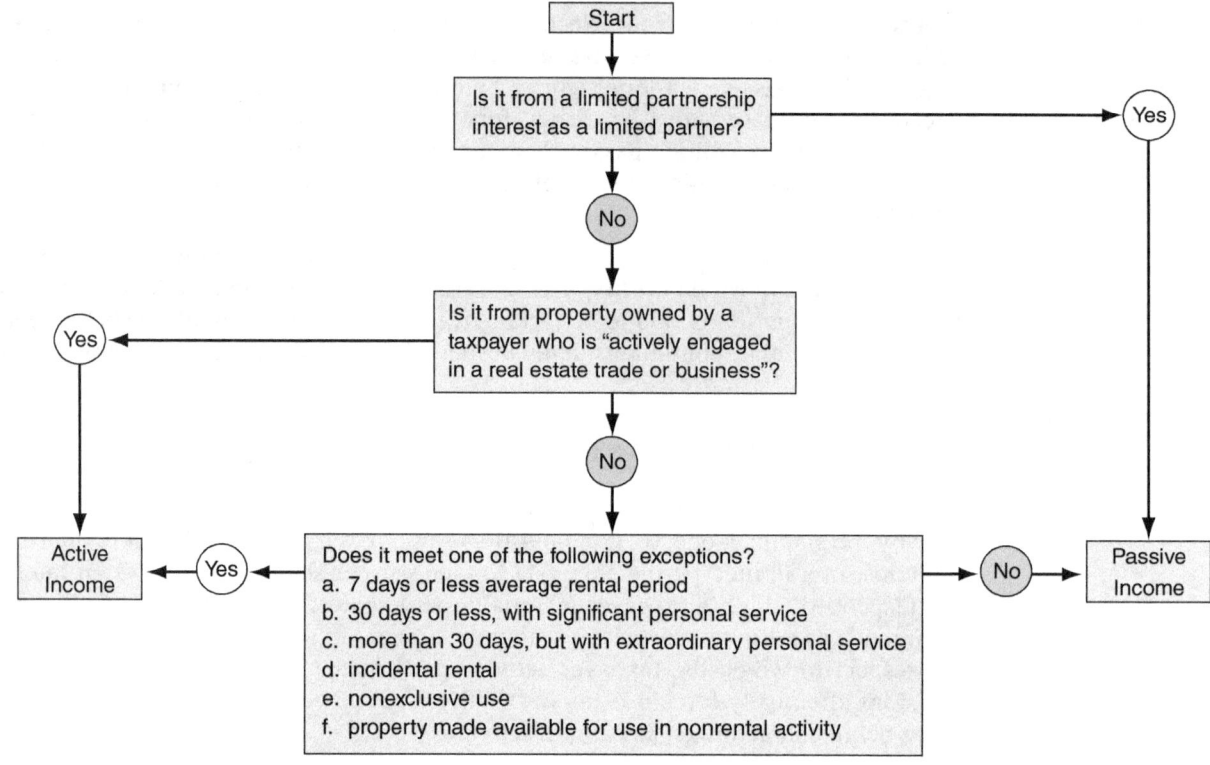

AN EXCEPTION FOR SMALL-SCALE OPERATORS

One specific provision that applies only to real estate permits up to $25,000 annually of passive activity losses (and loss-equivalent tax credits) from operating rental real estate to be offset against otherwise taxable income such as wages and profits from business activities. But this exception is phased out ratably as adjusted gross income (computed *before* adjusting for net passive losses and loss-equivalent credits, and with some other modifications from the way taxpayers report their adjusted gross income on their annual tax returns) moves from $100,000 to $150,000. There are two exceptions to this phase-out rule:

- With respect to passive activity tax credits that are attributable to the rehabilitation tax credit described earlier, the exception is phased out ratably only as adjusted gross income (before adjusting for net passive losses and loss-equivalent credits) moves from $200,000 to $250,000.
- With respect to credits attributable to the low-income housing credit, there is no adjusted gross income limitation.

To qualify for the exception, a taxpayer must have at least a 10% ownership interest in the property and (other than for the pass-through of low-income housing or rehabilitation credits) must be an active participant in the real estate rental operation. The requirement of active participation is less strenuous than the material participation requirement described earlier. The Senate Finance Committee, in reporting on the enabling legislation, described *active participation* as making management decisions or arranging for others to provide services such as repairs and maintenance. Moreover, services performed by a taxpayer's spouse are attributed to the taxpayer in determining whether the active participation test is met.

TAXATION OF FOREIGN INVESTORS

Increased interest by foreign investors in United States real estate, as discussed in Unit 1, has prompted concern in the Treasury Department that some foreign investors might be escaping taxation on their gains. The U.S. Congress responded with the Foreign Investment Real Property Tax Act of 1980 (FIRPTA).

The act, as amended, requires any person acquiring a U.S. real property interest from a seller who is not a U.S. citizen to withhold and remit to the IRS 10% of the gross sales price.

Any buyer who fails to withhold the correct amount may be liable for the amount in question, plus interest and penalties. There are certain other, rather esoteric exceptions, but the withholding is generally required unless any of the following conditions exists:

- The property is worth no more than $300,000 and is for the purchaser's use as a personal residence.
- The transaction is protected from taxation pursuant to a U.S. tax treaty with another country, and the buyer and the seller are unrelated.
- The seller or the buyer obtains a "withholding certificate" from the IRS, which reduces the amount to be withheld.

Reporting and withholding requirements are extensive and complex, and their specifics are beyond the scope of this text. They are designed to ascertain that taxes are paid before assets are moved beyond the reach of the United States Treasury.

THE ALTERNATIVE MINIMUM TAX

In addition to determining their taxable income and income tax obligation using the regular computational procedure, taxpayers must compute an alternative minimum taxable income and alternative minimum tax (AMT). As the name implies, taxpayers must pay the larger of the alternative or the regular tax. TCJA did increase the alternative tax minimum significantly.

Many taxable and tax-deductible items are treated less leniently under the alternative minimum computation than under the regular tax computation. Among these are cost recovery allowances; the cost must be recovered over a greater number of years. Moreover, certain gains on disposal that can be deferred or are treated preferentially under the regular tax computation method are treated as regular taxable income under the alternative method. As a consequence, some of the anticipated tax advantages associated with real estate investment might be jerked away due to the AMT. Though it is beyond the scope of this text, prudent investors will always consider the AMT consequences of their investment initiatives.

TAX CONSEQUENCES OF PROPERTY SALES

Recall that an investor's adjusted tax basis in a property is the initial tax basis adjusted for cost recovery allowances and property improvements, plus certain other adjustments that may sometimes apply. The gain or loss on disposal is simply the difference between the amount realized from sale or exchange and the adjusted basis at the time of the transaction. The tax consequences depend in part on how the transaction is structured. Unit 11 addresses this issue in more detail.

SUMMARY

Real estate investors have an initial tax basis in all newly acquired property. If two or more assets are acquired in a single transaction, the initial basis must be allocated between assets in accordance with their relative market values. Periodically, the basis is adjusted, sometimes upward and sometimes downward, but it can never fall below zero. When the property is sold, the gain on disposal is computed by deducting the adjusted tax basis from the selling price.

Owners of real property held for use in a trade or business or for production of income are allowed to deduct a depreciation allowance to provide for recovery of their investment in buildings and other improvements. All depreciation allowances represent downward adjustments to the tax basis.

Taking title to property in one's own name or jointly with another investor has the attraction of legal simplicity—the deed merely conveys property to the investors by name. If title is to be held jointly by two or more people, the wording in the deed of conveyance is a major determinant of the exact nature of the cotenancy.

Corporations are legal entities and thus may hold title to property in their own names. Corporations are also taxable entities and must file income tax returns in much the same fashion as individuals. Income is first taxable to the corporation, and then any earnings distributed as dividends are taxable to the shareholders. Moreover, any tax-deductible losses on corporate-owned real estate accrue to the corporation rather than to the corporate shareholders; corporations (other than those qualifying for and electing S corporation status) are not tax conduits.

Partnership entities offer indirect ownership without the double taxation problem associated with corporations. Title is recorded in the partnership name, but individual partners report income and losses from partnership operations on their personal income tax returns. If properly documented and reported, income is not taxable to the partnership. Each item of partnership income and expense retains its character when reported on the tax returns of the individual partners. For this reason, partnerships are said to be *tax conduit*s.

Numerous incentives are incorporated into the Internal Revenue Code to induce taxpayer actions that are considered socially desirable. Investors who exploit these provisions may be able to significantly reduce their income tax liability. Real estate–related opportunities include tax-oriented use of financial leverage, earning tax credits by acquiring and rehabilitating older or historically significant structures, or structures that house low-income tenants.

Borrowing is not a taxable event, and interest expense incurred on loans that encumber real estate is generally deductible when incurred and paid. By releveraging their position when they desire to liquidate a portion of their equity, investors can avoid the tax liability that would result from selling.

With significant exceptions, operating losses on rental real estate cannot be used to offset otherwise taxable income from salaries, wages, or profit from business or portfolio operations. Key exceptions are for modest losses reported by individuals with limited adjusted gross income, losses on certain low-income rental housing, and losses incurred by persons actively engaged in a real property trade or business.

The increase of foreign investment in U.S. real estate has prompted tax code provisions designed to ensure payment of income tax liability on foreign-company transactions. To a substantial extent, the burden of enforcement has been imposed on taxpayers who buy real estate from foreign owners.

RECOMMENDED READING

Commerce Clearing House. *U.S. Master Tax Guide*. Riverwoods, Ill.: Commerce Clearing House. Published annually.

Hoven, Vernon. *The Real Estate Investor's Tax Guide: What Every Investor Needs to Know to Maximize Profits.* 5th ed. Chicago: Dearborn Real Estate Education, 2008.

Journal of Real Estate Taxation. A quarterly periodical published by Warren, Gorham & Lamont, 210 South St., Boston, MA 02111.

Smith, Brent C. "If You Promise to Build It, Will They Come? The Interaction between Local Economic Development Policy and the Real Estate Market: Evidence from Tax Increment Finance Districts." *Real Estate Economics,* 37:2, 2009, 209–234.

Turnbull, Geoffrey K, Bennie D. Waller, Scott A. Wentland, Walter R.T. Witschey and Velma Zahirovic-Herbert. "This Old House: Historical Restoration as a Neighborhood Amenity." Land Economics, forthcoming

INTERNET REFERENCES

For information on income tax issues:
www.irs.gov

Guide to the alternative minimum tax:
www.fairmark.com/amt

For information on interest expense:
www.treasurydirect.gov/govt/reports/ir/ir_expense.htm

REVIEW QUESTIONS

1. How is a taxpayer's initial tax basis in a property determined?
2. Describe three common methods of allocating the tax basis between land and other assets.
3. List the basic conditions under which depreciation allowances are permitted.
4. List several adjustments that decrease the basis of a property and several that increase the basis.
5. Describe the differences between joint tenancy and tenancy in common.
6. List the major advantages and disadvantages of the corporation as an ownership form.
7. Describe the major advantages of an S corporation.
8. How does the tax treatment of expenditures for interest on borrowed money differ from that on expenditures to repay the loan?
9. When is prepaid interest deductible?
10. Explain the tax treatment of construction-period interest expense.
11. How do tax credits differ from tax deductions?
12. Describe the general criteria for exemption from the passive activity loss rules for persons engaged in real property trade or business.

DISCUSSION QUESTIONS

1. In view of the increasing frequency of income tax legislation, discuss the wisdom of relying on favored income tax treatment as a major element in the flow of benefits from property ownership.
2. Explain why a corporation whose shares are traded publicly might wish to show one measure of depreciation or cost recovery when reporting taxable income to the IRS and an entirely different measure when reporting operating results to shareholders.
3. Why has Congress provided shorter cost recovery periods for residential than for nonresidential property?
4. Suggest reasons why the IRS might resist setting forth precise rules for determining whether an expenditure will be treated as a repair or an improvement.
5. Should government policy be designed to influence the choice between partnership and corporate ownership forms? Explain your reasoning.
6. Are tax credits the best way to subsidize property rehabilitation? Explain why or why not.

PROBLEMS

1. An investor buys a property for $1 million, with 40% of the purchase price attributable to the land and the balance to a single structure. The purchaser incurs transaction costs equal to 5% of the purchase price (these must be capitalized). The investor then spends $400,000 to rehabilitate the structure (she is entitled to no tax credits). Subsequently, she claims $110,000 of cost recovery allowances. She then sells the land but retains title to the building and a long-term leasehold interest in the land. The sale price is $600,000, including transaction costs, which equaled 10% of the selling price.

   What is the investor's adjusted tax basis in the remaining asset after accounting for all of these transactions?

2. A residential rental property is acquired during the first month of the taxable year, at a total cost (including transaction costs) of $1.2 million. Of this amount, $200,000 is properly attributable to the land. Determine the annual depreciation allowance for the first year and for each of the ensuing nine years.

3. Assume that during the last month of the 10th year of ownership, the property in Problem 2 is sold for $1.5 million. Assume also that the seller incurs transaction costs equaling 6% of the sales price. What is the amount of the gain or loss on the sale?

4. A 50,000-square-foot parcel of land (which has equal value per square foot) is purchased by a developer who pays $10,000 in cash, takes title subject to an existing $70,000 first mortgage note that she assumes and agrees to pay, and signs a note and purchase-money mortgage for an additional $20,000 (transaction costs are zero). The developer constructs a building on the easternmost 25,000 square feet at a total construction cost of $75,000. The westernmost 25,000 square feet is improved with sewers, grading, and parking facilities at a total cost of $18,000. The developer then borrows $100,000 from a mortgage lender and uses the loan proceeds to retire the existing first mortgage loan, the purchase-money mortgage note that was created when the land was purchased, and a short-term personal loan that was used to help finance construction. This new $100,000 loan is secured by a new first mortgage on the easternmost 25,000 square feet of property, leaving the westernmost 25,000 square feet clear of all liens (all promissory notes call for interest at current market rates). At this point, the developer sells the westernmost 25,000 square feet of property for $80,000, net of transaction costs. The developer also claims an $8,333 cost recovery (depreciation) allowance on the building that she has constructed on the easternmost 25,000 square feet of property. What is the developer's adjusted tax basis in this property after accounting for all of this activity?

UNIT 11

Tax Consequences of Property Disposal

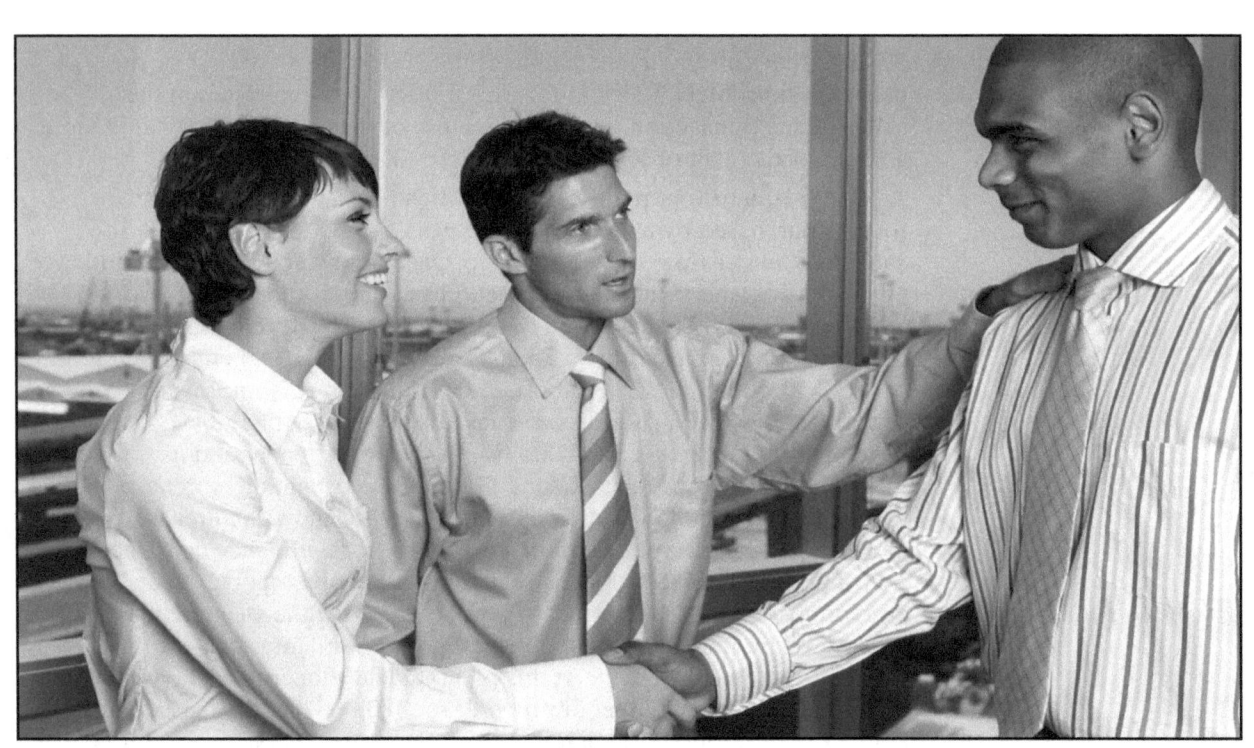

UNIT PREVIEW

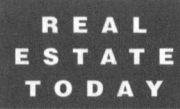

The tax consequences of property disposal depend in part on the amount and nature of the gain or loss (if any), and in part on how the transaction is structured. This unit demonstrates how to compute gains and losses and explains what determines the nature of the gain or loss. It then considers the tax consequences of special deal structures.

COMPUTATION OF REALIZED GAIN OR LOSS

Everything of economic value received in exchange for a property constitutes the *consideration*. This includes the balance due on any mortgage to which a property remains subject, whether or not the purchaser assumes personal liability. If the seller receives other property or services as a part of the deal, these must be included at their fair market value. The principle is illustrated in Example 11.1.

> **Example 11.1**
>
> A taxpayer transfers title to a vacant commercial lot (which is owned free and clear) in exchange for $50,000 in cash at the time of the transaction and a note for $100,000 due in 12 months. The purchaser also transfers title to another vacant lot (market value $80,000) and a pickup truck (market value $8,000). In addition, the purchaser, who is an attorney, agrees to represent the seller without cost in divorce proceedings that are scheduled in the near future. The value of this legal service is $12,000. The buyer takes title subject to an existing mortgage-secured note, which has a remaining balance of $300,000. Total consideration involved in the transaction is $550,000.

The realized gain or loss on a transaction is the difference between the consideration received and the adjusted tax basis at the time of the transaction, as Example 11.2 illustrates.

> **Example 11.2**
>
> Suppose the seller in Example 11.1 incurred transaction costs of $3,000 and had an adjusted basis (just prior to the sale) of $48,000. The gain on disposal is $499,000, computed as follows:
>
> | | | |
> |---|---:|---:|
> | Sales price | | $550,000 |
> | *Less*: Adjusted tax basis: | | |
> | Basis prior to sale | $48,000 | |
> | *Add*: Selling costs | 3,000 | 51,000 |
> | Realized gain on disposal | | $499,000 |

TAX TREATMENT OF REALIZED GAIN OR LOSS

A realized gain may be treated as ordinary income or as capital gain. If it is capital in nature, it is accorded special tax treatment. Likewise, a loss may be a reduction in ordinary taxable income for the year or may be treated as a capital loss and offset only ordinary taxable income to a limited extent.

When Is a Gain Treated as Ordinary Income?

A gain is ordinary income when it results from recapture of depreciation or cost recovery allowances. It is also ordinary income when it results from selling assets that are held for resale in the ordinary course of business.

Recapturing depreciation or cost recovery allowances

Investors who put their properties into use before the effective date of 1986 tax law changes had the option of computing depreciation or cost recovery allowances using an accelerated method. A gain on disposal of property written off on an accelerated schedule will often be characterized as recapture. To the extent they are so characterized, it will be recognized as ordinary income rather than a capital gain.

Property held primarily for Resale

People who hold real estate for resale in the ordinary course of business are called *dealers*, and property held primarily for that purpose is called *dealer property*. The sale of dealer property results in ordinary income rather than capital gains. The only exception to this rule involves large-block sales of inventory for liquidation purposes—such sales may give rise to capital gains or losses.

Unrecaptured depreciation or Cost recovery allowances

A gain on disposal occurs when property is sold at a price in excess of its adjusted tax basis. Because depreciation allowances reduce the adjusted tax basis, they increase the potential for gains on disposal. The amount that must be recaptured is equal to the lesser of the total depreciation allowable on the asset (except that for home offices, only depreciation for periods after May 6, 1997 counts), and the total gain realized. If the total gain realized is more than the amount that must be recaptured, the excess may be reported as a capital gain provided that the asset has been held for more than one year. If the total of the depreciation deductions is greater than the gain realized, the entire amount of the gain is taxed at the 25% rate. To illustrate, consider a property that would have an adjusted tax basis of $1 million (after adjusting for selling costs of $55,000), had it not qualified for depreciation deductions. If this property is sold for $1.1 million (and continuing the assumption that it did not qualify for a depreciation allowance), the gain on disposal would be $100,000.

Sales price	$1,100,000
Less: Adjusted tax basis (remember, no depreciation)	1,000,000
Gain on sale (long-term capital gain)	$ 100,000

But suppose straight-line depreciation has accumulated in the amount of $220,000, reducing the owner's adjusted tax basis to $800,000. Any gain on disposal that does not exceed the $220,000 of accumulated depreciation will be characterized as *unrecaptured depreciation* and taxed at a 25% rate. Gains in excess of the $220,000 of accumulated depreciation will be treated as long-term capital gains and taxed at a 20% rate if the owner is in the maximum tax bracket.

Assuming the same $1.1 million sales price as before, but incorporating the assumption that the owner has claimed cumulative tax-deductible depreciation allowances in the amount of $220,000, the gain on the sale will be $320,000. This occurs because the owner's adjusted tax basis will have been reduced by the amount of the depreciation allowances. Here are the numbers:

Sales price		$1,100,000
Less: Adjusted tax basis:		
Basis before claiming depreciation	$945,000	
Less: Cumulative depreciation allowances	220,000	
Basis prior to sale	$725,000	
Add: Selling costs	55,000	780,000
Gain on sale		$320,000

The $300,000 gain will be broken into two layers for tax purposes: the portion that stems from having taken the depreciation allowances and the portion that results from the property having gone up in market value. If the investor was in the maximum tax bracket (over $479,000 in income), her tax would be as follows:

Total gain	$320,000
Less: Unrecaptured depreciation (to be taxed at 25%)	220,000
Long-term capital gain (to be taxed at 20%)	$100,000

The tax liability due to the sale would be $65,000, determined as follows:

Income tax:	
Due to recovery of depreciation (0.25 × $220,000)	$55,000
On long-term capital gain (0.20 × $100,000)	20,000
Total income tax liability	$75,000

When Do Capital Gain or Loss Rules Apply?

Gains realized from the sale or taxable exchange of long-lived assets held for use in a trade or business or for production of income (not intended primarily for resale in the ordinary course of business) are treated as capital gains unless characterized as recapture of depreciation or cost recovery allowances. The capital gain is long term if the asset was held for more than 12 months. Otherwise, it is short term.

Long-lived assets (i.e., those that ordinarily last more than one year) intended for personal use (a personal residence, household furnishings, autos, and so forth) are also considered capital items when there is a gain on disposal. Losses on the sale of personal assets, however, have no income tax consequences.

A special rule applies to assets used in a trade or business, as opposed to those held for investment purposes or for personal use. Reflecting the applicable section of the Internal Revenue Code, these are called *Section 1231 assets*. Gains on the sale of Section 1231 assets are treated as capital gains, to the extent they exceed losses on the sale of other Section 1231 assets during the same taxable year; losses (net of offsetting gains) are treated as reductions in ordinary income for the year. Rental real estate with respect to which the owner is actively engaged in management and which has been owned more than 12 months is considered a Section 1231 asset.

Why Is the Difference Important?

The Tax Code places an upper limit on the rate at which long-term capital gains will be taxed. The rate varies, depending on the nature of the property and the calendar period during which it was owned. (Congress revises the capital gains rules with every shift in the political winds. For the most current tax rules and a detailed explanation, visit the IRS website at *www.irs.gov.*) In December 2017, the Tax Cuts and Job Act (TCJA) was signed into law by President Donald Trump making significant changes to the capital gains rate. The new law provides zero capital gains for those in the 10% or 15% tax bracket, but a maximum of 15% for most taxpayers. For those in the 37% tax bracket, capital gains is 20%.[1] Moreover, there is a limit to the amount of capital losses that can be deducted from ordinary income during any one taxable year.

Computation of Net Capital Gains or Losses

Transactions involving capital assets or Section 1231 assets are cataloged according to whether they result in gains or losses. Capital gains and losses are further subdivided according to whether they are long term or short term. (A long-term capital gain or loss is incurred from the sale or exchange of a capital asset that has been held for more than one year; a short-term capital gain or loss is from an asset that is held for one year or less.)

Gains and losses are offset against each other within each category: Section 1231 gains and losses are offset against each other, short-term gains and losses are offset against each other, and long-term gains and losses are offset against each other. The ultimate tax consequences of each depend on whether gains or losses are greater.

Net Section 1231 gains or losses

If there is a net Section 1231 loss, it is offset against ordinary income. If there is a net Section 1231 gain, it is treated as ordinary income to the extent that net Section 1231 losses have been used to offset ordinary income during the previous five years. Any remaining net Section 1231 gains are treated as long-term capital gains.

Net capital gains or losses

When there are net capital losses in one category (long-term or short-term) and net capital gains in the other, the two are offset against each other.

- If what remains is a net capital loss, it is offset against ordinary income, but only to the extent of $3,000. Any remaining net capital loss must be carried forward to the next taxable year. The carried-forward losses retain their identity as short term or long term in the next taxable year.
- If what remains is a net short-term capital gain, it is taxed as ordinary income for the year.
- If the net long-term capital gains (including net Section 1231 gains) exceed offsetting short-term capital losses, the remainder is defined by Code Section 1222(11) as *net capital gains.*

---

[1] *https://www.irs.gov/taxtopics/tc409* (last visited 6-17-2018)

ESTIMATING CASH FLOW FROM SELLING MAEGAN'S MAGIC MANOR

In Unit 6, we estimated the future value of a 280-unit apartment complex called Maegan's Magic Manor. By capitalizing the projected sixth-year income, we estimated that the property would have a market value of $17.8 million at the end of an anticipated six-year holding period. In Unit 9, we developed a loan amortization schedule, which was presented in Figure 9.6. Then, in Unit 10, we projected annual depreciation allowances, which were presented in Figure 10.1. Using this information and incorporating an estimate of transaction costs incurred in selling, we can project after-tax cash flow from disposing of Maegan's Magic Manor at the end of an anticipated six-year holding period.

The realized gain on disposal is simply the selling price minus the adjusted tax basis at the time of sale. The tax basis before the sale is the initial tax basis (computed in Unit 10) minus cumulative depreciation allowances (also computed in Unit 10 and presented in Figure 10.1). Transaction costs incurred on disposal (assumed here to be 5%) are added to derive the adjusted tax basis at the time of sale. The calculations are shown in Figure 11.1.

FIGURE 11.1: Estimate of Investor's Adjusted Tax Basis in Maegan's Magic Manor at Time of Disposal*

Purchase price	$13,596,700
Add: Transaction costs	150,000
Initial tax basis	$13,746,700
Less: Cumulative depreciation allowances (from Figure 10.2)	2,366,600
Adjusted basis prior to sale	$11,380,100
Add: Selling costs (0.05 × $17,800,000)	890,000
Adjusted basis at time of sale	$12,270,100

*All values have been rounded to nearest $100.

The taxable gain on disposal is the selling price minus the adjusted tax basis at the time of sale. The portion of the gain that stems from the adjusted tax basis, having been reduced by claiming depreciation deductions, will be characterized as unrecaptured depreciation and taxed at a 25% rate. The remaining portion is a long-term capital gain and will be taxed at a 20% rate. Applying these rates to the two layers of gain yields the expected income tax consequences of the sale. This is shown in Figure 11.2. The anticipated after-tax cash flow is the sales receipts minus all disbursements associated with the sale. These are shown in Figure 11.3.

FIGURE 11.2: Estimated Income Tax Consequences of Selling Maegan's Magic Manor Apartments*

Selling price	$17,800,000
Less: Adjusted basis (from Figure 11.1)	12,270,100
Gain on disposal	$5,529,900
Less: Gain attributable to unrecaptured depreciation (from Figure 11.1)	2,366,600
Long-term capital gain	$3,163,300
Tax:	
On recovery of depreciation (0.25 × $2,366,600)	591,600
On long-term capital gain (0.20 × $3,163,300)	632,700
Total tax liability	$1,224,300

*All values have been rounded to nearest $100.

FIGURE 11.3: Estimate of After-Tax Cash Flow from Disposal of Maegan's Magic Manor Apartments*

Selling price		$17,800,000
Less: Selling costs (from Figure 11.1)	$890,000	
Income taxes (from Figure 11.2)	1,224,300	
Mortgage balance (from Figure 9.6)	8,015,800	10,130,100
After-tax cash flow		$7,669,900

*All values have been rounded to nearest $100.

WHEN ARE REALIZED GAINS OR LOSSES RECOGNIZED?

A distinction has been made between *realized* and *recognized* gains or losses. Recall that a gain or loss is realized at the time of asset disposition. Whether the gain or loss is recognized for income tax purposes, and tax consequences thereby incurred in the taxable year of the transaction, depends on how the transaction is structured.

If a transaction is a cash sale (regardless of how the buyer arranges financing) and the seller realizes a gain, the gain will be recognized in the year of the transaction. If the seller realizes a loss, we have seen that a portion may have to be carried forward and recognized in future taxable years.

When a seller takes back a promissory note in partial payment or receives assets of like-kind (i.e., real estate traded for real estate), all or a portion of a gain or loss might be deferred. The deferral is sometimes mandatory, sometimes optional, as explained later in this unit.

USE OF THE INSTALLMENT SALES METHOD

When a seller receives only partial payment for real property during the year of sale, reporting the transaction under the *installment sales method* permits a portion of the income tax liability to be deferred until the balance of the cash is collected. Tax liability is incurred only on a pro rata basis with each year's collection of sales proceeds.

Advantages of Installment Sales Reporting

When interest rates on third-party mortgage loans are high or the mortgage loans are difficult to obtain, sellers who provide a substantial portion of the necessary financing can greatly facilitate property disposal. Installment sales provisions in the Internal Revenue Code are intended to make this possible without the unfortunate side effect of having income tax liability exceed cash collections in the year of the transaction.

A possible by-product of the installment sales method, of great potential benefit, is that taxes on the gain may be deferred until the seller is in a lower tax bracket. If the investor's income dropped below $479,000, he would save 5% on the long-term capital gain. A sale might be arranged during peak income-earning years, for example, with payment spread over the seller's retirement years. The amount of taxable gain and the nature of the gain (ordinary income and/or capital gain) are determined at the time of the transaction. But the applicable tax rate is that which is in effect when taxes become due. The decline in marginal tax rate in recent years has added another incentive to defer gains by using the installment method. An example of this is TCJA. Another benefit of the installment sales method is that payments can be kept small enough to prevent the seller from being put into a higher tax bracket.

What Gain Qualifies

Owners who have used an accelerated method to compute depreciation or cost recovery allowances may find a portion—sometimes all—of their gain characterized as ordinary income due to recapture of these allowances. The portion of a gain that represents recapture does not qualify for reporting under the installment method. The *installment method gain*, therefore, is the total gain on a transaction, minus the portion that represents recapture. This is illustrated in Example 11.3.

Example 11.3

Residential income property that has an adjusted tax basis of $1.6 million is sold for $2 million. The buyer takes title subject to the $1.5 million balance of an existing mortgage-secured promissory note, pays $50,000 in cash at the closing, and agrees to pay the $450,000 balance of the purchase price in 10 equal annual installments payable at the end of each succeeding year, with interest at 8% on the unpaid balance. The seller pays a broker's commission of $80,000. Other closing costs incurred by the seller total $20,000. As a consequence of his having used an accelerated cost recovery method, $100,000 of the seller's gain on disposal is characterized as ordinary income due to recapture. The gain on the sale is $300,000, of which only $200,000 qualifies for reporting under the installment method:

Selling price		$2,000,000
Less:		
Adjusted basis prior to sale	$1,600,000	
Broker's commission	80,000	
Other transaction costs	20,000	1,700,000
Gain on sale		$300,000
Less: Recapture		100,000
Installment method gain		$200,000

The Contract Price

The *contract price* is the total selling price (i.e., the market value of all consideration tendered by the buyer), less the balance of any mortgage note payable by the purchaser to a third party. Keep in mind, however, that if the property is sold subject to such a mortgage (whether or not the buyer assumes personal liability for the balance to which the transfer is subject), then the contract price is reduced by only that portion of the mortgage note that does not exceed the seller's adjusted tax basis in the property. The contract price for the transaction in Example 11.3 is $500,000:

Selling price	$2,000,000
Less: Balance of old note, to be paid by buyer	1,500,000
Contract price	$500,000

If the existing mortgage note had exceeded $1.7 million (the seller's adjusted tax basis after adjusting for transaction costs incurred on the sale), then the excess would have to be included in the contract price.

The Recognized Gain

The relationship between installment method gain and the contract price determines the portion of each year's collections on the contract that must be recognized as a taxable gain. Divide the installment method gain by the contract price to derive this percentage figure. Then multiply the year's collections on the principal amount of the contract by this ratio. The product is the currently taxable installment method gain. The balance of the year's collections (other than the interest, which is taxable as ordinary income in the year received) represents recovery of capital and has no tax consequences.

These instructions can be reduced to a six-step procedure:

1. Compute the realized gain just as if the installment sales method were not to be used.
2. Divide the realized gain into two portions: recapture and installment method gain.
3. Compute the contract price by subtracting from the total selling price the balance of any mortgage note that calls for payments by the purchaser to a third party and adding back any amount by which any pre-existing note (to which the property remains subject) exceeds adjusted tax basis of the seller.
4. Divide the installment method gain (from step 2) by the contract price (from step 3) to determine the portion of annual collections on the principal amount of the contract that represents collection of the installment method gain.
5. Determine the amount of the principal collected during the year. Be careful to exclude from this calculation any amount collected that represents payment by the purchaser of interest on the indebtedness. Only the principal portion is included.
6. Multiply the principal collected (from step 5) by the percentage that represents the gain (from step 4). This is the amount of receipts that is to be recognized as installment method gain for the year. The balance of the principal collected represents a return of the taxpayer's investment and is not taxable.

Recall from Example 11.3 that payments on the new note are to be made annually. It follows that no payments will be collected in the taxable year of the transaction. The recognized gain that year will be based on the collections at the time of the transaction itself. The gain to be recognized is $119,000:

Initial payments	
Down payment	$50,000
Additional principal payments during year	0
Amount of mortgage assumed by buyer in excess	
of seller's adjusted tax basis	0
Total initial payments	$50,000
Gross profit ratio	
Installment method gain (computed earlier)	$200,000
Total contract price (computed earlier)	500,000
Ratio ($200,000 / $500,000)	–.40
Recognized gain in the year of the transaction:	
Installment method gain to be recognized ($50,000 × 0.40) =	$20,000
Plus: Recapture (computed earlier)	100,000
Recognized gain in year of transaction	$120,000

The Imputed Interest Problem

A buyer usually signs a note as evidence of obligation for the unpaid portion of the purchase price. Credit terms ordinarily provide for periodic payments to retire the note, plus interest payments on the unpaid balance. The principal portion of these payments is considered a part of the purchase price. The interest payments, in contrast, are simply additional income taxable to the seller and generally have no impact on recognition of the gain on sale.

The IRS insists that any installment sales contract or mortgage note include a provision for a reasonable rate of interest. If no such provision exists, the IRS imputes interest by reducing the total selling price to an amount representing the value of the down payment plus the present value of the obligation to make future payments, when the future payments are discounted at a minimum rate of interest as stipulated by the commissioner of the IRS.

The Outstanding Indebtedness Problem

The benefits of the installment method are greatly reduced when sellers use the installment method of reporting gains yet still owe substantial debt. The Internal Revenue Code incorporates complex rules requiring a seller to recognize progressively greater portions of an installment method gain as the total amounts of the taxpayer's own indebtedness grows.

Example 11.4

An investor has been investing all available savings in small parcels of real estate such as single-family dwellings, duplexes, and small stores. Over the years, a substantial equity in those properties has accrued, so the investor is considering moving into a large property that can be managed professionally and will yield economies of scale.

The properties have an aggregate market value of $1.5 million and are subject to mortgages totaling $1 million. The investor has an adjusted tax basis of $700,000 and has accumulated depreciation of $200,000. Cash available for reinvestment if the investor sells these properties (and assuming, for simplicity, that transaction costs are zero) will be $360,000, calculated as follows:

Taxable gain on transaction:		
Selling price		$1,500,000
Less: Adjusted tax basis		700,000
Gain on disposal		$800,000
Less: Gain attributable to unrecaptured depreciation		200,000
Long-term capital gain		$600,000
Tax:		
On recovery of depreciation (0.25 × $200,000)		50,000
On long-term capital gain (0.20 × $600,000)		120,000
Total tax liability		$170,000
Cash flow available for reinvestment:		
Selling price		$1,500,000
Less:		
Income taxes	$170,000	
Mortgage balance	1,000,000	1,170,000
Net cash flow		$330,000

LIKE-KIND EXCHANGES (1031 EXCHANGES)

Otherwise taxable gains or tax-deductible losses realized on an exchange of like-kind assets are not recognized in the year of the transaction. Rather, they are deferred until a future, taxable transaction occurs with respect to the substitute property. When gains are involved, a series of such exchanges can pyramid one's real estate holdings by retaining wealth that would otherwise be reduced by tax liability with each transaction. The government in effect extends an interest-free loan in the amount of taxes so deferred.

Enabling legislation for like-kind exchanges, sometimes (erroneously) called *tax-free exchanges*, is contained in Section 1031 of the Internal Revenue Code. Reflecting this, they are sometimes simply called *Section 1031 exchanges*. The 2017 American Tax Relief Act preserved like-kind exchanges for real estate, but not for personal property.

In Example 11.4, the investor pays a heavy price for moving into an alternative investment opportunity: His $500,000 equity is reduced to $360,000 due to the income tax. If the investor negotiates tax-deferred exchange instead of selling and reinvesting the after-tax net proceeds, the entire $500,000 equity will transfer to the new property.

Exchange vs. Sale and Purchase

In order to qualify under Section 1031, there must have been a bona fide exchange of the assets involved. It appears that the question of whether a transaction is treated as an exchange or as a sale and purchase is more a matter of form than of intent. Investors must ascertain that proper steps are taken by all parties to document transactions as bona fide exchanges. The other parties might not be in a position to have their tax liability deferred under Section 1031, regardless of the form of the transaction. They may therefore be considerably less motivated to structure the transaction appropriately.

Purpose for Which Property Is Held

To qualify as a like-kind exchange, property conveyed must have been held for productive use in a trade or business or as an investment and must be exchanged for like-kind property that is also to be used in a trade or business or held as an investment. Properties may qualify if they fall into either of these categories: property held for use in a trade or business may be exchanged for investment property and vice versa.

Certain types of property, however, are specifically excluded by statute. These include securities or evidence of indebtedness (stocks, bonds, notes, and so forth), beneficial interests in trusts, and inventory. For real estate investors, the latter category is likely to prove the most troublesome because inventory includes one's stock in trade or other property (including real estate) held primarily for resale.

The Definition of Like-Kind Property

Only like-kind property qualifies for tax-deferred exchange treatment. The like-kind concept relates to the nature of the property, not to its quality or grade. The implication for real estate investors is that real estate may be exchanged for other real estate without regard for the type of realty involved, so long as it is held as an investment or for use in a trade or business. Examples issued by the Treasury to amplify this point include the following[2]:

- Property held for use in trade or business, together with cash, for other property intended for use in a trade or business
- Urban real estate for a farm or ranch
- Improved for unimproved real estate held for investment purposes
- A leasehold (with not less than 30 years to run) for a freehold
- Mineral interest in land (not merely an assignment of payments) for a fee title in real estate

---

[2] Treasury Regulation 1.1031(a)–1.1031(b).

An additional exception to the general rule has been more recently written into the Internal Revenue Code: real estate in the United States and real estate in foreign countries are not like-kind under Code Section 1031.

Tax Consequence of Like-Kind Exchanges

If all property involved in an exchange qualifies as like-kind and all parties qualify, then no party to the exchange may recognize any gain or loss on the transaction. Note that this is mandatory, not elective. Any gain or loss realized in an exchange but not recognized for income tax purposes, is reflected in the tax basis of the newly acquired property.

When some of the property involved in an exchange fails the like-kind test, then some portion of a gain (but not of a loss) must be recognized in the year of the transaction. This unlike property that is recognized for tax purposes is called boot. The balance of the realized gain is deferred as before and is reflected in the adjusted basis of acquired property.

Because they can have a major impact on the income tax consequences of adjusting a real estate portfolio, real estate analysts need to become familiar with the details of the like-kind exchanges. A more extensive treatment is presented in Appendix D.

SECTION 1033 ROLLOVER: CASUALTY AND EMINENT DOMAIN

Section 1033 provides another tax-free exchange for the receipt of proceeds from eminent domain or casualty. To qualify for a Section 1033 rollover or involuntary conversion, the investor must have destruction of the property beyond the control of the taxpayer or taking of the property through condemnation or eminent domain. The taxpayer has two years after the close of the taxable year in which the gain is realized to roll over the proceeds into a new investment that is similar or related in service or use. The Section 1033 rollover does not require that the technical rules of Section 1031 apply, including the use of a qualified intermediary.

GIFTS OF PROPERTY

When property is owned free and clear and is given to someone else, no consideration is involved in the transaction and there is no realized gain or loss. Because no gain or loss has been realized, of course none is recognized. There may, however, be gift tax consequences.

The Unified Gift and Estate Tax

All bona fide gifts and all property passed as a legacy at death is subject to a unified and graduated gift and estate tax. The tax is imposed on the giver or, in the case of a legacy, on the estate of the deceased. There are several exemptions and exclusions:

- In 2018, following the TCJA, taxpayers can give up to $15,000 per person per year to as many individuals as they wish, with no gift tax implications (the amount changes through time). This is an increase from the previous $14,000. The gifts must be present interests (i.e., the recipient must have immediate access to the gift), unless the recipient is a minor. If the recipient is a minor, the gift can be placed in trust until the recipient becomes an adult. If spouses jointly make gifts, they may give up to $30,000 per recipient per year without incurring gift tax liability, but they must file an information gift tax return in the year of the gift.

- There is an unlimited exemption for gifts or legacies to one's spouse, provided the spouse is a U.S. citizen at the time of the gift. For spouses who are not U.S. citizens, tax-exempt gifts were limited (in 2012) to $139,000 per annum.
- There is an unlimited exemption for payment of tuition and medical expenses for others, provided payment is made directly to the education or health care provider.

In addition to the exclusions and exemptions previously listed, every taxpayer as a lifetime credit against the unified gift and estate tax. The amount of tax on estates that is offset by the credit increased through time, reaching $11.18 million in 2018. Owners can gift up to $11.18 million with no gift tax due if they subtract it from estate tax lifetime exclusion.

What If the Property Is Subject to a Mortgage?

If a property is transferred subject to a mortgage, there will be both sale and gift elements to the transfer because relief from indebtedness is valuable consideration (even though the giver may be liable for the debt, the recipient must pay it to retain control of the mortgaged property). If the mortgage balance exceeds the giver's adjusted tax basis, the difference will be a realized gain. The difference between the property's market value and the mortgage balance is a gift and is potentially subject to the gift tax.

The Tax Basis of Property Received as a Gift

The tax basis of a gift recipient's interest in a property will be the same as the giver's interest, unless the giver incurred a gift tax liability. In that case, the recipient's tax basis will be increased by the portion of the gift tax that results from the property's value having grown during the giver's period of ownership.

A Gifting Strategy for Highly Appreciated Property

If the sale of a property will result in a substantial realized gain, considerable tax savings may be realized by using a gifting strategy. When two individuals who consider themselves an integral economic unit (so that it doesn't really matter who holds title) are in different income tax brackets, consider transferring property to the party in the lower bracket, and letting that party sell. The gain on disposal will then be taxed at that party's lower marginal bracket, and the after-tax proceeds will be greater.

This strategy is defeated, of course, if the transfer results in gift tax liability. The gift tax may be avoided by exploiting the unified credit, which offsets the gift tax. Otherwise, consider transferring title in small enough annual increments to avoid gift tax liability.

Alternatives May Be Less Taxing

Alternatives to an outright gift may be advisable even when two parties who consider themselves an integral economic unit are in substantially different income tax brackets. If a highly appreciated property is transferred as a legacy instead of being transferred as a gift, the recipient gets a stepped-up tax basis equal to the value on which estate taxes are based. This means that all appreciation during the lifetime of the deceased owner escapes income taxes altogether. It is wise, therefore, to consider holding highly appreciated real estate so that it will benefit from the stepped-up basis rule. If a portion of the equity needs to be liquidated during the interim, this can be accomplished by additional borrowing against the property. As noted earlier, borrowing is not a taxable event, yet it liquidates equity as surely as an outright sale does.

Should property owners desire to defer recognition of taxable gains during their lifetimes but nonetheless wish to adjust their portfolios, they should consider like-kind exchanges, as previously discussed. There is no limit to the number of substitute properties that can be acquired in a series of such exchanges, with all gains being deferred. When the property owners die, their heirs take title with stepped-up tax basis, and all the deferred gains are permanently avoided.

SUMMARY

If sellers take back promissory notes in partial payment for property, they may defer recognition of taxable gains until they collect proceeds from the notes. The gain is recognized on a pro rata basis as the principal portion of the note is collected. Deferral does not affect the recognized gain's status as ordinary income or a capital gain.

Taxes due to gains on disposal of real estate are deferred if the property is exchanged for other property in a qualifying like-kind exchange. The tax liability is deferred until the property received in the trade is itself disposed of in a transaction that does not qualify as like-kind. To qualify as a like-kind exchange, both the old and the substitute property must be held for use in a trade or business or for production of income. Certain types of property are specifically excluded from like-kind exchange treatment. These include securities and evidence of indebtedness, beneficial interests in trusts, and inventory.

If some unlike property (boot) is received in an otherwise qualifying like-kind exchange, then any realized gain must be recognized for tax purposes, to the extent of the value of the unlike property received. The balance of the gain is deferred until the substitute property is sold. No part of a realized loss may be recognized, however, if the transaction qualifies even in part as a like-kind exchange.

When property is given away, the tax basis in the hands of a new owner is the same as it was in the hands of the previous owners. The only exception is when the previous owners incurred some gift tax liability due to increases in property value during their ownership period. If property is transferred subject to mortgage indebtedness, the amount of the debt is considered to be consideration for the transaction. Only the remaining value is a gift.

RECOMMENDED READING

Commerce Clearing House. *U.S. Master Tax Guide*. Riverwoods, Ill.: Commerce Clearing House. Published annually.

Guggenheim, Joseph. *Tax Credits for Low-Income Housing*. 13th ed. Glen Echo, Mass.: Simon Publications, 2006.

Hoven, Vernon. *The Real Estate Investor's Tax Guide: What Every Investor Needs to Know to Maximize Profits*. 5th ed. Chicago: Dearborn Real Estate Education, 2008.

Irwin, Robert. *Buy or Sell Real Estate After the 1997 Tax Act: A Guide for Homeowners and Investors*. New York: John Wiley & Sons, 1998.

Journal of Real Estate Taxation. A quarterly periodical published by Warren, Gorham & Lamont, 210 South St., Boston, MA 02111.

Turnbull, Geoffrey K, Bennie D. Waller, Scott A. Wentland, Walter R.T. Witschey, and Velma Zahirovic-Herbert. "This Old House: Historical Restoration as a Neighborhood Amenity." Land Economics, forthcoming.

INTERNET REFERENCES

For information on income tax issues:
www.irs.gov

For information on historical properties tax credits:
www.nps.gov/tps/tax-incentives.htm
www.dhr.virginia.gov/tax_credits/tax_credit.htm

REVIEW QUESTIONS

1. What is the principal advantage of using the installment sales method of reporting property sales?
2. List the qualifications necessary for an exchange of property to be considered a like-kind exchange for tax purposes.
3. How are gains and losses in a like-kind exchange treated?
4. Under what circumstances will giving away property be considered in part a sale or exchange?
5. What is the relationship between federal gift taxes and federal estate taxes?
6. How large a gift can be made to an individual other than one's spouse during a single calendar year, without the gifts being subject to gift taxes?

UNIT 11 Tax Consequences of Property Disposal

DISCUSSION QUESTIONS

1. Why are the taxes on installment sales permitted to be deferred? Does this provision seem to represent good public policy? Why or why not?

2. From a public policy perspective, what is a reason to accord like-kind exchanges different income tax treatment from that associated with selling the old property and buying the substitute? In either instance, are there compelling public policy reasons to permit income taxes to be deferred?

PROBLEMS

1. The Griggs Hotel was sold for $5 million. The investors originally purchased the hotel for $3.5 million five years ago. During their ownership of the hotel, the investors accumulated depreciation of $600,000. Calculate the tax bill on the sale for the investors.

2. Ben Bigalow is considering selling an apartment building that he bought several years ago for $820,000, including transaction costs. He has claimed total (cumulative) depreciation (cost recovery allowances) of $255,000. He has made no capital improvements during his holding period.

   Bigalow has been offered $900,000 for this property ($300,000 over the existing $600,000 mortgage note, to which the property will remain subject when sold). Terms of the offer are $90,000 in cash at the closing. Buyer assumes the $600,000 balance on the existing first mortgage note and signs a note and purchase-money mortgage for the remaining $210,000 of the purchase price. The $210,000 note provides for three equal annual payments including principal and interest, with interest at 12%.

   If Bigalow accepts this offer and incurs $45,000 of sales costs, what will be the resultant increase in his taxable income in the year of the transaction and in each of the three succeeding years, assuming he uses the installment method of reporting the sale? Bigalow has no imputed interest problem, and the property would generate zero taxable income each year if it is not sold. Bigalow has no other outstanding debts.

PART FOUR

Case Problem

1. Please refer to the Case Problem for Part Three. Assignment 2 of that case required you to develop a seven-year projection of before-tax cash flows from the St. George Apartments. If you have not yet completed that assignment, please do so now. Using the format illustrated in Figure 10.2 (or an alternative format prescribed by your instructor), incorporate income tax consequences and extend the forecast to include after-tax cash flow from operation. In developing your projection, make the following assumptions:
   a. Eighty percent of the purchase price is attributable to the buildings, and the taxpayer is in the 40% marginal income tax bracket.
   b. Because she is engaged full time as a real estate practitioner, she is not subject to the passive activity rules.
   c. She will incur no liability for the AMT during the projection period.

2. Assignment 4 of the Case Problem for Part Three asks you to estimate before-tax cash from the disposal of the St. George after seven years. If you have not yet done so, please complete that assignment now. Using the format illustrated in Figures 11.1, 11.2, and 11.3 (or the format recommended by your instructor), extend the forecast to include after-tax cash flow from disposal, assuming that the gain on disposal will be taxed at 25% (if it represents unrecaptured depreciation) or 15% (if it is long-term capital gain).

Save your work from Case Problems 1 and 2. It will be needed to solve subsequent cases.

Case Problem

3. Shirly Chase, a founding partner in the firm of Dean and Howe, has a prospering professional practice. Chase has decided to investigate real estate as an estate-building mechanism and has asked you for advice concerning the property described below. You promptly arrange a consultation, at which time you obtain a retainer and determine the following facts:

   a. Chase's earnings from her professional practice are sufficient to place her firmly in the 35% marginal income tax bracket (combined federal and state). She expects this situation to continue into the indefinite future.

   b. Long-term capital gains are expected to be taxed at a 15% marginal tax rate.

   c. Chase has other investments but is in no danger of incurring liability for the AMT.

You investigate several properties that seem to fit Chase's needs and conclude that one seems particularly well suited to her investment picture. Information on the property, an apartment building, is as follows:

- Market value (and asking price) = $2,150,000
- Next year's expected gross income = $425,000
- Next year's expected operating expenses = $210,000
- Building value/total property value = 0.80
- Available mortgage = $1,600,000
- Mortgage terms: 9% interest, 25-year, fully amortizing note with monthly payments and a seven-year call provision. There is no penalty for prepayment and no loan origination fee.
- Operating forecast: Operating income and operating expenses alike are expected to increase at a compound annual rate of 3% for an indefinite period.
- Holding period: If Chase acquires the property, she will most likely sell after six years and pay off the balance of the mortgage note out of the sales proceeds.
- The gross income multiplier, which is expected to remain constant over the transaction costs associated with disposal after six years (at the end of her sixth year of ownership), are expected to be about 6% of the sales price.

Develop a comprehensive six-year after-tax cash-flow forecast for this property, including estimated after-tax cash from disposal.

PART FIVE

Measures of Investment Performance

Forecasting of after-tax cash flows from investment proposals, as discussed in Part One through Part Four, is a necessary step in rational investment decision making. In itself, however, forecasting is not sufficient. Investors must apply decision criteria to the forecasts.

Unit 12 surveys traditional approaches to the task. It explains the virtues and weaknesses of traditional techniques, which range from simple ratios between price and expected first-year revenue to more complex attempts that incorporate considerations such as income tax consequences and equity buildup.

Contemporary techniques require a basic understanding of the mathematics of compound interest and discount. Readers who lack this background should study Appendix A before venturing further into Part Five. Units 13 and 14 use the mathematical techniques from Appendix A to present a state-of-the-art investment decision model.

UNIT 12

Traditional Measures of Investment Worth

UNIT PREVIEW

Investment analysts must sift through a veritable mountain of informational chaff to glean intelligence for rational decision making. Approaches range from snap judgments based on little more than hot tips to careful and time-consuming analysis of reams of financial and economic data. Investors often compromise by using rules of thumb based on past experience or benchmark measures of profitability based on market observation.

This unit introduces the most traditional techniques. It proceeds from popular ratios measuring profit/price relationships and operating results to more complex tools used extensively by those educated in traditional real estate investment analysis. It then introduces more advanced techniques that are explored at length in subsequent units.

RATIO ANALYSIS

Ratios are widely used to gauge the reasonableness of relationships between various measures of value and performance: income multipliers express the relationship between market value and operating income; operating ratios highlight the relationship between gross income and operating expenses; break-even ratios show the percentage of gross income required to meet cash expenditure requirements; and debt-coverage ratios show the relationship between NOI and debt-service obligations.

Income Multiplier Analysis

Income multiplier analysis is a simple technique whose contemporary usefulness belies its antiquity. It highlights the relationship between price and either gross or net income. For single-family rental properties, monthly income is often used in the analysis; for all other properties, the convention is to use annual income.

Multipliers do not serve as sufficient tools of analysis in isolation, but they enable analysts to quickly and inexpensively weed out obviously unacceptable proposals. More extensive (and more costly) analysis can then be concentrated on properties that show greater promise. To use multiplier analysis as a filter, first determine the relationship prevailing in the market area. Then automatically reject all opportunities whose multipliers exceed this benchmark figure. Subject only those opportunities that pass the preliminary screening test to further analysis.

Example 12.1

An investment opportunity that costs $100,000 and requires a 25% down payment is expected to yield the following operating results during the first year:

Potential gross rent	$27,000
Less: Allowance for vacancies and rent loss	1,000
Effective gross income	$26,000
Less: Operating expenses	13,000
Net Operating income	$13,000

Other relevant information includes the following:

- There is a $75,000, 25-year mortgage loan available that requires equal monthly payments with interest at 6% per annum (monthly payments are $483.23; annual debt service is $5,798.76).
- Best estimates indicate that the property will increase in market value at a compound rate of about 5% per annum.
- The investor is subject to a combined federal and state marginal income tax rate of 40%.

Gross Income Multipliers

Also referred to as *gross rent multipliers*, *gross income multipliers* highlight the relationship between a property's price and its gross income. The effective gross income multiplier in Example 12.1 is 3.85:

$$\text{gross income multiplier} = \frac{\text{market price}}{\text{effective gross income}} = \frac{\$100{,}000}{\$26{,}000} = 3.85$$

Analysts who use gross income multipliers must decide whether to focus on potential gross rent or effective gross income. The determining factor is likely to be data availability. When information on vacancy rates and credit losses is unreliable and difficult to verify, the most appropriate measure might be potential gross rent. Using potential gross rent, the gross multiplier in Example 12.1 is approximately 3.7:

$$\text{gross income multiplier} = \frac{\text{market price}}{\text{potential gross income}} = \frac{\$100{,}000}{\$27{,}000} = 3.7$$

Net Income Multipliers

Calculated the same way as gross multipliers, *net income multipliers* express the relationship between value and NOI. They differ from gross multipliers only in their use of net instead of gross income. For Example 12.1, the net income multiplier is 7.69:

$$\text{net income multiplier} = \frac{\text{market price}}{\text{net operating income}} = \frac{\$100{,}000}{\$13{,}000} = 7.69$$

Financial Ratio Analysis

To facilitate comparisons between properties, ratio analysis is frequently used. Commonly encountered examples include the operating ratio, the break-even ratio, and the debt-coverage ratio.

Operating ratio

The percentage of effective gross income consumed by operating expenses is expressed as an *operating ratio*. However, the operating ratio can be misleading because it reflects, in part, the efficiency of management as well as of the property itself. An extremely low operating ratio may be an indication that managers have not spent proper monies to keep the property maintained, which means repairs are necessary; this is also known as deferred maintenance. Some investors look for properties with high operating ratios, intending to reduce the ratios through efficient management and thereby increase indicated property values. The operating ratio for Example 12.1 is 52%:

$$\text{operating ratio} = \frac{\text{operating expenses}}{\text{effective gross income}} = \frac{\$13,000}{\$26,000} = 0.50 \text{ or } 50\%$$

Break-even ratio

Sometimes called *default ratios*, *break-even ratios* are most useful when used on a before-tax cash-flow basis. They indicate the relationship between cash inflows and outflows from all sources. The lower the break-even ratio, the greater the decline in gross revenue (or the increase in operating expenses) can be before investors experience negative cash flow from a project. Applying the formula to the project in Example 12.1, the ratio is 72.30%:

$$\text{break even ratio} = \frac{\text{operating expense} + \text{debt service}}{\text{effective gross income}} = \frac{\$13,000 + \$5,798.76}{\$26,000}$$
$$= 0.723 \text{ or } 72.3\%$$

Debt-coverage ratio

The *debt-coverage ratio* expresses the extent to which NOI can decline before it becomes insufficient to meet the debt-service obligation. This gives an indication of safety associated with the use of borrowed funds. The debt-coverage ratio in Example 12.1 is 2.24:

$$\text{debt coverage ratio} = \frac{\text{net operating income}}{\text{annual debt service}} = \frac{\$13,000}{\$5,798.76} = 2.24$$

TRADITIONAL PROFITABILITY MEASURES

A shared characteristic of all traditional profitability measures is an attempt to relate cash investment to expected cash returns in some systematic fashion. The techniques differ in the degree to which they incorporate available data. They differ also in that some ignore the issue of risk and others make rudimentary attempts to adjust for risk differentials.

Overall Capitalization Rate

Also known as the *free-and-clear rate of return*, the *overall capitalization rate* expresses the first year's expected NOI as a percentage of market price. The rate in Example 12.1 is 13%:

$$\text{overall capitalization rate} = \frac{\text{net operating income}}{\text{market price}} = \frac{\$13,000}{\$100,000} = 0.13 \text{ or } 13\%$$

Recall that the net income multiplier is price divided by NOI. The overall capitalization rate, therefore, is simply the reciprocal of the net income multiplier. The reciprocal of 0.13 is 7.69, which we saw earlier as the net income multiplier for Example 12.1.

In a typical negotiating session, there is an acknowledged trade-off between price and financing terms. Because this trade-off is not reflected in the overall capitalization rate, comparison of rates between properties with significantly different financing arrangements can be misleading. This limits the usefulness of overall capitalization rates as an investment analysis tool.

Equity Dividend Rate

A measure that does, to some extent, incorporate the effect of using borrowed money is the *equity dividend rate*. It compares equity cash flow with the amount of the equity investment. As generally calculated, the equity dividend rate expresses before-tax cash flow (NOI minus debt service) as a percentage of the required initial equity cash outlay (purchase price minus borrowed funds).

Calculating the equity dividend rate for the property in Example 12.1 requires prior determination of the *equity dividend* (NOI minus debt service) and the *initial equity investment* (purchase price plus purchase expenses minus mortgage loans). These calculations are as follows:

Equity dividend (before-tax cash flow):
Net operating income	$13,000
Less: Debt service	5,799
Equity dividend	$7,201

Initial cash outlay:
Purchase price	$100,000
Plus: Purchase expenses	5,000
Less: Available mortgage	75,000
Initial equity	$30,000

Using these values, the equity dividend rate applicable to Example 12.1 can be determined. It is 24%:

$$\text{equity dividend rate} = \frac{\text{before-tax cash flow}}{\text{initial cash outlay}} = \frac{\$7,201}{\$30,000} = 0.24 \text{ or } 24\%$$

The equity dividend rate's usefulness is limited because the analysis does not incorporate income tax considerations. Cash flow measured on a before-tax basis will be helpful in discriminating between investment opportunities only if the alternatives have reasonably similar income tax consequences.

To render it more useful, the measure, also called the *cash-on-cash rate of return*, can be calculated on an after-tax basis. The modified equation expresses the first year's expected net spendable cash (after all financing costs and income taxes) as a percentage of the initial cash investment.

If the property in Example 12.1 is acquired on the first day of the year, interest expense for the first year will be $4,464 (the procedure for determining this is explained in Unit 8). As explained in Unit 10, the depreciation or cost recovery allowance depends on several factors not given in the current example. For this illustration, simply assume the allowance to be $2,700. Combining these two bits of information with the projected NOI from Example 12.1 permits an estimate of the first year's income tax obligation:

Net operating income		$13,000
Less:		
Interest expense	$4,464	
Cost recovery allowance	2,700	7,164
Taxable income		$5,836
Times: Marginal tax rate		0.40
Income tax obligation		$2,334

After-tax cash flow to the equity position is the NOI minus debt service and income tax payments:

Net operating income	$13,000
Less: Debt-service obligation	5,799
Before-tax cash flow	$7,201
Less: Income tax (computed above)	2,334
After-tax cash flow	$4,867

With this information, the cash-on-cash rate of return for Example 12.1 can be calculated on an after-tax basis. The computation is:

$$\text{cash-on-cash return} = \frac{\text{after-tax cash flow}}{\text{equity investment}} = \frac{\$4,867}{\$30,000} = 0.16223 \text{ or } 16.22\%$$

Even with the inclusion of income tax consequences, this measure's usefulness is limited, because it fails to incorporate the impact on investment performance of changes in the property's value and of changes in after-tax cash flow through time. Rational analysis demands that all consequences for the projected holding period be included in the analysis.

Broker's Rate of Return

Seeking to cast the best possible image of a property they are trying to sell, brokers sometimes argue that the cash-on-cash rate of return should be modified to reflect the buildup of an investor's equity. The *broker's rate of return* adjusts the equity dividend or cash-on-cash rate to include both income tax consequences and equity buildup resulting from amortization of mortgage debt. This increases the indicated return to the equity position, making the property appear more attractive.

For the property in Example 12.1, the broker's indicated rate of return is 15.67%, determined as follows:

$$\text{broker's return} = \frac{\text{after-tax cash flow} + \text{equity buildup}}{\text{initial equity}} = \frac{\$4{,}867 + \$1{,}335}{\$30{,}000}$$
$$= 0.2067 \text{ or } 20.67\%$$

To after-tax cash flow plus equity buildup, some brokers add the anticipated rate of increase in property value. Making the broker's rate of return even higher further enhances the apparent attractiveness of the investment proposition.

Though widely used, the broker's rate of return is misleading. The important measure of potential cash flow from disposal is the difference between market value and remaining balance on mortgage indebtedness, less estimated brokerage commission and other transaction costs. Because this cash flow is not realized on an annual basis, but only on property sale, it is inconsistent to include equity buildup in the measure of annual cash flow.

Ratio Analysis for Maegan's Magic Manor

The ratios to analyze Maegan's Magic Manor Apartments can be developed from the figures in Figure 12.1.

FIGURE 12.1: Ratio Analysis for Maegan's Magic Manor

Ratio	Formula	Values	Result
Gross income multiplier	= Market price / Effective gross income	= $13,596,700 / $2,272,100	= 5.98
GIM using PGI	= Market price / Potential gross income	= $13,596,700 / $2,346,100	= 5.80
Net income multiplier	= Market price / Net operating income	= $13,596,700 / $1,265,700	= 10.74
Operating ratio	= Operating expenses / Effective gross income	= $1,006,400 / $2,272,100	= 44.29%
Break-even ratio	= (Operating expenses + Debt service) / Effective gross income	= (1,006,400 + 784,200) / 2,272,100	= 78.81%
Debt-coverage ratio	= Net operating income / Annual debt service	= $4,265,700 / $784,200	= 1.61
Overall capitalization rate	= Net operating income / Market price	= $1,265,700 / $13,596,700	= 9.31%
Equity dividend rate	= Before-tax cash flow / Initial cash outlay	= $481,500 / $4,246,700	= 11.34%
Cash-on-cash	= After-tax cash flow / Equity investment	= $334,900 / $4,246,700	= 7.89%
Broker's return	= (After-tax cash flow + Equity buildup) / Initial cash outlay	= ($260,300 + $200,800) / $4,246,700	= 10.86%
Equity buildup	= Annual debt service − Interest expense	= $784,200 − $515,800	= $268,400

Payback Period

One of the simplest and perhaps most common rules of thumb is to estimate the number of years required to recoup one's initial cash investment in a project. In *payback-period analysis*, alternative opportunities are ranked according to the time required for the anticipated cash proceeds to equal the initial cash investment.

When anticipated cash flow from a project is the same amount each year, the payback period can be calculated simply by dividing initial cash outlay by the expected annual cash flow. Thus, for a project that requires an initial cash outlay of $10,000 and is expected to yield an annual cash flow of $2,500, the payback period is four years:

$$\text{payback period} = \frac{\text{cash outlay}}{\text{annual cash flow}} = \frac{\$10,000}{\$2,500} = 4 \text{ years}$$

Of course, expected cash flow from real estate is seldom the same from year to year. Consequently, payback-period calculations are not as straightforward as the example suggests. In most instances, the period must be determined by summing expected proceeds from year to year until the total equals initial outlay.

Example 12.2 illustrates the procedure. The third column is simply the summation of all after-tax cash-flow estimates from the second column. With required equity investment of $48,330, the initial equity expenditure is expected to have been fully recovered at some point during the sixth year. Therefore, the payback period (expressed in whole years) is six years.

Example 12.2

A property can be acquired with an initial equity expenditure (i.e., a down payment) of $48,330. Annual after-tax cash flows are expected to be as indicated in the second column below. Anticipated cumulative cash flows are indicated in the third column.

Year	After-Tax Cash Flow	
	Current Year	Cumulative
1	$7,145	$7,145
2	$8,185	$15,330
3	$9,222	$24,552
4	$10,171	$34,723
5	$11,115	$45,838
6	$12,054	$57,892
7	$12,895	$70,787

The appeal of payback-period analysis is its apparent simplicity and its adaptability as a policy tool. Investors can specify a maximum payback period for real estate of a specific type or in a given location, based on their perceptions of associated risks. Many investors still use the payback period before calculating other more complex measures. If all the cash flows of an investment, including sale proceeds, never pay back its initial investment, it is not a good investment and needs no further analysis. Payback period is also a good technique for investors who are in a hurry to get cash flows.

One major shortcoming of this method is that it ignores all cash flows beyond the payback period. This failure will cause assets with poor appreciation prospects to look more promising than those with potential for growth in value over the holding period. A second problem is that the method fails to discriminate among cash flows with different timing, even during the payback period. A project with most of the benefits in the early years would look no better than one offering the same total benefit spread evenly over the entire payback period, or with the bulk of its cash flow in later years. The time value of money is thus ignored, and the project with the greatest potential return may not be chosen. A solution to the time value drawback is discounted payback where the initial cash investment is paid back with discounted (present value) annual cash flows.

ADJUSTMENTS FOR MORE RATIONAL ANALYSIS

In order to understand the shortcomings of traditional investment performance measures, we need first to review the major components of expected return. There is of course an initial equity cash commitment, for which the investor expects to receive cash flow from operations during the holding period and cash from disposal on termination of the investment position. Five major factors interact to govern the relative attractiveness of investment proposals:

- The amount and timing of the initial cash commitment
- The amount and timing of expected net cash inflows
- The certainty with which expectations are held
- Yields available from other investments
- The investor's attitude toward risk

Regardless of particular investor predispositions, anticipated investment benefits must be adjusted for quantity, quality, and timing. *Quantity* refers to the amount of expected net cash flows, after incorporating all income tax consequences and adjusting for debt-service obligations arising from financial leverage. *Quality* refers to the certainty with which these expectations are held. *Timing* refers to when the forecasted net cash flows are expected to be received. These factors must be evaluated in terms of risk-adjusted yields available from other investments (the opportunity cost of capital) and the investor's attitude toward bearing risk.

The ideal measure of profitability would incorporate all these elements. A common weakness of traditional profitability measures is that they ignore the question of timing of net cash inflows. For this reason, they have become mere adjuncts to time-adjusted measures.

Time-Adjusted Return Measures

Time-adjusted techniques discount expected future cash flows to make them more nearly comparable with those receivable in the present. Some techniques adjust purely for the time value of money, while others include an adjustment for risk. One popular version takes the adjustment factor as a variable that equates future and present cash flows. All these measures are considered in Unit 13.

SUMMARY

Traditional techniques for evaluating investments include ratios for comparing income with market price and ratios for evaluating profitability and financial risk. They also include several measures of profitability designed to compare anticipated cash flows with required initial cash expenditures. These traditional techniques are useful as filters, but none of them properly accounts for the time value of money. This is a serious flaw because the timing of cash inflows and outflows is a major element in the comparative desirability of investment alternatives. Time-adjusted measures of return are an essential tool of rational investment analysis.

RECOMMENDED READING

American Institute of Real Estate Appraisers. *The Appraisal of Real Estate.* 14th ed. Chicago: Appraisal Institute, 2013.

Fisher, Jeffrey D., and Robert S. Martin. *Income Property Appraisal*, 3rd ed. Chicago: Dearborn Real Estate Education, 2008.

Ventolo, William L., and Martha R. Williams. *Fundamentals of Real Estate Appraisal.* 12th ed. Chicago: Dearborn Real Estate Education, 2015.

INTERNET REFERENCES

For information on worth measures:
www.appraisalinstitute.org

REVIEW QUESTIONS

1. How are income multipliers used in measuring investment worth?
2. Why might some investors search out properties with high operating ratios?
3. What is a characteristic common to all traditional profitability measures? What are the weaknesses in these forms of measurement?
4. Compare the concept of the overall capitalization rate with the equity dividend rate.
5. How is the broker's rate of return calculated? What is its major drawback?
6. List major factors governing the relative attractiveness of a real estate investment.
7. List the advantages and disadvantages of using the payback period as a measure of investment worth.

DISCUSSION QUESTIONS

1. Which traditional ratios used in real estate analysis are most closely related to the following concepts used in stock market analysis?
   a. Dividend yield
   b. Price-earnings ratio
2. What impact might the inflation rate have on the usefulness of traditional profitability measures such as the cash-on-cash return, payback period, and equity dividend rate?

PROBLEM

1. A 28-unit apartment building is offered for sale at $325,000. If it is purchased for the asking price, subject to its existing $204,500 mortgage loan balance, an investor in the 28% marginal income tax bracket can expect the following outcome during the first full year of ownership:

Potential gross rent	$74,760
Plus: Miscellaneous income	420
	$75,180
Less: Vacancy allowance	3,759
Effective gross income	$71,421
Less: Operating expenses	40,060
Net operating income	$31,361
Less: Debt service	25,334
Before-tax cash flow	$6,027
Plus: Principal paid	837
Less: Cost recovery allowance	9,060
Taxable income (loss)	($2,196)
Times: Marginal tax rate	0.28
Income tax (tax savings)	($615)
Before-tax cash flow	$6,027
Plus: Tax savings	615
After-tax cash flow	$6,642

Based on the first-year forecast and assuming the property is purchased for the asking price, compute the following:

a. The potential gross income multiplier
b. The net income multiplier
c. The operating ratio
d. The break-even ratio
e. The debt-coverage ratio
f. The overall capitalization rate
g. The cash-on-cash rate of return
h. The broker's rate of return

UNIT 13

Discounted Cash-Flow Analysis

UNIT PREVIEW

Modern investment analysis is a practical application of the economic theory of the firm, which states that one should operate at the point where marginal revenue equals marginal cost. Translated into the language of investment analysis, this means ventures are acceptable as long as the rate of return on an investment at least equals the cost of investable funds.

This unit considers at length two common applications of the basic decision criterion: present value and IRR. Both have merit as investment analysis techniques, both can be supported with compelling logical arguments, and several variations of each have been developed in the literature.

PRESENT VALUE

Present value, discussed in detail in Appendix A, is the value today of benefits that are expected to accrue in the future. It is derived by adjusting all anticipated future cash flows at a predetermined rate per time period. A present value in excess of the required initial equity cash outlay means a project is expected to yield a rate of return in excess of the discount rate used. If the discount rate is the minimum acceptable rate of return, this implies that the project is worthy of further consideration. A present value that is less than the required initial equity expenditure results in automatic rejection.

To use this approach, discount all anticipated future cash flows at the minimum acceptable rate of return. The result is the present value of expected cash flows:

$$PV = \frac{CF_1}{(1+i)} + \frac{CF_2}{(1+i)^2} + \frac{CF_3}{(1+i)^3} + \cdots + \frac{CF_n}{(1+i)^n}$$

where i is the minimum acceptable (required) rate of return, n is the number of years in the projection period, $CF1$ is the cash flow expected in the first year, $CF2$ that for the second year, and so on, through the cash-flow expectation for year n. Alternatively, the formula can be expressed as

$$PV = \sum_{t=1}^{n} \frac{CF_t}{(1+i)^t}$$

where Σ simply means add together the values of $CF_t (1 + i)^t$, where the values of t range from one through n.

Example 13.1

An investment proposal is expected to generate $15,000 of after-tax cash flow each year for eight years and $35,000 of after-tax cash flow from disposal at the end of the eighth year. The required equity cash outlay to acquire the asset is $90,000. The minimum acceptable rate of return is 10%.

UNIT 13 Discounted Cash-Flow Analysis

In Example 13.1, the present value is approximately $98,684:

Year	Expected Cash Flow	Present Value Factor (Rounded)	Present Value at 10% (Rounded)
1	$15,000	0.909091	$13,636
2	$15,000	0.826446	12,397
3	$15,000	0.751315	11,270
4	$15,000	0.683013	10,245
5	$15,000	0.620921	9,314
6	$15,000	0.564474	8,467
7	$15,000	0.513158	7,697
8	$50,000	0.466507	$23,325
Total			$96,351

CALCULATOR APPLICATIONS

$PMT = 15{,}000$
$FV = 35{,}000$
$n = 8$
$i = 10$

Solve for present value:
$PV = 96{,}351.65$

NET PRESENT VALUE

Subtracting the required initial equity expenditure from the present value of projected cash flows yields net present value (NPV). A positive NPV means a project increases the investor's wealth in current value dollars and is expected to yield a rate of return in excess of the discount rate and therefore merits further consideration. An NPV of less than zero means that the project is expected to yield a rate of return less than the minimum acceptable rate and therefore should be rejected.

Discounting at the minimum acceptable rate of 10%, the NPV of anticipated cash flows from the investment opportunity described in Example 13.1 is approximately $8,684:

Present value of future cash flows (rounded)	$96,351
Less: Initial cash outlay	90,000
Net present value	$6,351

Because this is greater than zero, the expected rate of return exceeds the 10% minimum acceptable rate, and the project merits further consideration.

INTERNAL RATE OF RETURN

Because—as explained in Appendix A—there is an inverse relationship between discount rates and present value, there must be some rate that will exactly equate the present value of a projected stream of cash flows with any positive initial cash investment. This rate is known as the *internal rate of return,* or IRR. The equation for the IRR is:

$$0 = \sum_{t=1}^{n} \left[\frac{CF_t}{(1+k)^t} \right] - \text{initial cash outlay}$$

where CF_t is the cash flow projected for year t and k is the discount rate that satisfies the equality condition. All the terms in the equation are taken as known except k, for which the appropriate value is determined.

Consider a project expected to yield a cash-flow stream, CF_1, CF_2, ..., CF_n over n future periods. The IRR is simply a rate k such that if the initial cash outlay were deposited at an interest rate equaling that rate for each period, withdrawing the amount CF_1 at the end of period 1, CF_2 at the end of period 2, and so on through CF_n at the end of period n would exactly exhaust the fund at the end of the nth period.

If the IRR is equal to or greater than an investor's required rate of return, a project warrants further consideration. If the IRR is less than the minimum acceptable rate of return, the project is rejected.

In Example 13.1, the IRR is approximately 11.6%. This is determined by trial and error, using successive approximations of the appropriate discount rate. Cash flows are discounted using a financial calculator or financial tables. Tables are considerably more awkward to use than calculators because the calculator program of successive approximations must be replicated manually by table users.

CALCULATOR APPLICATIONS

PMT = 15,000
FV = 35,000
n   = 8
PV = −90,000

Solve for interest rate:

i = 11.63%

Because annual cash flow from operations in Example 13.1 represents a level annuity, an annuity table would be used if a financial calculator were not available. The table would be used to calculate the present value of the final sum expected in year eight.

Discounting at 11%, the present value of all expected cash flows equals approximately $92,379. This is somewhat more than the initial cash outlay required, so the IRR must be slightly more than 11%. Discounting again at the next higher rate for which the table provides factors, the present value at 12% is seen to be approximately $88,651, slightly less than the initial cash outlay. Interpolating between 11% and 12%, as described in Appendix A, reveals the rate that equates the present value of expected future cash flows with the required initial outlay, approximately 11.6% (some error is introduced in the interpolation process).

Having calculated IRR based on expected cash flows in Example 13.1, the investor compares the result with the required rate of return. Because the IRR exceeds the required rate (11.6% versus 10%), the project is further considered. Ultimate acceptance or rejection depends on estimates of relative riskiness and on the relative attractiveness of alternative investment opportunities.

The major distinction between the IRR approach and the present value approach is that the latter requires that a predetermined discount rate be introduced early in the analysis. This difference, however, is more illusory than substantive as an argument for one method over the other. Those who use the IRR technique must specify some minimal threshold rate against which the internal rate of return is measured, to determine its acceptability. IRR users, therefore, delay but do not escape the necessity of estimating an investor's required rate of return.

Decision criteria based on IRR analysis can easily be expressed in present value or NPV terms. IRR thus appears to have little to recommend it over alternative techniques based on the same discounting concept.

Problems with the Internal Rate of Return

While the IRR has no substantive advantage over alternative methods of applying discount rates to projected cash flows, it does have serious weaknesses not found in the alternatives. Persistent support of a flawed technique might be admirable were there no substitutes that possessed equal power to discriminate between acceptable and unacceptable opportunities. Such is not the case, however, with the IRR approach. Its continued advocacy is therefore somewhat curious. Austin Jaffe has suggested a possible explanation. He notes that research and debate in the real estate literature tend to lag behind general financial analysis literature by a number of years. Real estate analysts are perhaps now debating an issue that has long been resolved by those in the financial and economics mainstream.[1]

Problems associated with the IRR can result in conflicting decision signals from this and other discounted cash-flow approaches. Generally, such a conflict arises

---

[1] Austin Jaffe, "Is There a 'New' Internal Rate of Return Literature?" Real Estate Economics, 5:4, 482–502.

because the IRR signal is distorted. If heeded, it might result in serious investment error. Potential dissonance stems from peculiarities of the IRR equation, which can yield more than one solution, and from problems associated with the reinvestment assumption inherent in choices among alternative investments that exhibit different patterns of anticipated after-tax cash flows.

The reinvestment rate problem

Interproject comparisons using IRR analysis involves an implicit assumption that funds are reinvested at the IRR. The IRR method reliably discriminates among alternatives only if other acceptable opportunities expected to yield an equally high rate are available. This, of course, is an unlikely prospect when the IRR is considerably above the opportunity cost of capital.

Example 13.2

An investor must select from two alternatives that require equal initial cash outlays and have identical time horizons. Expected cash flows from the alternatives are as follows:

	Investment Alternative	
	A	B
Initial equity expenditure	$10,694	$10,694
Net cash inflow, Year 1	$7,000	$0
Net cash inflow, Year 2	$7,000	$14,890

Consider the investment alternatives in Example 13.2. IRR analysis makes alternative A seem more desirable than B. This is because alternative A has an IRR of approximately 20%, whereas B's internal rate of return approximates only 18%. To satisfy yourself that this is so, discount the cash flows from each project at these rates and note that the present value of anticipated future cash flows in each case approximates the required $10,694 initial equity expenditure.

CALCULATOR APPLICATIONS

A
PMT = 7,000
FV = 0
n   = 2
PV = −10,694

Solve for interest rate:
i = 20.00%

B
PMT = 0
FV = 14,890
n   = 2
PV = −10,694

Solve for interest rate:
i = 18.00

If cash flows during the holding period can be reinvested at 20%, then alternative A will indeed result in a total return of 20% per annum over the two-year period. To see this, consider the cumulative cash that results if the first year's $7,000 cash flow is in fact reinvested at 20%. It will grow to $8,400 in one year. When this is added to the $7,000 to be received at the end of the second year, the cumulative total is $15,400. Discounting this amount over a two-year period at 20% yields a present value equal to the $10,694 initial equity expenditure. Here are the computations (terminal value is the future value of all intermediate cash flows when compounded forward, at a designated rate, to the end of the investment holding period):

Terminal value of cash inflow with 20% reinvestment rate:

Year 1 (cash Inflow $7,000)	$8,400
Year 2 (cash Inflow $7,000)	7,000
Cumulative terminal value at 20%	$15,400
Times: Present value factor at 20%	0.6944
Present value of $15,400 due in two years	$10,694
Less: Initial cash outlay	10,694
Net present value at 20%	$0

CALCULATOR APPLICATIONS

PV = 7,000
n = 1
i   = 20

Solve for future value:
FV = 8,400

FV = 15,400
n = 2
i   = 20

Solve for present value:
PV = 10,694

If the first year's net cash flow from alternative A is reinvested at any rate less than 12.7%, the yield on invested funds over the two-year period will be less than the IRR on alternative B. Suppose, for example, that the best return available on funds reinvested at the end of the first year is 10%. The total return on alternative A for the two-year period will then be only 17.24%. Here is the arithmetic:

Terminal value of net cash flow with 10% reinvestment rate:

Year 1 (net cash flow $7,000)	$7,700
Year 2 (net cash flow $7,000)	7,000
Cumulative terminal value at 10%	$14,700
Times: Present value factor at 17.24%	0.7275
Present value of $14,700 due in two years	$10,694
Less: Initial equity outlay	10,694
Net present value at 17.24%	$0

> **CALCULATOR APPLICATIONS**
>
> PV = 7,000
> n = 1
> i = 10
>
> **Solve for future value:**
> FV = 7,700
> FV = 14,700
> n = 2
> i = 17.24
>
> **Solve for present value:**
> PV = 10,694.63
>
> (Calculator is more accurate due to rounding in the present value factor table)

The reinvestment rate problem also limits the usefulness of the IRR technique when choosing between alternatives that have different useful lives or different holding periods. If the indicated IRR is unrealistically high, reinvestment at that rate is not a reasonable assumption and the IRR will give an ambiguous decision signal.

Example 13.3 demonstrates this problem. Both investment alternatives have an expected 15% IRR, but they are equally desirable only if the reinvestment rate is also 15%. In that case, the yield over the five-year investment horizon will be exactly 15% with either alternative, as the following computations indicate:

	A	B
Terminal value of cash flow with 15% reinvestment rate		
Year 1 (reinvested for 4 years)	$17,490	$17,490
Year 2 (reinvested for 3 years)	15,209	15,209
Year 3 (reinvested for 2 years)	13,225	13,225
Year 4 (reinvested for 1 year)	0	11,500
Year 5 (reinvested for 0 years)	0	10,000
Totals	$45,924	$67,424
Times: Present value factor at 15%	0.49718	0.49718
Present value of terminal value at 15%	$22,832	$33,522
Less: Initial cash outlay	22,832	33,522
Net present value at 15%	$0	$0

CALCULATOR APPLICATIONS

A

$PV = 10{,}000$
$n = 4$
$i = 15$

Solve for future value:
$FV = 17{,}490$

$FV = 45{,}924$
$n = 5$
$i = 15$

Solve for present value:
$PV = 22{,}832.34$

B

$FV = 67{,}424$
$n = 5$
$i = 15$

Solve for present value:
$PV = 33{,}521.64$

(Calculator is more accurate due to rounding in the present value factor table)

Example 13.3

An investor must select from alternatives having the following cash-flow characteristics:

	Investment Alternative	
	A	B
Required initial cash outlay	$22,832	$33,522
Annual cash inflow first 3 years	$10,000	$10,000
Annual cash inflow years 4 and 5	$0	$10,000

UNIT 13 Discounted Cash-Flow Analysis

If the reinvestment rate is less than 15%, then alternative A will not offer an equally high total return over the five-year investment horizon. At a reinvestment rate of 10% per annum, for example, total return over the entire five-year period will be approximately 11.9% per annum for alternative A and approximately 12.7% for B. These computations are shown as follows:

	A	B
Terminal value of cash flow with 10% reinvestment rate		
Year 1 (reinvested for 4 years)	$14,641	$14,641
Year 2 (reinvested for 3 years)	13,310	13,310
Year 3 (reinvested for 2 years)	12,100	12,100
Year 4 (reinvested for 1 year)	0	11,000
Year 5 (reinvested for 0 years)	0	10,000
Terminal value of all cash flows	$40,051	$61,051
Approximate discount rate to equate Terminal value with initial cash outlay	11.9%	12.7%

CALCULATOR APPLICATIONS

A
$PV = 10,000$
$n = 4$
$i = 10$

Solve for future value:
$FV = 14,641$
$FV = 40,051$
$n = 5$
$PV = -22,832$

Solve for interest rate:
$i = 11.8958\%$

B

$FV = 61,051$
$n = 5$
$i = -33,522$

Solve for interest rate:
$i = 12.7386\%$

The multiple-solutions problem

Generally, a project's NPV is a decreasing function of the discount rate used. With successively higher discount rates, a point is reached where the NPV becomes zero. This rate is the IRR, and any higher discount rate will result in a negative NPV. When the discounting equation is well behaved in this fashion, there is but one IRR, one discount rate that equates all cash inflows with all cash outflows.

Unfortunately, not all cash-flow forecasts are this accommodating. Investment proposals may have any number of IRRs, depending on the pattern of anticipated cash flows. It is possible to have as many IRRs as the number of reversals in sign (positive to negative or vice versa) of the cash-flow stream. Yet sign reversals are a common characteristic of cash-flow streams from real estate projects. Junior mortgage financing often requires a balloon payment (i.e., a final payment—substantially larger than the regular debt service—that retires the remaining balance). Net cash flow will usually be negative in the year the junior mortgage note matures. For each sign reversal, there is an additional solution to the IRR equation. Most of these alternative solutions will be outside the realm of real numbers, and there is but one IRR solution. It is possible, however, for multiple solutions to fall within the realm of real numbers.

Eugene F. Brigham presents a simple illustration by citing a coal-mining firm's analysis of an open-pit mining operation that requires an initial cash outlay of $4.4 million and is expected to generate positive cash flow of $27.7 million during the first year of operations. During the second year, in accordance with state and federal regulations, land will be returned to its "natural" state at an estimated cost of $25 million. This cash-flow pattern generates two IRR solutions: 9.2% and 420%.[2]

---

[2] Eugene F. Brigham and Michael C. Ehrhardt, *Financial Management: Theory and Practice*, 11th ed. (Ft. Worth, Texas: South-Western College Publishers, 2004).

COMPARING NET PRESENT VALUE AND INTERNAL RATE OF RETURN

Under most circumstances, the IRR and NPV approaches will give the same decision signals. When this occurs, there is little significance in the choice of one over the other. The rules are as follows:

- When using IRR, reject all projects whose IRR is less than the minimum required rate. Projects with an IRR equal to or greater than the minimum acceptable rate (the *hurdle rate*) are further considered.
- When using NPV, discount at the minimum acceptable rate of return and reject all projects with an NPV of less than zero. Projects with an NPV of zero or greater are further considered.

The essential similarity of these decision criteria is reflected in their mathematical formulation. The only structural difference is the discount rate. Remember that the discount rate used in the IRR is the effective yield; the NPV will be exactly zero when the IRR equals the minimum required rate of return.

There are, however, some conditions under which contradictory signals emerge. We have seen that the two techniques may rank alternatives in different order. Because investors must often choose among alternatives rather than make a simple choice to accept or reject one investment, this can be a serious problem. Limited equity funds frequently dictate choice from among several opportunities, all of which may meet minimum acceptance criteria. Inconsistent rank-ordering can occur where projects differ in the size of the initial investment or in the timing of cash receipts and disbursements.

Where IRR and NPV analysis give different decision signals, results of NPV analysis are usually preferred. This follows from most financial analysts having accepted the idea that investors should strive to maximize their wealth. Doubters are referred to an extensive discussion of the relative merits of these approaches by authors generally acknowledged as eminent authorities as well as pioneers in the theoretical aspects of capital budgeting methodology.[3]

APPROACHES TO SHORE UP INTERNAL RATE OF RETURN

Numerous attempts have been made to modify the IRR to eradicate the multiple solutions and reinvestment rate dilemmas. Three approaches are particularly worth noting for their ingenuity, if not for their usefulness. None eliminates the serious problem of failure to consistently give solutions consonant with the objective of maximizing investor wealth.

Modified Internal Rate of Return

One approach, called a *modified internal rate of return* (MIRR), solves the multiple root problem by discounting all negative cash flows back to the time at which the investment is acquired and compounding all positive cash flows forward to the end

---

[3] See, for example, Harold Bierman, Jr., and Seymour Smidt, *The Capital Budgeting Decision,* 9th ed. (Upper Saddle River, N.J.: Prentice Hall, 2007).

of the final year of the holding period. This eliminates all sign changes and allows a unique solution.

Example 13.4 incorporates a numerical illustration developed by James H. Lorie and Leonard J. Savage to demonstrate the problem.[4] Discounting future cash flows at either 25% or 400% yields an NPV of exactly zero; both are indicated IRRs. Because there is no unique solution, there is no "correct" IRR.

Example 13.4

An investment proposition requires an initial cash expenditure of $1,600 and is expected to generate a net cash flow of $10,000 at the end of one year. Due to income tax and mortgage financing factors, the venture is expected to yield a negative $10,000 when terminated at the end of the second year.

Proponents of the MIRR would eliminate the double-solution problem by discounting negative cash flows back to year zero and compounding positive cash flows forward to the end of the investment holding period. For Example 13.4, if we assume an opportunity cost of capital (the presumed appropriate rate for the discounting) of 20%, there results an 18.51% discount rate, which equates the positive terminal value with the negative initial amount. First, discount the second year's anticipated negative cash flow back to the time of the initial cash outlay and sum its (negative) present value with the $1,600 expenditure actually encountered at that time:

Cash expected in year 2	($10,000)
Times: Present value factor for two years at 20%	0.69444
Present value of second year's cash flow	($6,944)
Plus: Initial cash flow	(1,600)
Initial value	($8,544)

Now compound the first year's anticipated positive cash flow forward to the end of year two, again at the presumed 20% opportunity cost of capital. This yields a terminal value of $12,000 (see Figure 13.1).

Cash expected in year 1	$10,000
Times: Compound value factor for one year at 20%	1.2
Terminal value	$12,000

There remains only to find a discount rate that will make $12,000 due in two years have a present value of $8,544. A quick calculator computation yields a MIRR of approximately 18.5%.

---

4   James H. Lorie and Leonard J. Savage, "Three Problems in Rationing Capital," *Journal of Business* (October 1955): 229–39.

CALCULATOR APPLICATIONS

FV = 12,000
n = 2
PV = –8,544

Solve for interest rate:
i = 18.51%

In addition to its intimidating complexity, this technique is extremely sensitive to variations in the rate chosen for preliminary discounting and compounding. To see this, repeat the exercise related to Example 13.4, using 10% as the appropriate rate. Now try 15%. You will find the MIRRs to be approximately 5.6% and 12%, respectively.

FIGURE 13.1: MIRR Example Using 20% Discount Rate

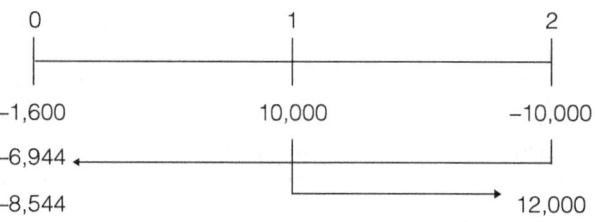

CALCULATOR APPLICATIONS

FV = 10,000	FV = 10,000
n = 2	n = 2
i = 10	i = 15
Solve for present value:	**Solve for present value:**
PV = 8,264 + 1,600 = 9,864	PV = 7,561 + 1,600 = 9,161
FV = 11,000	FV = 11,500
n = 2	n = 2
PV = –9,864	i = –9,161
Solve for interest rate:	**Solve for interest rate:**
i = 5.60%	i = 12.04%

Adjusted Rate of Return

Adjusted rates of return are particularly well explained by Donald Valachi.[5] Assuming cash flows as described in Example 13.4, Valachi suggests that an investor has in essence "borrowed" $10,000 from the project at the end of year one and repaid the "loan" at the end of year two. Assuming a reinvestment rate of 20%, the first year's $10,000 cash flow will have grown to $12,000 by the end of the second year. Offsetting this against the $10,000 net outflow at the end of the second year yields a net terminal value of $2,000. The discount rate that gives this $2,000 terminal value a present value equal to the $1,600 initial cash expenditure is approximately 11.8% (there are actually two roots; the other is a negative 2.1%).

CALCULATOR APPLICATIONS

$FV = 2,000$
$n = 2$
$PV = -1,600$

Solve for interest rate:
$i = 11.80\%$

This technique works well for the cash flows illustrated in Example 13.4, but consider the following series.[6]

Initial cash outlay	$1,000
Cash flow in year 1	$6,000
Cash flow in year 2	($11,000)
Cash flow in year 3	$6,000

This cash-flow pattern produces IRR solutions of 0%, 100%, and 200%. Because it is unlikely that year one's cash flow will be compounded at a rate high enough to allow it to cover year two's negative cash flow, some other course of action is necessary. One might "borrow" from year three by discounting part of that cash flow back to year two. Or one might discount all of year three's cash flow back to year two and compound only part of year one's cash flow forward. The results of these alternatives are two drastically different adjusted IRRs. As VRMs became increasingly commonplace, cash flows more frequently alternated between negative and positive, and rules needed to apply the adjusted rate of return became devilishly complex.

---

[5] Donald J. Valachi, "More on the Arithmetic of Multiple and Imaginary Rates of Return," *Real Estate Appraiser and Analyst* (September-October 1980): 19–20.

[6] These numbers are taken from an example propounded by James C. Van Horne in *Financial Management and Policy*, 4th ed. (Englewood Cliffs, N.J.: Prentice Hall, 1977), 105.

Financial Management Rate of Return

M. Chapman Findley and Stephen D. Messner have developed a widely publicized variation on the IRR, called the *financial management rate of return*. Their version incorporates two intermediate rates, one a cost of capital rate used to discount negative cash flows back to year zero and the other a specified reinvestment rate for compounding positive cash flows to the end of the projection period. Interested readers will do well to start their research with a study of articles by Michael Young and H. S. Kerr, both of whom provide definite critiques of the model.[7]

Discounted Cash-Flow Analysis of Maegan's Magic Manor

NPV and IRR can be calculated from the figures in Figure 10.2 and assuming the investor has a hurdle rate of 15%. After-tax cash flows are assumed to occur at the end of each year. Monthly cash flows would require discounting at a monthly rate.

	After-Tax Cash Flow	Present Value at 15% (rounded)
Year 1	$334,900	$291,217
Year 2	$439,300	332,174
Year 3	$490,500	322,512
Year 4	$445,300	254,602
Year 5	$476,900	237,104
Year 6	$8,172,700*	$3,533,284
Total present value of future cash flows:		$4,970,893
Less: Initial cash outlay		4,246,700
Net present value		$724,193

*Combined Year 6 after-tax cash flow ($502,800) plus after-tax sales proceeds ($7,669,900).

Because the NPV is positive, the expected rate of return exceeds the 15% minimum acceptable rate, and the project is a good one. With an NPV greater than zero, we know that the IRR is greater than the hurdle rate of 15%. The IRR is 18.64% when solved on a financial calculator.

---

[7] Michael Young, "FMRR: A Clever Hoax?" *Appraisal Journal* 47 (July 1979): 359–69; H. S. Kerr, "A Final Word on FMRR," *Appraisal Journal* 48 (January 1980): 95–103.

SUMMARY

Modern investment evaluation techniques generally involve some variation of a discounted cash-flow model expressing the present value of all anticipated future cash flows. Most common are the IRR and the present value/net present value models. The IRR model is conceptually appealing to many, but it contains flaws that make it less desirable than the present value/net present value approach.

RECOMMENDED READING

Besley, Scott, and Eugene F. Brigham. *Essentials of Managerial Finance.* 14th ed. Ft. Worth, Tex.: South-Western College Publishers, 2007.

Bierman, Harold, Jr., and Seymour Smidt. *The Capital Budgeting Decision.* 9th ed. Upper Saddle River, N.J.: Prentice Hall, 2007.

Karathanassis, G.A. "Re-Examination of the Reinvestment Rate Assumptions." *Managerial Finance* 30, no. 10: 63–69.

INTERNET REFERENCE

For information on performance measures:
www.appraisalinstitute.org

REVIEW QUESTIONS

1. Under what conditions will a project be rejected when using present value in investment decision making?
2. Describe the internal rate of return.
3. What assumption is made about reinvestment of cash flows in net present value calculations? In internal rate of return calculations?
4. What is the major difference between the internal rate of return approach and the present value approach?
5. Under what conditions might the internal rate of return yield multiple solutions?
6. List some conditions under which the present value and the internal rate of return might yield conflicting decision signals. When this occurs, which should be selected?
7. What are the advantages and disadvantages of the modified internal rate of return, the adjusted rate of return, and the financial management rate of return?
8. What is the difference between present value and net present value?

DISCUSSION QUESTIONS

1. What is the relationship among present value, net present value, and internal rate of return? Is there a consistent relationship at all possible values for these measures? Explain.

2. If you were judging the extent to which a financial consultant exercised due diligence in evaluating an investment proposal, would you be influenced by the consultant's choice between internal rate of return and present value as an evaluation methodology? Explain why or why not.

3. Because cash-flow projections and cost of capital estimates are, at best, inexact in most cases, does it make a practical difference whether an analyst uses present value or internal rate of return as a decision criterion? Explain why or why not.

PROBLEMS

1. Henry can purchase a piece of land for $45,000 and lease it for a paintball range to net $4,000 a year. If Henry's opportunity cost/discount rate is 11% and he can sell the land in seven years for $60,000 net of selling expenses, is the land a good investment for Henry? Use NPV.

2. Use IRR to see if Henry's investment in Problem 1 is a good one.

UNIT 14

Investment Goals and Decision Criteria

UNIT PREVIEW

This unit examines methods for selecting a discount rate. It then explains how the discounted cash-flow technique might be applied to various categories of investment decisions and to the development of an investment negotiating strategy that uses the investment value concept introduced in Unit 1.

THE CHOICE OF A DISCOUNT RATE

Choice of the proper discount rate is critical when selecting among investment alternatives as well as when deciding which opportunities merit additional consideration. Analysts who use the IRR approach need not select a discount rate, but cannot totally avoid the issue. They still must decide on a minimum acceptable rate of return as a yardstick against which to measure the IRR.

Minor adjustments in the rate used to discount the cash flows can result in dramatic changes in NPV. The further into the future cash-flow projections are made, the greater the influence of discount rate variations. Moreover, relative rankings of opportunities can be changed by altering the discount rate when opportunities differ in the timing of anticipated cash flows.

Example 14.1 illustrates how relative rankings can be altered when a different discount rate is used. At a 15% discount rate, respective NPVs are $25,469 and $23,592 and project A appears preferable to project B. But at a rate of 14% the relative rankings are switched, with project B's revised NPV of $34,872 being preferable to project A's new NPV of $30,403. Thus, with a discount rate of 14% or less, project B appears more desirable, while project A is more desirable with discount rates of 15% or more.

Example 14.1

An investor must choose between two projects, both of which require an initial equity expenditure of $100,000. Project A is expected to generate $25,000 of after-tax cash flow each year for 10 years, after which the assets will be worthless. Project B offers a projected $500,000 of after-tax cash flow, all of which is expected to be received at the end of the 10th year of ownership.

The Summation Technique

One of the earliest methods proposed for developing discount rates is the *summation technique* and is based on the proposition that investors seek compensation for deferring consumption, for bearing risk, for sacrificing liquidity, and for portfolio management. The sum of the compensation rates for each of these items is held to comprise the appropriate discount rate.

Figure 14.1 illustrates how the summation technique might be used to derive an estimate of a discount rate, if one knew the appropriate values for the various factors.

FIGURE 14.1: Real Estate Comparisons

Safe rate (risk-free)	0.120
Compensation for risk	0.020
Compensation for liquidity	0.015
Compensation for burden of management	0.001
Discount rate	0.156

The difficulty of estimating appropriate values is the major weakness of this technique. The greater the number of factors used, the greater is the opportunity for error.

The Risk-Adjusted Discount Rate

Realistic problems associated with estimating appropriate compensation for various components render the summation technique impractical. A frequently advocated alternative lumps compensation for all elements other than waiting (the safe, or risk-free, rate) into one "reduced form" rate, called a *risk premium*. The sum of the risk-free rate and the risk premium is held to be the appropriate discount rate.

The risk-free rate

The risk-free rate is compensation solely for waiting, with no premium for risk. The yield on extremely short-term Treasury bills issued by the federal government is frequently taken as a reasonable approximation of the risk-free rate. The risk of default is virtually zero, and the risk of loss in purchasing power due to inflation or loss of interest income due to illiquidity is small because of the short maturities.

The risk premium

The risk premium, an additional rate of return increment required to compensate for bearing risk, differs according to the investor's conception of a project's riskiness. The greater the perceived risk, the higher the discount rate used. The risk premium will typically consider risk issues and incorporate premiums for liquidity, maturity, and default. The acceptable trade-off between risk and return is a function of the individual investor's attitude toward risk.

The Marginal Cost of Capital

Textbooks in corporate finance generally advocate using *marginal cost of capital* as the appropriate discount rate.[1] The marginal cost of anything is the cost of one additional unit of the item. The marginal cost of capital, therefore, is the cost of an additional dollar of new funds. A problem arises in trying to apply this concept when funds are raised from more than one source because marginal cost from each source differs. Under such circumstances, some authorities recommend using several different

---

[1] See, for example, Eugene F. Brigham and Michael C. Ehrhardt, *Managerial Finance*, 11th ed. (Ft. Worth, Tex.: South-Western College Publishers, 2006).

discount rates, depending on the circumstances surrounding the decision.[2] Perhaps the most common solution is to apply a weighted average rate that incorporates the marginal cost of all sources, with the cost of each weighted in accordance with the percentage of total new capital to be generated from that source.

For most real estate projects, the cost of debt is easily identifiable, and this cost (expressed as annual debt service) is subtracted from gross income to arrive at an estimate of after-tax cash flow to equity investors. When treated in this manner, the cost of borrowed capital should not be incorporated into the discount rate. The marginal cost of equity capital then becomes the appropriate determinant of the discount rate.

The marginal cost of equity for corporations whose shares are actively traded is estimated by comparing earnings per share with the market price of the shares. For privately held corporations or noncorporate investors, no such market index is available, and marginal cost of capital is a difficult concept to apply. Under those circumstances, the opportunity cost of equity capital is a more meaningful basis for determining the appropriate discount rate.

The Opportunity Cost of Capital

The question facing an analyst is this: What rate of return can be earned on the best available alternative use of funds that does not appreciably increase an investor's exposure to risk? This is the investor's *opportunity cost of capital*. It serves admirably as a minimum acceptable rate of return, or *hurdle rate*, because investors are unlikely to accept any project with an expected rate of return below that available elsewhere with the same degree of risk.

Using opportunity cost as a discount rate permits direct comparison among projects in the same general risk category. This eliminates difficulties that might otherwise arise when cash-flow projections from alternative proposals differ drastically in amount or timing.

Lastly, a uniform discount rate for all competing projects greatly facilitates risk analysis of the type discussed in Part Six. It permits risk analysis to be incorporated into policy guidelines and enables subordinates or analysts to screen investment proposals in much greater detail than is otherwise possible.

INVESTMENT DECISIONS AND DECISION RULES

Precise rules for making investment decisions necessarily depend on the nature of the problem. While general principles are universally applicable, their specific application depends on situational factors. This section examines a number of situations and the appropriate application of general principles for each.

---

2 Harold Bierman, Jr., and Seymour Smidt, *The Capital Budgeting Decision*, 9th ed. (Upper Saddle River, N.J.: Prentice Hall, 2007).

Comparing Projects of Different Sizes

Net present value can give an ambiguous decision signal when projects require different levels of initial cash outlay. Furthermore, large projects might have large NPVs, and bigger is not always better. However, the measure can be converted to a cost/benefit ratio, which does this task admirably. This cost/benefit ratio, called a *profitability index* (PI), is calculated by dividing the present value of expected future cash flows by the amount of the initial cash outlay. The quotient represents present value per dollar of initial cash expenditure. The general decision rule, then, is to accept the project with the greatest PI (assuming, of course, projects are of equal risk).

Example 14.2

The present value of expected cash flows from an investment is $74,340, when discounted at the opportunity cost of capital. The required equity cash outlay to acquire the asset is $60,000.

Applying the PI technique to Example 14.2 results in a tentative decision to accept the project. This project offers $1.24 of present value for every $1 of initial cash investment. The calculation is as follows:

$$PI = \frac{\text{present value}}{\text{cost}} = \frac{\$74,340}{\$60,000} = 1.24$$

When using the PI as an initial screening device, reject all projects with an index of less than one. This is, of course, a simple variant of rejecting any project whose NPV is less than zero. Only projects with a PI equal to or greater than one are subjected to additional analysis.

The PI is simply an alternate way of expressing NPV data, because instead of subtracting initial cash outlay from present value, we divide by that amount. Therefore, when present value minus initial cash outlay equals zero, the PI will equal one. It follows that when NPV is less than zero, the PI will be less than one; and when NPV is more than zero, the PI will be more than one.

Choosing Among Mutually Exclusive Opportunities

Investors often must select from among nominally desirable investment alternatives. They must, for example, decide among alternative allowable capital recovery methods (depreciation). Financing alternatives, lease or buy choices, decisions to accept or reject offers to buy or sell, selection from among alternate lease terms or tenants, and alternate forms of ownership all constitute examples of mutually exclusive choices. Investors deciding among mutually exclusive alternatives should accept the one producing greater NPV.

We have seen that the PI expresses the relative profitability and thus is useful for comparing projects that require differing amounts of cash outlay. For choosing among mutually exclusive projects, however, the NPV approach is preferred because it expresses in absolute terms the project's expected economic contribution.

To illustrate, consider the mutually exclusive uses of the building site described in Example 14.3. Using the PI, the shopping center alternative appears preferable, but the NPV approach shows the office building to be preferable. Because the NPV criterion shows the net economic contribution of the project, we would prefer the office building on the site. Figure 14.2 summarizes the computations.

FIGURE 14.2: Summary of Investor's Development Alternatives

	Shopping Center	Office Building
Present value of net cash flows	$90,000	$108,000
Less: Initial equity outlay	60,000	75,000
Net present value	$30,000	$33,000
Profitability index	1.50	1.44

Example 14.3

An investor owns a site worth $60,000. Using her equity in the land (which she owns on a free-and-clear basis) as collateral, she can secure a mortgage loan to cover the cost of constructing a strip shopping center. Alternatively, she can construct a small multiple-story office building. The office project, however, will require that she invest an additional $15,000 of equity funds to bridge the gap between construction cost and available mortgage funds. The present value of after-tax cash flows from the strip shopping center is estimated to be $90,000; from the office building, $108,000.

Mutually Dependent Investment Decisions

Investment proposals are mutually dependent if acceptance of one forces the investor to accept the other. If investment decisions are related in this fashion, group the mutually dependent ventures into consolidated units and treat each unit as a single investment venture. Accept the mutually dependent combination having the highest NPV, provided it is greater than zero. If the consolidated units differ in the amount of initial equity commitment, compare the combinations' PIs.

INVESTMENT VALUE AND INVESTMENT STRATEGY

Investment value was defined in Unit 1 as the value of an income-producing property to a particular investor. Prospective investors will be motivated to buy if they believe investment value is greater than market price. Owners will be motivated to sell if they believe they will receive more than their properties are worth to them as elements in their personal investment portfolios.

> **Example 14.4**
>
> An investor estimates that a property has a present value of anticipated future cash flows of $250,000. He suspects he can acquire the property for about $725,000, paying $225,000 in cash and financing the balance via a first mortgage loan. The present owner believes she can sell for about $725,000 and that the present value of future after-tax cash flows if she continues to hold the property in her portfolio is about $400,000. An existing mortgage loan on the property has a remaining balance of $200,000. If the owner, in fact, sells for $725,000, she estimates that her taxes and transaction costs will total about $100,000.

Look at the position of the prospective buyer in Example 14.4. Summing the $250,000 present value of anticipated after-tax cash flows (the value of the expected equity cash expenditure) and the expected $500,000 mortgage loan (the cost of which is incorporated into the present value computations) yields an investment value of $750,000 to the prospective purchaser. If, as the investor suspects, the property can be acquired for $725,000, only $225,000 of equity cash will be required. Present value of future cash receipts less required equity (the cost to acquire the future cash flows) yields an NPV of $25,000. Buying this property is expected to increase the investor's net worth by $25,000. These relationships are summarized in Figure 14.3.

FIGURE 14.3: Summary of Buyer's Position

Present value of equity	$250,000
Add: Available financing	500,000
Buyer's investment value	$750,000
Expected purchase price	$725,000
Less: Available debt financing	500,000
Expected equity investment	$225,000
Present value of equity position	$250,000
Less: Expected equity investment	225,000
Net present value	$25,000

Now consider the current owner's position. Summing the $400,000 present value of anticipated future after-tax cash flows and the $200,000 remaining balance of the existing mortgage produces an investment value of $600,000 if she continues her ownership. She can sell for $725,000 and net $625,000 after taxes and transaction costs. Therefore, she can improve her position by selling.

The sale of the property for the expected $725,000 will net her $425,000 of after-tax cash flow (sales price minus loan balance, transaction costs, and income taxes). In effect, she exchanges the $400,000 present value of future cash flows for $425,000 in net cash proceeds from selling. The NPV of a decision to sell is therefore estimated to be $25,000. These relationships are summarized in Figure 14.4.

FIGURE 14.4: Summary of Seller's Position

Investment value:		
Present value of equity position		$400,000
Add: Mortgage loan balance		200,000
Seller's investment value		$600,000
Net present value:		
Expected sales price		$725,000
Less: Mortgage loan balance	$200,000	
Taxes and transaction costs	100,000	300,000
Expected after-tax cash flow from sale		$425,000
Less: Present value of equity position		400,000
Net present value of seller's position		$25,000

Marked differences in investment value, like those for the prospective buyer and seller in Example 14.4, occur because investors differ in their access to debt capital and the opportunity cost of equity. They occur also because of different perceptions of a property's potential and due to differences in income tax positions.

The relationship between subjective investment values in Example 14.4 is diagramed in Figure 14.5. The greater the spread between investment value and transaction price for both buyer and seller, the greater the possible increase in both investors' net wealth. Keep in mind that neither party will know the other's investment value. Because the buyer does not know the minimum amount the seller will accept and the seller does not know the maximum amount the buyer will pay, both parties bargain with incomplete information. This uncertainty increases the importance of good bargaining strategy.

FIGURE 14.5: Buyer's and Seller's Investment Value (from Figures 14.3 and 14.4) and the Transaction Range

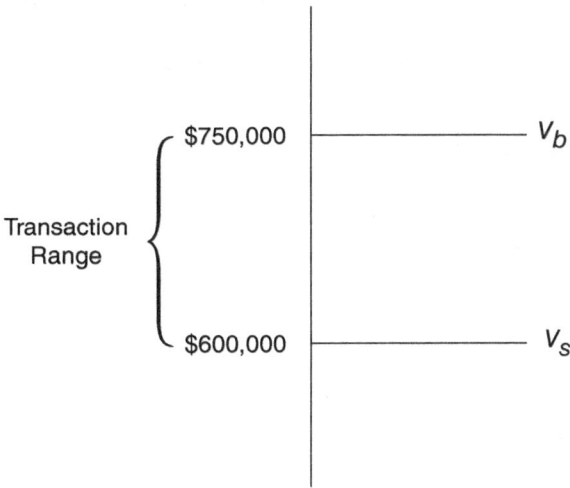

APPLICATION OF THE DISCOUNTED CASH-FLOW TECHNIQUE

This final section applies previously discussed procedures for developing after-tax cash-flow projections and discounts them at the minimum acceptable rate of return. Space limitations require that several assumptions be made about key variables that, in a realistic situation, would be subject to debate and judgmental variation. Now examine Example 14.5.

> **Example 14.5**
>
> A married couple investment team is considering a 48-unit apartment complex, expected to be available for $1.3 million. The couple expects to be able to arrange an $840,000, 8%, 25-year, fully amortizing first mortgage loan, which will require monthly payments. Whether or not they make this commitment, they will be in the 40% (combined federal and state) marginal income tax bracket throughout the contemplated investment period (they file a joint tax return). Taxes on gains from the sale of the apartment complex are expected to be levied at 25% to the extent the gain represents recapture of straight-line depreciation and at 15% on the balance. If the couple invests, they expect to hold the property for approximately six years and then to sell for cash to finance their retirement plan. The investors' minimum acceptable rate of return on investments of this type is 12% per annum.
>
> The investors note that the area is fully developed, with no land available for significant new, competing buildings, and they detect no discernible trend of either rapid growth or decline. They conclude that both rents and expenses over the next few years are likely to move approximately in concert with the general change in consumer prices. They expect the consumer price index to increase at about 4% per annum (compounded) over the next few years, and they take this as the expected rate of increase in both rents and operating expenses.

The first step in analyzing the opportunity in Example 14.5 is to forecast revenue and expenses for the property over the expected holding period. Starting with the previous owner's operating statement, adjusting as explained in Part Three, the investment team generates the forecast of first-year operating figures shown in Figure 14.6.

FIGURE 14.6: First-Year Operating Forecast

Potential gross rent		$262,000
Less: Allowance for vacancies		17,500
		$244,500
Plus: Other income (parking)		1,600
Effective gross income		$246,100
Less: Operating expenses		
Management fee	$12,300	
Salary expense	22,500	
Utilities	26,500	
Insurance	12,500	
Supplies	3,200	
Advertising, legal, misc.	1,500	
Maintenance and repairs	20,000	
Property tax	30,700	
Total operating expenses		$129,200
Net operating income (annual)		$116,900

Having determined that operating results are most likely to increase at an average rate of 4% per annum over the holding period, forecasting becomes a mechanical projection at that rate. The forecast must be made on an after-tax cash-flow basis, however. This requires that taxable income or tax-deductible losses also be forecast for each year of the prospective holding period. To calculate interest expense for this purpose, an amortization table for available financing must be developed. This information is shown in Figure 14.7.

The investors' expected taxable income from the investment for each year consists of the expected NOI minus interest expense and depreciation allowances. Because the investors expect to be in the 40% marginal income tax bracket with or without this investment, the tax (or tax savings) for each year will be computed at the 40% rate. These calculations are presented in the upper half of Figure 14.8.

Depreciation allowances reduce taxable income, but they do not affect before-tax cash flow from an investment. Conversely, reduction of the principal amount of mortgage indebtedness reduces cash flow without affecting taxable income. The lower half of Figure 14.8 contains after-tax cash-flow forecasts, which start with NOI and are adjusted for debt service and income tax effects.

FIGURE 14.7: Mortgage Amortization Schedule*

Year	Interest	Principal	Total Debt Service	Ending Balance
1	$66,803	$10,996	$77,799.12	$829,004
2	$65,890	$11,909	$77,799.12	$817,095
3	$64,901	$12,898	$77,799.12	$804,197
4	$63,831	$13,968	$77,799.12	$790,229
5	$62,672	$15,127	$77,799.12	$775,102
6	$61,415	$16,384	$77,799.12	$758,718

*Computed with a financial calculator. Computations assume a mortgage loan of $840,000, to be repaid in equal monthly installments over 25 years, with interest at 8% per annum.
  Monthly payment = $6,483.26
  Annual debt service = 12 × $6,483.26 = $77,799.12

FIGURE 14.8: After-Tax Cash-Flow Forecast

	Year 1	Year 2	Year 3	Year 4	Year 5	Year 6
Effective gross income	$246,100	$255,900	$266,200	$276,800	$287,900	$299,400
Less: Operating expenses	129,200	134,400	139,700	145,300	151,100	157,200
Net operating income	$116,900	$121,500	$126,500	$131,500	$136,800	$142,200
Less: Interest expense	66,803	65,890	64,901	63,831	62,672	61,415
Depreciation*	36,242	37,818	37,818	37,818	37,818	36,242
Taxable income	$13,855	$17,792	$23,781	$29,851	$36,310	$44,543
Times: Marginal tax rate	0.40	0.40	0.40	0.40	0.40	0.40
Income tax	$5,542	$7,117	$9,512	$11,940	$14,524	$17,817
Net operating income	$116,900	$121,500	$126,500	$131,500	$136,800	$142,200
Less: Debt service	77,799	77,799	77,799	77,799	77,799	77,799
Before-tax cash flow	$39,101	$43,701	$48,701	$53,701	$59,001	$64,401
Less: Income tax	5,542	7,117	9,512	11,940	14,524	17,817
After-tax cash flow	$33,559	$36,584	$39,189	$41,761	$44,477	$46,584

*Assumes that 80% of the $1.3 million purchase price is properly attributable to the building, and that purchase closes during the first month and sale closes during the last month of the respective taxable years. See Unit 10 for details.

If the current gross rent multiplier continues to apply, this property will have a market value of approximately $1.65 million when sold at the end of the sixth year of ownership. Subtracting estimated transaction costs (5% of the sales price) and the owners' adjusted basis before the sale (cost minus accumulated depreciation allowances) yields the anticipated gain on disposal. Figure 14.9 summarizes the expected income tax consequences of disposal.

Figure 14.10 converts the expected selling price and income tax consequences into a forecast of after-tax cash flow from disposal. This involves subtracting the estimated transaction costs, income tax liability, and mortgage balance from the forecasted selling price of the property.

FIGURE 14.9: Income Tax Consequences from Disposal

Sales price		$1,650,000
Less:		
Transaction costs (at 5%)	$82,500	
Adjusted basis (cost minus depreciation)	1,076,244	1,158,744
Gain on sale		$491,256
Tax on sale:		
Tax on recapture of straight-line depreciation (0.25 × $223,756)		55,939
Tax on long-term capital gain (0.15 × $267,500)		40,125
Total tax on sale		$96,064

FIGURE 14.10: Forecast of After-Tax Cash Flow from Disposal

Sales price	$1,650,000
Less:	
Transaction costs (from Figure 14.9)	$ 82,500
Income tax (from Figure 14.9)	96,064
Mortgage balance (from Figure 14.7)	758,718
Net cash flow	$712,718

Anticipated after-tax cash flows are discounted in Figure 14.11 to adjust for differences in timing of the expected receipts. Because the present value of all anticipated future cash flows exceeds the required initial equity investment ($523,485 present value compared with an investment of only $460,000), we conclude that the venture is expected to generate a yield in excess of the investors' 12% minimum acceptable rate.

FIGURE 14.11: Present Value of Anticipated After-Tax Cash Flows

Year	After-Tax Cash Flow	Present Value Factor at 12%	Present Value (Rounded)
1	$33,559	0.892857	$29,963
2	$36,584	0.797194	29,165
3	$39,189	0.711780	27,894
4	$41,761	0.635518	26,540
5	$44,477	0.567427	25,237
6	$46,584	0.506631	23,601
6 (from disposal)	$712,718	0.506631	361,085
Present value of all anticipated cash flows			$523,485
Plus: Available mortgage loan			840,000
Investment value			$1,363,485

Estimating Investment Value

An alternative presentation of the data from Example 14.5 involves estimating the maximum purchase price to yield the lowest acceptable rate of return. This approach is a particularly valuable source of intelligence for improved negotiating. With the mortgage financing assumed to be available for the property in Example 14.5, the investors can pay the present value of cash flow to the equity position plus the amount of the available mortgage and still expect to receive a 12% return on equity funds. Investment value for this couple is therefore equal to the $523,485 present value plus the $840,000 mortgage, which gives a total of $1,363,485. This computation is shown at the bottom of Figure 14.11.

The effect of mortgage financing assumptions on investment value serves to emphasize the most valuable use of this computation—its contribution to negotiating position. Because present value differs with the amount and cost of available financing, investment value will also vary. There is, therefore, a different investment value for every possible set of financing arrangements. When a seller finds a prospective purchaser's investment value unacceptably low, there is the possibility of a trade-off between price and credit terms.

Preparatory to negotiating price and terms, an investor should compute investment value under a variety of potential prices with attendant terms for partial seller financing. These alternatives give the investor a basis for counteroffers, as well as a means to quickly evaluate the other side's proposals.

> **CALCULATOR APPLICATIONS**
>
> | FV = 33,559 | 36,584 | 39,189 | 41,761 | 44,477 | 759,302 |
> |---|---|---|---|---|---|
> | n = 1 | 2 | 3 | 4 | 5 | 6 |
> | i = 12 | | | | | |
>
> **Solve for present value:**
>
> | PV = 29,963 | 29,165 | 27,894 | 26,540 | 25,237 | 384,486 |
> |---|---|---|---|---|---|
>
> Total present value = 523,485

Note that computing the investment value requires a presumption of a purchase price. This is because the depreciation allowance, an integral element in the cash-flow forecast, depends on the price. If investment value proves to be less than the presumed purchase price, do the calculations again, using the initial calculation as the revised purchase price. This will yield a closer approximation between presumed price and tentative investment value. A third calculation will yield an even closer approximation. Successive approximations quickly generate an investment value so close to the presumed price that the difference will be inconsequential. Using an electronic spreadsheet makes the successive approximations as simple as loading a revised price into a personal computer and *recomputing*.

SUMMARY

Decision signals generated by discounted cash-flow models are extremely sensitive to differences in the discount rates used. A minor shift in the rate can alter the rankings of investment alternatives. For this reason, choosing a discount rate is a vital element in the usefulness of an analytical model.

One approach, now largely abandoned, to deriving a discount rate is the summation technique. This involves choosing a risk-free rate, a risk premium, and rates to compensate for illiquidity and for the burden of investment management. The sum of these separate rates is held to be the appropriate discount rate. Difficulty in determining the rates for each of these elements renders the summation technique more a historical curiosity than a helpful tool for analysis.

Many analysts do use a risk-adjusted discount rate, usually derived from observation of rates available in the marketplace. Conceptually, the rate is the sum of a risk-free rate and a risk premium. The most commonly used proxy for a risk-free rate is the yield on short-term government securities. To this must be added a premium that will vary, depending on the amount of risk perception associated with a particular investment venture.

Marginal cost of capital is the cost of procuring one more unit. Many analysts believe this to be the appropriate rate to use when considering the advisability of an investment venture. Because cash-flow forecasting generally yields a forecast of the cash flow to the equity investor, the marginal cost of equity capital is the most appropriate measure. Opportunity cost—the benefit forgone by not accepting the best available alternative investment proposition—is frequently taken as the best estimate of the marginal cost of equity capital.

Investment decision rules that use discounted cash-flow analysis must be adjusted to accommodate varying circumstances facing an investor or an analyst. When projects require different amounts of initial equity cash expenditure, the present value can be expressed as a PI. This measure indicates the present value per dollar of equity investment.

When comparing mutually exclusive projects, choose the one with the largest NPV. When evaluating mutually dependent projects, group them into sets of mutually dependent alternatives and evaluate each set as if it were a single investment venture.

Investment value is the most an investor is justified in paying for an asset, given the anticipated after-tax cash flows the asset will generate and the investor's minimum acceptable rate of return. To estimate investment value, add the available mortgage loan to the present value of anticipated after-tax cash flows to the equity position.

RECOMMENDED READING

Brigham, Eugene F., and Joel F. Houston. *Fundamentals of Financial Management,* 13th ed. Ft. Worth, Tex.: South-Western College Publishers, 2013.

Institute of Management and Administration. "Analyzing New Products: Choice of Hurdle Rate and Cash-Flow Assumptions Key to Decision Making." *IOMA's Report on Financial Analysis, Planning and Reporting* 3, no. 10 (October 2003): 10–13.

INTERNET REFERENCE

For the Institute of Management and Administration:
www.ioma.com

REVIEW QUESTIONS

1. What is the significance of the discount rate chosen when evaluating investment opportunities?
2. What is the basis for the summation technique? What is assumed to be the appropriate rate of return in this technique?
3. What is a risk-free rate of return?
4. When is the opportunity cost of capital an appropriate discount rate?
5. How is the profitability index calculated, and when is it most useful?
6. Describe mutually dependent investment decisions. How should mutually dependent investments be treated?
7. What are mutually exclusive investment opportunities? Give some examples. When is a choice between mutually exclusive alternatives likely to occur?

8. What role does investment value play in the investment strategies of a buyer and seller?

9. What effect do the amount and cost of mortgage financing have on the present value and investment value of a property? How might this relationship be used in the negotiation process?

DISCUSSION QUESTIONS

1. Because the opportunity cost of equity capital changes over time, should long-term and short-term commitments be evaluated using different opportunity costs? Explain why or why not.

2. When discounting long-term cash-flow forecasts using the opportunity cost of capital, should the rate used reflect costs at the time the commitment is to be made or should it reflect anticipated average capital costs over the forecast period? Explain.

3. Why do some investors use a discount rate higher than their cost of capital?

PROBLEMS

1. William Smith, the junior partner in the firm of Jones, Brown, and Smith, has been offered, for $2.15 million, an apartment complex that is expected to generate after-tax cash flows from operations as indicated in the following chart. The forecast incorporates a first mortgage loan of $1.5 million. Smith expects to sell the property after seven years, and the best estimate of after-tax cash flow from disposal is $740,000.

Year	Expected After-Tax Cash Flow from Operations
1	$60,000
2	$70,000
3	$80,000
4	$87,000
5	$93,000
6	$99,000
7	$105,000

Using a 10% discount rate, compute the following:
a. Net present value
b. Profitability index
c. Approximate investment value

2. What is the expected internal rate of return on the project in Problem 1?

PART FIVE

Case Problem

1. Byron Bass is a commercial real estate broker who also has a keen eye for personal investment opportunities. He has an opportunity to buy Academic Arms, an apartment building that caters to students. He estimates that he can acquire the asset for $1.3 million with purchase costs of 2% and that the seller will take back a $1.2 million first mortgage note with the annual debt service and principal payments reflected on the following schedule of projected cash flows. Bass plans to sell the project when the loan balance falls due at the end of the seventh year.

   Bass has researched Academic Arms and has generated the following schedules, in which he has considerable confidence.

Academic Arms Apartments Projected After-Tax Cash Flows from Operations

	Year 1	Year 2	Year 3	Year 4	Year 5	Year 6	Year 7
Effective gross income	$286,442	$295,035	$303,877	$313,004	$322,393	$332,067	$342,029
Less: Operating expenses	157,543	162,269	167,138	172,152	177,316	182,637	188,116
Net operating income	$128,899	$132,766	$136,739	$140,852	$145,077	$149,430	$153,913
Less: Debt service	126,370	126,370	126,370	126,370	126,370	126,370	126,370
Before-tax cash flow	$2,529	$6,396	$10,369	$14,482	$18,707	$23,060	$27,543
Less: Depreciation	36,967	38,575	38,575	38,575	38,575	38,575	36,967
Plus: Principal paid	6,671	7,369	8,141	8,993	9,935	10,975	12,124
Taxable income (loss)*	($27,767)	($24,810)	($20,065)	($15,100)	($9,933)	($4,540)	$2,700
Times: Tax rate	0.28	0.28	0.28	0.28	0.28	0.28	0.28
Tax (tax saving)	($7,775)	($6,947)	($5,618)	($4,228)	($2,781)	($1,271)	$756
Before-tax cash flow	$2,529	$6,396	$10,369	$14,482	$18,707	$23,060	$27,543
Less: Tax (Plus: Savings)	(7,775)	(6,947)	(5,618)	(4,228)	(2,781)	(1,271)	756
After-tax cash flow	$10,304	$13,343	$15,987	$18,710	$21,488	$24,331	$26,787

*Bass has adequate passive income to offset these losses.

Academic Arms Apartments Anticipated Income Tax Consequences of Disposal (at the end of seventh year of ownership)

Sales price		$1,700,000
Less: Adjusted tax basis before sale		1,195,191
Taxable gain		$504,809
Income tax on sale:		
Tax on recapture of straight-line depreciation (0.25 × $266,809)		$66,702
Tax on long-term capital gain (0.15 × $238,000)		35,700
Total tax on sale		$102,402

Academic Arms Apartments Anticipated After-Tax Cash Flow from Disposal (at the end of seventh year of ownership)

Sales price		$1,700,000
Less:		
Income taxes	$102,402	
Transaction costs (0.08 × $1,700,000)	136,000	
Mortgage balance	1,135,792	1,374,194
After-tax cash flow		$ 325,806

a. Using the first-year operating forecast, compute:
- Gross income multiplier (using effective gross income)
- Net income multiplier
- Operating ratio
- Break-even, or default, ratio
- Debt-coverage ratio
- Overall capitalization rate
- Equity dividend rate
- Cash-on-cash return

b. Using a 12% rate, discount the expected after-tax cash flows from this investment and determine the following:
- Present value
- Net present value
- Profitability index
- Investment value

c. Determine the project's anticipated IRR.

2. Please refer to the Case Problems for Part Four. Assignments 1 and 2 of that case required you to develop projections of after-tax cash flows from operations and from disposal of the St. George Apartments. If you have not completed that assignment, please do so now. Using your after-tax projections, compute the following:

   a. The present value of the opportunity, discounting at 14%
   b. The investment value, discounting at 14%
   c. The internal rate of return

PART SIX

The Risk Element

Traditional real estate investment literature fell behind related fields such as corporate capital budgeting and portfolio analysis by not systematically incorporating risk considerations into the investment equation. We now shift focus to address this critical element.

The purpose of Part Six is to demonstrate that specific investment objectives can be related to probabilistic estimates of possible investment outcomes. Investors can compare expected outcomes with the probability that a particular venture will produce a yield equal to or greater than some predetermined minimum acceptable threshold. Faced with quantified risk and return trade-offs, investors will be well positioned to make rational investment decisions.

Unit 15 discusses risk in general terms, with the objective of acquainting readers with the issues involved in comparing risk-return combinations of alternative investment opportunities. Unit 16 reviews traditional approaches to dealing with the problem. Unit 17 then introduces contemporary alternatives and demonstrates their application to real estate. Unit 18 concludes the section by introducing risk management in a portfolio context.

UNIT 15

Risk in Real Estate Investment

UNIT PREVIEW

Previous units discussed investment evaluation based on a single best estimate of net cash flows over the projection period. The illusion of exactness in these point estimates is seductive, but failing to appreciate the significance of possible forecasting errors can cause serious investment miscalculations. All forecasts are probabilistic in nature, and the implication of precision found in statements with values rounded to the nearest whole dollar should be questioned.

This unit introduces risk as an investment analysis issue. It distinguishes among major risk elements and discusses methods for controlling risk. It considers the relationship among risk, risk-taker, and profit expectations. The unit concludes with an introduction to problems in measuring risk and incorporating risk perception into the investment decision.

KEY RISK ELEMENTS

The elements of risk can be usefully characterized according to their origins. Risk stemming from the possibility of making inappropriate business decisions or of misjudging the economic consequences of one's actions is labeled *business risk*. The risk inherent in the use of borrowed funds, and thus determined by choice of financial arrangements, is called *financial risk*. Environmental risk is the negative impact on value caused by environmental problems. Risk of loss from natural hazards (fire, flood, storm, and so forth) can be transferred to insurance companies and so is characterized as *insurable risk*.

Business Risk

Even the most precisely calibrated operating projections are subject to gross errors. The likelihood that actual operating results will vary from expectations is sometimes called *business risk*.

Business risk stems both from factors internal to the investment equation and from circumstances attributable to the economic environment surrounding a project. For example, management inefficiencies may cause operating expenses to exceed expectations or result in an inordinately high vacancy rate. Sloppy credit investigation and lax rent collection practices may spawn unexpectedly high credit losses. Any of these events, all internal to the investment equation, will cause NOI to fall below the forecast.

The economic environment may be less favorable than anticipated and cause an unexpectedly low level of demand for real estate services. This means either a higher-than-expected vacancy rate or reduced rental rates. In either event, an unfortunate by-product will be gross rental revenue below that anticipated at the time an investment commitment was made. This in turn means that NOI will fall below expectations.

Financial Risk

Part Three pointed out that financial leverage (using borrowed funds) increases the yield on an equity investment (and is therefore considered positive, or favorable) so long as the cost of borrowed funds is less than the yield on assets. Unfavorable leverage, in contrast, decreases the yield on an investor's equity funds. Financial leverage also amplifies the variability of possible returns to equity investors. Increased variability represents additional risk due to the financing decision and so is part of the financial risk associated with the investment.

Consider a property with an expected NOI of $125,000 and a market value of $1 million. Assume the range of possible NOI is $100,000 to $150,000. If an investor purchases this asset without using borrowed funds, the expected current yield (before income taxes) is 12.5% ($125,000 / $1,000,000). Possible annual pretax yields (cash-on-cash) range from 10% ($100,000 / $1,000,000) to 15% ($150,000 / $1,000,000).

Assume that our investor finances $700,000 of the purchase price via a mortgage loan that requires equal monthly payments over 25 years with interest at 7%. The payments will be $4,947.45 per month and the annual debt-service obligation will be

12 times this amount, or approximately $59,369. Before-tax cash flow to the equity investor is, of course, reduced by the amount of the annual debt-service obligation. With the loan, the range of possible before-tax cash flows is $100,000 minus $59,369, or $40,631, at the low end and $150,000 minus $59,369, or $90,631, at the high end. The expected before-tax cash flow becomes $125,000 minus $59,369, or $65,631. These computations are presented in Figure 15.1.

Of course, the mortgage loan also reduces the size of the required equity investment from $1 million to only $300,000. The expected annual pretax yield therefore becomes the expected before-tax cash flow of $65,631 divided by the $300,000 equity investment, or 21.877%. The range of possible annual pretax yields with the mortgage loan is from 13.5% to 30.2%, also shown in Figure 15.1.

FIGURE 15.1: Range of Possible Outcomes with Financial Leverage

	Lower Bound	Expected	Upper Bound
Net operating income	$100,000	$125,000	$150,000
Less: Debt service	59,369	59,369	59,369
Pretax cash flow	$40,631	$65,631	$90,631
Current yield*	13.5%	21.9%	30.2%

$$\text{*current yield} = \frac{\text{pretax cash flow}}{\text{equity investment}}$$

$$\text{lower bound} = \frac{\$40,631}{\$300,000} = .135 \text{ or } 13.5\%$$

$$\text{expected} = \frac{\$65,631}{\$300,000} = .219 \text{ or } 21.9\%$$

$$\text{upper bound} = \frac{\$90,631}{\$300,000} = .302 \text{ or } 30.2\%$$

Alterations in the range of possible outcomes due to financial leverage are illustrated in Figure 15.2. Leverage raises the expected annual pretax yield (depicted by the small vertical bars) from 13.5% to 30.2%, but it also increases the range of possible annual yields rather impressively. As depicted by the horizontal bars in Figure 15.2, annual yields with leverage can fall significantly below the range of possible yields without leverage. The graph also illustrates that the upper end of the range of possible yields is greatly increased by the leverage. This possibility is sometimes referred to as *upside risk* and is a much-desired consequence. Whether the enhanced yield expectation and the greater upside risk justify the amplified downside risk attendant to financial leverage depends on investor risk preferences, as discussed later in this unit.

FIGURE 15.2: Most Likely Current Yield and Range of Possible Variation

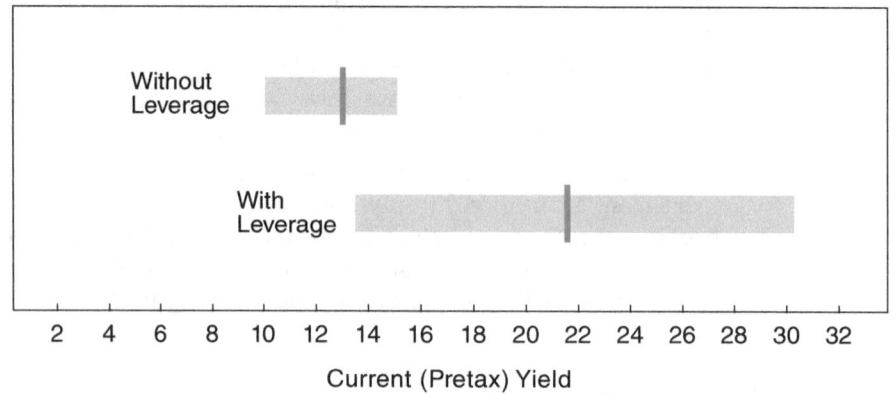

Because mortgage lenders have a prior claim on NOI, with investors' before-tax cash flow being a residual, increasing the amount of borrowed funds (and thus the debt-service obligation) also increases the probability that NOI will be insufficient to meet the debt-service obligation. This is an additional dimension of financial risk.

To illustrate, consider a 28-unit apartment project expected to generate $10,000 per unit of gross income. Assume the units require annual expenditures of approximately $5,000 per unit for variable operating expenses. An expected $5,000 per unit remains to cover fixed expenditures—including debt service—and to provide a return to the investor. If all the units are rented for the entire year at the expected rental rate, annual cash flow will be $140,000 before debt service and other fixed costs. Further assume that fixed charges other than debt service (these comprise insurance and property taxes) total $20,000. Expected rental revenues net of variable costs, at various occupancy levels, are depicted in Figure 15.3.

The occupancy levels are measured on the horizontal axis of Figure 15.3. Fixed costs are by definition the same regardless of occupancy level. Revenue varies directly with occupancy. Because, as we have seen, each unit generates $5,000 above its variable costs of operation, 100% occupancy will generate $140,000 to cover fixed costs and profit. Of this amount, $20,000 is applied to cover fixed costs, with the balance accruing to the investor. Therefore, with 100% occupancy the investor will earn before-tax cash flow of $140,000 minus $20,000, or $120,000.

Reductions in occupancy levels diminish revenue available for fixed costs and profit without affecting the fixed-cost element. The entire reduction, therefore, is reflected in reduced profits. At a 14% occupancy level (four of the 28 units rented for the entire year) revenue minus variable costs exactly equals the $20,000 of fixed costs; pretax profits are zero. The before-tax break-even occupancy level with no debt financing is therefore 14%.

FIGURE 15.3: Break-Even Occupancy Levels With and Without Financial Leverage

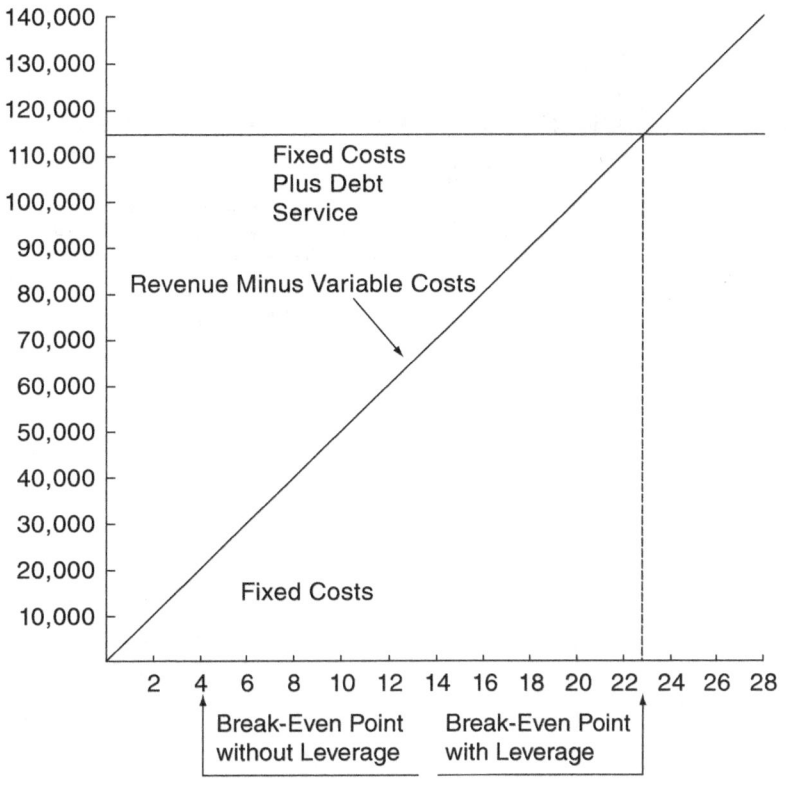

Now see what happens when debt financing is used. Assume our investor borrows $750,000 at 12% interest, with the debt to be paid in equal monthly installments of principal and interest over 25 years. The monthly payment will be approximately $7,900, and the annual debt-service obligation will be 12 times this amount, or $94,800. As with other fixed costs, the debt-service obligation remains invariant regardless of occupancy levels.

Figure 15.3 also illustrates this revised financial picture. As before, when fully occupied, the project will generate $140,000 above variable costs. Every vacant unit (if it remains vacant for a full year) will reduce this amount by $5,000. Because fixed costs and debt service are prior obligations, the entire reduction in revenue represents diminished before-tax cash flow to the investor. A full year's revenue from 23 units is required to meet fixed costs plus debt service. This represents an 82% occupancy level just to break even on the project (before taxes). Financial leverage has increased the occupancy level necessary to maintain solvency from 14% to 82% and has thereby greatly increased the probability (i.e., the risk) of insolvency.

Figure 15.4 illustrates the same point but assumes rents are varied to maintain a target occupancy level. This alternative presentation places per-unit rental rates on the horizontal axis.

FIGURE 15.4: Break-Even Rental Rates With and Without Financial Leverage

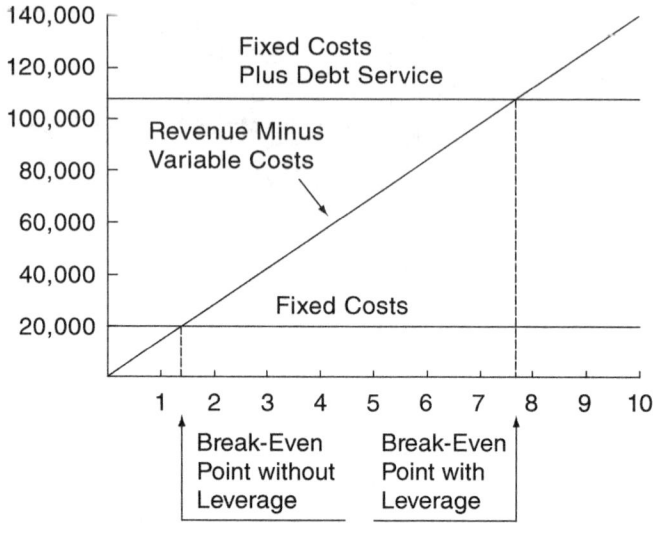

Environmental Risk

Environmental risk can affect the value of real estate because the cost of cleaning up an environmental problem can greatly exceed the total value of the property. One example in commercial real estate vividly illustrates the impact of environmental risk. In the 1980s, it was estimated that 10% of the gas stations in the United States had gas leaks that would require cleanup costs of more than $1 million. Most of the contaminated sites were purchased for less than $100,000 in order to be converted into other retail uses. Lenders learned not to foreclose on contaminated property and now require an environmental assessment before approving a loan. This environmental assessment involves an expert inspection of the property and the chain of title, known as a Phase I Report. If environmental problems are suspected, a Phase II Report may be required with other tests, such as soil borings. Investors should obtain environmental assessments even if not required by a lender because potential environmental contamination can destroy investment return. Environmental problems from such former uses as dry cleaners or photo developing shops can have cleanups as costly as extensive asbestos removal.

Insurable Risk

Accurate prediction of losses due to fire, flood, and other natural hazards is virtually impossible for any particular building or property. It is possible, of course, to calculate the odds of such a loss, based on statistical sampling techniques. But to an investor who has just been wiped out by fire or flood, how significant is the fact that the likelihood of the occurrence was, perhaps, 1 in 10,000?

Predictability based on statistical averages is the foundation of the insurance industry. Because their dollar losses are relatively predictable, insurers can develop fee schedules that compensate for all projected losses plus a premium for expenses and profits and a reserve for the unexpected. For large firms, the degree of uncertainty involved in the insurance function is very small. Investors can transfer many risk elements to insurance firms that specialize in bearing statistically predictable risk.

Fire and extended-coverage insurance shifts the risk of property damage by fire, smoke, wind, hail, lightning, and so on, from the property owner to an insurance company. Liability insurance protects against claims resulting from injuries sustained on the property. Damage to plate glass can be covered, as can damage due to malfunctions in sprinkler systems. Other types of insurance that property owners frequently obtain include protection against loss or damage to building contents and coverage on mechanical equipment such as boilers, water heaters, and air-conditioning units. If building owners have employees working on the premises, workers' compensation insurance may also be necessary.

CONTROLLING RISK

Risk analysis, after years of virtual neglect, has become a popular topic in real estate literature. Unit 18 synthesizes much of current writing on the subject and consolidates generally accepted contemporary techniques into a comprehensive approach. These sophisticated techniques, however, are inappropriate when the additional cost of analysis more than offsets the benefit from avoiding selection error. For relatively inexpensive projects, or where outcomes are highly predictable, less complex analysis might be in order. Moreover, risk can often be greatly reduced with relatively simple risk management procedures.

Reduction of Risk Through Judicious Investment Selection

One way to reduce risk is simply to invest in less risky projects. Accepting only those opportunities whose outcomes are fairly well ascertainable reduces default risk essentially to zero and virtually eliminates uncertainty associated with the outcome of the investment itself (though not the uncertainty and risk of purchasing power loss through an inflation rate that exceeds the rate of return on the investment).

An unfortunate by-product of this strategy is that opportunities for extraordinary profits are also eliminated. The tendency for expected return to increase or decrease along with associated risk is an inevitable characteristic of free markets. Should opportunities for anticipated gains unaccompanied by commensurate risk appear, investors will quickly enter the market and drive expected returns down to a level approximating those available in other investment opportunities of the same general risk category.

There is, of course, a whole spectrum of risky investment opportunities in the economy. Financial markets allow investors to interact in competitive bidding so that an appropriate level of return is assigned by the market to each opportunity, commensurate with the level of risk perceived by market participants. Figure 15.5 depicts the trade-off between risk and expected return necessary to attract a potential investor into a project or projects. As risk increases, the investor requires a higher expected return to compensate for the additional risk exposure. Keep in mind that this diagram reflects investor *expectations* only. Expected profits may never materialize—the investor may in fact suffer substantial losses. But for the investor to accept a project in the first place, potential reward must be sufficiently high to justify bearing the perceived risk.

FIGURE 15.5: Risk-Reward Indifference Curve

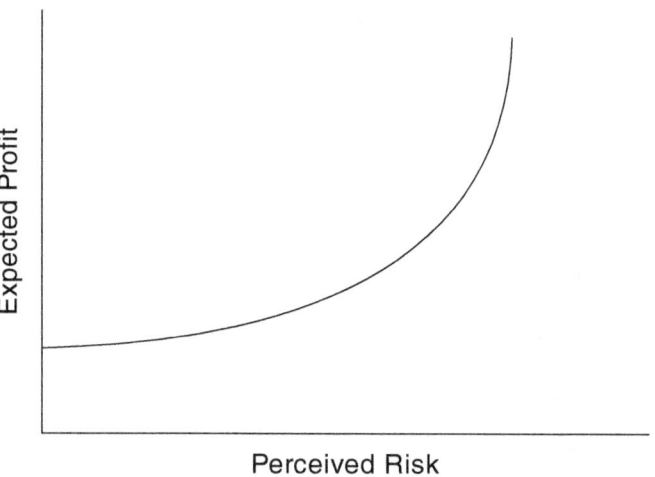

Whereas Figure 15.5 depicts expectations of an individual market participant, actual outcomes are more likely to be as illustrated in Figure 15.6. The dots in the diagram depict actual outcomes of market ventures as they relate to expectations of participants (depicted by the solid line *rr*). If the market is efficient, then actual outcomes will vary randomly about expected outcomes reflected by the market line (market efficiency is discussed in Unit 2). Unusually high or low gains relative to expectations will occur randomly and will tend to cancel each other out. Because all participants in an efficient market have approximately the same information and draw approximately the same conclusions from that information, outcomes for individual participants will also vary randomly in approximately the same proportion as do outcomes for the entire market.

The significance of all this is that, in an efficient market, the only way to reduce risk associated with single investment ventures is to choose a venture with a lower expected return. We noted in Unit 2, however, that real estate markets tend to be somewhat less efficient than organized securities markets. As a consequence, real estate investors who exploit market inefficiencies are able to reap extraordinary profits without shouldering commensurately greater risk. To do this, they must consistently identify opportunities whose outcomes lie to the left of line *rr* in Figure 15.6. They might accomplish this by attaining a monopoly position within certain locations or with respect to significant market information.

FIGURE 15.6: Perceived Risk and Actual Investment Returns When Market Is Inefficient

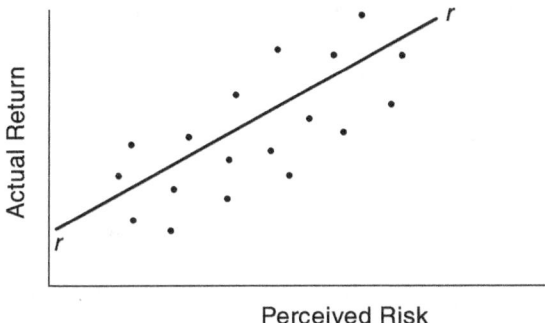

Diversification as a Risk Management Tool

Investors can further control risk exposure by considering the relationship between assets already held and potential new acquisitions. Because factors influencing profitability and market value do not uniformly impact all properties, holders of diversified portfolios can expect a more stable (and predictable) pattern of earnings than would result from concentrating all wealth in a single project. Diversification does not ensure risk reduction unless properties are chosen to avoid high correlation between investment performance among the various assets.

Portfolio diversification is a relatively simple proposition for multimilliondollar real estate investment corporations. They can diversify geographically to reduce the impact of regional shifts in economic activity. Likewise, they can easily acquire any desired mix of apartment complexes, office towers, suburban office parks, and so on. Unit 19 addresses this concept more extensively.

However, most investors face budget constraints that complicate diversification efforts. If it means sacrificing economies of scale by investing in smaller properties, diversification may entail forgoing some expected return.

One solution is to pool equity funds with other investors facing the same dilemma. This rather popular approach to the problem is often called *syndication*. A frequent arrangement involves a promoter who organizes the syndicate and manages the venture for a fee plus a percentage ownership, while passive investors contribute all or most of the equity funds.

Most syndicates are organized as limited partnerships. Another alternative is to buy shares in equity real estate investment trusts (REITs). Because major income tax legislation in 1986 radically altered the tax shelter benefits from real estate limited partnerships, equity REITs have become relatively more significant as an investment vehicle. REITs are discussed in greater detail in Unit 23.

It is important to note that diversification can reduce risk, but it cannot eliminate all risk. Systematic or market risk is nondiversifiable and cannot be eliminated. When the price of oil collapsed in the mid-1980s, all real estate properties in such oil-dependent cities as Houston, Texas, suffered devaluation. When an entire system is negatively affected, diversification does not help. During the Great Depression and Great Recession (financial and housing crisis in late 2008) all properties were negatively affected.

Market Research as a Risk Control Tool

Real estate investors make assumptions about a venture's ability to generate income over an extended period. Risk can usefully be viewed as the possibility of variance between assumptions and actual outcomes. One of the best methods of reducing that variance is to make more accurate assumptions.

Part Two of this text discusses techniques for generating better information on which to base assumptions. Meticulous study of market data permits better estimates of current operating results and more reliable forecasts.

Property Management to Control Risk

Professional property managers are uniquely positioned to enhance the accuracy of cash-flow projections. Their access to market data and their knowledge and experience regarding the economics of property operations are valuable forecasting ingredients. Competent management also plays a vital role in making outcomes conform to assumptions. Resident managers are a critical element, as they control day-to-day operations. They may be able to enhance revenue by controlling vacancy and rent losses and reducing tenant turnover. They can hold expenses down by monitoring all operations and through astute preventive maintenance.

Shifting Risk to Tenants

Lease agreements often permit landlords to shift some risk to tenants. *Expense stops* commit tenants to pay specified operating expenses above some contractual level. *Triple-net leases* make tenants responsible for all expenses.

An additional strategy frequently used with long-term leases pegs rental rates to changes in a price-level index such as the consumer price index, the wholesale price index, or average rents for that type of property in the district. This effectively shifts purchasing power risk (the risk that future receipts will have less purchasing power due to general price inflation) to tenants.

Hedging to Control Risk

Hedging, a common practice in securities and commodities markets, may also reduce risk for real estate investors. *Purchase options* are a common form of hedging used in real estate. When contemplating a development project, for example, a developer might purchase an option to buy a selected site. This provides time to plan, to obtain required governmental approvals, and to secure needed financing. Soil and engineering studies may also be completed while property is under option. Purchase options thus provide time to eliminate some of the uncertainty associated with the development process.

Interim or "standby" financing commitments are another hedging mechanism used by investor-developers. To avoid being committed to an unfavorably high interest rate, a developer who believes rates will decline during the construction period may purchase a loan commitment that is binding on the lender but is an option to the developer. The commitment is exercised only if better terms cannot be obtained.

RISK PREFERENCES AND PROFIT EXPECTATIONS

After all viable risk control techniques are exploited, a core of unavoidable risk remains. Attitudes toward this residual risk will vary with the personalities of investors and with their capacities to absorb financial reverses, as well as with personal investment objectives.

Typical investor attitudes toward risk are illustrated in Figure 15.7. Rational investors prefer a higher to a lower return for a given level of risk; for a specified level of return they prefer less risk to more risk. They accept additional risk only if accompanied by additional expected investment rewards.

Figure 15.7 also demonstrates increasing risk aversion as total risk exposure increases. To induce the investor whose attitude is depicted in Figure 15.7 to accept an increase in risk exposure from r_1 to r_2, there must be the expectation that returns will increase from P_1 to P_2. To persuade the same investor to accept another increment of risk (from r_2 to r_3), expected rewards must be increased by a substantially larger amount. The investor becomes so risk-averse when total risk exposure reaches r_4 that no amount of expected additional reward can induce further movement into the realm of risk. Because the investor will be equally satisfied by all risk-reward combinations depicted by the line in Figure 15.7, it is sometimes called a *risk-reward indifference curve.*

Recall the earlier observation that rational investors prefer less risk for a given level of expected return. This behavioral trait is depicted in Figure 15.7 by the arrow extending to the left from the risk-reward indifference curve, indicating that the investor will prefer any combination of risk and return that can be plotted on the figure in that direction. Because rational investors also prefer a greater return with a given level of risk, the arrow extending upward from the curve indicates a direction in which risk and reward combinations will leave our investor feeling better off than will any combination found on the curve. In fact, a whole set of indifference curves could be plotted, filling the entire plane on which values from the two axes of Figure 15.7 intersect. Any curve above that shown in Figure 15.7 will represent a series of risk-reward combinations that will leave the investor more satisfied than the combinations on the illustrated curve. Because we have posited that the depicted curve illustrates minimum acceptable risk-reward combinations, it follows that all combinations above the one illustrated are even more acceptable. For this reason, the area above the curve in Figure 15.7 is labeled "acceptable risk-reward combinations."

Similarly, it can be demonstrated that the investor will be less satisfied with more risk for a given level of return (depicted by the right-facing arrow in Figure 15.7) or less expected return for a given level of risk (depicted in Figure 15.7 by the arrow extending downward from the curve). No combination of risk and expected return below the curve depicting minimum acceptable combinations will satisfy the investor whose attitude is reflected in Figure 15.7. The area below the minimum acceptable set of combinations is therefore labeled "unacceptable risk-reward combinations."

FIGURE 15.7: Attitudes Toward Risk Differ

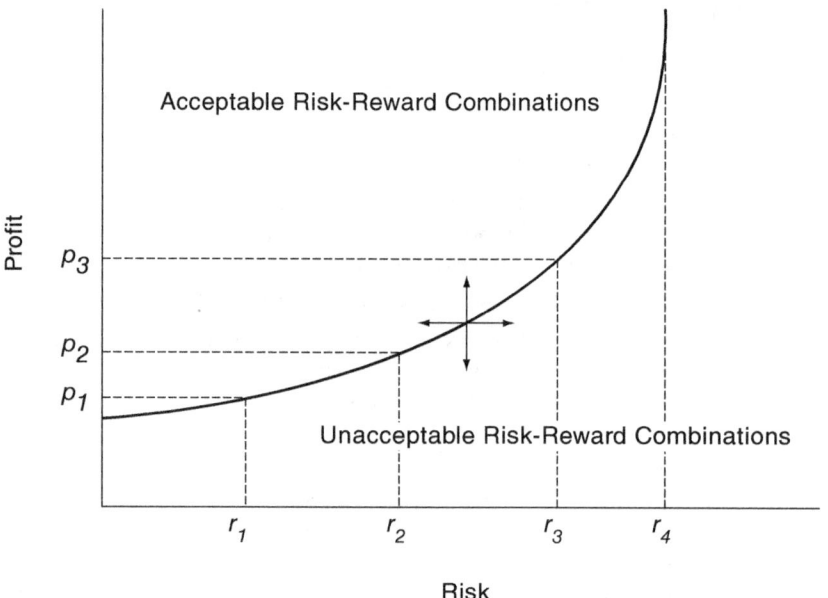

Degrees of Risk Aversion

Of course, the precise configuration of risk-reward indifference curves will depend on the individual investor's personal attitude toward risk. Functions depicting various investors' attitudes will not necessarily have the same shape. The more risk-averse the individual, the more steeply sloped the indifference curve showing that person's preferences. The indifference curve of an investor who is completely indifferent toward risk would have no curvature at all; some investors may even be willing to trade expected return for the opportunity to bear greater risk and will therefore have a downward-sloping risk-reward indifference curve.

Rational Risk Taking

Rational risk taking is epitomized by successful insurance firms. This industry turns a handsome and highly predictable profit by allowing insured parties to substitute the certainty of a small loss (the insurance premium) for the uncertainty of a larger loss from catastrophes. Insurance companies can do this through astute risk management. They calculate the odds and charge a premium sufficient to compensate for the chance of loss.

Insurance companies might be characterized as risk takers by design. So might rational and knowledgeable real estate investors. Before committing substantial resources, such investors will do the following:

- Specify investment objectives concerning return on investment, timing of return and acceptable risk levels.
- Identify major risks involved and quantify them as completely as possible.
- Eliminate some risks, transfer others via insurance or other techniques, and constrain remaining risks to acceptable levels.
- Make decisions to accept or reject specific investments, based on whether expected returns justify bearing the remaining risks in view of the contribution the venture makes toward overall investment objectives.

MEASURING RISK

Instead of quantifying risk perceptions, real estate analysts and investors have traditionally developed subjective impressions and attached a return premium in addition to that required in the absence of "above normal" risk. Traditional approaches to incorporating the risk premium have included shorter payback periods, higher required rates of return, or downward adjustments to projected cash flows. All these techniques result in smaller investment values—the amount an investor is willing to pay for a project.

Traditional risk-adjustment techniques share a serious shortcoming: they do not permit quantification of the risk element. This makes interproject comparisons difficult even for the analyst estimating the risk; it renders completely impossible the task of communicating risk perception to a second party. When analysts are working with client investors, the dilemma becomes more important. Of what avail is an analyst's excellent grasp of the risk element if it cannot be communicated to the client?

Techniques are available for communicating risk assessment without incorporating the analyst's personal risk-bearing proclivities. Such techniques are discussed in Unit 17. They are offered as alternatives to the traditional methods that are explored in Unit 16.

SUMMARY

Risk is a ubiquitous problem in real estate investment analysis. Some risks can be shifted to other parties or minimized through investment-management techniques. But risk avoidance has a price. Many investors purposely shoulder risk because the expected rewards outweigh potential costs.

Risk must be made amenable to measurement and quantification before it can be properly incorporated into the analysis. Only then can trained analysts communicate their perceptions to clients, enabling the latter to make informed decisions.

Traditional means of adjusting for risk inextricably intertwine the analyst's risk perception and personal risk preference. These techniques are appropriate only on the rare occasions when analysts and clients share a common attitude toward risk. Because risk preference is influenced not only by wealth and pre-existing risk exposure but also by subtle psychological factors, common attitudes toward risk are about as likely as identical fingerprint patterns.

RECOMMENDED READING

Brigham, Eugene F., and Joel F. Houston. *Fundamentals of Financial Management.* 13th ed. Ft. Worth, Tex.: South-Western College Publishers, 2013.

INTERNET REFERENCE

For information on environmental risk:
www.environmentalriskmanagers.com

REVIEW QUESTIONS

1. What is the effect of financial leverage on the pretax yield of a property? What is its effect on the level of risk associated with the venture?
2. What is insurable risk?
3. What is business risk, and how can it be reduced for the investor?
4. Are real estate markets efficient? Why or why not?
5. How is diversification used as a risk management tool?
6. How do landlords shift risk to tenants?
7. What steps are involved in rational risk taking?
8. List some of the traditional risk-adjustment techniques and their common shortcomings.

DISCUSSION QUESTIONS

1. Risk can be characterized as diversifiable or nondiversifiable, depending on whether it is possible to eliminate the risk by holding a sufficiently diversified portfolio. Insurable risk is diversifiable. Why, then, don't real estate investors simply eliminate such risks by diversifying rather than paying an insurance company to handle the risk?

2. Because diversification, appropriately pursued, reduces risk, should investors extend their diversification until all diversifiable risk has been eliminated? Why or why not?

3. Diversification has been described as "not putting all of one's eggs in one basket," with the connotation that this is a good policy. Mark Twain's response was, "Put all of your eggs in one basket and watch that basket." Comment on this.

4. How might risk be shifted by the wording of tenant leases? How might it be avoided by choice of organizational entity?

UNIT 16

Traditional Risk-Adjustment Methods

UNIT PREVIEW

This unit explores traditional risk-adjustment and analysis practices with a view toward demonstrating their major strengths and weaknesses. Adjustments to the payback period, adjustments to the discount rate, and adjustments to projected cash flows are discussed. In each case, both theoretical and practical objections to the techniques are presented. Partitioning and sensitivity analysis are then introduced as useful tools that have more recently found their way into common practice.

REAL ESTATE TODAY

THE PAYBACK-PERIOD APPROACH

Recall from Unit 12 that the payback period is the time required for cash inflows from an investment to equal the original cash outlay. If, for example, an investment requires a down payment of $15,000 and is expected to yield $3,000 per annum, the payback period is five years. This is determined by dividing the down payment by the annual net cash inflow:

$$\frac{\$15,000}{\$3,000} = 5$$

One way that proponents of this technique adjust for risk is by varying the minimum acceptable payback period. Risky investments are expected to have a shorter payback period than those that embody less risk. The precise amount of the adjustment is necessarily subjective, because risk itself is generally not measured. Analysts simply state how much shorter a particular investment's payback period is required to be, based on a subjective impression of risk.

Payback-period analysis is an inadequate method of evaluation, even in the absence of risk, and adding risk renders it even less useful. Desirability of real estate opportunities often depends heavily on expected gain from disposal. Risk, in those cases, is primarily a function of the certainty associated with the anticipated sales price. But if the disposal point extends beyond the payback period, neither anticipated benefit nor attendant risk will be included in the analysis.

Consider Example 16.1. A four-year payback period is virtually certain. But how can the required payback period be adjusted for the uncertainty associated with anticipated cash flow from sale of the property five years later?

THE RISK-ADJUSTED DISCOUNT RATE

Discounted cash-flow analysis techniques are discussed in Unit 13 and explained in Appendix A. Given the appropriate rate, discounting anticipated cash flows to arrive at an opportunity's present value is a mere mathematical exercise. Left unanswered is the question of which discount rate is appropriate. The answer depends on how the risk-adjustment problem is handled.

Example 16.1

A warehouse, available for $800,000, is almost certain to yield a net annual cash flow of $200,000 for the next five years, after which it is expected to have a market value such that the net cash flow from disposal will be $1 million. The annual cash flow during the holding period is secured by a tenant with an impeccable credit rating, who has five years remaining on her lease. The expected selling price after five years is predicated on the tenant's renewing the lease—an eventuality that is far from certain. If the tenant does not renew, then the selling price will depend on the investor's ability to find a comparable tenant at the same rental rate.

Traditionally, the discounted cash-flow model has incorporated a risk-adjusted discount rate. A risk-free rate is proposed to represent the pure time value of money. To this a premium is added to compensate for risk. The risk-free rate is (presumably) the same, regardless of the nature of the proposal under consideration, changing only to reflect variation in the disutility of waiting. Risk premiums, in contrast, vary with each proposal. The amount of the premium depends on attendant risk and the investor's attitude toward the risk.

The Risk-Free Discount Rate

Choosing an appropriate risk-free rate is more a theoretical than a practical problem. Most analysts simply select a risk-adjusted rate without bothering to stipulate values separately for the risk-free rate and the risk premium.

Analysts who wish to demonstrate the derivation of their risk adjustments do, of course, have this problem. Most adopt the convenience of using the rate available on short-term federal securities. Because they are short term and highly secure, interest rates on Treasury bills are nearly devoid of premiums for default risk or interest rate risk.

The Risk Premium

Any adjustments for perceived risk should be based on an investor's risk-return trade-off function, as discussed in Unit 15. In practice, real estate analysts who use this approach have generally chosen a risk premium that embodies their perceptions of the risk and their personal risk-return trade-off functions. But because trade-off functions reflect individual attitudes toward risk, this will be appropriate only if an analyst's attitude corresponds exactly to that of the client-investor. Because attitude is determined by factors such as total wealth, pre-existing risk exposure, and personal psychological preferences, there is no reason to suppose that an analyst's attitude will ever exactly match a client's. Indeed, even the analyst's attitude will likely differ when applied to an investment analyzed for a client rather than where the analyst's own resources are at risk. Making this approach operational by determining the appropriate risk premium presents a seemingly insurmountable hurdle.

Theoretical and Practical Problems

In spite of its problems, the risk-adjusted discount rate is probably the most commonly used approach. It is, nevertheless, fraught with both theoretical and practical difficulties.[1]

If riskless and risk premium portions of the discount rate are considered separately, the risk-free rate accounts for the pure time value of money. But when an additional discount factor is introduced for risk, it also incorporates an adjustment for time.

---

[1] For an extended discussion of these difficulties, see A. A. Robichek and S. C. Myers, "Conceptual Problems in the Use of Risk-Adjusted Discount Rates," *Journal of Finance* 21 (December 1966): 727–30.

As a consequence, future risk is discounted more heavily than near-term risk. Yet it is possible that near-term risk may be greater than more distant risk.

Consider, for example, a new apartment project. The probability of construction cost overruns and of an unexpectedly lengthy rent-up period is generally far higher than the probability of significantly misestimating subsequent operating results. Yet the risk premium during the latter period is greater than that of the former. Each subsequent year of operation is discounted more heavily than the preceding, in spite of the fact that as neighborhoods mature, operating outcomes generally become more predictable.

> **Example 16.2**
>
> A 10-year project is under consideration, for which the appropriate risk premium is estimated to be 6% and the risk-free discount rate is estimated to be 5%. The overall discount rate, the sum of the risk-free rate and the risk premium, is therefore 11%. Discounting involves dividing each year's cash-flow projection by a number derived by raising the discount-rate-plus-one to a power equaling the number of years before the cash is expected to be received.

Example 16.2 illustrates the problem. Discount factors for the first three years (discounting at 11%) are, respectively, 1.11, $(1.11)^2$, and $(1.11)^3$. Were there no risk involved, the discount rate would be simply one plus the riskless rate, or 1.05. The factors for the first three years then would be 1.05, $(1.05)^2$, and $(1.05)^3$. The factor by which anticipated cash flow for each year is divided to account for perceived risk is the differences between the risk-free and the risk-adjusted factors. For the first three years, the risk adjustments are:

Year	Risk-Adjusted Discount Factor	Riskless Discount Factor	Risk-Adjustment Factor
1	1.1100	1.0500	0.0600
2	1.2321	1.1025	0.1296
3	1.3676	1.1576	0.2100

Because the risk-adjustment factor grows through time, investment desirability is more greatly impaired the further into the future the anticipated risk lies. This holds true in spite of the fact that the riskless discount rate has already accounted for the time value of money. A problem of double accounting for time is clearly evident.

For some investment ventures, risk might appropriately be viewed as increasing with the length of time involved in the forecast. H. Y. Chen and others have shown that when risk is viewed as an increasing function of time, the risk-adjusted discount rate is theoretically sound.[2] However, for projects where risk is not a function of time, the technique is seriously flawed.

A second shortcoming is the impracticality of expressing risk-adjusted discount rates as policy statements. A policy that specifies minimum risk-return combinations permits subordinates to screen out obviously unacceptable investment projects. Only those opportunities that meet minimum standards are passed for review by final decision makers. Because risk premiums must be determined individually for each project, they are not well suited to a policy of delegating preliminary investment decisions.

THE CERTAINTY-EQUIVALENT TECHNIQUE

Double accounting for risk in the risk-adjusted discount rate can be eliminated by adjusting projected cash flows instead of discount rates. The risk-adjusted cash-flow projections are then discounted at the risk-free rate. This approach, called the *certainty-equivalent technique*, also neatly sidesteps the need to quantify risk perceptions. It does introduce other practical problems, however. These include the cost of determining appropriate certainty-equivalent adjustments and the increased risk of client alienation. When final decisions are made by a committee instead of an individual, these new problems become challenging.

Certainty equivalents, in effect, translate risk-preference functions such as those discussed in Unit 15 into risk-indifference functions. Determining numerical values for these certainty-equivalent factors is the principal difficulty associated with applying the approach. The values can be estimated by presenting an investor with a series of combinations of risky and risk-free cash flows and asking for a stated preference between each set. An extended series of such experiments will result in a preference map representing the investor's attitude toward risk. From this map, certainty-equivalent factors can be extracted. Getting an investor to state preferences in this fashion, however, is difficult and time-consuming. The time and the associated expense might cause the investor to rebel.

PARTITIONING PRESENT VALUES

We have seen that real estate is valued solely for the anticipated future stream of benefits that ownership bestows. Real estate investment, therefore, can be seen as the purchase of a set of assumptions about a property's ability to produce a benefit stream. The generally accepted measure of benefits is after-tax cash flow. Factors contributing to this flow include annual pretax cash flows, income tax consequences, loan amortization, changes in property value over the projected holding period, and so forth.

In Part One, investment value was divided into present value of equity and present value of debt. Similarly, the present value of the equity position can be partitioned into its component parts. Expressing each component as a percentage of the total permits the relative importance of each to be assessed. Components that comprise major segments of the total present value of the equity position will merit extended analysis.

---

2 H. Y. Chen, "Valuation Under Uncertainty," *Journal of Financial and Quantitative Analysis* 2 (September 1967): 313–26.

Consider the investment proposal in Example 16.3. Figure 16.1 contains after-tax cash-flow projections based on the data in the example, using procedures discussed in Part Three. Figure 16.2 details the after-tax cash-flow forecast from disposal at the end of the anticipated holding period. Tax due on sale is calculated as illustrated in Unit 11.

FIGURE 16.1: Simon's Sylvan Setting: Six-Year Cash-Flow Projection

	Year 1	Year 2	Year 3	Year 4	Year 5	Year 6
Effective gross income	$393,000	$405,000	$417,000	$429,000	$442,000	$455,000
Less: Operating expense	177,000	194,000	200,000	205,000	212,000	220,000
Net operating income	$216,000	$211,000	$217,000	$224,000	$230,000	$235,000
Less: Debt service	222,180	222,180	222,180	222,180	222,180	222,180
Before-tax cash flow	($6,180)	($11,180)	($5,180)	$1,820	$7,820	$12,820
Plus: Principal	6,532	7,360	8,294	9,346	10,531	11,866
Less: Depreciation	69,697	72,727	72,727	72,727	72,727	69,697
Taxable gain (loss)	($69,345)	($76,547)	($69,613)	($61,561)	($54,376)	($45,011)
Tax (tax saving)	($27,738)	($30,619)	($27,845)	($24,624)	($21,750)	($18,004)
Before-tax cash flow	($6,180)	($11,180)	($5,180)	$1,820	$7,820	$12,820
Tax consequences	$27,738	$30,619	$27,845	$24,624	$21,750	$18,004
After-tax cash flow	$21,558	$19,439	$22,665	$26,444	$29,570	$30,824

Example 16.3

Simon's Sylvan Setting, a luxury apartment complex, can be purchased for $2.3 million, inclusive of transaction costs. The venture requires an equity investment of $500,000, with the $1.8 million balance of the purchase price to be financed via a fully amortizing, 30-year mortgage note. Interest on the borrowed funds will be at 12% per annum. Payments on the mortgage note will be made monthly. Depreciation allowances are based on a building value of $2 million, using the straight-line method over 27.5 years. The property is expected to be worth $2.9 million, net of transaction costs, at the end of an expected 6-year holding period. The investor is in the 40% marginal income tax bracket (federal and state combined) and expects to remain in that bracket throughout the investment period. If the property is acquired, it is expected that the closing will occur early in the first month of the tax year and that the subsequent sale will close late in the last month of the sixth year of the investment period. This information is incorporated with estimates of rental revenue and operating expenses to generate the six-year cash-flow forecast presented in Figure 16.1.

Figure 16.3 illustrates the technique of discounting to express expected after-tax cash flows in terms of present value equivalents. To estimate the importance of each element in the analysis in Figure 16.3, discount each element separately. For example, note in Figure 16.3 that the first year's expected after-tax cash flow of $21,558 has a present value equivalent of $19,598 when discounted at 10% and rounded to the nearest whole dollar.

FIGURE 16.2: Simon's Sylvan Setting: After-Tax Cash Flow from Sale

Sales price (net)		$2,900,000
Less:		
Mortgage balance	$1,746,072	
Tax due on sale	197,576	1,943,648
After-tax cash from sale		$956,352

Reference to Figure 16.1 reveals that the first year's after-tax cash-flow estimate comprises the following elements:

Effective gross income	$393,000
Less: Operating expenses	177,000
Net operating income	$216,000
Less: Annual debt service	222,180
Before-tax cash flow	($6,180)
Plus: Income tax savings	27,738
After-tax cash-flow forecast	$21,558

CALCULATOR APPLICATIONS

$FV = 956{,}352$
$n = 6$
$i = 10$

Solve for present value:
$PV = 539{,}836$

Discounting each of the elements separately and summing the present value equivalents yields the same present value estimate shown in Figure 16.3. The alternative computations are as follows:

	Present Value Amount	×	Present Factor	=	Value
Gross income	$393,000		0.909091		$357,273
Less:					
Operating expenses	(177,000)		0.909091		(160,909)
Debt service	(222,180)		0.909091		(201,982)
Plus: Tax savings	27,738		0.909091		25,216
Present value of after-tax cash flow					$19,598

FIGURE 16.3: Simon's Sylvan Setting: Measures of Investment Performance

Year	After-Tax Cash Flow	Discounted Cash Flow @ 10%
1	$21,558	$19,598
2	$19,439	16,065
3	$22,665	17,029
4	$26,444	18,062
5	$29,570	18,361
6	$30,824	17,399
Sales proceeds	$956,352	539,836
Present value of equity		$646,350

Component parts of the after-tax cash-flow forecast for each year can be discounted separately in this manner. Figure 16.4 shows present value equivalents in this fashion. Note that the final column of Figure 16.4 is the same as the present value estimates computed in Figure 16.3, except for a small cumulative rounding error.

The present value of each component part of the expected after-tax cash flow, as computed in Figure 16.4, is presented in summary form in Figure 16.5. The final column of Figure 16.5 presents each element as a percentage of the total present value estimate. These measures give the analyst valuable clues concerning the seriousness of errors in the forecast.

Note, for example, that the anticipated outcome is almost totally dependent on cash flows from tax savings and appreciation during the holding period. Approximately 17% and 52% of the present value, respectively, is expected to be generated from these sources. Consequently, results will be disproportionately dependent on appreciation, placing a premium on accurate forecasting of increases in market value during the holding period.

FIGURE 16.4: Simon's Sylvan Setting, Present Value of Partitioned Cash Flows*

Year	Gross Rent $\times 1/(1+i)^t$	−	Operating Expense $\times 1/(1+i)^t$	−	Debt Service $\times 1/(1+i)^t$	+	Tax Consequence $\times 1/(1+i)^t$	=	After-Tax Cash Flow $\times 1/(1+i)^t$
1	$357,273		$160,909		$201,982		$25,216		$19,598
2	334,711		160,331		183,620		25,305		16,065
3	313,298		150,263		166,927		20,920		17,028
4	293,013		140,018		151,752		16,819		18,062
5	274,447		131,635		137,956		13,505		18,361
6	256,836		124,184		125,415		10,163		17,400
Totals	$1,829,578		$867,340		$967,652		$111,928		$106,514

Add present value of cash flow from disposal:
Loan amortization $\times 1/(1+i)^n = \$53,929 \times PVF^* = \$30,441$
Appreciation $\times 1/(1+i)^n = \$600,000 \times PVF^* = 338,684$
Taxes $\times 1/(1+i)^n = \$197,576 \times PVF^* = (111,526)$
Capital recovery† $\times 1/(1+i)^n = \$500,000 \times PVF^* = 282,237$ 539,836
Present value of equity position $646,350

* Present value factors at 10%.
† Original equity investment (down payment).

FIGURE 16.5: Simon's Sylvan Setting: Sources of Present Value

Source of Present Value	Amount of Present Value	Percent of Total
Effective gross income	$1,829,578	283.1
Operating expenses	(867,340)	(134.2) } (0.8)
Debt service	(967,652)	(149.7)
Tax consequences of operations	111,928	17.3
Loan amortization	30,441	4.7
Increase in market value	338,684	52.4
Tax liability on sale	(111,526)	(17.3)
Capital recovery on sale	282,237	43.7
Totals	$646,350	100.0

SENSITIVITY ANALYSIS

Sensitivity analysis is a logical extension of partitioning to determine which portions of the forecast merit further refinement. Whereas partitioning emphasizes the relative importance of various sources of cash flows, sensitivity analysis reveals how forecasting errors will affect the present value of actual after-tax cash flows. The technique consists of altering components of the forecast one at a time and studying their impact on investment value or present value of the equity position.

To see how sensitivity analysis works, consider again the venture in Example 16.3. Suppose we wanted to appraise the impact of a plus-or-minus 10% error in the forecasted selling price.

The after-tax cash flow under each of these alternatives is computed in Figure 16.6. Substituting these alternative after-tax cash proceeds into Figure 16.3 alters the expected present value and the investment value of the venture rather significantly.

There is, of course, an alternative expected present value and investment value for every possible assumption about the rate of appreciation (and thus the sales price) of the property. Figure 16.7 illustrates the relationship between percentage changes in the sales price and percentage changes in the equity value. A 10% change in expected selling price, either plus or minus, produces a corresponding 22% (approximately) change in the venture's equity value.

If we suppose the appreciation rate has been forecasted correctly, but the annual NOI has been overstated by 10%, what impact will this have on investment value?

Because the taxpayer in our example is assumed to be in the 40% marginal income tax bracket, after-tax cash flow will be changed by 60% of the amount of the change in taxable income. Discounting yields the dollar change in present value that results from forecasting error. These calculations are shown in Figure 16.8.

FIGURE 16.6: Simon's Sylvan Setting: Impact of ± 10% Variation in Sales Price on After-Tax Cash Flow From Disposal

	After-Tax Cash Flow From Disposal		
	With −10% Variation	Expected	With +10% Variation
Sales price	$2,610,000	$2,900,000	$3,190,000
Less:			
Loan balance	$1,746,072	$1,746,072	$1,746,072
Tax on sale	$154,076	$197,576	$241,076
After-tax cash flow	$709,852	$956,352	$1,202,852

Change in Selling Price	Present Value Cash Flow from Disposal	Investment Value of Equity
No change (See Figure 16.3)	$539,836	$646,350
10% decrease	$400,693	$507,207
10% increase	$678,979	$785,493

FIGURE 16.7: Relationship Between Changes in Forecast Variables and Changes in Equity Value

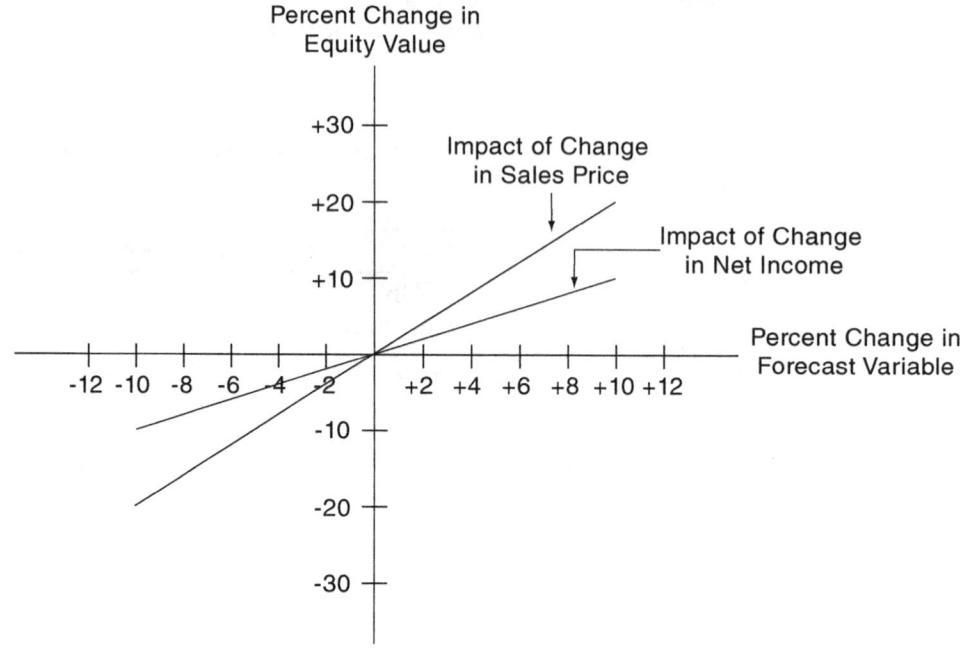

The present value and investment value of the venture after incorporating this change are shown in the following.

Change in Gross Revenue	Present Value of ATCF	Equity Value
No change (see Figure 16.3)	$0	$646,350
10% decrease (see Figure 16.8)	–$57,735	$588,615
10% increase (see Figure 16.8)	+$57,735	$704,085

The relationship between percentage changes in annual NOI and percentage changes in investment value is also illustrated in Figure 16.7. That the investment outcome is less sensitive to errors in the operating income forecast than in the appreciation forecast is reflected in the steeper slope of the line depicting the latter relationship. A similar graph could be constructed to show the relative impact of error in each segment of the forecast.

In general, the steeper the graph of the relationship, the more significant the error in the forecast; therefore, the greater the amount of time and expense the analyst is justified in expending to refine the forecast. If anticipated cash flows prove sensitive to variations in the vacancy allowance, for example, the analyst might wish to generate a more refined analysis of marketability; if results are sensitive to variations in the operating expense ratio, one might experiment with lease clauses that shift any upward variations to the tenants.

FIGURE 16.8: Simon's Sylvan Setting: Impact of ± 10% Variation in Net Operating Income on Present Value of Future Cash Flows

Year	Change in Annual After-Tax Cash Flow*	Present Value of Change @ 10%
1	$12,960	$11,782
2	$12,660	10,463
3	$13,020	9,782
4	$13,440	9,180
5	$13,800	8,569
6	$14,100	7,959
Total		$57,735

*Ten percent of net operating income from Table 16.1, adjusted by the investor's 40% marginal income tax bracket.

Figure 16.9 summarizes the strengths and weaknesses of the various risk-adjustment methods discussed in this unit.

FIGURE 16.9: Strengths and Weaknesses of Risk-Adjustment Methods

Risk-Adjustment Method	Strength	Weakness
Payback period	Simplicity	Unknown disposal point
		Failure to consider all cash flows
		Failure to consider time value
Risk-adjusted discount rate	Accounts for time value	Double accounting for time
	Appropriate discount rate increased with perceived risk	Impracticality of expressing rates as policy
Certainty-equivalent technique	Accounts for time value	Cost of determining adjustments
	Adjusts for increased risk	Difficult to determine appropriate adjustment factor
	Eliminates double accounting for risk	Increased risk of client alienation
	Sidesteps need to quantify risk perceptions	Difficult and time-consuming
Partitioning present values	Designates importance of cash flows	Complex present value computations
Sensitivity analysis	Reveals how forecasting errors affect cash flows	Complex computations

SUMMARY

Traditional techniques used to adjust for perceived risk associated with real estate investment have proven inadequate. They fail to produce a risk measure separate from the analyst's personal attitude toward risk, and thus are not amenable to precise communication of risk perception. In addition, they cannot readily be incorporated into a policy statement enabling delegation of preliminary decision-making tasks.

The payback-period method of analysis is not, strictly speaking, a risk-adjustment technique. But risk perception, interfaced with attitude toward risk, can be expressed in terms of the maximum acceptable payback period for a particular venture.

A technique that does explicitly consider risk and is widely used within the industry is the risk-adjusted discount rate. Users add to the risk-free rates of return premiums based on their perceptions of attendant risk. Thus, the appropriate discount rate increases directly with perceived risk. The technique fails, however, to divorce risk perception from the analyst's personal attitude toward risk. It also contains a technical flaw in that it discounts risk more heavily the farther into the future the risk lies.

Risk-adjusted discount rates adjust for increased risk by increasing the size of the divisor in the discounting equation. The certainty-equivalent technique accomplishes the same goal by decreasing the size of the dividend. Both approaches result in a lower present value for a given expected future cash flow as perceived risk increases.

The certainty-equivalent technique avoids some of the objections associated with the risk-adjusted discount rate but introduces new problems. Principal among these are difficulty in determining the appropriate adjustment factor and need to remake the determination for each project and each decision maker. Time and expense make this approach generally impractical as a continuing risk-adjustment technique.

Partitioning and sensitivity analysis, although not methods of adjusting for risk, are useful means of sharpening risk perception. They do this by illustrating how varying degrees of error in different elements of a forecast result in discrepancies between estimated and actual cash flows.

Partitioning reveals the relative significance of each source of after-tax cash flow. Sensitivity analysis takes a speculative approach by postulating variance at different points in the analysis and recomputing outcomes with revised estimates.

RECOMMENDED READING

Brigham, Eugene F., and Joel F. Houston. *Fundamentals of Financial Management.* 13th ed. Ft. Worth, Tex.: South-Western College Publishers, 2013.

Gane, David. "A DCF Analysis of Market Price for Leasehold Investments." *Journal of Property Valuation and Investment* 13, no. 3 (1995): 42–48.

Pivo, Gary. "Responsible Property Investment Criteria Developed Using the Delphi Method." *Building Research & Information* 36:1, 2008, 20–36.

Tirtiroglu, Dogan. "Property Investment Analysis Using Adjusted Present Values: Modifications." *The Appraisal Journal* 66, no. 3 (July 1998): 298–304.

Wincott, D. Richard. "Normalized Discount Rates versus Risk-Adjusted Discount Rates." *Real Estate Issues* 17, no. 2 (Fall 1992/Winter 1993): 27–30.

REVIEW QUESTIONS

1. How do users of the payback-period approach adjust for risk? Why is the payback-period approach inadequate for evaluating real estate opportunities?
2. What does the risk-free rate mean? Is it really risk free? Explain.
3. What problems does the risk-adjusted discount rate have?
4. What is meant by partitioning the present value of the equity position?
5. Describe how sensitivity analysis works and how it is used in evaluating a real estate investment opportunity.

DISCUSSION QUESTIONS

1. Partitioning the present value of the equity position is described as a risk evaluation measure. Discuss the probable role of electronic spreadsheets in the growth of this procedure. Will dedicated computer programs that do not include this procedure nevertheless lend themselves to using partitioning? Why or why not?

2. How do partitioning and sensitivity analysis complement each other as risk measurement tools?

UNIT 17

Contemporary Risk Measures

UNIT PREVIEW

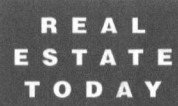

Cash-flow forecasting techniques discussed in Part Two, generate point estimates of revenue and expenditures that are, in effect, the single best estimates of most probable outcomes. They are, nonetheless, estimates; actual outcomes will almost certainly differ from the forecasts. Risk associated with cash-flow forecasting can conveniently be defined as the probability of variation between actual and expected outcomes. More formally, risk is the measurable likelihood of variance from the most probable outcome.

This operational definition forms the takeoff point for modern risk analysis. It permits risk estimates to be expressed quantitatively and enables analysts to rank investment opportunities in terms of investor risk-return preferences.

Probabilistic risk estimates are commonplace in corporate finance and capital budgeting literature. Real estate analysts have adopted the techniques somewhat more cautiously.

The defenders of the traditional risk measures discussed in Unit 16 pose the objection that modern quantification is simply not practical in real estate analysis. They argue that inefficient localized markets, sparse statistical data, and high information costs make real estate a special case in which generally accepted capital budgeting and risk analysis techniques are inappropriate.

These objections miss the point. Data are even more sparse and less reliable in corporate capital budgeting situations than in real estate. Yet modern risk analysis is an integral part of the capital budgeting process in most corporations. Techniques used there are directly applicable to real estate investment decisions.

Analysts do develop some subjective "feel" for the risk inherent in investment opportunities. This is the basis for the traditional adjustments described in Unit 16. All that is needed to accommodate modern risk analysis is a language that permits analysts to express their perceptions in numeric form and articulate a set of decision criteria against which to weigh the outcomes.

This unit provides these additional tools. After distinguishing between risk and uncertainty, the unit reviews basic probability concepts and demonstrates how point estimates of possible outcomes might be converted into probability distributions. It then applies traditional statistical decision rules in a real estate investment context.

PROBABILITY AS A RISK MEASURE

Probability is the chance of occurrence associated with any possible outcome. If, for example, a six-sided die is tossed onto a flat surface, there is an equal chance that any side might face up when the die comes to rest. The probability of any given side facing up is, therefore, one in six, or 0.1667.

The probabilities associated with any possible occurrence range from zero to one. If the probability of occurrence equals zero, the event certainly will not occur. A probability of one indicates certainty of occurrence. In our die-tossing example, one of the six sides must certainly face up. The sum of all associated probabilities must therefore equal 1.

Formally, this is expressed as

$$\sum_{i=1}^{n} P_{xi} = 1$$

where P_{xi} is the probability of occurrences of outcome x, and the summation of the values for i includes all possibilities. When all possible outcomes are arrayed over their associated probabilities, the result is a probability distribution.

Risk Is Different Than Uncertainty

Decision situations are conveniently divisible into *certainty, risk,* and *uncertainty.* With certainty, there can be only one possible outcome, and decisions are based solely on the decision maker's preference among the certain alternatives. Few decision makers, however, face such clear-cut choices. More typically, they must choose among alternatives whose outcomes incorporate elements of risk, elements of uncertainty, or both.

Uncertainty implies an unknown number of possible outcomes, with no significant information about their relative chances of occurrence. Because it is by definition unmeasurable, there is no way to communicate degrees of uncertainty. Under such conditions, almost anything can happen.

Risky events also have a number of possible outcomes, but the analyst is able to generate information on which to estimate the probability of occurrence of each. Some risk elements are susceptible to more or less precise measure, based on sampling techniques and statistical inference. Others are subject only to educated guesses about the range of possible outcomes from one extreme to the other. Formal risk analysis shapes these measures, estimates, and guesses into a concrete, standardized format, incorporating probability as the measure of risk.

The distinction between risk and uncertainty is that with uncertainty, probabilities are neither known nor estimable, whereas with risk, the probabilities associated with various possible outcomes are either known or estimable. Authorities differ regarding the importance of this distinction.[1] For our purpose, it is valuable because decision makers exercise some control over the category into which certain elements fall. Uncertainty can sometimes be resolved with additional research or the passage of time. As better information becomes available, many uncertain elements can be converted to risk factors by incorporating their associated probability distributions into the analysis.

Estimation of Probabilities

When the influence of all factors bearing on an outcome can be held relatively constant, experience provides a reliable indication of future events. In such circumstances, experimentation or observation of sample data permits inferences about future outcomes.

This is illustrated by the earlier example of a (presumed fair) six-sided die. The intuitive deduction that each side has an equal chance of facing up can be verified by observing the outcome of repeated tosses. Various sides may face up with unequal frequency during early tosses, but (if the die is fair) these are mere chance variations. The greater the number of tosses, the smaller the role played by chance and the greater the tendency for each side to be equally represented.

Weight one side of the die or shave a corner, and the probability of each side facing up will no longer be equal. A new set of probabilities can be estimated quickly, however, by recording the outcome of repeated tosses. A sizable sample of such tosses yields a highly reliable indication of the average outcome of any future series of tosses, so long as major determinants of the outcome (such as the playing surface and the degree to which the die is weighted or shaved) remain constant. Varying any factor produces a whole new set of probabilities.

Investment analysts are not blessed with such reliable probability estimating techniques. Estimating future cash flows from real estate ventures might best be described as part art and part science. It involves studying all factors that significantly influence outcomes, making estimates of or assumptions about the level of each factor, and relating these to a specific investment forecast and its associated probability.

Point estimates of cash flow, such as those discussed in Part Two, necessarily assume some specific economic environment. Were the analyst to anticipate a different environment, a revised forecast would be required. A series of such revisions will generate a whole spectrum of net cash-flow forecasts, each reflecting a slightly modified set of assumptions about economic and social conditions during the projection period.

---

[1] For contrasting approaches, compare the distinction made by Steven E. Bolten, *Managerial Finance,* 2nd ed. (Boston: Houghton Mifflin, 1981), with that of J. Fred Weston and Eugene F. Brigham, *Managerial Finance,* 9th ed. (Ft. Worth, Tex.: The Dryden Press, 1992). For a more detailed treatment of the distinction, see R. Duncan Luce and Howard Raiffa, *Games and Decisions* (New York: John Wiley, 1957).

There is, of course, no way to determine precisely what the future portends. Yet we can develop informed estimates, which enable us to say with relative confidence that various possible outcomes will materialize. In some instances, estimates can be derived objectively by applying statistical techniques to accumulated data. In other instance, lack of objective data might force reliance on the distilled wisdom of an analyst's experience as a basis for estimating which of the alternative economic environments is most likely.

Regardless of how estimates are generated, relative confidence in various potential outcomes can be expressed by coupling each with a probability estimate. This procedure produces a probability distribution of possible cash flows. If estimates are derived objectively with statistical techniques, risk is said to be measured by *objective probability distributions*.

If statistical measuring techniques cannot be applied, estimates will represent a quantification of the analyst's subjective impression of the risky nature of anticipated cash flows. Such risk estimates are expressed as *subjective probability distributions*. They represent the quantified perception of a trained analyst and are only as reliable as the judgment of the person whose opinion they incorporate. Subjective probability measures do not simplify the analyst's task in any way; they do add precision to the communication of conclusions.

Opinions expressed in precise, readily understandable terms permit investment decisions consistent with the analyst's assessment, yet reflecting the decision maker's personal investment philosophy and risk preference. This is the special virtue of using subjective probability distributions to communicate risk. The adjective *subjective* is appended to indicate that the probability estimates are statements of opinion or beliefs held by an individual analyst.

Example 17.1

A shopping center analyst develops estimates of annual net cash flow from percentage leases under economic conditions ranging from good to poor, both with and without the existence of a competing center. The analyst's estimates are as follows:

Competing center built?	Cash Flow under General Business Conditions		
	Good	Fair	Poor
No	$250,000	$200,000	$150,000
Yes	$225,000	$175,000	$125,000

Consider Example 17.1. Multiple cash-flow projections in the example reflect an analyst's estimate of the influence of general business conditions and of the presence or absence of a competing shopping center. Regardless of general business conditions, construction of a competing center will have an adverse impact on cash flows and thus on the investment's profitability. The better the general economic environment during the lease period, the more cash a lease will generate, whether or not the competing center is built.

Example 17.1 could be extended to incorporate as many additional possibilities as circumstances warrant. A different set of cash-flow possibilities could be developed to reflect the expected impact of labor strife or major change in the general level of employment. Additional sets of possibilities might be shown, depending on what happens to tax laws, whether a proposed highway interchange is actually built, and so on. Expansion possibilities are virtually endless. The analyst's task is to identify those possible events that have a significant likelihood of actually transpiring and that will have a measurable impact on investment outcome. Separate forecasts are then made to reflect possible outcomes for all particularly crucial eventualities.

Conventional Probability Rules

By convention, the probability assigned to the likelihood of an event's occurrence must be a number between zero and one, where zero represents impossibility of occurrence and one represents absolute certainty. If events are mutually exclusive (only one of them *can* occur) and exhaustive (one of them *must* occur), then the sum of the probabilities associated with events in the set must equal 1.

To illustrate, on any given day, it will either rain or not rain. Therefore, the sum of the probabilities associated with these two possibilities must be 1. If the probability of rain is 0.40, then the probability that it will not rain must be 1.0 minus 0.40, or 0.60.

Application of Joint Probabilities

A very important probability rule is sometimes called the *multiplicative law of probability*. It is used to express the probability of occurrence of an event whose outcome depends in turn on the outcome of some prior event. If we call these events A and B, then the probability of events A and B occurring is the product of the probability of event A times the probability of event B given that event A has occurred. In statistical notation:

$$P(A \text{ and } B) = P(A) \times P(BA)$$

If events A and B are independent of each other, that is one event does not impact the other, then the probability of event A and event B occurring is simply the product of the marginal probabilities, or

$$P(A \text{ and } B) = P(A) \times P(B)$$

To apply the concept to real estate investment, consider again the illustration in Example 17.1. The analyst assigns subjective probabilities to the likelihood of each specific event. (Accept, for the present, the convenient fiction that these are the only possible outcomes.)

Assessing the economic environment, the analyst arrives at the probabilistic estimates of most likely general economic conditions during the forecast period, as indicated in Figure 17.1.

FIGURE 17.1: Probabilistic Forecast of Various Economic States

Economic Environment	Associated Probability
Good	0.20
Fair	0.60
Poor	0.20
Total	1.00

FIGURE 17.2: Probability That Competing Shopping Center Will Be Built, Under Various Economic Conditions

Probability That Competing Center Will	Economic Environment		
	Good	Fair	Poor
Be built	0.80	0.50	0.20
Not be built	0.20	0.50	0.80
Total	1.00	1.00	1.00

Figure 17.2 expands Example 17.1 by relating various economic environments and the probability that a competing shopping center will be constructed. Note that the probabilities in Figure 17.2 are *conditional*: they depend on various economic conditions. For each possible set of economic conditions, a competitive center either will or will not be built. Therefore, the sum of the mutually exclusive probabilities under each set of possible conditions must equal 1.

Combining probabilistic estimates from Figures 17.1 and 17.2 generates joint probabilities concerning various possible economic environments and competitive conditions. For example, Figure 17.1 indicates a probability of 0.20 that economic conditions will be good, and Figure 17.2 reflects a probability of 0.80 that a competitive center will be built if economic conditions are good. The probability that economic conditions will be good *and* that a competitive center will be built is the product of these two underlying probabilities: 0.20 *times* 0.80, or 0.16. This, and all other joint probabilities generated from Figures 17.1 and 17.2, is shown in Figure 17.3.

Because Figure 17.3 exhausts all possible combinations of general economic conditions and competitive environments, the sum of the probabilities in the table must equal 1. Moreover, the probability of various general economic conditions can be determined by summing the factors in the table vertically. Comparing the footings from Figure 17.3 with the probabilities in Figure 17.1 confirms that the probability of good economic conditions is 0.20; of fair conditions, 0.60; and of poor conditions, 0.20.

FIGURE 17.3: Probability Estimates of Economic Conditions and Related Competitive Environments

Probability That Competing Center Will Be	Economic Environment			
	Good	Fair	Poor	S
Yes	0.16	0.30	0.04	0.50
No	0.04	0.30	0.16	0.50
	0.20 +	0.60 +	0.20 =	1.00

Summing Figure 17.3 horizontally gives the probability of competition. Finally, because there either will or will not be competition, and some general economic condition must prevail, both vertical sums and horizontal crossfootings in Figure 17.3 must sum to 1.

INTERPRETING RISK MEASURES

Probabilistic estimates of possible outcomes provide valuable intelligence about relative risk. Projections can be made even more useful with additional manipulation of data to provide estimates of most likely outcomes and associated probability distributions of all possible alternatives.

Probability Distributions

An array of all possible outcomes and their related probabilities of occurrence is called a *probability distribution*. The probability distribution of possible net cash flows from the venture described in Example 17.1 is presented in Figure 17.4. The possible net cash flows from Example 17.1 are multiplied by their related probabilities as generated in Figure 17.3. The products are summed in column 4 of Figure 17.4 to generate an expected (i.e., most probable) cash flow from the shopping center project.

FIGURE 17.4: Expected Annual Cash Flow From Proposed Shopping Center Project

(1) Possible Economic Environment	(2) Related Cash-Flow Forecast (from Example 17.1)	(3) Probability of Occurrence (from Figure 17.3)	(4) Weighted Average (2) × (3)
Competing center built, and economic environment is			
Poor	$125,000	0.04	$5,000
Fair	$175,000	0.30	$52,500
Good	$225,000	0.16	$36,000
No competing center, and economic environment is			
Poor	$150,000	0.16	$24,000
Fair	$200,000	0.30	$60,000
Good	$250,000	0.04	$10,000
Total		= 1.00	$\overline{CF}$ = $187,500

Distributions such as that shown in Figure 17.4 are called *discrete* probability distributions, to reflect the assumption that possible outcomes are limited to specific point estimates presented in the computation. The bar graph in Figure 17.5 shows the same data.

Figure 17.4 incorporates an assumption that the six cash-flow alternatives from Example 17.1 exhaust all possibilities associated with the venture. This is, of course, merely a convenient fiction. Because net cash flow from percentage leases is a function of leaseholders' sales revenue, the actual distribution must encompass all intermediate values as well. This is descriptive of a continuous probability distribution.

The discrete probability distribution of Figure 17.5 can be converted to a *continuous* distribution by explicit recognition of values between and beyond the point estimates of Figure 17.4 as being in the realm of probabilities. This is illustrated in Figure 17.5 by the solid line tracing the outer range of the discrete estimates of possible outcomes.

FIGURE 17.5: Probability Distribution of Cash Flows

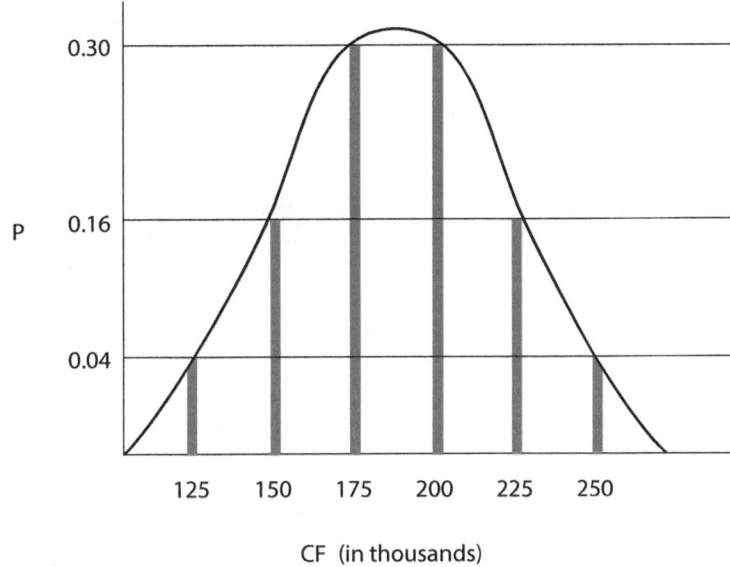

Expected Value

The *expected value* of a probability distribution of possible cash flows is the weighted average of the possible cash flows making up the distribution, with each value weighted by its associated probability of occurrence. The relationship can be expressed as:

$$\overline{CF} = \sum_{i=1}^{n} CF_i P_i$$

where $\overline{CF}$ is the expected value of the cash-flow distribution, CF_i is the value associated with the ith probability, and P_i is the probability associated with that value.

Figure 17.4 applies this formulation to compute the expected value of the cash-flow projections from Example 17.1. Column 2 of the table gives the various possible values of the CF_i, and column 3 expresses the values of the P_i. The product of $CF_i P_i$ is shown in column 4. The summation of column 4, and the solution to the above equation, is the expected cash flow from Example 17.1: $187,500.

Measuring Dispersion

Recall that risk is defined as the possibility of variation of actual outcomes from expectations. Expressing the expected outcome as a probability-weighted average permits using variance or standard deviation as a measure of risk.

Variance

Variance is the weighted average of the squared differences between each possible outcome and the expected outcome. Expressed algebraically, this relationship is

$$V = \sum_{i=1}^{n}\left(CF_i - \overline{CF}\right)^2 P_i$$

where V is the variance, CF_i is the value of the ith possible outcome, $\overline{CF}$ is the expected value, and P_i is the related probability. Applying this formula to the possible nth-year cash flow in Example 17.1 and combining the previously calculated expected value of $187,500 with probability measures from Figure 17.4 yields a variance estimate of $856,250,000. Computations are shown in Figure 17.6.

FIGURE 17.6: Variance of the Probability Distribution of Possible Cash Flows From Shopping Center in Example 17.1

Possible Cash Flow	Expected Cash Flow	$CF_i - \overline{CF}$	(P_i)	$(CF_i - \overline{CF})^2 P_i$
$125,000	$187,500	(62,500)	0.04	$156,250,000
$150,000	$187,500	(37,500)	0.16	$225,000,000
$175,000	$187,500	(12,500)	0.30	$46,875,000
$200,000	$187,500	12,500	0.30	$46,875,000
$225,000	$187,500	37,500	0.16	$225,000,000
$250,000	$187,500	62,500	0.04	$156,250,000
			$\Sigma = 1.00$	$V = \$856,250,000$

Standard deviation

Because variance uses squared differences between observed values and the mean of a distribution, the relationship is nonlinear. The square root of the variance, called *standard deviation*, provides a much more usable measure of dispersion, particularly when it is used to compare alternative investment opportunities with significantly different expected values. This eliminates the distorting effect of squaring differences that vary greatly in magnitude.

The formula for the standard deviation is

$$\sigma = \sqrt{\sum_{i=1}^{n}\left(CF_i - \overline{CF}\right)^2 P_i}$$

where σ is the standard deviation, the CF_i are the various possible values of the cash flows, $\overline{CF}$ is the mean of the distribution of possible cash flows, and P_i is the probability of occurrence of each possible value.

Standard deviation has mathematical properties that make it particularly useful as a measure of risk. So long as the underlying probabilities are symmetrically distributed about the mean of the distribution, approximately 68.3% of all possible values will lie within one standard deviation of the expected value. Two standard deviations encompass approximately 95% of all possible outcomes, and three standard deviations to either side of the expected values include virtually all possible outcomes. Figure 17.7 illustrates this relationship.

FIGURE 17.7: Percentage of Area Under Normal Curve Encompassed by X Standard Deviations From the Mean

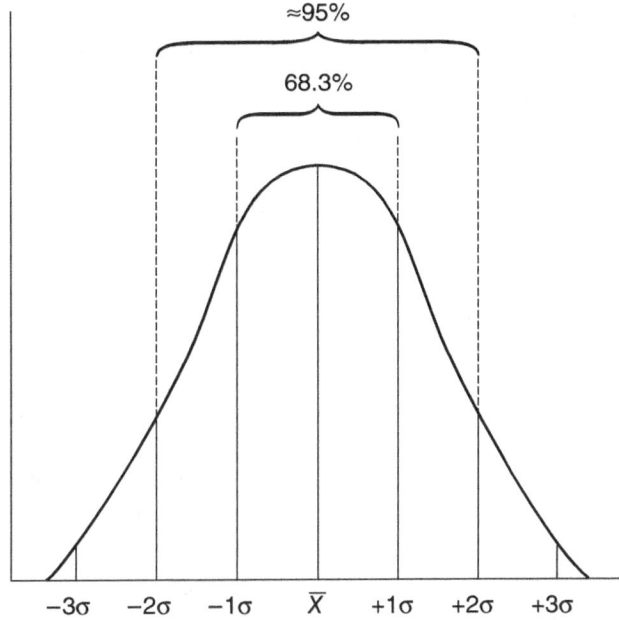

The drawing above is oversimplified because the tails come infinitely close without ever touching the horizontal axis.

Once the mean and the standard deviation are established, the probability of occurrence of values over any desired interval within the distribution can be determined by reference to a table of standardized values expressing the relationship. Such a table, sometimes called a table of *Z-values*, is given in Appendix C. It shows the portion of the area under the normal distribution lying to the left or right of various specified values. The Z-value from the table is simply the number of standard deviations from the mean to the value in question.

The relationship is frequently expressed algebraically as

$$Z = \frac{X - \overline{X}}{\sigma_x}$$

where X is some specified value under a symmetric distribution (often called a *normal curve*), $\overline{X}$ is the midpoint of the distribution (the expected value), and σ_x is the standard deviation.

Having earlier determined the variance of the distribution of possible net cash flows in Example 17.1 to be $856,250,000 (see Figure 17.6), the standard deviation can be computed by simply taking the square root of this amount, which is approximately $29,262. The expected value (i.e., the midpoint) of the distribution was previously determined to be $187,500 (see Figure 17.4). These two parameters, the expected value and the standard deviation, effectively determine the entire distribution of any normally distributed variable. Standard deviation serves well as the sole measure of risk only when the probability distribution is relatively symmetrical. If it is significantly skewed to either side, a measure of skewness may need to be incorporated into the model.

This is possible, but it vastly complicates the mathematics. Our analysis considers only the symmetric distribution.[2]

Figure 17.8 illustrates the relationship calculated for Example 17.1. The expected value of $187,500 is the midpoint of the distribution. One standard deviation is plus-or-minus $29,262, which we can determine (using the table of Z-values in Appendix C) encompasses approximately 68.3% of all possible values. The probability of the actual value falling within any range corresponds to the percentage of the total area under the curve that falls within that range. Therefore, the probability is approximately 0.683 that the actual cash flow will prove to be within plus-or-minus $29,262 of $187,500, which is to say between $158,238 and $216,762.

To determine this by reference to the table in Appendix C, first calculate the percentage of the total area *not* falling within one standard deviation of the midpoint (the unshaded area in Figure 17.8). Because this is a symmetric distribution (i.e., the sides of the probability distribution of possible cash flows are mirror images of each other, with 50% of the area under the curve lying on either side of the mean), we need to solve the problem for only one side of the curve. The same value will also apply to the other side. Refer to the table of Z-values in Appendix C to find the percentage of the total area under the curve to the left of point X. The area is 0.1587, or 15.87%. Now, because 50% of the total area under the curve lies to the left of the midpoint, it follows that the area from point X to the midpoint must be 50% minus 15.87%, or 34.13%. The total portion of the area under the curve that lies between one standard deviation and the midpoint, therefore, is two times 34.13%, or approximately 68.3%.

---

[2] For a discussion of probability estimation involving asymmetrical distributions, see John G. Kemeny et al., *Finite Mathematical Structures* (Englewood Cliffs, N.J.: Prentice Hall, 1959): 172–78.

FIGURE 17.8: Probability That Present Value Will Fall within Plus-or-Minus One Standard Deviation From the Mean

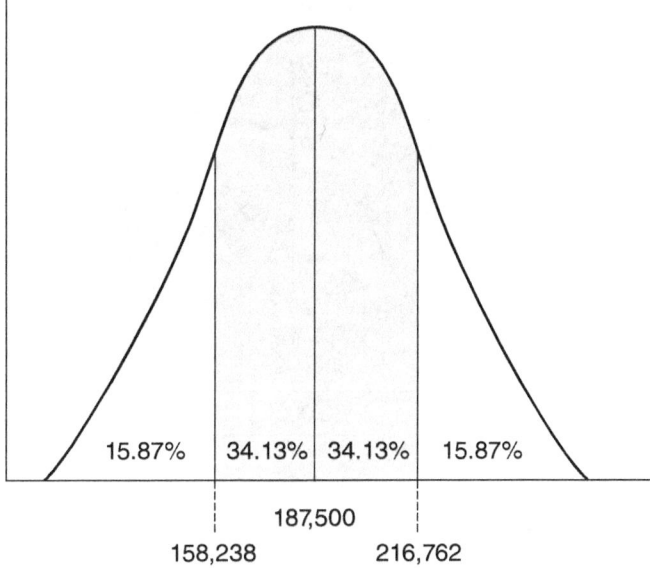

The drawing above is oversimplified because the tails come infinitely close without ever touching the horizontal axis.

As an exercise, use the table of Z-values to determine the probability that cash flow in Example 17.1 will equal or exceed $170,000. The first step is to determine how many standard deviations this variable, CF_i, lies from the mean, $\overline{CF}$:

$$Z = \frac{CF_i - \overline{CF}}{\sigma_{CF}} = \frac{\$170,000 - \$187,500}{\$29,262} = -0.60$$

From the table in Appendix C, determine that approximately 0.2743 of the total area lies to the left of the point associated with –0.60 standard deviations. Because 0.50 *minus* 0.2743 equals 0.2257, we can be 22.57% confident that the cash flow will actually be between $170,000 and $187,500, provided we have correctly specified the parameters of the problem. Moreover, we know that 50% of the possible outcomes are above $187,500. It follows that the probability of cash flow equal to or more than $170,000 is 0.50 *plus* 0.2257, or about 0.73 (see shaded area in Figure 17.9).

FIGURE 17.9: Probability of Cash Flows

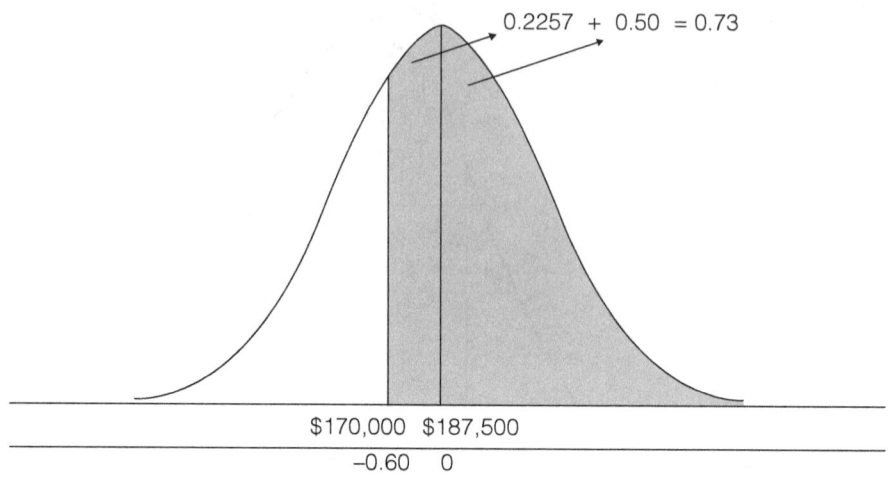

Coefficient of variation

Standard deviation serves admirably as a comparative measure of risk when evaluating alternatives involving approximately the same level of annual cash flow. When dissimilar cash flows must be compared, it is sometimes useful to go one step further and to calculate the *coefficient of variation*, which is the standard deviation of the cash flow divided by the expected cash flow.

In essence, it is a measure of risk per unit of return. That is the lower the ratio of risk to return, the better the risk-return trade-off. For the project in Example 17.1, the coefficient of variation is

$$\frac{\text{standard deviation}}{\text{expected cash flow}} = \frac{\$29,262}{\$187,500} = 0.156$$

When alternatives are being compared with respect to expected outcomes and relative riskiness rather than for derivation of a bid price, the coefficient of variation offers the advantage of permitting direct comparisons when the mean values of the cash-flow distributions vary.

STANDARD DEVIATION AND THE DISCOUNTED CASH-FLOW MODEL

A number of methods of incorporating risk into the investment decision have been used, the most appropriate being in part determined by the nature of the analysis. A second major factor is the pattern of the anticipated stream of investor benefits and the relationship between year-to-year forecasts.

Mean/Standard Deviation Approach

Perhaps the most useful approach to incorporating risk into an investment decision is to use the *mean/standard deviation* model. It involves developing both an expected cash flow and a standard deviation measure for each year of the projection period. The technique is best illustrated by using a single-period cash-flow forecast. This avoids complications introduced when annual cash flows are influenced by outcomes from previous years. After demonstrating the principle with this simplifying assumption concerning cash-flow patterns, we will examine more complex situations.

Example 17.2

A proposal requires an initial equity investment of $25,000. After three years, it is expected that the investment position will be liquidated with a net cash inflow of $50,000. The standard deviation of the cash flow in the third year is estimated to be $7,000, and the range of possible cash flows is assumed to be distributed symmetrically about the expected amount. Cash flow during the first two years is virtually certain to be zero. The investor's opportunity cost of equity capital (the appropriate discount rate) is 10%.

Consider Example 17.2. Though the forecast includes a point estimate of cash flow for the third year, there is in fact a whole spectrum of possible cash flows for that year. This is evidenced by the estimated $7,000 standard deviation of the cash flows. The standard deviation estimate, you will recall, is derived by comparing the range of possible outcomes with the expected outcome.

There is a present value associated with each possible cash-flow outcome in Example 17.2. Were it possible to discount every possible outcome, a probability distribution of possible present values would result. This distribution of present values also, of course, will have an expected value (the midpoint of the distribution) and a standard deviation.

Because the distribution of possible cash flows in Example 17.2 is assumed to be distributed symmetrically about its mean, the distribution of present values also will be symmetrically distributed. Moreover, the midpoint of the distribution of present values will be the discounted value of the midpoint of the distribution of cash flows. This expected present value is $37,566, calculated as follows:

$$\overline{PV} = \frac{\overline{CF}}{(1+i)^3} = \frac{\$50,000}{1.10^3} = \$37,566$$

UNIT 17 Contemporary Risk Measures

Where there is only one anticipated future cash flow (rather than a series of forecasted outcomes), computing the standard deviation of the present value distribution is equally uncomplicated. Simply discount the standard deviation of the cash-flow distribution at the same discount rate used in determining the midpoint of the distribution of possible present values. For Example 17.2, the computation is

$$\sigma_{PV}\hat{E} = \frac{\sigma_{CF}}{(1+i)^3} = \frac{\$7,000}{1.10^3} = \$5,259$$

Recall that when the rate of return equals the discount rate, the present value of future cash flows will equal the amount of the initial cash outlay. Should the actual cash flow from the project in Example 17.2 be such that its present value (discounting at 10%) proves to be $25,000 more, it follows that the actual rate of return on the project will have been 10% or better. The probability that this will occur equals the percentage of the total area under the probability distribution of possible present values lying to the right of the point where the actual outcome is $25,000.

Figure 17.10 depicts the probability distribution of possible present values of the cash flows from Example 17.2. The probability that the actual present value will be $25,000 or better (and thus, the rate of return will be 10% or more) is represented by the unshaded area under the curve. We can determine what percentage of the total area this represents by using the equation discussed earlier in the unit:

$$Z = \frac{PV_x - \overline{PV}}{\sigma_{PV}}$$

where:

Z = the standardized value
PV_x = minimum acceptable present value
$\overline{PV}$ = the expected present value (i.e., the arithmetic mean)
σ_{PV} = the standard deviation of the present value

Substituting values from Example 17.2 into the equation yields

$$Z = \frac{\$25,000 - 37,566}{\$5,259} = -2.39$$

Reference to the table of Z-values in Appendix C reveals that the area to the left of $PV = \$25,000$ is just slightly more than 0.8% of the total area under the distribution.

FIGURE 17.10: Probability of Acceptance Error (Probability That Actual Present Value Will Be Less Than Minimum Acceptable)

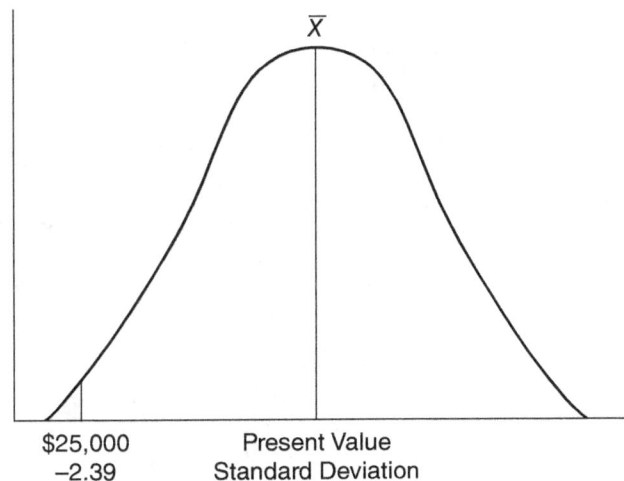

The drawing above is oversimplified because the tails come infinitely close without ever touching the horizontal axis.

The probability that this project will generate at least a 10% rate of return, therefore, is estimated to be more than 0.99. Expressed another way, the investor can be more than 99% confident of earning a rate of return equal to or greater than the opportunity cost of capital.

Establishing Acceptable Risk Profiles

The probability that a venture will generate less than the minimum acceptable rate of return and thus that its acceptance will prove to have been a mistake is called the *probability of acceptance error*. Having specified an absolute maximum probability of acceptance error beyond which no investment opportunity will be undertaken, there remains the problem of discriminating between acceptable and unacceptable risk-reward combinations that lie within the range of provisional acceptability. Within that range are gradients of risk. Investors expect compensation for all incremental risk assumed.

To facilitate choosing among risky opportunities, and to ensure consistency over time, investors may specify the maximum acceptable probability of acceptance error associated with various levels of present values per dollar of invested cash or with various expected rates of return. This permits a more refined preliminary screening by subordinates, further reducing the time spent by final decision makers on projects destined for ultimate rejection.

Before risk profiles can be constructed, expected outcomes must be expressed in terms that permit interproject comparisons of cost and benefit. Profitability indices (discussed in Unit 14) have this characteristic, inasmuch as they represent the ratio of present value to initial cash outlay. They convert absolute present value estimates to measures of relative present value per dollar of required initial cash expenditure. To illustrate, consider again the investment in Example 17.2. The midpoint of the distribution of possible outcomes, expressed in present value terms, is $37,566, and the initial cash outlay is $25,000. The expected value of the probability distribution of possible profitability indices, $\overline{PI}$ is

$$\overline{PI} = \frac{\$337,566}{\$25,000} = 1.50$$

Recall from Unit 14 that when present value just equals the initial cash outlay, the PI is exactly 1 and the NPV is 0. Also, recall that this means the IRR exactly equals the discount rate used to determine present value. Present value, NPV, and the PI, therefore, all measure the same relationship. An advantage of the PI is that it permits comparisons among projects of different magnitudes.

Figure 17.11 replicates Figure 17.10, with a second scale measured in terms of the PI. Note that at the point where the present value of future net cash flows equals the initial cash outlay of $25,000, the PI is 1, indicating that this corresponds to an IRR just equal to the 10% minimum acceptable rate.

FIGURE 17.11: Probability of Acceptance Error (Probability That Actual Probability Index Will Be Less Than Minimally Acceptable)

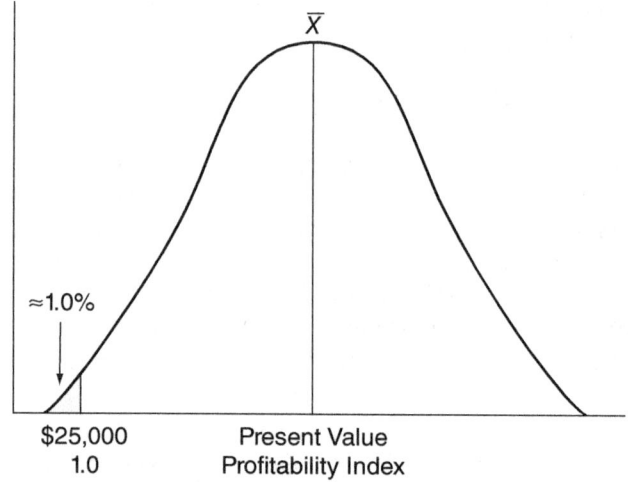

The drawing above is oversimplified because the tails come infinitely close without ever touching the horizontal axis.

The specification of maximum levels of risk for various values of profitability indices (expected benefits) permits project evaluation by reference to a risk profile that does not depend on the magnitude of the commitment. If the dispersion of possible outcomes indicates the project is too risky for the benefit it is expected to generate per dollar invested, the proposal is automatically rejected. If not, it is passed to the investor for a final decision. All projects passing this preliminary filtering process are considered, and final decisions are made according to portfolio risk-return considerations, with available cash acting as a constraint.

A tabulation of acceptable combinations of risk and expected benefits will reflect a positive relationship between expected profitability and dispersion of possible returns (risk). The exact trade-off depends on the investor's attitude toward risk. This permits interface of the investor's risk preferences with the analyst's informed opinion regarding the risk implicit in a particular project.

Risk profiles for two investors are presented in Figure 17.12 and illustrated in Figure 17.13. The table presumes that anticipated after-tax cash flows have been discounted at a rate representing the minimum acceptable yield on the investor's equity investment. If the actual yield falls below this minimum rate, the PI will be less than one (i.e., the present value of the cash flows will be less than $1 for each $1 of equity investment). Should this occur, the investment venture will prove to have been a mistake.

If the expected PI is greater than 1, indicating an expected rate of return in excess of the minimum acceptable rate, the investor is willing to accept some risk (measured as probability) that the actual rate of return will fall below the minimum acceptable level.

FIGURE 17.12: Risk-Return Profiles for Two Investors Who Express Risk in Terms of Probability of Earning Less Than a Specified Minimum Acceptable Rate of Return

Expected Profitability Index	Minimum Acceptable Probability That Profitability Index Will Be Equal or Less Than One	
	Investor A	Investor B
0.0	0.0000	0.0000
1.2	0.0150	0.0150
1.4	0.0230	0.0260
1.6	0.0290	0.0345
1.8	0.0330	0.0430
2.0	0.0350	0.0460
2.2	0.0350	0.0490
2.4	0.0350	0.0500

FIGURE 17.13: Risk-Return Profiles Expressed in Terms of Profitability Index

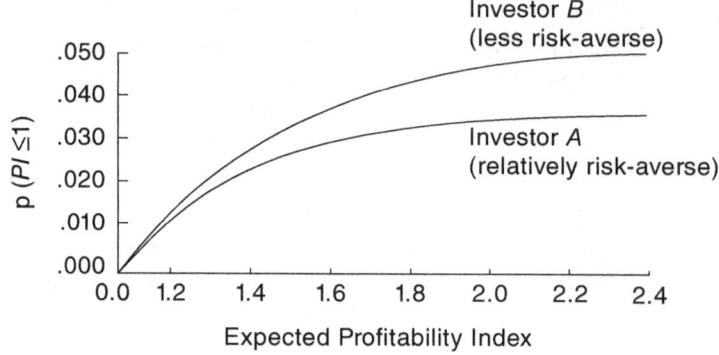

Thus, with an expected PI of 1.2 ($1.20 of present value for each $1 of equity cash invested), investor A in Figure 17.12 will accept a probability of as much as 0.0150 that the actual PI will be 1 or less and, therefore, that the rate of return will be equal to or less than the minimum acceptable rate. The higher the expected PI (and thus the expected rate of return), the greater the acceptable risk (probability) that the actual rate of return will fall below acceptable levels and the venture will prove to be a mistake.

Figure 17.13 graphically portrays the relationship between expected present value per dollar invested (profitability indices) and acceptable levels of risk for the investors whose risk-return preferences are charted in Figure 17.12. For each investor, the area below the lines in Figure 17.13 represents acceptable combinations of risk and expected profitability indices; the area above the lines represents unacceptable combinations.

DEALING WITH MORE COMPLEX CASH-FLOW PATTERNS

To avoid premature complications, our discussion thus far has assumed a single-period cash-flow pattern. This simplifies the dialogue but, for most real estate ventures, is highly unrealistic. Cash flows (both positive and negative) usually occur periodically over a number of years. It becomes necessary, therefore, to estimate the mean and standard deviation of the cash flows for each year in the projection period, including the cash flow from disposing of the project at the end of the holding period.

With multiple-year patterns, cash flow in subsequent periods will depend at least in part on what happens in earlier periods. If projections prove overly optimistic in early years, chances are that the same will hold for the entire life of the project. Likewise, if cash flows in early years are greater than anticipated, favorable deviations are likely to occur in future years as well, so long as the same causal influences are present. The extent to which causal factors influence cash flows over two or more periods is called *serial correlation*. It is measured by the *coefficient of correlation*, which can range from 0 to plus-or-minus 1. When the correlation coefficient equals zero, serial cash flows are completely independent of each other. A coefficient of plus-or-minus 1 indicates perfect correlation of the cash flows.

Serial correlation (or its absence) does not affect the expected present value of a series of cash-flow projections. It will, however, drastically alter the standard deviation of the probability distribution of possible present values. In general, the greater the degree of serial correlation of annual cash flows, the wider the dispersion of possible outcomes about the mean and the greater the standard deviation of the probability distribution of possible present values.

Perfectly Correlated Cash Flows

If serial cash flows are perfectly correlated, deviation from the expected outcome in one period will result in deviations in all future periods. If actual cash flows in one period are exactly one-half standard deviation to the right or left of the mean value of the probability distribution of possible cash flows for the period, then actual cash flows for all future periods will be exactly one-half standard deviation to the right or left of the probability distributions of all possible cash flows.

The standard deviation of the present value of a perfectly correlated stream of cash flows is:

$$\sigma_{PV} = \sum_{t=1}^{n}\left[\frac{\sigma_{CF_t}}{(1+i)^t}\right]$$

where σ_{PV} is the standard deviation of the present value distribution, σ_{CF} is the standard deviation of the cash-flow distribution for time period t, and i is the discount rate used to derive the expected present value. For perfectly serially correlated cash flows, therefore, simply discount the standard deviation of the cash-flow distributions to derive the standard deviation of the present value distribution.

To see how the degree of serial correlation affects the standard deviation of the probability distribution of present values, consider the series of cash-flow projections in Example 17.3.

Example 17.3

A real estate project requires an initial equity outlay of $50,000. An analyst develops the following estimate of the midpoints and standard deviations for annual cash flows over the projected life of the investment venture:

Mean of Cash-Flow Distribution	Standard Deviation
$15,000	$5,400
$15,000	$4,500
$40,000	$9,000

The probability distributions of annual cash flows are assumed to be symmetrical about the means, and the serial correlation coefficients are all assumed to be +1. The investor's minimum acceptable rate of return (and therefore the appropriate discount rate) is 12%.

Remember that the expected value (the *mean*) of the probability distribution of possible present values associated with a symmetrically distributed cash-flow distribution is simply the present value of the mean of the cash-flow distribution.

Discounting the means from Example 17.3 and summing the present values yields the mean of the probability distribution of possible present values of all cash flows from the venture. These computations are shown in Figure 17.14.

Recall also that the standard deviation of the probability distribution of possible present values for perfectly serially correlated cash flows is derived by simply discounting the standard deviations of the cash-flow distributions. These computations are also illustrated in Figure 17.14.

Uncorrelated Cash Flows

Expected present value does not change when the possibility of serially independent (uncorrelated) cash flows is introduced, but the standard deviation of the present value distribution may be greatly altered. In general, the greater the degree of serial correlation of the annual cash flows, the greater will be the dispersion—and thus the greater the standard deviation—of the probability distribution of possible present values.

To illustrate this relationship, consider again the cash-flow projections in Example 17.3, but recompute the standard deviation of the present value under the revised assumption that the actual cash flow for each year is considered to be completely independent of that for other years.

FIGURE 17.14: Mean and Standard Deviation of Probability Distribution of Present Values from Example 17.3

Year	Expected Cash Flow	Mean of Present Value @ 12%
1	$15,000	$13,393
2	$15,000	11,958
3	$40,000	28,471
		$53,822

Year	Standard Deviation of Cash Flow	Standard Deviation of Present Value
1	$5,400	$ 4,821
2	$4,500	3,587
3	$9,000	6,406
		$14,814

The formula for computing the standard deviation of the present value is

$$\sigma_{PV} = \sqrt{\sum_{t=1}^{n}\left[\frac{\sigma_{CF_t}}{(1+i)^{2t}}\right]}$$

where σ_{PV} is the standard deviation of the present value, σ_{CF} is the standard deviation of the cash flow for year t, and i is the discount rate used to derive the present value of the cash flows. Substituting the standard deviation of the cash flows and the discount rate from Example 17.3 yields a standard deviation of the present value of $8,784. Here is the calculation:

$$\sigma_{PV} = \sqrt{\frac{\$5,400}{1.12^2} + \frac{\$4,500}{1.12^4} + \frac{\$9,000}{1.12^6}} = \$8,784$$

Comparing this with the standard deviation of the present value under the assumption of perfect serial correlation, as derived in Figure 17.14, makes clear the consequence of serial correlation; moving from perfect to zero serial correlation reduced the standard deviation of the present value by $6,030, or almost 41%.

Partially Correlated Cash Flows

Shifting from an assumption of serial independence to one of perfect serial correlation changes the computation of standard deviation and thus the dispersion of the probability distribution of possible outcomes from an investment, but does not seriously complicate the arithmetic. Problems do arise, however, where there is *partial serial correlation*.

In situations involving less-than-perfect serial correlation, some of the expected cash flows may be highly correlated over time, while others may be more nearly independent. This is illustrative of most real-world circumstances. When this occurs, the standard deviation problem becomes complex.

To deal with the issue, Frederick S. Hillier has developed a model that is particularly applicable to real estate investment situations.[3] His model groups annual cash flows on the basis of whether they are more nearly independent or serially correlated over time. The two groups are then treated as if they were *completely independent* and *perfectly correlated*, respectively.

The present value of the segmented income streams is unaffected by the treatment afforded in Hillier's model. The formula for the revised standard deviation of the present value, however, becomes

$$\sigma_{PV} = \sqrt{\left[\sum_{t=1}^{n} \frac{\sigma_{CF_t}}{(1+i)^t}\right]^2 + \left[\sum_{t=1}^{n} \frac{\sigma^2_{CF_t}}{(1+i)^{2t}}\right]}$$

where the first bracketed term under the radical applies to the standard deviation for the cash flows assumed to be perfectly correlated and the second bracketed term applies to the standard deviation for the stream of net cash flows assumed to be serially independent (uncorrelated).

To illustrate the use of Hillier's model, consider the data in Example 17.4, which represent a breakdown of supporting data from Example 17.3.

The expected present value of the venture in Example 17.4 remains unchanged (except for rounding differences) from that of Example 17.3:

$$PV = \frac{\$27,000 - \$12,000}{1.12} + \frac{\$27,000 - \$12,000}{1.12^2} + \frac{\$27,000 - \$12,000}{1.12^3} = \$53,882$$

The standard deviation of the expected present value, however, is drastically altered by the assumption of serial correlation of gross revenues. Substituting standard deviation measures from Example 17.4 in the formula developed by Hillier gives

$$\sigma_{PV} = \sqrt{\left[\frac{\$3,780}{1.12} + \frac{\$3,500}{1.12^2} + \frac{\$6,000}{1.12^3}\right]^2 + \left[\frac{\$1,620^2}{1.12} + \frac{\$1,000^2}{1.12^4} + \frac{\$2,700^2}{1.12^6}\right]}$$

$$= \$10,739$$

---

[3] See Frederick S. Hillier, "The Derivation of Probabilistic Information for the Evaluation of Risky Investments," *Management Science* 9 (April 1963): 443–57.

Example 17.4

Attempting a better grip on the risk element associated with the investment in Example 17.3, the analyst separates net cash-flow projections into receipt and expenditure components. Separate standard deviation estimates are developed for each component.

Because rental revenues are so dependent on locational factors, the revenue stream is considered to be highly correlated over time. If the location is less desirable than anticipated, less-than-expected revenues will occur in each of the forecast years. The same factor will affect the selling price of the property at the end of the holding period, which is included in the expected cash flow for that year.

Operating expenses, on the other hand, are largely independent of locational influences. They are considered to be serially independent and are expected to vary from projected values only as a result of random factors.

Annual projections of revenue and expenditures and associated standard deviation estimates are determined to be as follows:

	Revenue Projections		Expenditure Projections	
Year	Projected Revenue	Standard Deviation	Projected Expenditures	Standard Deviation
1	$27,000	$3,780	$12,000	$1,620
2	$27,000	$3,500	$12,000	$1,000
3	$52,000	$6,000	$12,000	$2,700

SUMMARY

Modern risk-analysis techniques developed in the fields of corporate finance and capital budgeting can be applied to real estate investment analysis. The techniques allow risk to be expressed in terms of probability of variance from expectations. Because data are not available for statistical sampling of the type used in the physical and biological sciences, probabilities in real estate investment analysis are frequently subjective, reflecting the informed opinion of an analyst rather than being generated from objective information sources.

Techniques for expressing risk in probabilistic terms involve developing probability distributions of possible outcomes and estimating related standard deviations. This in turn permits expression of likely investment consequences as ranges of possible outcomes and accompanying levels of confidence. Probability distributions of possible outcomes may be expressed as present values, NPVs, profitability indices, or any number of other measures as desired by an analyst or client.

RECOMMENDED READING

Adair, Alastair. "Research Review." *Briefings in Real Estate Finance* 1, no. 1 (June 2001):88–95.

Brigham, Eugene F., and Joel F. Houston. *Fundamentals of Financial Management.* 13th ed. Ft. Worth, Tex.: South-Western College Publishers, 2013.

Peng, Liang, and Thomas Thibodeau. "Risk Segmentation of American Homes: Evidence from Denver," *Real Estate Economics* 41:3, 2013.

Weaver, William. "A Pedagogical Tool to Assist in Teaching Real Estate Investment Risk Analysis." *Journal of Real Estate Practice and Education* 7, no. 1 (2004): 43–52.

REVIEW QUESTIONS

1. What objections to modern techniques do users of traditional risk measures have? Why are their objections off target?
2. Describe the difference between risk and uncertainty.
3. How might one estimate probabilities related to real estate investments? What role do subjective probability measures play in the analysis?
4. Explain *discrete* and *continuous* probability distributions.
5. Explain the usefulness of variance and standard deviation in risk measurement.
6. Describe the calculation for the coefficient of variation and explain its purpose in the analysis.
7. How are profitability indices used in development of risk profiles?

DISCUSSION QUESTIONS

1. Is the probability distribution approach to risk measurement discussed in this unit more likely to be adopted as computer literacy becomes increasingly widespread? Explain your reasoning.
2. If probabilities cannot be measured using sample data, but must be expressed as subjective probabilities, is there any benefit in expressing them in quantitative terms? Why or why not?
3. What are some examples of events or contract provisions that could skew or attenuate the probability distribution of possible cash flows from a real estate development?

UNIT 18

Risk Management in a Portfolio Context

UNIT PREVIEW

Previous units explored the relationship between risk and expected return and defined risk as the expected variance in returns. To treat equally both positive and negative variance from expectations, without the distorting effect of simply squaring the variance, we used the square root of the sum of the squared variances—standard deviation. When more than one asset is included in a portfolio, a third dimension must be incorporated in the risk-return equation: covariance of returns.

Covariance measures the way the total portfolio variance is altered when additional assets are added to a portfolio. It is a function of the correlation between the returns on portfolio assets. The lower the covariance, the smaller the portfolio risk. This lumping together within the portfolio of assets that exhibit low covariance is the cornerstone of diversification to reduce aggregate risk.

MODERN PORTFOLIO THEORY AND RISK MANAGEMENT

Considered to be the father of modern portfolio theory, Harry Markowitz, was born in the middle of the 20th century. Most authorities mark its beginning in 1952 with the publication of Markowitz's seminal article, "Portfolio Selection."[1] The literature expanded exponentially during the 1960s and 1970s, and the proliferation continues today.

The essence of modern portfolio theory is that among the universe of possible investment portfolios, there is a subset that represents optimal combinations of expected return and risk, and the precise choice from among this subset depends on an investor's attitude toward risk. Contemporary literature on real estate portfolio management indicates that modern portfolio theory is the dominant influence that molds institutional portfolio managers' strategy.

Systematic and Unsystematic Risk

It is not possible to eliminate all risk through diversification. Some risk is inherent in the market itself. This *market risk* is inherent in the market system, and for that reason, is often called *systematic risk*. It exists without regard to selection of specific assets.

In contrast, risk associated with a specific asset (or a specific industry or geographic locale) can be eliminated in a portfolio by matching the asset with others that exhibit low or negative covariance. Because this risk element is asset-specific and not inherent in the system, it is sometimes called *unsystematic risk*.

The relationship between systematic and unsystematic risk, and the reduction in unsystematic risk through diversification, is illustrated in Figure 18.1. It is widely accepted that unsystematic risk accounts for roughly half the total risk in the stock market. There is a lack of data to support a generalization of this type regarding real estate markets, but the localized nature of real estate assets suggests that unsystematic risk probably accounts for a larger portion of total risk.[2] Variation in rent levels and vacancy rates due to market-wide changes in supply and demand variables are examples of systematic risk associated with real estate assets. Site-specific factors such as building defects and micromarket variables that affect rents and vacancy rates are unsystematic risks that can be largely eliminated by diversification without reducing expected returns.

Market prices, to the extent the market is efficient, reflect systematic but not unsystematic risk. This implies that investors are compensated by higher expected returns for bearing systematic risk but are not compensated for bearing unsystematic risk, and that holding a poorly diversified portfolio is more costly for real estate investors than for stock or bond investors. Stated another way, real estate investors stand to gain more in terms of risk reduction by diversifying their portfolios than do other investors.

---

1 Harry Markowitz, "Portfolio Selection," *Journal of Finance* (March 1952): 77–91.
2 Anthony B. Sanders, Joseph L. Pagliari, Jr., and James R. Webb, "Portfolio Management Concepts and Their Application to Real Estate," *The Handbook of Real Estate Portfolio Management* (Chicago: Richard D. Irwin, Inc., 1995): 131.

FIGURE 18.1: Eliminating Nonsystematic Risk Through Diversification

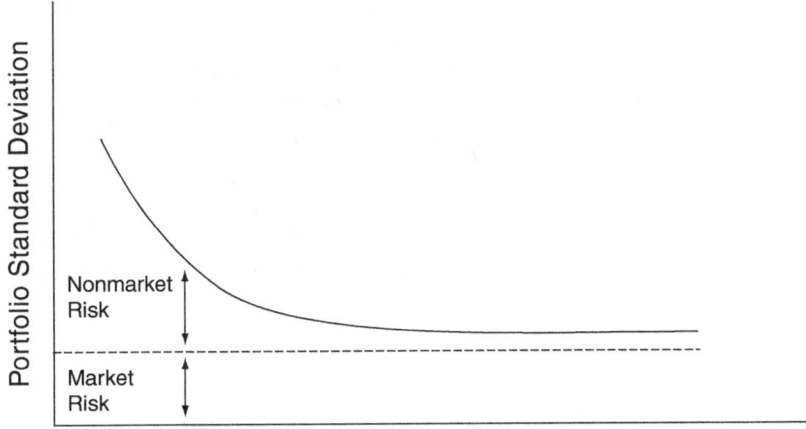

The Efficient Frontier

Figure 18.2 portrays various portfolios, measured in terms of their expected return and risk. If every possible portfolio of risky assets—every attainable combination of risk and return—were included in the figure, it would have course have more dots, but there is no reason to expect that it would differ in configuration. Of particular interest are the attainable combinations along the top border of the universe of attainable combinations. These embody the maximum returns obtainable with given levels of risk or the minimum risk possible for given levels of return. All portfolios located elsewhere in the universe of attainable combinations are suboptimal because it is possible to gain higher expected returns without assuming more risk or to reduce risk without sacrificing expected returns, by altering the portfolio.

FIGURE 18.2: The Efficient Frontier

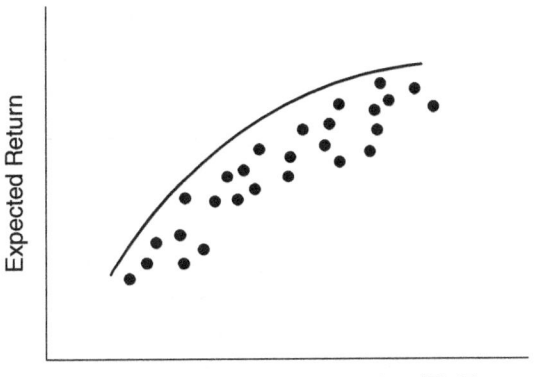

Modern portfolio theory identifies the sets of attainable combinations along the upper border as *efficient portfolios*, because no others offer higher expected returns for the same or lower levels of risk, or lower risk with the same or higher levels of expected return. In the aggregate, these efficient portfolios represent the *efficient frontier*. The idea is to select from among the efficient portfolios the one that maximizes investor satisfaction, given the investor's objectives, capital constraints, and attitude toward risk.

An important observation is that the set of attainable combinations contains not just real estate investments but the entire universe of risky investments. The optimal efficient portfolio will almost certainly include some real estate assets and some other risky assets as well.

Furthermore, modern portfolio theory posits that the efficient frontier changes when borrowing and lending opportunities are introduced. Investors can choose assets that have no default risk and that are so short term as to virtually eliminate interest rate risk. When these assets, called *risk-free assets*, are added to the portfolio, the efficient frontier becomes a straight line below point C on Figure 18.3. A highly risk-averse investor might choose to hold only the risk-free asset, in which case the risk would be zero and the expected return R_f. Alternatively, the risk-averse investor could choose to hold the portfolio indicated by point M, or any other portfolio along the efficiency frontier above point C.

FIGURE 18.3: The Efficient Frontier With a Risk-Free Asset

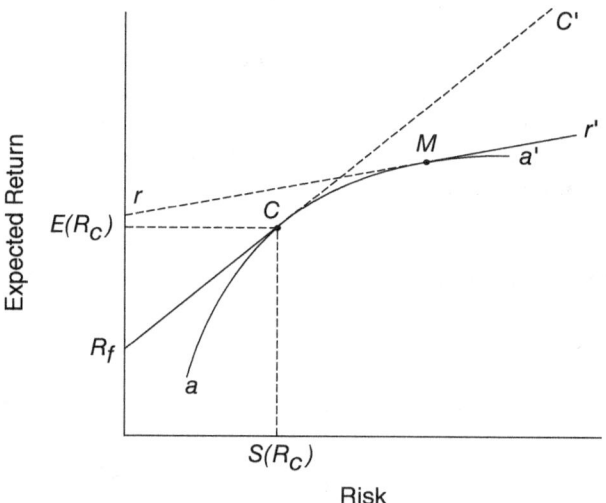

If the investor could borrow as well as lend at the risk-free rate, the set of efficient portfolios would extend beyond point C in Figure 18.3, along the broken line. Portfolios between R_f and C are combinations of the risky and the risk-free assets. Portfolio C comprises wholly risky assets. After committing all available funds to portfolio C, the investor could borrow at rate R_f to increase the size of the investment in portfolio C.

This would move the portfolio out into the risk-return plane along the broken line CC' in Figure 18.3.

It is highly unlikely, however, that an investor could borrow at the risk-free rate. When borrowing costs are higher than risk-free lending rates, the only part of the line R_fCC' that will be included in the set of attainable combinations is the segment R_fC. If the investor's borrowing rate is given by the point r on the vertical axis of Figure 18.3, then the risk-return combinations available through borrowing to increase the size of the portfolio are given by the segment Mr' of the line rMr'.[3]

Under these conditions, the set of attainable combinations in the efficient portfolio is given by the line R_fCMr' in Figure 18.3. This line is reproduced in Figure 18.4 without the broken segments. The efficient portfolio comprises a combination of the risk-free assets and portfolio C in varying proportions to the point where the expected return is $E(R_c)$, at which point the portfolio contains none of the risk-free asset. Beyond this point, expected returns can be increased by altering the portfolio of risky assets as indicated by the efficiency frontier from point C to point M.

On reaching the combination of risky assets represented by point M in Figure 18.4, the expected return is $E(R_m)$ and the perceived risk is $S(R_m)$. Higher levels of expected return with minimum risk can be obtained by borrowing at interest rate r and purchasing an ever larger quantity of the invariant portfolio of risky assets represented by point M. This moves the investor out into the risk-return plan along the line segment Mr'. The length of the line segment is determined by the amount of financial leverage the investor can undertake without increasing the cost of borrowing.

FIGURE 18.4: The Efficient Frontier With Borrowing and Lending

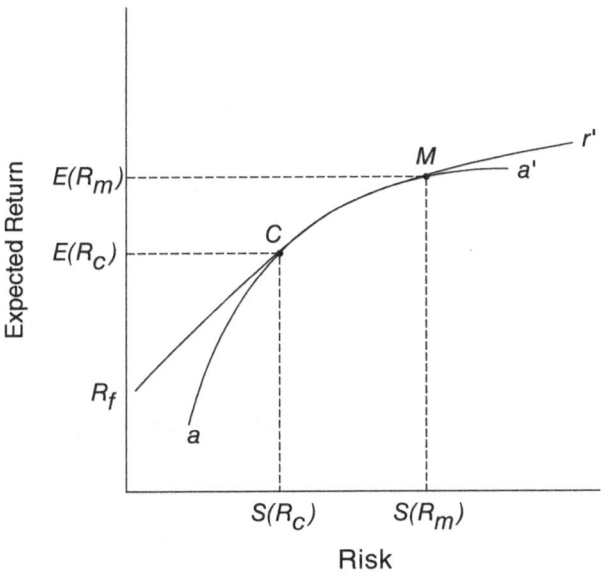

---

[3] Nicholas W. Schrock, "Asset Choice under Uncertainty with Borrowing Introduced," *Western Economic Journal* (March 1967): 201–10.

THE ROLE OF REAL ESTATE IN THE EFFICIENT PORTFOLIO

Recall that, given the assumptions underlying modern portfolio theory, any portfolio of risky assets other than those between points C and r' in Figure 18.4 represent inefficient combinations. Investors holding other combinations can increase return without shouldering more risk or reduce risk without sacrificing return by altering their portfolio until it represents a point along this line segment. Several research studies have indicated that real estate will represent a significant proportion of these efficient portfolios.[4]

No one knows exactly where the efficient frontier lies, of course, or exactly what assets it will encompass. Even if sufficient data were available, performing the mathematical computations to identify the frontier would be a prodigious task. Anthony Sanders, Joseph Pagliari, and James Webb note, for example, that to create an optimal portfolio of common stocks from the Wilshire 5000 Index would require estimating approximately 12.5 million paired correlation coefficients.[5] When real estate is added to the universe of possible investments, the problems of data availability and reliability are magnified several times over. The result has been described as a "fuzzy" efficient frontier.[6] This implies that instead of a single efficient portfolio occupying each point on the efficient frontier, representing a discrete return-risk expectation, numerous dissimilarly weighted portfolios offer the same expected risk-return combination.

Given these observations, it is not surprising to find widespread disagreement regarding the proper role of real estate in institutional portfolios. With only a few exceptions, studies suggesting particular portfolio allocations to real estate conclude that 10% to 20% is optimal. Yet research into actual real estate holdings among pension funds revealed an average of only 4.37% of assets committed to real estate equities in 1991 (the study was limited to funds that exceed $100 million in assets).[7] The commitment ranged from 0% to 17% of assets.

DIVERSIFICATION STRATEGIES FOR REAL ESTATE

Real estate's positive impact on portfolio performance has been well documented. There is widespread disagreement about how much real estate should be included in a diversified portfolio, but little dissension concerning the merit of its inclusion. Moreover, modern portfolio theory and its subsequent spinoffs argue uniformly for diversification to eliminate nonsystematic risk. There remains the question of how diversification should be pursued—geographically, across asset categories, and through time.

---

4   Vickie L. Bajtelsmit and Elaine M. Worzala, "Real Estate Allocation in Pension Fund Portfolios," *The Journal of Real Estate Portfolio Management* 1, no. 1 (1995): 25–38. The authors summarized 11 studies published between 1984 and 1991 that recommended substantial commitments to real estate in institutional portfolios.
5   Sanders, Pagliari, and Webb, "Portfolio Management Concepts," 139.
6   Richard B. Gold, "Why the Efficient Frontier for Real Estate Is 'Fuzzy'," *The Journal of Real Estate Portfolio Management* 1, no. 1 (1995): 59–66.
7   Bajtelsmit and Worzala, "Real Estate Allocation in Pension Fund Portfolios."

Joseph L. Pagliari, Jr., suggests categorizing product alternatives by the defining characteristics of geography, product type, and stage in product life-cycle.[8] He illustrates the alternatives using a diagram similar to Figure 18.5 and observes that each cell in the array has risk and expected return characteristics that are at least partially unique.

Stephen Lee and Simon Stevenson found that REITs do play a significant role over both different time horizons and holding periods. The findings of their study show that REITs' attractiveness as a diversification asset increase as the holding period increases.[9]

FIGURE 18.5: The Range of Diversification Alternatives

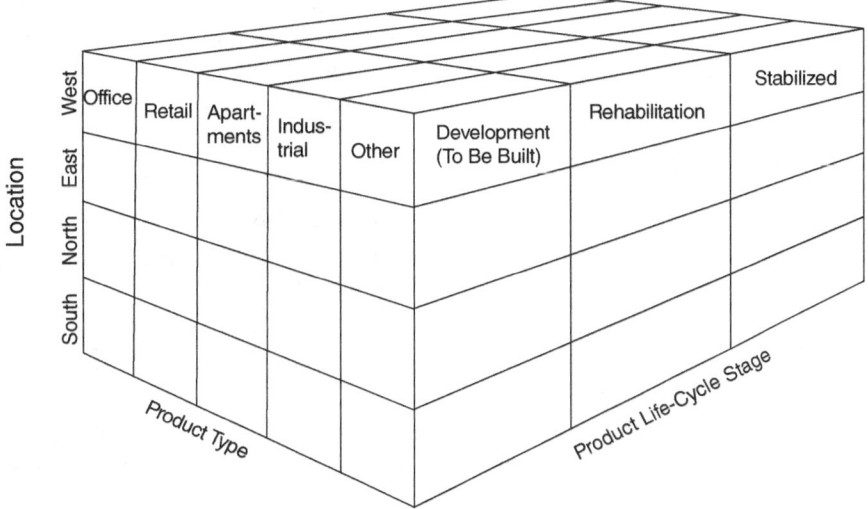

Geographic Diversification

Reducing risk by geographic diversification presupposes geographic locals where levels of economic activity are not highly correlated. Nothing is accomplished by acquiring widely separated assets that behave economically as if they were side by side. Owning property on the east and west coasts will not reduce the volatility of one's portfolio, for example, if the coastal cities are subject to roughly similar economic forces.

---

8   Joseph L. Pagliari, Jr., "Real Estate in 3-D: See It Now!" *Real Estate Issues* (Fall-Winter 1990): 16–19.
9   Stephen Lee and Simon Stevenson, "The Case for REITs in the Mixed-Asset Portfolio in the Short and Long Run," *Journal of Real Estate Portfolio Management* 11, no. 1 (January–April 2005): 55–80.

SUMMARY

When assets are considered in a portfolio context rather than individually, the focus shifts to risk and expected return for the portfolio. Risk associated with an individual asset is less important than the effect the asset has on total portfolio risk. An asset that, taken individually, is more risky than the total risk for the portfolio to which it is being added can actually reduce the aggregate riskiness of the portfolio.

Most portfolio managers address their task from the perspective of modern portfolio theory, which emphasizes identifying of the subset of portfolios that generate the maximum return for a given level of aggregate risk and selecting the specific subset that matches the profile of the investor in terms of return objectives and attitude toward risk.

Researchers generally agree that real estate is an essential component of efficient portfolios. They do not agree concerning the percentage of the portfolio that should be devoted to real estate. Portfolio managers appear skeptical of recommendations from academic researchers about how much real estate should be included in their portfolios.

RECOMMENDED READING

Coleman, Mark S. "Real Estate in the Real World: Dealing with Non-Normality and Risk in an Asset Allocation Model." *Journal of Real Estate Portfolio Management* 11, no. 1 (January–April 2005): 37–53.

Harding, William G., Kartono Liano, and Gow-Cheng Huang. "REIT Stock Splits and Market Efficiency." *The Journal of Real Estate Finance and Economics* 30, no. 3 (2005): 297–315.

Lee, Stephen L. "The Return Due to Diversification of Real Estate to the U.S. Mixed-Asset Portfolio." *Journal of Real Estate Portfolio Management* 11, no. 1 (January–April 2005): 19–28.

Louis, Hencock, and Amy X. Sun. "Growth in Housing Prices and Long-Term Abnormal Stock Returns." *Real Estate Economics*, 41:1, 2013.

Pagliari, Joseph L. Jr., editor. *The Handbook of Real Estate Portfolio Management.* Chicago: Richard D. Irwin, Inc., 1995.

Pagliari, Joseph L. Jr., James R. Webb, and Joseph J. Del Casino. "Applying MPT to Institutional Real Estate Portfolios: The Good, the Bad and the Uncertain." *The Journal of Real Estate Portfolio Management* 1, no. 1, 1995: 67–88.

Worzala, Elaine, and Vickie L. Bajtelsmit. "Real Estate Asset Allocation and the Decision-Making Framework Used by Pension Fund Managers," *The Journal of Real Estate Portfolio Management* 3, no. 1, 1997: 47–56.

Ziobrowski, Brigitte, and Alan J. Ziobrowski. "Higher Real Estate Risk and Mixed-Asset Portfolio Performance." *Journal of Real Estate Portfolio Management* 3, no. 2 (1997): 107–15.

INTERNET REFERENCES

www.REIS.com

REVIEW QUESTIONS

1. Describe the relationship between variance and covariance.
2. What is the relationship between covariance and portfolio riskiness?
3. In modern portfolio theory, how do portfolios on the efficient frontier differ from others in the universe of possible portfolios?
4. Distinguish between systematic and unsystematic risk.
5. How does the inclusion of a risk-free asset change the configuration of the efficient frontier?
6. What portion of an efficient portfolio do academic researchers generally conclude should consist of real estate equities?
7. Why is it unlikely that actual portfolios will in fact always lie along the efficient frontier?
8. Under what circumstances would geographic diversification not necessarily reduce portfolio risk?
9. In what sense is the efficient frontier "fuzzy"?

DISCUSSION QUESTIONS

1. Would the shape of the efficient frontier likely be different for a taxable and a nontaxable institutional investor? How might income taxes alter the configuration of the efficient frontier?
2. If you conclude that income taxes do alter the shape of the efficient frontier for some institutions and not for others, is this likely to affect investment decisions in a way that is beneficial to society at large, or is the effect likely to be harmful? Will the effect be neutral?

PART SIX

Case Problem

Refer again to the Academic Arms Apartments case problems at the end of Part Five.

1. Discounting at 12%, what will be the present value of the project if the investor's marginal income tax rate is increased to 33% for the third and all subsequent years of the investment period (including the tax levied on the gain on disposal)? Will this reduce the equity yield below the investor's 12% minimum acceptable expected rate of return?
2. Suppose the income tax rate does not change, but actual NOI and selling price are 5% below expectations? How will this affect the desirability of the investment outcome?
3. Suppose NOI and selling price are 5% above the expected level?
4. Would it be helpful to know something about the degree of confidence the forecaster has in the cash-flow forecast?

PART SEVEN

The Real Estate Investment Analysis Process Illustrated

Readers have by now been exposed to the entire real estate investment analysis process. The road has been long and involved, however, and our final objective has at times been obscured by emphasis on detail. This section is designed to bring together procedures from the preceding sections by applying the discounted cash-flow model to solve actual investment analysis problems. To demonstrate the basic model's flexibility and universal applicability, a variety of problems are introduced. Each example illustrates a separate aspect of the analysis process, and none should be omitted from the serious student's reading program.

UNIT 19

Investment Feasibility Analysis

UNIT PREVIEW

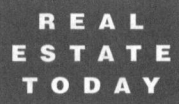

We have seen that real estate investors, whether they take a debt or an equity position (i.e., whether they are mortgage lenders or equity investors), place funds at risk in anticipation of receiving a future stream of cash receipts. They are, in effect, buying a set of assumptions about the project's ability to generate the anticipated revenue streams. Feasibility analysis addresses the likelihood that the specific course of action will be successful.

In simple terms, a proposal is feasible if there is a reasonable probability of achieving individual or organizational goals. Feasibility analysts seek to answer the question, "Will it work?" In an investment analysis context, this involves estimating the amount and timing of required cash expenditures and expected cash inflows, and assessing the degree of confidence that goes with the estimates.

More precisely, a real estate project is "feasible" when the real estate analyst determines that there is a reasonable likelihood of satisfying explicit objectives when a selected course of action is tested for fit to a context of specific constraints and limited resources.[1]

This definition implies a careful and explicit statement of objectives against which expected outcomes can be measured. It implies also that a proposed action fits the constraints imposed by the physical, financial, legal, and social environment in which the program will be carried out.

Rather than a single specific course of action, several alternatives may have been identified. Feasibility analysis seeks to determine whether all, none, or some of the alternatives offer an acceptable probability of achieving minimum investor objectives.

---

1 James A. Graaskamp, *A Guide to Feasibility Analysis* (Chicago: Society of Real Estate Appraisers, 1970), 4.

THE NATURE OF THE FEASIBILITY QUESTION

A *financial feasibility study*, whether formal or informal, addresses the question of whether the project's operating income will be adequate to service proposed mortgage indebtedness or whether a proposed offering price will result in a minimum acceptable investment outcome. For a proposed development or redevelopment, the study addresses the question of whether the relationship between development costs and market acceptance will enable the developer to meet minimum acceptable investment targets.

Relationship to Investment Analysis

That a proposed course of action is feasible does not imply that it is appropriate. There may be feasible alternatives that are more attractive. Feasibility analysis provides the investment analyst with only a point of departure. It answers the question of what an investor *can* do but not what an investor *should* do.

One widely used book explains the distinction this way: "Feasibility analysis is more reportorial than valuative or action-oriented. . . investment analysis, on the other hand . . . is concerned with *selection* from among alternative courses of action to achieve the 'best' results in terms of the client/investor's objectives."[2]

Valuation Analysis and Feasibility Analysis

Valuation analysis (appraisal) addresses the question of value. It seeks answers to the question, *what is the asset worth?* When the value being estimated is market value, the appraisal must incorporate the assumption that the asset will be used in its *highest and best use*, the use that generates the greatest value.[3]

Appraisers (valuation analysts) start with no preconceived notion of the use to which an asset will be put. Rather, they identify a set of alternatives thought to be nominally feasible: uses that offer a reasonable probability of meeting prevailing financial performance standards. From this set of feasible alternatives, the analyst seeks to identify one specific use that supports the greatest value indication for the property (the highest and best use).

This implies that even though valuation analysis and feasibility analysis differ in terms of the question they seek to answer, they use much of the same analytical data. In both cases, the analyst estimates the stream of net revenue a property is likely to generate. Therefore, both require careful study and analysis of market data, a subject covered in Unit 6.

---

2 Stephen D. Messner, Byrl N. Boyce, Harold G. Trimble, and Robert L. Ward, *Analyzing Real Estate Opportunities: Market and Feasibility Studies* (Chicago: National Association of Realtors®, 1977), 86.

3 On page 171, *The Dictionary of Real Estate Appraisal*, 4th ed. (Chicago: Appraisal Institute, 2002), defines "highest and best use" as the reasonably probable and legal use that results in the highest value.

The Dimensions of the Feasibility Question

Feasibility analysts are likely to approach their craft with a bias flavored by their professional backgrounds. Thus, engineers are likely to concentrate on physical characteristics of the site and the structure, while land planners might be especially concerned with land-use regulations and overall land-use plans. In like manner, investment analysts are inclined to approach feasibility questions from a financial perspective.

Yet for a proposal to be feasible, it must be physically possible, given the constraints of the site; legally feasible, given the constraints of laws, regulations, and land-use restrictions; and financially feasible.

Figure 19.1 illustrates this point. There is likely to be a broad range of physically feasible uses and a broad range of legally feasible uses. Similarly, there will be a significant set of alternatives that, if they were legally and physically feasible, would offer a reasonable probability of achieving the investor's financial objectives. Within each set, most of the alternatives are ruled out because they are not also in the other two sets. Only those alternatives in the shaded area in Figure 19.1 are simultaneously physically, legally, and financially feasible, such that it is attainable overall. The shaded area in Figure 19.1 reflects the overall attainability of the proposal.

FIGURE 19.1: Dimension of Project Feasibility

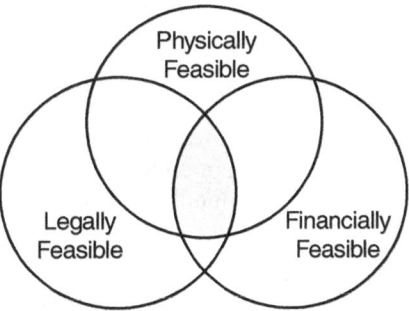

The Objective of the Analysis

Before feasibility analysts can address the question of individual or enterprise objectives and the likely outcome of a proposed course of action, the objectives themselves must be delineated. Expressed differently, the feasibility problem must be defined. James Graaskamp has argued that real estate feasibility analysis divides conveniently into three problems:

1. *With a predetermined site, investigate alternative uses.* The enterprise has identified a specific site and is searching among alternative possible uses for one that offers the best probability of meeting enterprise objectives. The physical and legal characteristics of the site and its location with reference to its economic environment become the takeoff point for the analysis.

2. *With a predetermined use, investigate alternative sites.* The enterprise has a specific activity in mind and is searching for the most appropriate site or set of existing improvements. The needs of the specific use and the economics of its locational needs are the takeoff point for feasibility analysis under these circumstances.

3. *With predetermined funds, investigate alternative investment opportunities.* The enterprise wishes to identify the subset of available opportunities that fit its investment objectives so that it can choose the most promising alternative.

Limitations

All economic activity is undertaken with the restriction of limited resources, and these constitute a constraint on the range of feasible alternatives. Values, goals, and objectives also place limitations, as do attitudes toward bearing risk.

Physical characteristics of sites limit the range of improvements they will support or the nature of activity they will tolerate. Society, through ordinances (zoning codes, building codes, fire codes, housing codes, and so forth) and regulatory oversight, places limits by stating what must be done and what may not be done at specific sites. Limitations should be identified and defined explicitly early in the feasibility analysis process.

STEPS IN THE FEASIBILITY ANALYSIS PROCESS

Whether undertaken on a formal or an informal basis, feasibility analysis proceeds through distinctly identifiable steps. The general steps in the process are listed here as if they take place in sequence. However, the process is iterative and continuous through the period of development or acquisition.

1. Assess physical and legal aspects of the site. Appropriate specialists are employed as required to ascertain the adequacy or physical capability of the site in terms of zoning, sewer, water, subsoil, drainage, freedom from contaminants, and so forth.

2. Estimate demand for the proposed real estate services. Determine required amenities and users' basic space requirements. Depending on the type of improvements, determine the need for transportation, accessibility, services, taxes, and so forth.

3. Analyze competitive space. Consider present and future competitive sites to estimate the degree of pressure on rents and likely vacancy rates.

4. Estimate the cost of construction, alteration, rehabilitation, or fix-up, as proposed in the initial concept, and the cost of facility operations. If several alternative proposals are involved, estimate the costs associated with each.

5. Estimate the cost of financing for various possible combinations of equity and debt financing packages. This includes an estimate of likely mortgage loan ratios, amortization periods, interest rates, front-end fees, and income tax consequences.
6. Estimate the rate at which units will be rented or sold (*absorbed*).
7. Develop a schedule of cash inflows and outflows. This involves projecting the cost and timing of development or redevelopment expenditures, the cash receipts from financing and from rental operations, and the cost of operations and debt service. The output from this process is a multiple-year operating cash-flow projection such as that illustrated in earlier units.
8. Evaluate the anticipated cash flows for adequacy, given the investor's minimum acceptable rate of return and the degree of risk the investor is prepared to accept vis-a-vis the market rate of return for similar projects.

PRELIMINARY FINANCIAL FEASIBILITY

A full-scale feasibility study is time-consuming and expensive. Investors, therefore, need a simplified process for identifying projects that can be eliminated early in the analysis. Consequently, feasibility analysis should be viewed as a continuous process that becomes progressively more involved as the investor approaches the final decision. Projects may be dropped anytime an overwhelming obstacle or "knock-out blow" is discovered.

Remember that a project is feasible if it has a reasonable probability of achieving the goals of participating individuals and organizations. If the venture is a new development or a redevelopment, this includes regulatory authorities who must approve the project. For both new and existing projects, it will include an investor or group of investors who will take an equity position and a separate investor or group of investors who will take a debt position.

Regulatory Authorities

Real estate is highly regulated. The public sector is a partner in every development or redevelopment project, whether the private developer likes it or not. Just as the private investor approaches the development or redevelopment project with a set of explicit goals, so does the public sector. Approval for a project—rezoning or zoning variances, building permits, and occupancy permits—will not be granted unless the regulatory authorities believe it has a reasonable expectation of meeting the public sector's goals.

The Objectives of Lenders

Simply stated, the objectives of lenders are that the project generate sufficient cash flow to permit repayment of interest and principal on the mortgage loan and that the project's most probable selling price will be sufficient, in the event of default and foreclosure, to generate through a forced sale the cash necessary to retire the mortgage loan. Two common measures of this ability are the debt-coverage ratio and the loan-to-value (LTV) ratio, both of which were introduced in Unit 7.

The debt-coverage ratio (also known as the debt-service coverage ratio) is the relationship between a project's expected NOI and the annual debt-service obligation. Lenders specify a minimum acceptable ratio that varies with the degree of confidence they have in the project and with the availability of funds. A minimum debt-coverage ratio of 1.20 is common.

The loan-to-value ratio (LTV) is the relationship between a project's estimated market value and the amount of the mortgage loan. Lenders specify maximum acceptable LTV ratios, and these typically range between 70% and 80%, depending on the nature of the project, the availability of borrowed money, and the borrower's personal credit rating.

Equity Investors' Objectives

The objectives of the equity investors' objectives are often stated in terms of minimum acceptable rates of return on equity funds. They often also specify a minimum acceptable current yield: the relationship between current-year cash flow to the equity investors and the amount of equity funds invested.

Solvency Testing—The Equity Investor's Perspective

Preliminary financial feasibility deals with threshold questions concerning a proposed venture: will initial operating results satisfy the threshold criteria of both debt and equity investors? This type of investigation has been characterized as solvency testing. It enables a quick look at the impact of alternative revenue sources for a project and of alternative financing structures. Two common approaches to preliminary solvency testing have been called *front-door* and *back-door* approaches.[4]

When project cost is given or assumed, the front-door approach involves estimating the minimum gross rent that will be required to meet investors' threshold criteria. To see how the approach is applied when there are both equity and debt investors, both of whom have specified minimum threshold criteria, consider Example 19.1.

---

[4] James A. Graaskamp, *Fundamentals of Real Estate Development, ULI Development Component Series* (Washington, D.C.: ULI-The Urban Land Institute, 1981), 13–23.

Example 19.1

A small office building (27,200 square feet of net leasable area) is available for $2.88 million. A one-year operating forecast for the property has yielded the following operating estimates:

Market rent, per square foot	$23.50
Vacancy and uncollectible rent (as a percentage of potential gross)	8%
Operating expenses, per square foot	$10.20

A check with likely mortgage lenders reveals that the best available loan terms are interest at 9.5% per annum on a partially amortizing 20-year loan whose rate will be subject to renegotiation after 7 years. Moreover, the investor is unlikely to be able to borrow more than 75% of the purchase price, and the minimum acceptable debt-coverage ratio appears to be 1.20.

The prospective equity investors are a small group of partners in a professional practice, and they have agreed that their minimum acceptable pretax current yield is 6%. The maximum acceptable default ratio (the occupancy level at which the NOI is just sufficient to cover the debt service) is 81%.

Information from Example 19.1 is incorporated into Figure 19.2, which illustrates the approach. Consider first the lender's criteria. Because the lender has specified a maximum LTV ratio of 0.75, the maximum mortgage loan is 75% of the project's cost, or $2.16 million (cost in this case serves as a proxy for market value— the two are not necessarily the same). The lender has also cited loan terms: a partially amortizing 20-year loan with interest at 9.5% per annum, with a seven-year call. The loan constant associated with these terms is 0.111855556, and this implies maximum annual debt service of $241,608. Here are the calculations in summary:

Project cost	$2,880,000
Times: Loan-to-value ratio	0.75
Maximum mortgage loan	$2,160,000
Times: Annual debt service constant	0.111855556
Maximum annual debt service	$241,608

CALCULATOR APPLICATIONS

n = 240 (12 months × 20 years)
i = 791667 (9.5 ÷ 12)
PV = 2,160,000

Solve for payment:
PMT = 20,134.03
× 12
DS = 241,608

FIGURE 19.2: Preliminary Feasibility Analysis Solvency Testing—Equity Investor's Approach

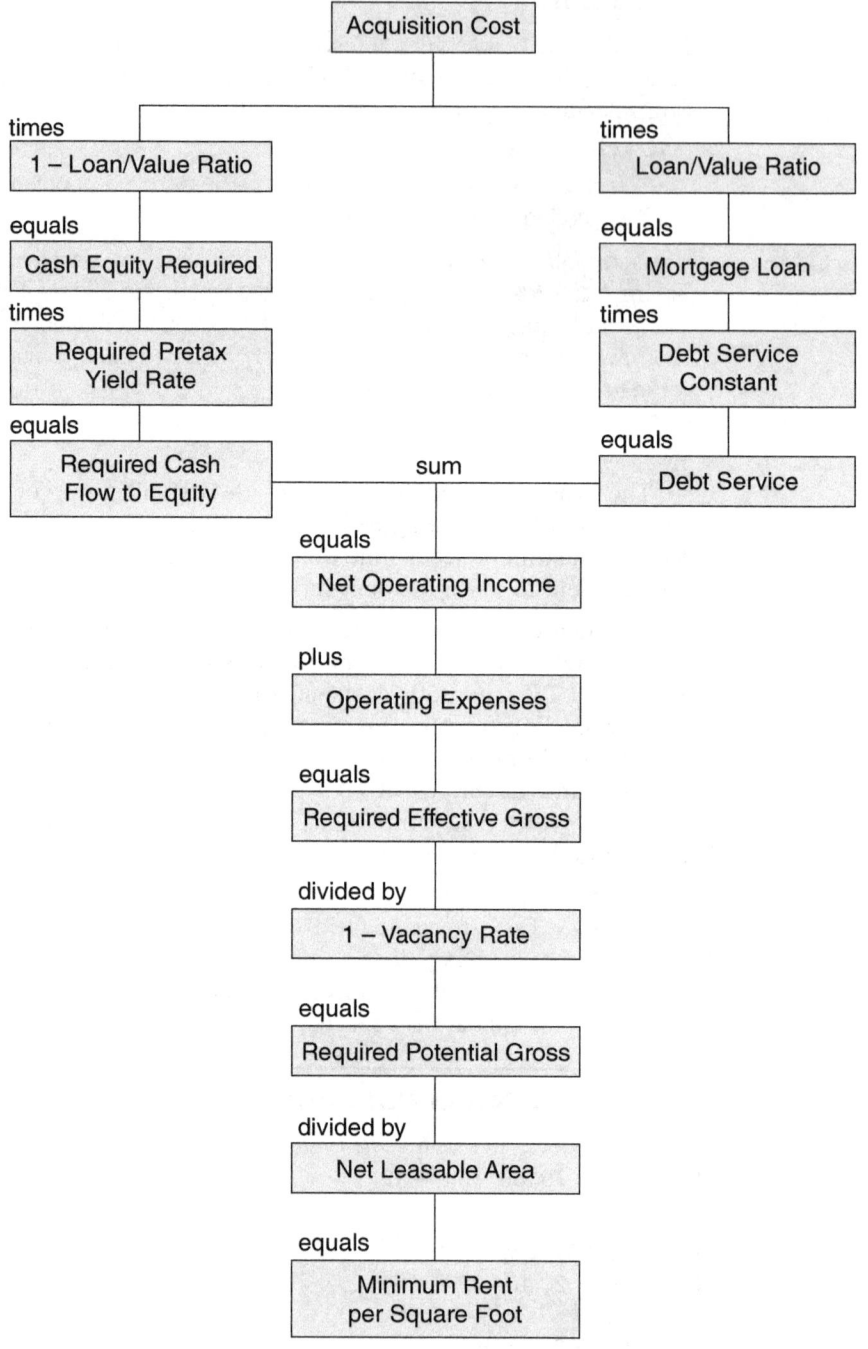

Equity funds are required to bridge the gap between project cost and the available mortgage loan. Because the lender will provide no more than 75% of project cost, equity investors must provide the remaining 25%: $720,000. The equity investors who will be involved in this project require a 6% annual yield on equity funds. This implies a minimum annual cash flow to the equity investors of $43,200.

Project cost	$2,880,000
Times: One minus loan-to-value ratio	0.25
Equity funds required	$720,000
Times: Minimum annual yield	0.06
Minimum annual cash flow to equity investors	$43,200

Debt service and before-tax cash flow to equity investors necessarily come from NOI (unless, as is sometimes the case, the investment starts with cash reserves to make up the annual shortfall). The first year's NOI, therefore, must be equal to these two amounts: $241,608 + $43,200 = $284,808.

Effective gross income must cover operating expenses (including reserves for repairs and replacements if any are planned) and NOI requirements. The first year's effective gross, therefore, must be $569,859.

Net operating income	$284,808
Plus: Operating expenses ($10.20 × 27,200 sq. ft.)	277,440
Effective gross income	$562,248

Because Example 19.1 indicates an estimated vacancy and bad-debt loss equaling 8% of potential gross income, it follows that effective gross income will be (1 − 0.08), or 0.92 times the potential gross. The minimum potential gross, therefore, is (effective gross / 0.92): $562,248 / 0.92 = $611,139. Dividing the minimum potential gross revenue by the 27,200 square feet of net leasable space yields a minimum acceptable rent of $22.47 per square foot. This compares favorably with the market rent of $23.50 per square foot cited in Example 19.1, a number that would have been generated with reference to the rate in comparable units in the market area.

The front-door preliminary analysis can be extended to determine the default ratio, the occupancy level below which NOI will be insufficient to cover operating expenses and debt service, and the debt-coverage ratio. Both of these ratios are dimensions of risk analysis.

The default ratio, or break-even occupancy level, is determined by adding the operating expense to the debt service and dividing by the gross potential revenue. For the project in Example 19.1, the ratio is 81.2%, low enough to satisfy the equity investors who required under 85%. Here is the computation:

$$\text{default} = \frac{\text{operating expenses} + \text{debt service}}{\text{gross potential revenue}} = \frac{\$277,440 + \$241,608}{\$639,200}$$

$$= 0.81203 \text{ or } 81.2\%$$

The debt-coverage ratio is 1.16, too low to satisfy lender requirements:

$$\text{debt-coverage ratio} = \frac{\text{net operating income}}{\text{debt service}} = \frac{\$284{,}808}{\$241{,}608} = 1.17$$

Because the front-door approach to preliminary feasibility satisfies the equity investors but not the lenders who require a DCR of 1.20, we need to look at the project from the lender's perspective. This involves a back-door approach.

Solvency Testing—The Lender's Perspective

As presented in Example 19.1, a survey of comparable projects in the market area has generated an estimate of possible gross rents and operating expenses that can be used to estimate the maximum supportable mortgage loan. From this, we can back into the maximum amount the equity investors can commit to the project, given their minimum acceptable current yield. Figure 19.3 illustrates relationships involved in the back-door approach.

If the space is leased at the average rate in the market area for comparable properties ($23.50 per square foot, as shown in Example 19.1), the cash flow available to service the debt and provide cash (dividends) to the equity investors will be $337,824. Here are the numbers:

Potential gross (27,200 sq. ft. @ 23.50)	$639,200
Less: Vacancy loss @ 8%	51,136
Effective gross income	$588,064
Less: Operating expenses (27,200 sq. ft. @ $10.20)	277,440
Net operating income	$310,624

Because lenders have indicated that they will insist on a debt-coverage ratio of at least 1.20 ($1.20 of NOI for every $1.00 of annual debt service), the maximum supportable debt service is $310,624 / 1.20, or $258,853. For the loan terms given in Example 19.1, this implies a mortgage loan of no more than $2,314,172 (about $2.3 million), determined as follows:

Net operating income	$310,624
Divided by: Minimum debt-coverage ratio	1.20
Maximum supportable debt service	$258,853
Divided by: Debt service constant, 9.5%, 20 years	0.111855555
Maximum mortgage loan	$2,314,172

FIGURE 19.3: Preliminary Feasibility Analysis—Lender's Approach Perspective

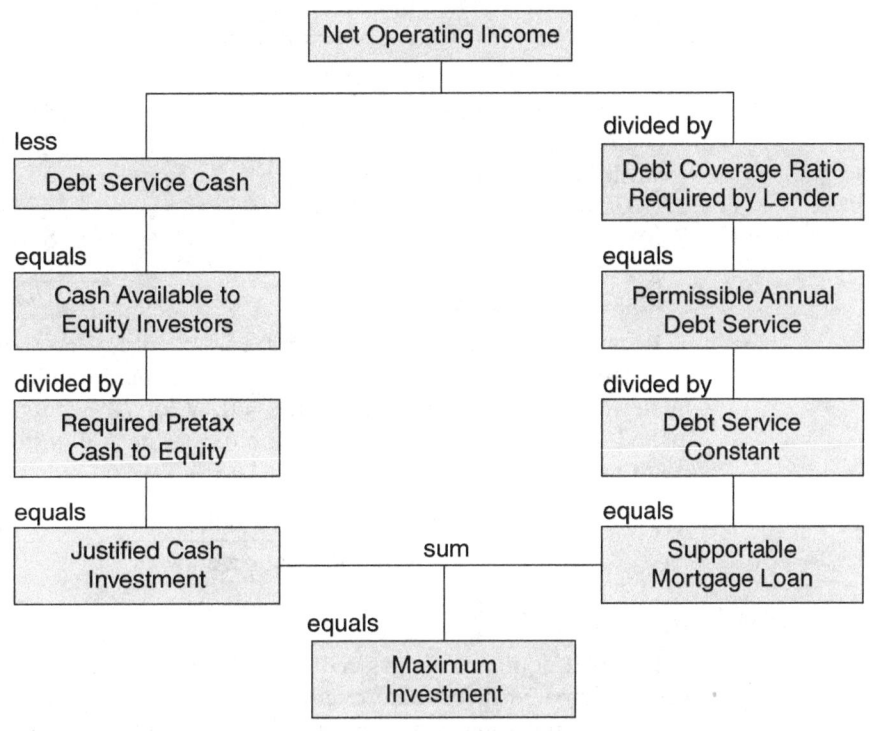

CALCULATOR APPLICATIONS

PMT = DS ÷ 12 = $258,853 ÷ 12 = 21,571.08
n   = 240 (20 × 12)
i   = 0.7916667 (9.5 ÷ 12)

Solve for present value:
PV = $2,314,168

A mortgage loan of $2,314,168, consuming $258,834 of the annual NOI, will leave just $51,790 available for the equity investors. Earning a current yield of 6% implies an equity investment of no more than $863,167 and a total cost of no more than $3,177,167, calculated as follows:

Net operating income	$310,624
Less: Annual debt service	258,853
Cash flow to equity investors	$51,771
Divided by: Equity yield rate	0.06
Maximum equity investment	$862,851
Plus: Available mortgage	2,314,168
Maximum project cost	$3,177,018

Recall that the lenders will accept a LTV ratio of no more than 75%, we note the relationship between the mortgage loan and the maximum project cost in the preceding calculations: $2,300,000 / $3,177,018 = 0.72, or 72% (rounded); the LTV criterion is satisfied. Note also that this formulation meets the equity investors' insistence that the default ratio not exceed 85%:

$$\text{default} = \frac{\text{operating expenses} + \text{debt service}}{\text{gross potential revenue}} = \frac{\$277,440 + \$258,853}{\$639,200}$$

$$= 0.839 \text{ or } 83.9\% \text{ (rounded)}$$

Rational equity investors will also have an after-tax rate of return target for the entire anticipated investment cycle. We have seen in prior units, however, that developing such an estimate involves an extensive and somewhat involved forecasting and discounting operation. Committing time and money to accomplish the more detailed and complete analysis will be justified only if the investment proposal meets the preliminary screening criteria just investigated. Those that meet the preliminary criteria are subjected to a long-term forecast and analyzed on an after-tax cash-flow basis.

FORMAT FOR A FEASIBILITY REPORT

The organization of the report should reflect its purpose and facilitate its use, not merely meet some predetermined criteria for appropriateness. Thus the format suggested here is not in any way definitive. Figure 19.4 presents the suggested format in summary form. Here is a description of each element:

- *Title page*. In addition to being laid out attractively, the title page should identify the nature of the report and the property involved, as well as the analyst who has prepared the report. It may also identify the party for whom the report is prepared and the date of preparation.

- *Table of contents*. The table of contents is designed to facilitate finding material in the report. A very short report might have no table at all. Longer reports should have a table of contents that, as a minimum, tells the page number on which each major report section begins.

FIGURE 19.4: Format for a Feasibility Report

- Title page
- Table of contents
- Lists of tables and exhibits
- Executive summary
- Scope and limitations
- Regional and city analysis
- Location and site analysis
- Market analysis
- Financial analysis and cash-flow projections
- Conclusions and recommendations

The extent of detail in the table—the levels of subheadings for which page numbers are provided—will depend on the report's length and complexity. The issue is easily resolved if you keep in mind the purpose of preparing the table: to facilitate finding specific information in the report.

- *Lists of tables and exhibits.* Most feasibility reports are liberally sprinkled with tables, maps, and—in many cases—photographs. This is as it should be; well-designed tables and exhibits communicate masses of information economically. For tables and exhibits to be useful, however, the reader must be able to find them. This is best ensured by separate lists of tables and exhibits immediately following the table of contents.

- *Executive summary.* Executive summaries are of two basic types: narrative and outline. Both should be brief and succinct. They should give their reader key information, including the analyst's findings and conclusions, devoid of all explanatory or substantiating detail. Readers who want further detail will look to the body of the report.

- *Scope and limitations.* Cost or time considerations often impose limits on feasibility analysts. Clients may prefer that the analyst simply accept that certain assumptions are correct, for example, or may wish that data collected for some alternative use be incorporated without having the earlier research replicated. This section tells what the analyst did and did not do. It specifies the extent of the investigation and clearly and unequivocally describes any unsubstantiated premises or assumptions such as the physical nature of the soil, the legal character of property title, or any other pertinent item that the analyst did not personally verify.

- *Regional and city analysis.* Only information about the region and city that bears directly on the feasibility analysis is reported. Analysts are often tempted to include everything that they know or can find, whether or not it has any direct bearing on the project's feasibility. Resist this temptation by forcing yourself to observe the discipline of directly relating each piece of information to the feasibility analysis and showing its pertinence in the report. Then, after completing a semifinal draft of the report, go over this section and see how much you can edit out without reducing the report's usefulness. The principal types of information included in regional and city analysis are growth trends and economic base analysis.

- *Location and site analysis.* Include physical characteristics that bear on the feasibility of the proposed site use. Examples include width and depth, topography, drainage, soil composition, utilities, and so forth. Also include relevant legal characteristics: easements, zoning, setback requirements, and other restrictions that might limit the feasible uses of the site. Do not include irrelevant information.

- *Market analysis.* This section should explain the overall market conditions for the type of property being considered and the direction and strength of market trends. Supply and demand analysis, an integral part of the market analysis, will include an extensive analysis of supply considerations: the current supply of competing space, developments now in progress, and the prospects for future development. Demand will also be analyzed: current vacancy rates, the absorption rate under current market conditions, and the prospects for future absorption rates. From these supply and demand projections should flow a forecast of future rental rates and/or prices for competing space.

- *Financial analysis and cash-flow projections.* Market analysis provides the input for projecting cash flow from the proposed development or acquisition. The cash-flow section requires consideration of financing arrangements, cost, and operating expenses. The cash-flow model should include estimates of income tax consequences of ownership and operation (and of disposal, if applicable) and anticipated equity buildup through paying down the balance of mortgage indebtedness and of appreciation. This section of the report will include computation of appropriate investment indices such as operating ratio, break-even cash throw-off ratio, payback-period ratio, and debt service coverage ratio. Investment risk should be evaluated in terms of possible market changes, investment rate movements, legal exposure, changes in the political environment, and natural hazards.

- *Conclusions and recommendations.* This section may include a set of recommendations. It should summarize the findings in such key areas as security and risk, current cash-flow prospects, future cash flow and appreciation, investment liquidity, inflationary hedge, tax consequences, and nonmonetary objectives if applicable.

SUMMARY

Feasibility analysis addresses the question of whether a planned course of action is likely to achieve individual or enterprise objectives, given the available resources and specific constraints. Key issues are the legal, physical, and financial feasibility of a project proposal. Feasibility typically addresses the issue of the most appropriate use for a particular site, the most appropriate site for a predetermined use, or the most appropriate outlet for investment funds.

Feasibility analysis is iterative and continuous. It involves the following eight steps:

1. Assessing the physical and legal aspects of the site
2. Estimating demand for the space
3. Analyzing competitive space
4. Estimating costs of acquisition, construction, or rehabilitation
5. Estimating the cost and availability of borrowed funds
6. Estimating absorption rates
7. Developing cash-flow schedules
8. Evaluating the estimated cash flows in terms of acceptability of the expected outcome

Financial feasibility presumes that both equity investors' and lenders' financial objectives will be met if the project goes forward. Before undertaking a full-scale financial feasibility analysis, it is prudent to use a screening technique to identify with minimum cost projects that obviously are not feasible. The preliminary analysis should proceed from both the equity investors' and the lenders' points of view.

RECOMMENDED READING

Barrett, G. Vincent, and John P. Blair. *How to Conduct and Analyze Real Estate Market and Feasibility Studies,* 2nd ed. New York: Van Nostrand Reinhold Company, 1988.

Davis, Joseph M. "Project Feasibility Using Break-even Point Analysis." *The Appraisal Journal* 66, no. 1 (January 1998): 41–45.

Derbes, Max J. "Feasibility Income Deficiency." *The Appraisal Journal* 57(1) (January 1989): 88–89.

Etter, Wayne E. "Financial Feasibility Analysis for Real Estate Development." *The Journal of Real Estate Development* 4, no. 1 (Summer 1988): 44–55.

Graaskamp, James A. *Fundamentals of Real Estate Development, ULI Development Component Series.* Washington, D.C.: ULI-The Urban Land Institute, 1981.

Miles, Mike E., Gayle Berens, Mark J. Eppli, and Marc A. Weiss. *Real Estate Development, Principles and Process.* 4th ed. Washington, D.C.: ULI—The Urban Land Institute, 2007, Chapter 16.

INTERNET REFERENCES

For information on real estate development:
www.uli.org

REVIEW QUESTIONS

1. What question does feasibility analysis address?
2. What are the key dimensions of the feasibility question?
3. What are the steps in feasibility analysis?
4. How does a preliminary feasibility inquiry differ from a full-scale feasibility analysis? Why bother with a preliminary investigation?
5. How do equity investors' and lenders' objectives differ with respect to a project?
6. Describe the solvency testing approach to preliminary financial feasibility analysis from both the equity investor's and the lender's approach. How do they differ?

DISCUSSION QUESTIONS

1. How does feasibility analysis differ from investment analysis?
2. As long as the present loan-to-value ratio is sufficient to ensure adequate current collateral for a mortgage loan, should the lender be concerned about future cash flows or the trend of values for property of the type being financed? Discuss.

PROBLEMS

1. The following data, objectives, and constraints have been provided with respect to a proposed investment venture:

   Cost (including transaction costs) $3,200,000
   Net leasable area (square feet)   29,000
   Financing specifications:

   a. Mortgage loan terms: 12% interest; 25-year amortization schedule; renegotiable after 10 years

   b. Minimum acceptable current yield on equity funds: 6%

   Operating forecast for first year:
   Market rent per sq. ft.
   (based on analysis of comparable properties) $23.50
   Vacancy rate (percent)   10
   Operating expenses, per sq. ft. of leasable area $9.50

   If the maximum available loan-to-value ratio is 75% and the minimum acceptable debt-coverage ratio is 1.15, what is the minimum gross annual rental revenue that would make this project financially feasible?

2. If the minimum acceptable debt-coverage ratio is 1.20 and the maximum loan-to-value ratio is 70%, what is the maximum total investment (combined debt and equity funds) that will make the proposal in Problem 1 financially feasible?

UNIT 20

Subdivision Proposal Analysis

UNIT PREVIEW

Subdivision, in the generally accepted sense, consists of purchasing large tracts of land, dividing and developing it, and selling off smaller parcels. From an analytical perspective, subdividing vacant land, converting large buildings into condominium or cooperative units, and converting buildings into time-share units all have a great deal in common. These latter activities might profitably be thought of as vertical subdivision. All require initial cash outlays for property purchase and improvement, and all are expected to produce cash inflows as individual units are sold. Subdivision is considered an ongoing business activity, and profits are generally taxed as ordinary income from operating a business.

Proliferating land-use controls and increasingly complex regulatory provisions have transformed land development operations, commonly called *subdivision*. What was once a simple process of "buying by the acre and selling by the square foot" has become a sophisticated business operation requiring skilled legal, financial, and marketing talent combined with adept community planning ability. Business operations vary in scale from part-time subdividers who control only a few acres to multimillion-dollar corporations that subdivide land tracts extending over several square miles.

REAL ESTATE TODAY

THE SUBDIVISION PROCESS

Subdivision ventures grow out of a developer's perception of unsatisfied demand for certain types of buildable sites. If the contemplated use conforms to current zoning laws and government land-use plans, the developer may order a feasibility study to determine the probability that subdivision operations will be successful.

Whereas development objectives require extensive government approvals, the subdivider may acquire an option to purchase the land. With a secure option, the subdivider might analyze the feasibility of the project and create a detailed plan. If the intended use appears feasible and all necessary government permits prove obtainable, the option is exercised and the development plan is put into operation.

Title acquisition and land planning are followed by a land survey. Street locations are laid out, boundaries of individual lots are plotted, and utility easements are delineated in the survey.

Physical improvements follow completion of the surveying process. Major land grading, streetbeds, and utilities installation usually come first. Curbs, sidewalks, and street surfacing follow. These latter improvements are often accomplished concurrently with building construction. Many subdividers are reluctant to finish streets and add curbs and sidewalks while heavy construction equipment is active in the subdivision.

Sales, the final step in subdivision development, may begin on completion of the land plan and run concurrently with all other activities. Prospective residents, builders, and investors may be willing to purchase sites prior to completion of land improvements. They may receive some discount for purchasing at this stage and will have their pick from among the premier sites. In times of high demand, subdividers may be able to sell their entire inventory before land improvements are completed.

Subdivision is not limited to creating residential building sites. Whereas some subdividers specialize in residential projects, others create industrial parks and office parks. Apartment building sites, shopping centers, recreational parks, hospitals, cemeteries, and many other projects are created through the initiative of real estate subdividers.

Location Decisions

Subdivision location decisions must be responsive to needs of ultimate users. Residential subdivisions require convenient access to schools, shopping facilities, and transportation. Industrial subdivisions benefit from convenient access to materials sources and to markets. Availability of truck and rail transportation facilities, therefore, frequently plays an important role in industrial site location decisions.

Subdividers also need to consider current and potential uses of neighboring or adjoining sites. Large-scale subdividers frequently seek to control sufficiently large tracts of land so that they can successfully buffer their improvements from incompatible abutting uses.

Coping with Regulatory Requirements

Local government land-use control is exercised through zoning laws and master land-use plans. Government agencies also exercise control through enforcement of building codes and environmental protection statutes. Many small-scale subdividers limit their land acquisition to appropriately zoned tracts. This strategy minimizes necessary interaction between developer and public agencies. Large-scale subdividers, in contrast, frequently develop plans requiring extensive rezoning and myriad government approvals. Such plans are presented for consideration by appropriate agencies and may require substantial revision before final approval.

Municipalities often seek to influence the level of subdivision activity through their control over public utilities. Subdivision may be encouraged if sewer and water are readily available and deterred when such utilities are not in place. In many cases, additional capacity must be developed if these services are to be provided to a new subdivision which can be prohibitively expensive. Some municipalities pay all costs to provide such services. Others require developers to pay all or a substantial portion. Municipalities sometimes seek, by levying special assessments, to pass these costs to ultimate purchasers.

Creating the Subdivision Plan

Contents of land plans vary with the size of developments. Large-scale plans typically divide the area by specialized use categories, provide detailed street layouts, plot individual sites, and provide a utility distribution plan with appropriate easements. At the other extreme, a modest subdivision plan might entail nothing more than plotting individual sites and making provision for utility easements. In all cases, however, the plan should be detailed enough so that working drawings for streets and utilities may be developed and individual lots and streets may be surveyed.

Financing the Project

Subdividers generally use land acquisition and development loans to raise capital for their projects. These loans provide funds to purchase unimproved land as well as to improve it before resale. Lenders usually disburse loan proceeds on a piecemeal basis as improvements are completed. They regularly inspect projects to verify the existence and quality of improvements. Before disbursing any funds, lenders often require that subcontractors waive their rights to file liens against the project.

Most lenders view subdivision loans as riskier than construction loans. Lenders know that subdividers depend on proceeds from land sales for funds to repay loans. Lenders, therefore, are vitally concerned with project marketability. For the same reason, lenders should be more interested in subdividers' record of past successes than in their current net worth. Good market research and thorough investigation of subdivider credentials are essential to intelligent underwriting decisions.

INDUSTRIAL SUBDIVISION: A CASE STUDY

Subdivision encompasses a variety of projects. Some subdividers specialize in creating residential building sites; others create industrial, commercial, or office sites. Apartment building sites, shopping centers, industrial parks, recreational parks, cemeteries, and hospitals are all prospective uses for developable land. Subdividers must choose the most appropriate project from the spectrum of alternatives that may appear economically and legally feasible.

To illustrate major land development issues, the balance of the unit is devoted to analyzing an industrial subdivision proposal. Property to be developed is currently owned by a railroad and was previously used as a rail switching yard. Having recently abandoned local switching operations, the railroad considers the land surplus and has offered it for sale.

Site Characteristics

Site dimensions are approximately 3,733 feet by 3,733 feet, comprising 320 acres. The property is currently zoned for heavy industrial use, and surrounding uses are primarily manufacturing. Consequently, few government approvals are needed for the proposed project. Desirable features of the location include good railroad and truck access. Moreover, proximity of reliable public transportation allows area businesses to draw on the surrounding labor pool.

Prior to declaring this property surplus, the railroad itself launched an industrial subdivision project. Before corporate financial difficulties led it to abandon its development plans, it had completed a site plan. The railroad also procured written assurances from appropriate sources that the site can be provided with sewers, water, natural gas, and electricity in capacities adequate to support industrial usage. It conducted traffic studies that indicate existing public streets are adequate to handle vehicular traffic to and from buildings to be located on the site. As a consequence of predevelopment activity already completed by the railroad, a would-be developer need only purchase the property, complete necessary improvements, and sell off the subdivided parcels.

Of the total 320 acres, 64 acres will be needed for streets, rail spurs, storm water retention, and so forth. The remaining 256 acres will be incorporated into subdivided parcels. The site plan provides a street pattern that allows maximum flexibility regarding size of individual sites. This allows the developer to meet the needs of a wide variety of prospective industrial users.

The railroad has agreed to remove all existing improvements, which consist primarily of rail and a few small buildings. Further site preparation will be the responsibility of the purchaser or developer. A detailed survey will be required to locate streets and identify boundaries of individual parcels. Installation of underground utilities, curbs, gutters, streets, and street lighting will complete site preparation activities. As part of its own development plans, the railroad has prepared a detailed schedule, based on local contractors' estimates, of all subdivision costs. The projections include legal and survey expenses but exclude financing costs. Total estimated development costs are $3.84 million, or an average of $15,000 for each of the 256 salable acres.

Market Research

The real estate department of the railroad did an excellent job of preparing the site plan and estimating development costs but undertook no research to estimate marketability of the industrial sites. To generate this essential information, the prospective purchasers hired a real estate consulting firm to estimate market demand and probable absorption rates for this project. (*Absorption rates* refer to the rate at which units of a product are purchased in the marketplace. The relationship between anticipated absorption rates and rates at which competitors will place new units on the market indicates the degree of balance between quantities demanded and quantities supplied.)

Interviews with local industrial brokers indicate major competition from two other large industrial parks in the area. Investigation reveals that one of these projects, the Swampy Knolls Industrial Park, has recently sold its last available parcel. The other, Tri-City Industrial Park, has an estimated five-year supply of sites. Some brokers expect sales in the Tri-City project to increase now that Swampy Knolls is sold out.

Sales information regarding the competing parks, gleaned from a search of the county records, is presented in Figure 20.1. Note that 43 sales, ranging in size from 2.8 to 25 acres, occurred between 2008 and 2018 in the Swampy Knolls project. Forty-five sales ranging in size from 3 to 35 acres occurred in the Tri-City project between 2001 and 2011. Data from Figure 20.1 are summarized in Figure 20.2, which indicates that an average of 35.89 acres was sold each year in Swampy Knolls and that the Tri-City project had average annual sales of 64.91 acres. Thus, combined sales of comparable industrial land in the market area between 2010 and 2018 have totaled 896.28 acres, representing average annual absorption of 99.59 acres during the nine years during which both subdivisions were selling.

Interviews with management in local industrial firms indicate that the proposed industrial park will enjoy substantial locational advantages over major competitors. The Tri-City appears to be the second most desirable and Swampy Knolls the least desirable of the three. Local industrial brokers generally agree with these conclusions. They report that parcels in Swampy Knolls have been somewhat less attractive to potential purchasers than those in the Tri-City. They also point out, however, that Tri-City has attracted users of larger sites.

Sales prices in Swampy Knolls and Tri-City for the last two years are also examined. It is noted that land in both projects sold at an average price of $2.50 per square foot during this period. Given the competitive nature of the local industrial land market, and noting that Swampy Knolls has completely sold out, the consulting firm concludes that $2.50 per square foot will make the proposed project competitive. At that price, the firm estimates that the proposed project can capture 40% of the market currently shared by Swampy Knolls and Tri-City. Therefore, it projects average annual sales for the new industrial park at 40 acres per year.

FIGURE 20.1: Historic Absorption Rates: Industrial Park Properties

Year	Parcels Sold					
	Swampy Knolls Individual Sales (Acres)			Tri-City Individual Sales		
2008	14.00	15.60	11.10		No Sales	
	4.60	5.40				
2009	14.30	7.60	10.17		No Sales	
20010	15.04	16.30	10.05	18.70	20.00	15.30
				7.60	10.50	
2011	7.50	9.30	4.60	14.80	15.30	18.90
	15.60	4.70	5.40	7.03		
2012	16.30	8.30		18.20	15.30	10.01
2013	5.60	4.30	6.10	5.40	8.30	6.20
	5.24			3.03	3.00	
2014	12.50	8.40	5.30	30.00	25.00	9.50
	7.70			3.07	5.00	
2015	16.03	5.80	4.30	8.50	4.50	9.30
	4.60	5.40		8.20	6.40	9.40
				8.32	8.00	
2016	18.00	10.10	5.00	15.80	18.67	
2017	25.00	5.90	8.70	35.00	15.70	10.30
	3.20	7.20		11.06		
2018	14.30	7.50	2.80	25.00	17.50	14.60
				27.00	34.20	5.40
				3.20	8.50	6.53

FIGURE 20.2: Sales Records of Industrial Park Properties

	Total Sales (Acres)	
Year	Swampy Knolls	Tri-City
2008	50.70	0
2009	32.07	0
2010	41.39	72.10
2011	47.10	56.03
2012	24.60	43.51
2013	21.24	25.93
2014	33.90	75.57
2015	36.13	62.62
2016	33.10	34.47
2017	50.00	72.06
2018	24.60	141.93
Totals	394.83	584.22

Investment Analysis

A group of 10 real estate practitioners is considering purchase and subdivision of this property. They plan to use a general partnership, with each partner holding an equal interest in the project. Because subdivision is an ongoing business enterprise, all profits will be taxed as ordinary income.

The industrial broker who originally presented this property to the investors is willing to supervise all phases of the subdivision project for a fee of $75,000 per year. Financial projections are based on anticipated sales of 40 acres per year for six years and sale of the remaining 16 acres in the seventh year of the marketing program.

The railroad is asking $8 million for the property. A lender is willing to provide a mortgage loan for 80% of the purchase price, or $6,400,000, and an additional $3,840,000 to cover the cost of planned improvements. Borrowers will be required to pay interest at 9% per annum on the outstanding loan balance and to repay $40,000 of principal for each acre of land sold. Figure 20.3 shows a repayment schedule based on the assumption that 40 acres will be sold during each of the first six years of the project, with the remaining 16 acres sold in the seventh year.

FIGURE 20.3: Loan Repayment Schedule; Industrial Subdivision

Year	Beginning Balance	Principal Repaid	Interest Paid	Ending Balance
1	$10,240,000	$1,600,000	$921,600	$8,640,000
2	$8,640,000	$1,600,000	$777,600	$7,040,000
3	$7,040,000	$1,600,000	$633,600	$5,440,000
4	$5,440,000	$1,600,000	$489,600	$3,840,000
5	$3,840,000	$1,600,000	$345,600	$2,240,000
6	$2,240,000	$1,600,000	$201,600	$640,000
7	$640,000	$640,000	$57,600	$0

As land is sold, total annual real estate taxes are expected to decrease. Taxes need not be paid on the 64 acres dedicated to streets, rail, etc. Tax liability will accrue on the 256 acres owned during year one, the 216 acres owned during year two, and so forth. Tax rates for vacant land in this area produce a liability of about $0.10 per square foot. Multiplying the number of square feet owned by $0.10 produces an estimate of the partners' annual property tax liability. These computations are illustrated in Figure 20.4.

FIGURE 20.4: Calculation of Real Estate Taxes: Industrial Subdivision

	Year 1	Year 2	Year 3	Year 4	Year 5	Year 6	Year 7
Sq. ft. owned*	11,151,360	9,408,960	7,666,560	5,924,160	4,181,760	2,439,360	696,960
Times	×	×	×	×	×	×	×
Property tax per sq. ft.	$0.10	$0.10	$0.10	$0.10	$0.10	$0.10	$0.10
Estimated property taxes	$1,115,136	$940,896	$766,656	$592,416	$418,176	$243,936	$69,696

*Acres in inventory times square feet per acre.

Annual gross revenue projections are derived by simply multiplying the expected sales price per acre by anticipated sales volume for each year. Annual expenditures for brokerage commissions are expected to total 5% of gross sales. Administrative expenses of $75,000 per year will be incurred in years one through six. The agreement with the managing broker provides that this expense will decline to $25,000 in the seventh year. Advertising expenses are expected to be $50,000 the first year, $25,000 in years two through six, and $8,250 in year seven. Advertising expenses for the first year include the cost of maps, brochures, and signs, which do not represent recurring expenditures. Insurance expenses are based on a quotation obtained from a local insurance broker. Figure 20.5 consolidates income, expense, and mortgage loan information to produce estimates of annual before-tax cash flows for each year of the project.

FIGURE 20.5: Calculation of Before-Tax Cash Flows: Industrial Subdivision

	Year 1	Year 2	Year 3	Year 4	Year 5	Year 6	Year 7
Gross sales revenue	$4,356,000	$4,356,000	$4,356,000	$4,356,000	$4,356,000	$4,356,000	$1,742,400
Less: Brokerage fees	217,800	217,800	217,800	217,800	217,800	217,800	87,120
Net sales revenue	$4,138,200	$4,138,200	$4,138,200	$4,138,200	$4,138,200	$4,138,200	$1,655,280
Less:							
Administrative expenses	75,000	75,000	75,000	75,000	75,000	75,000	25,000
Advertising expenses	50,000	25,000	25,000	25,000	25,000	25,000	8,250
Insurance expenses	2,000	2,000	2,000	1,000	1,000	1,000	1,000
Real estate taxes	1,115,136	940,896	766,656	592,416	418,176	243,936	69,696
Net operating income	$2,896,064	$3,095,304	$3,269,544	$3,444,784	$3,619,024	$3,793,264	$1,551,334
Less:							
Interest	921,600	777,600	633,600	489,600	345,600	201,600	57,600
Loan repayment	1,600,000	1,600,000	1,600,000	1,600,000	1,600,000	1,600,000	640,000
Before-tax cash flow	$374,464	$717,704	$1,035,944	$1,355,184	$1,673,424	$1,991,664	$853,734

Figure 20.6 illustrates the calculation of annual taxable income. Cost of land sold is subtracted from total sales revenue to derive gross profit. Deducting operating expenses and financing costs from this amount yields taxable income.

Cost of land sold includes the original purchase price and all expenditures to prepare the land for sale.

FIGURE 20.6: Annual Taxable Income: Industrial Subdivision

	Year 1	Year 2	Year 3	Year 4	Year 5	Year 6	Year 7
Income	$4,356,000	$4,356,000	$4,356,000	$4,356,000	$4,356,000	$4,356,000	$1,742,400
Less: Cost of land sold							
Purchase price	1,000,000	1,000,000	1,000,000	1,000,000	1,000,000	1,000,000	400,000
Improvements	600,000	600,000	600,000	600,000	600,000	600,000	240,000
Dedicated land costs	250,000	250,000	250,000	250,000	250,000	250,000	100,000
Gross profit	$2,506,000	$2,506,000	$2,506,000	$2,506,000	$2,506,000	$2,506,000	$1,002,400
Less: Operating expenses							
Brokerage commissions	217,800	217,800	217,800	217,800	217,800	217,800	87,120
Administrative	75,000	75,000	75,000	75,000	75,000	75,000	25,000
Advertising	50,000	25,000	25,000	25,000	25,000	25,000	8,250
Insurance	2,000	2,000	2,000	1,000	1,000	1,000	1,000
Real estate taxes	1,115,136	940,896	766,656	592,416	418,176	243,936	69,696
Interest	921,600	777,600	633,600	489,600	345,600	201,600	57,600
Taxable income	$124,464	$467,704	$785,944	$1,105,184	$1,423,424	$1,741,664	$753,734

It also includes the purchase price and site preparation costs of land dedicated for public utilities and thoroughfares. Although many of these expenditures are incurred during the first year of operations, they must be allocated to the inventory of salable land and are not deductible for tax purposes until the land is sold.

The investors are all assumed to be in the 40% marginal income tax bracket both before and after considering the consequence of this investment. (Our demonstration includes state and local income taxes in the 40% estimate.) It is also assumed that their federal income tax position will allow them to use any losses produced by this venture. Figure 20.7 shows anticipated after-tax cash flow from the project. Annual taxable income (or tax-deductible loss) is simply multiplied by the investors' presumed 40% marginal tax rate. Before-tax cash flows are then adjusted for tax consequences to produce annual after-tax cash-flow forecasts.

FIGURE 20.7: Calculation of Before-Tax Cash Flows: Industrial Subdivision

	Year 1	Year 2	Year 3	Year 4	Year 5	Year 6	Year 7
Taxable income	$124,464	$467,704	$785,944	$1,105,184	$1,423,424	$1,741,664	$753,734
Times: Tax rate	0.40	0.40	0.40	0.40	0.40	0.40	0.40
Tax liability	$49,786	$187,082	$314,378	$442,074	$569,370	$696,666	$301,494
Before-tax cash flow	$374,464	$717,704	$1,035,944	$1,355,184	$1,673,424	$1,991,664	$853,734
Less: Income tax	49,786	187,082	314,378	442,074	569,370	696,666	301,494
After-tax cash flow	$324,678	$530,622	$721,566	$913,110	$1,104,054	$1,294,998	$552,240

After-tax cash-flow estimates are discounted at a rate of 20% and summed, producing a $2,528,482 present value of the equity position. Required equity equals land cost of $8 million less available financing of $6.4 million, or $1.6 million. NPV is equal to present value of the equity minus required equity, or $928,482. Positive NPV indicates a profitable venture if income and expenses occur as expected.

Investment value can also be calculated. Figure 20.8 illustrates this computation. Because available financing includes the cost of subdivision improvements, funds intended for this purpose must be subtracted to isolate financing available for land. To this is added the present value of the equity position. Investment value of $8,928,482 is greater than the asking price of $8 million, indicating a desirable project.

From these data, each partner's individual interest can be analyzed. Figures 20.9 and 20.10 split before-tax cash flows and taxable income into an individual partner's share. This involves dividing before-tax cash flows and taxable income, shown in Figure 20.6 and 20.7, respectively, by the number of partners. Because partners have equal interests, simply divide by ten. If individual partners had unequal interests, the total would be allocated in accordance with the partnership agreement.

If the investors used a pass-through entity, such as a Sub S corporation, for their ownership and their total income was less than $479,000, the result would be that 20% of the taxable income will be excluded from taxes. Therefore, in this example $24,893 would be excluded, yielding a tax savings of $9,957 for the first year.

FIGURE 20.8: Cash-Flow Analysis: Industrial Subdivision

Year	After-Tax Cash Flow	Present Value @ 20%
1	$324,678	$270,565
2	530,622	368,487
3	721,566	417,573
4	913,110	440,350
5	1,104,054	443,695
6	1,294,998	433,692
7	552,240	154,120
Present value of equity		$2,528,482
Less: Initial equity investment		1,600,000
Net present value		$928,482
Available financing		$10,240,000
Less: Cost of improvements		3,840,000
Financing for land		$6,400,000
Plus: Present value of equity		2,528,482
Investment value of land		$8,928,482

FIGURE 20.9: Allocation of Before-Tax Cash Flows: Industrial Subdivision

Year	Before-Tax Cash Flow	Individual Partner's Share
1	$374,464	$37,446
2	$717,704	$71,770
3	$1,035,944	$103,594
4	$1,355,184	$135,518
5	$1,673,424	$167,342
6	$1,991,664	$199,166
7	$853,734	$85,373

FIGURE 20.10: Allocation of Taxable Income: Industrial Subdivision

Year	Taxable Income	Individual Partner's Share
1	$124,464	$12,446
2	$467,704	$46,770
3	$785,944	$78,594
4	$1,105,184	$110,518
5	$1,423,424	$142,342
6	$1,741,664	$174,166
7	$753,734	$75,373

SUMMARY

Subdivision is a term applied to the land development process. It consists of purchasing raw land, adding necessary improvements, and selling the property in piecemeal fashion. The scale of subdivision projects may range from individuals dividing small parcels into a few building sites to large organizations dividing large tracts into areas devoted to multiple uses. Acquisition and development loans are used to finance subdivision.

RECOMMENDED READING

Barrett, G. Vincent, and John P. Blair. *How to Conduct and Analyze Real Estate Market and Feasibility Studies,* 2nd ed. New York: Van Nostrand Reinhold Company, 1988, 71–133.

Rabinowitz, Alan. *The Real Estate Gamble: Lessons from 50 Years of Boom and Bust.* New York: Amacom, 1980, 235–59.

INTERNET REFERENCES

For demographic information:
www.demographia.com
www.census.gov/ces/dataproducts/demographicdata.html

REVIEW QUESTIONS

1. Explain the concept of subdivision and some of the major concerns of the subdivider.
2. Describe the process used to determine the best-selling price for the subdivision of the proposed industrial park and to determine the projected annual sales.
3. Explain the considerations incorporated in the development of the revenue and expense projections over the selling period.
4. Figure 20.8 illustrates the calculation of the net present value and the investment value of the project. Do both values indicate the same investment decision?
5. What does the analysis of the individual partner's shares show? Is this project worthwhile from an individual standpoint?
6. What would be the effect of the use of a lower discount factor on the cash-flow analysis shown in Figure 20.8?

DISCUSSION QUESTIONS

1. In what ways are residential subdivision and condominium developments similar from the prospective of the developer, and in what important ways might they differ?
2. If you were offering individual investors an opportunity to invest in a subdivision project under your direction, would you provide them with detailed worksheets showing the reasoning behind your cash-flow projections? Why or why not?

UNIT 21

Development and Rehabilitation

UNIT PREVIEW

Unit 20 revealed that subdivision consists of improving and shaping land into usable parcels by grading, paving, installing utilities, and other necessary work. In contrast, development involves placing improvements—usually buildings—on the land. Rehabilitation is the renovation and, in some cases, remodeling of existing structures.

Many developers, particularly residential homebuilders, construct buildings primarily for resale. Others complete construction projects not for resale but as additions to their own property portfolios. Regardless of their specific strategies, creative developers are often able to satisfy an unmet demand and thereby reap the economic benefits of short-term monopoly. As other developers produce competing projects, the innovative pioneer usually moves on to exploit other unfilled market niches.

This unit provides an overview of the development process. Concepts are illustrated with a case study of a small shopping center development project. Because rehabilitation of existing structures is a development opportunity of growing importance, this topic is also considered. The unit concludes with a case study analyzing a proposal to rehabilitate a building that qualifies for an investment tax credit as a historic commercial structure.

OVERVIEW OF REAL ESTATE DEVELOPMENT

Real estate development projects range in size and complexity from single-family residences completed according to stock plans to entire new cities carved from decaying segments of older urban areas or from agricultural acreage or wasteland. At the lower end of the size spectrum, a developer might acquire a single-building lot and construct a house on a speculative basis. Proceeds from sale of the first house often provide necessary capital for the next single-residence venture. At the other end of the scale, developers may collaborate with major institutional leaders and with local, state, or federal government agencies to complete grandiose construction schemes designed to overcome urban blight or to provide badly needed new living or working environments.

Projects often originate with a concept for finished urban space and a perception of unmet demand. This situation has been described as "an idea in search of a site." The developer who identifies an entrepreneurial opportunity seeks out a site upon which the demand can be satisfied. In most situations, the site will be controlled through an option agreement until all details of the development can be worked out.

An equally likely motivation for a new development project is a developer or an investor seeking an appropriate use for a previously acquired site. This has been appropriately described as "a site in search of an idea." Whether development originates with a site to be exploited or a vision to be fulfilled, the common denominator is a need for the particular blending of talent and organizational skill that characterizes successful real estate developers.

Feasibility Analysis

When a development proposal has been created, a detailed feasibility study may be commissioned. Results of the market research phase of this study are relayed to the developer's architect for incorporation into a physical design. Architects and engineers provide cost estimates that are incorporated into the financial phase of the feasibility analysis. (Large-scale developments may require a master plan, as described in the subdivision discussion. Planning efforts will be closely coordinated with the work of feasibility analysts, architects, and engineers.)

Feasibility studies are generally divided into two major sections. The first consists of market research and attempts to determine the physical and locational characteristics that will have the greatest consumer appeal, as well as to determine what pricing structure the market will bear. The second section analyzes the economics of a proposed project. Construction costs are measured against project value to determine whether the proposed development is financially or economically viable.

Market research will vary with the situation. If a developer has a specific site in mind, researchers will seek to determine the type of improvements demanded at that location as well as the prices consumers are willing to pay. Consideration should be given to area demographics, to local trends, and to competitive supply. Researchers might go a step further and use survey techniques to measure consumer desires for specific amenities. If a developer is not tied to a specific site, the researchers may also analyze the area in search of some unmet space demand.

The cost of a project is always a major feasibility consideration. Architects are frequently commissioned to provide cost estimates. Alternatively, estimates might be derived from a firm that specializes in providing such information. Many developers generate their own cost estimates based on a combination of data from these sources and from their own past experiences.

Value estimates also require detailed information. Sales price or rental rates for competitive properties are collected and analyzed. Income-producing properties require a detailed estimate of operating expenses. If projections are being made over longer time horizons, trend data will also be studied.

Economic estimates are always based on assumptions derived from market research and can be no better than the research or the assumptions they incorporate. Adequate research should result in reliable estimates, which then form the foundation for sound development decisions.

Financing Real Estate Development

In most large-scale developments, the site will be controlled through an option agreement rather than an outright purchase. After determining that a planned use is feasible, and after receiving all necessary municipal approvals and an acceptable environmental audit, the developer is ready to exercise the option to purchase a site. At this stage, financial arrangements become a major consideration. The scarcity and cost of financing are hurdles that trip up many grandiose development schemes.

Developers generally look to construction lenders for the bulk of their development capital. Responsive lenders shoulder a substantial burden of risk. Builders may be unable to complete projects or may fall far behind schedule. Construction costs are difficult to estimate, and projects often run considerably over budget. This forces construction lenders to advance additional funds and thereby increase their risk exposure.

Lenders can reduce risk considerably by insisting that developers acquire end-loan commitments. These are agreements from other lenders to provide long-term financing on project completion. An end-loan commitment ensures that funds with which to repay the construction loan on completion of the project will be available.

When a developer cannot obtain an end-loan commitment before arranging a construction loan, standby or gap financing may be used. Under this arrangement, a lender agrees to provide funds for the gap between the time a project is completed and the time an end loan is secured. In most cases, the end loan is secured before any funds are actually drawn in connection with a standby loan commitment. A complete description of development financing, including a detailed case study, can be found in Chapter 12 of *Real Estate Finance, Third Edition* by Kolbe, Greer, and Waller.

The Construction Phase

Construction is one of the most important sectors in our economy. It is the largest single contributor to the gross national product, it employs more people than any other industry, and it uses more capital than most other industries. Construction, like other economic activity in a capitalistic economy, depends on the relationship between supply and demand, as discussed in Unit 2.

Construction projects are carried out on either a custom or a speculative basis. Custom building takes place on land owned by the ultimate purchaser, and the structure is built to the purchaser-user's exact specifications. Speculative construction is limited primarily (but not exclusively) to single-family residences. In this situation, a developer-builder sees a demand for certain types of homes in a particular location. The builder will start construction before any homes are sold. On completion, the homes are sold to users.

The nature of the construction process makes the industry unique. Construction takes place on site—that is, where the product will be used—imposing a special set of managerial and technological problems. A successful construction company is able to expand and contract its size in response to economic conditions and differences in the scale of construction projects.

General contractors are the prime operatives on most construction projects. They look to subcontractors for excavating, cement work, brick work, plumbing, heating, electrical work, roofing, and so forth. A user might enter into a contract with a general contractor for construction of a building. The general contractor then enters into agreements with subcontractors for the necessary labor and materials. General contractors coordinate the work of subcontractors and oversee construction progress.

Construction work is often put out for bid, with the job awarded to the lowest bidder. Many people, however, are more comfortable working with contractors who have proven track records, regardless of their fees. They may choose a contractor who charges for all labor and material and adds a predetermined fee to cover overhead and profit, sometimes referred to as cost-plus pricing. The alternative of a fixed-price contract is much riskier for the builder. New union agreements may cause labor costs to increase, or building material prices may rise unexpectedly. The larger the job and the longer the time necessary to complete it, the greater the risk associated with a fixed-price contract.

The modes of operation for building contractors vary greatly. A small-scale home-builder may employ only a few carpenters and own no equipment other than a small truck. On the other hand, an excavating contractor may have an enormous capital investment in such equipment as cranes, tractors, and a fleet of trucks. Large-scale developers may employ artisans from all building trades and own the equipment necessary to complete massive construction projects.

Construction, unlike most other industries, is not dominated by large firms. Given the wide variety of functions involved in building construction, and the fact that general contractors and subcontractors typically do not form lasting relationships, it is unlikely that substantial economies of scale can be achieved. This implies that large firms do not gain a competitive advantage by size alone.

A DEVELOPMENT CASE STUDY

A developer recently purchased a commercially zoned site on which to build a 75,000-square-foot neighborhood shopping center. The feasibility study revealed that best use would be a food store as the anchor tenant, with the remainder of the space devoted to smaller specialty shops. (Shopping centers are designated as community, regional, or superregional according to the sizes of their market areas. Anchor tenants are major stores whose customer drawing power is expected to generate shopper traffic that will benefit other merchants in the center. These and other shopping center concepts are discussed in Unit 22.) The anchor tenant has already signed a lease, and approximately 20,000 square feet of the specialty shop space has been taken. An investment group has agreed to purchase the shopping center on completion and lease-up. The developer expects to deliver a fully occupied shopping center within 16 months.

Plans and specifications for the building have been drawn by an architectural firm and several general contractors have submitted construction bids. The selected general contractor did not present the lowest bid, but did have the most experience in shopping center construction. It is the developer's opinion that the selected contractor should be able to complete the project on time and within the budget constraints set by estimated building costs, as illustrated in Figure 21.1.

FIGURE 21.1: Estimated Building Costs for Shopping Center Project

Excavating	$111,000	Electrical fixtures	61,015
Cement work	240,000	Tile and carpet	50,850
Masonry	279,000	Paving	150,850
Steel and bar joists	142,000	Parking lot striping	3,500
Metal door frames	23,000	Outdoor lighting	8,500
Carpentry work	172,385	Sprinkler system	110,000
Roofing	88,000	Roof paneling	30,500
Plumbing and sewer work	116,000	Plate class	68,315
Electrical Work	169,000	Gyp roof material	83,350
Heating and air-conditioning	368,320	Weather stripping	2,000
Insulation	2,400	Architect fees	93,525
Drywall	80,000	Permits	35,665
Acoustical ceiling	42,965	Environmental audit	5,000
Hardware	8,200	Surveys	2,000
Cabinets and mirrors	2,050	Contractor's overhead and profit	285,000
Painting	12,200	Estimated total cost	$2,846,590

Financing Arrangements

Total project costs include $1.5 million for land purchase and $2,846,590 for development and construction, for a total of $4,346,590. A lender is willing to advance funds for the construction phase but requires that the developer acquire the land from equity resources. Construction funds will be advanced in three installments (draws) as work progresses. For financial planning purposes, it is assumed that three equal draws of $948,863.33 will be made.

The first draw will be outstanding for 12 months, the second for 8 months, and the third for 4 months, as indicated in Figure 21.2. Interest on construction loan funds will accrue at a rate of 9% per annum on the outstanding balance. Total interest on the construction loan is expected to be $107,796.

FIGURE 21.2: Financing Costs for Shopping Center Project

First draw	
$948,863.33 at 9% for 12 months	$85,398
Second draw	
$948,863.33 at 9% for 8 months	56,932
Third draw	
$948,863.33 at 9% for 4 months	28,466
Estimated total financing costs	$170,796

Estimating Project Cost

Figure 21.3 summarizes total estimated project costs. Development and building costs were estimated at $2,846,590, as illustrated in Table 21.1. Total land cost equals $1.5 million, and financing costs were estimated at $170,796. The total of these items, or total project cost, is estimated at $4,517,386.

FIGURE 21.3: Total Project Costs for Shopping Center Project

Building construction	$2,846,590
Land cost	1,500,000
Financing costs	170,796
Total construction costs	$4,517,386

Net Operating Income Estimates

The results of a survey of rental rates in similar shopping centers are summarized in Figure 21.4. After considering this information, the developer has entered into lease agreements with a food store, which will serve as the center's anchor tenant and occupy 40,000 square feet. Approximately 20,000 of the remaining 35,000 square feet have been rented to smaller tenants.

FIGURE 21.4: Competitive Rental Survey for Shopping Center Project

Shopping Center	Anchor Tenants' Rental Rates (per sq. ft.)	Other Tenants' Rental Rates (per sq. ft.)
Marshy Valley	$6.50	$7.00–13.00
Lakemoor Commons	$6.25	$6.50–13.00
Floating Bogs	$6.50	$7.00–13.00
Swampy Basins	$6.00	$6.00–13.00

Rental rates will be $6.50 per square foot occupied per year for the food store and $10.00 per square foot for the smaller tenants. Rentals are on a net basis, with the tenants paying all expenses, including repairs, maintenance, insurance, and real estate taxes. Tenants will also pay a pro rata share of any common area maintenance costs, such as parking lot repairs.

NOI estimates are shown in Figure 21.5. Effective gross income is estimated by multiplying the amount of space devoted to a particular use by the rental rate for that type of space.

FIGURE 21.5: Pro Forma Income and Expense Statement for Shopping Center Project

Food store	
40,000 sq. ft. at $6.50/sq. ft.	$260,000
Other space	
35,000 sq. ft. at $10.00/sq. ft.	350,000
Estimated effective gross income	$610,000
Less: Management fee, at 7%	42,700
Estimated net operating income	$567,300

The food store lease contains a clause calling for increased rentals based on sales (percentage leases), but the tenant is not expected to reach this sales volume within the next three years. The prospective purchaser has decided to ignore the possibility of percentage rentals and will have the property managed by a firm that charges 7% of gross income. Based on these considerations, NOI is estimated at $567,300.

Sales Price

Data from recent shopping center property transactions, gathered by the prospective purchaser of this project, are summarized in Figure 21.6. The intended buyer notes that sales one and five in the table involved newly constructed centers and that sale four was an almost new center. Dividing NOI by the sales prices of these properties indicated that they were all purchased on the basis of a 10% overall rate of return.

Based on this information, the buyer agrees to purchase this shopping center at an overall rate of return of 10%. Dividing the projected NOI of $567,300 by 0.10 yields an expected sales price of approximately $5,673,000.

FIGURE 21.6: Recent Neighborhood Shopping Center Sales

Sale	Age (Years)	Sales Price	Net Operating Income	Indicated Capitalization Rate
1	New	$8,525,000	$852,500	10.00%
2	2	$5,650,000	$621,500	11.00%
3	3	$3,888,000	$486,000	12.50%
4	0.5	$6,069,000	$606,900	10.00%
5	New	$6,060,500	$606,050	10.00%
6	2	$4,065,000	$396,338	9.75%

The Developer's Profit

Figure 21.7 illustrates calculation of the developer's total expected profit. Estimated total construction costs are subtracted from expected sales price, producing a before-tax net profit estimate of $1,155,614. Income tax consequences are estimated by multiplying expected profit by the developer's marginal tax rate. Adjusting expected pretax profit for tax consequences produces a developer's profit estimate of $693,368.

FIGURE 21.7: Estimated After-Tax Profits

Sales price	$5,673,000
Less: Total construction costs (Table 21.3)	4,517,386
Before-tax profits	$1,155,614
Less: Taxes (40% marginal bracket)	462,246
After-tax profits	$693,368

The developer's profit is frequently expressed (on a before-tax basis) as a percentage of the initial equity investment (in this case, the cost of the land). For the project under analysis, this measure is expected to be $1,155,615 / $1,500,000, or 77% (rounded).

Net present value (NPV) of expected cash flows can also be calculated. The developer must expend $1.5 million of equity cash resources to purchase the land. Positive cash flows consisting of return of invested funds plus after-tax profit occur at the end of construction. If the project takes 16 months to complete, and the developer uses a 15% discount rate, NPV is calculated as shown in Figure 21.8.

FIGURE 21.8: New Present Value Estimate for Shopping Center Project

Sales price of shopping center		$5,673,000
Less: Loan balance (Figure 21.2)		
Principal amount	$2,846,590	
Interest	170,796	3,017,386
Cash Flow before income taxes		$2,655,614
Less: Income tax consequences (Figure 21.7)		462,246
After-tax cash flow		$2,193,368
Times: Discount factor at 15%		0.8281573
Present value of future cash flows		$1,816,454
Less: Initial investment		1,500,000
Net present value		$316,454

REHABILITATION

Unlike new construction, where developers begin with vacant sites and create buildings, rehabilitation begins with existing structures in need of extensive renovation. The rehabilitator takes a deteriorated or functionally obsolete (i.e., inappropriately designed by today's standards) building and improves its physical condition or brings it up to modern design standards. Many rehabilitation projects involve both of these changes.

Gentrification, or the recovery of residential areas containing physically deteriorated buildings, has provided much of the stimulus for recent rehabilitation activity. Structurally sound buildings of interesting architectural styles are prime targets for rehabilitation. Such buildings can often be acquired at bargain prices due to their deteriorated condition or the nature of the surrounding area. As rehabilitation efforts develop in a neighborhood, property values and rental rates often soar.

The prime areas for rehabilitation seem to be older inner-city neighborhoods with convenient transportation links to places of employment. These areas should have buildings with unique or unusual architecture and should contain single-family or two-unit to three-unit buildings. Smaller buildings allow entry by the first wave of rehabilitators: the urban pioneers. These individuals are willing to take the risk of purchasing in older areas. They are also willing to perform many of the rehabilitation tasks themselves. As they and others build "sweat equity" in their properties, the neighborhood often gains a reputation for economic resurgence. This reputation eventually attracts professional profit-oriented rehabilitators.

Rehabilitation Incentives

Various incentives induce people to undertake real estate rehabilitation efforts. Urban pioneers can often acquire property inexpensively. They are also able to build equity by performing many of the rehabilitation tasks themselves. The risks they bear as pioneers are often rewarded with high returns.

Real estate is a unique commodity in that it allows builders and rehabilitators the opportunity to create lasting monuments to their entrepreneurial abilities. Just as a developer might claim "that building is there because I put it there," the rehabilitator might claim "that building escaped the wrecking ball through my efforts." A rehabilitator may also enjoy the satisfaction of making a great impact on the destiny of an area or a neighborhood.

Profit expectations are, of course, among the more compelling motives for undertaking rehabilitation projects. Congress has enhanced these expectations by enacting tax legislation to reward qualifying rehabilitation efforts. Investment tax credit may be earned for rehabilitating older structures or structures that have been designated historically significant. In some states, federal as well as state rehabilitation tax credits may be available.[1] Turnbull et al. (2018) find that properties that are rehabilitated through the use of tax credits increase the value of nearby properties. Tax credits are also available for low-income housing. Because anticipated credits generate reductions in quarterly tax payments, they are usually treated for analytical purposes as a reduction in initial cost outlays.

Judging the Feasibility of Rehabilitation Proposals

Intelligent analysis of rehabilitation proposals begins with consideration of the value or expected selling price of the completed project. Once expected value of the completed project has been estimated, rehabilitation costs must be considered. Subtracting all costs and expected profit from estimated value as completed leaves the amount available for purchase of the property. If the property can be purchased for less, the project is feasible; if the cost is greater, the project is not feasible.

Consider the two projects illustrated in Example 21.1. Estimated value after rehabilitation for both projects is $200,000. Subtracting construction costs and expected profit leaves $80,000 available for purchase. Because the asking price for project A is $60,000, this project is feasible. Project B has similar completed value and costs. However, the asking price of $100,000 is greater than the amount the rehabber can afford to pay. If $100,000 is paid, the rehabber's expected profits are reduced to zero.

---

[1] Virginia Department of Historic Resources, "Federal and State Rehabilitation Tax Credits," www.dhr.virginia.gov/tax_credits/tax_credit.htm.

Example 21.1

	Project A	Project B
Completed value	$200,000	$200,000
Less:		
Construction costs	100,000	100,000
Expected profit	20,000	20,000
Available for purchase	$80,000	$80,000
Asking price	$60,000	$100,000

COMMERCIAL REHABILITATION: A CASE STUDY

Dr. Reggie Habam's office is located on a busy commercial street next to a 60 year-old frame residence. This 60-year-old structure has been vacant for two years, is in need of extensive repair, and is currently available for $30,000. An architect has inspected the building and determined that it can be rehabilitated in about three months at a cost of $130,000. Two general contractors have submitted bids for the rehabilitation work; both bids were for $130,000.

Habam is aware that a 10% investment tax credit is available if this building is rehabilitated as a commercial structure. Ten percent of estimated rehabilitation costs of $130,000 equal a credit of $13,000. Because a local financial institution is willing to make a loan covering total rehabilitation costs (see the following discussion of financing), the doctor figures his initial investment is reduced by the amount of the investment tax credit. Total equity investment (net of the investment tax credit) is therefore expected to be only $17,000. Here are the computations:

Acquisition cost		$30,000
Rehabilitation costs		130,000
Total costs		$160,000
Less:		
Mortgage loan	$130,000	
Tax credit	13,000	143,000
Required equity investment		$17,000

While working with the architect, Dr. Habam has also been negotiating a lease with a medical laboratory for the 2,400 square feet of space his rehabilitation efforts will produce. A tentative rental agreement has been reached at $8.50 per square foot for three years and $9.50 per square foot for three additional years. The lease will be on a net basis; the tenant will pay all operating costs. These costs include utilities, repairs, maintenance, insurance, real estate taxes, and so forth.

Financing Possibilities

A real estate appraiser has estimated the value of the completed project at $185,000. Using a 70% LTV ratio, a financial institution is willing to make a $130,000 loan on this project. Loan terms are 9% interest for 25 years, with payments to be made monthly. The lender has retained the right to renegotiate loan terms after 5 years. Figure 21.9 splits annual debt service into interest and principal components.

FIGURE 21.9: Loan Amortization Schedule for Commercial Rehabilitation Project

Year	Annual Debt Service	Interest	Principal
1	$13,091	$11,641	$1,450
2	$13,091	$11,505	$1,586
3	$13,091	$11,356	$1,735
4	$13,091	$11,193	$1,898
5	$13,091	$11,015	$2,076

Cost Recovery (Depreciation) Allowances

The straight-line method of computing the cost recovery (depreciation) allowance must be used. The basis for the allowance equals rehabilitation expenditures of $130,000 plus the $10,000 of the purchase price properly allocable to the building shell, minus the amount of tax credit. Had this building been designated a historic structure, the rehabilitation tax credit would have totaled 20% of qualifying rehabilitation expenditures, however, it is important to keep in mind that these properties may have certain restrictions or requirements as a result of their historical designation.

This amount, $127,000, will be recovered via the cost recovery allowance over a 39-year period.

The monthly cost recovery allowance is $127,000 divided by (39 × 12), or $271.37. During each full year of operation, therefore, Dr. Habam can claim an allowance of 12 times $271.37, or $3,256 (rounded). He can claim the allowance for only part of the first year, however, because the property will not be put into service until the fourth month. He expects to sell the property during the final month of the fifth year. The half-month convention applies to the month the property is put into service and to the month of disposal. Figure 21.10 illustrates the capital cost recovery allowance schedule.

FIGURE 21.10: Depreciation Allowances for Commercial Rehabilitation Project

Year	Beginning Balance	Depreciation Allowance	Ending Balance
1	$127,000	$2,307	$124,693
2	$124,693	$3,256	$121,437
3	$121,437	$3,256	$118,181
4	$118,181	$3,256	$114,925
5	$114,925	$3,121	$111,804

Calculating Annual After-Tax Cash Flows

The calculation of annual after-tax cash-flow projections is shown in Figure 21.11. A 5% management fee is subtracted from estimated gross income to arrive at estimated NOI. Subtracting annual debt service from NOI yields before-tax cash-flow estimates. Principal payments are added to before-tax cash flows, and cost recovery allowances are subtracted, to generate estimates of annual taxable income.

FIGURE 21.11: Calculation of After-Tax Cash Flows for Commercial Rehabilitation Project

	Year 1	Year 2	Year 3	Year 4	Year 5
Gross income	$15,300	$20,400	$20,400	$22,800	$22,800
Less: Management fee (5%)	765	1,020	1,020	1,140	1,140
Net operating income	$14,535	$19,380	$19,380	$21,660	$21,660
Less: Interest	11,641	11,505	11,356	11,193	11,015
Depreciation	2,307	3,256	3,256	3,256	3,121
Taxable income	$587	$4,619	$4,768	$7,211	$7,524
Times: Tax rate	0.28	0.28	0.28	0.28	0.28
Tax liability	$164	$1,293	$1,335	$2,019	$2,107
Net operating income	$14,535	$19,380	$19,380	$21,660	$21,660
Less: Debt service	13,091	13,091	13,091	13,091	13,091
Before-tax cash flow	$1,444	$6,289	$6,289	$8,569	$8,569
Less: Income tax	164	1,293	1,335	2,019	2,107
After-tax cash flow	$1,280	$4,996	$4,954	$6,550	$6,462

Tax consequences are then estimated by multiplying expected taxable income by the investor's 28% marginal income tax bracket (federal and state combined). After-tax cash flows are calculated by adjusting expected before-tax cash flows for tax consequences. Of course, if Dr. Habam owned his real estate with a pass-through entity, such as a Sub S corporation, the 2017 Tax Act would allow him to exclude 20% of the taxable income, a savings of $81 in the first year.

Estimating the Selling Price

Dr. Habam expects to sell the property after five years. Because the initial lease is for a period of 10 years, Dr. Habam thinks a purchaser will be getting a good building with a good tenant. If it is assumed that the relationship between income and value remains constant, a gross income multiplier can be used to estimate selling price. The current gross income multiplier is calculated by dividing the first full year's gross income into the purchase price:

$$\frac{\$160,000}{\$20,400} = 7.84$$

A sales price can then be estimated by multiplying the sixth year's expected gross income by the calculated gross income multiplier. This yields a calculated sales price of $178,752:

$$\$22,800 \times 7.84 = \$178,752$$

Calculated selling price is rounded, producing an estimated selling price of $180,000.

Estimating Income Tax and Cash Proceeds from Sale

The first step in estimating tax consequences from selling the property is to estimate the gain on sale. This is simply the estimated sales price minus the adjusted basis at time of sale and minus selling costs incurred. The gain on sale is treated as ordinary income in the year in which it occurs. Multiplying the estimated taxable income by the investor's 28% marginal tax rate (although the gain could put the investor in a higher tax bracket, we will assume that he is still in the 28% bracket) produces estimated taxes on sale of $13,495. Subtracting transaction costs, income taxes, and the mortgage balance from the estimated sales price yields the expected after-tax cash flow from the sale. These computations are illustrated in Figures 21.12 and 21.13.

FIGURE 21.12: Calculation of Tax on Sale for Commercial Rehabilitation Project

Estimated sales price (net)		$180,000
Less: Adjusted basis		
Land (cost)	$20,000	
Building	111,804	131,804
Gain on sale		$48,196
Times: Marginal tax rate		0.28
Tax on sale		$13,495

FIGURE 21.13: After-Tax Cash Flow from Disposal for Commercial Rehabilitation Project

Sale price	$180,000
Less:	
Loan balance	121,254
Tax on sale	13,495
After-tax cash flow from disposal	$45,251

Evaluating Expected After-Tax Cash Flows

Investment value is calculated by adding the present value of the equity position to the present value of available financing. In a rehabilitation project, the investor receives an additional benefit from the investment tax credit; this must also be added to the present value of the after-tax cash flows. Figure 21.14 illustrates analysis of expected after-tax cash flows for Dr. Habam's proposed project, given an appropriate discount rate (i.e., target rate of return) of 15%.

FIGURE 21.14: Analysis of After-Tax Cash Flows for Commercial Rehabilitation Project

Year	Expected After-Tax Cash Flow	Present Value @15%
1	$1,280	$1,113
2	4,996	3,778
3	4,954	3,257
4	6,550	3,745
5	6,462	3,213
(From disposal)	45,251	22,498
Present value of equity		$37,604
Plus:		
Tax credit		13,000
Available financing		130,000
Investment value		$180,604
Present value of equity		$37,604
Less: Required equity		17,000
Net present value		$20,604

Figure 21.14 illustrates the present value of expected after-tax cash flows as $37,604. Adding the tax credit and available financing to this amount yields an investment value of $180,604.

NPV can be obtained by subtracting the required equity investment from the present value of equity cash flows. Recall that the initial investment of $30,000 is reduced by a $13,000 investment tax credit to $17,000. This project is expected to produce positive NPV of $37,604 minus $17,000, or $20,604. If all assumptions hold, undertaking this project will increase Dr. Habam's net wealth by $20,604.

SUMMARY

Development involves placing improvements—usually buildings—on the land. Rehabilitation is the renovation and, in some cases, remodeling of existing structures. Many developers engage in both development and rehabilitation activities.

Development projects range in size and complexity from single-family residences built one at a time to entire cities carved from agricultural land or from decaying segments of older cities. Ventures might originate from a developer with an idea who looks for an appropriate site, from an investor with funds looking for an investment outlet, or from a site owner looking for an appropriate way to use a property. The project might be developed on a custom basis (designed to exact specifications of a purchaser/user) or on a speculative basis (built in the expectation that a purchaser can be found after the project is completed).

Rehabilitation projects spring from existing structures in need of extensive renovation. The rehabilitator starts with a building that is physically deteriorated or functionally obsolete and improves its physical condition or brings it up to modern design standards.

RECOMMENDED READING

Alenick, Jerome B. *Real Estate Development Manual.* Boston: Warren, Gorham and Lamont, 1990.

Beyard, Michael D. *Business and Industrial Park Development Handbook.* Washington, D.C.: ULI—The Urban Land Institute, 1988.

Casazza, John A., and Frank H. Spink, Jr. *Shopping Center Development Handbook.* 3rd ed. Washington, D.C.: ULI-The Urban Land Institute, 1998.

Kolbe, Phillip T., Gaylon E. Greer, and Bennie D. Waller, Jr. *Real Estate Finance.* 3rd ed. Chicago: Dearborn Real Estate Education, 2012: Chapter 12.

Martin, Thomas J., et al. *Adaptive Use, Development Economics, Process and Profiles.* Washington, D.C.: ULI—The Urban Land Institute, 1980.

Miles, Mike E., Gayle L. Berens, Mark J. Eppli, and Mark A Weiss. *Real Estate Development, Principles and Process.* 4th ed. Washington, D.C.: ULI—The Urban Land Institute, 2007.

O'Connor, Joseph W. "Real Estate Development: Investment Risks and Rewards." *Rea Estate Issues* 11, no. 1 (Spring-Summer 1986): 6–11.

O'Mara, Paul W. *Office Development Handbook, Second Edition.* Washington, D.C.: ULI—The Urban Land Institute, 1998.

Pederson, Rick. "Downtown Development: Why and How?" *Real Estate Issues* 12, no. 2 (Fall-Winter 1987): 49–51.

Turnbull, Geoffrey K, Bennie D. Waller, Scott A. Wentland, Walter R.T. Witschey and Velma Zahirovic-Herbert. "This Old House: Historical Restoration as a Neighborhood Amenity." Land Economics, forthcoming

INTERNET REFERENCES

For information on economic development:
www.eda.gov

For information on renovation of real estate:
www.realestaterenovations.com

The Urban Land Institute provides information on current issues in land use and financing:
www.uli.org

REVIEW QUESTIONS

1. How does the development concept of "an idea in search of a site" relate to "a site in search of an idea"?
2. How are feasibility studies used in the development process?
3. What types of financing are generally used in new development?
4. How do custom building and speculative construction differ?
5. Who bears the greatest risk in a fixed-price contract?
6. Describe an area that would be considered prime for rehabilitation.
7. Why are people willing to take on a rehabilitation project?
8. Outline the process of judging the feasibility of a rehabilitation proposal.

DISCUSSION QUESTIONS

1. In general, would you expect cost estimates to be more precise for new development projects or for rehabilitation projects? Explain your reasoning.
2. What is the minimum size for a project (measured in dollar terms) below which a feasibility study would not be warranted prior to undertaking development efforts?
3. How does a general contractor differ from a real estate developer?

UNIT 22

Industrial Property, Office Building, and Shopping Center Analysis

UNIT PREVIEW

Unit 22 demonstrates analysis of investment proposals involving industrial property, office buildings, and small shopping centers. Examples of each are presented to illustrate differences as well as similarities. Demand factors and locational considerations are discussed for each property category. Brief case studies demonstrate differences in procedure dictated by variations in institutional arrangements or market characteristics. The industrial building case study, for example, involves a property leased on a net basis to a single tenant. The office building case study illustrates a multitenant operation with expenses paid by the property owner. Percentage leases are introduced in the shopping center case study.

INDUSTRIAL BUILDING INVESTMENTS

Industrial buildings continue to be perennial favorites among real estate investors. Reliable, creditworthy tenants, long-term leases, and opportunities to shift many if not all operating expenses to tenants account for the popularity of these structures among investors. For their part, business operators frequently find themselves short of operating capital and prefer to channel available resources into business expansion rather than real estate ownership. Investors and business tenants thus find in leased industrial buildings a symbiotic relationship.

Demand for Industrial Space

Demand for industrial space is strongly linked to the demand for products produced by the industrial sector. Forces that increase demand for manufactured goods also increase demand for industrial space, and conversely, any situation that causes a decrease in demand for manufactured goods will result in a decrease in demand for industrial space; economists refer to this as a *derived demand*. Of course, changes in demand for space are not as volatile as changes in demand for industrial goods. Manufacturers generally adjust their space needs based on long-term projections of product demand.

Periodic shifts in demand for industrial space of various types and in different locations reflect alterations in composition of the industrial sector. Growth in service and technology-based industries in recent years has sparked increased demand for light assembly and research facilities. A decrease in demand for the products of heavy industry has greatly reduced the demand for structures used in these manufacturing processes.

Locational Factors

Processing industries have a wide degree of locational discretion. They may choose sites near their raw materials sources, near markets for their finished products, near their major sources of labor supply, or at some intermediate point. Their choices are usually conditioned by the economics of moving people, materials, or products between various sites. Industries that process heavy or bulky raw material into light or compact products may gain significant transportation economies by locating near their raw materials sources.

Location proximate to fuel or power supply

For some industries, raw materials can be moved less expensively than other factors of production. Examples include processors that consume large quantities of fuel or power. The first U.S. steel-making centers were located near coal mines because of the large quantities of that fuel required in early steel-making processes. High electrical power requirements favor the location of aluminum and electrometallurgical processors near sources of relatively inexpensive hydroelectric power.

Location proximate to markets

Commercial baking, beverage bottling, and home building are examples of industries where transportation costs increase as the product approaches the end of the production process. Accordingly, these products are generally fabricated near the location of their final use. This tendency to choose a location to reduce the cost of transportation to the final marketplace is sometimes offset by a desire to concentrate manufacturing to gain economies of scale in production.

Location of footloose industries

Many industrial location decisions defy all the preceding classifications. Because transportation is not a major item in their production costs, some manufacturers base location decisions on other criteria. They frequently choose locations remote from both raw materials and markets, thus incurring double transfer costs, to gain reductions in other processing costs. These have been described as *footloose industries*.

Labor is the most expensive productive factor for many footloose industries. Labor-intensive firms find it economical to seek sites that minimize labor-related costs. If they need predominantly unskilled or semiskilled labor, they are likely to choose locations where there is an abundant supply of such labor at comparatively low wage rates. If they require ready access to a pool of highly skilled workers, they will probably prefer a location near other employers who require similar skills or a locale that prospective employees will find particularly attractive.

Types of Industrial Buildings

There is no official classification system for industrial buildings. Yet a building can be characterized usefully according to the nature of its construction or the type of tenant it attracts. Approached from this perspective, most industrial structures can be classified as heavy industrial, loft, modern single-story, or incubator buildings.

Heavy industrial buildings

Steel, petroleum, and rubber processing facilities, as well as truck and auto manufacturing facilities, are all examples of heavy industrial buildings. Structures containing such industries are usually custom-designed to accommodate specific needs. These types of properties are typically owner-occupied and of little or no interest to investors.

Loft buildings

One of the earliest types of industrial buildings in the United States was loft buildings. They are multistory structures, usually with wood or concrete frames and masonry exterior walls. Loft buildings were designed to accommodate manufacturing processes as they existed in the early 1900s. Many loft buildings are located near central business districts, and many have been converted to uses other than manufacturing.

Modern one-story structure

The most common industrial structure built today is the modern one-story facility, typically located in a suburban industrial park. These buildings are usually designed for occupancy by a single tenant and are frequently owner-occupied. Yet many are owned by investors and leased to manufacturing firms. Such buildings are attractive to institutional investors because tenants are often responsible for all upkeep and operating expenses.

Incubator buildings

Incubator buildings are smaller multitenant structures. New firms rent space in such buildings and, as business expands, they move to larger quarters. Incubator buildings are usually owned by investors, who collect rents and pay many operating expenses. Tenants are usually responsible for their own utility bills and may be required to compensate the owners for any operating expense increases during the period of the lease.

AN INDUSTRIAL BUILDING CASE STUDY

Single-story net-leased industrial buildings are among the simplest types of investment properties to analyze. Net leases require that tenants pay all or most of the expenses associated with operating the leased property; that is, most of the responsibilities of real estate ownership are transferred to tenants. Investors merely collect rents and make debt-service payments. This simple arrangement makes these types of buildings a favorite among institutional investors. In simplicity of operation, such investments resemble the purchase of bonds or long-term notes. Net-leased properties, however, provide income tax benefits not available with securities.

To illustrate the analytical procedures associated with net-leased industrial buildings, consider the case of a new one-story structure containing 35,000 square feet of rentable space. A developer recently signed a creditworthy tenant to a six-year lease calling for rentals of $3.50 per square foot annually for three years and $4 per square foot for the remaining three years of the lease. The tenant is to pay all operating expenses, including insurance and property taxes. The prospective purchaser of this net-leased property expects to sell after a five-year holding period.

Income and Expenses Forecast

NOI is simple to forecast in this situation. Rental income will be $3.50 per square foot, or $122,500 ($3.50 times 35,000 square feet) annually for the first three years; thereafter, it will be $4 times 35,000 square feet, or $140,000. Because the investor will acquire title subject to an existing lease, there will be no rental expense, such as tenant improvements or leasing commissions, and no need to investigate market rental rates.

Financing

A loan of $700,000 (requiring monthly payments) is available. The interest rate will be 9% per annum. Figure 22.1 presents a loan amortization schedule for the first 5 years of a 20-year amortization period. The remaining balance at the end of the anticipated 5-year holding period will be approximately $620,949.

FIGURE 22.1: Loan Amortization Schedule for One-Story Industrial Building

Year	Annual Debt Service	Annual Interest	Principal
1	$75,577	$62,468	$13,109
2	$75,577	$61,238	$14,339
3	$75,577	$59,893	$15,684
4	$75,577	$58,422	$17,155
5	$75,577	$56,813	$18,764

Annual Income Tax Consequences

For income tax computations, the investor will use the straight-line cost recovery (depreciation) method over a 39-year period. (See Unit 10 for details of depreciation rules and the income tax consequences of alternative tax strategies available to investors.) Ten percent of the $875,000 anticipated purchase price is properly attributable to the land, with the remaining $787,500 attributable to the building. Annual depreciation allowances, therefore, are $787,500/39, or $20,192. Because of the half-month convention, the depreciation allowance in the first and last years of the holding period (assuming the property is acquired during the first month of the tax year and sold during the last month) is $19,351. Figure 22.2 summarizes these computations.

FIGURE 22.2: Depreciation Allowance Schedule for One-Story Industrial Building

Year	Beginning Balance	Depreciation Allowance	Ending Balance
1	$787,500	$19,351*	$768,149
2	$768,149	$20,192	$747,957
3	$747,957	$20,192	$727,765
4	$727,765	$20,192	$707,573
5	$707,573	$19,351*	$688,222

*Assumes purchase during the first month of the year, sale during the last month.

Figure 22.3 combines operating income, mortgage financing, and cost recovery allowance data to estimate annual after-tax cash flows. Annual debt service is subtracted from NOI to yield before-tax cash flow. Taxable income is derived by subtracting the depreciation allowance and interest expense from NOI.

FIGURE 22.3: After-Tax Cash-Flow Forecast for Single-Story Industrial Building

	Year 1	Year 2	Year 3	Year 4	Year 5
Net operating income	$122,500	$122,500	$122,500	$140,000	$140,000
Less:					
Interest expense	62,468	61,238	59,893	58,422	56,813
Depreciation allowance	19,351	20,192	20,192	20,192	19,351
Taxable income	$40,681	$41,070	$42,415	$61,386	$63,836
Times: Tax rate	0.40	0.40	0.40	0.40	0.40
Tax liability	$16,272	$16,428	$16,966	$24,554	$25,534
Net operating income	$122,500	$122,500	$122,500	$140,000	$140,000
Less: Debt service	75,577	75,577	75,577	75,577	75,577
Before-tax cash flow	$46,923	$46,923	$46,923	$64,423	$64,423
Less: Income tax	16,272	16,428	16,966	24,554	25,534
After-tax cash flow	$30,651	$30,495	$29,957	$39,869	$38,889

Note that this property is expected to produce positive taxable income in each year of the holding period. The prospective investor expects to be in the 40% marginal tax bracket both before and after considering the impact of this investment opportunity. Thus, income tax consequences are calculated by multiplying taxable income by 40%. Adjusting expected before-tax cash flows for anticipated tax consequences produces annual after-tax cash-flow forecasts as shown at the bottom of Figure 22.3.

Sales Proceeds Forecast

The final cash flow to the equity investor in a real estate venture is the after-tax proceeds from disposal. Forecasting these proceeds starts with an estimate of the sales price. Expected income tax consequences of disposal are computed under the assumption that current income tax laws will still be in effect.

The relationship between a property's market value and anticipated NOI for the forthcoming year can be expressed as a ratio called a *capitalization rate*. The relationship is

$$R = I/V$$

where R is the capitalization rate, I is the NOI, and V is the property value. Substituting the purchase price and the first year's forecast NOI for the property under analysis yields a capitalization rate of 14%:

$$0.14 = \frac{\$122,500}{\$875,000}$$

UNIT 22 Industrial Property, Office Building, and Shopping Center Analysis

Assuming that this relationship still prevails when the property is sold in five years, the value at that time can be estimated by dividing the sixth year's anticipated NOI (which is identical to that for year five) by the capitalization rate:

$$0.14 = \frac{\$140,000}{V}$$

Therefore:

$$V = \frac{\$140,000}{0.14} = \$1,000,000$$

Subtracting the adjusted basis at time of sale from the expected sales price yields the anticipated gain on disposal. The property's adjusted basis immediately before the sale will be initial cost minus cumulative depreciation allowances. (Any additional capital expenditures during the holding period will have been added to the property's basis. Basis computations and adjustments are discussed at length in Unit 10.) Figure 22.4 shows the expected income tax consequences of the sale.

Subtracting the anticipated income tax liability and the remaining balance of the mortgage loan from the net sales proceeds generates an estimate of the after-tax cash flow from disposal. As shown in Figure 22.5, the expected after-tax cash flow from selling this property after five years is $329,231.

FIGURE 22.4: Tax on Sale of One-Story Industrial Building

Sales price		$1,000,000
Less: Adjusted basis		
Land (cost)	$87,500	
Building	688,222	775,722
Taxable gain		$224,278
Income tax:		
On recapture of straight-line depreciation (0.25 × $99,278)		24,820
On long-term capital gain (0.20 × $125,000)		25,000
Total tax		$49,820

FIGURE 22.5: After-Tax Equity Reversion for One-Story Industrial Building

Sales price		$1,000,000
Less:		
Tax on sale	49,820	
Loan balance	620,949	670,769
After-tax equity reversion		$329,231

Evaluating After-Tax Cash Flows

The final step in the analysis is to estimate investment value and NPV of the equity position. Investment value is calculated by discounting expected annual after-tax cash flows and the anticipated after-tax proceeds of sale and adding the amount of the mortgage loan that was incorporated into the cash-flow forecast. Assuming the investor is seeking a 15% rate of return on equity funds, investment value is $975,225. Figure 22.6 illustrates the computations. Because investment value is greater than the expected purchase price, equity funds expended for this project are expected to yield more than the investor's desired rate of return.

FIGURE 22.6: Investment Value of One-Story Industrial Building

Year	Annual After-Tax Cash Flow	Present Value Factor @ 15%	Discounted Cash Flow
1	$30,651	0.869565	$26,653
2	30,495	0.756144	23,059
3	29,957	0.657516	19,697
4	39,869	0.571753	22,795
5	38,889	0.497177	19,335
(From disposal)	329,231	0.497177	163,686
Present value of equity			$275,225
Add: Available financing			700,000
Investment value			$975,225
Present value of equity			$275,225
Less: Required equity			175,000
Net present value			$100,225

An alternative way to show expected investment consequences is to compute the NPV of the venture. Acquiring the property at the asking price involves an equity investment of $175,000. NPV is simply the present value of expected after-tax cash flows minus the required equity investment. Because the NPV of $100,225 is greater than zero, the project is expected to yield a rate of return in excess of the 15% discount rate. This computation is also illustrated in Figure 22.6.

OFFICE BUILDING INVESTMENTS

Demand for office space has greatly increased in recent years because of dramatic growth in the service sector of the economy. Modern highrise structures are rapidly replacing older, smaller buildings in central business districts. Many office centers have also sprung up in suburban locations. These are usually highrise buildings or one-story and two-story structures in office parks.

The demand for office space, like that for industrial space, is a derived demand. It is related to the demand for services supplied by occupants of office buildings. Increases in the number and size of service industries such as law firms, accounting firms, and financial institutions are translated into expanded demand for space to house these activities. Moreover, total demand for office space has expanded due to the trend among employers to provide more working space per employee.

Owner-occupied office buildings are often designed to project the desired image of the owner-occupant. Investor-owned buildings, in contrast, tend to be somewhat more functional and less luxurious. Highrise buildings usually have multitenant floors located near the base and single-tenant floors near the top. This minimizes space utilization problems that might otherwise be created by the need to accommodate elevator core space. Full-floor occupants usually pay for all space on their floors, including washrooms and corridors.

Tenants in office buildings typically enter into multiyear leases. Office building owners learned long ago that if they are unable to raise their rents annually, increases in operating expenses will greatly erode their profits. As a result, they pioneered the process of passing increases in expenses on to their tenants. Leases often contain a clause stating that the landlord will pay operating expenses up to some specified amount per square foot, known as an expense stop. Any increases above this amount are passed to the tenant. This represents a significant decrease in the risk that office building ownership would otherwise impose.

Tenants often take options to renew leases on occupied space. Such lease arrangements inevitably contain a formula for computing increased rental rates for the renewal period, based on changes in the general price level. Such a provision spares the tenant the expense and bother of finding new quarters and spares the landlord the expense of locating a new tenant.

AN OFFICE BUILDING CASE STUDY

The property to be analyzed is a two-story, multitenant office building containing 10,000 square feet of rentable space. The building is situated on a 25,000 square-foot site that is partially landscaped and contains parking for about 35 automobiles. The property is being offered for $500,000. An investor who will remain in the 40% marginal tax bracket after the effects of purchase is considering acquisition.

Reconstruction of the Income and Expense Statement

Multitenant office buildings are generally leased on a gross rental basis. In this case, the property owner pays all operating expenses, with the exception of the tenants' heat and electricity. The landlord pays for heat and electricity to common areas only. Most leases also contain real estate tax stops, which require that tenants pay property taxes above a stipulated base amount.

Current income from the building is $10.51 per square foot of gross rentable area, for a total of $105,100 per annum before vacancy losses. Comparable buildings in the area are generating per-square-foot rentals of between $10.25 and $10.75 for similar space. Considering competition, current rentals seem appropriate. Office buildings in the area also experience a vacancy rate equal to about 7% of gross income. Reducing gross income by a vacancy allowance of approximately 7% produces effective gross income of approximately $97,700.

Figure 22.7 contains a reconstructed income and expense statement for the property. Expenses were estimated after studying the building's operating history and that of comparable buildings in the area. Estimates appear reasonable when compared with averages in the Building Owners and Managers Association International's current *Downtown and Suburban Office Building Experience Exchange Report* and with the Institute of Real Estate Management's current edition of *Income-Expense Analysis: Suburban Office Buildings*.[1]

Financing

A loan of $375,000 is available at 9% interest with a 20-year amortization schedule and monthly payments. The rate is renegotiable after 5 years, which is beyond the investor's expected holding period. Figure 22.8 presents an amortization schedule for this loan. Annual debt-service payments are $40,488, and loan balance at the end of the expected holding period is $322,651.

---

[1] *The Downtown and Suburban Office Building Experience Exchange Report* (Washington, D.C.: Building Owners and Managers Association International) is published annually, as are editions of *Income-Expense Analysis: Suburban Office Buildings* (Chicago: Institute of Real Estate Management).

FIGURE 22.7: Reconstructed Income and Expense Statement for 10,000-Square-Foot Office Building

Potential gross income		$105,100
Less: Vacancy at 7% (approximate)		7,400
Effective gross income		$97,700
Less: Operating expenses		
Electricity	$2,000	
Water	400	
Sewer fees	100	
Heating fuel	3,600	
Payroll /contract cleaning	7,600	
Cleaning supplies	700	
Janitorial payroll	4,300	
Janitorial supplies	400	
Heating/air-conditioning	2,100	
Electrical repairs	400	
Plumbing Repairs	500	
Exterior repairs	400	
Roof repairs	400	
Parking lot repairs	200	
Decorating (tenant)	1,800	
Decorating (public)	400	
Miscellaneous repairs	1,100	
Management fees	4,500	
Other administrative fees	1,000	
Landscaping maintenance	400	
Trash removal	600	
Window washing	200	
Snow removal	2,200	
Real estate taxes	15,800	
Miscellaneous services	500	
Total operating expenses		51,600
Net operating income		$46,100

FIGURE 22.8: Loan Amortization Schedule for 10,000-Square-Foot Office Building

Year	Annual Payment	Annual Interest	Principal
1	$40,488	$33,465	$7,023
2	$40,488	$32,807	$7,681
3	$40,488	$32,086	$8,402
4	$40,488	$31,297	$9,191
5	$40,488	$30,436	$10,052

Depreciation Allowance

The investor will use the straight-line depreciation computation method over a 39-year period. Expected purchase price of $500,000 is allocated 85%, or $425,000, to the building and 15%, or $75,000, to the land.

This allocation is supported by the local tax assessor's records. Annual depreciation allowance deductions will be $425,000 / 39, or $10,897. Because of the half-month convention, recovery allowance for the first and last years of the holding period is $10,443, assuming the property is acquired during the first month of the taxable year and sold during the last month. Computations are summarized in Figure 22.9.

FIGURE 22.9: Depreciation Schedule for 10,000-Square-Foot Office Building*

Year	Beginning Balance	Depreciation Allowance	Ending Balance
1	$425,000	$10,443	$414,557
2	$414,557	$10,897	$403,660
3	$403,660	$10,897	$392,763
4	$392,763	$10,897	$381,866
5	$381,866	$10,443	$371,423

*Assumes purchase during first month of taxable year, sale during last month.

Forecasting Annual After-Tax Cash Flows

Figure 22.10 contains calculations of forecasted annual after-tax cash flows. Income and expense estimates come from the reconstructed income and expense statement contained in Figure 22.7. Income and expenses are expected to grow at 5% per year. This rate appears justified after analysis of the local office market. Note that the tax stops require real estate taxes to remain stable over the expected five-year holding period.

Debt service is subtracted from NOI to produce before-tax cash flows. Taxable income or loss is multiplied by the investor's marginal tax rate to produce expected annual income tax consequences of ownership. Before-tax cash flows are adjusted for tax consequences to produce annual after-tax cash flows.

Forecasting After-Tax Cash Flow from Disposal

A capitalization rate based on the current relationship between income and market value is computed and applied to expected income from the property five years from the current date. This constitutes the basis for estimated market value five years later. The current rate is

$$\frac{\$46,143}{\$500,000} = 0.092286$$

FIGURE 22.10: After-Tax Cash-Flow Forecast: 10,000-Square-Foot Office Building

	Year 1	Year 2	Year 3	Year 4	Year 5
Potential gross rent	$105,100	$110,355	$115,873	$121,666	$127,750
Less: Vacancy (7%)	7,357	7,725	8,111	8,517	8,943
Effective gross income	$97,743	$102,630	$107,762	$113,149	$118,807
Less:					
Other operating expenses	35,800	37,590	39,470	41,443	43,515
Property tax	15,800	15,800	15,800	15,800	15,800
Net operating income	$46,143	$49,240	$52,492	$55,906	$59,492
Less:					
Interest expense	33,465	32,807	32,086	31,297	30,436
Depreciation allowance	10,443	10,897	10,897	10,897	10,443
Taxable income	$2,235	$5,536	$9,509	$13,712	$18,613
Times: Tax rate	0.40	0.40	0.40	0.40	0.40
Tax liability	$894	$2,214	$3,804	$5,485	$7,445
Net operating income	$46,143	$49,240	$52,492	$55,906	$59,492
Less: Debt service	40,488	40,488	40,488	40,488	40,488
Before-tax cash flow	$5,655	$8,752	$12,004	$15,418	$19,004
Less: Income tax	894	2,214	3,804	5,485	7,445
After-tax cash flow	$4,761	$6,538	$8,200	$9,933	$11,559

Based on projected growth rates for revenue and expenses, the sixth year's NOI is expected to be $63,347. The sales price at the end of year five can be estimated by dividing the sixth year's operating income forecast by the calculated capitalization rate:

$$\frac{\$63,257}{0.092286} = \$685,445$$

This estimate is rounded to $685,000. Subtracting an estimated selling cost equaling 11.5% of the sales price yields an expected net sales price (rounded) of $606,200. The property's adjusted basis (initial cost minus cumulative depreciation allowances) is subtracted from the expected net sales price to derive expected gain on disposal. This expected gain and the anticipated income tax liability are presented in Figure 22.11.

FIGURE 22.11: Tax Consequences of Sale of 10,000-Square-Foot Office Building

Sales price		$685,000
Less: Selling expenses		78,800
Net sales price		$606,200
Less: Adjusted basis		
Land (cost)	$75,000	
Building	371,423	446,423
Gain on sale		$159,777
Income tax:		
On recapture of straight-line depreciation (0.25 × $53,577)		13,394
On long-term capital gain (0.20 × $106,200)		21,240
Total income tax		$34,634

Subtracting the expected income tax liability and the remaining mortgage balance from the anticipated net sales price of the property yields the $238,915 forecast of after-tax cash proceeds from disposal. Figure 22.12 shows the details of this arithmetic.

FIGURE 22.12: After-Tax Cash Flow from Disposal of 10,000-Square-Foot Office Building

Sales price		$685,000
Less:		
Selling costs	$78,800	
Loan balance	332,651	
Tax on sale	34,634	446,085
After-tax cash flow		$238,915

Analysis of After-Tax Cash-Flow Forecasts

Anticipated after-tax cash flows are discounted at the investor's required rate of return on equity capital. Subtracting the required equity investment of $125,000 from the present value of expected future net cash flows generates NPV. Because the NPV is greater than zero, we conclude that the project offers an expected yield in excess of the investor's required rate of return. These computations are shown in Figure 22.13.

Alternately, we sum the present value of the anticipated future cash flows and the mortgage loan that was incorporated into the cash-flow forecast. The resulting investment value is the most the investor is justified in paying for the property (assuming, of course, that actual financing is the same as that incorporated into the forecast). Because this amount exceeds the asking price for the property, the project offers the prospect of earning more than the required yield on equity funds. Figure 22.13 also summarizes these calculations.

FIGURE 22.13: Present Value Analysis for 10,000-Square-Foot Office Building

Year	Annual After-Tax Cash Flow	Present Value Factor @ 10%	Discounted Cash Flow
1	$4,761	.909091	$4,328
2	6,538	0.826446	5,403
3	8,200	0.751315	6,161
4	9,933	0.683013	6,784
5	11,559	0.620921	7,177
(From disposal)	238,915	0.620921	148,347
Present value of equity			$178,200
Less: Required equity			125,000
Net present value			53,200
Present value of equity			$178,200
Add: Available financing			375,000
Investment Value			$553,200

SHOPPING CENTER INVESTMENTS

The relationships between landlords and tenants in shopping centers differ from those in freestanding stores and other structures. Major stores in shopping centers, called *anchor tenants*, attract shoppers to the center and thereby create customers for smaller specialty shops. Investors and developers have long provided favorable lease terms to anchor tenants and achieved their greatest returns on rentals received from specialty tenants. More recently, developers have allowed major tenants to construct their own buildings on sites leased from the owners or have sold sites and portions of the parking lots to the anchors. This reduces the owners' investment and often increases their return because they no longer own space subject to rental rates favoring tenants.

Lease arrangements also differ in shopping centers. A shopping center owner sets a base rental rate and often increases the rental rate as the tenant's sales volume increases. This is known as a *percentage clause* in a lease. Percentage clauses have the effect of making the shopping center owner a partner in the business of the tenants. For this reason, tenant selection as well as tenant mix is very important.

Large shopping center tenants typically lease space on a net basis; that is, they pay all expenses associated with operation of their spaces. Smaller tenants often pay their own utility expenses, while the landlord pays other operating expenses. Because these leases often extend for a number of years, landlords pay operating expenses up to some specified amount, and the tenant pays any excess costs. Expense stops are often a part of commercial net leases, so that the pass-through of excess expenses will be limited. Many leases have expense stops that are capped at 5% outside of property taxes. Therefore, such operating expenses as utilities and insurance will be controllable at no more than a 5% increase per year. Shopping center tenants also often pay a common area maintenance fee. This fee reimburses the owners for maintenance of common areas such as parking lots or mall space.

Shopping centers are usually classified according to the size of the trade area from which they draw customers and according to the types of merchandise sold by their major tenants. Categories include neighborhood centers, community centers, regional centers, and superregional centers.

Neighborhood Shopping Centers

Neighborhood centers serve a relatively small trade area, roughly that to which customers can commute by automobile within five to ten minutes. As anchor tenants, neighborhood centers usually have a food store and drugstore, which may occupy a combined total area of 35,000 to 50,000 square feet. The food store is expected to generate customer traffic from which other tenants—mostly purveyors of convenience goods—will benefit. Total area within neighborhood shopping centers ranges between 50,000 and 100,000 square feet.

Community Shopping Centers

In addition to a major food store, most community centers feature a junior department store or a major discount department store as an anchor tenant. The department store, typically ranging in size from 50,000 to 100,000 square feet, is usually located at the opposite end of the center from the food store, with specialty shops in between. This layout maximizes customer traffic past the specialty shops and distributes customer automobiles more evenly throughout the parking area. Having two anchor tenants increases the range of a community center's trade area, which may extend from 10 to 15 minutes in driving time from the center.

Regional Shopping Centers

Considerably larger than community centers, regional shopping centers may encompass 200,000 to 400,000 square feet of retail space. They are usually enclosed malls, and feature one or two major department stores as anchor tenants. They provide facilities to a variety of retailers, ranging from convenience goods to shopping goods such as furniture and appliances. As in community centers, anchor tenants at regional centers are considered the major attractive force for customers and are usually located at opposite ends of the center. Regional shopping centers have a trade area extending from 15 to 30 minutes in driving time from the facility.

Superregional Malls

Superregional shopping malls are a by-product of the nation's high-speed, limited-access freeway system. Ease and speed of travel have greatly expanded the trade areas of centers with good freeway access, enabling them to support much larger concentrations for retail facilities. In contrast to their regional counterparts, superregional malls may feature as many as four major department stores as anchor tenants. They tend to be very large, often encompassing from 500,000 to 750,000 or more square feet of retail space.

Lifestyle Centers

Some upper-middle-income consumers (those with annual household incomes of more than $75,000) do not like to shop at regional malls. Frequently, these households have children and two wage earners, so time is at a premium. Lifestyle centers cater to such consumers by housing retail shops in a high-quality, open-air setting near neighborhoods where upper-middle-income consumers live. The appeal is short driving time, easy access by automobile, and convenient parking near the consumer's store of choice. This type of center typically has a number of restaurants, which encourages more frequent visits by consumers.

A SHOPPING CENTER CASE STUDY

A property to be analyzed is a community shopping center containing a discount department store that occupies 105,000 square feet, a food store occupying 30,000 square feet, and a savings and loan association occupying 3,000 square feet. A fast-food operation has leased 30,000 square feet of the center's 435,600 square-foot site and constructed a restaurant building. All leases in the center are on a net basis, with tenants paying a pro rata share of any common area maintenance expenses.

Six real estate practitioners are contemplating purchase of this center for $3.8 million. They are intrigued by real property ownership and plan to hold the center for five years. They plan to purchase the property through a general partnership with each investor acquiring a one-sixth interest. The group will also incur an annual management fee representing 5% of base rentals.

Financing

Title will be transferred subject to an existing first mortgage loan, which has a remaining balance of $1,640,042 and requires no assumption fee. Annual payments of approximately $160,876 include interest on the outstanding balance at a rate of 7.5% per annum. Sellers will take back a promissory note (to be secured by a second mortgage) for $1,511,970, leaving a balance of $647,988 to be paid in cash at the closing. Terms of seller financing will be 10.5% interest and annual payments of approximately $167,116 (representing a 30-year amortization schedule), with the remaining balance of $1,484,170 due at the end of 3 years. Prospective purchasers believe that they will be able to refinance the outstanding balance of the second mortgage note when the balance becomes due. They anticipate refinancing terms to involve 13.5% interest with a 25-year amortization period. They realize that this new loan may have a variable interest rate or requires a balloon payment, but they believe that they will have disposed of the property before any such provisions are reflected in annual cash flows.

Figure 22.14 provides an amortization schedule for the existing first mortgage note, for the second mortgage note to be supplied by the sellers, and for the anticipated refinancing after three years. Figure 22.15 combines these amortization schedules into a consolidated debt-service schedule.

UNIT 22 Industrial Property, Office Building, and Shopping Center Analysis

FIGURE 22.14: Loan Amortization Schedules for Community Shopping Center

	Existing Loan			
Year	Annual Payment	Annual Interest	Principal	Balance
1	$160,876	$123,003	$37,873	$1,602,169
2	$160,876	$120,163	$40,713	$1,561,456
3	$160,876	$117,109	$43,767	$1,517,689
4	$160,876	$113,827	$47,049	$1,470,640
5	$160,876	$110,298	$50,578	$1,420,062

	Seller Financing			
Year	Annual Payment	Annual Interest	Principal	Balance
1	$167,116	$158,759	$8,357	$1,503,613
2	$167,116	$157,880	$9,236	$1,494,377
3	$167,116	$156,909	$10,207	$1,484,170

	Refinancing of Seller Financing			
Year	Annual Payment	Annual Interest	Principal	Balance
4	$209,186	$200,363	$8,823	$1,475,345
5	$209,186	$199,171	$10,015	$1,465,330

FIGURE 22.15: Combined Loan Amortization Schedule for Community Shopping Center

Year	Annual Payment	Annual Interest	Principal	Balance
1	$327,992	$281,762	$46,230	$3,105,782
2	$327,992	$278,043	$49,949	$3,055,833
3	$327,992	$274,018	$53,974	$3,001,859
4	$370,062	$314,190	$55,872	$2,945,987
5	$370,062	$309,469	$60,593	$2,885,394

Depreciation Schedule

For income tax purposes, the investment group will use straight-line depreciation over a 39-year period. The expected purchase price of $3.8 million is properly allocable 80% to the building and 20% to the land. Therefore, the annual allowance will be $3,040,000 / 39, or $77,949. The first and last years' allowances, assuming purchase during the first month of the taxable year and sale during the last month, will be $74,701, due to the half-month convention. Figure 22.16 contains a depreciation schedule indicating an adjusted basis for the building of $2,656,751 at the projected time of sale.

FIGURE 22.16: Depreciation Schedule for Community Shopping Center

Year	Beginning Balance	Depreciation	Ending Balance
1	$3,040,000	$74,701	$2,965,299
2	$2,965,299	$77,949	$2,887,350
3	$2,887,350	$77,949	$2,809,401
4	$2,809,401	$77,949	$2,731,452
5	$2,731,452	$74,701	$2,656,751

Forecasting Income

When the property is acquired, title will be transferred subject to existing leases. Examination of these leases reveals that base rentals for the department store and the food store will be $183,750 and $50,000, respectively, over the anticipated five-year holding period.

Rental for the fast-food restaurant will be $30,000 annually in the first three years and $32,000 in years four and five. The savings and loan association will pay $50,000 per year.

Leases for the department and food stores also contain percentage clauses. These require that the department store pay percentage rental equal to 1.5% of the net sales to the extent this exceeds the $700,000 base sales. The food store must pay 1% of gross sales when the percentage exceeds its $50,000 base rent. Prospective purchasers have been supplied with audited sales figures for both stores for the past 10 years. Year-to-year sales receipts have fluctuated rather widely, but both stores have experienced average annual sales growth rates of about 5% per year. Purchasers believe this rate will continue over the anticipated holding period. Figure 22.17 shows projected percentage rentals based on these estimates.

FIGURE 22.17: Percentage Rentals for Community Shopping Center

	Year 1	Year 2	Year 3	Year 4	Year 5
Department store					
Estimated annual sales	$2,200,000	$2,310,000	$2,425,500	$2,546,775	$2,674,114
Less: Base sales	700,000	700,000	700,000	700,000	700,000
Percentage sales	$1,500,000	$1,610,000	$1,725,500	$1,846,775	$1,974,114
Times: Percentage	0.015	0.015	0.015	0.015	0.015
Percentage rental	$22,500	$24,150	$25,882	$27,702	$29,612
Food store					
Estimated annual sales	$6,050,000	$6,352,500	$6,670,125	$7,003,631	$7,353,813
Times: Percentage	0.01	0.01	0.01	0.01	0.01
	$60,500	$63,525	$66,701	$70,036	$73,538
Less: Base rent	50,000	50,000	50,000	50,000	50,000
Percentage rental	$10,500	$13,525	$16,701	$20,036	$23,538

Annual Cash Flows and Taxable Income Forecast

Figure 22.18 combines operating income, financing, and cost recovery allowance data into an estimate of annual after-tax cash flows. NOI is simply anticipated rental revenue minus the management fee. Subtracting annual debt service from this amount yields before-tax cash flows. Adding back the principal portion of the debt service (the nondeductible part) and subtracting annual cost recovery allowances results in a forecast of taxable income or tax-deductible losses for each year of the anticipated holding period.

FIGURE 22.18: Calculation of Annual After-Tax Cash Flows for Community Shopping Center

	Year 1	Year 2	Year 3	Year 4	Year 5
Base rentals					
Department store	$183,750	$183,750	$183,750	$183,750	$183,750
Food store	50,000	50,000	50,000	50,000	50,000
Savings and loan	50,000	50,000	50,000	50,000	50,000
Out-parcel	30,000	30,000	30,000	32,000	32,000
Total base rentals	$313,750	$313,750	$313,750	$315,750	$315,750
Percentage rentals					
Department store	22,500	24,150	25,882	27,702	29,612
Food store	10,500	13,525	16,701	20,036	23,538
Total rentals	$346,750	$351,425	$356,333	$363,488	$368,900
Less: Management fee	15,687	15,687	15,687	20,036	20,036
Net operating income	$331,063	$335,738	$340,646	$343,452	$348,864
Less: Debt service	327,992	327,992	327,992	370,062	370,062
Before-tax cash flow	$ 3,071	$ 7,746	$ 12,654	$ (26,610)	$ (21,198)
Plus: Principal	46,230	49,949	53,974	55,872	60,593
Less: Depreciation	74,701	77,949	77,949	77,949	74,701
Taxable income (loss)	($25,400)	($20,254)	($11,321)	($48,687)	($35,306)

Estimation of Taxable Income and Cash Proceeds from Sale

As in previous examples, computing a capitalization rate facilitates estimating the market value of the property as of the anticipated sales date. The implied capitalization rate at the time of purchase is calculated by dividing the first year's NOI by the purchase price:

$$\frac{\$331,063}{\$3,800,000} = 0.087122$$

The market value at the anticipated selling date is estimated by dividing the sixth year's NOI by the capitalization rate calculated for year one. Projecting operating results for an additional year results in a sixth year NOI estimate of $354,546. Therefore, the estimated sales price at the end of year five is

$$\frac{\$354,546}{0.087122} = \$4,069,535$$

UNIT 22 Industrial Property, Office Building, and Shopping Center Analysis

The estimated sales price, rounded to $4,070,000, is reduced by estimated selling expense of $220,180. Net sales price is then gross selling price of $4,070,000 minus $220,180, producing $3,849,820.

Figure 22.19 illustrates calculation of the taxable gain on sale of the property. Adjusted basis is subtracted from net sales price, producing the gain on sale of $433,069. Subtracting the outstanding loan balance at the sale date from the net sales price yields the expected before-tax cash proceeds from disposal. Figure 22.20 illustrates this calculation, which produces a before-tax cash-flow estimate of $964,428. Tax consequences for partners are discussed later.

FIGURE 22.19: Taxable Gain on Sale of Community Shopping Center

Estimated sales price		$4,070,000
Less: Selling costs		220,180
Net sales price		$3,849,820
Less: Adjusted basis		
Land cost	$760,000	
Building*	2,656,751	3,416,751
Gain on sale		$433,069

*Cost minus accumulated cost recovery allowances

FIGURE 22.20: Before-Tax Cash Flow from Disposal of Community Shopping Center

Estimated sales price		$4,070,000
Less:		
Selling costs	$220,180	
Mortgage balance	2,885,392	3,105,572
Before-tax cash-flow estimate		$964,428

Evaluating After-Tax Cash Flows

Each partner is assumed to be in the 40% marginal tax bracket during the first four years of the investment period. Long-term capital gains generated from selling the property will be taxed at the 20% rate. Recaptured depreciation will be taxed at 25%. Figure 22.21 shows the distribution of expected before-tax cash flows and income or loss from the investment for this partner. Because the partners have not arrived at a contrary agreement, all items are distributed evenly. Figure 22.22 illustrates adjustments for income tax consequences to yield after-tax cash-flow estimates for the partner.

Figure 22.23 shows estimation of after-tax proceeds from sale for this partner, and Figure 22.24 illustrates computation of present value of the partner's equity position, with a 10% target rate of return.

FIGURE 22.21: Partner's Share of Cash Flows and Income or Loss on Community Shopping Center

Year	Total Before-Tax Cash Flow (Table 22.18)	Individual Partner's Share
1	$3,071	$512
2	$7,746	$1,291
3	$12,654	$2,109
4	($26,610)	($4,435)
5	($21,198)	($3,533)

Year	Taxable Income (Loss) (Table 22.18)	Partner's Share
1	($25,400)	($4,233)
2	($20,254)	($3,376)
3	($11,321)	($1,887)
4	($48,687)	($8,115)
5	($35,306)	($5,884)

Year	Before-Tax Cash Proceeds from Sale (Table 22.20)	Partner's Share
5	$964,428	$160,738

Year	Taxable Gain on Sale (Table 22.19)	Partner's Share
5	$433,069	$72,178

FIGURE 22.22: Annual After-Tax Cash Flows to Partner in 40% Bracket on Community Shopping Center

	Year 1	Year 2	Year 3	Year 4	Year 5
Partner's taxable income (loss) (Figure 22.21)	($4,233)	($3,376)	($1,887)	($8,115)	($5,884)
Times: Tax rate	0.40	0.40	0.40	0.40	0.40
Tax (savings)	($1,693)	($1,350)	($755)	($3,246)	($2,354)
Partner's before-tax cash flow (Figure 22.21)	$512	$1,291	$2,109	($4,435)	($3,533)
Tax consequences	1,693	1,350	755	3,246	2,354
Partner's after-tax cash flow	$2,205	$2,641	$2,864	($1,189)	($1,179)

UNIT 22 Industrial Property, Office Building, and Shopping Center Analysis

FIGURE 22.23: Partner's After-Tax Cash Flow from Disposal of Shopping Center

Partner's share of sale proceeds (Figure 22.21)	$160,738
Taxes on partner's share of gain	
Tax on recapture of straight-line depreciation (0.25 × $63,875)	15,969
Tax on long-term capital gain (0.20 × $8,303)	1,661
Partner's after-tax cash flow	$143,108

FIGURE 22.24: Present Value of Partner's After-Tax Cash Flow on Shopping Center Project

Year	Partner's After-Tax Cash Flow	Present Value of Cash Flow @10%
1	$2,205	$2,005
2	2,641	2,183
3	2,864	2,152
4	(1,189)	(812)
5	(1,179)	(732)
(From disposal)	$143,108	$88,859
Total present value		$93,655

Because the present value of expected after-tax cash flows is less than the individual partner's share of the required equity investment ($93,655 present value versus equity investment of $107,998), the partner cannot expect this project to generate a yield in excess of the discount rate. Remember, however, that the cash-flow projections and present value computations presuppose a specific purchase price and set of financing arrangements. The project can be made more attractive by lowering the price or offering more favorable mortgage terms. Financing terms can be enhanced by lowering the interest rate, lengthening the repayment period, or reducing the size of the down payment.

SUMMARY

Investment analytical procedures can be applied in a similar fashion to evaluate different types of real property. This has been demonstrated by applying the discounted cash-flow model to analyze an industrial building, an office building, and a shopping center. In each case, the procedure begins with demand analysis and proceeds to an after-tax cash-flow forecast. The anticipated cash flows, including the forecast after-tax cash flow from disposal at the end of the anticipated holding period, are discounted at the appropriate discount rate to generate a present value of the anticipated future flow of benefits.

RECOMMENDED READING

Kinnard, William N., Jr., Stephen D. Messner, and Byrl N. Boyce. *Industrial Real Estate,* 4th ed. Washington, D.C.: Society of Industrial REALTORS®, 1984.

McMahon, John. *Professional Property Development.* New York: McGraw-Hill, 2007.

Miles, Mike E., Gayle L. Berens, Mark J. Eppli, and Marc A. Weiss. *Real Estate Development: Principles and Process,* 4th ed. Washington, D.C.: The Urban Land Institute, 2007.

INTERNET REFERENCES

For information on commercial real estate:
www.ccim.com

For information on industrial and office real estate:
www.naiop.org
www.cbre.com
www.boma.org

For shopping center information:
www.icsc.org

REVIEW QUESTIONS

1. Why are investors attracted to industrial buildings as investment vehicles?
2. How do locational factors influence the choice of an industrial building site?
3. Consider the cash-flow projections of the industrial property illustrated in Figure 22.3. In year four, the owner will have to pay taxes on income from operations. Does this mean there is no longer a tax shelter associated with the property?
4. What is the major determining factor in the demand for office space?
5. Describe the structure of most office building leases.
6. A capitalization rate was used to estimate the sales price of the office building in the case study. What other method might have been used to estimate the probable selling price?
7. Outline the lease arrangements commonly found in shopping center properties.
8. Describe the various types of shopping centers.
9. Is the community shopping center analyzed in this unit a good investment for all the partners?

UNIT 22 Industrial Property, Office Building, and Shopping Center Analysis

DISCUSSION QUESTIONS

1. If demand in your market area were about the same for rental apartments and industrial space, would you generally prefer to develop apartments or industrial buildings? What are some key factors that would affect your choice?

2. If demand factors were about equal, what would be some other considerations determining your preference for developing and owning single-tenant industrial buildings or incubator-type buildings?

3. Compare and contrast management functions in major shopping centers with those in large office buildings.

4. If demand were about equal, what are some factors that would affect your choice between developing a major regional shopping center and committing an equal amount of funds to developing a string of neighborhood or community shopping centers?

PART SEVEN

Case Problem

Gary Goldberg asks your advice concerning a perplexing situation. Having recently read a book about how someone turned $1,000 into $2 million in real estate in his spare time, Goldberg is anxious to participate in this bonanza. His job as an executive assistant in a major commodities brokerage firm is secure but offers no opportunity for advancement. Goldberg feels, therefore, that real estate investment is his best chance to build a personal fortune.

Goldberg talked with three real estate brokers, each of whom presented him with a different investment opportunity. Because his funds are limited to $500,000 recently presented to him by a relative, he cannot accept all of these alternatives. He therefore discussed all three ventures with each broker and became extremely confused. Although they used the same financial data and operating projections, the brokers drew conflicting conclusions about probable rates of return on the investments.

THE INVESTOR

Further questioning reveals that Goldberg is employed by his father under a long-term contract at a salary that puts him in the 28% marginal income tax bracket (his state income tax is expected to go up as the federal rate comes down, thereby keeping him in the 28% bracket). His employment contract (which requires him to stay away from his father's place of business, to avoid public identification with the firm, and to remain unmarried throughout the contract period) provides for no salary increases, so Goldberg expects that his income from sources other than real estate will remain essentially unchanged for the next 10 years.

Goldberg tells you he is interested in tax shelter, cash flow, capital appreciation, and security of principal. He asks you to study data concerning the three investment opportunities. He would like you to reconcile conflicting yield expectations reported by different brokers and to make a definitive recommendation concerning his best course of action.

THE PROPERTIES

Industrial Building

The first broker offered a three-year-old, 35,000-square-foot industrial building for which the owner is asking $35 per square foot, or $1,225,000. The broker feels the property can be acquired for $1 million, or just under $30 per square foot. The building is under lease to a Class A tenant for $3.50 per square foot, or $122,500 per year, on a net lease basis. Based partly on the tenant's financial standing, a lender will provide a mortgage loan for 80% of the purchase price. The loan will be interest only (at 8.5%), payable monthly, with the principal amount due in 10 years.

Seven years remain on a ten-year lease. The tenant has an option to buy the property for $1.2 million when the lease expires, and is expected to do so. The building accounts for 90% of total property value.

Apartment Building

Broker number two recommended a 55-unit apartment building that currently generates a gross income of $297,000. The property is listed at $25,000 per unit, for a total price of $1,375,000. The owners are desperate, however, and the broker reports the property can almost certainly be acquired for $1.2 million. Of this amount, $960,000 is attributable to the improvements.

Operating expenses and vacancy losses are currently running about 50% of gross income. Both gross income and expenses are expected to remain constant over the (anticipated) seven-year holding period. At the end of the seventh year, the property is expected to have a market value of $1.2 million.

A 25-year, 8% mortgage loan is available for 75% of the purchase price. There will be no origination fee or prepayment penalty. Level payments will be made monthly.

Office Building

The final alternative is a 20,000-square-foot office building that is advertised for sale at $60 per square foot ($1.2 million total), but can probably be bought for $1.1 million. Buildings and other improvements account for 90% of the property's total value.

During the first year of the prospective holding period, this property should yield gross rent of $10 per square foot and incur operating expenses of about $4 per square foot. Both gross revenue and operating expenses are expected to increase thereafter at a compound annual rate of 5%. If the building is acquired, Goldberg will probably hold it for seven years. At that time, he should be able to sell it for about $1.25 million.

A lender has indicated willingness to make a 25-year, 8% mortgage loan for 75% of Goldberg's purchase price (with a 10-year call provision). There will be no origination fee and no prepayment penalty. Payments must be made monthly.

THE ANALYSIS

For each investment opportunity, develop an after-tax cash-flow projection for the anticipated seven-year holding period. Project after-tax cash proceeds from disposal at the end of the holding period. Which of these propositions, if any, seems appropriate for Goldberg? What will you advise? (In your analysis, assume that expected purchase prices include transaction costs and that expected sales prices are net of transaction costs.)

PART EIGHT

Real Estate as a Security

Real estate analysts who must evaluate specific investment proposals or choose among alternative real estate ventures will find the analytical model developed in Parts One through Seven universally applicable. Many people, however, have neither the time nor the inclination to undertake extensive analysis of specific ventures. Others have inadequate equity funds to exploit the intelligence such analysis generates. Share ownership in real estate limited partnerships or REITs represents a possible alternative for such investors. Fulfilling these investor needs enables syndicators and trusts to marshal large amounts of investor funds and thereby generate both unusual market strength and economies of scale in investment operations.

Real estate limited partnership syndications have in the past been a major intermediary for channeling funds from individual investors into real estate equities. The syndicates provided many of the tax-advantaged investment opportunities available to those who make direct investment in real estate ventures, plus the additional advantages of limited personal financial liability and freedom from management responsibilities. Changes to the Internal Revenue Code have virtually obliterated the syndicates' role in securitizing real estate. Leadership has passed to REITs.

Unit 23 explores the operation of real estate investment trusts, commonly called REITs (pronounced "reets"). Readers with long memories may consider REITs to be yesterday's news. Yet, REITs have reemerged as a convenient and popular way to incorporate real estate into securities portfolios.

UNIT 23

Real Estate Investment Trusts

UNIT PREVIEW

REAL ESTATE TODAY

Real estate investment trusts (REITs) are long-term investment vehicles that channel funds from passive investor-shareholders into real estate. Section 856 of the Internal Revenue Code provides tax-free status to qualifying REITs. This permits shareholders to enjoy many of the benefits associated with direct real estate investment, while also exploiting the limited liability and enhanced liquidity of publically traded corporate stock.

REITs are especially well-suited investments for the small investor. Investors with limited resources can easily invest in REITs just by opening a stock account with a brokerage firm. The ease of stock investing today opens the door to real estate investing through the purchase of just a few shares of REITs. The individual investor can also take advantage of the long-term investment strategy of the dividend reinvestment plan (DRIP), where the monies received from dividends are automatically reinvested by purchasing more shares of the REITs. This plan is particularly well suited for retirement and other long-term goals. REITs work very well in DRIPs because of their high-dividend yields.

REITs have become more attractive relative to real estate limited partnerships since passive income and loss rules were incorporated into the Internal Revenue Code in 1986 (see Unit 10); REITs are treated for tax purposes as portfolio assets rather than passive assets. In recent years, REITs have become a popular way for pension trusts to include real estate in their portfolios.

REIT REGULATION

Organized as corporations or trusts, REITs are chartered in the state(s) in which they are headquartered and are subject to the regulations and statutes of that state. They are also subject to federal law: Internal Revenue Code provisions specify minimum conditions under which they will be granted the special income tax status to which they owe their popularity with investors; SEC rules govern their relationship with the investing public.

Tax-Exempt Status

To qualify for tax-exempt status, REITs must conform to a staggering array of conditions, the most significant of which are the following:

- Shares must be held by at least 100 persons, and five or fewer shareholders cannot own 50% or more of the shares during the last half of any tax year. Since 1993, a pension fund trust has not been considered a single individual for purposes of applying the "five or fewer" rule. Code Section 856(h) provides that pension trust beneficiaries are considered to be holding the REIT shares in proportion to their interest in the pension trust.
- At least 75% of assets must consist of real estate, mortgage notes, cash, cash items, or government securities. Income from stocks and bonds purchased with the proceeds of new capital may qualify as part of this 75% during the first year after raising the funds.
- At least 90% of ordinary income (as distinguished from capital gains) must be distributed to shareholders within one year after the end of each fiscal year. This requirement is eased for certain types of noncash income.
- No more than 30% of gross annual income can represent gains from the sale of securities held for less than a year or real estate held less than four years.

Shareholder Rights

Shareholders of REITs have approximately the same rights as stockholders in any other corporation. They elect the trustees or directors. They also have the right to vote on proposed changes in the charter, declaration of trust, or bylaws, as well as on major decisions such as new stock issues, voluntary changes in tax status, or changes in investment policy.

Trustees and Directors

Shareholders elect trustees or directors who are responsible for conducting REIT investment and business activities. Guidelines enforced by the SEC dictate that the majority of trustees or directors be independent of the business activities and affiliates of the trust. Mortgage REITs usually draw trustees from the real estate lending industry; equity REITs draw from the general real estate community.

REIT MANAGEMENT

Because the REIT itself must be a passive investor, trustees or directors hire managers to conduct the general affairs of the REIT. Some REITs have internal managers, while others use external managers, called advisors. The managers or advisors are responsible for property acquisition and disposition, financing arrangements, property management or loan servicing, and all other functions associated with day-to-day operations.

The majority of REITs elect to engage outside advisors to handle day-to-day operations. Advisory companies may be owned by financial conglomerates or by individual business people. In almost all cases, the advisory company is a subsidiary of the individual or firm that originally sponsored the REIT.

Advisor Responsibilities

In addition to overseeing day-to-day operations, advisors frequently provide investment counsel. For this service, they may engage outside professionals such as investment bankers or securities underwriters, lawyers, real estate brokers, accountants, or mortgage companies to supplement their own abilities and efforts. Advisors also select property managers to oversee operation of rental property owned by the trust. Trust advisors handle property purchases and dispositions and may supervise loan origination operations or mortgage portfolio purchases and sales (in the case of REITs engaged in mortgage lending). They may also service loans on behalf of their REIT client and administer mortgage loan foreclosure or "workouts" of problem loans. REIT advisors also perform clerical functions and prepare quarterly and annual financial reports for REIT shareholders.

Advisor Compensation

The North American Securities Administrators Association's guidelines for setting advisory fees specify that independent trustees must determine at least annually that fees paid are "reasonable" for the nature and quality of services performed. Some advisory firms are paid on a fee-for-service basis, whereby compensation depends entirely on the volume of services performed. This approach became prevalent in the mid-1970s amid widespread financial disarray among REITs. In addition to fee-for-service and expense reimbursement, some advisors receive an annual fee computed as a percent of REIT assets. Compensation might also be a fixed fee, a percentage of net income, or a percentage of cash flow.

REIT ASSETS

Total REIT market capitalization was approximately $1.134 trillion at the end of 2017. Approximately 6% was in mortgages. Real estate equities accounted for the rest, led by the retail sector with 18%.

REITs are classified as equity or mortgage, according to the type of investments they favor. *Equity REITs* take equity positions in real estate projects. Some *mortgage REITs* make primarily long-term loans; others specialize in short-term loans to finance real estate construction.

Equities accounted for slightly more than 50% of total REIT assets in the late 1960s. This percentage decreased steadily during subsequent years (although equities continued to grow in absolute terms), while REITs concentrated on mortgage lending as their primary vehicle for growth. After reaching an all-time low of 16% of total assets in 1974, equities began growing in their importance to REIT portfolios. By 1977, they again constituted more than half of total REIT assets, but declined once more—to about 40% of the total by 1992—before reversing direction once more and reaching 94%. Equity investments run the gamut of imaginable ventures, from residential rental projects through massive office towers and shopping centers to special-purpose properties.

REITS AS INVESTMENT VEHICLES

REITs are a beguiling alternative to direct investment in real estate assets. Actively traded REIT shares are highly liquid, virtually eliminating one of the most serious objections to real estate investment. They are also a predictable, reliable generator of cash dividends at a rate higher than most stocks.

Shareholders of REITs are in a position somewhat analogous to that of the limited partners in real estate limited partnerships. Shareholders may incur income tax liability as a consequence of cash distributions, but they avoid the double taxation to which distributed corporate earnings are generally subject. They thereby benefit from such corporate attributes as limited liability, centralized management, continuity of life, and free transferability of interests, without incurring associated tax disadvantages.

REIT shareholders benefit from REITs' investments in real estate equities in much the same manner as they would from taking a position directly in real estate assets. They receive the annual cash flows and equity buildup from retirement of mortgage debt, as well as growth in property value. Because they are required to distribute the majority of their income each year, REITs provide a steady source of cash dividends. This makes REITs particularly attractive to investors who desire substantial current cash flow coupled with the inflation protection afforded by assets that have appreciation potential. As illustrated in Figure 23.1, equity REITs have in recent years offered a consistently higher dividend yield than Treasury bonds. Yet, unlike equity REITs, Treasury bonds have no appreciation potential and are especially subject to the ravages of inflation.

FIGURE 23.1: Equity REITs Generate Cash Dividends

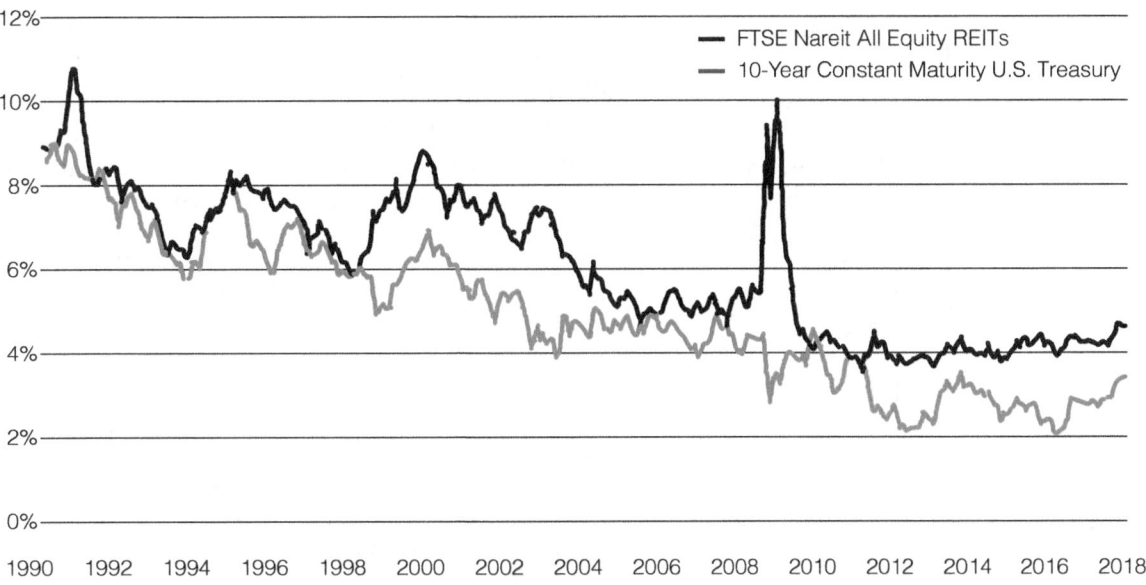

Income Tax Consequences

Because they are not taxed, REITs themselves do not benefit from tax shelter benefits frequently associated with real estate equity investment. Instead, REIT shareholders report their distributive shares of REIT taxable income on their personal income tax returns. A portion of the cash distributed to shareholders, therefore, is sheltered from income tax liability by deductions for cost recovery or depreciation allowances. Net losses, however, are not passed through to shareholders as they are in real estate limited partnerships. Because REITs are not double taxed as C corporations are (C corporations must pay corporate income taxes and then shareholders must pay individual income taxes on the dividends), the dividends for REITs are fully taxed at the investor's marginal tax rate, unlike C corporation dividends, which are currently taxed at a lower rate (15%).

REIT ownership subjects investors to the investment interest limitation rules explained in Unit 11. Interest incurred to acquire or carry portfolio assets, including REIT shares, can be offset only against income from portfolio assets. If portfolio interest expense exceeds portfolio income, the excess is carried forward to be offset in future years.

Diversification and Liquidity

Ownership of REITs enables investors of limited means to acquire indirect interests in large-scale real estate ventures. They thereby benefit from economies of scale that may not be available from smaller operations. Because REITs spread their investments over a large number of assets, investment risk is reduced through diversification.

REIT shares are generally more liquid than shares in real estate limited partnerships or direct ownership of real estate assets. Most REIT shares are traded on organized stock exchanges or in the over-the-counter market and are traded reasonably actively. Their market prices are thus readily ascertainable, and they can be sold without incurring prohibitive transaction costs. In contrast, real estate limited partnership shares may not be marketable at all.

Professional Guidance

Individual investors may lack the time or the knowledge necessary to search out properties, negotiate purchases, secure financing, oversee management, and supervise disposition. Investment in REIT shares provides indirect access to professionals who perform these services. REIT advisors or managers (discussed earlier) engage professional property managers and monitor their performance. They also arrange financing and supervise property disposition. Investors indirectly pay for these services, but the cost per REIT share is generally modest. The same services might be prohibitively expensive for individuals committing a small amount of capital to direct ownership.

Investment Risk

REIT shareholders face the same risks as owners of common stock. Dividend distributions may vary from year to year, reflecting fluctuations in the performance of REIT assets. Share resale values are affected by general market conditions and by changes in performance of REIT asset portfolios.

Equity REIT's dividends and share values of equity REITs may decline due to decreasing occupancy levels or unforeseen increases in operating expenses in their real estate portfolio. Operating performance and asset values may also be adversely affected by ill-chosen or poorly timed investments.

Mortgage REITs face all the risks generally associated with real estate mortgage lending, including interest rate risk. Borrowers may default on loan payments, reducing trust income, which in turn reduces ability to pay dividends. Foreclosures may result in loan losses, depressing both cash distributions and net asset value of REIT shares. Any events adversely affecting REIT revenue or net worth will ultimately be reflected in the value of shares.

An Additional Layer of Risk

Volatility associated with an individual REIT's shares can be diversified away. There remains the nondiversifiable, or systematic, risk that can be reduced only by accepting a lower rate of expected return. A comparison of returns and return variation between equity REITs and unsecuritized real estate shows that swings in REIT returns (primarily due to changes in market value) are more highly correlated with changes in the stock market than with changes in the market for unsecuritized real estate.[1] Because the stock market responds quickly (and, some would argue, exaggeratedly) to daily events, REIT returns—dividend yields plus-or-minus changes in share prices—swing widely from year to year.

Figure 23.2 illustrates this by showing the annual returns generated by a broad cross-section of REITs for the years 2009 through 2017. The Index, compiled by the National Association of Real Estate Investment Trusts (NAREIT®) includes all REITs traded on the New York and American Stock Exchanges and the Nasdaq National Market List. Though the average annualized rate of return for the nine years is 13.18%, year-to-year returns ranged from 2.29% in 2015 to 27.58% in 2010. Dividends tend to be fairly stable from year to year, so most of the return volatility is due to price swings.

FIGURE 23.2: Total Returns (Dividend Yield Plus-or-Minus Price Changes) of REITs Tracked by the National Association of Real Estate Investment Trusts

Year	Return
2017	9.27%
2016	9.28%
2015	2.29%
2014	27.15%
2013	3.21%
2012	20.14%
2011	7.28%
2010	27.58%
2009	27.45%
Nine-year average	8.82%

Source: NAREIT®

---

[1] F. C. Neil Myer, and James R. Webb, "Return Properties of Equity REITs, Common Stocks, and Commercial Real Estate: A Comparison," *The Journal of Real Estate Research* 8, no. 1 (Winter 1993): 87–106.

Relative returns to REITs and other assets reflect ephemeral investor interests and concerns, and fluctuate wildly. This is evident in Figure 23.3, which shows average annual returns to a cross-section of REITs for various time periods and compares them with the S&P 500 Stock Index. Over the 3-, 5-, and 10-year periods included in Figure 23.3, the average annual yield on REITs has been less than that on stocks, but for the 15- and 20-year periods, the REITs have outperformed stocks.

FIGURE 23.3: Comparative Performance Measures

	Average Annual Returns for Periods Ending May 31, 2018					
	1 Year	3 Years	5 Years	10 Years	15 Years	20 Years
REITs	-0.91	4.96	5.44	6.46	9.75	8.54
S&P 500 index	13.27	10.57	12.96	9.02	9.55	6.42

Source: NAREIT®

As noted earlier, share values do not necessarily reflect current operations of the underlying property portfolio. There is superimposed on that relationship a layer of investor interpretations of future industry prospects, and the market value of REIT shares will fluctuate with the level of investor optimism or pessimism. After analyzing the performance of securitized and unsecuritized real estate portfolios, Steven Kapplin and Arthur Schwartz concluded that, "once real estate is securitized, risk/return performance becomes more dependent on the behavior of securities' markets and less a function of the underlying assets in the securitized investment portfolio."[2]

REIT MUTUAL FUNDS

One simple and relatively inexpensive way to gain portfolio diversification on a limited budget is to purchase shares in a mutual fund. Like REITs, mutual funds avoid income taxes by distributing the bulk of their earnings to their shareholders each year. Whereas REITs invest in real estate or mortgage-secured debt, mutual funds invest in bonds or the stock of other companies. Open-ended mutual funds buy or sell their own shares on demand, with the price determined daily by the value of the mutual fund's portfolio at the close of business on the previous day. (Closed-end funds operate more like REITs: their shares are traded on the secondary market and are not routinely bought or sold by the fund itself.)

A number of open-ended mutual funds hold portfolios almost entirely made up of REIT shares. Some specialize in equity REITs, others in mortgage REITs, and some hold both in a blended portfolio. Most have diversified holdings in many states, and a few are diversified internationally. By buying shares in a REIT mutual fund, investors

---

[2] Steven D. Kapplin and Arthur L. Schwartz, Jr., "Recent Performance of U.S. Real Estate Securities," in Arthur L. Schwartz, Jr., and Steven D. Kapplin, eds., *Alternative Ideas in Real Estate Investments* (Boston: Kluwer Publishers, 1995), 17.

acquire fractional ownership in a more diversified portfolio with a smaller total financial commitment than they could achieve by investing directly in the REITs. They also get the benefit of specialized, and presumably informed, portfolio selection and management. REITs are highly specialized and relatively complex. The cost is an annual management fee expressed as a percentage of portfolio value.

HOW REITS ARE EVALUATED

The value of REITs is calculated just as we have calculated the value of other real estate assets in earlier units—the present value of future cash flows to be produced by the asset. For REITs, the future cash flows are designated as *funds from operations* (FFO). NAREIT adopted the term *FFO* in 1991 to provide an accurate measure of REIT cash flows or income performance. Analysis of common stock companies relies on net income figures. However, net income includes some items that distort cash flows, including depreciation, the noncash flow that affects taxes. In 2000, Graham and Knight found that FFO have higher information content than net income for REITs. They proposed that FFO were better measures of cash flows for REITs than net income because REITs have a greater impact on depreciation due to their very high proportion of fixed real assets. Furthermore, those real assets are depreciated to calculate net income, but are actually appreciating in value. They also attributed the greater relevance of FFO because REITs also depreciate tenant improvements, defer leasing costs such as commissions, and use straight-line rental calculations instead of the actual increased rent over time. Because FFO is a reflection of earnings before depreciation, it is a better measure of cash flows than earnings/net income and, therefore, best explains share value for REITs.[3]

SOURCES OF REIT INFORMATION

Because REITs are relatively new phenomena and constitute a small slice of the total securities market, sources of reliable REIT information have been slow to develop. Here are six sources that provide up-to-date information:

- *REIT Annual Report* (Washington, D.C.: National Association of Real Estate Investment Trusts). Published annually, the handbook contains industry statistics and data on approximately 300 REITs.
- *Lehman Brothers Equity REIT Index*. Published by Shearson Lehman Brothers (American Express Tower, World Financial Center, New York, NY 10285-1400), this index tracks the performance of the REIT industry and of individual industry segments.
- *SNL REIT Weekly*. This newsletter, published by SNL Securities, L.P., (410 East Main Street, Charlottesville, VA 22902), tracks the performance of approximately 225 REITs and reports industry happenings.

---

[3] Carol M. Graham and John R. Knight, "Cash Flows vs. Earnings in the Valuation of Equity REITs," *Journal of Real Estate Portfolio Management* 6, no. 1 (2000): 17–25; Ronald A. Stunda and Eric Typpo, "The Relevance of Earnings and Funds Flow from Operations in the Presence of Transitory Earnings," *The Journal of Real Estate Portfolio Management* 10, no. 1 (January–April 2004): 37–45.

- *Value Line Investment Survey.* Value Line (220 East 42nd Street, New York, NY 10017) includes 18 REITs in the list of securities covered on a regular basis.

- *REIT Score Property Directory.* This quarterly publication reports on more than 100 REITs, including property acquisitions and property holdings by metropolitan area. It is published by National Real Estate Index, 2200 Powell Street, Suite 700, Emeryville, CA 94608.

- *REIT Watch.* This is a monthly statistical report on the real estate investment trust industry and is available from *www. reit.com.*

SUMMARY

REITs use the corporate form of ownership to channel funds from passive investor-shareholders into real estate. They issue common stock, commercial paper, and debt securities, and invest the proceeds in real estate debt or equities. They were one of the first intermediaries to tap the stock, bond, and commercial paper markets for funds to invest in real estate.

REITs are often characterized by the type of real estate assets in which they specialize, and are called mortgage, equity, or hybrid trusts. Mortgage trusts make real estate loans, and equity trusts purchase properties outright. Hybrids do both.

By distributing most of their earnings to shareholders each year, REITs can avoid income tax liability. REIT shareholders thus avoid the double taxation that characterizes investment in corporate shares, yet benefit from the limited liability, centralized management, free transferability of interest, and other characteristics that make corporate stock attractive. Investors often gain some degree of diversification, as REITs frequently invest in a number of projects. Further diversification can be achieved with a limited budget by investing in REIT mutual funds.

REITs give investors access to economies of scale in real estate management and the expertise of real estate professionals that is generally unaffordable by small-scale investment directly in real estate equities. REIT ownership, though, exposes investors to fluctuations in the market price of stock as well as the possibility of variations in annual dividend distributions.

REITs are organized much like corporations. Shareholder owners elect trustees or directors. Trustees or directors appoint managers or use outside managers known as advisors. Managers or advisors oversee the day-to-day operations of the trust.

RECOMMENDED READING

Ambrose, Brent W., and Peter Linneman. "REIT Organizational Structure and Operating Characteristics." *The Journal of Real Estate Research* 21, no. 3 (May/June 2001): 141–62.

Ambrose, Brent W., and Xun Bian. "Stock Market Information and REIT earnings management." *Journal of Real Estate Research*, 2010, 32:1, 101-137.

Chen, K. C., and Daniel D. Tzang. "Interest-Rate Sensitivity of Real Estate investment Trusts." *The Journal of Real Estate Research* 3, no. 3 (Fall 1988): 13–22.

Chiang, Kevin C. H., Ming-Long Lee, and Craig H. Wisen. "Another Look at the Asymmetric REIT-Beta Puzzle." *The Journal for Real Estate Research* 26, no. 1 (January–March 2004): 25–42.

Gilbert, Michael S. "Equity Real Estate Investment Trusts and Real Estate Returns." *The Journal of Real Estate Research* 5, no. 2 (Summer 1990): 259–64.

Gyourko, Joseph, and Todd Sinai. "The REIT Vehicle: Its Value Today and in the Future." *The Journal of Real Estate Research* 18, no. 2 (September/October 1999): 355–75.

Hardin, William G., and Zhonghua Wu. "Banking Relationships and REIT Capital Structure." *Real Estate Economics*, 2010, 38:2, 257-284.

Kuhle, James L., Carl H. Walther, and Charles H. Wurtzebach. "The Financial Performance of Real Estate Investment Trusts." *The Journal of Real Estate Research* 1, no. 1 (Fall 1986): 67–76.

Lee, Ming-Long, and Kevin C. H. Chiang. "Substitutabilty between Equity REITs and Mortgage REITs." *The Journal of Real Estate Research* 26, no. 1 (January–March 2004): 95–113.

Lin, Crystal Y., and Kenneth Yung. "Real Estate Mutual Funds: Performance and Persistence." *The Journal of Real Estate Research* 26, no. 1 (January–March 2004): 69–93.

Myer, F. C. Neil, and James R. Webb. "Return Properties of Equity REITs, Common Stocks, and Commercial Real Estate: A Comparison." *The Journal of Real Estate Research* 8, no. 1 (Winter 1993): 87–106.

Webb, James R., and Willard McIntosh. "Real Estate Investment Acquisition Rules for REITs: A Survey." *The Journal of Real Estate Research* 1, no. 1 (Fall 1986): 77–98.

INTERNET REFERENCES

For information on REITs from the National Association of Real Estate Investment Trusts:
www.reit.com

For REIT data:
www.snl.com

REVIEW QUESTIONS

1. What is a real estate investment trust?
2. What are the major differences among mortgage, equity, and hybrid real estate investment trusts?
3. How do investor tax benefits in a real estate investment trust differ from those of a partner in a real estate partnership?
4. Describe the functions of real estate investment trust advisors.
5. Describe the conditions that must be met for a real estate investment trust to retain its trust status under the Internal Revenue Code.
6. Describe the sources from which real estate investment trusts draw funds for investment.
7. Explain the reasons why a group of investors might want to gain control of a real estate investment trust through common stock acquisition.

DISCUSSION QUESTIONS

1. From an individual investor's perspective, describe the relative merits of mortgage REITs, equity REITs, and hybrids.
2. Buying a REIT mutual fund subjects investors to an additional layer of management fees. Wouldn't it therefore make more financial sense to invest directly in a variety of REITs, thus gaining the advantages of diversification without incurring the additional expense? Explain your reasoning.

PART EIGHT

Case Problem

Several friends are debating the pros and cons of various approaches to real estate investment:

Terry Taylor (age 40) is a vocational education specialist who teaches woodworking and blueprint reading at a local high school. Taylor's school does not offer summer classes, so he is employed for only nine months each year. Taylor is married and has three children, all of whom are in secondary school. The Taylor family's annual income averages about $42,000, and their net worth is about $100,000.

Sharon Shafer (age 40) is a stockbroker. She earns more than $160,000 annually and works about 60 hours each week. She has a portfolio of common stocks worth more than $1 million and thinks real estate is an ideal way to diversity her portfolio. Shafer is unmarried and has no dependents.

Gary Groves (age 60) recently inherited $3 million from his father, whereupon he resigned his job as a clerk at the local library. Though he has little education beyond high school, Groves intends to invest his inheritance and manage his own portfolio.

Faye Hyde is a 34-year-old physician who works about 50 hours weekly and earns about $120,000 per year. Hyde is the sole source of support for three dependent children, whose ages range from 3 to 12. Her assets have a net value of about $200,000.

These friends are arguing over the relative merits of REITs, shares of stock in real estate corporations, and direct investment as a sole owner of rental property.

1. To what extent might differences of opinion be attributable to personal circumstances?
2. To what extent might differences of opinion be attributable to personal education and background or professional experience?
3. To what extent might differences of opinion stem from varying attitudes toward risk?
4. Make the necessary assumptions where information is lacking and suggest possible avenues for real estate investment by each of these friends.

APPENDIX A

Mathematics of Compounding and Discounting

Economic rationale for time adjustments is the first topic of Appendix A. The appendix then addresses how to measure growth of money through the compounding of interest income. Present value of a future sum is closely related to how a present amount grows and is logically the next topic of exploration. The text then moves a step further in complexity by considering the present value of a series of future amounts. Because payments to retire a loan are reciprocal to the present value of a series of future receipts, these topics are presented back to back. A final topic addressed is techniques for extending the usefulness of compound interest and discount tables.

CONCEPTUAL BASIS FOR COMPOUNDING AND DISCOUNTING

Compound interest and *discount* are based on two fundamental propositions: more is better than less, and sooner is better than later. From these propositions, it follows that people will insist on being compensated for waiting and that there will be a trade-off between the amount received and timeliness of receipt.

That more of a good thing is better than less is not a matter for serious dispute. Economists have considered this a self-evident proposition since the dawn of their discipline. If one bottle of champagne is gratifying, two will be even more so, three are even more desirable than two, and so forth. Fundamental to this concept (and certainly to our example) is that one need not consume the greater quantity if one does not wish to do so. Increased gratification stems from certain knowledge that more is readily available if desired. Two bottles thus provide the same option as one, plus the intoxicating choice of still more refreshment.

A preference for present over future receipt is only a small step further into abstraction. Who would not (other things being equal) prefer $500 today to the certain promise of $500 next month? Choosing the promise of future receipt reduces one's option for present consumption without offering anything in return. Current receipt, in contrast, provides the option of consumption now, next month, or at any time in the distant future. Clearly, the want-satisfying power of a good is generally enhanced by current receipt.

The more intense the desire for immediate gratification, the greater will be the rate of trade-off, as illustrated in Figure A.1. This relationship is sometimes called *time preference for money*, or the *time value of money*. The topmost line in Figure A.1 represents an individual who has a very high time preference. The individual's strong preference for immediate receipt indicates that she will insist on handsome compensation for waiting. The lower line in the figure represents the trade-off function of someone who has relatively low time preference and can therefore be induced to wait with very little compensation. The middle line represents the trade-off function of one with only a moderate time preference.

Growth in the amount available for consumption, as a consequence of waiting, is called *compound interest*. Reducing the amount available, as a consequence of opting for more immediate receipt, is called *discounting*. The greater the rate of compound interest or discount, the steeper will be the slope of the trade-off functions in Figure A.1.

FIGURE A.1: Time Preference for Money

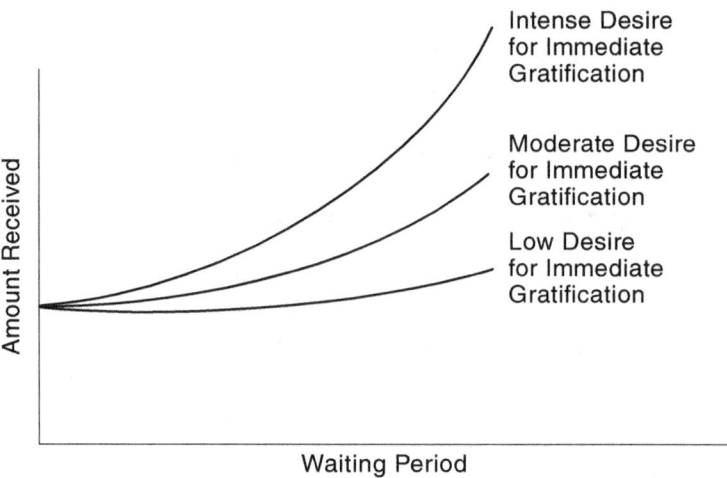

HOW MONEY PLACED ON DEPOSIT WILL GROW

If $1,000 placed on deposit for one year earns 7% interest, the amount of interest will be 0.07 times $1,000, or $70. The amount on deposit at the end of the year (assuming no withdrawals of either principal or interest) will be $1,000 plus $70, or $1,070.

APPENDIX A Mathematics of Compounding and Discounting

This simple example incorporates all the elements of compound interest. The general relationship can be expressed as

$$\text{final amount} = \text{original amount} + \text{interest earned}$$

Because annual interest is usually expressed as a rate or percentage of the amount on deposit (the principal), the same relationship can be expressed as

$$\text{final amount} = \text{original amount} + (\text{original amount} \times \text{interest rate})$$

Rearranging terms on the right-hand side of the equation yields

$$\text{final amount} = \text{original amount} \times (1 + i)$$

where i is the interest rate. In the illustration of \$1,000 placed on deposit for one year at 7% interest, this becomes

$$\$1,070 = \$1,000 \times 1.07$$

Suppose now that the \$1,000 principal amount is left on deposit for three years, with interest at 7% per year compounding annually. Annual compounding means that accumulated interest itself earns interest in all subsequent periods. Figure A.2 illustrates how compound interest accumulates so that the final amount after three years (hereafter called the *compound value*) totals \$1,225.04. Expressed in terms of the preceding equation, the compound value at the end of three years is

After 1 year: $\$1,000 \times 1.07$
After 2 years: $(\$1,000 \times 1.07)(1.07)$
After 3 years: $(\$1,000 \times 1.07)(1.07)(1.07)$
$= (\$1,000)(1.07)^3$
$= \$1,000 \times 1.22504$
$= \$1,225.04$

FIGURE A.2: How a Debt Accumulates at Compound Interest

Year	Amount Owed at Start of Current Year	Plus Interest at 7%	Amount Owed at Year End
1	\$1,000.00	0.07 × \$1,000.00	\$1,070.00
2	\$1,070.00	0.07 × \$1,070.00	\$1,144.90
3	\$1,144.90	0.07 × \$1,144.90	\$1,225.04

This relationship among principal, compound interest, and time is summarized in more general fashion as

$$V_n = PV(1 + i)^n$$

where V_n is the compound value, also known as the future value (FV), PV is the initial amount deposited (or borrowed), i is the interest rate, and n is the number of time periods involved.

The only laborious arithmetic in the formula is raising $(1 + i)$ to the nth power. For the problem illustrated, there are only three periods over which to calculate the compound value. But suppose there had been 75 periods! In the absence of a good calculator or a set of tables, the calculation of $(1 + i)^n$ would be tedious in the extreme.

Fortunately, inexpensive financial calculators will quickly handle the computational chores. Also, tables are readily available that give solutions to $(1 + i)^n$ for various values of both i and n. An excerpt from such a table, showing representative values of i and n, is reproduced here as Figure A.3. Time periods in the table are expressed as years, but they could just as well be days, months, quarters, or any other period appropriate to the problems being considered.

The solution shown on Figure A.2 can be derived quickly by referring to Figure A.3. Simply extract the value for $(1 + i)^n$ by reading down the column in Figure A.3 under the 7% rate and across the row indicating value after three years.

FIGURE A.3: Compound Value of $1 Left on Deposit $[(1 + i)^n]$

Year	6%	7%	8%	9%	10%	12%	14%
1	1.0600	1.0700	1.0800	1.0900	1.1000	1.1200	1.1400
2	1.1236	1.1449	1.1664	1.1881	1.2100	1.2544	1.2996
3	1.1910	1.2250	1.2597	1.2950	1.3310	1.4049	1.4815
4	1.2625	1.3108	1.3605	1.4116	1.4641	1.5735	1.6890
5	1.3382	1.4026	1.4693	1.5386	1.6105	1.7623	1.9254
6	1.4185	1.5007	1.5869	1.6771	1.7716	1.9738	2.1950
7	1.5036	1.6058	1.7138	1.8280	1.9487	2.2107	2.5023
8	1.5938	1.7182	1.8509	1.9926	2.1436	2.4760	2.8526
9	1.6895	1.8385	1.9990	2.1719	2.3579	2.7731	3.2519
10	1.7908	1.9672	2.1589	2.3674	2.5937	3.1058	3.7072
15	2.3966	2.7590	3.1722	3.6425	4.1772	5.4736	7.1379
20	3.2071	3.8697	4.6610	5.6044	6.7275	9.6463	13.7435
25	4.2919	5.4274	6.8485	8.6231	10.8347	17.0001	26.4619

That factor (1.2250) is the compound amount of $1 left on deposit for three years at 7%. Multiplying this factor by the $1,000 initial payment yields the value for V.

Now consider a real estate application of compound interest. Suppose a vacant residential building lot, currently worth $5,000, is expected to increase in value at a compound annual rate of 10% for at least the next six years. The lot's expected FV after six years is expressed by the following equation:

$$V_6 = PV \times (1.10)^6$$
$$= \$5,000 \times 1.7716$$
$$= \$8,858$$

where V_6 is the expected value at the end of the sixth year, and PV is the initial investment at point zero on the timeline. The factor (1.7716) can be derived by solving for $(1.10)^6$, or it can be taken from a table such as Figure A.3. Multiplying the factor by the initial $5,000 market value of the property gives its expected value of $8,858.

PRESENT VALUE OF A FUTURE AMOUNT

The equation for the FV of an initial amount can easily be altered to solve for the present value of a known future amount. The restructured equation is

$$PV = \frac{FV}{(1+i)^n}$$

where the symbols have the same meaning as before, but the initial amount PV is the unknown. In this form, the equation is used to solve problems involving the present value of known or estimated future amounts or the interest (discount) rate required to equate known present values with known or estimated future amounts.

Example A.1

A parcel of land is expected to be worth $1,500 per acre when water mains are extended five years later. How much can an investor pay for the land today and still expect to earn 12% per annum on his investment before considering transaction costs and income taxes, assuming carrying costs (the cost to maintain the land) exactly equal rental revenue from the property?

Example A.1 illustrates. To solve the problem, first express it as

$$PV = \frac{FV}{(1+i)^n}$$
$$= \$1,500 / (1.12)^5$$
$$= \$1,500 / 1.7623$$
$$= \$851$$

With simple algebraic sleight of hand we can reconfigure $PV = FV/(1 + i)^n$ to read $PV = FV \times 1/(1 + i)^n$. Note that performing the multiplication in our restructured equation (this is, multiplying FV by 1) takes us right back to the original formulation. With this restructured format we are able to consistently multiply by factors in compound interest or discount tables. Figure A.4 is an excerpt from tables that provide values for $1/(1 + i)^n$, used when solving for present values of single sums due in the future.

To use Figure A.4 to answer the question posed in Example A.1, we restate the equation as

$$PV = FV_5 \times \frac{FV}{(1+i)^n}$$

The value of $1/(1+i)^n$ can be solved with a calculator or taken from a table such as Figure A.4. To use the table, read down the 12% column and across the five-year row. The factor at the intersection of the column and row is 0.5674. Multiplying this factor by the $1,500 expected FV of the land gives the present value per acre (rounded to the nearest dollar) of $851 when the FV is discounted at 12%.

Note the distinction between Figures A.3 and A.4. The first gives values for $(1+i)^n$, while the latter gives values for $1/(1+i)^n$. Because these are reciprocals of each other, separate tables are not really needed. All the values for either table can be derived by dividing the corresponding values from the other table into one.

FIGURE A.4: Present Value of $1 Due at a Future Date [$1/(1+i)^n$]

Year	6%	7%	8%	9%	10%	12%	14%
1	0.9434	0.9346	0.9259	0.9174	0.9091	0.8929	0.8772
2	0.8900	0.8734	0.8573	0.8417	0.8264	0.7972	0.7695
3	0.8396	0.8163	0.7938	0.7722	0.7513	0.7118	0.6750
4	0.7921	0.7629	0.7350	0.7084	0.6830	0.6355	0.5921
5	0.7473	0.7130	0.6806	0.6499	0.6209	0.5674	0.5194
6	0.7050	0.6663	0.6302	0.5963	0.5645	0.5066	0.4556
7	0.6651	0.6227	0.5835	0.5470	0.5132	0.4523	0.3996
8	0.6274	0.5820	0.5403	0.5019	0.4665	0.4039	0.3506
9	0.5919	0.5439	0.5002	0.4604	0.4241	0.3606	0.3075
10	0.5584	0.5083	0.4632	0.4224	0.3855	0.3220	0.2697
15	0.4173	0.3624	0.3152	0.2745	0.2394	0.1827	0.1401
20	0.3118	0.2584	0.2145	0.1784	0.1486	0.1037	0.0728
25	0.2330	0.1842	0.1460	0.1160	0.0923	0.0588	0.0378

This reciprocal relationship is illustrated in Figure A.5, with reference to Example A.1. The FV of the land ($1,500) is the compound amount of $851 growing at 12% per annum for five years. Conversely, the value to the investor ($851) is the present value of $1,500 to be received in five years, when discounted at 12% per annum.

A by-product of the convenience of separate tables for present and FVs is the problem of determining which to use. One way to keep this straight is to remember that the solution to factors on the future-value table is always greater than that for the percent value at the same interest rate (so long as the rate is greater than zero). This reflects the basic idea that an amount received in the present is always more valuable than the promise of receiving the same amount at a future date. The future amount must be larger to induce one to wait.

FIGURE A.5: Relationship Between Present Value and Future Value When Compounding and Discounting at 12%

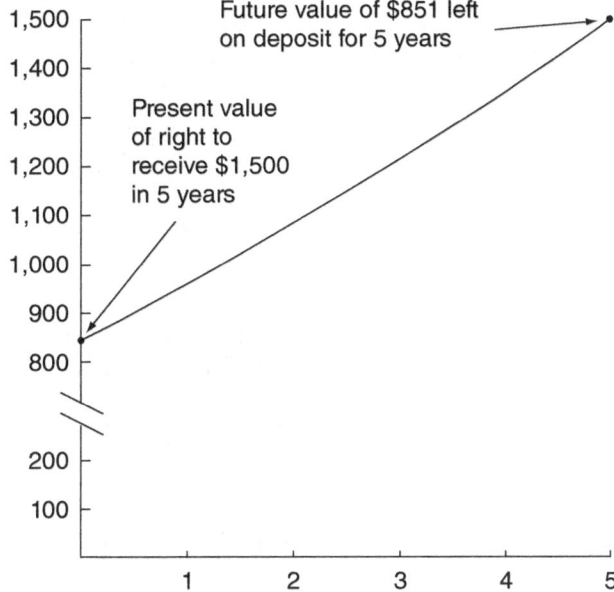

HOW A SERIES OF DEPOSITS WILL GROW

Our discussion so far has focused on the present and the FV of a single sum: how a deposit grows or the present value of a single amount due in the future. But suppose a series of amounts is to be left on deposit or the present value of a series of payments or receipts must be determined.

Consider first the case of a series of fixed payments left on deposit. Any series of equal periodic amounts is called an *annuity*.

Conventionally, annuity payments are assumed to be made at the end of each period, though this is not a necessary assumption. Tables can be designed with any desired assumption about the timing of periodic cash flows. As a matter of convention, however, most annuity tables are designed with the assumption that all cash flow occurs instantaneously at the end of each period. For example, payments of $500 per annum made at the end of each year for five years constitute a five-year annuity. If these payments were deposited into an account paying 7% per annum, how much would be in the account at the time the last payment is made?

APPENDIX A Mathematics of Compounding and Discounting

The first payment draws interest for four years, the second for three years, the third for two years, and the fourth for one year; the final payment draws no interest at all. If the compound values of all these payments are summed, the total is the compound value of the annuity. The problem is expressed algebraically as

$$S = PMT_1(1+i)^{n-1} + PMT_2(1+i)^{n-2} + PMT_3(1+i)^{n-3} + \ldots + PMT_{n-1}(1+i) + PMT_n$$
$$= PMT_k[(1+i)^{n-1} + (1+i)^{n-2} + (1+i)^{n-2} + \ldots + (1+i) + 1]$$

where S is the compound value of the series of payments, PMT is the amount of the level annual payment, i is the compound annual interest rate, n is the number of payments to be made, and k indicates that PMT is a constant. For convenience, the previous expression is frequently condensed as follows:

$$S = PMT_k \left[\sum_{t=1}^{n-1} (1+i)^t + 1 \right]$$

where $\sum_{t=1}^{n-1}$ simply means add together the value of $(1+i)^t$ for n minus one periods, and t indicates the time periods from one through n minus one.

Substituting $500 for PMT_k, 7% for i, and five years for n, we solve for the compound value of $100 per year for five years:

$$S = 500 \left[\sum_{t=1}^{4} (1.07)^t + 1 \right]$$
$$= \$500 \left[(1.07) + (1.07)^2 + (1.07)^3 + (1.07)^4 + 1 \right]$$
$$= \$500 \times 5.75074$$
$$= \$2,875.37$$

The solution can be reached much more conveniently by referring to tables that give the value of the bracketed term in the preceding equation. Values for the bracketed term can be derived with a financial calculator or extracted from a table such as the excerpt presented here as Figure A.6. Read across the top of the table to the 7% column and down the left margin to the five-year row. The value found at the intersection of the column and row is 5.75074. Substituting this value for the bracketed term in the preceding equation, we determine the compound amount to be $500 × 5.75074 = $2,875.37. This solution is diagramed in Figure A.7.

APPENDIX A Mathematics of Compounding and Discounting

FIGURE A.6: How $1 Deposited at the End of Each Year Will Grow

$$\left[\sum_{t=1}^{n-1}(1+i)^t + 1\right]$$

	Annual Interest Rate						
Year	6%	7%	8%	9%	10%	12%	14%
1	1.00000	1.00000	1.00000	1.00000	1.00000	1.00000	1.00000
2	2.06000	2.07000	2.08000	2.09000	2.10000	2.12000	2.14000
3	3.18360	3.21490	3.24640	3.27810	3.31000	3.37440	3.43960
4	4.37462	4.43994	4.50611	4.57313	4.64100	4.77933	4.92114
5	5.63709	5.75074	5.86660	5.98471	6.10510	6.35285	6.61010
6	6.97532	7.15329	7.33593	7.52333	7.71561	8.11519	8.53552
7	8.39384	8.65402	8.92280	9.20043	9.48717	10.08901	10.73049
8	9.89747	10.25980	10.63663	11.02847	11.43589	12.29969	13.23276
9	11.49132	11.97799	12.48756	13.02104	13.57948	14.77566	16.08535
10	13.18079	13.81645	14.48656	15.19293	15.93742	17.54874	19.33730
15	23.27597	25.12902	27.15211	29.36092	31.77248	37.27971	43.84241
20	36.78559	40.99549	45.76196	51.16012	57.27500	72.05244	91.02493
25	54.86451	63.24904	73.10594	84.70090	98.34706	133.33387	181.87083

FIGURE A.7: How $500 Deposited at the End of Each Year for Five Years Will Grow

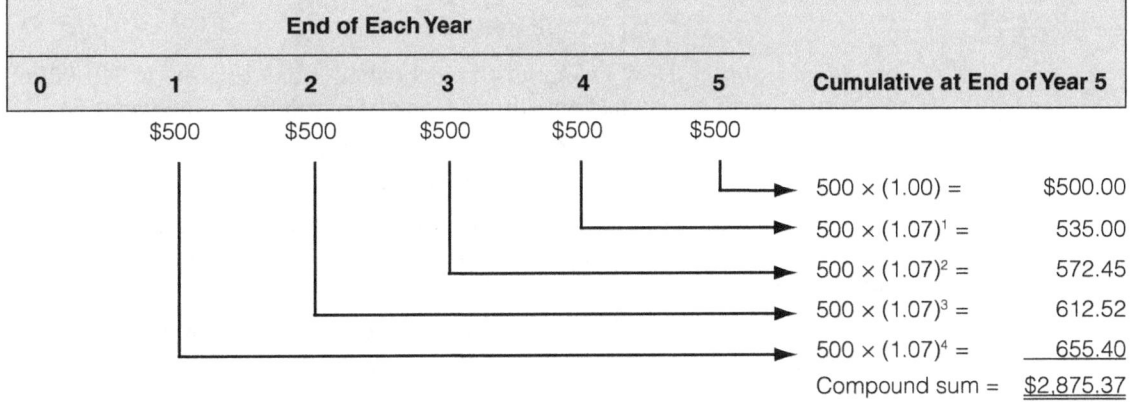

PRESENT VALUE OF AN ANNUITY

We have seen that any series of periodic payments received or paid at regular intervals may be called an *annuity*. Examples include pension checks from a retirement fund or payments on a fully amortized installment note. While all such regular periodic streams of cash technically qualify as annuities, not all are popularly known as such. The present value of an annuity is best thought of as the amount that, if invested today at a given interest rate, will provide the known periodic payments for the prescribed period.

To illustrate, suppose funds are to be placed on deposit with interest at 6% per annum, sufficient to permit withdrawals in $1,000 increments at the end of each year for three years. To determine the amount of the required initial deposit (assuming there is to be a balance of exactly zero after the third annual withdrawal), the problem might be broken into three separate subquestions:

- *Subquestion 1*: How much must be deposited today to accumulate $1,000 in one year? To solve this question, first restructure the basic equation to solve for the present value of a single future amount:

$$PV = PMT_1 \times 1 / (1 + i)$$

where R_1 is the first periodic withdrawal, i is the interest rate, and there is just one compounding period. The $1/(1 + i)$ is taken from Figure A.4 or derived with a calculator. Substituting the appropriate numerical values into the equation, we have

$$PV = \$1,000 \times 1 / (1.06)$$
$$= \$1,000 \times 0.9434$$

- *Subquestion 2:* How much must be deposited today to accumulate $1,000 in two years? Again, substituting the appropriate numbers into the basic equation, we have

$$PV = \$1,000 \times 0.1 / (1.06)^2$$
$$= \$1,000 \times 0.8900$$

- *Subquestion 3*: How much must be deposited today to provide $1,000 in three years? Numerical substitution results in the following equation:

$$PV = \$1,000 \times 1 / (1.06)^3$$
$$= \$1,000 \times 0.8396$$

The total amount to be deposited to provide for the three annual withdrawals is the sum of the three values just calculated. Therefore, the total present value PV, the amount to be placed on deposit, is

$$PV = [\$1,000 \times 1 / (1.06)] + [\$1,000 \times 1 / (1.06)^2] + [\$1,000 \times 1 / (1.06)^3]$$
$$= \$1,000 [1 / (1.06) + 1 / (1.06)^2 + 1 / (1.06)^3]$$

APPENDIX A Mathematics of Compounding and Discounting

Values for $(1/1.06)^t$, where t ranges from one through three, were derived in subquestions one through three. Summing these three values, we get

$$PV = \$1,000 \times (0.9434 + 0.8900 + 0.8396)$$
$$= \$1,000 \times 2.6730$$
$$= \$2,673$$

The general form of the preceding computation can be expressed as

$$PV = PMT_n \times [1 / (1 + i) + 1/(1 + i)^2 + \ldots + 1 / (1 + i)^n]$$

where PMT_n is the amount of a level periodic receipt, PV is the initial deposit, and i is the discount (interest) rate.

Alternatively, the same concept can be expressed as:

$$PV = PMT_k \left[\sum_{t=1}^{n} \frac{1}{(1+i)^t} \right]$$

The practical problem in solving these calculations is the time required to do the computations when the number of compounding periods and thus the number of values to be summed is very large. Precomputed tables for the cumulative values simplify the problem, as does the availability of a financial calculator (procedures using a financial calculator are explained in Appendix B). An excerpt of these cumulative values is presented here as Figure A.8.

Returning to the problem of a three-year annuity of $1,000 per year with a 6% per annum discount (interest) rate, determining the present value (i.e., the required initial deposit) involves finding the annuity factor in Figure A.8, which lies at the intersection of the 6% column and the three-year row. This factor (2.6730) multiplied by the $1,000 annual annuity payment equals the amount of the initial deposit ($2,673):

$$PV = PMT_k \left[\sum_{t=1}^{3} \frac{1}{(1.06)^t} \right]$$
$$= \$1,000 \times 2.6730$$
$$= \$2,673$$

FIGURE A.8: Present Value of an Annuity of $1 per Year

$$\left[\sum_{t=1}^{n}\frac{1}{(1+i)^t}\right]$$

Year	Annual Discount Rate						
	6%	7%	8%	9%	10%	12%	14%
1	0.9434	0.9346	0.9259	0.9174	0.9091	0.8929	0.8772
2	1.8334	1.8080	1.7833	1.7591	1.7355	1.6901	1.6467
3	2.6730	2.6243	2.5771	2.5313	2.4869	2.4018	2.3216
4	3.4651	3.3872	3.3121	3.2397	3.1699	3.0373	2.9137
5	4.2124	4.1002	3.9927	3.8897	3.7908	3.6048	3.4331
6	4.9173	4.7665	4.6229	4.4859	4.3553	4.1114	3.8887
7	5.5824	5.3893	5.2064	5.0330	4.8684	4.5638	4.2883
8	6.2098	5.9713	5.7466	5.5348	5.3349	4.9676	4.6389
9	6.8017	6.5152	6.2469	5.9952	5.7590	5.3282	4.9464
10	7.3601	7.0236	6.7101	6.4177	6.1446	5.6502	5.2161
15	9.7122	9.1079	8.5595	8.0607	7.6061	6.8109	6.1422
20	11.4699	10.5940	9.8181	9.1285	8.5136	7.4694	6.6231
25	12.7834	11.6536	10.6748	9.8226	9.0770	7.8431	6.8729
30	13.7648	12.4090	11.2578	10.2737	9.4269	8.0552	7.0027

PRESENT VALUE OF A PERPETUAL ANNUITY

A *perpetuity* is a never-ending stream of payments or receipts. For such a cash-flow pattern to exist, it must necessarily be the case that each installment represents only accrued interest. If some principal were retired with each payment, then the principal would eventually be exhausted and the stream would end; there would not be a perpetual flow.

This being the case, it follows that each payment is simply the interest rate per period multiplied by the principal amount of the annuity:

$$PMT_k = PV \times i$$

where PMT_k is the periodic payment or receipt, PV is the present value (principal amount) of the annuity, and i is the rate of interest per period. To solve for the present value, simply transpose the symbols in the equation:

$$PV = PMT_k / i$$

APPENDIX A Mathematics of Compounding and Discounting

To illustrate, consider a perpetual annuity of $10,000 per annum, with interest at 8% per annum. The present value of the perpetuity is:

$$PV = PMT_k / i$$
$$= \$10,000 / 0.08$$
$$= \$125,000$$

Suppose the appropriate discount rate associated with the above annuity moves to 10% per annum. This reduces the present value of the perpetuity to $100,000:

$$PV = PMT_k / i$$
$$= \$10,000 / 0.10$$
$$= \$100,000$$

This result leads to the generalized observation that there is an inverse relationship between the discount rate and the present value of any future series of payments or receipts.

PAYMENTS TO AMORTIZE A LOAN

Suppose you were to receive a lump-sum educational grant of $10,000 to be spent during four years of university study. How much could you withdraw at the end of each year, in four equal installments, to exactly exhaust the fund with the last annual withdrawal if the balance in the fund draws interest at 6%? This is an annuity problem not unlike those investigated earlier. Recall the general expression for a level annuity, which is

$$PV = PMT_k \left[\sum_{t=1}^{n} \frac{1}{(1+i)^t} \right]$$

The essential difference here is that the initial payment PV is known and the periodic receipt PMT_k is the unknown quantity. The problem can be solved with a financial calculator or by using factors from Figure A.8. To use the table, find the value for the summation of $1/(1+i)^t$, where the interest rate, i, is 6% and the time periods range from one through four years. The factor is 3.4651. The problem can thus be expressed as

$$PV = PMT_k \left[\sum_{t=1}^{4} \frac{1}{(1.06)^t} \right]$$
$$= PMT_k \times 3.4651$$

and, as the value of PV is known to be $10,000,

$$\$10,000 = PMT_k \times 3.4651$$

Solving for PMT_k yields

$$PMT_k = \$10,000 / 3.4651$$
$$= \$2,885.92$$

Note that the final solution involves dividing by an annuity factor. Recall that division is the same as multiplying by a reciprocal (i.e., $a/b = a \times 1/b$). Tables can easily be generated that incorporate reciprocals of values from an annuity table. Such a table (incorporating monthly, rather than annual, payments) is included here as Figure A.9.

The factors in Figure A.9 are often called *loan amortization factors*, or *debt constants*. The table itself is then referred to as an *amortization table*. It gives the equal periodic payment necessary to repay a $1 loan, with interest, over a specified number of payment periods. (A table showing the distribution of a specific payment schedule between principal and interest is frequently called an *amortization schedule*.) Because Figure A.9 gives repayment factors based on monthly payments, it is not reciprocal to Figure A.8. A table of annual payments, however, would be.

To see how an amortization table works, consider a $100,000 loan that calls for interest at 8% per annum on the unpaid balance. If the loan is to be repaid in equal monthly installments (including both interest and principal) over five years, monthly payment obligations can be determined by multiplying the $100,000 face amount by the amortization factor from Figure A.9, which lies at the intersection of the 8% column and the five-year row. The product, $2,027.60, is the amount the lender must receive each month for five years to recover the initial $100,000 outlay and receive 8% per annum interest on the outstanding balance of the loan.

FIGURE A.9: Monthly Payment to Amortize a $1 Debt

Year	Annual Discount Rate						
	6%	7%	8%	9%	10%	12%	14%
1	0.086066	0.086527	0.086988	0.087451	0.087916	0.088849	0.089787
2	0.044321	0.044773	0.045227	0.045685	0.046145	0.047073	0.048013
3	0.030422	0.030877	0.031336	0.031800	0.032267	0.033214	0.034178
4	0.023485	0.023946	0.024413	0.024885	0.025363	0.026334	0.027326
5	0.019333	0.019801	0.020276	0.020758	0.021247	0.022244	0.023268
6	0.016573	0.017049	0.017533	0.018026	0.018526	0.019550	0.020606
7	0.014609	0.015093	0.015586	0.016089	0.016601	0.017653	0.018740
8	0.013141	0.013634	0.014137	0.014650	0.015174	0.016253	0.017372
9	0.012006	0.012506	0.013019	0.013543	0.014079	0.015184	0.016334
10	0.011102	0.011611	0.012133	0.012668	0.013215	0.014347	0.015527
15	0.008439	0.008988	0.009557	0.010143	0.010746	0.012002	0.013317
20	0.007164	0.007753	0.008364	0.008997	0.009650	0.011011	0.012435
25	0.006443	0.007068	0.007718	0.008392	0.009087	0.010532	0.012038
30	0.005996	0.006653	0.007338	0.008046	0.008776	0.010286	0.011849

Had the $100,000 loan in the preceding example called for annual payments, Figure A.9 would not have been usable. No table of annual amortization payments is given because loans seldom provide for this repayment pattern. But an amortization factor can be derived easily by calculating the reciprocal of the factor for an 8%, five-year annuity. Divide the annuity factor, 3.9927, from Figure A.8, into one. The quotient, 0.25046, is the annual payment to retire a five-year, 8% loan of $1, with annual payments. Multiplying this factor by a $100,000 loan amount gives the annual payment necessary to retire the loan in five years: $25,046. The problem also can be solved without reference to tables. With annual payments, the equation is

$$\text{payment} = \text{loan amount} \times \left[\frac{i}{\left(1 - \left[\frac{1}{(1+i)^n}\right]\right)} \right]$$

If payments are made monthly, the equation is revised accordingly:

$$\text{payment} = \text{loan amount} \times \left[\frac{\left(\frac{i}{12}\right)}{\left(1 - \left[\frac{1}{\left(1+\frac{i}{12}\right)}\right]^{12n}\right)} \right]$$

Note that an annual payment is somewhat more than the sum of 12 monthly payments on a loan of the same size with the same amortization period and interest rate ($25,046 versus $24,331.20 in the preceding example). This is because interest on the outstanding balance is greater for the annual payment note as a result of the balance not having been "paid down" at monthly intervals during the year. In general, the more frequently payments are made, the less the total interest obligation will be and thus the less the total debt-service payment.

EXTENDING THE USEFULNESS OF FINANCIAL TABLES

Even though they are rapidly being rendered superfluous by inexpensive financial calculators, tables can be used to solve a wide variety of real estate investment and financial problems. Several applications are illustrated here to provide additional exercise in using the tables, as well as to demonstrate their versatility. These extended uses are by no means exhaustive. They are intended rather to demonstrate the flexibility of compound interest and discount concept, the total usefulness of which is limited only by imagination and inventiveness.

Finding Values Not in the Tables

Interest and discount tables give factors for values at intervals over a wide range. Sometimes, however, the rate under consideration falls at an intermediate point between those in a table. When this happens, estimate the actual value by *interpolating* between table values most nearly approximating the rate being sought.

Interpolation involves assuming a linear relationship between tabular values. This introduces a degree of error, because the actual relationship is quadratic rather than linear. The convenient assumption greatly simplifies calculations, however, and the error will generally be insignificant if interpolation is between those tabular values closest to the unknown factor.

The problem is illustrated in Figure A.10. The curved line shows the relationship between values from Figure A.8 for discount rates of 7% and 8% and for all intermediate discount rates. Interpolation results in estimates of values not in the table, as indicated by the straight line in the illustration. Distance between the curved (actual) function and the straight (estimated) line represents error introduced by interpolation. Obviously, the wider apart the known values from which an unknown factor is estimated, the greater the error introduced by the assumption of linearity.

Figure A.10 depicts the consequence of using straight-line interpolation to estimate the appropriate present value factor for a five-year annuity when the discount rate is 7.25%. Figure A.8 gives annuity present value factors for discount rates of 7% and 8% but for no intermediate rates.

FIGURE A.10: Interpolating Between Known Present Value Factors

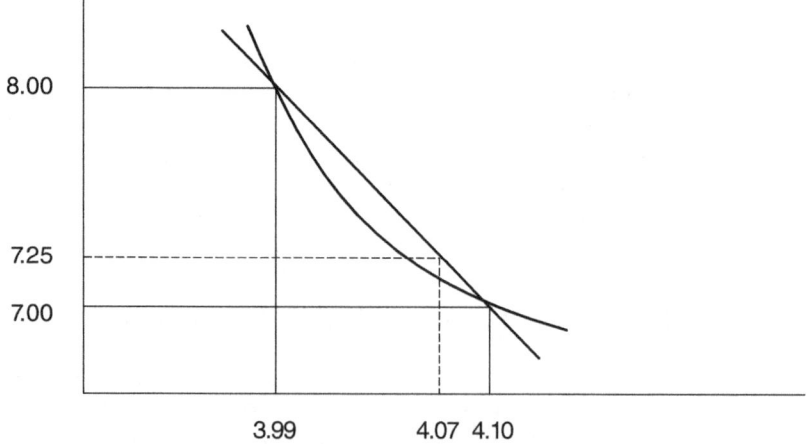

Because 7.25% falls one-fourth of the way between these given factors, approximate an appropriate factor by moving one-fourth of the distance between the factor for 7% and that for 8%. The 7% factor is 4.1002, and that for 8% is 3.9927. Multiply the difference by 0.25 and subtract this amount from the factor of 7%. The result is a factor of 4.0733, determined as follows:

$$4.1002 - 0.25 (4.1002 - 3.9927) = 4.0733$$

Figure A.11 diagrams the preceding calculations. The total number of percentage points between 7% and 8% is 8 minus 7, or one point. The distance between discount rates of 7% and 7.25% is 7.25 minus 7, or 0.25 point. Because 0.25 point is 25% of one point, the "target" discount rate lies 25% of the distance between the known values. Assume a linear relationship and estimate the discount factor for the 7.25% rate by moving 25% of the distance between the discount factor for 7% and that for 8%.

The total distance between the factor for 7%, 4.1002, and that for 8%, 3.9927, is 0.1075. Twenty-five percent of this distance is 0.25 × 0.1075, or 0.0269. Moving this far from the 4.1002 value associated with the 7% discount rate results in an estimate of 4.0733 for the factor associated with a discount rate of 7.25%.

FIGURE A.11: Interpolating to Find Values Not on the Tables

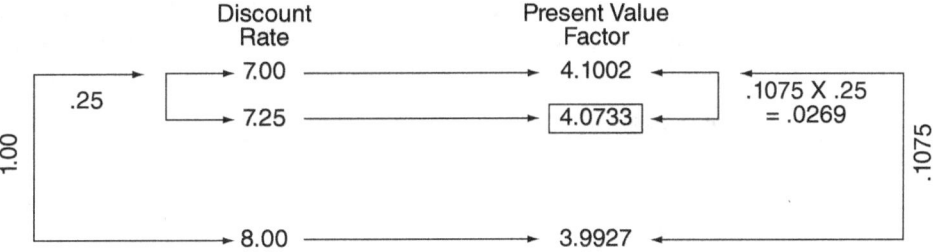

Remaining Balance of a Note

Understanding the reciprocity of annuity tables and amortization tables (with the same time period between payments) sets the stage for easily determining the remaining balance on a fully amortizing note. The face amount of a note can be thought of as the present value of an annuity whose periodic receipts are the debt-service payments. But amortization tables are used because the present value is known and the future payments are unknown, whereas with conventional annuity problems, the known factors are the future payments and the present value is unknown.

To see this relationship clearly, consider a $100,000 loan calling for level monthly payments to fully amortize the loan over 25 years, with interest at 9%. Referring to the amortization table (Figure A.9), multiply the factor found at the intersection of the 9% column and the 25-year row by the $100,000 face amount of the loan.

The monthly payment is found to be $839.20. The same answer results from solving the equation, as discussed earlier, or using a financial calculator.

Now, remembering the reciprocal relationship between annuity and amortization factors, treat the remaining payments as a level monthly annuity and discount (the annuity period will be the number of monthly payments remaining, and the discount rate will be 1/12th the contract rate of interest). You can also use the amortization table to determine the present value of a monthly annuity of $839.20 that extends for 25 years, when discounted at 9%. To derive the present value factor for the monthly annuity using the table, go back to the intersection of the 9% column and 25-year row of the amortization table and divide the factor into one. The result (1 / 0.008392 = 119.16), when multiplied by the monthly payment, yields the remaining balance of $100,000. We, of course, already knew this to be the present value, because that is the amount of the original loan. The approach, however, can be used to determine the remaining balance at any future date by simply substituting the remaining number of payments for the period.

Present Value of a Deferred Annuity

To find the present value of an annuity that does not start until sometime in the future, find the value of the annuity at the beginning of the first year of payments or receipts and then discount this amount to the present as a single sum. Alternatively, solve for an annuity that extends over both the annuity payment period and the period of the deferral and subtract the present value of the annuity for the period of the deferral; the remainder is the present value of the deferred annuity.

Example A.2

Determine the present value, when discounting at 6% per annum, of a five-year annuity of $1,000 per annum (paid at the end of each year), with the first annuity payment due four years later.

Example A.2 illustrates the problem. The first annuity payment or receipt is due in four years. Because payments are made at the end of each year as in an ordinary annuity, the annuity period actually starts at the beginning of the year in which the first payment is made. There is, therefore, a three-year lapse before the annuity period starts.

Solution alternative A

The first step is to solve for the value of the annuity at the beginning of the annuity period (three years hence). At that point, there is a straightforward five-year annuity of $1,000 per annum. The value at that point (which we will call V_3) is $4,212.40, determined as follows:

$$V_3 = PMT_k \left[\sum_{t=1}^{5} \frac{1}{(1.06)^t} \right]$$
$$= \$1,000 \times 4.2124$$
$$= \$4,212.40$$

The second step is to discount V_3 as a single sum due three years later. The present value is $3,537. Here is the calculation:

$$PV = V_3 \times 1 / (1.06)^3$$
$$= \$4,212.40 \times 0.8396$$
$$= \$3,536.73$$

These two steps can, of course, be combined into a single mathematical operation, with the same results. Here is the combined computation:

$$PV = PMT_k \left[\sum_{t=1}^{5} \frac{1}{(1.06)^t} \right] \times \left[\frac{1}{(1.06)^3} \right]$$
$$= \$1,000 (4.2124 \times 0.8396)$$
$$= \$1,000 \times 3.53673$$
$$= \$3,536.73$$

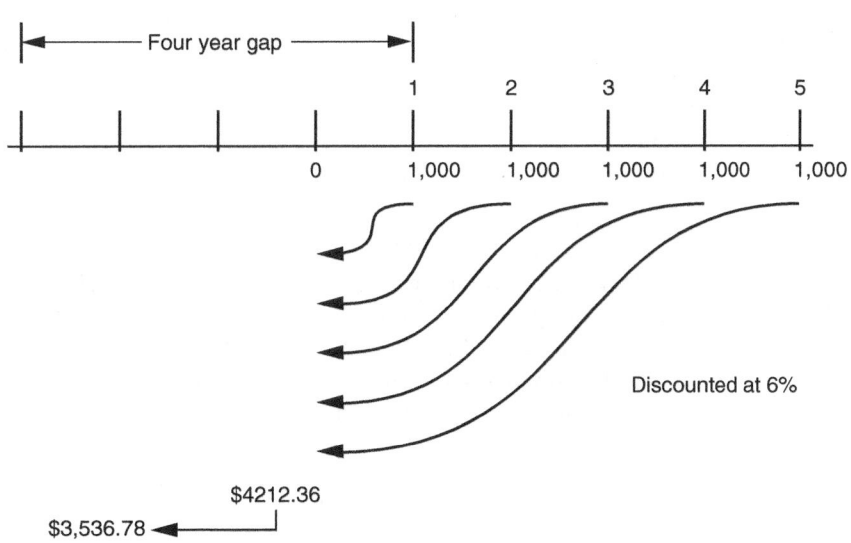

On a financial calculator the entries are as follows:

$$1000 \, PMT$$
$$6 \, i$$
$$5 \, N$$
$$PV = 4212.36$$

This PV is then treated as a FV to be discounted back 3 years @ 6%, such that

$$4212.36 \, FV$$
$$6 \, i$$
$$3 \, n$$
$$PV = \$3536.78$$

Solution Alternative B

Determine what the present value would be if the annuity extended over both the deferral period and the payment period (three years + five years = eight years). From this value subtract the value of the annuity for the first three years (the period of the deferral). The remainder is the present value of the annuity for the period in which it is actually to be received.

For the annuity in Example A.2, the present value would be $6,209.80 if payments extended over the entire eight-year period:

$$PV = PMT_k \left[\sum_{t=1}^{8} \frac{1}{(1.06)^t} \right]$$
$$= \$1{,}000 \times 6.2098$$
$$= \$6{,}209.80$$

From this amount subtract the value of the annuity for the period of the deferral. This is three years, and the value to be subtracted is $2,673, determined as follows:

$$PV = PMT_k \left[\sum_{t=1}^{3} \frac{1}{(1.06)^t} \right]$$
$$= \$1{,}000 \times 2.6730$$
$$= \$2{,}673$$

The present value of the five-year annuity that will be received, starting after three years, is simply the present value of the last five years of the eight-year annuity. To find this amount, subtract the present value of the three-year annuity (the portion of the eight-year annuity that will not be received) from the present value of the eight-year annuity. The computation yields the same solution as before, except for a small rounding error. Here are the numbers:

$$PV = \$6{,}209.80 - \$2{,}673$$
$$= \$3{,}536.80$$

APPENDIX A Mathematics of Compounding and Discounting

These computations can also be consolidated into a single equation, with the same results:

$$PV = PMT_k \left[\sum_{t=1}^{8} \frac{1}{(1.06)^t}\right] - \left[\sum_{t=1}^{3} \frac{1}{(1.06)^t}\right]$$
$$= \$1,000(6.2098 - 2.6730)$$
$$= \$1,000 \times 3.5368$$
$$= \$3,536.80$$

Annuities in Advance

Our earlier statement that annuity payments or receipts are treated as if the transaction occurred at the end of each period needs further elaboration. This is not a necessary assumption for using discounting and compounding; it is merely a convention adopted when constructing annuity tables. A table incorporating the assumption that cash flow occurs at the beginning of each period, or at any intermediate point within the periods, could easily be developed.

Such tables are not frequently available. Existing tables must therefore be modified when working with cash flows that occur at the beginning of each period. Annuities with this sort of schedule are conventionally called *annuities in advance, or annuities due*.

To find the present value of annuities in advance, simply multiply the annual amount by

$$\sum_{t=1}^{n-1} \frac{1}{(1+i)^t}$$

and add one more payment. Example A.3 illustrates.

Example A.3

Determine the present value of an annuity of $1,000 per annum for five years when the appropriate discount rate is 6% per annum and when the annuity payment is made at the beginning of each year. (Values are rounded to the nearest whole dollar.)

$$= (\$1,000 \times 3.4651) + \$1,000$$
$$= \$3,465 + \$1,000$$
$$= \$4,465$$

$$PV = PMT_k \left[\sum_{t=1}^{4} \frac{1}{(1.06)^t}\right] + R$$

APPENDIX A Mathematics of Compounding and Discounting

To find the compound value of an annuity when payments are made at the beginning rather than the end of each period, multiply the amount of the annual annuity payment by

$$\sum_{t=1}^{n+1} \frac{1}{(1+i)^t}$$

where n is the actual number of payments, and subtract the amount of one payment. Example A.4 demonstrates these calculations.

Example A.4

Determine the compound (future) value of an annuity of $1,000 per annum for five years when the compound interest rate is 6% per annum and when payments are made at the beginning of each year. (All amounts are rounded to the nearest whole dollar.)

$$S = PMT_k \left[\sum_{t=1}^{6} \frac{1}{(1.06)^t} \right] - R$$

$$= \$1,000(6.9753) - \$1,000$$

$$= \$6,975 - \$1,000$$

$$= \$5,975$$

APPENDIX B

Compounding and Discounting with Financial Calculators

Financial tables such as those discussed in Appendix A have for many years been a major labor-saving device for analysts by greatly simplifying computational chores. The tables themselves are well on their way to being outmoded, however, by the ready availability of low-cost electronic calculators programmed to do financial computations. Many of these calculators are not much larger than a standard business card (some are even incorporated into wristwatches), and many of them cost less than a book of financial tables.

This appendix is intended to demonstrate the use of financial calculators to solve problems such as those explained in Appendix A. To show comparability of calculator solutions with those derived from tables, each example demonstrates how table values themselves may be derived by using calculators. Illustrations then show how calculators can be used to find other values that are not found in the tables.

FUTURE VALUE OF A DOLLAR

The future-value interest factor is used to calculate how a sum left on deposit at a compound rate of interest will grow. The compound interest formula is

$$FV = PV (1 + i)^n$$

where

FV = Future value
PV = Present value (amount invested today)
i = Rate
n = Number of periods

Example B.1

The future-value interest factor for three years at 8% is calculated as follows:

$$FV = (1 + 0.08)^3$$
$$= 1.2597$$

The future value, interest factor in Example B.1 can be determined by using a calculator with the keys n, i, PV, PMT, and FV by entering $n = 3$, $i = 8$, $PV = 1$, and solving for FV. To calculate the factors for Example B.1 and all following examples in this appendix, use the following substitutions:

1. *Monthly Factors*

    n = Number of months

    i = Annual rate / 12

2. *Quarterly Factors*

    n = Number of quarters

    i = Annual rate / 4

3. *Semiannual Factors*

    n = Number of half years

    i = Annual rate / 2

APPENDIX B Compounding and Discounting with Financial Calculators

Example B.2

1. FV of $1 for three years at 8% per annum, compounded monthly.

$$FV = (1 + 0.006667)^{36}$$
$$= 1.270237$$

Calculator solution:
n = 36   i = 8/12
PV = 1   FV = ?

2. FV of $1 for three years at 8%, compounded quarterly.

$$FV = (1 + 0.02)^{12}$$
$$= 1.268242$$

Calculator solution:
n = 12   i = 8/4
PV = 1   FV = ?

3. FV of $1 for three years at 8%, compounded semiannually.

$$FV = (1 + 0.04)^{6}$$
$$= 1.26532$$

Calculator solution:
n = 6   i = 8/2
PV = 1   FV = ?

COMPOUND VALUE OF AN ANNUITY

The compound value of an annuity equation is used to calculate how much an amount invested periodically will be worth at some future date if it earns interest at a compound rate. The compound value formula is

$$FV = PMT \times ([(1 + i)^n - 1] / i)$$

where

FV = Future value
PMT = Payment (amount invested periodically)
i = Rate
n = Number of periods

Example B.3

The future worth of an annuity factor for three years at 8% is calculated as follows:

$$FV = ([(1 + 0.08)^3 - 1] / 0.08)$$
$$= 3.2464$$

The factor in Example B.3 can be determined with a financial calculator by entering $n = 3$, $i = 8$, $PMT = 1$, and solving for FV.

> **Example B.4**
>
> 1. FV of $1 per month for three years at 8% per annum, compounded monthly.
>
> $$FV = \$1 \times ([(1 + 0.00667)^{36} - 1] / 0.00667)$$
> $$= \$40.54$$
>
> Calculator solution:
>
> $n = 36$ $i = 8/12$
> $PMT = 1$ $FV = ?$
>
> 2. FV of $1 per quarter for three years at 8% per annum, compounded quarterly.
>
> $$FV = \$1 \times ([(1 + 0.02)12 - 1] / 0.02)$$
> $$= \$13.41$$
>
> Calculator solution:
>
> $n = 12$ $i = 8/4$
> $PMT = 1$ $FV = ?$
>
> 3. FV of $1 semiannually for three years at 8% per annum, compounded semiannually.
>
> $$FV = \$1 \times ([(1 + 0.04)^6 - 1] / 0.04)$$
> $$= \$6.63$$
>
> Calculator solution:
>
> $n = 6$ $i = 8/2$
> $PMT = 1$ $FV = ?$

PRESENT VALUE OF A DOLLAR

The present value of a dollar formula is used to calculate how much some amount to be received in the future is worth today considering compound interest. The formula is

$$PV = FV \times 1 / (1 + i)^n$$

where

PV = Present value
FV = Future value
i = Rate
n = Number of periods

APPENDIX B Compounding and Discounting with Financial Calculators

Example B.5

The present value interest factor for three years at 8% is calculated as follows:

$$PV = 1 / (1 + 0.08)^3$$
$$PV = 0.7938$$

The present value interest factor in Example B.5 can be determined using a calculator by entering $n = 3$, $i = 8$, $FV = 1$, and solving for PV.

Example B.6

1. PV of $1 at the end of three years at 8% per annum, compounded monthly.

$$PV = 1 / (1 + 0.00667)^{36}$$
$$= 0.7873$$

   Calculator solution:
   $n = 36$ $i = 8/12$
   $FV = 1$ $PV = ?$

2. PV of $1 at the end of three year at 8% per annum, compounded quarterly.

$$PV = 1 / (1 + 0.02)^{12}$$
$$= 0.7885$$

   Calculator solution:
   $n = 12$ $i = 8/4$
   $FV = 1$ $PV = ?$

3. PV of $1 at the end of three years at 8% per annum, compounded semiannually.

$$PV = 1 / (1 + 0.04)^6$$
$$= 0.7903$$

   Calculator solution:
   $n = 6$ $i = 8/2$
   $FV = 1$ $PV = ?$

PRESENT VALUE OF A LEVEL ANNUITY

The present value annuity formula is used to calculate how much an amount to be received periodically in the future is worth today, for a given rate of interest or discount. The formula is

$$PV = PMT \times [(1 - [1/(1 + i)^n]) / i]$$

where

PV = Present value
PMT = Payment per period
i = Rate
n = Number of periods

Example B.7 can be solved using a calculator by entering $n = 3$, $i = 8$, $PMT = 1$, and solving for PV.

Example B.7

The present value interest factor of an annuity for three years at 8% is calculated as follows:

$$PV = [(1 - [1 / (1 + 0.08)^3]) / 0.08]$$
$$= 2.5771$$

Example B.8

1. PV of $1 per month for three years at 8% per annum.

    $$PV = 1 \times [(1 - [1 / (1 + 0.0066667)^{36}]) / 0.0066667]$$
    $$= 31.9118$$

    Calculator solution:
    n = 36 i = 8/12
    PMT = 1 PV = ?

2. PV of $1 per quarter for three years at 8% per annum.

    $$PV = 1 \times [(1 - [1 / (1 + 0.02)^{12}]) / 0.02]$$
    $$= 10.5753$$

    Calculator solution:
    n = 12 i = 8/4
    PMT = 1 PV = ?

3. PV of $1 per period semiannually for three years at 8% per annum.

    $$PV = 1 \times [(1 - [1 / (1 + 0.04)^6]) / 0.04]$$
    $$= 5.2421$$

    Calculator solution:
    n = 6 i = 8/2
    PMT = 1 PV = ?

AMOUNT TO AMORTIZE $1 (MORTGAGE CONSTANT)

The *mortgage constant* or loan constant is the percentage of the mortgage paid periodically for principal and interest, and is used to calculate the payment on a fully amortizing loan. It is the percentage of the original loan that must be paid periodically in order to fully repay principal and interest over the term of the loan. The formula is

$$MC = i/(1 - [1/(1+i)^n])$$

where

MC = Mortgage constant
i = Rate
n = Number of periods

Example B.9

The mortgage constant for a three-year loan at 8% interest, with annual payments, is calculated as follows:

$$MC = (0.08)/(1 - [1/(1+0.08)^3])$$
$$= 0.3880$$

The constant in Example B.9 can be derived using a financial calculator by entering $n = 3$, $i = 8$, $PV = 1$, and solving for *PMT*.

Example B.10

1. Payment (PMT) per period to amortize $1 over three years at 8% per annum, with monthly payments.

$$PMT = 0.006667 / (1 - [1 / (1 + 0.006667)^{36}])$$
$$= 0.0313$$

Calculator solution:
- $n = 36$
- $PV = 1$
- $i = 8/12$
- $PMT = ?$

2. Payment (PMT) per period to amortize $1 over three years at 8% per annum, with quarterly payments.

$$PMT = 0.02 / (1 - [1 / (1 + 0.02)^{12}])$$
$$= 0.0946$$

Calculator solution:
- $n = 12$
- $PV = 1$
- $i = 8/4$
- $PMT = ?$

3. Payment (PMT) per period to amortize $1 over three years at 8% per annum, with semiannual payments.

$$PMT = 0.04 / (1 - [1 / (1 + 0.04)^{6}])$$
$$= 0.1908$$

Calculator solution:
- $n = 6$
- $PV = 1$
- $i = 8/2$
- $PMT = ?$

RECOMMENDED READING

White, Mark A. "Financial Problem Solving with an Electronic Calculator." *Financial Practice and Education* (Fall 1991): 73-88.

APPENDIX C

Normal Distribution Table

FIGURE C.1: Areas Under the Standard Normal Curve

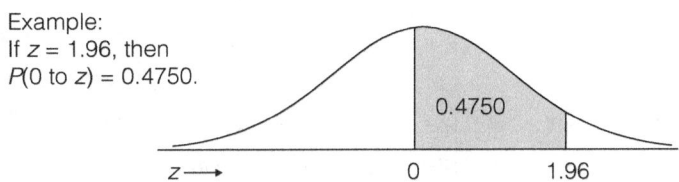

Example:
If z = 1.96, then
$P(0$ to $z) = 0.4750$.

This table presents the area between the mean and the Z-score. When Z=1.96, the shaded area is 0.4750.

z	0.00	0.01	0.02	0.03	0.04	0.05	0.06	0.07	0.08	0.09
0.0	0.0000	0.0040	0.0080	0.0120	0.0160	0.0190	0.0239	0.0279	0.0319	0.0359
0.1	0.0398	0.0438	0.0478	0.0517	0.0557	0.0596	0.0636	0.0675	0.0714	0.0753
0.2	0.0793	0.0832	0.0871	0.0910	0.0948	0.0987	0.1026	0.1064	0.1103	0.1141
0.3	0.1179	0.1217	0.1255	0.1293	0.1331	0.1368	0.1406	0.1443	0.1480	0.1517
0.4	0.1554	0.1591	0.1628	0.1664	0.1700	0.1736	0.1772	0.1808	0.1844	0.1879
0.5	0.1915	0.1950	0.1985	0.2019	0.2054	0.2088	0.2123	0.2157	0.2190	0.2224
0.6	0.2257	0.2291	0.2324	0.2357	0.2389	0.2422	0.2454	0.2486	0.2517	0.2549
0.7	0.2580	0.2611	0.2642	0.2673	0.2704	0.2734	0.2764	0.2794	0.2823	0.2852
0.8	0.2881	0.2910	0.2939	0.2969	0.2995	0.3023	0.3051	0.3078	0.3106	0.3133
0.9	0.3159	0.3186	0.3212	0.3238	0.3264	0.3289	0.3315	0.3340	0.3365	0.3389
1.0	0.3413	0.3438	0.3461	0.3485	0.3508	0.3513	0.3554	0.3577	0.3529	0.3621

FIGURE C.1: Areas Under the Standard Normal Curve (continued)

z	0.00	0.01	0.02	0.03	0.04	0.05	0.06	0.07	0.08	0.09
1.1	0.3643	0.3665	0.3686	0.3708	0.3729	0.3749	0.3770	0.3790	0.3810	0.3830
1.2	0.3849	0.3869	0.3888	0.3907	0.3925	0.3944	0.3962	0.3980	0.3997	0.4015
1.3	0.4032	0.4049	0.4066	0.4082	0.4099	0.4115	0.4131	0.4147	0.4162	0.4177
1.4	0.4192	0.4207	0.4222	0.4236	0.4251	0.4265	0.4279	0.4292	0.4306	0.4319
1.5	0.4332	0.4345	0.4357	0.4370	0.4382	0.4394	0.4406	0.4418	0.4429	0.4441
1.6	0.4452	0.4463	0.4474	0.4484	0.4495	0.4505	0.4515	0.4525	0.4535	0.4545
1.7	0.4554	0.4564	0.4573	0.4582	0.4591	0.4599	0.4608	0.4616	0.4625	0.4633
1.8	0.4641	0.4649	0.4656	0.4664	0.4671	0.4678	0.4686	0.4693	0.4699	0.4706
1.9	0.4713	0.4719	0.4726	0.4732	0.4738	0.4744	0.4750	0.4756	0.4761	0.4767
2.0	0.4772	0.4778	0.4783	0.4788	0.4793	0.4798	0.4803	0.4808	0.4812	0.4817
2.1	0.4821	0.4826	0.4830	0.4834	0.4838	0.4842	0.4846	0.4850	0.4854	0.4857
2.2	0.4861	0.4864	0.4868	0.4871	0.4875	0.4878	0.4881	0.4884	0.4887	0.4890
2.3	0.4893	0.4896	0.4898	0.4901	0.4904	0.4906	0.4909	0.4911	0.4913	0.4916
2.4	0.4918	0.4920	0.4922	0.4925	0.4927	0.4929	0.4931	0.4932	0.4934	0.4936
2.5	0.4938	0.4940	0.4941	0.4943	0.4945	0.4946	0.4948	0.4949	0.4951	0.4952
2.6	0.4953	0.4955	0.4956	0.4957	0.4959	0.4960	0.4961	0.4962	0.4963	0.4964
2.7	0.4965	0.4966	0.4967	0.4968	0.4969	0.4970	0.4971	0.4972	0.4973	0.4974
2.8	0.4974	0.4975	0.4976	0.4977	0.4977	0.4978	0.4979	0.4979	0.4980	0.4981
2.9	0.4981	0.4982	0.4982	0.4983	0.4984	0.4984	0.4985	0.4985	0.4986	0.4986
3.0	0.4987	0.4987	0.4987	0.4988	0.4988	0.4989	0.4989	0.4989	0.4990	0.4990
3.1	0.4990	0.4991	0.4991	0.4991	0.4992	0.4992	0.4992	0.4992	0.4993	0.4993
3.2	0.4993	0.4993	0.4994	0.4994	0.4994	0.4994	0.4994	0.4995	0.4995	0.4995
3.3	0.4995	0.4995	0.4995	0.4996	0.4996	0.4996	0.4996	0.4996	0.4996	0.4997
3.4	0.4997	0.4997	0.4997	0.4997	0.4997	0.4997	0.4997	0.4997	0.4997	0.4998

APPENDIX D

A Closer Look at Like-Kind Exchanges

Section 1031 of the Internal Revenue Code, which provides for deferral of income tax gains or losses on transactions that meet the Code's criteria for like-kind exchanges, is introduced in Unit 11. Because like-kind exchanges are so potentially beneficial for real estate portfolio adjustments, the issue is further explored in this appendix.

TAX CONSEQUENCES

Recall from Unit 11 that gains or losses on transactions that wholly qualify as like-kind must be deferred until the substitute property is disposed of in a taxable transaction. To qualify, both the old and the substitute property must be held for productive use in a trade or business or as an investment. If they meet these criteria, virtually any real estate will be considered like-kind with any other real estate.

Not All Parties Need Qualify

The test of whether a transaction qualifies as a tax-deferred exchange is applied separately to each party to the trade. To qualify, individuals must not have been holding their property for resale or for personal use. A property must have been held either as an investment or for use in a trade or business (but not as inventory). If one party's motive for ownership was inappropriate under Section 1031, the other party to the transaction may nevertheless qualify.

Example D.1

Alice Alt wants to acquire Larry D. Lundberg's property in an exchange. Lundberg is willing to sell outright but has no interest in Alt's property. The broker finds a third party who is willing to buy Alt's property. The deal is completed by an exchange of property interests between Alt and Lundberg and a purchase by the third party of the property acquired by Lundberg from Alt. Alt has a tax-deferred exchange; Lundberg does not.

In Example D.1, Alt may defer any gain on the transaction because she acquired like-kind property to be held as an investment. Lundberg, however, does not qualify and so must recognize any realized gain. Lundberg is disqualified because the property acquired from Alt is held for resale. The flow of assets between the parties is illustrated in Figure D.1.

FIGURE D.1: A Two-Way Exchange with a Third-Party Buyer

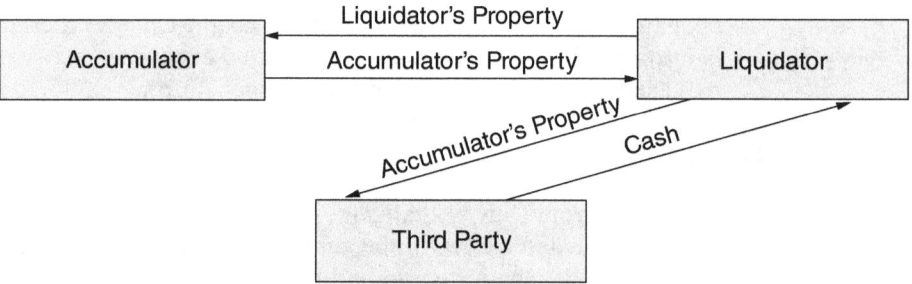

Even if Lundberg had not found an immediate buyer for property acquired from Alt in Example D.1, it is possible that recognition of gains could not be deferred under Section 1031. Had the property traded to Alt been listed for sale for a period of time immediately before the exchange, this would have established that it also was held primarily for sale. The important point here is that the tax consequences to Alt are independent of those to Lundberg.

Effect of Receiving Unlike Property

Receipt of property that does not meet the like-kind definition has the effect of partially disqualifying a gain from deferral under Section 1031. The person receiving unlike property, or boot, must recognize any gain realized on the transaction to the extent of the boot received.

Boot includes anything of economic value other than like-kind assets involved in the transaction. Examples include cash, services rendered or an obligation to render services, debt forgiveness, and a promise to convey something of value in the future.

A special rule applies to one category of unlike property: the transfer of like-kind property subject to mortgage indebtedness. The amount of debt relief involved in such a transfer is treated as receipt of unlike property, whether or not the other party assumes and agrees to pay the indebtedness. However, when each party takes title subject to an outstanding mortgage, only the party that receives net debt relief is considered to have received boot, and the amount is the difference between the two mortgages. Example D.2 illustrates.

Example D.2

Smith and Jones agree that their respective equities are equal in value. They agree to trade equities, each party taking title subject to the mortgage note on the property received. Their positions before the exchange were as follows:

	Smith	Jones
Market value of property	$750,000	$1,400,000
Less: Balance of mortgage	250,000	900,000
Value of equity	$500,000	$500,000

Jones has received boot of $650,000 in the form of net debt relief (the old debt of $900,000 minus the new debt of $250,000). Therefore, Jones incurs an income tax liability for any gain realized on the transaction, to the extent of the $650,000 of net debt relief.

An investor may receive net debt relief and yet have to pay cash to balance the market value of assets exchanged. In that case, only the difference between net debt relief and the cash paid is treated as boot received. However, receipt of cash or other unlike assets is not offset against net mortgage liability assumed. Example D.3 illustrates.

> **Example D.3**
>
> Fred Frasier and Betty Boyd agree to exchange properties. Each party is to assume the balance of the outstanding mortgage note on realty received in the exchange, and Boyd agrees to pay cash to Frasier to "balance the equities." Their positions before the exchange were as follows:
>
> | | Front | Back |
> |---|---|---|
> | Market value of realty | $1,100,000 | $1,100,000 |
> | Less: Balance of mortgage | 600,000 | 700,000 |
> | Market value of equity | $500,000 | $400,000 |
>
> Based on this analysis, Boyd agrees to pay Frasier $100,000. Even though she receives net debt relief in the exchange, Boyd has not received boot as defined in Section 1031 and need not report a taxable gain. This is because the net debt relief is offset by payment of cash boot. The effect is the same as if the $100,000 cash had been applied instead to reduce the mortgage balance before the trade. Offsetting the $100,000 of net debt relief against the $100,000 cash paid by Boyd results in an even trade from Boyd's point of view.
>
> When cash is received, however, it is not offset by mortgage liability assumed. Frasier, therefore, has received $100,000 boot in the form of cash, notwithstanding the fact that he has assumed $100,000 of additional mortgage liability.

A party who receives unlike property in an exchange must recognize any gain to the extent of the value of boot received. Note that this applies only to gains. Losses realized in a transaction may not be recognized if the exchange qualifies even partly as like-kind.

Treatment of Transaction Costs

Transaction costs include such items as brokerage commissions, recording fees, transfer taxes, and attorney's fees. Transaction costs may be thought of as a reduction in proceeds from the old property or an addition to the purchase price of the new. In either case, they reduce the realized gain and thereby become a part of the tax basis of newly acquired property. Transaction costs may also be offset against any unlike property (boot) received and thereby reduce the portion of the realized gain that must be recognized.[1]

---

[1] Revenue Ruling 72-456.

TAX BASIS OF ACQUIRED PROPERTY

Property acquired in a like-kind exchange has a substitute tax basis that reflects the deferred gain or loss. It consists of the adjusted basis of the property conveyed, with further adjustments reflecting the circumstances of the exchange.

> **Example D.4**
>
> Ronald Ryan exchanges property that has an adjusted tax basis of $900,000 for like-kind property with a market value of $1.5 million. He pays transaction costs of $1,500 but neither receives nor pays any boot. Both properties are exchanged on a free-and-clear basis.

To see how this rule works, consider Example D.4. Ryan has a realized gain of $598,500 and a substitute tax basis of $901,500. His realized gain is computed as follows:

Market value of property received		$1,500,000
Less:		
Transaction costs	$1,500	
Adjusted basis of old property	900,000	901,500
Realized gain on transaction		$598,500

Ryan's substitute tax basis is determined by adding to his old adjusted tax basis his transaction costs and any additional consideration he paid, then subtracting any additional consideration received and any recognized gain:

Basis of old property		$900,000
Plus:		
Additional consideration paid	0	
Transaction costs incurred	$1,500	1,500
		$901,500
Less: Additional consideration received		0
Tax basis of substitute property		$901,500

The same result can be reached by subtracting from the fair market value of the property Ryan received the amount of any gain realized but not recognized:

Market value of substitute property		$1,500,000
Less: Deferred gain		
Realized gain	$598,500	
Minus: Recognized gain	0	
Amount Deferred		598,500
Tax basis of substitute property		$901,500

When Ryan sells the substitute property acquired in Example D.4, his taxable gain is computed on the difference between the net proceeds and adjusted basis at that time. And because the basis of the substitute property reflects the deferred gain, selling the substitute property triggers recognition of the gain.

We have deliberately kept examples simple to better illustrate how the basis of a newly acquired property is computed. Example D.5 is a more complex exercise designed to demonstrate how the same rules can carry an analyst through the computational thicket.

Example D.5

Irma Gonzalez owns income property with a market value of $2 million and a mortgage of $750,000. Her adjusted basis before the transaction is $1.2 million. She exchanges this for another income property with a market value of $3.5 million that is subject to a mortgage of $1.5 million. Gonzalez pays $750,000 cash for the difference in equities, and each party takes title subject to existing mortgages. Gonzalez pays transaction costs of $20,000.

Gonzalez's realized gain is the difference between the market value and the adjusted tax basis of her original property, minus transaction costs:

Market value of assets received		$3,500,000
Less: Tax basis of assets tendered		
Real estate (basis before exchange)	$1,200,000	
Transaction costs	20,000	
Cash	750,000	
Net debt assumed	750,000	2,720,000
Realized gain		$780,000

Having received only like-kind property in the exchange, however, Gonzalez defers recognition of the entire gain. The initial basis of the new property is determined as follows:

Adjusted basis before the exchange		$1,200,000
Add:		
Transactions costs	$20,000	
Mortgage assumed	1,500,000	
Cash paid	750,000	2,270,000
		$3,470,000
Less: Old mortgage (debt relief)		750,000
Tax basis of substitute property		$2,720,000

Note that the basis of the substitute property in Example D.5 is simply its fair market value less any unrecognized gain: $3,500,000 minus $780,000, or $2,720,000.

If, due to receiving unlike property, some portion of a realized gain must be recognized, the basis of substitute property is increased by the amount of the recognized gain. This is illustrated in Example D.6.

Example D.6

Dudly Dean, D.D.S, exchanges his dental office building (market value of $1,528,000) for another office and a used cabin cruiser (market value estimated to be $28,000). Dean owes a mortgage balance of $800,000 on his building, and his adjusted tax basis is $1 million. Each party agrees to assume the existing mortgage on property received in the exchange. The building received by Dean has an outstanding mortgage balance of $700,000 and a fair market value of $1,400,000. Transaction costs to Dean are $50,000.

Dean has a realized gain, part of which must be recognized because he receives unlike property in exchange. The realized gain is $478,000, computed as follows:

Market value of assets received		
Real estate		$1,400,000
Personalty		28,000
Net debt relief		100,000
Total		$1,528,000
Less: Basis of assets tendered		
Real estate (basis before exchange)	$1,000,000	
Transaction costs	50,000	1,050,000
Realized gain on exchange		$478,000

The realized gain generates tax liability to the extent of any unlike property received in the exchange, net of transaction costs. Dean must therefore recognize $78,000 of the realized gain as currently taxable.

Mortgage on old property	$800,000
Less: Mortgage assumed	700,000
Net debt relief	$100,000
Value of other unlike property received	28,000
Total value of unlike property received	$128,000
Less: Transaction costs	50,000
Net boot received	$78,000

Example D.6 (continued)

The tax basis of the new property received by Dean is the adjusted basis of his old property, increased by any additional payments made and any recognized gain and reduced by any other value received:

Adjusted basis of old property		$1,000,000
Plus:		
Transaction costs	$50,000	
Debt assumed	700,000	
Recognized gain	78,000	828,000
		$1,828,000
Less:		
Old mortgage	$800,000	
Personalty received	28,000	828,000
Basis of new property		$1,000,000

The substitute tax basis in Example D.6 can be proved by reducing the market value of the new property by the amount of the unrecognized gain. The results should be the same as in the example. The calculations are as follows:

Market value of property received		$1,400,000
Less: Unrecognized gain		
Realized gain (Example D.6)	$478,000	
Minus: Recognized gain	78,000	
Unrecognized portion of gain		400,000
Basis of new property		$1,000,000

EFFECT OF LOSSES IN SECTION 1031 EXCHANGES

So far, all examples have assumed a gain on the exchange, with the discussion centering on whether a portion of the gain must be recognized and on the resulting tax basis of substitute property. But what happens if there is a loss on an exchange?

If a transaction qualifies fully under Section 1031 as like-kind, then neither a gain nor a loss may be recognized. We have seen, however, that if an investor realizes a gain and receives any unlike property, then a portion of the gain must be recognized. This partial recognition relates only to gains; receipt of some unlike property in an otherwise like-kind exchange never triggers partial recognition of a loss.

Example D.7

Samuel Smart trades income-producing real estate for like-kind property. The property received by Smart has a fair market value of $80,000 and is subject to a mortgage of $55,000. Smart's old property has an adjusted basis of $95,000 and is subject to a mortgage of $60,000. The parties exchange equities, each assuming the mortgage on the property received. Transaction costs are zero.

The transaction in Example D.7 qualifies under Section 1031 as a like-kind exchange, but Smart has received unlike property in the form of net debt relief. Had there been a gain, it would be recognized to the extent of Smart's net debt relief ($5,000). In this example, though, Smart has experienced a loss rather than a gain:

Market value of property received	$80,000	
Mortgage assumed by other party	60,000	$140,000
Less:		
Mortgage assumed by Smart	55,000	
Adjusted basis of old property	95,000	150,000
Gain (Loss) on the exchange		($10,000)

Although Smart may not recognize her loss in the year of the transaction, it is reflected in her tax basis for the new property. Thus, its recognition is merely deferred until the new property is sold. Smart's basis for the new property is her old basis, adjusted for the other property involved in the transaction. The illustration assumes there are no transaction costs. Were such costs incurred, they would be added to the new basis. Smart's new basis is as follows:

Basis of old property	$95,000
Plus: Mortgage assumed	55,000
	$150,000
Less: Mortgage assumed by other party	60,000
Basis of new property	$90,000

Note that the basis of Smart's new property is simply its market value adjusted by adding any additional value given by Smart and subtracting any value received plus any unrecognized loss or less any unrecognized gain:

Market value of property received	$80,000
Plus: Unrecognized loss	10,000
Basis of new property	$90,000

Note also that the substitute basis of Smart's new property exceeds its fair market value by the amount of the unrecognized loss. It would also include any transaction costs incurred by Smart. If she subsequently sells the property, her recognized loss on the sale will reflect this substitute basis in excess of fair market value. The deferred loss will be recognized at that time.

ALLOCATING THE SUBSTITUTE BASIS

Just as the initial basis of purchased property must be allocated between land and improvements to determine cost recovery allowances, so must the substitute basis of property acquired in a Section 1031 exchange be allocated. The basic rule remains invariant: allocate on the basis of relative market values.

Example D.8

Gary and Smith trade like-kind properties. Both parties own their properties on a free-and-clear basis. Relative values before the exchange are agreed to be as follows:

	Adjusted Basis	Market Value Dollar Amount	Market Value Percentage of Total
Geltloss			
Land	$200,000	$200,000	40%
Improvements	100,000	300,000	60
Total	$300,000	$500,000	100%
Smith			
Land	$50,000	$50,000	10%
Improvements	200,000	450,000	90
Total	$250,000	$500,000	100%

Consider Example D.8. To keep the illustration simple, assume there are no transaction costs. Because no boot is involved, Gary will have a substitute basis equaling the adjusted basis of his old property: $300,000. This basis is allocated to the acquired land and improvements in the ratio of their relative market values: 10% to the land and 90% to the improvements. Gary's basis after the exchange is as follows:

Land (10%)	$30,000
Improvements (90%)	270,000
Total basis (100%)	$300,000

Our illustration assumes relative market values are known. In a real situation, these values must be determined. This may be accomplished by agreement between the parties in an arm's-length transaction, by an independent appraisal, or by using relative values as determined by the property tax assessor. These do not exhaust the potential means of arriving at an estimate of relative market values, but they are all approaches that have been accepted in the past.

If more than one property is received in an exchange, the substitute basis is allocated among acquired properties in the ratio of their relative market values as of the date of the exchange. The allocated substitute basis of each property is in turn allocated between land and improvements on the basis of relative values. To illustrate, assume the property received from Smith in Example D.8 consists of a store building on one small plot of land and an adjoining vacant lot. Assume further that each of the lots is worth $25,000 if unimproved, and the store building alone is worth $450,000 before considering the value of the site. Gary's $300,000 substitute basis is first allocated to the two separate properties in the ratio of their relative values: 5% to the vacant lot and 95% to the store and site. The substitute basis of the store and site (0.95 × $300,000 = $285,000) is then allocated to site and improvements based on their relative values. The resulting substitute basis is as follows:

	Market Value	Percentage of Total Value	Substitute Basis
Vacant lot	$25,000	5%	$15,000
Store			
Site	25,000	5	15,000
Improvements	450,000	90	270,000
Total	$500,000	100%	$300,000

NONSIMULTANEOUS EXCHANGES

When exchanges do not involve simultaneous transfers of ownership, there are strict time requirements within which the entire transaction must be completed. To qualify for tax deferral, the substitute property must be identified within 44 days following the day of the initial property transfer, and the final transfer must be completed by the earlier of (a) 179 days following the day of the initial property transfer or (b) the due date for the taxes that would be imposed if the transaction did not qualify for tax deferral.

When titles are not transferred simultaneously, the usual arrangement is to use a qualified intermediary, an escrow account or a trust, that receives the taxpayer's relinquished property, acquires the like-kind substitute, and then transfers the replacement property to the taxpayer. The IRS has issued a regulation (Reg. 1.1031(k)-1(g)(4)) that sets forth rules governing the responsibilities of an intermediary.

EXCHANGES BETWEEN RELATED PARTIES

If a like-kind exchange is between related parties, then both parties must hold their substitute properties for at least two years after the date of the exchange. If either party disposes of the substitute property early, then the party who qualified for and claimed a deferred gain under the like-kind exchange rules must recognize the deferred gain in the year that the disposition occurs. Exceptions to this general rule are provided in the following cases:

- The death of either party
- Involuntary disposal due to the property's destruction, seizure, condemnation, or imminent threat of condemnation

RECOMMENDED READING

Briskin, Robert A. "Like-Kind Exchanges—Common Problems and Solutions." *The Tax Advisor* 36, no. 4 (April 2004): 204–12.

Brown, William P., and Evelyn C. Hume. "Tax-Free Exchanges Complicate Depreciation Calculations." *Practical Tax Strategies* 74, no. 1 (January 2005): 4–13.

Carman, Paul D. "Like-Kind Exchanges of MACRS Property Clarified in New Regulations." *Real Estate Taxation* 31, no. 4 (Third Quarter 2004): 167–78.

Heller, Richard M. "Reverse Real Estate Exchanges—Inside and Outside the Safe Harbor." *Journal of Financial Service Professionals* 57, no. 6 (November 2003): 12–15.

Sacks, Jeffrey, and Jonathan Black. "Like-Kind Exchange As an Exit Strategy for Investors in LIHTC Housing." *Multi-Housing News* 40, no. 2 (February 2005): 18–21.

REVIEW QUESTIONS

1. How is the tax basis of property acquired in a like-kind exchange determined?
2. Describe the allocation of the basis of property acquired in a like-kind exchange.
3. How is the tax basis of property received as a gift determined?

PROBLEMS

1. Ben Bicker owns rental property worth $1 million and subject to a mortgage of $250,000. His adjusted tax basis in the property is $400,000. He trades for a like-kind property worth $1.5 million, which is subject to a mortgage balance of $600,000. Bicker pays $150,000 cash to balance the equities, and each party takes title subject to existing mortgages. Bicker pays transaction costs of $45,000. What is Bicker's substitute tax basis?

2. David Driver D.D.S., exchanges an office building (market value = $1,528,000) for an apartment building (market value = $1.4 million). Driver owes $800,000 on a note secured by a mortgage on his office building, which has an adjusted tax basis of $1 million. The building he will receive in the exchange is encumbered with a mortgage that has a balance of $700,000. Driver incurs transaction costs of $50,000. Each party agrees to take title subject to the existing mortgage on the substitute building; cash will be tendered to balance the equities. What will be Driver's substitute tax basis after the exchange?

3. Mr. Vicker owns income property with a market value of $1 million that is subject to a mortgage of $250,000. The adjusted basis is $400,000. He exchanges the property for another that has a market value of $1.5 million (land value is $250,000; the rest is the value of the improvements) and is subject to a mortgage of $600,000. Vicker pays $150,000 cash for the difference in equities, and each party takes title subject to existing mortgages. Vicker pays transaction costs of $6,500. What is the substitute tax basis of Vicker's new building and other improvements (excluding the basis of the land)?

GLOSSARY

A

absolute monopoly A market that has only one supplier of a good or service for which there are no reasonably acceptable substitutes.

absorption rates Rates at which the market will "absorb" a product; the rate at which units will be purchased.

abstract and opinion A summary of the chain of past title transfers for real property and an attorney's written opinion that the title contains no defects.

abstract of title A brief summary of each recorded document pertaining to title to a specified parcel of land.

accelerated method A method of computing depreciation or cost recovery allowances whereby large annual allowances are claimed in the early years of ownership, offset by smaller allowances in later years.

acceleration clause A clause that permits the mortgagee to declare the full amount of a debt due and payable if the mortgagor defaults on any of the agreed-on terms.

acceptance The act of a party to whom a thing is offered by another, whereby the offeree receives the thing with the intention of retaining it.

accredited purchasers Investors who either (1) are sufficiently wealthy so that a contemplated securities purchase (of $150,000 or more) will not exceed 20% of their net worth, (2) have a net worth in excess of $1 million, or (3) have a two-year earnings record of more than $200,000 per annum and expect their current earnings to exceed $200,000.

accretion A gradual increase in land area adjacent to a body of water because of soil deposited by wave and current action.

accrued depreciation A loss in value due to physical deterioration, functional obsolescence, and economic or locational disadvantages.

acknowledgment Certification by a notary public or other appropriate public official that the grantor has stated before the official that he executed the acknowledged document.

ad valorem A Latin term used to describe the taxing of property according to value.

adjusted basis The amount paid for property, plus all subsequent capital expenditures made to improve it, minus all tax deductions for depreciation or cost recovery allowances.

adjusted gross income Gross taxable income minus a set of specific deductions spelled out in the Internal Revenue Code.

adjusted rate of return Modified version of the internal rate of return, designed to eliminate problems associated with negative cash flows.

adverse possession Wrongful occupancy of real estate in a manner and for a time period described in state statutes. Title then vests in the adverse possessor by operation of law and is independent of any previously recorded title to the property.

affirmative covenant A mutual promise between neighbors that a property will be used in some specified manner.

after-tax cash flow Cash flow generated from a property after accounting for all operating expenses, all debt-service obligations, and all income tax consequences for the current period.

agglomeration economies An amorphous term referring to cost reductions ascribed to proximity.

all-inclusive mortgage *See* wraparound mortgage.

alternative minimum tax A provision that specifies the minimum amount of federal income tax for which all taxpayers are liable. After computing tax liability the regular way, taxpayers must perform the alternative computation. They are required to pay the greater of the regular or the alternative minimum tax.

alternative minimum taxable income The income on which liability for the alternative minimum tax is computed.

amortization table A schedule of equal periodic payments necessary to repay a $1 loan, with interest, over a specified number of payment periods.

amortize To claim an expenditure, which is incurred at the beginning of the period, as an annual expense or income tax deduction over an extended period of years.

anchor tenants Tenants who are expected to attract customers to a shopping center and thereby generate business for other merchants in the center.

annual compounding Accumulated interest that in and of itself earns interest in all subsequent periods.

annual mortgage constant The percentage of the original principal amount that must be paid annually in order to fully repay interest and principal over the term of the loan.

annuity Any series of periodic payments received or paid at regular intervals.

annuity table A schedule providing factors used to calculate the present value of a compound level annuity.

articles of agreement *See* installment sales contract.

asset liquidity *See* liquidity.

assignment Transfer of contractual rights from one contracting party (the assignor) to another person (the assignee) who is not a party to the contract.

assumption clause A clause whereby mortgagors agree not to sell mortgaged property subject to the mortgage or to have a buyer assume an existing mortgage without prior approval of the mortgagee.

assumption fee A fee charged by a lender as a condition for permitting assumption of mortgage indebtedness by a party other than the original mortgagor. This permits mortgagees to adjust their rates of return to the current market when interest rates have risen.

atomistic markets A market in which no one person or group can measurably affect market prices. Market participants are simply price takers, in that they have a choice of accepting prevailing prices or of not participating in the market at all.

avulsion A sudden and perceptible shift in land boundaries due to floods or sudden alterations in the course of rivers or streams.

B

back-door approach A type of preliminary financial feasibility study that involves estimating the maximum amount of equity financing that investors can commit to a project, given their minimum acceptable current yield.

band of investment technique A technique used to calculate the weighted average cost of capital for a property. The cost of each source of funds is weighted by a factor equal to the proportion of total funds that will be derived from that source.

base lines A set of imaginary lines running east and west used by surveyors for reference in locating and describing land under the government survey method of property description.

basic rate The sum of the weighted average cost of capital and the equity buildup factor used in order to determine the appropriate overall capitalization rate.

bid-rent curve A functional relationship that depicts the absolute maximum rent a firm with a specific profit profile can pay and still find remaining in business a worthwhile endeavor.

blanket mortgage The pledge of two or more parcels of property as security for a single loan.

blind pool syndication A form of limited partnership in which the promoter assembles a group of investors with the purpose of acquiring an undesignated asset of a specific type.

book value The value at which assets are recorded on a firm's books of account (i.e., its accounting records); usually cost minus accumulated depreciation or cost recovery allowances.

boot (*See also* like-kind exchange) Assets received as consideration in what would otherwise be an exchange of entirely like-kind assets. Receipt of boot may trigger tax liability in what would otherwise be a tax-deferred transaction.

break-even ratio The relationship between cash expenditure requirements and gross revenue from an investment project. Sometimes called a *default ratio*.

broker's rate of return A rate of return measure that adjusts the cash-on-cash return to include equity buildup from debt amortization and thereby shows a slightly more favorable return than does the cash-on-cash measure.

building codes The set of laws that establishes minimum standards for constructing new buildings or altering existing structures. Building codes are intended to ensure minimum protection against fire damage and to safeguard against faulty design in construction.

business risk Risk stemming from the possibility of making inappropriate business decisions or of misjudging the economic consequences of actions.

C

capital assets All assets held by a taxpayer (whether or not connected with the person's trade or business) except those specifically enumerated by the Commissioner of Internal Revenue. Generally, assets of a fixed or permanent nature or those used in carrying on a business or trade.

capital expenditure An expenditure of funds that extends the useful life of a capital asset or adds to its value.

capital formation The raising of debt or equity funds for real estate projects.

capital goods Products destined to be used in the production of other goods or services.

capitalization rate The relationship between net income from a real estate investment and the value of the investment. This relationship is usually expressed as a percentage.

capitalize To add an amount to the tax basis of a property.

capital recovery The portion of an overall capitalization rate composed of recovery of the owner's capital outlay.

cash-on-cash rate of return The first year's expected after-tax cash flow, divided by the initial cash outlay required to acquire the investment.

central business district The focal point of urban places where goods and services are exchanged.

central place theory The postulate that if the surrounding countryside were a flat, undifferentiated plane, central places would be located so as to minimize the distance from all points in the tributary area. It states further that the larger the city, the larger its tributary area must be.

certainty equivalents Substitute cash flows determined by the certainty-equivalent technique.

certainty-equivalent technique A procedure that seeks to establish substitute cash flows that leave an investor indifferent between absolutely certain receipt of the substitute amounts and the expectation of receiving the point estimates, along with attendant risk.

certificate of limited partnership A document that must be filed with the appropriate state agency to create a limited partnership.

certified historic structure (*See also* registered historic district) Any structure that is either listed in the National Registry of Historic Places or located in a registered historic district and certified as being of historic significance to the district.

ceteris paribus A Latin term used by economists to mean that demand schedules are applicable only as long as all factors other than price that influence buyer behavior do not change.

city planning A procedure for formulating land use schemes, used by municipalities in their efforts to reach specified goals in the utilization of land within the municipality.

coefficient of correlation A measure of the extent to which the values of variables in a sample or a population are interdependent.

coefficient of determination A measure of the percent of variation in the dependent variable associated with variation in the value of the independent variable. In regression analysis, designated by the term *r-square* (r^2).

coefficient of multiple correlation A measure of the percentage of variance in the dependent variable that is "explained" by variation in the independent variables.

coefficient of serial correlation A measure of the degree to which outcomes in subsequent periods are related. Possible coefficients range from zero to plus-or-minus one.

coefficient of variation Standard deviation of the distribution of possible outcomes, divided by the expected outcome.

collective goods *See* public goods.

commitment letter A letter to a prospective borrower, wherein a lender states terms and conditions under which it will provide the requested funds. A precise period is usually specified during which the commitment remains effective. Commitment letters generally state conditions under which the lender may revoke the commitment and set forth any further provisions on which the commitment is contingent.

community shopping center A shopping center that typically draws most of its customers from an area extending from 10 to 15 minutes in driving time. Community shopping centers usually feature a food store and a junior department store or a discount store as anchor tenants. Size may range from 50,000 to 100,000 square feet of retail space.

comparative advantage An economic principle developed by the economist David Ricardo that provides an explanation of why some areas tend to concentrate on producing a limited number of goods and seek much of what they consume from other areas.

comparative sales approach An appraisal procedure that analyzes recent sales data from similar properties and draws inferences about the value of the property being appraised.

comparative unit method A valuation approach that estimates costs by comparison with similar buildings whose construction costs are known. To render buildings of slightly different size more directly comparable, costs are expressed on the basis of some standardized unit of measure such as per square foot or per cubic foot.

complements Goods or services whose consumption occurs in tandem with that of the item in question. A change in the price of one good or service can cause a shift in the demand curves for its complements.

compound amount The summation of principal and compounded interest over a specified holding period.

compound interest Interest income attributable to previously accrued interest that has been left on deposit.

concentric zone model An urban economic model developed by Earnest W. Burgess in the 1920s. The concentric zone model was designed to explain urban development through the use of transitional zones.

concessions *See* rent concessions.

condemnation proceeding The consequence of a property owner's refusal to voluntarily convey title at a price offered by a governmental agency seeking to convert the property to public use.

condominium An ownership arrangement whereby title to specified portions of a property vests in individual users, and title to a common area vests in all users jointly.

condominium association An association, composed of all those owning interest in a condominium, that serves as a governing and managing body, usually through an elected board of directors.

condominium declaration The enabling document that creates a condominium. The declaration desires both individual and common areas of the premises and provides for assessment of owners for costs of maintaining and insuring common areas.

conduit *See* tax conduit.

consideration Under contract law, the impelling reason to enter into a contract. Something of value given in exchange for a promise.

constructive notice A legal doctrine under which notice may be attributed even though a party may be completely ignorant of the facts. Recording statutes provide that recording a document in the public record constitutes constructive notice to the world.

consumer good The end product of the production process.

consumer price index An index of changes in the price of a representative "market basket" of consumer goods, relating the current price to that in designated base year.

contract for deed *See* installment sales contract.

contract price Total selling price minus any pre-existing mortgage to which a property will remain subject when sold under conditions permitting the transaction to be reported for tax computation purposes under the installment sales method. If the pre-existing mortgage exceeds the seller's adjusted basis in the property, the excess of the mortgage over the seller's basis must be added to the contract price.

cooperative An apartment the tenant purchases by buying stock in the corporation that owns the building rather than simply buying the apartment.

corporations Artificial entities, created under state laws, that are empowered to own property and transact business in their own names. They may buy, sell, and otherwise enter into contracts. As legal entities, corporations have an identity separate and distinct from that of their owners.

cost approach An appraisal technique whereby an estimate of land value is added to the estimated cost of reproducing existing improvements on the land (net of accrued depreciation) to derive a value estimate for the entire property.

cost recovery allowance An income tax rule that provides for recovery of capital expenditures on property having a finite useful life, acquired on or after January 1, 1981, and used in a trade or business or for production of income.

cost recovery assets Assets on which tax-deductible cost recovery allowances may be claimed.

cotenancy Real property title held in the name of two or more owners.

counseling Providing competent, unbiased advice on diversified problems in the broad field of real estate involving any or all segments of the business, such as merchandising, leasing, management, planning, financing, appraising, court testimony, and other similar services.

covenant against removal A restriction imposed by the mortgagee prohibiting the mortgagor from removing or demolishing any part of the building without the lender's consent.

covenant against waste A restriction imposed by a mortgagee prohibiting the mortgagor from allowing the building to deteriorate during the period of the mortgage.

covenant of insurance A mortgage clause in which the mortgagor promises to maintain adequate insurance coverage against fire and other specified hazards.

covenant of seizin (*See also* seizin) A mortgage clause whereby the mortgagor warrants that she is the lawful owner of the property being mortgaged.

covenant of title A promise or assurance made by the grantor in connection with title transfer.

covenants Promises that property will, or will not, be used in some specified manner.

covenant to pay taxes A common mortgage clause in which the mortgagor promises to pay all property taxes and assessments levied against the property during the period of the mortgage.

cross-sectional surveys Surveys involving one-time sampling from a population of research interest. All elements are measured at a single point in time. Cross-sectional surveys provide a "snapshot" of the variables under observation as of the time of the survey.

curtesy A husband's interest in his wife's property.

custom construction A construction project that takes place on land owned by the ultimate purchaser, involving a structure built to the exact specifications of the purchaser-user.

D

dealer In real estate, one who is in the business of buying and selling property interests for one's own account. Gains on dealers' sales are reported as ordinary income rather than as capital gains.

debentures Bonds secured by the borrower's income stream.

debt amortization The process of gradually extinguishing a debt by a series of periodic payments to the creditor.

debt constant The percentage of the original principal amount that must be paid annually in order to fully repay interest and principal over the term of the loan. The constant can be expressed as an annual percentage or monthly percentage. Sometimes called a *debt-service constant*.

debt-coverage ratio The relationship between a project's annual net operating income and the obligation to make principal and interest payments on borrowed funds. Debt-coverage ratios are often used to evaluate a lender's margin of safety regarding mortgage loans.

debt service Payments to a lender. Debt-service obligations may involve payment of interest only or both principal and interest so as to fully or partially amortize a debt over a specified term.

debt-service constant *See* debt constant.

debt-to-equity ratio The ratio between borrowed funds and equity funds.

decision model A systematic process for identifying opportunities that show promise of contributing adequately to predetermined investment goals.

declining balance method A method of computing annual depreciation or cost recovery allowances that provides the greatest allowance in the first year of ownership and progressively smaller allowances for each successive year.

decree The judgment of a court of equity, ordering execution of the provisions of that judgment.

deed A legal document that conveys title in real property from one party to another. The document must be signed, witnessed, delivered, and accepted.

deed of trust A deed passing title to property from an owner to a trustee, who holds that property as collateral for a mortgage loan advanced by another. Also called a *trust deed* or *trust indenture*.

default A mortgagor's failure to fulfill any of the agreed-on terms in a security agreement.

default ratio *See* break-even ratio.

defeasance clause Mortgage provisions intended to render nominal conveyance void on satisfaction of the mortgagor's obligation.

deficiency judgment A judgment against a debtor's personal assets beyond those assets owned on a defaulted debt instrument.

delivery The legal act of transferring ownership of real estate.

demand An economic term that refers to the entire range of relationships between price and quantity.

demand curve A graphic illustration of the relationship between price and the quantity of a good or service buyers will take off the market. Also called a *demand function*.

demand function *See* demand curve.

demand schedule A table that relates quantity demanded to a good's or service's price, at all relevant prices.

demand to purchase Desired increase in a market participant's inventory of a product, at a specific price.

dependency exemption An amount of adjusted gross income that taxpayers may exempt from taxable income for each person dependent on them for financial support.

dependent variable In regression or correlation analysis, a variable whose value is thought to be affected by the value of other variables (independent variables) included in the analysis.

deposit insurance An insurance program that protects depositors from loss due to bank failures.

depreciable asset *See* depreciable property.

depreciable property Property on which a tax-deductible depreciation allowance may be claimed.

depreciation Decline in an asset's value or useful life, due to wear, tear, action of the elements, or obsolescence.

depreciation allowance A tax-deductible allowance to account for the decline in value or useful life of an asset due to wear, tear, obsolescence, or action of the elements.

derived demand Demand for a good or service that stems from the use of that good or service in the production of something else.

descriptive statistics A statistical application that uses quantitative expressions to describe characteristics of a sample or an underlying population.

development A real estate activity that involves adding improvements such as buildings.

differentiated product Products that are sufficiently different from competitive products to reduce the degree of substitutability. Producers of differentiated products have some degree of control over price.

diminishing marginal utility The economic principle that as additional units of a good are possessed or consumer per unit of time, the additional (marginal) utility of each successive unit is less than that of the preceding unit.

discounted cash-flow approach An investment evaluation technique that incorporates adjustments for both volume and timing of anticipated future cash flows and is generally accepted as the most desirable approach to evaluating opportunities.

discounting Expressing anticipated future cash flows as present-worth equivalents.

discount points A reduction in net loan proceeds to make the effective interest rate equal the current market rate.

discount rate A rate that measures return on investment after the recovery of invested capital.

discrete probability distribution A probability distribution in which possible outcomes are limited in number.

disintermediation The situation where people, seeking better yields, withdraw their savings from major institutional lenders and participate directly in financial markets.

diversification The reduction in total risk through holding a variety of property types and spreading ownership over a wide geographic area.

dominant tenement Land that reaps the benefit of an easement.

dower A wife's interest in her husband's property.

dram shop insurance Insurance against liability arising from incidents related to liquor consumption.

due process Proceedings in accordance with legal precedent, statutes, and constitutional provisions, designed to protect the rights of all parties to a dispute.

E

earnest money Money paid as evidence of good faith or actual intent to complete a transaction, usually forfeited by willful failure to complete the transaction.

earnest money deposit A good-faith deposit into an escrow account (or into a broker's trust account), typically accompanied by a purchase offer.

easement Nonpossessory interest that permits limited use of someone else's land. Conveys only a right to use the land.

easement appurtenant An easement created on one parcel of land (the servient tenement) for the benefit of an adjacent parcel (the dominant tenement).

easement by expressed grant Easement created by a specific agreement between the affected parties.

easement by implication An easement created as a consequence of a landowner selling property to which access requires crossing other property that the landowner also owns. Easements by implication are created when reasonably necessary, when the need is apparent at the time property is conveyed, and when the need appears to be permanent in nature.

easement by prescription An easement acquired through the open, continuous, adverse use of real property for a specified period of time.

easement in gross An easement that constitutes personal property, independent of any related land interest.

economic base analysis A study that divides economic activity into domestic and export sectors and seeks to determine the degree to which activity in the domestic sector is dependent on the level of activity in the export sector.

economic base theory An explanation of urban growth that postulates that total economic activity in an urban area is a function of the level of activity in its export sector.

economic obsolescence Loss in value due to inappropriate location.

Economic Recovery Tax Act of 1981 A major revision of the Internal Revenue Code, enacted into law in 1981.

economic rent Profit generated by a good or service in excess of the profit necessary to induce firms to produce the good or service. Sometimes referred to as *pure profit*.

effective gross income Potential gross rental revenue, minus losses for vacancies and uncollectible accounts, plus income from related sources.

effective interest rates Rates actually paid for the use of borrowed funds. Effective rates are a function of the amount borrowed and the amount and timing of the required repayment.

efficient markets Markets in which all relevant information is immediately and fully reflected in market prices. Participants in efficient markets are unable to consistently achieve above-average market yields. The hypothesis that a market is completely efficient is referred to as the *strong form* of the efficiency hypothesis.

eminent domain Authority vested in both federal and state governments allowing them to take private property for public use without the owner's consent.

encumbrances A lien, charge, or claim against real property that diminishes the value of the property but does not prevent the passing of title.

end loan A loan secured by a mortgage on a completed building, terminating a chain of loans to finance land acquisition and construction. Also called a *permanent loan* or a *takeout loan*.

end-loan commitment An agreement by a lender to provide an end loan on satisfaction of all contingencies specified by the lender.

equilibrium In economics, a stable, balanced, or unchanging system. A situation in which there is no tendency for anything to change.

equilibrium price The price at which there will be sufficient quantity of a product to satisfy the desires of all consumers at that price but with no surplus remaining on the market; the market-clearing price.

equitable right of redemption The legal right of a borrower, or the borrower's heirs or assigns to redeem mortgaged property for a limited period of time after default. Also called *equity of redemption*.

equity The concept of fairness and justice applied to the portion of common law relating to the rights and duties of individuals. Also the money value of what is owned, arrived at by subtracting all that is owed from the value of the ownership to arrive at a net ownership value figure.

equity buildup The accumulation and growth of the money value of what is owned. That is, an increase in the net financial interest in a specific property.

equity dividend rate Before-tax cash flow expressed as a percentage of the required initial equity cash outlay.

equity of redemption *See* equitable right of redemption.

equity REIT A type of real estate investment trust that concentrates its resources on equity interests in real property.

equity yield rate Interest earned on recovered capital.

escalator clause Lease clause that requires tenants to pay all operating expenses above amounts specified in the lease.

escheat The legal principle that property title reverts to the state when an intestate owner (one with no will) dies with no heirs.

escrow The holding by a third party of something of value that is the subject of a contract between two other parties until the contract has been consummated.

escrow agent A disinterested third party who acts as agent for parties to an escrow agreement.

escrow agreement A contract between parties to a transaction and a third party who functions as an escrow agent. The agreement contains written escrow instructions, which govern the agent's action in performance of his escrow duties.

estate for years A leasehold interest that extends for an exactly specified period, after which the interest automatically expires.

estate subject to a condition precedent An estate created (rather than terminated) on the happening of some specified contingency.

excess accumulated earnings tax A penalty tax levied on corporations that accumulate earnings in excess of corporate needs.

excess cost recovery allowance Cost recovery allowance actually claimed, minus what would have been claimed had the taxpayer used the straight-line cost recovery method from the beginning.

executory A contract that lacks some necessary performance by one of its parties and is therefore not yet completed.

expected value The midpoint of a symmetric probability distribution; the most likely outcome.

explicit transfer costs (*See also* implicit transfer costs) Costs measurable in dollars; specifically, cost per mile of chosen transportation mode, plus the dollar value of the time spent en route.

external costs (*See also* external diseconomies) Costs incurred by the public from the act or nonact of a private party.

external diseconomies External costs where benefits accrue to the decision maker while costs are borne by others.

external economies (*See also* externality) A good side effect of production or consumption, for which no payment is received or made.

externality A good or bad side effect of production or consumption, for which no payment is received or made.

F

facilities management Overseeing the physical upkeep of properties as well as keeping records of income and expenses associated with their operation.

factor of production Goods or services that are themselves intended to be used in producing other goods or services.

feasibility analysis An analysis of the likelihood of success of a specific proposed course of action.

feasibility study A study of the costs and benefits of a proposed course of action, to determine the likelihood of achieving project goals within the context of specified constraints and available resources. A proposal that has a reasonable probability of satisfying explicit objectives is considered feasible. A financial feasibility study addresses the question whether the proposed course of action will meet financial objectives.

Federal Deposit Insurance Corporation (FDIC) An independent federal agency that insures deposits up to a certain amount in all national banks and in all state banks that have been accepted as FDIC members.

fee simple absolute The greatest real property interest recognized by law. This term expresses the idea that the interest is held with no preconditions or qualifications.

fee simple defeasible A qualified fee estate that may be subject to a condition subsequent or determinable, depending on the nature of the qualification. Some states also permit creation of fees subject to conditions precedent.

fee simple estate Any real property interest.

fee splitting Analogous to life estates and remainders whereby title passes to or reverts on the occurrence of some event.

fee subject to a condition subsequent A fee that extends only until the happening of some specified act or event.

fee tail A carryover from the feudal system, requiring that title pass to lineal descendants of the property owner.

fiduciary One who is in a position of trust or confidence with respect to another person.

financial assets Assets such as promissory notes, bonds, and commercial paper that represent financial claims rather than ownership of physical assets.

financial intermediaries Institutions such as commercial banks, savings and loan associations, credit unions, and so on that act as go-betweens from savers to user-borrowers.

financial leverage The impact of borrowed money on investment return. That is, the use of borrowed money to amplify consequences to equity investors.

financial management rate of return A modification of the internal rate of return, designed to eliminate problems encountered when negative cash flows are included in the forecast.

financial risk Risk that cash flow from a project will be insufficient to meet the investor's debt-service obligation.

fiscal policy Exercise of influence on the economy by controlling government spending and taxation.

footloose industries Industries in which firms are not restricted geographically by transportation cost considerations. Such firms frequently seek locations with a ready supply of labor or minimal labor costs.

forecasting Predicting a future value from known, related data.

foreclosure by sale Sale of mortgaged property at public auction as a consequence of default by the mortgagor. Foreclosure by sale extinguishes the equitable right of redemption.

foreclosure decree A court order specifying an exact time period (a period determined by state laws) during which the equity of redemption will exist.

free-and-clear rate of return *See* overall capitalization rate.

freehold An estate in real property that, unless assigned or otherwise conveyed, remains in perpetuity, or for life.

front-door approach A type of preliminary financial feasibility study that involves estimating the minimum gross rent required to meet investors' threshold investment acceptability criteria.

fully amortized The ultimate retirement of a mortgage debt through installment payments that include both interest and principal over the term of the loan.

functional efficiency A measure of how well a property performs its intended function.

functional obsolescence The loss of functional efficiency due to defective or dated design. This reduces a building's competitive position relative to more functionally efficient structures and may eventually lead to abandonment or succession of use.

fundamental analysis An investment analysis technique that emphasizes investigation of the underlying business activity being undertaken by the firm whose securities are being considered.

G

gap financing *See* standby financing.

general contractor A contractor who takes full responsibility for construction of a project by formal agreement with the owner or developer and hires others as subcontractors to perform specific tasks.

general partner *See* limited partnership.

general partnership An entity in which all partners have equal rights to management and conduct of the firm; each partner is, in effect, an agent for the partnership.

gentrification Reclamation of residential areas containing physically deteriorated buildings and restoration of a deteriorated neighborhood for the use of predominantly middle-class residents.

goods or services (*See also* product) Items offered for sale in the marketplace.

graduated-payment mortgage (GPM) A mortgage that allows a borrower, in effect, to borrow additional money during the early years of the mortgage to reduce the monthly mortgage payment obligation during those early years. This additional loan is added to the mortgage and is repaid by increased debt-service obligations in the later years.

grantee A person to whom a grant is made; the purchaser.

grantor A person who conveys real estate by deed; the seller.

gross income For income tax computation purposes, all revenue generated from any source, unless specifically excluded by provisions of the Internal Revenue Code.

gross income multiplier (*See also* income multiplier analysis and net income multiplier) Evaluation technique that describes the relationship between most probable sales price and gross revenue. Sometimes called a *gross rent multiplier*.

gross rent multiplier *See* gross income multiplier.

H

health and safety codes Rules and regulations designed to promote public health and safety in the construction and/or demolition of improvements to real property.

hedging Taking an investment position that will pay off if the investor's primary investment does not. Hedging reduces aggregate investor risk.

historic structure *See* certified historic structure.

holdover tenant A tenant who remains in possession of real estate after the expiration of the lease.

housing codes Laws specifying minimum building standards, with the objective of promoting public health, safety, or welfare.

hurdle rate The minimum acceptable yield on investment funds. Projects that are not expected to yield at least the investor's hurdle rate are rejected.

hybrid REIT A real estate investment trust that mixes mortgage and equity instruments in its portfolio.

I

implicit transfer costs (*See also* explicit transfer costs) Indirect costs of moving goods or people between linked sites. Although they are often more difficult to identify than are explicit transfer costs, they may also be larger.

income For purposes of determining federal income tax liability, all revenue generated from any source unless specifically excluded by provisions of the Internal Revenue Code.

income multiplier analysis (*See also* gross income multiplier *and* net income multiplier) A technique for expressing the relationship between price and either gross or net income.

incubator buildings Relatively small, multitenant structures in which new or small but growing firms rent space on an interim basis until growth generates a need for larger quarters.

independent variable In regression or correlation analysis, a variable whose value is thought to be determined by factors other than those under analysis, but which is thought to affect the value of one or more other variables (the dependent variables) in the analysis.

indifference curve A graphic presentation of combinations of values for two variables, representing the preferences of an individual who will be indifferent among the various combinations.

inferential statistics The drawing of conclusions from evidence contained in statistical data.

inferior goods Consumer goods for which demand decreases as purchasing power rises.

information search costs The cost of generating relevant market information. High information search costs tend to reduce market efficiency.

initial tax basis The tax basis of a property at the time of acquisition. Usually, cost plus any additional outlays required to ensure good and defensible title.

installment method gain The difference between gain on disposal of an asset that qualifies for installment method reporting and the recapture of accumulated depreciation or cost recovery allowances. Only this portion of the gain may be reported using the installment method. The remainder must be recognized in the taxable year of the transaction.

installment sales contract Contract that sets forth terms and conditions under which a seller is obligated to render deeds of conveyance to the buyer at some future date. Also called a *land contract, contract for deed*, or *articles of agreement*.

installment sales method A method for reporting sales to the IRS whereby a portion of the resulting income tax liability may be deferred when some of the proceeds from the sale are not collected during the current taxable year.

insurable risk Risk of loss from natural hazards such as fire, flood, storm, and so forth that can be transferred to an insurance company.

interim financing Financing used during the construction phase, to be superseded by takeout financing after construction is completed.

intermediate goods Goods combined with other goods to create consumer products.

internal rate of return (IRR) A financial analysis technique that involves setting net present value at zero and finding a discount rate to satisfy the equality condition; that is, the discount rate that makes present value exactly equal to required initial cash outlay.

Internal Revenue Code Public Law 591-Unit 736 This law (as subsequently revised) constitutes the statutory authority for income, employment, estate, and gift taxes levied by the IRS. Generally referred to by tax practitioners more simply as *the Code*.

interpolation A procedure for estimating values that fall between tabular amounts.

intrastate offering A security issue offered for sale solely within one state by an issuer resident in or a corporation incorporated and doing business in that state. A qualifying intrastate offering is exempt from requirements for federal registration.

investment Commitment of money or other assets in expectation of financial gain.

investment income *See* portfolio income.

investment interest limitation Provision of the Internal Revenue Code that places a dollar limit on the amount of investment interest that can be deducted in any one taxable year on loans used to finance investments.

investment tax credit A credit against income tax liability, earned as a consequence of investing in qualifying assets.

investment value The summation of the present value of the equity position plus the present value of the debt position. The present value of the equity position is calculated on an after-tax basis and considers the tax consequences to a specific investor.

investor Any person or entity who takes an equity position in real estate for use in a trade or business or for production of income.

itemized deductions Taxpayer expenditures, listed in Sections 161 through 195 of the Internal Revenue Code, that may be deducted from adjusted gross income to arrive at taxable income.

J

joint probabilities The probability of joint occurrence of two or more events. The probability that both event A and event B will occur equals the probability that A will occur times the probability that B will occur, given that A occurs. This relationship is sometimes referred to as the *multiplicative law of probability*.

joint tenancy (*See also* right of survivorship) An estate held jointly by two or more persons under the same title in which each has the same degree of interest and the same right of possession. Joint tenancy usually entails the right of the surviving tenant(s) to take title to a decedent's interest (right of survivorship).

joint tenants Parties who hold equal and undivided interests under joint tenancy.

judgment samples A sampling technique that regards individual observations, with respect to certain characteristics, as typical of the underlying universe.

judicial partition A court proceeding to terminate a cotenancy arrangement when the co-owners are unable to agree on terms for sale or physical division of jointly owned real estate.

junior mortgage A mortgage that is legally subordinate to another (senior) mortgage.

L

land contract *See* installment sales contract.

land development The business activity of acquiring large tracts of land, subdividing, and selling off individual smaller tracts. Also frequently called *subdivision*.

land-use controls Publicly imposed controls on land usage aimed at assuring orderly development.

lease Legal document conveying limited right to use a property. Document generally specifies all terms of lease a well as permitted use.

leasehold Right of a tenant in leased property.

leasehold estate Estate of a tenant in a leased property.

leasehold interest Interest of a tenant in a leased property.

lessee The holder of a leasehold interest in a property. Generally referred to as a *tenant*.

lessor A property owner who transfers certain rights for a limited period to a tenant. Generally referred to as a *landlord*.

license Privilege to enter onto the land of a licenser in order to do certain things that would otherwise be considered trespassing.

lien Claim against a property that allows the proceeds from a forced sale of the property to be used to satisfy the debt.

life estate Grants life tenants full property rights for the remainder of their life.

life tenants Individual possessing full property rights in a specific property for the remainder of their life.

like-kind exchange Exchanges of assets deemed under Internal Revenue Code Section 1031 to be of like-kind. Gains or losses on exchanges that involve only like-kind assets must be deferred until the newly acquired (substitute) asset is disposed of. Transactions that are only partially like-kind may result in total or partial recognition of gains or losses. Also frequently called *tax-free exchanges* or *Section 1031 exchanges*.

limited partner *See* limited partnership.

limited partnership An ownership arrangement involving one or more general partners and one or more limited partners. General partners assume full liability for debts of the partnership and exercise control over operations, while a limited partner's liability is limited to the extent of actual capital contribution to the partnership or additional liability voluntarily assumed.

linkages Relationships requiring the movement of goods or people from one location to another.

linked sites Sites that are interrelated by linkages; that is, related by the need to move goods or people from one site to the other.

liquidation damages Monetary award specified in a contract to be awarded to the damaged party in the event of a breach by either party.

liquidity Ability to convert an asset to cash without incurring loss.

loanable funds Monies hold by financial intermediaries in excess of required reserves; monies available to borrowers.

loan broker Individual who places loans with primary lenders for a fee.

loan commitment Obligation of a lender to provide specific funds at some future date. Terms may be specified, or they may be those prevailing on the date funds are advanced.

loan origination fee A charge by a lender, assessed at the time a loan commitment is made or at the time funds are advanced.

loan proceeds The face amount of a loan minus amounts deducted by the lender for items such as loan origination fees or discount points.

loan-to-value ratio Relationship of debt funds to total project value, stated as a percentage.

locational advantages Advantages, garnered by an occupant, due solely to the locational desirability of a site.

locational benefits The benefits derived from the use of real estate that are properly attributable to the desirability of the site location.

longitudinal studies Studies of relationships among variables, measuring changes in the variables through time. They involve repeated measures of the same phenomena to record any variation through time. Also called *time series studies*.

long run Economic term used to describe the length of time necessary for the operation of market forces to produce equilibrium.

long-term capital gains Term used in tax accounting to refer to gains realized on disposal of assets held for more than six months.

M

marginal benefits Economic term used to describe the benefits derived from an additional unit of production. In a financial sense, it might be used to describe the financial rewards of additional investment.

marginal cost Economic term used to describe the cost associated with production of each additional unit of a good or service.

marginal cost of capital The cost of an additional dollar of new capital funds.

marginal cost of production The cost of adding one more unit per period to one's rate of production.

marginal revenue Economic term used to describe revenue derived from an additional unit of a good or service sold.

marginal utility Satisfaction derived from the consumption of an additional unit of some economic good or service.

market Institutional arrangement that facilitates the exchange of good and/or services.

market data approach One of the three traditional appraisal approaches. Produces an indication of value through the analysis of recent sales of similar properties.

market demand curve Curve showing the amount of an economic good or service that will be demanded at various price levels. Demand curves are typically downward sloping, indicating that as price increases, demand decreases.

market price *See* transaction price.

market rent The rent a property would command on the open market if it were currently vacant and available.

market research Activity undertaken to determine consumer attitudes; attempts to determine what consumers want, where they want it, and how much they are willing to pay for it.

market simulation An attempt to replicate the actions of buyers and sellers in the marketplace. In real estate, it would be an attempt to estimate the outcome of a transaction involving real property by simulating the actions of "most probable" buyers and sellers.

market value The price at which a property can be acquired on the open market in an arm's-length transaction under all conditions requisite to a fair sale. The generally accepted definition presumes that both buyer and seller act prudently and knowledgeably and that the price is not affected by undue stimulus experienced by either party.

materialman's lien Claim arising from having supplied materials in connection with construction or improvement of real property.

materialmen Suppliers of materials in connection with construction or improvements of real property.

mean In statistics, the arithmetic average.

mechanic's lien Lien securing a claim that stems from having provided services in connection with construction or improvement of a property.

metes and bounds A method of delineating real property boundaries by references to enduring landmarks.

microeconomic theory Theory of small economic units. Generally referred to as the *theory of the firm*.

modified internal rate of return (MIRR) A variant of the internal rate of return, intended to eliminate the multiple root problem by discounting all negative cash flows back to the time an investment commitment must be made and by compounding all positive cash flows forward to the end of the final year of the investment holding period. The modified internal rate of return is the discount rate that equates the present value of all negative cash flows with the future value of all positive cash flows.

modified pass-throughs Ginnie Mae security backed by a pool of insured mortgage loans. A pro rata share of the repayment of interest and principal is "passed through" to holders of the pass-through securities.

Modified Uniform Limited Partnership Act A modified version of the Uniform Limited Partnership Act, which carefully specifies actions limited partners can take without endangering their limited liability.

monetary policy Use of control over the money supply to stimulate or dampen economic growth.

monopolistic competition A market arrangement whereby any number of competitors sell goods or services sufficiently differentiated that buyers will not be entirely indifferent among them, so that selection will be affected by elements other than price alone.

monopoly elements A characteristic of a good or service that differentiates it from other goods or services and thereby makes the others less acceptable as substitutes.

monthly constant The monthly debt-service obligation expressed as a percentage of the amount borrowed.

mortgage A document that pledges real estate as collateral for a loan.

mortgage-backed securities Securities backed by real estate mortgages as collateral.

mortgage bankers Individuals or firms that originate real estate loans. They may either hold such loans in their own investment portfolios or sell them in the secondary market.

mortgage commitment Obligation on the part of a lender to provide funds at some future date. Loan terms may be fixed or are those that prevail at the time the funds are to be advanced.

mortgage correspondents Individual mortgage bankers or brokers representing an institutional lender in a specified geographic location.

mortgagee Party to whom real estate is pledged under the terms of a mortgage. Typically, the lender in a real estate transaction.

mortgage participation certificates A bond backed by real estate as collateral. Bondholders participate in the proceeds of a group of mortgages that back the certificates.

mortgage REIT A real estate investment trust that invests primarily in real estate loans secured by first mortgages.

mortgage warehousing The process of inventorying real estate loans. Mortgage bankers or brokers sometimes inventory loans while assembling pools of loans for subsequent transfer to larger institutional real estate lenders.

mortgagor Party pledging real estate under the terms of a mortgage. Borrower who pledges real estate as collateral for a loan.

most fitting use Real estate use that optimally reconciles all public and private interests.

most probable selling price A probabilistic estimate of the price at which a future property transaction will occur; a prediction of the transaction price that will emerge if a property is offered for sale under current market conditions for a reasonable length of time at terms of sale currently predominant for such properties.

most probable use Use to which a property is most likely to be put. Recognizes that use is not certain. Most probable use is that use having the highest probability of occurrence. Recognizes the possibility of other uses while assigning lower probabilities to them.

multiple nuclei The theory that once a metropolitan area's major central business district is completely developed, a series of miniature central business districts will spring up throughout the metropolitan area.

multiple regression Statistical technique used to measure the association between a dependent variable and multiple independent variables.

multiplicative law of probability *See* joint probabilities.

N

natural price Adam Smith's concept of long-run, market-determined price. Smith held that the price of all goods and services will, over the long run, equal the cost of production.

neighborhood Sometimes referred to as a grouping of similar buildings, residents, or business enterprises.

neighborhood influences Factors influencing the desirability of a neighborhood. These include physical, economic, and locational characteristics.

neighborhood shopping centers Shopping centers that serve a trade area from which customers can commute by automobile within roughly five to ten minutes. Anchor tenants are usually food stores and drugstores, which may occupy a combined total area between 35,000 and 50,000 square feet.

net cash flow Net monetary benefits an individual or group of individuals receive as a reward for committing funds to an enterprise. Net cash flow before taxes ignores the tax effect of investments, and net cash flow after taxes accounts for the tax effects of investment.

net income multiplier (*See also* gross income multiplier *and* income multiplier analysis) Property market value expressed as a multiple of its net operating income.

net lease Lease arrangement under which tenants are required to pay all property operating costs.

net operating expenses Total expenses associated with the operations of a real estate project.

net operating income Effective gross revenue minus operating expenses.

net present value (NPV) Current capital value of all the benefits of an investment, minus the required initial cash outlay.

nominal interest rates Quoted cost of borrowing. Actual or effective interest rates may be substantially higher due to charges such as loan origination fees and the cost of maintaining required compensating balances.

normalized expenses An appraisal term for the operating expenses of a property as they would occur in a typical year.

normalized net operating income The net income figure that results when a typical year's operating expenses are subtracted from a typical year's effective gross income.

O

obligee Individual who makes a promise to pay a specified sum under the terms of a promissory note. Typically a borrower.

obligor Individual to whom a promise is made to pay a specified sum under the terms of a promissory note. Typically a lender.

offering memorandum A document intended to fully disclose the nature of a private offering of a security.

oligopoly A market arrangement characterized by few producers, into which entry by new producers is extremely difficult.

operating expense ratio Operating expenses expressed as a percentage of effective gross income.

operating expenses Cash expenditures required to maintain property in sufficient condition to generate effective gross revenue.

operating ratio *See* operating expense ratio.

operative words of conveyance Words used to indicate the intention to transfer title to real property.

opportunity cost of capital Forgone opportunity to earn interest on funds committed to other investments.

option agreement An agreement giving one party the right to buy or sell an asset within a specified time period at a fixed or determinable price.

overall capitalization rate Net operating income divided by a property's market value. Also called the *free-and-clear rate of return*.

P

partial release A mortgage clause providing for segments of a property to be released after specified lump-sum payments on the loan. Typically used in subdivision and development financing.

partnership An association of two or more people who join together to carry on a business for profit.

partnership agreement Document that specifies the rights and responsibilities of individuals who join together to carry on a business for profit. May be oral, but is usually written.

party wall An exterior wall common to two contiguous structures, each under different ownership.

passive activity Any trade or business is a passive activity for a taxpayer who is not actively involved in operations on a "regular, continuous, and substantial (year-round) basis."

passive activity income (*See also* passive activity) Income from passive trade or business activities. Income from passive activities can be used to offset losses from other passive activities. Any passive activity income not offset by losses is merged with taxable income from other sources.

passive activity losses (*See also* passive activity) Losses from passive trade or business activities. Passive activity losses can generally be offset against only passive activity income. Any remaining passive activity losses, with certain important exceptions, must be carried over and applied against future years' passive activity income, even though a taxpayer may have substantial taxable income from nonpassive sources during the year of the loss.

pass-through certificates Certificates backed by a pool of insured mortgages. Interest and principal collected are used to pay interest on the certificates as well as retire them.

payback period The amount of time required for an investor to recover the capital committed to a venture.

payee Individual to whom a promise has been made to repay a specified sum at some future date under the provisions of a promissory note.

percentage clause Lease provision that specifies rental based on some base rate, plus a percentage of the tenant's gross sales.

percentage lease Lease that provides for rental payments based on the tenant's gross sales.

permanent loan *See* end loan.

perpetuity A never-ending stream of payments or receipts.

personal consumption expenditures Economic term used to describe individual spending on such items as food, shelter, and clothing.

personal property Ownership interests in all properties other than real property. Examples include securities, partnership interest in a business, and ownership of an automobile. Also called *personalty*.

personalty *See* personal property.

physical deterioration Term used by appraisers to describe any loss in value due to physical wear.

physical durability Ability of a building to withstand physical wear and tear.

plat Diagram of a proposed subdivision, showing the location of all streets, sites, and easements.

police power Power of a municipality to enforce laws designed to promote health, safety, morals, and general welfare. Building codes, planning objectives, and zoning ordinances are all enforced through the exercise of police power.

population In statistics, the entire universe of data from which samples are drawn.

portfolio income Income from interest, dividends, rents, royalties, gain from disposition of investment property, passive activity income that is treated as portfolio income under the phase-in rules of the Tax Reform Act of 1986, and income from a trade or business in which the taxpayer does not materially participate (unless the activity is a "passive activity" under the passive loss rules).

portfolio risk Overall risk associated with ownership of a group of assets. Risks associated with one investment may decline when combined with another investment having offsetting risk patterns.

possibility of a reverter Residual interest in a property that becomes effective when a life estate terminates.

potential gross income The maximum amount of revenue a property would produce if fully rented at market rates.

potential gross rent The amount of rental revenue a property would generate if there were no vacancies.

preliminary prospectus Memorandum providing full disclosure of all items pertinent to a public security offering. A preliminary prospectus must be submitted to and approved by the Securities and Exchange Commission prior to any advertising of the offering.

prepaid interest Interest paid prior to the date on which it is due. In real estate loans, prepaid interest is often deducted from the loan amount when funds are advanced.

prepayment clause Typically a clause in a mortgage specifying penalties to be paid by the borrower in the event a loan is prepaid.

present value The value today of anticipated future receipts or disbursements.

present value approach Technique used to express anticipated future cash flows in terms of their current worth by adjusting for the opportunity cost of capital.

present value of an annuity Present worth of a series of level payments received at even intervals. Current value reflects the compounded opportunity cost of capital.

price elasticity A measure of the responsiveness of supply (price elasticity of supply) or demand (price elasticity of demand) to changes in price of a product or service.

price inelastic (*See also* price elasticity) A market condition in which price reductions cause a decline in total revenue and price increases result in increased total revenue.

price makers Economic units operating on a large enough scale to have some control over the price of their goods or services in the marketplace.

price searchers Economic units that recognize that they cannot completely control the price at which goods are exchanged, but also understand that they do affect market prices. Price searchers must be constantly aware of the impact their pricing decisions will have on the decisions of competitors.

price takers Economic units operating on such a small scale that they have no control over the price of their goods or services in the marketplace.

primary data Data gathered by researchers specifically for the problem with which they are currently grappling.

primary mortgage markets Markets in which real estate loans originate.

principal In finance, the amount on which interest liability is computed.

principal meridians Imaginary lines extending north and south between the Earth's poles, used as reference lines in property surveys.

principle of substitution Valuation principle stating that a person is not justified in paying more for a property than the cost to construct or acquire a substitute property.

private goods Economic goods where consumption by one individual reduces the amount available for consumption by others.

private grants Voluntary transfer of title to real property. These include transfer for consideration, gifts, and bequests.

private offering *See* private placement.

private placement Sale of a securities offering to a small group as opposed to a public offering, where sale is advertised to the general public. Sometimes called a *private offering*.

private placement memorandum Prospectus for a private placement. Does not have to be submitted for SEC approval, but must provide full disclosure.

probability A measure of the chance of occurrence associated with any possible outcome.

probability distribution An array of all possible outcomes and their related probabilities of occurrence.

probability of acceptance error The probability that accepting a proposed investment will prove to have been a mistake.

processing costs The cost of converting unfinished goods to finished goods.

product (*See also* goods and services) The end result of the production process.

productivity The ability of a property to generate utility or want-satisfying power. A property's ability to command rent is a measure of its productivity.

profitability index Measure of present value per dollar of cash outlay, calculated by dividing the present value of expected future cash flows by the initial cash outlay.

promissory note Agreement containing promise to pay a specified sum at some specific future date.

property management Overseeing the operations of real property for others. Includes renting space, collecting rentals, supervising maintenance, budgeting, etc.

prospectus A document that fully discloses the nature of a securities offering.

public goods Economic goods or services for which consumption by one individual does not reduce the amount available for consumption by others. Also called *collective goods*.

public infrastructure In real estate, the systems used to deliver public services to a site. Includes streets, sidewalks, sewer pipes, water pipes, etc.

public issue Securities issue offered for sale to the general public. Such an issue requires registration of a prospectus with the SEC. Also referred to as a *public offering*.

public offering *See* public issue.

purchase-money mortgage Mortgage given by a buyer to a seller to secure part payment of the purchase price. A purchase-money mortgage is typically recorded when deed is passed, establishing its precedence over all other claims.

purchase option The right to purchase a property within a specified time and at a predetermined price.

pure profit. *See* economic rent.

Q

quantity demanded Amount of an economic good or service purchasers will buy per period of time at a specific price.

quantity survey method A technique used to estimate the cost of new real property improvements. Costs are estimated in the same way an architect or builder figures construction costs.

quarter sections Squares resulting from the intersection of guide meridians and standard parallels are divided into 36 sections, each containing 640 acres. Sections are then divisible into four quarter sections containing 160 acres each.

quiet title suit Suit filed by an adverse possessor to gain title to property by adverse possession.

quitclaim deed A deed that purports to convey only those rights in a property that are possessed by the person making the conveyance, with no warrants that any such rights in fact exist.

R

radial/axial development Theory of urban development based on the idea that businesses locate along major arterial streets, creating a radial or axial pattern of growth outward from the central business district.

real assets Physical things with economic value, such as land, buildings, machinery, gold, antiques, and so forth. In contrast with financial assets such as promissory notes, bonds, and commercial paper, real assets tend to hold their value during periods of price inflation.

real estate investment Acquiring an ownership or a leasehold interest in real property, with a profit motive.

real estate investment trusts (REITs) Untaxed corporate entities organized to pool the resources of individual investors for investment in real estate. Some REITs invest in mortgages while others take ownership positions.

real estate service Benefits of use of real property. Real estate provides shelter and location for users.

Real Property Administrator (RPA) Professional designation conferred on property managers by the Building Owners and Managers Association International. Designation is a sign of professional achievement for those who completely fulfill prescribed educational and experiential requirements.

recording statutes Statutory provisions for permanent records of all transactions involving real property.

recovery property Property subject to the cost recovery allowance provisions first introduced into the tax system by the 1981 revision of the Internal Revenue Code.

rectangular survey system Use of a grid-type arrangement to identify land in a branch area by reference to a single geographic point.

redevelopment Process of clearing older structures in an area and replacing them with new buildings.

red herring Term sometimes used for a preliminary securities prospectus, which must be submitted to and approved by the SEC before any advertising is undertaken for a public issue.

redlining Term used to describe the unwillingness of certain financial institutions to provide real property financing in certain areas; derived from the practice of delineating areas with red lines on city maps.

regional planning Setting standards for the overall development of large geographical areas. Standards apply to land use, transportation systems, infrastructure, etc.

regional shopping center A shopping center that draws the majority of its customers from a trade area extending from 15 to 30 minutes in driving time from the center. It may encompass 200,000 to 400,000 square feet of retail space and usually features one or two major department stores as anchor tenants.

registered historic district Any area listed in the National Registry of Historic Places. Also includes any area so designated by appropriate state or local statute, provided that the secretary of the interior certifies that the statute will substantially achieve its purpose of preservation and rehabilitation and that the district meets substantially all the requirements for listing in the National Registry.

regression analysis Statistical technique used to measure the association among two or more variables.

Regulation B Implementing regulation of the Federal Reserve to enforce provisions of the Equal Credit Opportunity Act enacted in 1974.

Regulation Z Implementing regulation of the Federal Reserve to enforce provisions of the Truth in Lending Act enacted in 1969.

rehabilitation Process of refurbishing older or physically deteriorated buildings for current use.

reliction Recession of the water line of a lake or river resulting in the exposure of additional dry land.

remainderman Individual possessing a remainder interest in real property. Remainder interest becomes operative on expiration of a life estate.

remainders (*See also* reversion) Residual interests that become effective when the life estate of another ends.

renegotiable-rate mortgage Mortgage with an interest rate subject to redetermination at fixed intervals, as specified in the body of the mortgage or the accompanying promissory note.

rent concessions Agreements between landlord and tenant that reduce actual rental payments or receipts below those specified in a lease. A landlord might, for example, give one month's free occupancy, thereby reducing the effective rental rate over the entire occupancy period. Also simply called *concessions*.

rent escalator clauses Lease provisions that require tenants to pay all operating expenses above amounts specified in their leases.

rent roll A record of all tenants, showing the rent paid by each.

replacement cost Appraisal term used to describe the cost of building a structure similar in utility to the one for which value is being estimated. Replacement cost assumes construction at current standards.

reproduction cost Appraisal term used to describe the cost of building a structure identical to the one for which value is being estimated.

reservation Clause used in a deed to withhold some portion of the grantor's property rights.

reserve for repairs and replacements Appraisal adjustment used in the normalization of operating expenses to account for repairs or replacements that do not occur on an annual basis.

residential member (RM) Professional designation conferred by the American Institute of Real Estate Appraisers on individuals specializing in residential valuation. Designation signifies satisfaction of prescribed educational and experiential requirements.

residential specialists Real estate brokers who concentrate on the sale of single-family detached dwellings, town houses, condominiums, or cooperatives.

residual capitalization Appraisal technique that splits income between land and building. If building value is known, remaining income is capitalized to estimate land value, and if land value is known, remaining income is capitalized to estimate building value.

restrictive covenant Promise to refrain from using land or buildings for purposes specified in the clause creating the covenant.

revenue bonds Securities used to finance revenue-generating projects where the income produced by the undertaking will be used for interest payments and retirement of securities.

reversion Term used to describe the interest of one who will receive title if a conditional fee is extinguished.

right of survivorship (*See also* joint tenancy) A right unique to joint tenancy. Should one joint tenant die, the deceased's interest passes to the remaining joint tenants.

right to rescind Right of an individual to terminate an agreement, returning all parties to the legal position or relationship existing prior to the agreement.

riparian lands Lands abutting waterways or lakes. Title may extend to the water's edge or to the center of the water, depending on whether the waterway is navigable.

risk Measurable likelihood of variance from an expected outcome. Risk is generally measured as variance or standard deviation.

risk-adjusted discount rate A discount rate that includes the minimum acceptable yield on a riskless investment, plus a premium to compensate the investor for perceived risk associated with the venture under consideration.

risk averters Refers to the economic concept that individuals prefer less risk to more at a given level of return. Most individuals avoid risk and will assume additional risk only if it is accompanied by expectations of additional return.

risk-free discount rate Opportunity cost of capital based on riskless alternative investments.

risk premium Incremental return necessary to induce investors to assume additional risk.

risk-reward indifference curve A graphic representation of the relationship between perceived risk and acceptable rates of expected return where the investor will be equally satisfied by all risk-reward combinations.

r-square (r^2) *See* coefficient of determination.

S

S corporation *See* tax option corporation.

sample A group of observations drawn from a larger body of data (called a *population* or *universe*) and thought to be representative of the larger body.

secondary data Data used in a research project that were previously gathered for some other purpose.

secondary financial markets Markets comprising arrangements for buying and selling existing financial instruments.

secondary mortgage market A market in which existing mortgage notes are traded.

Section 1031 exchange *See* like-kind exchange.

sector theory A theory developed by Homer Hoyt and based on the observation that successive waves of residential development within a given socioeconomic class tend to continue outward from the urban center in a wedge-shaped pattern.

seizin A covenant found in a warranty deed whereby the grantor warrants that she does in fact possess the rights or interest being transferred.

senior mortgage A mortgage that takes priority over all other mortgages.

Senior Real Estate Analyst (SREA) A professional designation awarded by the Society of Real Estate Appraisers.

Senior Real Property Appraiser (SRPA) A professional designation awarded by the Society of Real Estate Appraisers. The SRPA designation is awarded to commercial and industrial appraisers.

Senior Residential Appraiser (SRA) A professional designation awarded by the Society of Real Estate Appraisers.

sensitivity analysis Financial analysis in which all variables but one are held constant and the result of a change in the remaining variable on the outcome is analyzed.

serial bonds Secured debt instruments that are retired in the sequence of their individual serial numbers.

serial correlation A measure of the extent to which causal factors influence outcomes over two or more time periods.

servient tenement Land bearing the burden of an easement appurtenant.

shift in demand The result of a shift in the relationship between price and quantity.

short-term capital gains Taxable gains on the sale of capital assets that have been owned for six months or less.

simple linear regression A statistical technique used to measure the association between two variables.

simulation The construction of a model intended as a simplified representation of realty, within which the impact of various factors can be isolated and quantified.

sinking fund payments Payments drawn from a fund set aside from the income of property that, with accrued interest, will eventually pay for replacement of the improvements.

sinking fund recapture technique A recapture computation that involves computing the recapture rate such that the sum of recovered capital and compound interest thereon will, over the useful life of the wasting asset, accumulate an amount equal to its cost.

space-time A four-dimensional concept combining the three dimensions of space with a fourth dimension of time. Real estate services are typically sold in space-time units.

special agent One whose authority to act is limited to a particular job or a specific task. Typically, a real estate broker acts in the capacity of a special agent.

special assessment A legal charge against real estate by a public authority to pay the cost of public improvements such as streetlights, sidewalks, and other street improvements.

special warranty deed A deed in which the grantor warrants or guarantees title only against defects arising during her ownership of the property and not against pre-existing defects.

specific asset syndication A type of syndication where the promoter gains control of a property and then assembles a group of investors.

speculation Assumption of business risk in hope of gain; purchase or sale of assets in hope of benefiting from market fluctuations.

speculative construction A business strategy where a developer/builder starts construction before any homes are sold, in anticipation of sufficient market demand to render the project profitable.

spread The difference between interest earned on mortgage loans and interest paid to depositors by financial intermediaries.

standard deviation A measure of dispersion about the mean of a probability distribution, frequently used as an indication of risk associated with an investment venture. The square root of the variance.

standard error of the forecast The degree of confidence to be placed in a forecast value for a dependent variable. Conceptually similar to the same measure as calculated in simple linear regression.

standard metropolitan statistical area A federally designated geographically described urban area with cohesive patterns of trade, communication, employment, and transportation.

standard parallels Imaginary lines running parallel with base lines (east-west lines) at 24-mile intervals, used as reference points in surveys using the rectangular survey method.

standby financing An arrangement whereby a lender agrees to keep a certain amount of money available to a prospective borrower for a specified period of time.

standby forward commitment An agreement for future purchase of mortgage notes at yield rates specified in advance. These commitments are sold by and binding on Fannie Mae but are optional for holders of the commitments.

standby loan commitment A binding option sold for a nonreturnable standby fee by a lender to a borrower, providing that the lender will loan a specific amount on stated terms to a borrower at any time within a stated future period. The borrower may or may not exercise the option.

statistical induction Drawing conclusions about an underlying population from data contained in a sample.

statistical inference Drawing conclusions about the future from a measured record of the past.

statutory exemption The portion of income that is exempt from the alternative minimum tax.

statutory right of redemption A statutory right granting a defaulting mortgagor an additional opportunity to recover foreclosed property. Limited in time by state statute.

straight-line method A method of computing depreciation or cost recovery allowances whereby the allowance is claimed in equal annual increments.

strict foreclosure Foreclosure accomplished by transferring a defaulting mortgagor's title directly to the mortgagee.

strong form efficiency hypothesis *See* efficient markets.

subagent One appointed by an agent to perform some duty, in whole or in part relating to the agency.

subcontractor A person who contracts to do work for someone who has a larger contract to do the job. For example, electrical work on a new house might be done on a subcontract for the contractor who has overall responsibility for building the house.

subdivider One who buys undeveloped acreage wholesale, segments it into smaller parcels, and sells it retail.

subdivision *See* land development.

subdivision controls Regulations imposed by various levels of government to regulate or control subdivision operations.

subjective value The value of an asset to the present owner or to a prospective purchaser. Similar to the economic concept of value in use.

subordination agreement A clause in a mortgage or lease stating that the right of the holder will be secondary or subordinate to a subsequent encumbrance.

subscription agreement A document that specifies the relationship between limited partners and the sponsoring general partner in a limited partnership arrangement.

substitute basis The initial tax basis of property acquired in a like-kind exchange. The substitute basis reflects any deferred gain or loss on the property tendered in the exchange.

summation technique A method used for developing capitalization rates, based on the idea that investors must be compensated to induce them to invest their wealth and that additional compensation is required for risk bearing and for illiquidity.

superregional shopping center A shopping center that draws customers from an extremely wide geographic area and supports very large concentrations of retail facilities. Superregional centers frequently feature as much as 500,000 to 750,000 square feet of retail space. They may have as many as four major department stores as anchor tenants.

supply The relationship between price and the quantity of a product suppliers place on the market during a specified time period, for all possible prices.

supply to sell Desired decrease in a market participant's inventory of a product, at a specific price.

symmetric probability distribution A probability distribution in which each side is a mirror image of the other.

syndicate A group of two or more people united for the purpose of making and operating an investment. A syndicate may operate as a corporation, a general partnership, or a limited partnership.

T

table of residuals A listing of differences between actual values for a variable and those values predicted by a regression equation.

takeout loan *See* end loan.

tax auction A procedure for selling tax-delinquent land or real property where verbal or written offers are taken and the property is sold to the highest bidder.

tax basis *See* initial tax basis.

tax conduit A partnership characteristic whereby tax-deductible losses "pass through" the partnership "conduit" and are reported by each partner in accordance with his or her individual ownership interest in the partnership.

tax credits Direct offsets against a taxpayer's income tax liability, provided as tax incentives to induce action thought to be in the best interests of the nation.

tax deductions (*See also* itemized deductions) Reductions in taxable income.

tax deed A deed to property taken by government for nonpayment of taxes and resold at auction pursuant to law.

tax-deferred exchange *See* like-kind exchange.

tax-free exchange *See* like-kind exchange.

tax lien A lien placed on a taxpayer's property by government for nonpayment of taxes.

tax option corporation A qualifying corporation whose shareholders have elected to be taxed directly for their shares of corporate income, rather than having the corporation itself incur income tax liability. Provisions are found in Subchapter S of the Internal Revenue Code. Sometimes called an *S corporation*.

tax preference item Tax deductions or exemptions that are added back to adjusted gross income for purposes of computing the alternative minimum tax liability.

tax schedule income The amount of taxable income used as a reference for computing income tax liability when using tax rate schedules provided by the IRS.

tax stops Lease provisions that require tenants to pay all property taxes beyond some specified level.

technical analysis Attempting to estimate future changes in market values by investigating the past market behavior.

tenancy at sufferance Wrongful occupancy, which can be terminated by a property owner at any time.

tenancy at will A tenancy stating no fixed period and that either landlord or tenant may terminate at any time, or in the time specified by statute, usually 30 days.

tenancy by the entirety A type of joint tenancy that can exist only between spouses, in which the married couple takes conveyance of the tenancy interest in common, with that interest being treated as a single, indivisible unit and with the survivor continuing to hold the tenancy as a matter of right.

tenancy from period to period A tenancy by one who holds a leasehold interest for an unstated period and pays rent each period, each payment serving as renewal for an additional period. This often results from the holding over of a previous specified-term tenancy on which rental was paid each period.

tenancy in common Tenancy by two or more parties holding an interest in the same property, that interest being undivided, although not necessarily equal in each holder.

theorems Fundamental mathematical rules from which various mathematical operations are derived.

time preference for money Preference for more immediate rather than delayed receipt of funds, so that investment benefits are more valued the sooner they are received.

time series surveys *See* longitudinal studies.

time value of money *See* time preference for money.

title closing The meeting of parties to a sales contract at a designated place and time for the purpose of executing the contract.

title defect A possible legal difficulty that may limit the marketability of the title.

title insurance Insurance against losses resulting from the passage of legally invalid title, issued by a title insurance company after a title search by that company has established that legally valid title exists in the seller, who then is able to pass that title to the insured.

title insurance policy A contract wherein the title insurer agrees to indemnify the insured against losses resulting from imperfect title.

title search A circumspect review of all documents and records in the recorder's office pertaining to a property to determine if the seller has good title to the property.

title transfer To convey or relinquish title to another party.

Torrens system A system of registering title to real property that accurately determines the ownership of land and every lien and claim on it. Under this system, land title is registered in much the same way as is title to an automobile.

township A six-mile-square area containing 36 sections, each one mile square, used in the rectangular survey system of land description.

trade area The geographic area from which a store or shopping center draws the majority of its patronage.

transaction costs Items such as brokerage fees, recording fees, transfer taxes, and attorney fees incurred in connection with a real estate transaction.

transaction price The price at which a transaction actually occurred; the outcome of a bargaining process between buyer and seller. Sometimes called *market price*.

transaction range The range of prices at which a transaction can occur between an owner and a prospective purchaser. The owner's subjective value determines the lower level of the transactions range; the prospective buyer's subjective value determines the upper level.

transactions balances The quantity of money required to finance general business operations and satisfy day-to-day demands of householders.

transfer costs (*See also* implicit transfer costs and explicit transfer costs) Costs of transportation between linked sites.

transport breakpoints Points along major transportation routes where the mode of transport must change.

trust account A bank account separate and apart and physically segregated from a broker's own funds, in which a broker is required by state law to deposit all monies collected for clients. Similar to an escrow or special account.

trust agreement A document that sets forth terms of security arrangements and instructs the trustee in the event of default.

trust deed *See* deed of trust.

trustee The person in a trust relationship who holds property for the benefit of another person (the beneficiary).

trust indenture *See* deed of trust.

Truth in Lending Act One of a series of modern consumer protection acts, requiring lenders to fully disclose the rates of interest, other charges, and all terms and conditions of each loan, in writing and clearly stated.

U

uncertainty An environment holding an unknown number of possible outcomes, where there is no significant information about the relative chance of occurrence of each.

unfavorable financial leverage Use of borrowed funds when their cost exceeds the rate of return on assets being financed.

Uniform Limited Partnership Act A model law to govern creation and operation of limited partnership entities that has been enacted (in some cases, in substantially revised form) by every state except Louisiana.

unit-in-place method A means of assessing replacement costs, in which an appraiser estimates the cost of building components separately, developing a unit cost for each component, and including overhead and profit allocation estimates as well as direct labor and materials cost, and then adds all costs together to reach total cost and thereby replacement cost.

universal agents Agents who are empowered to perform all legal acts for their principals.

universe In statistics, the entire population of data from which samples are drawn.

urban growth An increase in the intensity of use of land resources. This may or may not entail an increase in population of an urban land area. It usually includes higher capital investment per unit of land employed and increased productivity associated with urban economic processes.

useful life The period over which a property will benefit the owner's trade or business.

utility An economic term for the want-satisfying power embodied in a good or service.

V

value in exchange The value an asset can command in the marketplace.

value in use The value of an asset to its owner or to a prospective owner.

variable-rate mortgage A financing instrument that permits the lender to alter the interest rate, with a certain period of advanced notice, based on a specific base index.

variance A measure of dispersion of possible values about the midpoint of a probability distribution of possible outcomes, frequently used as a measure of risk. The square of the standard deviation.

vendee The purchaser of real estate under articles of agreement or a contract for deed.

vendor The seller of real estate under articles of agreement or a contract for deed.

void To have no force or effect; that which is unenforceable.

voidable That which is capable of being adjudged void but is not void unless action is taken to make it so.

voluntary conveyance Voluntary transfer by a defaulting mortgagor of the mortgaged property to the mortgagee, to avoid a foreclosure suit and a possible deficiency judgment.

W

warranty deed A deed that contains a clause warranting that title to real property is clear and the property is unencumbered.

weighted average cost of capital Capital cost computed by weighting the cost of each component in accordance with the proportion of total capital it comprises.

wholesale price index An index of changes in the wholesale price of a representative "basket" of goods, referenced to a specified base period.

worker's compensation insurance Insurance against claims for injuries sustained by employees.

wraparound lender (*See also* wraparound mortgage) Assumes responsibility for meeting debt-service obligations on the mortgage note that has been "wrapped."

wraparound mortgage A mortgage subordinate to, but still including, the balance due on a pre-existing mortgage note, in addition to any amount to be disbursed on the new note. Also called an *all-inclusive mortgage*.

Z

zoning ordinance The fixing by government of geographic areas in which specified kinds of buildings and businesses may be developed.

zoning regulations *See* zoning ordinance.

INDEX

100 percent location 55
150 percent declining balance method 194

A

absolute monopoly 39
absorption rate
    definition 387
    historic 388
acceleration clause 152
acceptance error 341, 342
acquired property 499
acquisition cost 190
active investor 8
active participation 207
adjusted rate of return 263
adjusted tax basis 218
after-tax borrowing costs 172
after-tax cash flow 198
    analysis 431
    anticipated 281
    commercial rehabilitation 411, 413
    community shopping center 438, 441
    disposal 219, 280, 317
    evaluation 424, 439
    forecast 124, 197, 279, 280, 422, 429
    industrial building 422, 424
    industrial subdivision 392
    office building 429, 430
    projections 18
    sale 313
after-tax equity reversion 423
after-tax profits 406
agricultural bid-rent curve 58
amortization
    alternatives 155
    factor 167, 169
    of dollar 491
    schedule 180, 279, 476
    table 476

analysis paralysis 71
annual taxable income 392
annuity
    compound value 484, 487
    definition 469
    in advance 483
    present value of 472, 474
asset
    market for 34
atomistic market 39, 42

B

basis 193
before-tax borrowing cost 172
before-tax cash flow
    community shopping center 439
    from operations 180, 181
    industrial subdivision 391, 393, 394
benefit stream
    perceived risk 14
    value of 14
bid-rent curve 58
blanket mortgage 154, 161
boot 228, 497
borrowing cost 172
break-even ratio 238
broker's rate of return 240
business risk 292
buyer
    investment value 277
    position summary 275
    value relationships 11

C

Canadian rollover loan 157
capital gain/loss
    rules 216
    Section 1231 217
    tax consequences 217

capitalization rate
    for apartment building 123
    formula 422
carrying cost 137
cash flow
    analysis 394
    complex patterns 344
    correlated 344
    disposal estimate 218, 219
    expected annual 332
    financing consequences 135, 137, 141
    partially correlated 347
    present value of 316
    probability 333, 338
    projections 312, 378
    shopping center 437
    sources of 7
    summary 107
    uncorrelated 345
    value relationships 15
    wraparound note 177
cash-on-cash rate of return 239
casualty 226
census data 77, 88
central business district 52
central place theory 52
centripetal forces 54
certainty-equivalent technique 311, 321
coefficient of variation 338
commercial banks 144
communication 78
community shopping center 433
    annual after-tax cash flow calculation 438
    cash-flow to partner 440
    depreciation schedule 436
    disposal 439
    loan amortization schedule 435
    partner's share 440
    percentage rentals 437
    taxable gain on sale 439

index **535**

comparable properties 104
comparative performance measures 456
complexity 71
compound interest
    conceptual basis for 463
    debt accumulation 464
    formula 486
    value of $1 466
compound value formula 487
concentric ring model 52
conduits 144
consideration 214
construction bonds 161
construction period interest 203
consumer/resident profile 79
continuous distribution 332
contract price 221
corporation
    ownership 201
    tax consequences 208
cost
    benefits versus 69, 70
    revenue relationship 42
cost recovery
    allowable periods 193
    basis adjustment 193
    commercial rehabilitation project 410
    recapture 215
    tax shelter 136
co-tenancy arrangement 200
credit
    government-sponsored 160
    instruments for 152
cross-sectional surveys 79

D

data
    collection techniques 72
    Internet 91
    sources 76, 88, 89
dealer property 215
debt
    amortization schedule 180
    constants 476
    investor 8
    service constant 135
debt coverage ratio
    available financing and 139
    formula 138, 238
    operating projection 179
debt-to-equity ratio
    definition 137
    function 138

decision process 13
deed of trust 154
deferred annuity 480
demand
    closed market system 36
    determinants of 29
    function 28
    revenue forecasts and 125
    schedule 28
    shifters 31
demand curve
    definition 28
    illustration 29
    movement along 32
deposit growth 469, 471
depreciation 215
depreciation allowance
    commercial rehabilitation project 410, 411
    computation 193
    definition 193
    industrial building 421
    office building 428
    projection 196
    recapture 215
    tax consequences 136, 208
    unrecaptured 215
depreciation schedule
    apartment building 195
    office building 428
    shopping center 436
derived demand 418
descriptive research 79
development
    alternatives 274
    building cost estimates 403
    case study 403
    construction costs 400
    construction phase 402
    feasibility analysis 400
    financing 401, 404
    market research 400
    NOI estimates 404
    overview 400
    patterns 51
    present value estimate 407
    profit 406
    pro forma income and expense statements 405
    project cost estimate 404
    recent sales 406
    rental survey 405
    sales price 405

discounted cash-flow
    analysis 264
    standard deviation and 338
    technique application 277
discounting 463
discount rate
    risk-adjusted 282, 308, 321
    risk-free 309
    summation technique 270, 282
discrete probability distributions 332
diseconomies of scale 43
dispersion measurement 333
diversification 355, 359
Dodd-Frank Act 155
DRIP (dividend reinvestment plan) 449

E

economic rent 43
effective gross income 102
effective interest rate
    comparison of 173
    full-term loan 174
    prepayment after five years 175
efficient frontier 355, 356, 357
efficient portfolios 356, 358
eminent domain 226
environmental audits 115
environmental risk 115, 292, 296
equilibrium price 31
equity dividend 239
equity investor 8, 370
equity participation mortgage 158, 161
equity real estate investment trust (REIT) 300
equity value 318
estate settlement procedure 202
excess accumulated earnings 201
exchange rate 6
executive summary 377
exhibits 377
expected value 333
expense stops 300
explicit costs 96, 142

F

feasibility analysis
    development 400
    equity investor approach 372
    objective 367
    report format 376, 377
    steps in 368, 379
    valuation analysis and 366
financial analysis 378

financial feasibility study 366
financial leverage
    amount of 139
    and borrowing costs 142
    definition 292
    measuring 137
    operating projection 178
    optimal amount of 143
    range of possible outcomes 293
    risk and 140
    tax consequences of 203
financial management rate of return 264
financial ratio analysis 237
financial risk 292
financial tables 477
financing
    alternatives 172, 173
    industrial building 420
    office building 426
    shopping center 434
footloose industries 419
forecast
    matrix 73
    NOI 119
    operating expense 117
    variables 318
foreign investor 6
four-quadrant forecasting market 74
free-and-clear rate of return 238
functional efficiency 100, 114
functional obsolescence 114
future value
    of dollar 486
    present value relationship 469

G

gain
    community shopping center sale 439
    on disposal 136
geographic diversification 359
geographic information systems (GIS) 81, 91
gift
    alternatives 228
    strategy 227
    tax basis 227
government census 89
gross income 114
gross income multiplier 124, 237

H

heavy industrial buildings 419
hedging 301
housing census 88
hurdle rate 260, 272

I

implicit costs 96, 142
imputed interest 223
income/expense forecast 420
income/expense statement 425, 427
income multiplier analysis 236
income tax
    disposal consequences 280
    industrial building 421
    sale consequences 219
incremental cost of borrowing 142
incubator buildings 420
individual ownership 201
industrial bid-rent curve 58
industrial building
    after-tax cash-flow 422, 424
    after-tax equity reversion 423
    case study 420
    demand for 418
    depreciation allowance 421
    financing 420
    footloose industries 419
    fuel/power supply 418
    income/expense forecast 420
    income tax consequences 421
    investment 418
    investment value 424
    loan amortization schedule 421
    location factors 418
    market proximity 419
    sales proceeds forecast 422
    tax on sale 423
    types of 419
industrial subdivision
    after-tax cash flows 393
    annual taxable income 392
    before-tax cash flows 391, 393, 394
    case study 386
    cash-flow analysis 394
    investment analysis 389
    investment value and 393
    market research 386
    repayment schedule 390
    sales records 389
    site characteristics 386
    taxable income 395
    tax calculation 390

industrial use 56
inefficiency 41
inferential analysis 80
inferential statistics 80, 85
information
    cost factor 42
initial equity investment 239
initial tax basis 191
installment method gain 220
installment sales
    advantages of 220
    contract 161
    interest provisions 223
institutional investors 4
insurable risk 292, 297
insurance companies 143
interest
    deductibility limits 204
    definition 182
interest-only (IO) loans 156
interest rate
    relevance of 6
internal rate of return (IRR)
    explanation 252
    formula 252
    NPV comparison 260
    problems with 253
    reinvestment 254
Internal Revenue Code
    installment method gain 223
    installment sales 220
    private activity bonds 160
    REIT provisions 449
    Section 1031 exchange 226
    Section 1231 assets 216
internet 91
interpolation 478, 479
investment
    adjustments 243
    decision rules and 272
    factors 243
    performance 8, 314
    shopping center 432
    strategy implications 204
    variety in 7
investment analysis
    feasibility questions 366
    industrial subdivision 389
investment value
    computation 282
    definition 275
    estimation of 281
    formula 15
    industrial building 424
    industrial subdivision 393

index

overview 13
transaction range and 277
investor
   categories 7
   traits 20

J

joint tenancy 200
junior mortgage 159

L

land
   availability 117
land-use
   economic factors 50
   location and 51
lease 95
lenders 370
level annuity 490
lifestyle center 433
like-kind exchange
   acquired property 499
   nonsimultaneous 505
   related parties and 506
   substitute basis 504
   tax consequences 226, 495
   tax-deferred 228
like-kind property 225
limited liability 202
linkage
   analysis of 115
   changes 116, 125
   industry location and 55
   market area 96
   transfer cost and 54
liquidity 202
loan
   amount 180
   payments to amortize 475, 476
loan-amortization factors 167, 476
   available financing and 140
   definition 138
   function 139
   operating projection 179
loan amortization schedule
   apartment building 182
   commercial rehabilitation 410
   community shopping center 435
   industrial building 421
   office building 427
location
   analysis 378
   commercial 56

decisions 52
industrial use 56
retail decisions 57
subdivision 384
locational characteristics 115
locational factors 418
loft building 419
longitudinal, studies 80
long-lived assets 216

M

macro level forecast 74
manufacturers 88
marginal cost of capital 271, 282
marginal revenue 42
market
   adjustment process 43, 57
   area 96, 98
   clearing price 41
   definition 37
   economic function of 41
   efficiency 37, 41
   equilibrium 42
   rent 103
   rental space 57
   structure 39, 40
market analysis
   report 378
   sequential components of 72
market research
   analysis paralysis 71
   conditions and 70
   cost vs. benefits 69, 70
   design 71
   development 400
   extent of 69
   for risk control 300
   industrial subdivision 387
   need for 58
   planning for 79
   purpose 68
   report preparation 75
market value
   definition 10
   determination of 12
   formula 179
   future estimate 122
   physical basics of 13
material participation 205
mean/standard deviation approach 338
mineral industries 88
modern one-story structures 419
modified internal rate of return (MIRR) 260, 262

money 464
monopolistic competition 40
monopoly 125
month-to-month tenancy 95
mortgage
   amortization schedule 279
   constant 491
   provisions 153
   restructuring 155
most probable selling price 10
multiplicative law of probability 329
mutually dependent investment 274
mutually exclusive opportunities 273
mutually exclusive projects 274

N

natural zoning 54, 58
neighborhood
   definition 38
   environmental factors 116
   influences 96, 125
   shopping center 432
net capital gain/loss 217
net income multiplier 237
net lease 159
net operating income (NOI)
   development estimates 404
   forecasts 119
   rental property 94
net present value (NPV)
   discount rate and 270
   explanation 251
   IRR comparison 260
   mutually dependent investment 274
   mutually exclusive opportunities 273
nominal interest rate
   application 175
   real rate and 170
nonsimultaneous exchange 505
normal distribution table 493

O

objective probability distribution 328
observation 78
occupancy levels 294, 295
office building
   after-tax cash flow 428, 429
   case study 425
   depreciation allowance 428
   depreciation schedule 426
   financing 425
   income/expense statement 425, 427

investments 424
loan amortization schedule 427
market boundaries 99
nodal pattern 100
tax consequences of sale 430
oligopoly 40
open-ended mortgage 154, 161
operating expense
    estimates 101, 117
    reconstruction of 106
operating expense ratio
    forecasted 122
    formula 121
operating forecast
    first year 120, 278
    reconstruction of 106
    six-year 121
operating ratio 237
operating statement
    example 102
    illustration 94
    introduction to 94
    reconstruction of 105
    revised 106
opportunity cost 283
ordinary income 215
overall capitalization rate 238
owner-occupied office building 425

P

partially amortizing mortgage 155
partially correlated cash flow 347
partial release clause 154
partial serial correlation 347
partitioning 321
partnership 208
passive investor 8
payback-period
    analysis 308
    formula 242
    method 320
peer-group properties
    comparison with 95
    identification of 100
pension funds
    commercial mortgages 143
    real estate investment by 5
perceived risk 14
percentage rentals 437
periodic tenancy 95
perpetual annuity 474
physical characteristics
    definition 124
    impact of 114

physical durability
    declining 115
planning tools 68
population census 88
portfolio decisions 68
portfolio diversification 299
preliminary financial feasibility 369
prepaid interest 203
present value
    after-tax cash flow 441
    annuity in advance 483
    anticipated after-tax cash flow 281
    debt position 15
    deferred annuity 480
    definition 250
    development estimate 395
    dollar 468, 488
    equity position 15, 17
    formula 250, 488
    future value relationship 469
    interpolation between factors 478
    level annuity 490
    mortgage-financing assumptions 281
    NOI variation and 319
    of annuity 472, 474
    office building 431
    of future amount 467
    partitioned cash flows 311, 315
    perpetual annuity 474
    probabilities 337
    probability distribution 346
    standard deviation of 346
prevailing market conditions 70
price makers 40
price searcher 40, 41
primary data
    sources 78
private activity bonds 160
private data sources 89
probability
    as risk measure 326
    cash flow 338
    conventional rules 329
    definition 326
    distribution 328, 331, 334
    economic conditions and 330
    estimates 327
    forecast 330
    formula 326
    joint 329
    multiplicative law of 329
product differentiation 117
product substitutability 42

profit
    expectations 301, 408
    opportunities 37
profitability index (PI) 273
profitability measures 238
project comparison 273
project cost estimate 404
project feasibility analysis 368
promissory note
    purpose of 161
property
    highly appreciated 227
    physical characteristics 124
    rehabilitation tax credit 204
    resale 215
    subject to a mortgage 227
    tax basis 227
property management
    for risk control 300
    market research and 68
purchase-money mortgage 153, 161
purchase options 301
pure/perfect competition 39

Q

quality 243
quantity 243

R

ratio analysis 236, 241
real estate investment trust (REIT)
    definition 449
    evaluation 457
    information sources 457
    regulation 450
real interest 171
realized gain/loss 214, 219
recognized gain/loss 219, 222
recommendations 378
recordation 159
recovery
    unrecaptured cost 215
redevelopment bonds 160
regional/city analysis 377
regional shopping center 433
regulatory authorities 369
rehabilitation
    after-tax cash flow 411, 413
    case study 409
    cost recovery 409
    financing possibilities 410
    incentives 407
    loan amortization schedule 410

proposal feasibility 408
    selling price estimation 411
    tax on sale 412
reinvestment rate 256, 258
related party exchange 506
relative interest rates 6
relative scarcity 32
relative value 191
remaining balance 479
renegotiable-rate mortgage (RRM) 157
rent
    ability to command 95
    break-even rate 296
    increases 119
rental income
    characteristics of 206
    exemptions 205
rental market 57
rental terms 79
rental units 34
residential market area 97
retail market 88
risk
    adjustment 303, 310
    attitude toward 22, 302
    aversion 302
    controlling 297
    diversification and 355
    elements 292
    financial leverage and 140
    investor objective risk 20
    measures 303, 331
    preferences 301
    premium 271, 309
    profiles 341
    reduction 297
    shifting of 300
    taking 303
    tolerance 20
    uncertainty versus 326
risk-adjusted discount rate 271, 308, 320
risk-adjustment methods 320
risk-averse investor 21
risk-free discount rate 271, 309
risk management
    diversification and 299
    portfolio theory and 354
risk-return profiles
    minimum acceptable probability 343
    probability index 342
risk-reward indifference curve 298, 301
rollover loan 157

S

sale 208
sale-and-leaseback 159, 161
sales proceeds forecast 422
Section 1031 exchange
    effect of loss 502
Section 1231 216, 217
seller
    financing 153
    investment value 277
    position summary 276
    value relationships 11
sensitivity analysis 316, 321
serial correlation 344
service industry 88
shared appreciation mortgage (SAM) 158
shared equity participation (SEP) 158
shopping center
    annual cash flow 437
    case study 434
    cash proceeds from sale 438
    categories 432
    depreciation schedule 436
    financing 434
    income forecast 436
    investments 432
    taxable income estimation 438
    taxable income forecast 437
simplified transaction 202
site
    analysis 378
    characteristics 386
small-scale operations 206
solvency testing 370, 374
spatial modeling 81
standard deviation
    discounted cash-flow model 338
    dispersion measures 334
    formula 334
    of present value 346
Subchapter S corporation 202
subdivision
    definition 395
    financing 385
    plan creation 385
    process 384
    regulatory requirements 385
subjective probability distribution 328
substitute basis 504
summation technique 270
superregional malls 433
supply
    closed market system 36
    factor 117, 125
    of real estate 32
    time function relationship 37
supply analysis 117
    product differentiation 117
    time element 33
supply curve 34
syndication 299
systematic risk 354

T

take-back mortgage 153
tax
    commercial rehabilitation project 413
    credit 204
    deductions 136
    industrial building sale 423
    office building sale 430
    shelter 136
tax basis
    acquired property 499
    adjustments to 196
    initial 190, 191
    significance 190
tax option corporations 201
tenancy at will 95
tenancy in common 199, 200
tenant
    profile 79
    shifting risk to 300
terminal value
    definition 255
    example 258
time
    series 79
    supply function relationship 37
time-adjusted return measures 244
timing 243
title insurance 159
total yield 134
transaction cost 42, 197, 498
transaction price 10
transaction range
    definition 10
    investment value and 277
    value relationship 12
transfer cost
    alteration of 116
    analysis of 115
    linkages and 54
    market area 96
    neighborhood influences 96
transportation census 89
trend extrapolation 124

triple-net lease 300
trust agreement 154
trust deed 154
two-way exchange 496

U

uncertainty
    implications 326
    risk versus 326
uncorrelated cash flow 345
unfavorable leverage 292
Unified Gift and Estate Tax 226
unlike property 228, 497

unrecaptured 215
unsystematic risk 354
upside risk 293
urban development 51

V

vacancy rates
    comparable properties 104
    example 105
    historical data 119
valuation analysis 366

value relationship
    buyer perspective 11
    cash flows and 15
    seller perspective 11
    transaction range 12
variance 334

W

wholesale trade 88

Z

zone of transition 51
z-value 335